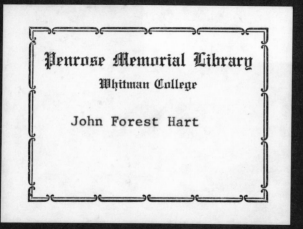

A Biography: Henry Cabot Lodge

WILLIAM J. MILLER left his native Asheville, N.C., at 17 (on finishing high school) for Cleveland, O., where he literally grew up on the famous "Press" whose Editor Louis B. Seltzer called him "one of the best newspaper writers Cleveland has ever had." Before he was old enough to vote he had covered Cleveland's bank crashes, NRA rallies, eviction riots, the Bonus March. Later he covered the auto sitdown strikes, the bloody Little Steel Strike, Father Coughlin's and Gerald L. K. Smith's hate rallies.

At 27, he was one of Harvard's early Nieman Fellows, covered World War II for the "Press," landing in Southern France in the same first wave as Lodge. At war's end he joined *Newsweek*, covered Henry Ford's funeral, wrote Eddie Rickenbacker's and John L. Lewis' "cover stories," went on to *Time* where he wrote such well-remembered covers as the Hartfords of the A & P, the DeWitt Wallaces of the *Reader's Digest*, the du Ponts of Wilmington, and Time's bull-market stories. As editorialist for *Life* and chief editorial writer of the New York *Herald Tribune* he often worked closely with Lodge, whom Miller—a political independent—admired for his own political independence and courage. Of prerevolutionary Carolina Scotch-Irish yeoman stock, Miller is the grandson of a Confederate officer.

Alfred Eisenstaedt, Life © Time Inc.

Henry Cabot Lodge

A Biography by William J. Miller

H

James H. Heineman, Inc.

New York

Library of Congress Catalogue Card No. 64–23625

© 1967, James H. Heineman, Inc., New York, New York
All rights reserved. No part of this book may be used
or reproduced in any manner whatsoever without written
permission of the publisher except in the case of brief
quotations embodied in critical articles and reviews.

For information address: James H. Heineman, Inc.,
60 East 42nd Street, New York 10017

Design and typography by Noel Martin.
Printed and bound in the United States of America.
First Printing 1967

*To my sons, Patrick, William, Thomas and
Michael, in the hope that the life of a
man of value may enrich their own; and
to my daughters, Marilyn, Carolyn, Victoria
and Madeline, to remind them that a good wife's
love and help make a gift beyond measure.*

CHAPTER ONE

America will cease to be a great nation whenever her young men cease to possess energy, daring, and endurance, as well as the wish and the power to fight the nation's foes. —Henry Cabot Lodge and Theodore Roosevelt, *Hero Tales from American History* (New York, 1895)

In the chill midmorning of February 1, 1944, a lanky figure clambered out of a taxi at the little-used east entrance of the White House, where reporters would not be apt to see him, and strode quickly inside. Senator Henry Cabot Lodge, Jr., of Massachusetts was carrying out the most important decision he had ever made.

At forty-one, he was a man of action in each rawboned inch of his six feet two and three-quarter inches, militarily erect as befitted a man who had spent many a summer on rough, tough maneuvers with the U.S. Cavalry, both horse and armor. His wideset, light blue eyes were grave, and his firm jaw grimly set.

He knew his way about the White House, and had since childhood. As he strode toward the President's office, a flow of memories stirred. He had come to dinner there with his parents, in the days when his grandfather was the most powerful senator in Washington, and President Theodore Roosevelt's closest friend. Grandfather Lodge had ordered a special door built in his own house, so the President could enter from the garden unobserved, at any hour. He remembered White House dinners with the jovial Taft. Coolidge—whose nomination he had covered as a reporter—had asked him to lunch with the young hero Lindbergh while he was covering the White House for the New York *Herald Tribune*. He had also covered Hoover's nomination, as well as that of the President now awaiting him— Franklin Delano Roosevelt.

As Lodge was ushered in, Roosevelt wore his familiar electric grin. Only a few years before he would have scowled fiercely; at that time he had broken all Presidential precedent by publicly denouncing Lodge. Moreover, Lodge had fought Roosevelt's early effort to "quarantine the aggressors" and help the Allies in the days before America awoke to its own danger. With his chief Senate friend and ally, Michigan's Arthur H. Vandenberg, Lodge had fought to the end for a Fortress America strong enough to stay aloof from the approaching world conflagration. Pearl Harbor had ended their isolationism, and whatever domestic quarrels Lodge may have had with Roosevelt were behind them both as the President changed from "Dr. New Deal" to "Dr. Win the War."

2   Moreover, the President, an old preparedness advocate from World War I, was well aware that Lodge, as much as any man, had fought for more than a decade—as journalist and author, as well as senator—for the sort of military strength which, had it come in time, might have averted World War II.

Now no trace of the old enmity remained.

Roosevelt waved his big hand in greeting: "Hello, Cabot!"

He had Press Secretary Steve Early with him, perhaps feeling he might need one veteran journalist's advice in dealing with another. Roosevelt had a great flair for dramatic stories and began telling both his listeners the details of the Battle of Kwajalein, then raging. At length he paused to give Lodge a chance to talk.

"Mr. President," said Lodge, "I have decided to resign my seat in the Senate and go into combat duty in the Army."

The President's eyebrows shot up in surprise and so did Early's. The surprise was understandable. It was the first time since the Civil War that a senator had chosen to give up his seat to fight for his country.*

"Cabot, that's splendid!" said the President. "I congratulate you! I wish I were going with you!"

Lodge had been pondering the action for some time. His only fear was that he might be assigned to some chairborne role. After all, the Commander-in-Chief could, if he wished, assign him to guard the Panama Canal or the Staten Island ferry.

Lodge explained to the President that he wanted to make sure that if he did resign he would be assigned to active combat duty: he had had most of his training with the Cavalry Brigade, which had become the Second Armored Division. He knew Patton, Crittenberger and many of the officers. Crittenberger had just left for England. Lodge told the President that he had checked before Crittenberger had left and that Crittenberger had assured him that he had a place for Lodge when they got into action.

"What I plan to do," Lodge added, "if you will give me your blessing, is to fly to England to join him before my resignation is announced in the Senate."

"Certainly you have my blessing," said the President. "I only wish I could go along with you." Later that afternoon, still nostalgic about the whole episode, the President sent Lodge this gracious, self-revealing note:

Dear Cabot:

I want you to know that I am awfully glad that you came to see me this

* There is only one statue in the great space under the Capitol dome in Washington which is not the statue of a President. It is of Senator Baker of Oregon who left the Senate for active combat duty in the army and was killed at Ball's Bluff, Virginia. He was a great friend of Lincoln, and the only senator ever to have been killed in action.

morning. And I am writing this note to tell you that I would do just what you are doing, if I could.

I missed being with the guns in 1917-18. It's too late now. I envy you the opportunity that is yours and I congratulate you upon the decision you have made.

> *Good luck and all best wishes.*

With this blessing, Lodge moved swiftly. Up to this point he had told no one of his plans but his wife, Emily, their two young sons, and his old army friend, General Willis Dale Crittenberger. Now he called in his administrative assistant, Maxwell Rabb, to ask Senator D. Worth Clark of Idaho, acting president of the Senate, to stop by. When he did so, Lodge told Clark and Rabb in confidence of his plans. "I'll never forget Clark's expression," Rabb recalls. "He was visibly awed. As a senator he knew what a tremendous job it is to get and keep a seat in the Senate and what a wrench it would be to give all that up voluntarily. After all, nothing like this had ever happened in any of our lifetimes. Cabot told Clark that he would send him a letter to be read to the Senate on Friday morning."

Lodge had seen the President on Tuesday. That Thursday evening, Lodge gravely shook hands with his sons, twelve-year-old George and nine-year-old Harry, and told them to be good while he was gone. He was wearing his major's uniform, but they had seen him go away in uniform so many times over the years that it was no surprise. He had already been out to Walter Reed Hospital to get the necessary shots. Toward midnight Rabb and Emily drove Lodge out to the National Airport just across the river. At the near-deserted field Emily, always brave and gay, gave him a big smile with her good-bye kiss. Cabot boarded an Air Transport Command C-87 transport, with other high-priority passengers bound for the preinvasion centers of England, for the arduous transocean flight to Bermuda first and then, after refueling, to Prestwick, Scotland, and London.

At eleven the next morning in the Senate, after Chaplain Frederick Brown Harris had prayed for the country as "the instrument of Thy providence to free the earth of tyranny," and eighty-nine senators had answered present, Acting President Clark asked the legislative clerk to "read a communication." He read:

Dear Mr. President:

The fact that the United States is entering the period of large scale ground fighting has, after grave thought, brought me to the definite conclusion that, given my age and military training, I must henceforth serve my country as a combat soldier in the Army overseas. In order to serve in combat, I hereby resign from the United States Senate. . . .

> *Henry Cabot Lodge, Jr.*

4   A hush, then a startled murmur met the news. Up rose aging David
Walsh, the senior senator from Massachusetts. He was a Democrat, but
in part he owed his election eighteen years before to the fierce support of
Cabot's Aunt Constance, the elder Senator Lodge's daughter. Now he
spoke his "mingled sentiments of regret and admiration for the high patriotic motives that prompted his decision. . . . Senator Lodge's service in
the Senate has been conspicuous. He has impressed his colleagues with
his unfaltering devotion to his Senatorial duties, and has made a lasting
impression upon the Senate for the readiness with which he has grasped,
as a young Senator, the problems of our day and time. In personality, in
his concept of public service, and in his conscientious devotion to duty, he
typified the highest traditions of New England. . . ."

Another elder statesman, White of Maine, then rose to express "great
regret and something of consternation. Senator Lodge came to this body
with an inherited tradition of public service. In the few short years he has
spent among us he has maintained that high character of service. By his
industry, by his intelligence, by his strict attention to the duties and demands of his office and of the Senate he has earned and commands the
respect of every Member of this body. . . . It means a distinct loss to the
Senate . . . a loss to his state and a loss to the public life of this country."

Senator Brewster of Maine also paid tribute. Only the summer before,
he related, he had flown with Lodge, together with three other senators,
to all the fighting fronts of the world, and was startled by how many of
the active commanders in the field were old friends and military associates
of Lodge. "He was of invaluable aid to the committee," said Brewster, "and
he added a global viewpoint to the knowledge which he had already acquired as a result of years of military service as a reserve officer. . . . [He]
goes out to add luster to a name already distinguished in the annals of
this Chamber and this country."

Now Michigan's gray, owlish Arthur Vandenberg rose slowly to his feet.
From the time Lodge first entered the Senate in January, 1937, Vandenberg
had liked his clean-cut appearance, quick and nimble mind and political
skill. (Years later Vandenberg would write in his diary of Lodge: "He has
more political assets than anyone I know. . . . He is a superb public servant. I fully expect him to be a Republican President of the United States—
and I hope I live long enough to have the chance to help put him in the
White House.") Now Vandenberg simply said, "This contemplation moves
me very deeply because I think it is the disclosure of a great and patriotic
soul at its best. I think it is a challenge to America. It seems to me this
resignation is simply the final and conclusive demonstration of a superb
character and an incorrigible courage." Shortly afterward Vandenberg
jotted down the depth of that day's impression: "In all my twenty years

in the Senate no single episode ever thrilled me so deeply as the quiet   5
drama which saw young Lodge in his usual Senate seat on a late afternoon
in February and the next morning heard his resignation read at the desk
after his overnight departure to the fighting front. No one, including myself, had any idea Cabot planned to quit the Senate and go to War. It was
typical of him. He made no valedictory speech to his colleagues and there
was no band to escort him to the station. He just quit the Senate and went."

Over in London that same day, at the U.S. Navy's preinvasion planning
headquarters in Grosvenor Square, a member of that staff, Lieutenant
Commander John Mason Brown, had just come back from lunch when
he saw some startling news clattering over the office's AP ticker. Brown,
former theater critic for the New York *Post* and gifted essayist, had been
one of Lodge's closest friends since their days at Harvard together. He had
scarcely finished reading what the Senate had just heard when someone
said, "There's an Army major here to see you." He stepped outside and
there was Cabot Lodge, his handsome face beaming in a well-remembered
smile ("Lodge smiles with his whole face," says Brown.)

"My God, Cabot!" Brown cried. "How can you be here when I just this
minute read about you resigning in Washington!" Brown recalled afterward: "I really thought I *was* seeing things."

That evening the two old friends had dinner and a long and garrulous
evening of reminiscing and catching up. A score of years had passed but
it seemed only yesterday, as they recalled it, when the two, clad only in
towels, one lazy summer day, had waved to the old senator on his porch
at Nahant as they walked down for a swim to the natural pool formed by
the sea and rocks below his secluded summer home. "That old house," says
Brown, "always reminded me of a ship putting out to sea."

Around that cavernous, gray clapboard house at East Point, the fabric
of Cabot's early life had been woven.

CHAPTER TWO

These are the men!
The North has given them name,
The children of God who dare . . .
These are the men!
In the strength of the primal song
As the increate world turned white
They descended and dwelt with the sea . . .
These are the men!

—George Cabot Lodge, *The Norsemen*
(Scribner's, 1896)

Sagamore Hill
July 6, 1902

Dear Bay,
We are overjoyed; best wishes for the boy, and warmest congratula-
tions for Bessie and you.

Affectionately yours,
Theodore Roosevelt.

Thus the President of the United States, writing to his young friend George
Cabot Lodge, then twenty-eight, at the Lodge summer home, greeted the
arrival on the day before of "Bay" Lodge's firstborn. The boy was soon
christened Henry Cabot Lodge, Jr., in honor of his grandfather, the senator
who was the President's closest friend and confidant.

Nahant, where the boy was born, is a peninsula, "thrust out into the
open ocean [the senator had observed] with nothing between it and Portugal, all rocks." A single square mile of granite finger jutting southward
from the Essex County shore, "as though," wrote Henry Adams, "directing
the Bostonian homeward," it is fourteen miles from Boston's Hub. Nahant's
own seamost protrusion, East Point, is girded almost completely by jagged
rocks against which the sea thuds and spumes beneath circling gulls crying
a lazy doom. There young Henry Cabot Lodge would spend his happiest
boyhood hours. The first regular sound to meet his ears was the steady
boom and thunder of the nearby sea, and all of his life that memory would
make him eager to be near the sea.

"The earliest and most prized memories of my life," he recalled years
later at Nahant's centenary, "are of Nahant, of its great cliffs and the roar
of the surf beating on the headlands, of its streets lined with elms, and

its houses in so many of which I have been. . . . I think of Castle Rock, Forty Steps Beach, Pulpit Rock and Swallow's Cove. . . . I remember the red light of Egg Rock and the horse-drawn carriages which used to take us from Lynn to Nahant."

When the boy was a year old, Henry Adams came to his first birthday party, and observed, "He looks like Thomas Aquinas." Adams was Bay Lodge's closest friend, and was like a member of the family, since his brother Brooks had married the sister of Senator Lodge's wife. Cabot came to call Henry Adams "Dawdy," after a fictional character the family thought he resembled with his bald head and boundless affection for children.

Cabot's early childhood was as pleasant and sunny as the summer days that seemed to last forever at Nahant. He grew up in an atmosphere of the deepest love. His young father and mother were so lost in love for one another that friends who had seen them on their honeymoon in Paris wrote home rather enviously about it. Bay was a poet, and he addressed his most lyrical poetry to Bessie, his beautiful, black-haired bride:

*She moves in the dusk of my mind, like a bell with the sweetness of
  singing.*
In a twilight of summer fulfilled with the joy of the sadness of tears.
*And the calm of her face, and the splendid slow smile are as memories
  clinging.*
Of songs and of silences filling the distance of passionate years.

Bay was a dashingly handsome man, blue-eyed with light-brown hair. He was always deeply tanned from constant sailing and riding. The second of Senator Lodge's three children, he devoured books as well as languages— he had mastered French, German, Italian—with insatiable scholarship. Yet he was also a lithe-muscled outdoor man. President Roosevelt idolized Bay. He was always eager to read Bay's latest poems, and often took him to his Dakota ranch for shooting and riding. Bay had no interest whatever in business, and cared nothing for the world of power in which his father moved in Washington. His nature, Henry Adams wrote of him, was "as elementary and simple as the salt water."

Young Cabot grew up in an atmosphere of constant intellectual stimulation. Bay and Bessie talked to one another in French almost as often as English. Cabot's Nanny, a Fräulein Schultz, taught the growing boy German. Bessie read to him constantly, and the old senator also would often sit reading sonorously aloud from favorite passages of Shakespeare or the Bible. The whole family was a small community of scholars.

Bay's older sister, Constance—who had called him "Ba-by" as a child and thus given him his nickname—was as sharp-witted, sharp-tongued

8   and opinionated as her friend Alice Roosevelt. She had married Augustus
Peabody Gardner, who now represented the North Shore in Congress, and
who was like another son to the senator. "Gussie" was usually present at
the talkfests. George Abbott James, Henry James' cousin and the husband
of Senator Lodge's elder sister, would drop in, as sometimes would Henry
James himself. The novelist Edith Wharton and her husband Edward were
often there. To young Cabot, this ambiance seemed to blur almost indis-
tinguishably into that which Grandfather Lodge would call up from his
boyhood memories, when his father's visitors at Nahant had included Longfellow and Senator Charles Sumner, and the gentle Louis Agassiz who
would show the boys strange and unknown specimens of sea life washed
up on the rocky shore.

Bay's younger brother, John Ellerton Lodge, could give as well as take
in the family repartee. He was a gifted painter, and many Nahanters remembered his lovely watercolor of Pulpit Rock. He was gifted enough at
music to set Aeschylus' *Agamemnon* to music and see it produced at Harvard Stadium. He mastered thirty-three languages, including Sanskrit, and
grew so expert in oriental art that he was made curator of the Japanese-
Chinese collection at the Boston Art Museum. Uncle John, as Cabot
came to know him, had a marvelous ironic wit. When there was a dispute
over whether the Boston Art Museum or Gussie's aunt, Mrs. Jack Gardner,
owned the genuine portrait of Philip IV by Velasquez, John, studying one
of the portraits, observed: "Just look at the expression on the dog's face,
how much more intelligent it is than Philip IV's. Of course, Velasquez did
that intentionally. He was taking his revenge for having to paint such
stupid people. Now Philip is remembered only because Velasquez painted
him." Once John and Bay spent a whole summer studying Egyptology together. They were also fond of disputing fine points of Buddhism with
Senator Lodge's classmate and lifelong close friend, Dr. William Sturgis
Bigelow, great-bearded and totally bald, who always shared their summers.*

The family liked nothing better than to spend long evenings reading to
one another from favorite books or disputing over the latest literary or dramatic works. Senator Lodge's pride and joy was his classical library of some
eighteen thousand beautifully bound books, some of which had come down
from his great-grandfather Senator George Cabot of Massachusetts, from

* Bigelow's beautiful house at 56 Beacon Street was always Boston headquarters for
the Lodge family. He had lived sixteen years in Japan, became a great friend of the
Mikado, who decorated him, and became a convert to Buddhism and a Buddhist priest.
He acquired the finest collection of Japanese art outside of Japan, and gave it to John
Ellerton Lodge's care at the Boston Museum of Fine Arts. After Dr. Bigelow died, and
Bishop William Lawrence conducted an Episcopalian service for him in Boston, his
ashes were taken to Kyoto on a Japanese cruiser and solemnly buried in the Buddhist
cemetery there.

Grandfather Henry Cabot, from paternal grandfather Giles Lodge, as well as from his wife Nannie's father, Admiral Charles Henry Davis, an outstanding scholar and scientist. The library completely dominated the senator's Washington home at 1765 Massachusetts Avenue (where the Brookings Institution now stands).

To this house, President Roosevelt came frequently, slipping in and out of the inconspicuous side entrance built especially for him. "Go to Senator Lodge and talk with him," Alice Roosevelt remembered her father telling a foreign diplomat. "There is no one who knows my mind better or whom I trust more." When young Quentin Roosevelt tried to keep a favorite White House policeman from being transferred, and the officer told him it would be impossible, Quentin piped: "I'm going to see Lodge. That's what Father tells everybody when he wants to have anything done."

The President consulted Lodge on most of his important decisions. In a letter from Oyster Bay hailing Cabot's birth, the President also discussed the senator's advocacy of Oliver Wendell Holmes for the Supreme Court. "Now as to Holmes," said Roosevelt, "the labor decisions which have been criticized by some of the big railroad men and other members of large corporations constitute to my mind a strong point in his favor. The ablest lawyers and greatest judges are men whose past has naturally brought them into close relationship with the wealthiest and most powerful clients, and I am glad when I can find a judge who has been able to preserve this aloofness of mind so as to keep his broad humanity of feeling and his sympathy for the class from which he has not drawn his clients." Lodge advocated Holmes for the same reason. Though a modestly rich man himself (his estate eventually totaled $1,200,000), he was no toady to business nor a worshipper of money for its own sake. He wrote savage indictments of the corrupting influence and misuse of great wealth, and advised his sons and grandson to judge people by their character and not by their wealth or ancestry. He told them what Grandfather Henry Cabot had told him: "My boy, we do not talk about family in this country. It is enough for you to know that your grandfather is an honest man."

Young Cabot's life was a familiar cycle of summers at Nahant, and winters back in Washington. After Cabot's birth, Bay and Bessie moved into a home of their own at Nahant, a square two-story stucco affair called "The Villa," by the rocky cliff leading down to Forty Steps Beach. He very early learned to swim, taking lessons from a muscular young man named Emerson, and almost as quickly learned to sail. He was soon joined in this by his brother John, who was born fifteen months after him.

At Nahant, life seemed endlessly warm and wonderful. It was still entirely a summer colony then, of clapboard or shingled unheated homes. They had many friends and playmates—Mallie Greenough, who would

10   become Cabot's lifelong confidant, Harrison Gray Otis, Jimmy Newell, Jimmy Bangs, Willis Beal, Alfred Codman, Pelham Curtis, Francis Gray. Their favorite sport was swimming naked at Cupid Rock, at the head of a deep inlet whence women had been barred as far back as any Nahanter's memory ran, and where males from six to sixty splashed in the raw.

Each boy had his own dory. They sailed up and down the whole relatively calm and sandy beach which Nahant's protrusion forms along the shore from Lynn to Marblehead, some four miles distant. At Marblehead the shore turns sharply westward into the great natural harbor formed by Salem and Beverly just beyond, circling eastward again to the great fishing port of Gloucester. The whole area abounds in islands with such beckoning names as Egg Rock, Great Misery, Little Misery, Little Haste and Great Haste, Great Gooseberry and Little Gooseberry, Cat Island, Eagle Island— all this enough to make any venturesome lad imagine himself Captain Kidd or the great Bluebeard himself. They sometimes searched for buried treasure, since legend persisted that Kidd had buried it along this coast. Failing to find it, they sometimes hid treasures of their own, to dig up later.

When the summer was over, family life centered in a rented house at 1925 F Street (where John was born, in what is now the ladies' room of the 1925 F Street Club) while the senator was building a handsome new three-story stone residence for his son at 2346 Massachusetts Avenue, just off du Pont Circle and not far from his own. Their last child and only daughter, Helena, was born July 8, 1905, at Southwest Harbor, Maine, where the family spent that summer.

Christmas was the most memorable time of those Washington winters. Henry Adams—"Dawdy"—would come, looking rather like a rotund elf as he helped hang their tree with ornaments and light the old-fashioned wax candles, clamped to the branches in their small metal holders. There was much gaiety and laughter.

On Christmas day itself, there was a family ritual, faithfully followed each year. All would gather at the old senator's house. Theodore and his wife Edith would come, often with some of their own family. President Roosevelt sat at one end of the table, carving roast pig, and Senator Lodge at the other, carving turkey, their wives among the children and relatives in between.

Senator Lodge would commence this ritual by reading Charles Lamb's essay, "The Origin of Roast Pig." The President would say grace. When the feasters could feast no more they moved into the great library, whose high walls were lined with books from floor to ceiling. There they basked before a roaring log fire, the senator sitting in a high armchair on the left, the President in another on the right.

Admiral Harry Davis, Nannie Lodge's brother, would usually be there. An

old seadog, like his admiral father, he had a seaman's clear blue eye, a   **11**
New England twang and a dry Yankee sense of humor. He had a pet name,
Daisy, for his sister Evelyn who had married Brooks Adams. After the
ceremony Brooks came over to Admiral Davis and told him:

"Harry, my wife's name is Evelyn, and hereafter I want you to stop calling her Daisy."

Uncle Harry thought this over, then took out his pipe and said, "My dear
Brooks, I cannot change the habits of a lifetime at the bidding of a com-
parative stranger."

When Uncle Harry's pipe was all but buried in his thick beard, to Cabot
and John the beard seemed to be smoking by itself. One Christmas afternoon he sat there by the fire, with smoke rising from his beard, and after
a long silence suddenly exclaimed:

"Pinky"—his name for Senator Lodge—"Pinky, Napoleon was a Frenchman."

Senator Lodge was outraged at such ignorance. "Why, Harry," he cried,
"you know very well Napoleon was a Corsican."

The talk passed on to other things and Uncle Harry seemed to doze.
Suddenly, he pointed his pipe firmly at Roosevelt and said, "Theodore,
Napoleon was a Frenchman." Grandpa Lodge leaped to his feet. "Don't be
an ass, Harry," he said, "everyone knows Napoleon was a Corsican." Lodge
and Roosevelt scurried around to find the books to show Uncle Harry he
was wrong, but the old seadog never cracked a smile.

Senator Lodge's home was an intellectual center of Washington, orbiting
in turn about that of Henry Adams. Adams' wife, whom he loved deeply,
had killed herself in a fit of melancholy by drinking poison in 1885 (his
monument to her in Rock Creek Park is one of Washington's loveliest
sights). He did not entertain formally after that, but his home at 1603
H Street was the heart of Washington's intellectual life. Just around the
corner from his house was the palatial new home at Sixteenth and H of
John Hay, Lincoln's secretary who had become Secretary of State for
McKinley and Roosevelt. "Theirs were almost the only houses," Edith
Wharton wrote, "where one breathed a cosmopolitan air, and where such
men as Sir Cecil Spring-Rice [later the British Ambassador], J. J. Jusserand
[the French Ambassador], and Lord Bryce [also British Ambassador] felt
themselves immediately at home. . . . My pleasantest hours in Washington were spent at their houses."

It was in this stimulating atmosphere that young Henry Cabot Lodge
began cutting his intellectual teeth. Adams, Bay's closest confidant, was
as often at their home as they were at his. Cabot roved at will from Adams'
house to that of John Hay, whose grandchildren, Jerry and Eva Wadsworth,
were his playmates.

12   One day the whole Lodge family went to the White House for dinner. Cabot's sister Helena stared about her with pleasure and exclaimed: "I like this hotel! I'm going to come here again." As for Cabot, he was most impressed by the President's military aide, Colonel Frank R. McCoy, a former Rough Rider whom Teddy had called "the finest soldier in the U.S. Army." The Colonel became at once Lodge's hero, the man he wanted to be.

It was impossible for anyone, even youngsters, to be around Henry Adams without absorbing a liberal education. "He has one of the most remarkable minds I have ever known," Senator Lodge observed. "He knows everything, historically and artistically." The boys were devoted to him. "He is queer to the last degree," Cecil Spring-Rice wrote of him; "cynical, vindictive, but with a constant interest in people, faithful to his friends and passionately fond of his mother and of all little children ever born; even puppies." (Adams, in turn, found Spring-Rice "mad of course but not more mad than an Englishman should be.")

By the time the Japanese cherry trees were in bloom, the boys began to look forward to the annual hegira to Nahant, where the senator would come up weekends until the Senate adjourned. The trip was sometimes arduous, on the unpredictable New Haven. The cars had to be ferried across New York Harbor, and on one crossing in 1909, when Cabot was nearly seven, fog made this alone a seven-hour event. Bay was carrying not only a manuscript by Henry Adams, but his own ambitious dramatic poem, *Herakles,* on which he had toiled long, endless nights. He had the three children, Fräulein Schultz, and their nurse as well. He wrote his mother, Nannie, an agonized account of the journey.

Instead of attaching a diner, the New Haven gave its suffering passengers fifteen minutes for refreshments at New Haven. "There, at ten o'clock, in the heartbreaking dingy dreadfulness of the waiting room, we thronged four deep round a vastly rectangular barrier like a shop counter, girdled, for the public, by high, greasy 'fixed' stools, covered with inedible pseudo-foods under fly-blown glass bells, and defended, so to speak, by an insufficient and driven horde of waiters and waitresses. . . . Fräulein and the nurse secured, by prodigious exertions, and wonderfully drank, cups of a dim grey fluid which they believed to be coffee, while I and the children got back to the train with some apples, oranges and sinister sandwiches, which all, later, and with every accompanying degradation of drip and slop and grease, all mixed with car dirt, we did devour—to avoid starvation."

It was a nightmare journey, climaxed by temporarily losing his bags after the arrival in Boston—bags containing both his and Adams' manuscripts—and finally, at the end of the journey in Nahant, by the further discovery that "they had given me, for the nurse's bag, the bag of a total stranger. In the nurse's bag beside her own effects, were some of Helena's, including a silver mug; and so as I lay, at last, in my own bath, I heard, 13 strangely concordant with the whole horrible day's experience, Fräulein and Hedwig moaning, in shrill German, the loss. So Monday I go to town to do some errands, to find if possible the damned bag. The children are none the worse for the journey and are already benefited by the good air."

Only a few weeks later Bay was dead, and Cabot lost his handsome, romantic father at so early an age that later it was a common mistake for people to assume that he was the son, not the grandson of the old senator. Cabot would always remember his father as at once a poet and a rebel (so Henry Adams thought) who could not locate the enemy. His appealing and magnetic figure—now rather blurred by time—deserves to be better known.

Bay Lodge was like some child of nature, a throwback to those Norman sailors named Cabot who, from the Isle of Jersey, for centuries had roved all seas. Adams termed him a "Norse faun," like those Norsemen of his poem. It is Adams who has written most understandingly of his young friend:

"Throughout life, the more widely his character spread in circumference, the more simply he thought, and even when trying to grow complex—as was inevitable since it was to grow in Boston—the mind itself was never complex, and the complexities merely gathered on it, as something outside, like the seaweeds gathering and swaying about the rocks. Robust in figure, healthy in appetite, careless of consequences, he could feel complex and introspective only as his ideal, the Norse faun, might feel astonished and angry at finding nature perverse and unintelligible in a tropical jungle. Since nature could not be immoral or futile, the immorality and futility must be in the mind that conceived it. Man became an outrage—society an artificial device for the distortion of truth—civilization a wrong. Many millions of simple natures have thought, and still think, the same thing, and the more complex have never quite made up their minds whether to agree with them or not; but the thought that was sufficient for the Norseman exploring the tropics, or for an exuberant young savage sailing his boat off the rude shores of Gloucester and Cape Ann, could not long survive the atmosphere of State Street. . . .

"The gap between the poet and the citizen was so wide as to be impassable in Boston, but it was not a division of society into hostile camps, as it had been in England with Shelley and Keats, or in Boston itself, a half-century before, with the anti-slavery outbursts of Emerson and Whittier, Longfellow and Lowell, which shook the foundations of the state. The Bostonian of 1900 differed from his parents and grandparents of 1850, in owning nothing the value of which, in the market could be affected by the poet. Indeed, to him, the poet's pose of hostility to actual conditions of

14 society was itself mercantile—a form of drama—a thing to sell, rather than a serious revolt. Society could safely adopt it as a form of industry, as it adopted other forms of bookmaking. . . . Society was not disposed to defend itself from criticism or attack. Indeed, the most fatal part of the situation for the poet in revolt, the paralyzing drug that made him helpless, was that society no longer seemed sincerely to believe in itself or anything else; it resented nothing, not even praise. The young poet grew up without being able to find an enemy. . . ."

At Harvard, Bay Lodge, learning French with that aptitude his whole clan shows for languages, was drawn to French literature and thought. "I have been reading an immense quantity from variegated authors, Balzac especially," he wrote to his mother when he was twenty-one, "also Flaubert, Alfred de Vigny, Leconte de Lisle, and Musset, Hugo and Renan. . . . Next time French literature is discussed ask them what living poet equals Sully Prudhomme." He began trying to perfect his own verse, offered "three efforts in a more lyrical strain. I find it rather a relief to be less trammeled, and unfettered to so concrete and absolute a form as the Petrarchan sonnet,—which is the only kind I write now. I have been looking over the few sonnets Shelley wrote. He had no form at all in them. . . . 'Ozymandias' . . . [has] no structure at all. Yet of course we know that the whole, as read, is superb. . . . Still I do think, other things being equal the Petrarchan form adds a dignity and beauty to a sonnet which no other form possesses. . . ." In his last college year he wrote, "I do so want to do something that will last. . . . I am never satisfied with what I do," and went off to seek perfection in Paris, then soon found himself torn by doubts and indecision: "The thing which tore me worst . . . was the continual thought of money and my crying inability to adapt myself to my time and become a money-maker. . . . I said to myself that I ought to go home in order to get into the tide of American life if for nothing else: that I oughtn't to be dreaming and shrieking inside and poetizing and laboring on literature here in Paris, supported by my father, and that I ought to go home and live very hard making money. I said to myself that I knew I could not be very quick at money-making, but that at any rate in the eyes of men I should lead a self-respecting life."

He conquered his despair and stayed another year, burrowing deep into Romance philology, Spanish and Italian, riding horses in the Bois for exercise. He wrote of pondering "a copy-book commonplace which is at the same time a metaphysical profundity, viz., that the present is all that *is* and it is not. . . . While you are uttering 'now', it is fled—it never existed. . . . And the past—that's the cruel thing, the killing memories. Memories of yesterday, of the moment just fled, which are as hopelessly dead, as impossibly distant as memories of ten years gone. The past is like a great

pit, and the present like a frittered edge which is continually crumbling   *15*
and falling utterly down into the pit. . . . I have a more vivid memory of
Sister with long hair, driving old Rab up the side-walk by the Gibsons' at
Nahant, on a gray autumn day, than of most things happened within the
year. And my memories are all sad—sad with an infinite hopeless regret;
that one of Sister for example has almost made me cry. And then the present is the past so facilely, so quickly, and I find myself sometimes when
I am not doing anything—talking perhaps or sitting idle or even reading,
in fact *un peu toujours*—suddenly turning sick and cold and saying to myself, 'See, your life goes, goes, goes. Every day you get more memories to
dwell about you like mourning creatures, and still nothing done—with your
youth, your strength, and every minute the memories thickening and the
pain of them increasing, and still nothing done. Man! Man! Your life is
very short, already twenty and two years: as many again, and you will be
hardened into your mould, and the mould yet unmade! Up, up and do
something! . . . And then did it ever occur to you that the present is like
a piece of paper on which experience writes in invisible ink, and that only
when the heat of the pain of memory and regret blows upon it, do the
characters come out and do you know how intensely alive, how happy, or
at any rate how miserable, or at least how unbored you *had been*.

"It seems to me all the happiness (except, of course, physical) which
we get is only the more or less incomplete suggestion or partial realization
of some remembered happiness. For instance, the slant of the western sun
through green leaves sometimes brings back one perfectly unimportant
afternoon when I was very small, and Sister sat on the grass under those
willows, behind the little toolhouse in front of Mr. Locke's, and read a story
aloud to me. She left off in the middle, and I can distinctly remember the
last words she said. Now when I can get a vivid suggestion of something
intensely happy in my memory, infinitely richer and more happy than I
had any idea of when it occurred, it makes me more happy than anything.
Happiness is a continual thinking backward or forward, memory or expectation."

Coming home in 1896, he went to Newport for a few days in August
and found himself in rebellion against all its standards. "I hate the philis-
tine-plutocrat atmosphere of this place, and it tends not to diminish my
views anent modern civilization and the money power. I sincerely thank
God I shall never be a rich man, and never will I, if my strength holds. . . .
If I haven't it in me to write a poem, what a sordid farce my life will be!"
He went off to punish himself with a year of spartan, dogged studying in
Berlin. "All my news is contained in the word work. Nearer ten hours than
eight of this have I done every day—written translations from German,
reading of German grammar, reading Schiller . . . talking, going to the

16 theater,—'Faust', 'The Winter's tale', very good, and a translation of the 'Dindon' etc. . . . It's wonderful how the soul clears itself up in this sort of solitude in which I am living. . . . I have acquired the ability to write over poetry and work it into shape, which is a great step forward. . . . I have never worked harder or lived more utterly simply. . . ."

In the spring of 1898 he felt ready to publish his first poems, a 135-page volume called *The Song Of the Wave*. One sonnet, "To Essex," sang of the haunts of home. It begins,

> *Thy hills are kneeling in the tardy spring*

and finds its echo in the last verse:

> *We know how wanton and how little worth*
> *Are all the passions of our bleeding heart*
> *That vex the awful patience of the earth.*

The book was well received. Bay Lodge undoubtedly had poetic talent. His greatest gift, however, to all who knew him, was in the total effect of his being, his enormous vitality and love of life which had a hypnotic effect upon everyone who met him. Edith Wharton was impressed from the moment she first saw him in Washington. She early drew Bay into her own circle of intimates who often gathered at her famed retreat, The Mount, at Lenox, Massachusetts, for disputations long into the night. Henry James was often there.

" 'Abundance', that is the word which comes to me whenever I try to describe him," Mrs. Wharton wrote of Bay. "During the 12 years of our friendship,—and from the day it began—I had, whenever we were together, the sense of his being a creature as profusely as he was finely endowed. There was an exceptional delicacy in his abundance, and an extraordinary volume in his delicacy.

"All this, on the day when he was first brought to see me,—a spring afternoon of the year 1898, in Washington—was lit up by a beautiful boyish freshness, which as the years passed, somehow contrived to ripen without fading. In the first five minutes of our talk, he *gave* himself with the characteristic wholeness that made him so rare a friend; showing me all the sides of his varied nature; the grave sense of beauty, the flashing contempt of meanness, and that large spring of kindly laughter that comes to many only as a result of the long tolerance of life. It was one of his gifts thus to brush aside the preliminaries of acquaintance, and enter at once, with a kind of royal ease, on the rights and privileges of friendship; as though—one might think—with a foreboding of the short time given him to enjoy them.

Chapter Two

". . . Then and to the end he lived every moment to the full, and the first impression he made was of a joyous physical life. His sweet smile, his easy strength, his deep eyes full of laughter and visions,—these struck one even before his look of intellectual power. I have seldom seen anyone in whom the natural man was so wholesomely blent, with the reflecting intelligence; and it was not the least of his charms that he sent such stout roots into the earth, and had such a hearty love for all he drew from it. Nothing was common or unclean to him but the vulgar, the base, and the insincere, and his youthful impatience at the littleness of human nature was tempered by an unusually mature sense of its humors.

"One is accustomed in enjoying the comradeship of young minds, to allow in them for a measure of passing egotism, often the more marked in proportion to their sensitiveness to impressions; but it was Cabot Lodge's special grace to possess the sensitiveness without the egotism."

Cecil Spring-Rice, who had known Bay well when he was Secretary of the British Embassy in Washington, and later during his year in Berlin, got the same deep impression:

"We bathed together [at Nahant] and I remember so well the immense joy he had in jumping into the water, and then lying out in the sun till he was all browned—as strong and healthy a creature as I have ever seen, and exulting in his life. Then we rode together at Washington and I can see him now galloping along in the woody country near Rock Creek.

"It wasn't until I saw a good deal of him in Berlin that I realized what a rare and extraordinary mind he had. He was then studying hard at philosophy. In an extraordinarily quick time he learnt German and seemed to take naturally to the most difficult books—just as he had done to the sea without any conscious effort. . . . I am quite sure with him there was no object except just the attainment and the presence of truth. . . . I never knew anyone so 'detached,' deaf to the usual voices of the world; and so determined to live in the light of Truth, taking nothing for granted till he had proved it by his own original thought. . . . I think he was the sort of stuff that in the middle ages would have been a great saint or a great heresiarch—I dare say we have no use for such people now."

Bay's first book of poems appeared just as the Spanish-American War began. The war gave him the opportunity to have, for the first time, a sense of meaningful action.

He was acutely conscious of the strong weight of naval tradition on his family—from the first George Cabot whose Essex privateers were the scourge of British sail, down through the graceful Yankee clippers of those China traders, the Lodges. He felt the tradition equally through his mother, Anna Cabot Mills Davis Lodge, whose father, Charles Henry Davis, was one of the most distinguished and revered officers ever to serve in the

18   U.S. Navy. Davis made the first geodetic survey of America's Atlantic coast, wrote learned treatises on its tides, knew the whole coast so well that it was he, under the command of Admiral Du Pont, who planned the Union capture of Port Royal, South Carolina. He was in command of the Union gunboats which defeated a Confederate flotilla at the Battle of Fort Pillow, on the Mississippi, and when this victory left Memphis with no alternative, went ashore to accept its surrender from the mayor. Davis, who became a rear admiral, was chosen to be a member of the special honor guard to accompany Lincoln's body from Washington to Springfield.

As the Spanish-American War began, the admiral's son, Captain Harry Davis, was in command of the U.S.S. *Dixie,* a passenger ship converted to an armed raider when war broke out. Up to this time Bay Lodge had been working in Washington as secretary to his father. Now he signed on the *Dixie* as a cadet, eager for action.

"We came down and on our way destroyed two blockhouses which were at the southern end of the Trochoa," he wrote his mother Nannie on June 25 off Cienfuegos, Cuba. "The next day we engaged a battery at a place called Trinidad, and yesterday we engaged the same battery, a gunboat in the harbor, and a gunboat that came out to us, and used them up pretty badly. So you see I am in it. Nothing very serious so far, but we still have been under fire and have killed a good many Spaniards."

"We came up from Cape Cruz on the 6th," he wrote in August, "and saw the wrecks of the Spanish fleet lying up on the beach below Santiago—a great sight. . . . I am very glad on the whole I came as a cadet and not as an ensign for as a cadet I am not supposed to know anything, which puts me in a true position and not in a false one. None of these militia officers know any more than I do, and they are in a false position. . . ."

The *Dixie,* together with the *Annapolis* and *Wasp,* with Captain Davis in charge, escorted the troop landings in Puerto Rico. Cadet Lodge went in under a flag of truce to demand the surrender of Ponce, then Puerto Rico's biggest town (forty thousand population). "We found that there was a Spanish colonel with about 300 men, who said he would 'die at his post.' He was back in the town, which is about two miles inland. However, during the night delegates came off and surrendered the town, on condition that the troops be allowed to withdraw, which we granted, and at six o'clock the next morning we went in again and I myself raised the flag over the office of the Captain of the Port, amid immense enthusiasm of the population. . . . The town had been deserted fearing a bombardment, and from every nook and corner crowds appeared cheering and crying, 'Viva los conquistadores Americanos'; 'Viva el Puerto Rico libre.' . . . The army, though supposed to be in possession of the town, had not taken the City Hall. . . . I got an American flag and went onto the roof, where the flagstaff was, taking with me the Mayor of Ponce. There with great solemnity, the Mayor and I bare-headed, I raised the flag. The whole square was swaying with people, and as the flag went up they cheered—such a noise as I never heard. . . . Then the Mayor and I went below and the Mayor presented me with his staff of office, the Spanish flag which flew over the City Hall, and the banner of Ponce, and formally delivered over to me his authority. . . . I then with great ceremony, gave back to the Mayor his badge of office and the town of Ponce."

Cadet Lodge proved to be a first-class sea warrior. "He shows unbounded zeal and unflagging industry," Captain Davis wrote to brother-in-law Senator Lodge, "and a great aptitude for the profession. He has already developed the real sailor's trick of being always the first on hand. No one has ever been known to say, 'Where is Mr. Lodge?' This is not the encomium of a fond uncle. I see very little of him on duty except in working ship, when his station is near mine. He is a daily companion to me in hours of leisure, but on duty he is the First Lieutenant's (Merriam) man, and I notice he is always called on for duty where promptness and intelligence are required. I could give you a much higher estimate of his usefulness if I quoted Merriam, than in recording my own observation."

On August 8, 1900, Bay was married to Elizabeth Davis, one of the loveliest belles of Washington society. Her grandfather, New Jersey's Senator Frederick Theodore Frelinghuysen, had been President Arthur's Secretary of State; her father, John Davis, was a brilliant lawyer who became judge of the U.S. Court of Claims at twenty-eight (his portrait adorns the dining room of Washington's Metropolitan Club, of which he was president). She was, Henry Adams noted, "another survival of rare American stock: Davis of Plymouth, Frelinghuysen of New Jersey, Griswold of Connecticut, with the usual leash of Senators, Cabinet officers and other such ornaments, in her ancestry." Despite these credentials, she cared no more than did Bay for the vanities and preenings of society, "greasy gossip [as he wrote her] of this world of little motives and little desires."

They showed their contempt for this world, when invitations for a formal wedding had been sent out and wedding presents were already arriving, by simply eloping, getting married at Boston's First Church of the Advent with none but the required witnesses present, then skipping off on their honeymoon to Tuckanuck, the island retreat of that boon family friend William Sturgis Bigelow, then off to Paris, for nearly a year, the following January. Elizabeth Sherman Cameron, beautiful niece of General Sherman and widow of General Grant's Secretary of War, caught up with them in Paris and wrote Bessie's maiden aunt, Lucy Frelinghuysen, of this "mad young couple." "Bessie," she wrote, "was lovely. There is something luminous, gay, fawn-like shining in her eyes. . . . Bay is in adoration be-

20 fore her, of course. And really, Lucy, when I see their youth and love and enjoyment of things, I forgive—and envy—their folly. Was there ever anything like it? Everyone shakes their head over them—but dear me! I came away so impressed that I believe it is they who are wise to live and love and enjoy without a thought of that awful tomorrow. Neither you nor I have ever tasted what they are now living on—don't you regret it?" Henry Adams gave them his apartment by the Etoile, and his manservant, for an idyllic summer. They came home in August to take up a familiar cycle of winters in Washington and summers at Nahant, where Cabot was born the following summer.

The years sped and Bay's small family grew. Each passing year seemed to oppress him anew with his sense of losing time in writing a lasting work which would measure up to his own demanding sense of excellence. He brought out a book-length poetic drama, *Cain,* and pressed on into a still more ambitious and serious one, a Promethean drama called *Herakles.*

"His most marked trait of mind," Henry Adams noted, "lay in his instinctive love of logic, which he was probably not even aware of, although often—as is seen everywhere in *Cain* and *Herakles*—the reasoning is as close and continuous as it might be in Plato or Schopenhauer." In the twelfth and last scene of the latter, Herakles has, by self-sacrifice, "made himself—and the whole of humanity within him—one with the infinite will which causes and maintains the universe. He has submitted to God by merging himself in God: he has, by his so-called labors, or miracles, raised humanity to the divine level."

> *I drew the Hound of Hell, the ravening Death*
> *Into the light of life, and held him forth*
> *Where the soul's Sun shed lightnings in his eye*
> *And he was like a thing of little meaning,*
> *Powerless and vain and nowise terrible . . .*
> *Yea, I have brought into the soul's dominion*
> *All that I am!—and in the Master's House*
> *There is no strength of all my mortal being*
> *That does not serve him now: there is no aim,*
> *There is no secret which he does not know:*
> *There is no will save one, which is the Lord's!*

Besides logic, Adams noted, Bay loved a good paradox and liked to chase it into its burrow. "When you are accustomed to anything, you are estranged from it"; and his supreme gift for liking was never to get accustomed to things or people. By way of a historical paradox he maintained that the Church was devised as a protection against the direct rays of

Christ's spirit, which, undimmed, would compel to action and change of character. By way of a poetical paradox he loved Walt Whitman to fanaticism, and quoted his favorite description of the world, Walt's "little plentiful mannikins skipping about in collars and tailcoats." Yet he sometimes declared that his favorite line in poetry was Swinburne's—

> *Out of the golden remote wild west where the sea*
> *without shore is*
> *Full of the sunset, and sad, if at all, with the*
> *fullness of joy.*

Perhaps, if he had chosen a verse of poetry to suggest his own nature, he might have found it in another line of Swinburne's:

> *Some dim derision of mysterious laughter.*

When Bay Lodge delivered his poem "The Soul's Inheritance" before the Phi Beta Kappa Society at Cambridge in 1906, Henry Adams felt that he had discovered "a new power that would probably have led him in time into a new field, where he could put himself in closer relations with the world. His delivery was good, his voice admirable, and his power over his audience was evident." He showed new growth and strength in his poem "The Pilgrims," delivered that same December to the annual dinner of the New England Society in New York, containing "three sonnets as beautiful as any he ever wrote."

Yet, for all his magnificent physique, Bay's heart, which he had tormented in so many punishing, night-long vigils of the most intense creation, was tiring. That August of 1909 he went to Tuckanuck Island with his father for a quiet, lazy rest at Bigelow's place: "I read a good deal and take my swim, and an occasional sail . . . life flows evenly and quietly and cheerfully." He was seized at night, on August 19, by violent indigestion, believed due to his eating a bad clam. He was up all night, but felt better in the morning and got some sleep. His father passed the time reading aloud to him. By nine that night the pains returned and he was racked by waves of nausea. Senator Lodge, now thoroughly alarmed, crossed the island and telephoned to Nantucket for a doctor, then rushed back to his son. When the doctor arrived in the morning, he gave Bay nitroglycerin and digitalis. After lunch, another doctor arrived. Bay's condition had become critical. Lodge again went to Nantucket, to wire his wife, Nannie, to come. When he got back he had been without sleep thirty-six hours and the doctor ordered him to rest. He lay down in his room. Suddenly the doctor called out. The senator rushed into the parlor. "There is a sudden

22 failure," said the doctor. Lodge held Bay's head in his arms. "Is he going?" he asked desperately as the doctor gave Bay a powerful injection and held a stethoscope to his chest. "He is gone," the doctor said. Lodge wrote to his friend and host Bigelow: "So he died. Perfectly quietly, without a gasp or a struggle, in my arms, sitting in your big chair in the parlor by the dining table. So he died in my arms. You will know the lonely agony of that moment for me. I cannot write of it even without wanting to cry out as I did then." Bay was only thirty-five. Like many of his young poet friends, he had died early. Harvard's philosopher George Santayana went so far as to suggest that all had been destroyed "by lack of air to breathe" in a materialist society.

A two-volume collection of all Bay's work was published by Houghton Mifflin after his death. Theodore Roosevelt wrote this introduction:

Of all the men with whom I have been intimately thrown, he was the one man to whom I would apply the rare name of genius. He was an extraordinary student and scholar: he walked forever through the arch of past experience of all the great minds of the ages. Any language which he cared to study was his, and he studied every language which held anything he wished. I have never met another man with so thorough and intimate a knowledge of so many great literatures. . . . He was more than a Book-man. He loved his friends, he loved the life of human interest, and the throbbing pulse-beat of cities. He loved also the breath of the open; and he knew the joy which comes in the strife of hardy adventure. As a boy and young man he was a bold and good rider; he was equally at home hunting alone on the vast Western plains, and, also alone, wild fowl shooting in the dangerous winter seas off the New England coast. His combination of idealism and bodily prowess made it inevitable that he should strain every nerve to get into the Spanish War. . . . He belonged to the gallant brotherhood of men who have written and fought, the brotherhood whose foremost figures number, among many, many others, Cervantes at Lepanto, Sydney in the Low Countries, Koerner, the man of sword and song . . .

Henry Adams wrote Bay's mother that "Bay was my last tie to active sympathy with men. He was the best and finest product of my time and hopes." Adams noted that Bay's sonnets "The Pilgrims" did not appear in print until after his death, "as though he had intended them for his epitaph: and perhaps he did."

They are gone . . . They have all left us, one by one;
Swiftly, with undissuadable strong tread,

Cuirassed in song, with wisdom helmeted,
They are gone before us, into the dark, alone . . .
Upward their wings rushed radiant to the sun:
Seaward the ships of their emprise are sped;
Onward their starlight of desire is shed;
Their trumpet call is forward;—they are gone!
Let us take thought and go!—we know not why
Nor whence nor where,—let us take wings and fly!
Let us take ship and sail, take heart and dare!
Let us deserve at last, as they have done,
To say of all men living and dead who share
The soul's supreme adventure,—"We are gone!"

Bay was cremated, as he had wished. He had loved Keats' "Ode on a Grecian Urn." On a clear summer day, by East Point's thudding spume, Bessie Lodge entered a rowboat by Forty Steps Beach, and John Ellerton Lodge rowed her well out into the open water. There she took the lovely Grecian urn which she had closely held, and, as Bay had wished, consigned it and his mortal ashes gently to the sea.

CHAPTER THREE

Work at your lessons & learn all you can. It is not so important what you learn as that you should work at your task, whatever it is. Whatever you try to do—do it with all your might & do your best.

So wrote the elder Henry Cabot Lodge to his namesake and grandson when Cabot was ten. With the father's death, the grandfather would become more and more tutor, preceptor and guide to young Cabot, almost as if a generation had not intervened and one was literally the other's successor. Uncle John also was a never-failing counselor.

In the early years it was Bessie Lodge who shaped and taught him most. Indeed her influence extended strongly throughout Lodge's life. "Mother told us in a gentle and lovely way that Father was gone," Cabot's brother John recalls. "I remember a tremendous feeling of desolation and bursting into tears. Mother was very brave. She faced up to all tribulations with complete courage. I never knew her to indulge in self-pity."

Bessie had wired the dread news to all their old friends—to the Roosevelts, who were in Paris, to dear old "Dawdy," Henry Adams, to Mrs. Wharton and to Henry James. Adams learned of the telegram on his arrival at his good friend Mrs. Cameron's house on Lake Thun, and turned back at once to Paris to find what had happened. "I could only seek Mrs. Roosevelt and Mrs. Wharton who could tell me nothing but the fact of the telegrams," he wrote Bessie from Paris on August 29, knowing only that Bay was dead. He was overwhelmed by memories of his own wife's tragic death: "Your miseries so acutely recall my own, of times that I shudder to remember, as to make me afraid to write at all. . . . You have been so much to me—so kind and sympathetic in these last, difficult years of growing age,—and I am so grateful to you for the gleams of sunshine you have brought that, if it were not for the recollections of my own craving for assurance of affection in my old sense of abandonment, I should feel as though you must know it all, and would want only to be left alone, to bear your own troubles as you could. But if you are like me, as I remember how my mind went to pieces under the shock, you will turn from one mood to another without rest, and will want affection at one moment as violently as you want solitude at the next. You will want to talk about Bay, and to listen to our assurances of love and admiration for him . . . you know that he had no greater admirer than I, but at the moment I am thinking most of you and of your constant goodness to me, and whether I have any means of returning it. He had all that was worth having in life, since he had you and his genius besides . . . When I think how intensely he must have enjoyed life at its best moments, I envy him with all my heart, but always I think of you as the most exquisite part of it, and of the children as your gift . . ."

After Bessie wrote Adams a full account of the tragedy, he wrote a much longer letter on September 27, saying he had forwarded her other letter, to Mrs. Cameron (his constant companion), on to Marienbad. "You know, without having to be told of it, how much you are in our thoughts, yet I remember well how hard I found it to feel that I was not alone, and how eagerly I wanted to be constantly assured that everybody was suffering or had suffered some such irreparable loss as made them understand what you are feeling." Adams then launched into a remarkable discussion of grief, reflecting his awareness that discussing it, though painful, is also a solace. "Even in the worst depths of solitude, I was surprised to find that almost everyone, beyond childhood, was nursing some memory, or hiding some wound, that was never spoken of, but made the deepest feeling in life. We are all together in that relation, and if it is not husband and wife, it is a lover or only child, that fills the background of life, and makes the interest and poetry of our age. What we really mourn most is our own youth and the love it brought. Sooner or later it passes for us all, and we say no more about it, but the memory lives on it and on nothing else, so that when we see some new victim suffer we feel it as ourselves." He assured Bessie that she would find half her friends who have reached middle life "quite ready to envy you for having had all that was best in the world, and even bow, in your solitude, for having more left to you than most of them have. Even if it is only a memory, most women would be glad to change with you." Adams reflected upon his discovery of "what an ocean of disappointment and despondency I lived on. We all hurry to disguise it and hide it from other people, but among ourselves it is a sort of secret society, with pass-words and nods and jests, that take for granted all the thoughts that won't bear repeating aloud. . . . When all the supports of one's existence suddenly give way, one writhes under it like a crushed worm. Nothing helps except to think of the happiness we have had, and even that is a kind of self-torture. I am old enough not to try to make the suffering less. The suffering is itself almost a pleasure that one does not want to forget. . . . All I care for is to help you to carry it."

Adams then closed with a striking passage which Bessie often read over and over again, and to Cabot and John, in later years: "You know how I felt Bay's genius and admired his art, and you will not be too jealous when I say that of all the poems he gave us, none approached the one he began with, first of all, when he gave us you. And I doubt whether all the genius that ever lived has ever produced poem or figure that could rival you when

26 you produced the children. You know that this is no new notion of mine, for I said it all, years ago, in print * and in solemn seriousness. The woman and the child are the wonder of my old age. You are the true poems, the best he ever did. Goodbye!"

Bessie now gave all her attention to the children. "She taught us not to think about ourselves," John recalls. "If one of us got preoccupied with some selfish interest, she would say, 'Don't you think we could find something more interesting to think about? There are so many interesting things happening in the world.' She never punished us. If she so much as frowned at anything we did we'd be conscience-stricken not to cause her any pain, and we wouldn't do that again. She didn't care how many things got broken, but the one thing she couldn't tolerate was not telling the truth."

That fall of 1909 they returned to Washington, which had always been Bessie's home. Cabot and John shared a room on the top floor of their three-story stone house at 2346 Massachusetts Avenue. They were not yet old enough to enter St. Alban's, the famous private school near their home. The boys went first to Miss Ward's classes in a big wooden structure across from the school. Both had already heard French spoken so often at home that it was almost a second language. At home, governess Fräulein Schultz, the same of Bay's epic train ride, continued teaching them German. Bessie Lodge was forever reading to them aloud, all the great children's stories and verses—especially Stevenson's—Lear's nonsense rhymes and Lewis Carroll. She read the complete Bible to the children, a verse each Sunday. Even before they could fully understand the meaning, the great majesty and beauty of the King James scripture sang in their heads.

Once Easter came, they could look forward to returning soon to the golden sun and sand of Nahant. To save money, thrifty Bessie would double up the four of them in two berths, she and Helena sharing the upper and Cabot and John the lower. Occasionally the silence would be broken by John's yell: "Hey, you're sticking your toe in my nose!" Then came the wonderful summers of swimming, sailing, playing. Old Senator Lodge would join their adventures.

The senator was sometimes thought aloof, austere or even arrogant by those who did not know him well. But he was a very warm and human man, particularly with children. He helped fire the imagination of his grandsons by relating tales of his own childhood quests for treasure. "I made up my mind," as he later recounted in his *Early Memories*, "that on the side of the cliffs near [my] house . . . there was a cave which had been closed up by the fall of a rock, suggested by a long crack and projecting shelf. I fixed the place in my memory by slipping there one day when I

* In his *The Virgin and the Dynamo.*

was pounding the rock and as I fell I brought my teeth sharply together, biting clean through my tongue, an incident as real as my cave was imaginary and a good deal more painful. But although I made no impression on the hard surface of the rock, I pictured the cave in my mind and fitted it up and filled it with treasure, greatly to my own satisfaction. I became finally so pleased with my invention that I confided an account of it to my companion and contemporary, Sturgis Bigelow, who . . . was so interested that I gave him to understand that I had seen all these wonders, and I produced an old and rusty shotgun which I had found in the garret as something which I had brought from the cave." The senator was fond of telling how Stevenson said, "Every child hunts for buried treasure," and when Henry James replied that *he* never had, Stevenson said: "Then you were never a child."

The old senator knew a great deal about boys and boyhood. Unlike so many men, he had not forgotten his own. He would tell the youngsters about his own boyhood adventures, around Boston as well as Nahant. Long before William Golding's *Lord of the Flies,* the elder Lodge shrewdly noted "the close resemblance of boys to savages . . . as shown by their queer adhesion to meaningless customs, such as doing certain things only at certain times of the year, their odd superstitions wholly unconnected with religion, their loyalty to some code peculiar to themselves and alien to everyone else, and their ready hero worship, often misdirected but at bottom generous and fine." He remembered how the boys he knew fought, got sick trying to smoke, and had "a large and ignorant curiosity as to sexual relations, not morbid, merely characteristic of the young animal." He was admittedly quite a hell-raiser. "A large part of the waking hours of my friends and myself was given up to mere mischief, from breaking windows and street lamps to much more serious undertakings. . . . I know that like Mr. Swiveler, the number of streets which were closed to me steadily increased, not as in his case on account of debts, but from the dread of just retribution at the hands of those whose property I had injured."

Any Boston brahmin who could confess how he had smashed windows and streetlights was bound to be a hero to his grandsons—and such the old senator was, and remained. So the summers passed.

When they returned to Washington in the fall of 1911, Cabot was old enough to enter St. Alban's. Like most boys who have lost their fathers, he tended to daydream, and seemed a bit solemn and sad. Uncle John called him "the wise old man." He also had a stammer. The school did not seem to be able to focus his attention and his energies. Bessie Lodge decided it would be good for the children to go to school the following year in France, where the disciplines and exactions of education were much more intense

28   than in America. Cabot was delighted at the news. "Just think, John," he told his brother, "next year we'll be able to wear Eton collars!" That would be a measure of being more grown-up.

Bessie, planning to go with them to Europe, looked forward to seeing again the old friends so beloved by her husband. She wrote to Adams and Mrs. Cameron of her plans, to Mrs. Wharton. She tucked a note of her own inside a letter that George Abbot James, (whose estate, Lowland, adjoined the Lodges') was writing to his cousin Henry James. From his Sussex home, Lamb House, at Rye, Henry James wrote her on September 27, 1912:

My dear Mrs. Bay:
How shall I tell you what a charming pleasure it is to receive your gentle note?—To find it nestle in the heart of my dear old G.A.J.'s large letter even as the very corolla (is that what the thing is called?) of that generous flower. It brings back to me those life-saving afternoons (as I kind of felt them) on the Nahant verandahs when you came across to tea and peopled to us, for the time, by your single beautiful presence, that immensity of nothing! Best boon of all is your prospect of really reaching at no distant date this convenient side of the world. You must absolutely celebrate that event when it takes place, by coming to see me here as soon as possible thereafter. I am only just on a small sweet loop-line the tiniest bit off your most appointed track. We get on to Dover so easily that breakfasting at this house at the ordinary hour we are (quite magically) in Paris by about five o'clock and so the other way around. May all good angels smooth your course and speed your start. The years go and the fates intermeddle and the wind rises (or too utterly falls) and we don't know where we are—even when we thought we did: the moral of which is Be about it in time! That's the kind of tone my antiquity finds it must take to you. It has a dread of having to wait for anything—there comes with that necessity an uncanny loss of interest and faith. Therefore was the advent of your note —unheralded and as it were sudden (even now) so very delightful to me. . . . go on being kind to dear G.A.J. for when I ask myself whom he sees I can think of nobody but you. He will immensely miss you when you cease to recur there—as sketched above; and then truly I shan't like to think of the unpeopled nothing—at all! . . . I bless our possession of a climate in this place which shall make it mild and sweet and cozy (when it really wants to) to hang on here till little short of Christmas—when there are sometimes a few roses still in my garden. . . . Give my bestest love at Lowland please. . . . I think ever so rememberingly of your exquisite, your appealing children, and tell myself what a much mixed savor they must give to your cup.

Chapter Three

*Little fear for you of that's not always tasting—! I send them my earn-
est blessing and am yours, dear Mrs. Bay, all faithfully,*

Henry James

In November Bessie sailed with the three children on the *Oceanic*. From
Cherbourg they took the train to Paris, where Edith Wharton met them at
the station, making it all seem very homelike. Mrs. Wharton—born Edith
Newbold Jones—sprang from a number of New York's old middle-class
families (Rhinelanders, Newbolds, Schermerhorns, Pendletons, Gallatins)
who had become wealthy merchants and bankers. She was already a successful novelist whose works were being translated in France. She was, in
her own way, a fugitive from her surroundings as Bay Lodge had been
from his. Writing novels, among her kinsmen, was scarcely regarded as
respectable. "None of my relations ever spoke to me of my books," she
wrote later, "either to praise or blame . . . the subject was avoided as
though it were a kind of family disgrace." When she married Bostonian
Edward Wharton, their summer home at Lenox, Massachusetts—The
Mount, atop Bear Mountain—became a haven for all such literary refugees.
Year after year Bay and Bessie Lodge had belonged to her "inner group"
whose common stock of allusions, cross-references, pleasantries became
almost a private language.

Seeing Edith Wharton brought back, for Bessie, all these treasured memories. Edith saw them settled at the Hotel de Tremoille on the Rue de Tremoille not far from the Etoile. For the boys, she bespoke a boarding school
at St. Cloud, where they were promptly entered. Such homelessness, however, was simply too much for boys so recently made fatherless. "We were
so homesick—in such despair," John Lodge recalls. Not surprisingly, they
did poorly in their studies, provoking a reprimand from the old senator to
his namesake. The senator seemed to fear that Cabot might, like Bay, become so fond of Europe as to lose his roots at home:

*1735 Massachusetts Avenue
Dec. 1, 1912*

*My dearest Boy—
It was a great happiness to find your postal card waiting for me when
we arrived on Thursday night. I am glad that you think of America &
want to come back to your own country. Remember always that your
father fought for his country in the Spanish War & that your grandfather whose name you bear & your ancestors on both sides for many
generations have served your country both in war & peace. So you
have an honorable tradition to maintain. But above all you are an
American & can be nothing else & if you remember this you will al-*

30   *ways want to live in America for in that way alone can you be a really useful man. At the same time as you are in Paris you must take advantage of it & learn to speak French well which will be of great value to you always. You know how at Nahant in Autumn we see those long lines of migratory birds flying South. Well one of those migratory birds as they are called came over the ocean the other day & whispered in my ear that you were lazy at school. I do not like to hear that & so I told the bird. You must not be lazy . . .* [the Senator closed with the injunction to work hard which begins this chapter]

> *Ever my dearest Boy,*
> *Your loving Grandfather*

By Christmas, Bessie decided to keep the boys with her. She took an apartment at 55 Avenue Marceau in the Etoile and placed them in a nearby school run by a M. Gory at 18 Rue Matignon. He taught them how to fence. He toughened them by teaching them all the niceties of that form of boxing called *savate,* in which besides the fists, the feet also are used, as devastatingly as a kangaroo's. Cabot managed to break an arm at these sports.

Although the boys could speak French, M. Gory mercilessly drilled them in all the mysteries of its verbs and tenses, and set them studying various aspects of French civilization and culture. It left on young Cabot a lasting memory of "hard work and long hours. I feel to this day such ability to concentrate as I have is due to a significant extent to the training I received there." The ocean-crossing birds now stopped dismaying the distant senator with their messages.

Two days after Christmas, the old senator, browsing among his beloved horde of books while preparing a Lincoln's Day address, found himself thinking of the boy who would some day inherit this great library.

Bemused, he sat down and penned young Cabot, in longhand, the longest note he would ever write to him, as if hoping to instill in him an enduring sense of family duty, love and tradition, which these books, going back so many generations, called up in his own memory:

You must come as soon as you can & I know you will be glad to be at Nahant once more where you will find the Hammond boys and have your houses and see good old Frank and ride & swim and go out in the boat with cousin Ellerton (James). I have been having some holidays too for you know Congress takes a vacation at Christmas time just like in school & Senators and Congressmen seem as glad as if they were boys themselves. . . . Best of all I have been spending much of my holiday in my library arranging my books, not reading but just looking them over and playing with them. I hope that you will like to do this same thing for all these books will be yours some day & my dearest wish is that you should love them & care for them as I do. I trust you will not only want to keep them but will be able to keep them for they make a very large family and need a very large house to shelter them. You will have to work hard & earn a good income in order to do so & hard work is the best thing for us all. I want you to keep these books, you see, because they belonged to your ancestors as well as to me. I will tell you whose books are in the library so that you may know & I will make a little table which you can understand

George Cabot—*your great-great-great-grandfather*
|

Giles Lodge   Henry Cabot—*your great-great-grandfather*
| |

John E. Lodge   Anna Cabot—*your great grandfather and grandmother*
|

Henry Cabot Lodge & Anna (Davis) Lodge—*your grandfather and*
| *grandmother*

George Cabot Lodge—*your father*
|

Henry Cabot Lodge—YOU

All those people from whom you are descended have books in this library—George Cabot and my father John Lodge had a great many. Then you will find too in this library a few books that belonged to your grandmother's father Admiral Davis and those you must especially value for he was one of the finest characters I have ever known. He was a distinguished naval officer and won two great fleet actions in the Civil War. He was an eminent man of science—a scholar of wide reading and a lover of books. Above all he was a brave, high-minded gentleman. "Integer vitae, scelerisque purus?"* Sometime you will know what those familiar Latin words mean but now your mother can translate them to you. Then your great-grandfather Davis was besides full of fun and humor and everybody loved him as you would if he were only alive with us now. As it is you must love his memory and when you read a book called the Newcomes you will find Colonel Newcome, not at all as able or as intelligent as your grandfather but with a beautiful and noble nature which is very like his. I had rather have you like your great-grandfather Davis than anyone else and so you must prize his books. The library has many rare books but it is not the library of a collector. It is a library gathered by people who liked to read. I

---

* "The man upright in his life, and free from crime, does not need Moorish javelin or bow." Horace, *Odes*.

have read most of the books in it that are not books of reference and that can be read. I have read many books because it was necessary to my work and many many more which have interested and instructed and delighted and amused me but that which never wearies or passes you will find in the great works of the imagination. Poetry comes first for great poetry is the highest work of the human intellect. But in the library you will find many friends—men and women I mean. Some of them the most real, never lived at all and live forever. I want you to have all these friends. They will never desert you and you will care for them more and more as you grow older. Some of these people were created by the great poets—Homer created a great many—Achilles and Hector are two of them. You will come to know them well. I like Hector best although he was slain by Achilles. But best of all Homer's men is Odysseus and the story of his wanderings. The Odyssey is one of the finest—I think the finest—story ever written. I used to read it in Greek and I hope you will always do so and not let your Greek go as I have mine because I have been so busy with other things. Then there are Hamlet and Falstaff and a whole world of men and women the creations of Shakespeare the greatest genius the world has ever seen. Faust is another great figure but one never quite feels as if he were a friend. Nor can you be friends with the awful figures in Dante's Inferno or the angelic ones in his Paradise but his Divine Comedy is one of the great books of the world of which you will never tire. But you will make warm friends with the Don Quixote and Sancho Panza of Cervantes—I used to read about them when I was a small boy like you and laugh as Cervantes laughed and all the world has laughed since at the things Don Quixote did. But as I have grown older I have discovered that Don Quixote is really one [of] the saddest, most pathetic and noblest figures among many friends. Then there are two other friends created for me by lesser men. Robinson Crusoe whom you know and Gil Blas whom Le Sage produced for us. They are delightful companions both. You must remember I am not talking about literature generally. There are hundreds of great books by men of great genius which you will I hope love and read and if not love, admire. I am speaking to you only of some of the real people created by genius whom I love and know and whom you will, I hope, love and know too because they all live in these books which will one day be yours. There is Dickens. He has created a whole world of people. I cannot name them there are too many. But I know him like Miss Snevillinni's Papa. I love them all. You must get someone to take you to see the statue of Alexandre Dumas. On the back is seated a figure of a very gallant gentleman named d'Artagnan. He is a fine figure. He is a great friend

of mine and so are his three friends Athos, Porthos and Aramis. I hope   33
that they will all be friends of yours. Also another Dumas man—
Chicot—I like to be with him and hear the lark trill and the mouse
cheep as he strides over the fields. Then there is Scott. He is not the
fashion now I believe but I don't mind telling you as a secret that I love
to go with Quentin Durward after the wild Boar of the Ardness and
wander the Highlands with Rob Roy. Just as I like to go with the
Squire and the rest to Treasure Island and Follow the Adventures of
the Capitaine Francoise and his Chevalier Des Tonchers who is almost
as good as an earlier hero Huon of Bordeaux. Then there are the real
men who lived in history but who had such genius that they made
themselves live in the books they wrote all about themselves—the great
autobiographers. You will read them later—St. Augustine and Rous-
seau and Samuel Pepys and Dr. Johnson and Benjamin Franklin and
George Borrow and Dumas. I could go on and on. There are many
many more too many to count. But they all live here among their books
which I hope you will learn to know and love them all. And when you
read of them in these same books I hope that you will feel the pleasure
which I now feel from knowing that the eyes now long closed, the eyes
of those who loved me rested on these same pages. You will feel the
same way I feel now and like to think that the eyes of those from whom
you descended and of your grandfather and grandmother who love you
dearly saw those same books and found in them the same undying
friendships as you have found. Your "Gammuzzy" sends her dearest
love and was delighted with your plant and still more by your thinking
of her. Give our bestest love to your mother and John and Helena.

> *Ever my beloved boy*
> *Your loving grandfather*
> *H. C. Lodge*

Bessie Lodge found amid the gay bustle and beauty of Paris a lifting of
her spirits. Picking up the same routine—after her sudden bereavement—
had served its own useful disciplines for her, but the complete change of
Paris was refreshing. The ability to renew the warm talk and presence of
Mrs. Wharton was like old days at The Mount, the golden afternoons and
long evenings of good talk, when everyone seemed to take inspiration from
each other. They talked much of Henry James, who had become Mrs.
Wharton's most revered friend. As she wrote, "I had never doubted that
Henry James was great, though how great I could not guess till I came to
know the man as well as I did his books." James himself watched her with
humorous irony and affection. In letters to friends he called her "The Angel
of Devastation," "The Angel of Paris," or the "Eagle" and spoke of "Our

34   great Edith" coming and going "with a great flap of her iridiscent wings."
He wrote to a friend, "Ah, my dear young man, you have made friends
with Edith Wharton. I congratulate you; you may find her difficult, but you
will never find her stupid, and you will never find her mean."

Edith and Bessie talked again about that one evening in particular when
James, who always seemed conversationally at his best at The Mount, was
asked to tell them about his Albany cousinship, "The Emmetry," as he
called it. For a moment he stood there, brooding in the darkness, murmur-
ing over to himself: "Ah, my dear, the Emmets—ah, the Emmets!"

"Then," as Edith recalled it, "he began, forgetting us, forgetting the place,
forgetting everything but the vision of his lost youth that the question had
evoked, the long train of ghosts flung with his enchanter's wand across the
wide stage of the summer night. Ghostlike indeed at first, wavering and
indistinct, they glimmered at us through a series of disconnected ejacula-
tions, epithets, allusions, parenthetical rectifications and restatements, till
not only our brains but the clear night itself seemed filled with a palpable
fog; and then, suddenly, by some miracle of shifted lights and accumulated
strokes, there stood before us as they lived, drawn with a million filament-
like lines, yet sharp as an Ingres, dense as a Rembrandt; or, to call upon
his own art for an analogy, minute and massive as the people of Balzac.

"I often saw the trick repeated; saw figures obscure or famous summoned
to the white square of his magic-lantern, flickering and wavering there,
and slowly solidifying under the turn of his lens; but never perhaps anything so ample, so sustained, as that summoning to life of dead-and-gone
Emmets and Temples, old lovelinesses, old follies, old failures, all long
laid away and forgotten under old crumbling gravestones."

Bessie often took the children to lunch or tea with Edith Wharton in her
lovely apartment, in a stately Louis XIV hotel on the Rue de Varenne. She
was full of stories of the evening Teddy Roosevelt spent there two years
before, on his triumphal tour of Europe after leaving the White House. She
remembered how, during one of her early visits to the Lodges in Washington, Roosevelt had summoned her to lunch at the White House. "At
last," he greeted her on the threshold, "I can quote 'The Hunting of the
Snark.' Would you believe it, no one in the Administration has heard of
Alice, much less of the Snark, and the other day, when I said to the Secretary of the Navy, 'Mr. Secretary, *what I say three times is true*,' he did not
recognize the allusion, and answered with an aggrieved air: 'Mr. President,
it would never for a moment have occurred to me to impugn your veracity.'"

They also often went to see Uncle Dawdy at his beautiful house on the
Bois de Boulogne. A true citizen of the world, he lived much of his time in
France. He was now in his seventy-fifth year and growing a bit wizened
with age. But it was an education in itself for the youngsters to hear the

man who had written *Mont St. Michel and Chartres* tell of the glories and   35
wonders that were theirs to see in France. He talked of his trip through
Europe with the senator and Bay in 1895, when he left them in Paris while
they went on to Madrid—and Bay walked out on his first bullfight ("I've
seen enough!"). Adams had gone with them to Salerno to see the burial
place of Pope Hildebrand, who had brought an emperor to his feet and
died a beaten exile. This remarkable man who, in his course on medieval
history at Harvard had first awakened the senator's own curiosity, now
helped stir that of his grandsons.

The children accompanied their mother to some of Paris' most fashion-
able salons. They lunched with the Contesse de Behague, and with the
Melchior de Vogues—he an *ancien* aristocrat who in his sixties would become a monk, his wife a nun. They sat and listened, nibbling their cookies
and sweetmeats.

In their first summer in France, Bessie took a house at Paris Plage, a
Normandy seaside resort. It was called the Villa de Genets d'Or. On Bas-
tille Day there was a carnival night where everyone dressed in costume,
and young Cabot went dressed as a Spahi and John as a Zouave, feeling
very military and important. They gorged themselves on *sucre d'orge*, a
particularly delicious candy sucker. The summer drifted by. Tanned and
refreshed for new ordeals at the hands of M. Gory, they returned to the
grind of school. Bessie relieved the monotony by taking them to Punch and
Judy shows along the Champs-Elysées and to carnivals where they could
ride ferris wheels and merry-go-rounds. So the winter months succeeded
one another. Then came the fateful summer of 1914, when a whole world
would end.

They went that summer to Dieppe, partly to be near Mrs. Wharton (now
divorced from Edward), who for years had spent her summers in a charming little stone manor house in the village of Offrannville. The whole countryside was bursting with flowers, and with orchards where newborn calves
cavorted under the apple blossoms. There Mrs. Wharton met "a passionately imaginative youth" named Jean Cocteau: "Excepting Bay Lodge I
have known no other young man who so recalled Wordsworth's 'Bliss was
it in that dawn to be alive!'"

Merely staying alive would soon be quite an achievement for the young
men of Europe.

Bessie's valet, Emile, whose sister Angelique was their cook, was mo-
bilized and went off to war. He would soon be killed at Soissons.

"I can remember the drum beat through the village," Cabot recalls, "summoning men to report for military service. I can remember the horses being
brought into the village from all the surrounding farms to have their hooves
branded with a number, so that they could be returned to their owners if

36 they ever survived the war." John, with fond dreams of becoming an ornithologist, had acquired several parakeets, a tame dove, some dozen birds all told. Bessie's maiden aunt, Lucy Frelinghuysen, was spending the summer with them. They got word the elder Lodges were in London, with Constance and her husband Gussie Gardner.

When the dreadful news of Sarejevo came, Gussie Gardner hurried straight over from London to help Bessie Lodge pack. "They were packing all night," John Lodge recalls. "We left Dieppe in two taxicabs. I had to leave my birds behind, and I was weeping. Angelique was with us, and our French governess. Uncle Gussie filled the cabs with gasoline cans so we could make Le Havre. We got on the first boat out. I'll never forget, as we left the dock, the people ashore were waving and singing the *Marseillaise*." Young Cabot took with him as a souvenir of this exodus a *laissez-passer* of the Ville de Dieppe, whose town seal is stamped across the photo of his pert young face, authorizing his departure from Havre at ten the night of August 5.

When they reached London, Bessie found a little flat on Half Moon Street, and the children explored nearby Green Park in their walks. While in England, Bessie took Cabot on the train down to Rye for the long-deferred visit to Henry James. She explained to Cabot that Rye had once been on the sea, but the sea had receded.

"We were received in his garden," Cabot recalls. "It was surrounded by a curved stone wall. The ground was covered with mulberries which had fallen from the trees. In the center was a little one-room house where he did his writing. He shook hands with me very gravely. He was a rather ponderous man, with a big, Romanesque face, rather sententious. He did a lot of er-rr-ring and ah-ing to get the right words as he talked—a good deal the same as he wrote. I wandered around the garden while he and mother sat in it and talked all afternoon. I sometimes sat and listened. It was all about old times and old friends."

Late in August, all the Lodges and their kin sailed on the *Olympic*. Vernon and Irene Castle were aboard. Cabot and John crept out of bed and hid behind a pillar in the big ballroom to watch the Castles do their famous waltz.

CHAPTER FOUR

*Dear Sir—Would you kindly let me know if you could take in my two
sons next Autumn? They will then be 12 and 13. Hoping for a favorable answer and for any information about the school which you can
give me . . .*

Thus wrote Bessie Lodge on April 26, 1915, to Mr. Frederick Winsor, headmaster of Middlesex School at Concord, Mass. It was time, she thought, for
Cabot and John to go off to prep school. Almost as a needless postscript she
added, "The boys are grandsons of Sen. Lodge."

Since returning from Europe the previous summer, Cabot and John had
been going to St. Alban's School in Washington. Bessie wanted them in the
same grade, to keep each other company, though Cabot, being a year older,
found the work easier than John.

They had renewed old friendships at the school, particularly with Jerry
and Evie Wadsworth, and often went to parties with them at Grandmother
Hay's house (Grandfather John Hay died in 1905). As before, Bessie sup-
plemented their instruction by reading aloud in the evening. She read them
all of Dickens, all of Walter Scott's romantic and chivalrous novels, all of
Thackeray.

The boys were often at the old senator's, who doted on them. They grew
accustomed early to meeting the many important people who came to see
him. Bay's brilliant young friend of old, Spring-Rice, was now Britain's
wartime ambassador. Another intimate of their circle, Jules Jusserand, who
had frequented the senator's house since his arrival as French ambassador
in 1902, was now in the prime of his great influence, and often came with
important Allied leaders. "I remember once hiding in the parlor," John
Lodge recalls, "listening to Grandpa and the French Prime Minister."

Cabot still had his stammer. John suffered from a tic, which, under
stress, set him batting his eyes furiously. The senator, as well as Uncle
John Lodge, began to feel that the boys needed more masculine authority,
such as a boarding school would provide. The senator liked everything he
had heard about Middlesex, a nonsectarian school founded in 1901 by
Winsor, a great friend of Lodge's own friend Thomas Wentworth Higginson. Winsor had invited Lodge to give the commencement address in 1909,
and Lodge had regretfully declined because "we shall be finishing work on
the tariff bill . . . and it will be out of the question for me to leave Washington."

He felt strongly that Cabot should go to school in his home state. It evidently never entered his mind that he and Bessie might have difficulty   37

38 getting the boys into Middlesex. They were quite startled when Winsor wrote Bessie that he already had ten or a dozen boys on his waiting list and, "It does not look very hopeful for your two boys. If you would be willing, however, to have them share a room, it would add distinctly" to their chances. He enclosed a catalog, calling attention to his "somewhat unusual requirements," adding that boys frequently did not have the required preparation in French.

Senator Lodge decided the time had come to speak strongly. He wrote the next letter to Winsor, stating, "I am extremely anxious that you should understand regarding my two grandsons. I want them educated in Massachusetts, and I am particularly anxious that they should prepare at your school, as their mother has now decided that she would like to send them there." Therefore, the senator assumed that they would go: "There will be no difficulty about their occupying one room," and as for French, "They both speak French freely and I cannot believe that they are not better prepared than most boys. I trust that you will be able to find places for them. . . ."

Winsor, however, was not easily intimidated. He repeated firmly that he would take them "if we possibly can" but only "if a sufficient number of vacancies occur between now and September for us to make room for them." However, their willingness to share a room would "certainly make it easier for us . . . because we have some rooms which have been used as single rooms which are really large enough to accommodate two boys." By late June, Bessie was inspecting Middlesex, with Nannie Lodge, still not sure of their admittance. Winsor suggested she also look over Mill Brook School, in case they had to wait another year. However, he showed them quarters in a farm house where the boys might possibly be quartered if admitted to Middlesex. "I must tell you," Bessie wrote him the next day, "that as the boys have never been north of Washington for the winter, I could not let them room in the farm house. I am afraid to introduce them to New England cold in a wooden house & oblige them to walk so far in all weather. The Chanlers are used to a cold climate but my boys are not." Teddy Chanler, son of old friends of the Lodges, was at Middlesex.

In the end, Winsor was able to find room for the boys—and a warmer room at that. Once they had taken their exams at St. Alban's, they went on to Nahant to start tutoring from one Frederick J. Manning* for their make-up exams at Middlesex. In late August, Manning wrote Winsor they were ready to take them: "They have had an hour's work a day since the first of July in Arithmetic and Geography, and John has been reading Mythology

---

* Lodge was getting very able instruction. Manning, an instructor in history at Yale, became professor of history at Swarthmore, married another noted historian, President Taft's daughter, Helen, later dean and president-emeritus of Bryn Mawr.

with his mother." Manning found the job harder than he had thought. "Their training in Arithmetic had been exceedingly poor—mainly consisting, it would seem, of unreasoning memory work. They were taught physical geography in France, but knew very little local geography. . . . Both have interesting minds, and deserve far better instruction than they have had until now. Cabot is perfectly capable of passing both his papers with a high stand. He has a decidedly mature mind, and concentrates easily. My task was to make him reason and realize the processes he used, and to awaken his interest." John was less able to concentrate and was "in sad need of the orderly discipline of a good school." Later, after giving them their exams, Manning sent the results on to their housemaster, Dr. Reginald Heber Howe, Jr., who had been coxswain on the Harvard rowing crew and later coached rowing at Harvard. He was one of several unusually able masters at Middlesex—including Winfield Brown and Archibald Galbraith —who later founded their own schools. "John," Manning wrote, "has been somewhat rebellious, and had to write his answers under constant compulsion; while both show the need of systematic school training in their struggles with self-expression. . . ." On the bottom of his letter, Dr. Howe wrily noted *"musculum partumeium,* (say),"* suggesting he thought the boys might need some physical as well as scholarly toughening. Bessie wrote off to Middlesex to find "what clothes, underclothes, etc., they should bring," and advice on her thought of "having their clothes washed in Boston with ours if possible." This was approved.

Before school began, tragedy once more struck the Lodge family. Nannie Lodge, Cabot's beloved "Gamuzzy," closer to him than anyone but Bessie, was stricken suddenly with a heart attack, and died at the old frame house at East Point. "The love and light of my life went out in an instant," the old senator wrote a friend. The boys went off to school wearing a mourning band on their sleeves.

The school was only twenty miles from Nahant. Both did well immediately. Their proficiency in French and German gave them a decided edge on other boys who were less well-trained. Cabot easily got a 96 in French his first term, an 88 in English, and an 83 in natural science, though his math was—and would remain—execrable (barely passing at 62). Nevertheless, with an average of 81, he ranked first in the sixth form class of nineteen boys. Both boys found themselves often incurring the form of punishment called "rounds" for infractions of discipline. A round consisted of walking around the oval driveway circling the school, about three-quarters of a mile. Being late to school brought five rounds. Cabot got 144 rounds during his first year—"too many," his report card noted.

The honor system prevailed, and students were trusted to complete all the rounds as ordered. Cabot and John got into a serious jam for "breaking

40   into" the Carlisle Library in a nearby town. They had gone there to return a book, and finding the library closed had gone through an unlocked window rather than waste the trip. They got the school's severest punishment —the six-mile walk to the top of Strawberry Hill and back.

The nearby woods abounded in garter snakes, and every boy felt duty-bound to have at least one snake in his pocket, to show on demand, and sometimes one in his bureau drawer as well. Often enough, a boy who jumped in bed without looking would find a snake in it. In winter groups of boys would go into the woods, make a lean-to, make a pot of chocolate, and have a feed. The incentive for good behavior was that, after two years of good conduct, one got his own study, where he could make chocolate, have snacks and the like.

Although Middlesex was not a church school, a nondenominational service was held each morning after breakfast, and all boys were required to attend Sunday School. Cabot and John, preferring to sleep late, begged Bessie to ask that they be excused. "Being very free in such matters," she wrote Mr. Winsor, "I see no reason why they should not unless you have something to say to the contrary." He did have something to say: "Attendance at Sunday School is required of all boys except those who go to the Catholic Church in Concord at the same time that our Sunday School comes, so that I cannot allow Cabot and John to be excused." At midyear, Cabot was still first in his class; Master Archibald Galbraith wrote Bessie: "I don't know whether I am more delighted at Cabot's holding his place and tightening his grip on it or at John's decided gain and his entrance into the honorable mention group."

By the end of the first year, John had displaced Cabot in first place. This indignity may have spurred Cabot to determine to get sufficient tutoring, during the summer of 1916, to skip a class and leave John behind entirely. Cabot was still showing "great weakness in arithmetic . . . and is not in the habit of thinking over his solutions to see if they accord with the given facts." Galbraith was "sorry to note that Cabot is at the foot of his class in the matter of rounds." Bessie, planning to attend commencement, asked if she might bring Senator Lodge. Winsor, delighted to snag him seven years after first inviting him, wired to ask Lodge "if he would be willing to say a few words to the graduating class in case he is to be present." The old senator gladly did so.

That summer Cabot buckled down to hard, earnest study of algebra, German and English in the hope of getting into the fourth form that fall. He got in, though again his worst showing was in the algebra exam. In spite of the stiffer work, he managed an average of 83 the first term, and was fourth in a class of nineteen. "You will see from Cabot's report," wrote Galbraith, "how fully he is justifying his promotion and weekly reports are improving. He has not yet found himself in his new class, but it is only **41** natural that the making of new and desirable friendships shall take time."

"Thus far," wrote Galbraith that December, "Cabot has devoted himself pretty exclusively to work; I shall welcome the time when he enters more into other activities. It will be good for him to have a wide circle of friends and more interests in which he can lose himself."

During the Christmas vacation in Washington, their grandfather, a formidable classicist, was distressed to learn that Middlesex did not even offer Greek—except in the last year as an extra—and then on special request. He fired off an injured note to Headmaster Winsor: "I had regretted always that only three years' instruction was allotted to the classics, but if the boys are correct in their statement about Greek instruction it seems to their Mother, as well as to me, very serious. I desire that my grandsons—and their Mother joins with me in the desire—should be well-grounded in both Latin and Greek. It is our wish also that they should be prepared to offer both Latin and Greek for entrance to Harvard. I believe very strongly that all boys who receive the highest education should know something of the great classical languages. I am unwilling to have my grandsons deprived of the opportunity, if they desire it, of reading Homer in the original."

Warming to his subject, the "scholar in politics" declared himself "one of those who think that education in the sciences and in purely utilitarian subjects has been carried altogether too far. No man can be described as a 'scholar,' nor even as a 'cultivated man,' unless he has at least a bowing acquaintance with the classics. They are the foundation of all our literature and, so far as the Greeks are concerned, of all abstract thought. Except possibly in the business courses now established at Harvard, I can conceive of no field of intellectual activity in which a knowledge of Greek and Latin are not of great value. . . ."

Mr. Winsor wrote to reassure him that the boys could have their Greek; "we always provide for an elective course in Greek where a boy wants to take it, and in the case of boys whose French is as thoroughly in hand as is Cabot's and John's, it is very easy to make this course in Greek cover the elementary Greek requirements for Harvard. The boys will thus be able to read Homer in college if they wish to and to go on and acquaint themselves with the great Greek tragedies as well." It was arranged that both would start Greek the following school year. Mr. Winsor, having no Greek master on his staff, would have to bring one from Boston, three times a week, by train.

He resented the snooping and prying of Middlesex masters, and sought to frustrate them, sometimes by resistance or disobedience. He was caught smoking, and very nearly expelled. "He shows from time to time an underhanded streak that worries me not a little," Heber Howe wrote Bessie.

42 "Though there were many calls on the boys for money this past term, Cabot was apparently unwilling . . . to give a small tip with his table to the maid in the dining hall. This has been a custom of the boys at Christmastime for many years and a thing they all gladly do. I know you agree with me that a boy cannot show his gentlemanly instincts better than in his respect and courtesy to servants." (What Cabot resented was not the tip, but being assessed without being consulted, being treated as a child and not as a person.) Cabot continued to draw too many rounds, and was punished for "wilful disregard of the privileges of going off the place." Bessie urged him to mend his ways.

"Always remember," she wrote him in February, 1917, "your resolution to be as straight as a ruler. It may be hard when you are very young to realize the harm caused by the lack of truthfulness but my experience has been that it grows into one of the most hateful things in the world because men and women who are not truthful about themselves soon become untruthful about others and cause much misery. I speak of what I myself have seen." She referred to Dickens' *Great Expectations*, which they had been reading: "You remember how different the two convicts are in 'Pip.' The reason we all like one and loathe the other is because, with all his faults, one was true at heart—the other crooked and false. I don't think there are many things that sound uglier that that word—false."

Cabot improved his behavior. His rounds fell, that next term, from 53 to 20—his lowest record yet.

His interest also was getting caught up by the developing war crisis, which was slowly, inexorably, drawing the U.S. into the European conflict. He listened more attentively to the old senator's account of his running battles with President Wilson. Grandfather and namesake were drawn closer also by Nannie's death. "An austere man," wrote John Mason Brown, who came to know both Cabot Lodges well, "he thawed completely when with his grandson. His eyes lighted up at the sight of him and his face, so often haughty in expression, creased into a hundred smiling wrinkles above his pointed beard and flowing mustache. His was the final flattery of treating his grandson not as a grandson but as an equal in knowledge and experience, and talking with him man to man about national and international affairs."

Young Cabot had long been aware that his grandfather was developing a growing distaste and distrust for President Wilson. In his early years this was merely an atmosphere which the boy accepted without fully understanding. Now he became more aware of the reasons, and felt a personal identity with the deepening struggle between these two historic enemies. To understand the elements that shaped the boy, it is helpful to see how the elder Lodge's distrust of Wilson began, and grew.

It started over a matter of principle, when the former president of Princeton University ran for governor of New Jersey. Only once in his life did
Senator Lodge break with his closest friend Roosevelt, and that was over
the same issue—the so-called initiative, referendum and recall. That was
a supposedly liberal reform, whereby the electorate itself could initiate
legislation, enact it by referendum, and recall unpopular judicial decisions.

Roosevelt had backed this reform in a speech at Columbus, Ohio, and
Lodge in a private letter split with him: "The most vital perhaps of all the
great principles embodied in the Constitution is that of securing the absolute independence of the judiciary. In the long course of the centuries
during which western civilization has developed it has been proved again
and again that whatever its defects there is nothing so essential, so vital
to human rights and liberty, as an independent court."

Lodge foresaw, with great prescience, what actually did happen years
later when California experimented with initiated referendum. He foresaw
that all sorts of cranks would use it to enact pet measures (as chiroprac-
tors, gamblers and faddists did in California) which uninformed voters
could not understand. "If people are unable to elect decent representatives," he wrote Roosevelt, "I doubt very much if they have either the intelligence or character to legislate intelligently. For it is a good deal easier
to elect a good representative than it is to pass a complicated law which
very few people understand unless they have given it particular attention."

Many years before, when the elder Lodge was editor, at twenty-nine, of
the *International Review,* he had published the first article of a Princeton
senior, Woodrow Wilson. A second article was brusquely marked "R.R.R."
—received, read and rejected—but the first formed the basis of Wilson's
first book, *Constitutional Government.* In this book, which Scholar Lodge
knew well, Wilson spoke disparagingly of popular democracy, bespoke
Edmund Burke's brand of conservatism, advocated a British-type cabinet
government, and deplored Jefferson's French Revolutionary radicalism as
severely as old George Cabot ever had done in the days when Jefferson was
his bête noire.

In later years, Wilson had dissociated himself completely from Bryan
populism (Bryan should be "knocked once and for all into a cocked hat"),
opposed labor unions as setting standards at the lowest common denomi-
nator, opposed Roosevelt's own trust-busting and opposed regulation of
business (he said what the country needed was a brains trust headed by
J. P. Morgan).

But, starting with his campaign for governor of New Jersey in 1910,
Wilson began turning every one of these principles upside down, attacked
the trusts, praised labor, advocated a powerful executive as a tribune of
the people, and fulsomely eulogized Bryan. Finally, Wilson—who had used

44 the same arguments as Lodge to denounce initiative and recall—now took these reforms to his bosom and sought to ride a reform wave to the Presidency. Lodge attacked him in April, 1912, and chose Princeton, where Wilson had so recently ruled, as the place to do it. "It was rather funny," he wrote Captain Alfred Mahan later, "I said that I was about to quote a distinguished ex-President of the University and the students cheered, evidently thinking I was going to assail him, knowing well my politics. When they had finished their applause. . . . I read [Wilson's past views] in support of my position and the quiet that fell upon them was quite something and the next time I mentioned him there wasn't a lisp from anybody." After the Democrats nominated Wilson, Lodge sized him up thus:

> *I think he is a man of ability but he has no intellectual integrity at all. A man can change one or two of his opinions for his own advantage and change them perfectly honestly, but when a man changes all the well-considered opinions of a lifetime and changes them all at once for his own popular advantage it seems to me that he must lack in loyalty of conviction. . . . I think he would sacrifice any opinion at any moment for his own benefit and go back to it the next moment if he thought returning to it would be profitable.*

Lodge, of course, was simply appalled when Wilson, who had denounced Bryan, made him Secretary of State. "One of the kindest-hearted and best meaning men in the world . . ." Lodge wrote of Bryan, "he is essentially a man of words and not only knows nothing about foreign relations, which is natural, but he does not know his ignorance and has no grasp whatever of his own situation. He has the stump-speaking mind. With him, words take the place of actions. He thinks that to say something is to do something, which is an imperfect view of administration."

However, Lodge kept a warily open mind on Wilson himself until the 1914 crisis with Mexico. In that country's three-cornered civil war between Huerta, Carranza and Pancho Villa, in which many Americans were killed and their property rights infringed, Wilson based his landing of Marines in Veracruz as a personal action against Huerta who had refused a Wilson demand. Lodge, terming it "a declaration of war against an individual," wanted to lift it up from the level of personal hostility and place it on the broad ground of national action. It seemed to him Wilson was determined to force Huerta out simply because Huerta had insulted Wilson, and Lodge thought this colossal egotism. But worse still, when U.S. Marines lost their lives at Veracruz and full-scale war seemed threatened, Wilson grew confused and indecisive. "What struck me most . . ." said Lodge, "was the President's evident alarm and his lack of determination as to his policy.

He ought never to have sent the fleet and the Marines to Veracruz unless he had been prepared not only for peaceful surrender of the city but also for the resistance. . . . All he seemed desirous of doing, the fighting having occurred, was to get out of the trouble in any way possible without continuing the war which he himself had begun." To Lodge, this smacked of indecision and weakness.

When World War I broke out, Lodge had the same aims as Wilson: He wanted the Allies to win, and he wanted America to keep out. But their views were miles apart as to means. Lodge wanted America to be so strong no one would dare fight it; Wilson thought America could best prove its peaceful intentions by failing to arm. "Armies and Navies organized to maintain peace serve the ends of peace," said Lodge in 1915, "because there is no such incentive to war as a rich, undefended, and helpless country, which by its condition invites aggression." He had been saying the same thing—backing Captain Mahan's views of seapower—since before the war with Spain. Keenly aware that the new British *Dreadnought* of 1906 had made our own battleships obsolete, he was elated to hear that Navy Secretary Josephus Daniels was "inclined to favor" the building of three modern battleships; Lodge informed Assistant Secretary Franklin D. Roosevelt he would "support such a policy to the utmost of my ability." Roosevelt, himself an ardent believer in a big navy, did his best to help Lodge and Lodge's son-in-law, Congressman Gussie Gardner, in their demand for naval expansion. Neither they nor Roosevelt got very far. "Wilson and Bryan are pushing us to a position which may bring war or humiliation and yet insist we shall remain defenseless," Lodge told Theodore Roosevelt. Lodge thought a stronger stand against the German use of U-boats would have averted the *Lusitania* tragedy; when it came, with heavy loss of American lives, he felt that German ships in U.S. ports should be seized as an indemnity, but predicted that Wilson would do nothing to make Germany respect American rights. T. R.'s sister, Corinne Robinson, saw Lodge standing on his steps that day holding the evening paper and on asking Lodge if Wilson would not be forced to take drastic action, he bitterly cried, "Words—words—words!" looking to her "like a Prophet of old." Wilson's succession of diplomatic notes, while the Germans played for time, seemed to bear him out. The fact that Secretary Bryan resigned rather than sign the second note to Germany, which was milder than his first one, mystified Lodge as much as Bryan's departure pleased him: "By no possibility could Wilson get a worse man but why Bryan should let his name go on the first note and then refuse to sign the mild one is difficult to understand."

As early as January, 1916, Lodge was calling for universal military training, a standing army of 210,000 men, with "1,000,000 men in reserve ready to come to the colors at all times." Wilson at first supported expan-

46 sion, then backed down to the extent that Secretary of War Lindley M. Garrison resigned in protest. By the time of the Republican convention that June, Lodge seemed like a whirling dervish, nominating one man (his colleague, Senator John Wingate Weeks, also of Boston), voting for another, letting himself be used as a possible candidate when Roosevelt urged him, then cordially welcoming the final victory of Charles Evans Hughes: "I am so anxious to defeat Wilson," he said, "that I should not hesitate to support any good man on whom we could unite." (To his delight that same June, Wilson's old enemy at Princeton, Dean Andrew West—who had called Wilson "the damnedest liar who ever stood in shoe leather"—cited Lodge, the scholar-senator, for an honorary degree).

Lodge had a reelection campaign of his own against Boston's Democratic Mayor John (Honey Fitz) Fitzgerald. He took the stump against Wilson with joyful savagery, crying that he had "vacillated and oscillated and paltered" with "unmeant words and empty bluster," was "without firmness or courage in foreign affairs" and was like Mr. Pickwick who said: "Hush, Don't ask any questions. It is always best on these occasions to do what the mob do." "But suppose there are two mobs," suggested Mr. Snodgrass. "Shout with the largest," replied Mr. Pickwick. Both Lodge and Wilson were reelected. By the following January, with Germany announcing full-scale resumption of submarine warfare, Wilson severed diplomatic relations. Lodge called for an end to partisanship in the crisis but privately wrote Roosevelt that Wilson "simply . . . is afraid . . . he flinches in the presence of danger, physical and moral." By March, with American ships being repeatedly sunk, Lodge was sure war would come "because I have some faith in the Germans and what they will do. I have none in Wilson, and I have been racking my brain . . . to see what crevice he can get out of. I have not found it yet."

At Middlesex, young Cabot Lodge loyally felt that all his grandfather's enmities and causes were his own. As the country moved toward war, even the younger boys at Middlesex got caught up in its excitement. On April 3, when the headlines blazoned Wilson's war message of the day before, young Cabot was alarmed at another story telling about a near-riot outside his grandfather's office, where some Boston pacifists—including a minister—gathered to harangue him.

The senator had stepped out into the corridor to talk to the delegation, headed by Alexander Bannwart, a young man of German extraction who had played baseball for Lowell under the name of Al Winn. To their questions, Lodge said he would support the President's expected request for a war declaration: "National degeneracy and cowardice are worse than war. . . . I must do my duty as I see it." Bannwart cried: "Anyone who

wants to go to war is a coward! You're a damned coward." The slender
Lodge, nearing sixty-seven, snapped: "You're a damned liar," and punched
Bannwart on the jaw. In the scuffle, Bannwart's companions were trying
to attack Lodge, but passersby rescued him, and Bannwart himself was
beaten and dragged off to jail (Lodge refused to press charges). Young
Cabot, approaching fifteen, worriedly wrote his grandfather:

"What an exciting time you must have had with that pacifist, what a
thing to ask you. . . . Are you badly hurt? Will you be able to go to the
Senate tomorrow or will you rest at home? My how I wish I was there with
you." But the senator, face slightly puffed, was able to take his seat that
historic evening and for once rose to applaud a Wilson speech that he
could find "first rate." He wrote to Mrs. Brooks Adams, Nannie's sister:
"For the first time, he spoke as a President ought to, and all his recommendations were good."

As the 1917 fall term at Middlesex began, the boys began taking both
Latin and Greek, as the old senator had insisted. At first things seemed
to go quite well. "Cabot has a steadily improving record," Heber Howe
wrote Bessie that November, "and should be congratulated. . . . Both
boys seem to be thoroughly welded into the school life." Before, Howe had
been worried about Cabot's tendency to be withdrawn; now suddenly he
had other worries: "I am sorry to have to notify you that Cabot will not be
allowed to have his Thanksgiving vacation on account of a punishment
. . . the boy's performance is difficult to fully explain by letter, but the
gist of it is that he made trouble by turning out the lights in the study room
and was put on bounds—and then went to the Harvard-Yale football game
in Cambridge." Howe could not conceal a certain glee at Cabot showing
his mettle. "I am glad the boy is to have a little jog for though I glory in
his more boyish attitude toward life in the school, yet he needs just such
a lesson."

This, it turned out, was partly the senator's fault. Bessie wrote Dr. Howe
that the senator told her, "Last Wednesday Cabot telephoned me and asked
me to get him two tickets for the Yale game. It is a great happiness to me.
Saturday, after the game, he came in here [to Dr. Bigelow's Beacon Street
home, where the senator now stayed when in Boston] and made himself
most agreeable."

Now Cabot was becoming better known for high jinks than high marks.
At midyear that December, he had piled up ninety-two rounds for mis-
deeds, and despite a 91 in French and an 82 in Latin, was still doing mis-
erably in math and little better in Greek; he stood fifteenth in a class of
twenty-five. The senator sent him stern rebukes, for this and other faults,
such as using "will" instead of "shall."

48   "You will never hear [that] mistake used in your own family. Now if you are going to write the sentence I have quoted from your letter you ought to say, 'Before I shall be home.' As it stands, it is slovenly." Cabot tried, very hard, wrote a new letter reeking with "shalls," and the senator responded: "I am glad to see that you have in mind what I said to you about using 'shall' and 'will.' . . . But in the sentence you write you have used 'shall' where it is imperative to use 'will.' . . . Bear in mind the old story of the Frenchman who fell in the water and cried out, 'I will drown and nobody shall save me!'"

Cabot pulled up his socks, managed to get back on the honors list in the first week of the 1918 term. "Your letter gave me the greatest possible pleasure," the senator wrote him. "It is not so much the place in the class that gratifies me although I am very much pleased by that. What pleases me far more is the knowledge that you have had the will and the determination to regain the place which you had lost through carelessness and indolence. You have shown, what I never doubted to be true, that you are able to control your mind and apply it to any subject that you choose. This is the most important thing in education."

Young Cabot had thrilled to his grandfather's accounts of Teddy Roosevelt's determination to raise a division of volunteers, like the old Rough Riders, and take them to France with his former White House aide, Colonel Frank McCoy— "the finest officer in the Army." Wilson's new Secretary of War, Newton Baker, frustrated the effort. But Cabot was equally thrilled that his Uncle Gussie Gardner, who had been a captain in the Spanish-American War and was now a major in the reserves, had gone off voluntarily to train in Louisiana, even though as a congressman he could not be called up with his outfit. Gussie took a voluntary reduction in rank to get a combat assignment. But he had sickened in the winter's flu epidemic, and died in January, 1918. "I know that you will feel the deep sorrow we all feel," the senator wrote Cabot, "and if you have not already done so I want you to write a most affectionate letter to your Aunt Constance, telling her how much you feel for her. I am anxious too that you should always remember him and never forget his example, in which you, as his nephew, must feel the greatest pride. . . . To his country he gave his life just as if he had fallen on the field of battle and as long as you live you must always think of this and try to live up to the high ideal of life and service which he has left to you." *

Easter of 1918 was a sad time for Cabot. He had come down with measles, and Bessie, fearing Helena might catch them, had him stay at

---

* The letter left a profound impression. Years later Cabot, responding to a newspaper's request to contribute to a series on "the man he most admired," devoted it to the story of Congressman Gardner's volunteering and his death in service.

Middlesex during the holidays. To make matters worse, the boys' beloved Dawdy, Henry Adams, died in his eighty-third year, and was buried in Rock Creek Park near the monument to his wife. Bessie wrote him about the funeral: "It was beautiful. I wish you had been there. It shows what a beautiful personality can do in life in spite of old age and physical infirmities. Dawdy's friends both men and women feel as bereft as if he was a young man & the three ladies who lived with him*——especially Miss Tone and Miss Adams——have shown the greatest feeling and devotion. I waited with them yesterday while the grave was filled in & then they covered it with flowers so lovingly & sweetly as if they were tucking dear Dawdy in for the night. And now he lies in the shadow of that beautiful monument by his wife's side, whom he loved so faithfully & whose death he mourned so bitterly 33 years ago."

With the Republican congressional victory of 1918, just as the war ended, Senator Lodge became majority leader. He also reached his apogee as chairman of the powerful Foreign Relations Committee. Soon the epic struggle over the League of Nations began. "It occurred just as I was beginning to pay attention to public events," Cabot recalled afterward. "I got tremendously caught up in the excitement of the whole thing."

"My outstanding recollection of Cabot," Instructor Galbraith recalled many years later, "was his firm but courteous rebuff of Charles Townsend Copeland, professor of English at Harvard, who came to the school to give one of the readings for which he was famous. As a preliminary to his reading, 'Copey' commented on the League controversy and deplored in no uncertain terms the stand Senator Lodge was taking." He tossed off a phrase, "Lodge, Ludendorf, Lippman and Lenin" which the youngster found as mystifying as it was insulting.

"At the close of the reading, Cabot walked up to Prof. Copeland and said, 'Professor Copeland, I am Senator Lodge's grandson. I think you have done him a great injustice, and I want you to know I resent your unfair criticism of him.' This from a boy of 16 to a highly regarded college professor with whom few undergraduates would care to match wits or engage in an argument. That episode raised Cabot many notches in my respect for his sturdiness of character, his fearlessness in expressing his views, his loyalty to his famous grandfather and the dignity with which he carried himself, all showing a maturity far beyond his years. It seemed to me a foreshadowing of the quality of man he was to become."

Cabot, if caught up by the war, was not nearly as caught up by his

---

* Mrs. Lodge referred to Miss Aileen Tone, who was Adams' secretary and companion; Miss Elizabeth Adams (Elsie)—daughter of his brother Charles Francis Adams Jr.,—who went to Europe with him every summer; and Miss Louisa Hooper, a niece of his wife who often stayed with him.

50 studies. "I am considerably disappointed with Cabot's achievement this year," Master Winfield Brown wrote Bessie that December, "for he fails in Geometry and barely misses failure in Greek. He is sitting back and taking things easy. Lessons have been too easy for him in the past. Very gifted mentally with a superb equipment in French and German, he has been able to keep along with half the work of the other boys. Now, confronted with Greek and mathematics, he applies the same easy-going methods and consequently fails. He will lose his ability to use his mind on tough problems unless he wakes up."

Senator Lodge joined in the waking up with new rebukes:

"All you need to do is to work. You do not do well with your geometry and your Greek simply because you do not work at them. You are entirely able to grasp them both but you must not be lazy. It would be a terrible disappointment to me if you should fail on any of your Harvard examinations. . . . You have only a few months so lose no time."

By June, 1919, Cabot had slipped from seventh to ninth in a class of twenty, with an average of 73.8. Though he had a year to go, under the system then prevailing he took his examinations for admission to Harvard that summer. He passed elementary and intermediate French and German, elementary Greek, and managed to squeak by in algebra and plane geometry.

Cabot had shot up like a string bean, and was skinny, as he would always remain. Bessie, doubtless thinking of Bay's early death, worried about his physique, wanted him to get more exercise, but worried lest he tax his heart. "I am very anxious that Cabot develop his chest," she wrote Dr. Howe. "He is hollow-chested and his head juts forward." Howe, the old rowing-master, set him to pulling sculls—a sport Cabot grew very fond of. John's eye-twitching had grown so severe, meanwhile, that Bessie decided to send him off to a school at Mesa, Arizona, where he could study Latin, Greek, history and geometry and at the same time learn to ride in the open. "I've got a horse of my own and ride a great deal," John wrote to a Mr. Taylor, a Middlesex master. "You have to do everything yourself: clean your horse, clean your house (each boy has a small house), make your bed, chop your own wood for your fire."

Taylor thought some of the same kind of life might be very good for Cabot that summer. A former pupil told him of a rancher in Melville, Montana, Blakeman, who might take Cabot in. Taylor wrote him, "Due to the family tradition and the family mode of life, the boy is apt to be a little soft physically and possibly in other ways. It is thought that a summer on a ranch in which there would be plenty of hard work to do and yet hard work tempered to the boy's strength might give him a stamina and a steadying influence. . . ." Blakeman wrote back that he would chance such "trouble and responsibility" only if it were "made well worth my while to do so." Evidently Bessie, who expressed a frequent concern over expenses, felt she could not afford it. Instead, Cabot got his exercise that summer at Bell Isle, a military camp at Portsmouth, New Hampshire, run by a tough former marine major, W. H. Parker. He trained there from July 1 to September 7, was six feet one and 155½ pounds when enrolled, had gained a half-inch and five pounds when "honorably disenrolled." Captain Parker assessed him thus:

Promotions and reductions—*appointed corporal, Aug. 18, 1919.*
Markmanship qualifications—*very good.*
Seamanship—*none.*
Swimming—*very good.*
Military efficiency—*excellent.*
Physical condition—*excellent.*
Remarks—*A splendid young soldier, zealous and most efficient in all duties.*

Cabot's interest in his grandfather's struggle with Wilson was growing deeper. He was among the crowds who, earlier that March of 1919, jammed Boston's Symphony Hall to hear Lodge debate the League of Nations with Harvard's President A. Lawrence Lowell. This contest between the scholar-senator and the head of his own college caught the popular imagination. The crowds flowed into the aisles, and thousands more outside strained against police ropes despite a cold mist and rain. Newsboys sold scorecards, listing each debater's accomplishments like the weight of rival prizefighters —lists of degrees, of books published, offices held (Lowell could trace his New England ancestry farther back).

A young man from the Boston Y led the crowd in "Onward Christian Soldiers" and the singing broke into a prolonged shout as Governor Calvin Coolidge led the two contestants to the stage. Coolidge, with laconic brevity, introduced Lodge as the first speaker. Cabot sat enthralled.

The old senator, except for the whiteness of his beard and deeper lines in his face, still looked very much as he did when John Singer Sargent caught him on his canvas in the 1890's—nearly six feet tall, but so thin as to seem smaller; a small, eager face, with a lingering boyishness to the bright blue eyes beneath the short curly hair, overall a faint expression of hauteur and aloofness. His voice was powerful, vibrant, but he spoke conversationally, right hand in his trouser pocket, left hand resting easily on the rostrum. Only three years before, Lodge had said "the peace of the world can be maintained only . . . by the forces which united nations are willing to put behind the peace and order of the world. . . . The great

52   nations must be so united as to be able to say to any single country, you must not go to war, and they can only say that effectively when the country desiring war knows that the force which the united nations place behind peace is irresistible."

Now, he asserted that he was not against *any* league—but Wilson's Covenant was poorly drawn. It failed to protect the Monroe Doctrine, American sovereignty over domestic issues was not properly asserted, and the Covenant was wrongly linked integrally with the Versailles Peace Treaty. If Wilson had sought the Senate's advice, its weaknesses would be corrected—and ratification follow as a matter of course. Waxing emotional, Lodge cried: "I am an American, I never had but one flag, and I am too old to learn to love another, an international flag."

Lowell's own moderate speech was the better argument, but this somewhat demagogic conclusion clearly won the evening's loudest applause. Young Cabot went back to Middlesex feeling that his grandfather certainly had the people with him, and had no question that he was right. Coolidge said, "Both men won."

The historic struggle came to its final showdown in early 1920, during Cabot's last year at Middlesex. The young man read each day's debates with the keenest interest. Wilson himself, who had collapsed while taking his case to the country the previous fall, lay ill and almost inaccessible in the White House.

When the showdown vote came on March 19, 1920, Lodge was trying to marshal his forces to ratify the League and the Treaty with his own Reservations—chiefly reasserting U.S. sovereignty, the Monroe Doctrine, and Congress's final power to decide on the use of American troops under Article X which called for collective action against aggressors. A quarter century later, Congress would make much the same reservations in joining another league—the United Nations—and a Democratic President would take them for granted. In 1920, some of Wilson's own most loyal supporters, including Herbert Hoover and Colonel House, urged him to accept the Treaty with the Lodge Reservations, feeling sincerely that they did not cripple the League.

Wilson stubbornly refused. The League was defeated—ironically, not by Lodge, who voted for it, but by Wilson who insisted that the loyal Democratic Senators vote *against* it, and they did so: twenty-three Democrats obeying Wilson combined with fifteen Republican irreconcilables who wanted no League. Thus they deprived it of the needed two-thirds majority. "Just as I expected to get my Democrats to vote with my Republicans on going into the League," Lodge told Corinne Roosevelt Robinson that afternoon, "a hand came out of the White House and drew back those Democrats."

Lodge thought this was more colossal egotism, like Wilson's "personal war" on Huerta: "He was so set upon having his own way that he was ready to destroy the Treaty of Versailles, which was framed to replace a victorious war with a victorious peace, rather than permit any modification in the terms of the League . . . which he identified with himself."

That last year, Cabot's studies improved markedly. He had been trying to carry too much, taking German tutoring in addition to his Greek and Latin. The school could not supply him his third year of Greek. With his load lightened, by February he had managed even to get his physics up to an 88, his Latin to 83, was back on the honors list and stood second in his class of eighteen. Moreover, he had cut his punishment rounds in half, to twenty, from the forty-two that had provoked this rebuke from Heber Howe in November: "A boy in the First Class should have better control of himself as rounds are contracted only for careless mistakes." At the term's end Howe could say, "The boy has . . . worked faithfully . . . and has in so many ways proved himself to be a dependable member of my household and the School, that I have only praise for him." In the final term, Cabot's physics slipped slightly but he managed to finish eighth in his class of nineteen with an average of 78. "I am sure he will prove a credit to the school," Howe could now write Bessie confidently. He had just missed honors. "I wish he might have had a 'frill' on his diploma, for I am quite sure he had the mental ability to do so."

Bessie proudly came to his commencement and heard Governor Coolidge deliver the address. Coolidge had been loath to come, had refused all invitations to speak at prep school commencements that busy political year. In fact his secretary had sent a routine refusal the same day Coolidge wired his own acceptance—after receiving a request from Senator Lodge. "The fact that he was not only willing to make an exception," Mr. Winsor wrote Bessie, "but to make it at the last moment, putting the engagement into a crowded week, shows how anxious he was to accede to any request the Senator might make of him." Coolidge's exhortations were lost to posterity. No record was made, and Cabot himself could remember nothing he said. As for the senator, he was not even there; he was off in Chicago preparing the Republican Convention of 1920, which he would chair, and to gleefully await the Republican victory which would give him his ultimate triumph over Wilson.

Cabot filled out his application for Harvard, then went off to Labrador to help Dr. Wilfred Grenfell in his famous medical mission. The English doctor's selfless work of taking supplies by dogsled and boat through icy seas, to isolated Eskimo fishing communities, had caught the imagination of New Englanders who helped him build schools and hospitals. Cabot went up to his headquarters at St. Anthony, helped him wheel supplies

54   from boats, helped tar the roofs of new buildings (work which his brother John repeated the following summer). He was an able seaman on the "Wop," the boat which brought supplies and medical care to the Labrador coast. He came back tanned and toughened.

That fall he went off to Harvard, preceded by this shrewd "estimate of character" from Headmaster Winsor:

> *H. C. Lodge Jr. is a grandson of the Senator and comes honestly by a real interest in intellectual things and in government and history. He is able, somewhat opinionated, and somewhat stubborn, but he has a winning smile and he intends to do right. I wish there were more fields of intellectual endeavor at Harvard outside the classroom, because he is one of the men who needs such fields to keep him stimulated.*

Cabot would find plenty to stimulate him.

CHAPTER FIVE

The Lodge some of us first met at Harvard . . . was a smiling young man of positive opinions. The fight over the League of Nations was still in the air, which meant that Lodge, though popular, was a center of controversy in the Yard inasmuch as he not only bore his grandfather's name but had inherited his convictions. Lodge did not duck the issue. He made himself heard in no uncertain terms, and it was just as certain that he would be heard from in the future. —John Mason Brown, *Through These Men* (Harper & Brothers, 1956)

Harvard was an accepted part of young Cabot's heritage. George Cabot had gone there, briefly, before sailing away on a codfishing boat to start the family fortune. One of Cabot's kinsmen, President Langdon, had prayed for the Yankee troops in Cambridge Common before they marched on Bunker Hill. Another, Elizabeth Cabot, became President Kirkland's wife; she was of such independent spirit that she distinguished herself as the first American woman to climb the Great Pyramid at Gizeh. The old senator had taught American history at Harvard—as Henry Adams' protege, and at his urging. And of course Bay had gone there.

Young Lodge majored in Romance languages. The senator had promised him a trip to Europe if he could finish in three years. Accordingly, he took on six full courses ("A very tough program indeed," Harvard's present dean, John Monro, says. "The ordinary Harvard load is four courses. Six is the maximum allowed.") He took English A (Rhetoric and English Composition); he took French 2 (French Prose and Poetry), German 2a (Introduction to German Literature of the 18th and 19th Centuries) and, in deference to the senator, continued his classics (Latin A, Cicero and Vergil). He took Professor C. H. Haskins' History 1 (European History from the Fall of the Roman Empire to the Present Time) and heard Professors J. H. Woods, Ralph Barton Perry and William E. Hocking give their Introduction to Philosophy.

Cabot worked hard at his studies, and did well. He had a good grasp of German, from Fräulein Schultz and his tutoring. His French, one classmate remembers, was better than the instructor's. "He was quick of mind, quick to laugh, and quick to plunge into an argument," recalls John Mason Brown, the soft-spoken Kentuckian who was in the class ahead of Lodge but became a close friend in spite of being a remorseless Democrat. "He was an extrovert, cocksure in a community of youths many of whom were equally confident. Although seldom seen studying, he always had the re-

56 quired knowledge. No one would have guessed from his relaxed manner and his undergraduate activities that he was carrying extra courses."

Brown, a man of great wit and charm, became a favorite of the old senator's, not only for himself but because Brown's grandfather and namesake had written a history, *Political Beginnings of Kentucky,* which the senator knew and admired. To clinch the bargain, Theodore Roosevelt had admired it too—and had once visited Grandfather Brown in Kentucky and spent the night at his home.

Young Lodge found time to play. During the winter Boston's eligible youths were expected to dance two or three times a week at debutante balls in the cream-and-gold hall of the Somerset Hotel. Cabot danced well, and liked parties. He drank very sparingly ("demon rum just never appealed to him," says old Nahant chum J. O. Bangs). He liked to act, especially in French dramas with the Cercle Français. He did so well in his studies that he made the dean's list, and was promptly applauded by Headmaster Winsor from Concord; Winsor, jealous of his school's reputation, kept a sharp eye on the work of his graduates, both prodding or hailing them as the situation required. He wrote Cabot in April, 1921, that his midyear record "comes so near being a distinguished one that I certainly hope you will be able to add some A's to it so that you may be a member at least of the second group of scholars, which certainly would be worth the extra effort that it would require." Cabot tried, but the best he could do was a B average. When his ranking was published on the Dean's list, his old headmaster wrote, "I want you to know that I appreciate very much the success of your last year's work, and the fact that you are enrolled in the group which is described as scholars of 'distinction.' " Winsor showed his appreciation by inviting Cabot, and the other Middlesex man who won the same distinction, to "dine with me quite informally at the Union at 7" one evening that January, 1922.

In the summer of 1921 Cabot and his brother John went to France to work for Anne Morgan's Committee for Devastated France. They lived in tents at Le Mieux la Croix St. Ouen, helping run a French Boy Scout camp for boys whose fathers had been killed or whose homes were destroyed in the war. They helped bring in supplies in a Model T truck, which would jackknife if one turned the wheel too sharply.

John was driving and Cabot sternly warned him: "Be very careful, John, you're not very good at driving, you know." Just then John turned the wheels too sharply and the truck jacknifed right through the window of a café, whose owner came out exclaiming shrilly: "That's the way Americans are! When they want a drink they drive right into the café in their car!"

The boys worked hard, and made many friends among the orphaned

French. They came away with a lasting sense of the hideousness of war.
They also perfected their French which now was as natural to them as
English. They returned to Harvard, where John had entered the year after
Cabot. They liked to sing together, and John Brown recalls an Easter at
East Point where Cabot and John "blew the roof off" with their barber-shop
rendition of "The Red Red Robin" and other ditties. Both sang in the Glee
Club.

In his second year Cabot was carrying seven subjects, including three
full courses—Prof. H. H. Burbank's Principles of Economics, Bliss Perry's
History of English Literature from Elizabethan Times to the Present, and
French 6 (General View of French Literature, by Professors C. H. Grand-
gent, J. D. M. Ford) and others. He also took four half-courses, J. A. Walz's
Influence of English Literature Upon German Literature in the 18th Century, George H. Chase's History of Ancient Art, Introduction to Geology,
and G. H. Edgell's History of Medieval, Renaissance and Modern Art.

Cabot became secretary of the Cercle Français. He was elected to Harvard's most erudite club, the Signet Society. "Some of the best talk I've
heard must have been at lunch there," John Brown recalls warmly. Thomas
Wolfe would be there, Philip Barry, the playwright, who was just writing
his first short stories, Donald Oenslager, who later distinguished himself
as a famous stage designer; Charlton MacVeagh, a brilliant writer and
talker. There was Cabot, Oliver La Farge, Ogden Nash, and young Corliss
Lamont, son of the Morgan banker. Cabot liked, above all, to talk. Talking
was his favorite exercise. Bull sessions were his meat, political arguments
his delight.

Lodge and Lamont were roommates throughout college, but poles apart
in their arguments. Lamont was as passionately pro-League of Nations as
Lodge was against. Lamont was fascinated by Lenin's beginning efforts to
build Communism; Lodge was as horrified by this sympathy as his forebear George Cabot had been of Jefferson's Jacobinism. But as often as they
hammered at each other, the two roommates never lost their temper. Instead, they formed a Debating Union where Lodge took the affirmative for
high tariffs and Lamont opposed them. Lodge also liked to write. He fired
a broadside at starry-eyed idealists—he regarded Lamont as one—in an
article for the *Advocate* called "Political Sentimentalists." Lodge was a
staunch member of both the Republican and Conservative Clubs. He was
not in Porcellian, his grandfather's top-drawer dining club, but the less
prestigious Fox Club instead.

Lodge no longer had many brushes with the school's authorities. He was
allowed to take off December 21, his freshman year, so as to go to Plymouth
to hear his grandfather deliver the Tercentenary Address in honor of New
England's founding. He had asked for two more days, so as to go on from

58 Plymouth to Washington with his grandfather, thus stretching the leave through Christmas. The dean ordered him to return for classes before Christmas recess. ("Deans never change," observes Harvard's John Monro, "we would do the same today.")

Cabot's favorite sport was rowing. He was on the freshman and sophomore crews, and was made captain of the junior crew. The egghead Signet chose him as its president in 1923, Cabot's final year. "Cabot liked or disliked people with the same intensity with which they liked or disliked him," says John Mason Brown.

His fellow eggheads were sometimes merciless in their flayings of Senator Lodge—he had helped nominate Harding, and had "notified" him at Marion—for President Harding's torturing of the English language, in a peculiar style which Mencken called "Gamalielese" and which Harding himself called "bloviating," a rambling, portentous mixture of platitudes, patriotism and nonsense. At a club dinner in Boston, when someone deplored that the French ambassador, M. Viviani, could speak no English, a catty Bostonian remarked: "Neither can Mr. Harding."

When Cabot relayed these complaints, the senator conceded that he could not share Harding's "affection for odd words . . . like 'normalcy.' . . . Perhaps I am less sensitive about it because I have been through eight years with a man who wrote English very well without ever saying anything."

Robert Lincoln O'Brien, editor of the Boston *Herald,* slyly sent the senator a note calling Harding "a student of Shakespeare's great play, 'Charles V.'" When the Senator replied that he knew no such play, O'Brien cited Harding's speech to some Boston actors, quoting lines from *Henry IV* and ascribing them to "Charles V." O'Brien regretted that "circumstances have not called to the great office someone of more bell-like mentality." The scholar-senator winced: "Charles V, of course, is mentioned in Shakespeare only in Henry VIII where there is an allusion to him because he was the nephew of Catherine of Aragon and was deeply interested in trying to protect his aunt against the divorce."

The senator doted on Cabot, and sought to have him with him as much as possible. They always tried to make the Harvard-Yale football and baseball games together. "My dearest Cabot," the senator wrote on May 18, 1922, raising a problem of great delicacy, "I can take two tickets for the Harvard baseball game at New Haven on June 20th and two for the boat race on June 23, but this privilege is given to me by Yale. I have the Yale LL.D. and for that reason the applications are sent to me. I do not know whether you want to take Yale tickets, because I suppose the Yale tickets would give seats with the Yale crowd and that you would prefer to be with your own." Shortly thereafter, Harvard sent the senator tickets of its own —and the problem was solved.

Lodge began trying out for a role in the Hasty Pudding Show, *Take a Brace* (it involved suspenders), and sought theatrical-minded John Mason Brown's coaching, but failed to get the part. However he went with the Hasty Pudding troupe when it put the show on for President Harding. The President died shortly thereafter, and The Hasty Pudding songwriter, Louis Silvers ["It isn't Raining Rain, You Know"], the play's outside "pro" advisor, remarked irreverently, "It took only one man to kill Lincoln."

Lodge got through Harvard with a minimum of escapades. One of the big events of the year was the Somerset ball, the night before the Harvard-Dartmouth football game. In 1922, such a mob was crushing to get inside that it was nearly a riot, and a beefy policeman was blocking off the crowd. Cabot, in white tie and tails, clutching his admission ticket imperiously, pushed his way through, causing the policeman to lose control of the crowd. In his wake pushed his friend and admirer, Thorwald Sanchez, son of the governor of Camaguey in Cuba, "You're under arrest!" cried the angry officer, whistling for his paddy wagon.

He shoved Lodge into it.

"Arrest me, too!" demanded Sanchez loyally.

He was shoved in after Cabot.

Both were booked for intoxication, though disorderly conduct was probably a fairer description. Senator Lodge was up for reelection, only five weeks away. A scandal could damage him.

"Name?" the booking officer asked Cabot.

"Henry Lodge," said the young man.

The officer wrote it down carefully, then did a double take.

"Any relation to the senator?" he asked sharply.

Lodge handled the problem brilliantly. He waited a long while, frowning, before replying. Finally he nodded, "I think so," unsurely—as if claiming an association which might prove helpful. It was just enough to convince the officer that he was claiming a relation not rightly his. The students spent the night in stir, and were released next morning—the papers happily missing the story.

Lodge made up for such high jinks by finishing Harvard, *cum laude*, in three years. In his third and final year, Cabot carried four full courses and four half-courses. His French advanced to Louis Allard's Romanticism and Realism in French Literature of the 19th Century, and his second course, French Comedy from Scribe Down to the Present Day, and in addition Professor L. J. A. Mercier's advanced course in French Composition during the spring term. He added Spanish to his languages, taking

60   a full course in Spanish Grammar, Reading and Composition. A fall half-course was Elementary Meteorology—the Weather and Weather Forcasting. In the spring he took Dr. Ralph M. Eaton's English Philosophy from Bacon to Mill, and found Eaton "a singularly luminous intellect." Eaton himself was so impressed by Cabot's love of philosophy that he invited him to stay on at Harvard and teach the subject. But Cabot asked for a year's leave of absence so he could be graduated with his class of 1924, and went to work as a reporter for the old *Transcript,* a paper as aristocratic as it was unprofitable (the Boston butler's supposed remark is legendary: "Sir, there are two reporters outside and a gentleman from the *Transcript*").

"My grandfather encouraged me to enter journalism instead of studying law," Lodge recalled later. "As one who was himself a member of the bar he felt that journalism was at least the equal of the law as training for political life." Moreover, the senator, whom Henry Adams made his assistant as editor of the *North American Review,* could pass on to Cabot Editor Adams' invaluable editorial advice: "Very early in my apprenticeship, I remember his handing me an article by an eminent local historian and antiquary, and saying, 'We shall print his article, of course, but I wish you to go over it and strike out all superfluous words, and especially all needless adjectives.' I faithfully performed my task and found to my surprise that without changing . . . the article I had shortened it by several pages."

As a cub reporter, young Lodge continued to room with Corliss Lamont at Holworthy Hall. He did whatever odd jobs the city editor assigned him. One day he covered the City Hall on the regular man's day off. At Mayor James M. Curley's noontime conference, a *Globe* reporter, as unaware as the mayor of the new reporter's identity, asked: "Have you heard anything further, your honor, from Senator Lodge about getting more navy contracts for the Boston Navy Yard?" "Why yes," said the golden-tongued Curley, "I had a letter from the old son of a bitch today, asking me to please lay off him in the public prints and saying he would do the best he could for the Yard." Lodge took notes unperturbed.

Young Lodge quickly showed a knack for writing the kind of human interest features which the *Transcript* spread across a half-page of the second section. He did one on Boston's first dial telephone ("Dramatically the first machine-made phone call was put through last Saturday night at the Aspinwall exchange. . . . Traffic manager William J. Lund who answered this first dialed call of Greater Boston was told by the caller that she had stayed up until after twelve in order to be sure that this new machine-switching, dial-using, operatorless telephone was a reality and not an idle dream".) Finding the phone system a promising news source, he did another feature in July, 1923, with a chart showing the peaks and valleys of telephoning in

Boston's various districts. At three in the morning, the lowest ebb, only Richmond Exchange, the market district was stirring ("already the vegetable dealers and the butchers are starting the day"). In the vagaries of University Exchange, he got in a playful swipe at his classmates. "There seems to be something loose, irregular and irresponsible about its line. Although it combines the features of a business and of a residential section, it seems as though it were uphill work for the Cambridge businessmen and housekeepers to make this chart wholly respectable. Note the abnormality of the 1:30 point when most people are having luncheon in the business sections. Here the telephone seems to be fairly humming with the calls which the Harvard student is making to his dean, his athletic manager, or his bootlegger."

He scooped all the Boston papers with a page one story about the Ku Klux Klan, having made his way into one of its secret meetings, and was flattered to receive a klansman's note warning him to keep quiet or else. His answer was to make some more investigations, pretend he wanted to join the Klan, interview some of its members who were jealous of each other, and print three more articles denouncing it. He tried his hand as critic, did a first-night review of Pavlova which so pleased the *Transcript's* theater and music critic, H. T. Parker, that he assigned Lodge to Pavlova for a whole week.

Roving the streets of old Boston, the young reporter found his ancestral blood stirred by such relics of the past as Thomas Hollis' apothecary shop, "a four story lopsided edifice with a gold mortar and pestle hanging over the door . . . the good old windows are pleasantly dirty, the floor is quaintly rough, the rafters are unhewn and the rows upon rows of bottles are covered with a venerable dust." It called up "the huge billowing sails of brigs and barkentines" which "once floated in and out of Boston harbor," and Cabot was glad to find the manager, Mr. Charles F. Lucy, "a fitting priest for this temple. When asked whether his was the first drug store in Boston, he looked up with a gentle, tolerating smile and said, 'It's the *only* drug store in Boston.'"

The scion of George Cabot, whom John Adams commissioned as America's first Secretary of the Navy, prowled the Charles Town Navy Yard, and boarded the battleship *Utah* to interview its commander, Captain Rufus Z. Johnston, a Medal of Honor winner whom he found "a living proof that military life does not make martinets," who "maintains contentment without laxity, order without friction and justice without tyrannical penalties," realizing that "in order to promulgate among others honor, virtue and patriotism, every man must show it in himself." He found that Captain Johnston "believes that there is some worthy side to every man's character." He told how Captain Johnston, instead of giving a disorderly discharge to a drunken old seaman who had offended again after repeated warnings,

62 kept him on as apprentice to the blacksmith, himself a reformed toper, on condition he never go ashore, and after two years the man was so totally reformed that when he transferred to another ship for a better job, "the crew lined up on the deck and gave him a cheer, for they had seen him raise himself from his former condition to one of universal respect." Such wisdom had brought the captain "the intense, loyal and unstinted devotion of his subordinates. He is a true example of what the articles for the government of the U.S. Navy demands of commanders—'to show themselves a good example of virtue, in honor and patriotism.'" The words are worth remembering, for despite their own tendency to "bloviate," they reflect a fine and simple streak in Lodge's character which would grow and deepen with the years.

Amid his prolific *Transcript* output, he found time to try his hand as a political speaker, praising the tariff and damning the League of Nations before a Young People's Club in a Roslindale church. He wrote John Mason Brown, who had graduated and gone off to Europe with Donald Oenslager, about his performance; walking slowly to the right side of the platform, pointing his finger at the audience, and saying quietly: "All of us here tonight are very young but the time is not so far when all the young women here will have children. I sincerely hope so." Then, raising his voice, he continued, "I ask any of you here whether you would be willing to send your boy to a distant province to fight for the crimes which some Oriental potentate may have committed." No one would be; Lodge confessed he enjoyed the performance as much as anything he had ever done, adding: "I received four dollars for it, so now I am a professional." Others found him so, too. Leverett Saltonstall, who was making his first run for the legislature, sought to get a little publicity in the *Transcript* and went to see Publisher George Mandell. "I'll send you down to see Cabot Lodge," said Mandell in his squeaky voice. "My heart sank about 40 miles," Saltonstall recalled long later, "I thought he meant the old Senator. Instead, I found this pink-cheeked youngster who began firing questions at me. 'When are you going to a meeting?' 'When are you making a speech?' 'How can I write anything if you don't make any speeches?'"

At the end of the year, Cabot decided to cash in his grandfather's promise of the trip to Europe. The senator took him to see President Coolidge, saying: "This young man finished Harvard in three years, but I had to bribe him to do it." Coolidge gave him a "To whom it may concern" letter for his trip and Secretary of State Hughes gave him another. Cabot cabled Brown he would catch up with him in Florence. He arrived in Italy, managed easily to get an interview with Mussolini (the *Transcript* played it as a scoop), and went on with Brown to Vienna, where he found the *lieder* and the *spritzer* of its cafes so congenial that he sang a solo in one, and was offered

a contract to become a salaried nightly performer. "He was really torn,"
John Brown recalls. They went on to Paris together, finding pleasant company there in some old Boston friends of the Lodges, Dr. and Mrs. Henry
Sears and their two attractive blond daughters, Emily and Jean. To know
the Sears family was, by the account of those who did, one of life's most
enjoyable experiences. They were remarkably close to one another, yet
joyously open to all their friends; they loved good talk, good music, good
wine, and were happiest watching young people enjoy themselves. Emily
had an irrepressible, bubbling gaiety and unaffected charm which captivated all who knew her. "Cabot, the dog," says Brown, "was courting
Emily that whole spring in Paris, but he kept us all in the dark. He'd see
Emily in the morning, then meet me for lunch and never let on where he'd
been."

The young reporter also kept on with his interviews. He had seen Austria's President Michael Hainisch. In Paris, he interviewed President Poincaré, and Gaston Doumergue, who was President of the Senate. He had a
good talk with an old family friend, the permanent head of the Foreign
Office, the Count de Chambrun* who coined the phrase, "To be a diplomat,
it is not enough to be stupid; one must also be polite." He saw the foreign
minister at a reception he was giving for an Indian prince who was in Paris
on his honeymoon. The prince invited Cabot to accompany him on the
town, and after many sights and considerable champagne, Cabot awoke
next morning to find the prince in the other bed at his hotel. "My God, the
bride will be frantic!" he thought, shaking the prodigal awake.

Cabot came home to the *Transcript*. His old roommate Corliss Lamont,
had gone off to England for a year at Cambridge. They resumed their political baiting of one another by mail, Lodge observing, "As far as I can see
there is nothing that we agree on. . . . It is a good thing to bear in mind,
I think, never to let a difference in views temper one's personal feeling.
. . . I am so interested in public questions and so are you that there is a
possibility that some day we may become violent in what we say to each
other. Let us always remember that that is our 'official side'—don't you
think so? The only thing that we do agree on is that better men are needed
in politics." Politics aside, the young scholars could meet on friendly ground.
Wrote Lodge:

> *I have read Lytton Strachey's recent book which you spoke of—"Land-
> marks in French Literature." It is below his previous works, in my*

* A descendant of Lafayette. When General Lafayette's son, George Washington du
Motier, took refuge in Boston, as M. Motier, when his father was imprisoned for five
years by the French Revolution, President Washington wrote George Cabot asking
him to provide him asylum.

judgment. His "Books and Characters" is much better. In that he shows a gift of criticism which no Englishman barring Matthew Arnold has possessed. There is no school of criticism in English literature the way there is in French. The French have a type of mind admirably adapted to it. The school of Sainte Beuve is justly famous and has many brilliant fellows now writing whose works it would pay you to read. If you are interested in Voltaire . . . Strachey's best account of him is in the "Books and Characters." . . . As you say he is "some man." The meeting between him and Benjamin Franklin when they kissed on the platform of the Academie at the time of Voltaire's triumph is probably one of the most amusing incidents of its kind in literary history. What would I have given to have seen it! . . . Harry Wheeler's usher's dinner is on the 8th. Shall you be there?

Cabot came home to find his grandfather preparing for the Republican convention in Cleveland, which would prove to be his last. His old antagonist, Woodrow Wilson, had died that February, and the senator would not long outlive him. Wanting Cabot to go to Cleveland with him, he asked the *Transcript* to assign him: "I could of course take him with me," the senator told its Washington chief, Theodore Joslin, "but I would prefer to have him go as a working newspaperman. Handle him as you would any other man. Be hard on him, for I want him to learn everything he possibly can there."

Cabot was scarcely awed by the assignment. He not only covered for the *Transcript,* with Joslin, but rewrote his own dispatches in French and cabled them to *Le Matin* of Paris, with the result that his byline appeared on page one of France's leading political newspaper when he was not yet twenty-two. His *Matin* file of June 12 begins:

. . . à part le groupe dissident du Wisconsin, qui à sa tête le Senateur La Follette, tout le parti est unanime a vouloir nommer M. Coolidge candidat à la presidence." [*Wrongly predicting General Harbord for Vice President, Lodge added:*] Cette candidature est chaleuresement accueillie par les anciens combattants Républicains, qui, à une récente reunion, ont rappellés les services rendu au Général Harbord dans la défense de Soissons et du Bois Belleau.

Cleveland was a humiliating experience for the old senator, who found himself reduced to an ordinary delegate. He had been both keynoter and chairman of the previous convention, presiding over it (so H. L. Mencken wrote) "from a sort of aloof intellectual balcony . . . his soul in some remote and esoteric Cathay. . . . For a while he would watch the show idly, letting it get more and more passionate, vociferous, and preposterous. Then, as if suddenly awakened, he would stalk into it with his club and knock it into decorum in half a minute." Now the old warrior was just part of the crowd. Coolidge in becoming President had taken over the political leadership of Massachusetts. He bore Lodge no malice, even though the senator had helped enact a soldiers' bonus over his veto. But Coolidge's political manager, William M. Butler, an old Lodge opponent, decided to freeze him out at the convention. "I have had every possible convention honor that could be given," Lodge wrote Editor Maurice Sherman of the Springfield *Union*. "They will not hurt my feelings by keeping me out of any place that I may be fitted for at Cleveland, and if it gives them any satisfaction to do it I shall hold no ill-feeling against anybody."

In Cleveland, when the Massachusetts delegation met with Butler in the chair, the senator in the front row, Lodge's name was not even mentioned as the various committee posts were voted on. The senator's face was impassive: "Without blinking an eye or moistening his lips," Butler himself recalled long after, "he stared politely before him and gave his foes no sign of his pain at the performance." He spent his evenings calmly reading Shakespeare in bed, from his favorite green-leather volume. Young Cabot, who shared his hotel room, was indignant at the treatment of his grandfather, but the old man brushed it aside. "I still remember him, lying calmly in his blue-and-white-striped pajamas, smiling and turning back to his Shakespeare." The senator was startled by a wire from Boston's Democratic Mayor Curley deploring his treatment and saying, "Your votes in favor of the soldiers' bonus . . . and of salary increases for post office workers merited the approval of patriotic citizens of Boston. At their request, I am forwarding to you a key to the city, under separate cover."

Shortly after the two Lodges came home, the old man was taken to Charles Gate Hospital in Cambridge to have his prostate removed. All seemed well. He was out on his porch at Nahant, convalescing, when Cabot and John Lodge and John Mason Brown, clad in their towels, walked by him for a naked plunge in the secluded seaside pool. "When he saw us," Brown remembers, "his face took on the most angelic expression. He rose to his full height, and threw his arm out in our direction, in the pantomime of beginning a speech. He looked like an old Roman Senator standing there, beaming down at us with his smile. It seemed like a sort of hail and farewell." The senator returned to the hospital in late October for a second operation, and wrote President Coolidge, who had telegraphed his best wishes: "I shall be back in Washington well and strong," but he was stricken by a cerebral hemorrhage on November 9 and died that evening. A few days later, Cabot followed the cortege out past Harvard to the rolling green cemetery of Mt. Auburn and the large brownstone crypt set in the hillside, with an

66 L carved in script above it. The great key was turned in the iron-latticed door through which other vaults could be seen. Creaking, the door swung open. The senator's casket was placed in a vault near those of his father, John Lodge, of his mother, Anna, and her father, Henry Cabot, whom she had had moved there when the crypt was built. (In the late afternoons she would sometimes come and sit in the tomb to keep him company.) The senator was at rest close to many friends who had often come to his home in his youth—Longfellow, Agassiz, Lowell, Holmes, the gentle Sumner—all these he had known and all now slept close by, on the green banks where the Charles flows to the sea.

There was only one Henry Cabot Lodge now, and he was on his own.

A social and political note in the Boston *Transcript* of July 10, 1925, marks the transition between the two Lodges. "President Coolidge," it reports, "was the guest of honor at a meeting of 1,000 Republican members of the Essex Club at their midsummer outing at Centennial Grove, Chebacco Lake, Essex, yesterday. Henry Cabot Lodge of Nahant moved that he be made an honorary member of the Essex Club—an honor now held only by former President Taft. After this motion had been voted unanimously, President Coolidge smiled and left." The "Junior" is left off Cabot's name; the younger man now honors a President in his own name and right.

Lodge resumed reporting for the *Transcript* after his grandfather's death. He moved over to Beacon Hill, to the gold-domed State House, the most important beat, and covered it better—so said a veteran clerk—than anyone in thirty years of his memory. Political buzzings began to sound about his own head. When a veteran congressman from Gloucester died, the Essex County Republican Council unanimously urged young Lodge to run for the Republican nomination to fill it, overlooking the fact that at twenty-two he was still three years shy of the Constitutional age. Nevertheless, the compliment was flattering.

Lodge was beginning to hunger for a bigger newspaper assignment. There was some talk that he might cover Coolidge's visit to the Black Hills of South Dakota to watch him inspect tall corn, and don Indian bonnets. The prospect was ridiculed by John Mason Brown, now a critic on *Theater Arts Monthly* in New York: "Personally, I can't think of anything more delightful than reporting the color of Mrs. Coolidge's hosiery. The size might make a revelation of social significance . . . it must be sickening watching Cal kiss the champion corn growers who were under 11 years of age and hugging the families of three children, because, by some deep symbolism, that gracious act may suggest that you would embrace a third term with the same avidity. I want you to get to Washington, and the sooner the better. Editorials, analytical articles and carefully considered weekly reports lie within the field of special training that would give you most profit."

Lodge took his advice. He stopped in at the *Herald Tribune* in New York and asked Managing Editor Julian Mason for a job. Mason liked his *Transcript* samples and offered Lodge a tryout at fifty dollars a week in the *Tribune's* Washington Bureau starting October, 1925. Lodge wired Brown the news. Brown wired back: A THOUSAND CONGRATULATIONS. AM DELIGHTED WITH WHAT YOU HAVE DONE. FROM NOW ON WILL BE AN ARDENT READER OF THE TRIBUNE. Lodge wrote farewell letters of deep thanks to Editor James Williams and Publisher Mandell of the *Transcript*. Mandell replied: "You made your own way and you did it well. You came into the office with everyone skeptical, you left it with everyone your friend. I am glad you came so quickly into a worthy job." Lodge plunged immediately into one of the crucial issues of the decade—the future of airpower as a weapon. In covering the hearings of the Air Board then in progress, and the court-martial of General Billy Mitchell, he got some shrewd advice from *Transcript* Editor Williams: ". . . the oligarchy in control of the War and Navy departments at this moment has not hesitated to use its full power to discredit every witness who did not echo the wish of the oligarchy. . . . General Patrick one of the airpower advocates does not wish to rob the land forces of their Air Service, or the sea forces of theirs. What he does ask, however, is that opportunity shall be given to build up a real air force whose mission it will be to fight the battle of the air, not the battle of the sea, and not the battle of the ground. . . ." Williams urged him, "in the language of the liturgy, to 'read, mark, learn and inwardly digest' the true nature of the issue." Lodge would soon be doing that, and with many another vital issue as well. He took life seriously—as classmate Charles Barnes had observed at Middlesex—and he did not come to Washington to waste time.

Shortly after he joined the *Tribune* Lodge exchanged some new letters with his old roommate, Corliss Lamont—then attending Harvard Law School. They give the clearest insight into how his views were maturing, and into the far-seeing realism of the role he thought America should be playing if it was to become the peacemaker that idealist Lamont longed for it to be. The exchange was provoked by Lamont's elation over Congress' approval for the U.S. to join the World Court, which he saw as a prelude to joining the League itself. Lamont began the exchange:

You want to make America great. All right. How are you going to do it? You can't neglect the economics of the situation . . . you will discover how important the political and economic stability of Europe and Asia are to America as a business matter. Forget the statement about our moral responsibility, and consider only our practical good, our enlightened selfishness, and then see if joining the League, with proper reservations, the old Lodge reservations, for instance, will not aid us in a practical, businesslike and unsentimental fashion. . . .

Of course, because of history, it will be extremely hard for you to change your views. But if you ever did so, that step alone would win you the respect and confidence of all intelligent persons. . . . It would prove that you were standing on your own feet and doing your own thinking. . . . I have presumed that you—like all of us—want to see war disappear from the earth. But the method you would use to achieve that end is different from mine. Yet sometimes I have an awful feeling that you don't really want war to go; that, with the U.S. big and strong enough to whip any whole continent leagued against it, you would rather like to see it put forth its power and 'show the world.' How else am I to explain the wild and whirling words you speak about Japan and England? . . .

On Feb. 26, 1926, Lodge took ten thoughtful pages to answer Lamont. It was the first time, he conceded, that he had been forced to try to put his present thinking in coherent order.

You are quite right in saying that "we have not argued about the League; we have gotten mad about it." That is true and natural and proper—considering our extreme youth and entire lack of first hand information. I am almost beginning to think that one cannot enjoy strong views if one knows anything about a subject. . . . I now know a little—a very little—more than I did when we used to argue in college. As a result I am in doubt as to what to think about any number of public questions. At any rate I am going to try, for the first time, to write you in a dispassionate tone, to resist the strong temptation to be abusive. . . . Of course, if you keep on talking to me about a "tiny, absurd, irreconcilable group," I shall retort with something about the "hirelings of the international bankers who prostitute their country's welfare to enhance the value of their employers' investments." But now that I know something of the merits of these questions I should like to confine myself to their merits. But before I become calm and dispassionate . . . you ask me whether I think I have done my "own thinking." . . . For the love of the good Lord, do you think you have? Do you think the influence of a grandfather on the foreign relations committee is any stronger than that of a father who's an international banker? Sweet God, Corliss, remember the proverb about throwing stones and glass houses. . . .

*I've seen such a lot in such a short time and I've had such remark-
able relations with such a number and variety of important people that
I must wait for several years before I can say with your admirable
and enviable definiteness: "Here is the trouble with the world and here
is the way to cure it." Foreign policy has been no exception to this uncertainty. I don't mean the Court . . . which I have never been able
to take very seriously. What I mean is the broad outlook for the United
States in the years to come. I feel, of course, that as long as we can
stay out of the mess the better. But I realize that the world is being
made smaller by modern inventions and that it is a question of time
before we will have to take some responsibility for something. We have
no responsibility for anything now and this beatific condition of having
our cake and eating it too cannot go on indefinitely. . . .*

*I think the case of England shows some points of similarity. Of
course we do not depend for our very existence on trade the way she
does and we are much more self-sufficient and much less interested in
the rest of the world than she is. But . . . we have ten billion dollars
worth of investments in Europe and these, as I think [your father] will
tell you, must be protected. Moreover they will increase and it will become the interest of the American people and not only the American
bankers to see to it that these investments are [protected]. You agree
with the bankers that they must be protected now. I am inclined to wait
until it is to the public's interest and not to that of any one class for us
to interfere. . . .*

*But assume . . . that distances will diminish and that foreign in-
vestments will increase until it becomes imperative for us to protect
them. What then? What did England do when that happened? She
built up her diplomatic machine until it attained a point of perfection
higher, probably, than that of any other country, and then with the
very best facilities for espionage and acquiring information, waited
for any trouble that might arise.*

*Then, whenever trouble arose, it was (and still is) her policy to be
represented at every conference, to worm herself in between every dispute and avert the war and keep things peaceful and the world safe for
British trade. Of course, she kept free all through the past sixty years
and is now rather better than free, for she bosses the only international political organization now existing—the League. Which, I suppose is the reason that the other big powers do not refer their disputes
to it anymore than they absolutely have to.*

*Wanting, as you say, "to make America great," I could want nothing
better than to see her in England's diplomatic position—with a high-
grade trained foreign service in the field; a sage and experienced class*

of "elder statesmen" in the shape of former ambassadors, governors, etc., at home whose influence was being exerted through politics, the platform and the press; and with the one international political club under her control.

But we are not in that position now . . . and it is perplexing to see how, when the time comes, we can be in as good a position. You may not believe it, but there are those who hold more unflinchingly to American political isolation than I do. To these, one argument against our taking a hand is that we have not the experience and equipment to hold our own at an international conference. I agree that we have neither the equipment nor the experience and I know from first hand that our facilities for acquiring information are simply pathetic, but I do not admit this as an argument.

We will never develop the kind of brains required, we will never acquire the experience, Congress will never be prodded into giving enough money—until our fingers have been burned and badly burned by the foreign countries. One cheering thing about our active entry into European politics will be the end of sentimentalism in this country about foreign affairs. This country is quite wise about and very much preoccupied with its internal development. Most Americans don't think about foreign affairs at all, those who do, think about it . . . between sobs and hysterical hiccoughs about brotherly love and so the politicians have a chance to play political football with it. This is unscientific and unintelligent, but it doesn't matter, because we're big and far away. But of course this can't last.

But assume that we do develop an adequate government service for interfering in European politics. The next question is: how shall we interfere? I think that our interest will always be peace and nothing more. I don't believe we'll ever want to run away with the booty after the fight is over, or get it even if no fight takes place. In this case our one interest will be to be free to act, as England always was. I doubt if we'll ever be imperialistic enough to demand the control of an organization, as England controls the League.

So all in all our best course will be, when the time comes that we have to take a hand, for us to build up our diplomatic equipment, nose our way into disputes and try to adjust them. And if the League is still going then—I mean going in fact and not in name—join it with such reservations as my grandfather offered. . . .

I do, Corliss, want to know the facts. That's one of the reasons I chose a profession where I see and write about facts. . . . One paragraph in your letter is not worth answering. It ranks with a remark

you made at the Signet last autumn that if the war department were　　**71**
abolished the U.S. at least would be kept out of war. . . . You wonder
whether or not I "don't really want to go to war." Can't you ever get
beyond the stage of talking about how horrible war is—which, natu-
rally, I agree to—and getting to the second stage of doing something
definite, possible and practical to stop it. . . .
　　Until we meet then—and can talk it over—I am

　　　　　　　　　　　　　　　　　　　　　　Ever yours, Cabot

For the *Trib,* he began covering the White House—and paid close attention, as well, to the War and Navy Department, which the press largely
ignored in the halcyon days of peace and prosperity.

He took a bachelor apartment at 1718 H Street, and found the Metropolitan Club a convenient place to entertain sources. It made him feel at home
to see its former president, Judge Davis, Bessie's father, look benignly down
upon him from his portrait in the dining room.

All of his grandfather's old friends and fellow warriors on the Hill—
Borah of Idaho, Hiram Johnson of California, and others—took him to
their bosom and helped him in innumerable ways. He tended to worship
heroes, and he particularly sought out Brigadier General Frank McCoy, who
had been wounded charging up San Juan Hill with Teddy Roosevelt, and
later served as his aide. McCoy had finally got overseas in World War I as
commander of New York City's Fighting Irish regiment. Lodge had long
talks with him at the Metropolitan, and was fired with a desire for a military career of his own.

A friend, Captain Philip Sherwood, younger brother of playwright
Robert Sherwood, and a superb horseman, had induced Cabot to join the
Cavalry Reserve in Boston. The time came for Cabot to seek promotion to
first lieutenant. Another good friend, Major Willis Crittenberger, a West
Pointer in charge of the press bureau of the War Department, encouraged
him and began spending hours with him at the club coaching Cabot on the
essentials for the first lieutenant's examination. He passed it easily and became attached to the Cavalry at nearby Fort Meyer, Virginia. He went out
there to get practice at jumps.

There and at the War Department he got to know Major George S. Patton,
who had done some spectacular work in tanks in World War I, in the
Argonne, but had gone back to horse cavalry when the Army's postwar
tank appropriation was cut to five hundred dollars.

Cabot also got great enjoyment out of his constant exchange of intimate
letters with John Mason Brown, in which the two shared their hopes and
plans. Cabot had just become engaged to Emily Sears. He wrote to Brown,

72 wishing that his friend could have his "glowing experience." Brown, still not engaged, "enjoyed every jubilant word of it . . . a buoyant and contagious thing, reflecting completely the joy which is now yours."

Brown was torn between trying to become a creative dramatist or seeking a post as a daily theater critic. "I grant you that the creator is the supreme person in the world of art. I think old William Dewitt Hyde stumbled on to truth when he wrote, 'One original line is worth all the able editing in this ably-edited world.'" Brown came down for a weekend with Cabot, Helena and Bessie Lodge. He was so delighted with it he wrote, "tell them that though I face daily the rushing millions of Manhattan; see their haggard faces as they swing from subway to shuttle, hear their weary voices as they chatter among themselves about the day's investments; and feel the cruel push of them as they start and end their daily dash for nickels . . . tell them (your mother and Helena) that over this hubbub I always feel their presence. They speak to me. And I take courage. 'Du courage,' says your mother. 'Du courage,' says Helena. And I lift my knapsack with fresh strength, smile widely to show the new spirit which has entered me, the dybbuk that has taken hold of my soul, and I am lost in a twinkling in the adjacent crowd. I am pushed on to a subway but as the doors slam, and the people breathe their hot breaths and groan with fatigue, a voice can be heard above the din. It is my voice. And it says, 'Thank you Mrs. Lodge and Helena.' And their visions bow and tears of happiness trickle from my eyes."

Brown was an usher and John Lodge the best man when Cabot and Emily were married that July, 1926. The wedding took place at Beverly's small Episcopal Church with a reception after at Beverly Cove, Dr. Sears' sixty-acre summer estate on the Beverly shore some twelve miles from Nahant. It was the North Shore's social event of the year. Great tents were spread on the green lawn, an orchestra played, several score guests toasted the young couple in prewar champagne from Dr. Sears' ample cellars. The wedding united the Cabots and Lodges with another famous old Boston family. Dr. Sears was the grandson of David Sears, who, in the words of one descendant, "owned half the West Coast and all of Alaska" and whose great mansion at 42 Beacon Street (now the Somerset Club) was one of the last great Georgian houses in America. The Searses were people of determination and action. When a daughter of David Sears grew unhappy in her marriage to a Swiss Baron, D'Hauteville, Mrs. Sears chartered a Cunard liner, kept it at Calais with steam up while she abducted her daughter and the two sons from Switzerland, fetched them home and got Daniel Webster to get the daughter a divorce—the first in Boston and in America. They built a second house, attached to theirs, where she could dwell without having to venture forth in public to shock and scandalize the community.

Chapter Five

Emily and Cabot went off to Europe on their honeymoon, spending much of it in Italy. (He carried a letter from the Italian ambassador in Washington praying for *"tutte le facilitazioni e cortesie"* for Signor Lodge *"accompagnato dall sua consorte"* and they got royal treatment.) They had easy entree to all the great salons of Rome and Paris, a good deal more, in fact, than they desired; apart from renewing old ties with Edith Wharton they were content simply to be together and reexplore remembered haunts. Paris was as familiar to Emily as to Cabot, she having gone to school there for three winters prior to her coming out party in Beverly where Cabot first met her in 1923 ("It took me two years to bring Cabot to the boil," she would laugh later on. "I exercised all my wiles, such as they were."). Cabot was on indefinite leave from the *Tribune,* but set on resuming that career. "I feel more enriched after this one year with the *Herald Tribune*," he wrote Helen Rogers Reid in thanks for her wedding present, "than I ever thought possible. . . . It has filled me with the desire to put all the originality and initiative at my command into my work and so do my humble bit toward the perpetuation and promotion of a great tradition."

He and Emily went home to live with the Searses at Beverly Cove in their huge old seaside, shingled house. (East Point, at Nahant now belonged to Uncle John Lodge.) Before returning to the *Trib,* however, Cabot would make his first plunge into politics. William M. Butler, the same Coolidge manager who had humiliated his grandfather at Cleveland, had been appointed to succeed Senator Lodge and was now running to be elected to that seat. "On returning from Europe last week," reported the Boston *Herald* October 1, Lodge "was asked by the Senator if he would not be willing to take the stump for him in every part of the state. . . . Mr. Lodge will comply with the request." He was undoubtedly torn between the anger he still felt for his grandfather's treatment and the grandfather's own admonion to be unfailingly loyal to the party. Lodge proved his loyalty, as well as his own political imagination and versatility.

He began calling up old friends of his from Harvard, particularly famous athletes, and quickly organized the Republican Associates, with the emphasis on youth. He lined up Alfred Chapin, Jr., amateur tennis champion who had played against Tilden, ex-football hero George Owen, Jr., ex-hockey star George Lee, Jr., 1924's football manager John Sherburne, Jr. "It's up to the young voters of the state, the leaders of tomorrow," he broadcast over WEEI. "Shall the State lose an administration so efficient as to be a model for other states of the union? . . . Shall the President be deprived of support from his home state?" He asked and got space in the Harvard *Crimson* to call young Republicans to arms: "If a well-known club after years of prosperous growth and accomplishments takes in no new members, what happens? It fails. . . . If a party no longer gains recruits

74 [the failure is] more dismal and far-reaching." Since only a third of qualified people vote, he said, two-thirds suffer a self-inflicted minority rule. The Boston *Herald* applauded him: "We have been hearing much . . . about the need for developing young men in the Republican party. Until the Republican Associates were organized . . . that talk had amounted to nothing. It now means business." At the Middlesex Club dinner, Lodge made headlines with a five-minute speech: "He read it quickly, clearly and sharply," said the *Herald*. "He gets his words out whole, sharp-edged and straight-aimed." ("If brevity is the soul of success in politics," echoed the Washington *Star*, "Henry Cabot Lodge, Jr. should go far.") On the night before the election he staged an old-fashioned parade, complete with red fire, torchlight and band, from Harvard Square across Harvard Bridge and up Massachusetts Avenue to Convention Hall. "With uniforms and drums and torches and fanfare," observed waggish Bob Washburn in the *Transcript*, "he and his marched for the cause. For it was as natural for him to cling to a Butler in the public service as to a butler in his domestic life. So he and his marched all the way, one wet night when spats lost their integrity, from Cambridge to Boston. It was the first time that a Lodge had played in the streets with the plain people, from a time to which the memory of man does not run."

It was, as it turned out, not quite enough. "That Senator Butler lost a considerable number of votes among the men and women who idolized Senator Lodge there can be no doubt," observed the Springfield *Union*. The senator's own daughter, Constance, had neither forgotten nor forgiven, and on election eve wired the Democratic nominee David I. Walsh, "wishing him all success on the following day. This undoubtedly [said the *Union*] offset everything the grandson had been able to do for Butler and the Lodge adherents voted nearly solidly for Walsh." Walsh won, 524,216 to Butler's 469,261. Nahant went Democratic for the first time in history.

The campaign over, Lodge went back to Washington to resume his job with the *Trib*'s bureau. He and Emily found an apartment. Coolidge had, of course, become President and Cabot, covering the White House, got to know him quite well.

He and the other correspondents swapped their Coolidge anecdotes with one another. There was the Dutch minister who, after three years in Washington, was reassigned, and called on Coolidge to say farewell. "Let me see," said Cal, "are you comin' or goin'?"

Coolidge was a very methodical man and always did everything at the same time every day. Every morning he would come into the oval office at two or three minutes before nine, sit and read his mail, and then, at six or seven minutes after nine, would buzz for his secretary—a beautiful blond girl, Miss Brigham, from Vermont.

She would sit in the accustomed chair without even looking up to see if the President was there, since he always was—waiting to dictate. There would be a long pause while he made up his mind what to say. One particular morning the pause went on longer and longer until she looked up to see whether he was there. He was, all right, squeaking to and fro in the swivel chair, kicking himself around by his toes so he could look at the Washington Monument, then kicking around again to face her, placing the tips of the fingers of each hand opposite one another.

"Miss Brigham," he said finally, "you're a very comely person."

She looked up astounded. More than astounded, she was shocked. She blushed to the roots of her hair. Coolidge looked up again and continued: "You're very personable, you're well-dressed, and altogether it's a pleasure to have you around."

"He's going crazy," Miss Brigham thought to herself. "This is the end."

Finally, in his nasal twang, Coolidge said: "I tell you this to put you in a good humor so that you may be more careful, in the future, about your spelling."

In 1927, after Lindbergh's epoch-making flight, the hero was brought back to the U.S. on a cruiser. It came up Chesapeake Bay and to Washington where the whole city was upside down with the greatest outpouring of hero worship Lodge would ever see.

The White House was undergoing repairs, and the Coolidges were temporarily living at the magnificent Patterson house on Du Pont Circle. They invited Lindbergh and his mother there as official guests. Any Washington hostess would have given an arm to be invited to meet them. Lodge's phone rang that morning, and he was startled to hear a voice announce: "This is Ike Hoover." (Hoover was the White House usher.) "The President and Mrs. Coolidge would like you and Mrs. Lodge to come to lunch today with Colonel Lindbergh and his mother." Lodge thought someone was playing a prank. Finally Hoover persuaded him the invitation was real, and at the appointed hour the young Lodges arrived. There were only six of them at lunch. The crowds were cheering outside and Lindbergh frequently had to get up and wave to appease them.

After lunch the three men retired to a little study, where the President sat in an office chair, tilting to and fro. The springs were squeaky. He got a white cigar-holder, inserted a large cigar, and lit up. Lodge lit a cigarette. Lindbergh didn't smoke. The three men looked at one another waiting for someone to speak.

Lodge, as the most undistinguished man there, did not feel that he should be the first to talk. Neither, apparently, did Lindbergh. It was one of Coolidge's peculiarities that he never felt under obligation to make conversation; in Massachusetts, this had often led others, embarrassed by the silence, to blurt out things they later wished they hadn't said. So the three sat there with Coolidge squeaking to and fro in his chair. Finally, in his nasal twang, Coolidge said: "Colonel, you were in the air mail service, weren't you?" "Yes sir," Lindbergh replied. "How did you like it?" asked Coolidge.

"It was very interesting," said Lindbergh, "and I learned a lot from it. But it got tiresome flying over the same mountains, the same rivers, and the same valleys all the time."

Coolidge rocked back and forth for quite a while longer.

"Well, Colonel," he said, "think of me out there on the *Mayflower* [the Presidential yacht] year after year—same Mayflower, same Potomac, same bank, same everything, except the changes in the seasons."

That August of 1927, during the short-handed vacation season, Cabot got his first crack at writing editorials for the *Trib*.

He came up to New York from his Washington beat to learn the game at the hands of a master, chief editorial writer Geoffrey Parsons, a genial, balding, gifted man who looked like a Rabelaisian friar, and was as charming a companion as he was a trenchant writer.

The combination of a Cabot and a Parsons had its historic flavor. Geoffrey was a direct descendant of Theophilus Parsons, a ringleader with George Cabot in the Essex Junto, which has been described as America's first political machine. Theophilus Parsons became Chief Justice of Massachusetts. His descendant and Lodge soon would form another Essex Junto, for a different reason.

At the moment, however, Lodge found himself doing editorials on the Sacco-Vanzetti case. The approaching execution sent his native Boston, and the world as well, into emotional upheavals, provoking angry divisions which sometimes seemed to have more to do with class against class than with the case itself. Considering Lodge's own Boston origins and class roots, his editorials were refreshingly fair-minded and objective. On August 16 ("The Last Hope") he speaks of the last-resort legal stratagems being tried by the defense, indicating "at least that counsel . . . are using every resource which the law permits. Nor does the law seem altogether destitute of resources. . . . There is, for instance, no written limit to the number of bills of exceptions which may be taken. . . ." On August 24, the execution brings a somber questioning of capital punishment itself. "There will be much searching of hearts," wrote Lodge, "in this solemn hour when the

Commonwealth of Massachusetts has executed its judgment upon Sacco   77
and Vanzetti. The whole vexed problem of capital punishment is involved.
. . . Some revision of the law would seem to be advisable expressly reserv-
ing the extreme penalty for those cases where punishment can be swift and
certain. . . . The time is not one for recrimination or hysteria but for a
sympathetic re-study of the problem of human justice in the light of these
men dead. . . ." And the following day, "while vandals are uprooting
saplings in Paris and hoodlums are hissing Mayor Walker in Berlin," he
urges "the doubters in this country" to "evince a sane and practical interest
in whatever new light can be thrown on the case" by a requested senatorial
investigation, and a suggested "commission of educators, publicists, attor-
neys and labor representatives . . . to inquire into the case."

Lodge showed that he could provide imaginative and scholarly "feature"
leaders such as "Rain After Battle," citing the World War belief that violent
rainstorms occurring after a battle were caused by the artillery. Scholar
Lodge quotes Plutarch: "In the year 101 B.C. after the battle of Aix, where
Caius Marius slew more than 100,000 Teutons, rain fell so hard . . . that
the inhabitants became enriched because the earth was fertilized by . . .
the putrefied bodies. It is an observation also that extraordinary rains pretty
generally fall after great battles, whether it be that some divine power thus
washes and cleanses the polluted earth . . . or that moist and heavy
evaporations, steaming forth from the blood and corruption, thicken the
air." Lodge is not convinced: "Rain after battle may simply be another mere
coincidence like so much else that is puzzling in life, attracting attention
when it comes, ignored when it fails to appear."

Lindbergh's conquest of the Atlantic, followed by other ocean flights, reminded this Nahant seaman of explorers who went "breaking the ice in
search of a northwest passage . . . founding colonies of Virginia and
Newfoundland. The enthusiasm over the news that some daring seaman,
like the captain of the *Buonaventure* for instance, had made the first crossing between the Cape and India surely must have resembled our enthusiasm for the first airman to traverse an equally dangerous stretch of water."

Thus young Lodge earned his spurs on the editorial page.

CHAPTER SIX

I first met him at the Al Smith convention in Houston in 1928. It was almost impossible to get an elevator in the Rice Hotel. I had waited a long while for an elevator in the lobby, and this tall, handsome young fellow beside me said, "I'm going to walk up," and I followed him toward the stairs. A Tammany thug was sitting there to keep anybody but Tammany delegates from the mezzanine, where they were meeting. "You can't go that way," said he, jumping up and blocking it. "Who says so?" asks the tall young man. "I say so," said the thug. The young man knocked him sprawling and we went on up the stairs. "Who are you?" I asked him. "I'm Cabot Lodge of the Herald Tribune," *he said.* —Arthur Krock of the *New York Times* to the writer.

Fresh from his editorial page tasks, Lodge plunged back into Washington reporting with heightened zest, his youthful vitality sharpened by the sense of power and drama at the center of affairs. "You were a most welcome visitor," Geoffrey Parsons wrote him, "and did the page, and all of us, good. When you feel like an editorial page job I shall count upon your letting me know. In the meantime, be sure to drop me a line when you have any ideas upon the political scene that you think I ought to know."

Lodge soon did so, in an episode revealing a trait which shows consistently throughout Lodge's life—a fierce loyalty to men whose character and deeds have caught up his admiration. It involved Leonard Wood, governor-general of the Philippines, who had died on Aug. 7, 1927. Lodge knew Wood as his grandfather's close friend and had often heard the senator relate how Wood, a doctor who volunteered in Cuba, had fought so well that he became a Regular Army brigadier in command of troops—an almost unheard-of accomplishment. Young Lodge had known Wood all his life, and like many had hoped to see him President. Now he sensed a cabal in Washington seeking to undo all Wood's work in the Philippines.

Lodge wrote Parsons that the sugar interests were working on President Coolidge to appoint a new governor who would back Manuel Quezon's independence movement. Wood had felt strongly that the Philippines had to build a self-sustaining economy before they could be cut loose from the U.S. "I have always admired General Wood so much," Lodge wrote, "that I hate to think that now that he is dead his work is going to be destroyed. . . . The plotting and scheming going on here now suggests an editorial to me: General Wood seems to be an exception to the rule—'They never die who fall in a good cause.' " He urged the *Trib* to back men like Henry Stimson, General Frank McCoy, or James Wadsworth, father of his boyhood friend. The *Trib* did so, and Stimson agreed to go. "Congratulations," wired Lodge, "on editorial . . . which averted a disaster and made possible Stimson appointment."

Cabot and Emily were now renting an apartment on Du Pont Circle, in easy visiting distance of his mother Bessie, who was living on with Helena in the old Massachusetts Avenue home. Helena continued to live there until 1929, when she met and married a handsome Belgian diplomat, Eduard de Streel (later chamberlain to Belgium's Queen Elizabeth) and went to live in Belgium, where she had three handsome children.

Cabot himself became a father on July 7, 1927, when Emily gave birth to a strapping son who was promptly christened George Cabot Lodge, after Bay. He had his father's broad brow and features but soon developed Emily's dark brown eyes. By now, Cabot was proving his ability not only to spot news but sometimes to make it as well. On the *Trib*'s front page, on Oct. 7, 1927, he reported that Assistant Secretary of the Treasury Seymour Lowman was in bad grace with the government and "might be forced to resign as a result of yesterday's muddying of Franco-American relations."

After France raised some tariffs, Lowman had announced an immediate stiff increase in duties on French auto and bicycle parts, saying: "The American policy is one of reciprocity . . . they go up, we go up. They go down, we go down." Other reporters simply noted the increases. Lodge, however, checked with Treasury Secretary Andrew Mellon as well as State Department officials and found that Lowman had acted without consulting either—that State's chiefs were "surprised and astounded." That week Lodge's brash young face appeared in the lead story of Henry Luce's fledgling *Time* magazine, which began its National Affairs section with an account of the news-behind-the-news made by this "pink-cheeked, Harvard-educated, quick-thinking grandson and namesake of the late Senator Henry Cabot Lodge . . . internationally-minded beyond his years (26) and . . . in training for a political career of his own." The *Trib* raised Lodge from fifty to sixty dollars a week, and soon he was working for *Time* as well: he was hired to be *Time*'s first Washington "bureau," i.e., to flag it on just such stories as the one his enterprise had produced on Lowman.

He was a chronicler of the dramatic history of his time. When Floyd Bennett died in Quebec, having caught pneumonia in a daring rescue mission to Greenely Island, Lodge followed the pioneer aviator to his grave: "Driving sheets of pitiless rain sounded the funeral dirge of Floyd Bennett, daring explorer and flyer, whom the Navy buried today among its great in Arlington National Cemetery."

By March, 1928, he was fulfilling John Mason Brown's hopes of doing

80 thoughtful background articles. In the Sunday section he did a half-page profile of Senator Tom Walsh of Montana, hero of the Teapot Dome inquiry, and, as "a Democrat, a Catholic and a Dry," a possible Democratic Presidential nominee that year. The portrait demonstrated Lodge's sharp eye for character-revealing detail, and an ability to bring a story to life with dramatic action:

> *On the afternoon of Jan. 18, Senator "Cotton Tom" Hefflin, purple in the face and with wild gestures, had just finished a long and savage attack on the whole Catholic Church, sparing neither Governor Smith nor the Senate leader of the Majority party. Men and women, crowded into the galleries, had been listening to the long torrent of abuse when finally the end came. Then there arose a rather short man of majestic bearing—a man with iron gray hair, penetrating eyes and a determined mouth under a close-clipped mustache. He had sat silently on the Democratic side throughout Hefflin's long vituperation. Now he arose, and in a dignified manner turned toward the Vice President's chair. In a quiet voice, he asked: "Mr. President, a parliamentary inquiry. What is the business before the Senate?" He was told that Senate Resolution 112, on the seating of Senator-elect Frank Smith, was before the Senate and he then addressed himself to that subject as though nothing had happened. No more effective rebuke could have been given Hefflin than this grand and restrained anti-climax.*

Lodge did not fail to note that Walsh, a believer in the World Court and the League, had nevertheless "voted for the Lodge reservations, thus disagreeing with the late President Wilson who held the view that the Covenant should be ratified without the dotting of an i or the crossing of a t." This profile brought the young Republican warm thanks from Democrat Walsh himself, and this accolade from the *Trib*'s own dean of Washington correspondents, Mark Sullivan: "For my own satisfaction, I want to tell you that I found pleasure in reading your account. . . . It is admirably proportioned between fact and interpretation." Lodge, now newsworthy to *Time*, now hailed by a sage of his own craft, could already count himself a pro.

As the time drew near for the 1928 presidential conventions, the *Trib* circulation men, preparing their Tribune Convention Scorecard, listed these "headliners" who would be covering them:

Mark Sullivan	*Wilbur Forrest*
Carter Field	*Theodore C. Wallen*
Grafton Wilcox	*Geoffrey Parsons*
Henry Cabot Lodge	*Arthur S. Draper*

By June 9, Lodge was getting front-page play from Kansas City. His **81** writing again showed his flair for action, drama and color: "Out here where the Kaw joins the winding Missouri and where the covered wagons passed before trudging over the plains, the brass bands are playing and gayly uniformed parades are marching up Main Street through festoons of bunting . . . California's Hoover delegation was the first to arrive this morning and startled Kansas City with its blue tam o'shanters and loud braying of its band to the tune of 'California, Here I Come.'" He reported that the Kansas delegation came with "huge three-inch sunflowers in their buttonholes," singing through "orange-colored megaphones . . . with becoming modesty: 'There may be flies on you but there are no flies on us.' Mounting the steps into the mezzanine of another hotel, they sang a series of songs to Senator Charles Curtis, their favorite son . . . 'in the White House roomy/the world's not gloomy/with Curtis.'" Lodge noted the arrival of Dr. Nicholas Murray Butler, Columbia University president, who "urged the Republican Party in his usual lucid fashion to 'nominate a man with G-U-T-S guts.'"

On June 11, as Lodge had predicted some weeks before to Parsons, "Andrew W. Mellon, strong man of the Republican Party who dominates Herbert Hoover's political future to a large extent," arrived to announce that he bore no last-minute word of Coolidge's willingness to be drafted, and then helped Hoover beat down Iowa's Governor Frank Lowden for the nomination, winning Kansas' support by naming the half-Indian Senator Curtis as Hoover's running mate.

Lodge found himself much too busy to file any carbons to Paris newspapers. Instead, he pushed on to the steamy precincts of Houston to cover Governor Franklin D. Roosevelt's memorable nomination of "the Happy Warrior," Alfred E. Smith. Despite Houston's inadequate facilities, the convention was held there because Publisher Jesse Jones had contributed heavily to the party's war chest. Instead of scattering delegates, press and candidate headquarters over various locations, the arrangers had concentrated all these into the overcrowded Rice Hotel. This created a fearful congestion, in heat that sometimes hit 120 degrees, mitigated only by puny electric fans. The elevators were so crowded that it was impossible to use them. People simply went from roof garden to lobby floor without a stop in between. To go up the main staircase from the lobby to the mezzanine took nearly half an hour.

Lodge and other reporters took to going up and down the service staircase. On one of these runs, the Tammany guard protecting a caucus attempted to stop him—with the results which left such a vivid impression on his companion, Arthur Krock.

Lodge had not given the encounter a second thought. His tribe has a

82 habit of being handy with its fists. At age sixty-seven, the old senator had used his own on a pacifist assailant. And in his *Early Memories* he relates how, as a boy, he was walking with his father, John, to the theater when "at a dark place on the Common, two men pushed into us; there were words. I saw something glitter in one man's hand, and then he was knocked down in the snow by my father, who merely said as we passed on: 'I think that fellow had a knife.' . . . I have no recollection of either fright or excitement. My faith in my father was too great to admit such emotions."

The Baltimore *Sun's* Henry L. Mencken, who had admired the elder Lodge, also found himself attracted to the grandson. Mencken, who was covering the Houston convention, invited Lodge up to his room to try some exquisite German beer, which he had somehow managed to obtain that morning from a North German Lloyd ship which came into Galveston from Bremen. In such Prohibition days, genuine *Münchener* was godlike nectar.

Amon Carter, publisher of the Fort Worth *Star-Telegram*, also had come to sample it—wearing two pearl-handled revolvers—and brought with him a large, pink-faced sheriff who wore a badge encrusted with rubies, sapphires and pearls. Carter and the sheriff after several rounds of the beer tried to get an elevator down, and three times were ignored as loaded elevators simply shot by their floors.

Carter became angry, pulled out both his pearl-handled revolvers, and fired them through the glass door of the elevator shaft. He turned, walked back into Mencken's room (which faced the elevators) and fired three or four volleys through the screens into the great outdoors. Then he and the sheriff departed.

While this was going on, Lodge bolted down the stairs, Mencken hid under his bed, and Henry M. Hyde, his *Sun* colleague, hid in the bathroom. At the sound of the shots, Texas Rangers came storming into the hotel, shouting that no one could leave until they discovered the perpetrators, fought their way up to Mencken's bedroom, and ordered him to come out from under the bed. He gave them no clues, but softened their ferocity with the remaining *Münchener*. So mollified, they left.

Lodge came back from the conventions to join Parsons once again on the editorial page. A report that Justice Holmes might resign gave him an opportunity to pay tribute to the man whose appointment got intertwined with news of his own birth: "Mr. Justice Holmes is far younger than most of us in mind and spirit. The terms 'old' and 'reactionary' are usually mentioned together, but certainly neither of them could be applied to Mr. Holmes. His opinions have such freshness, his mind is so penetrating and in tune with the age, and his general view of life has such tang and piquancy that we hope he will stay right where he is as long as his powers permit."

At the end of July, Secretary of State Frank Kellogg sailed for Paris to join in signing, with French Foreign Minister Aristide Briand and others, the Kellogg-Briand Pact to "outlaw war forever." This squiggling of signatures to a declaration of good intentions was universally hailed as an epochal milestone of man's progress toward peace. Lodge continued to think, as he had argued with Corliss Lamont, that strength is the best guarantor of peace. In what *Time* called "a truly amazing editorial in the usually 100% pro-Administration *Herald Tribune*," the young realist called it what it proved to be, an exercise in futility. "The conception of renouncing war by government fiat is inherently absurd." Kellogg, reading the editorial in the Paris edition of the *Trib*, was thunderstruck.

Lodge, faithful as always to the memory of his friends, prepared an editorial on the first anniversary of Leonard Wood's death "to reflect on the greatness of this man which he showed in intellect, in courage and in character." Both Wood's widow and his former Army aide were so moved that they wrote in appreciation. So did Helen Rogers Reid, the *Trib*'s co-owner, who informed him: "Did you know that it was read over the radio by Roxy on Sunday afternoon Aug. 12?"

Lodge had passed his twenty-sixth birthday writing these editorials. He was now a year past the minimum legal age to be a congressman, and was importuned by the Women's Republican Club of Lynn, hard by his birthplace of Nahant, to run against Democratic Congressman William P. Connery in that Essex district. A Republican pro also urged him to run. This was Congressman Charles L. Underhill's assistant, George H. Norton, who cited the many Lynn Democrats who had always voted for the elder Lodge, and would support Cabot, too.

"I have always felt and still feel," Lodge replied to Norton, "that the holding of public office is a great public trust and that, even if I could get elected, I should not aspire to office until I was wise enough and experienced enough to discharge the duties of whatever office I might hold in the best possible way. . . . This attitude has its selfish side: it is just as much to my own advantage to wait. It is just because I am so anxious to succeed and to hit the ball out fair and true every time that I want to wait until I am expert enough to tackle public problems with a sure hand. . . . At some future date, even with the chances very much against me, I might run—if there were an issue for me to espouse and if I were sufficiently experienced to deserve the people's confidence. My election this year would be a generous gesture on the part of my grandfather's friends for the sake of my grandfather's name. But in voting for me they would be voting for an uncertainty—as any man of my age is bound to be. At some future date I might be beaten, but I should not fear defeat if I entered the fight with my mind made up, secure in the knowledge that I was reasonably well equipped and was fighting for a good cause.

"I realize that as time goes by the roster of my grandfather's friends is bound to decrease and with it the political advantage which I have inherited. I shall regret to see this happen, but I fear it must be so. It will make the fight harder for me when I make it but it will be a fairer fight for the people of the district because the issue will not be confused by the desire to pay tribute to my grandfather's memory but will be based simply on the question as to whether I, as an individual, am qualified by ability and experience to represent them."

Norton was touched by this disclaimer. "I commend you for the exceptional attitude you have taken," he replied. "The position . . . is proof in itself that you are better qualified for Congress than a very large percentage of the membership of that body. . . . Your friends admire you all the more for your good sense and keen judgment."

Not long after this incident, in October, General Frank McCoy invited Lodge to come to Nicaragua and cover the forthcoming elections which Stimson had arranged the previous year. McCoy was very much at home in Nicaragua. As a result of his years of service in Cuba and the Philippines, he spoke Spanish fluently. In 1906 he had served as a member of the Peace Commission to Cuba, and in 1919 he had been a member of the Mission to Armenia. He had gone to the Philippines in 1921 with the special mission of investigation, and there he had become Leonard Wood's aide. Coolidge considered him a natural choice for Nicaragua because of his knowledge of Spanish peoples and language but even more for his skill as a mediator and his international reputation for fairness.

The *Trib*, glad to have an inside track in Nicaragua, sent Lodge, and Emily went along. They witnessed an election as "fair and free . . . as any that can be imagined," wrote Lodge who attributed it to McCoy's skill at handling the opposing sides in that explosive land:

General McCoy made it a point never to have a disagreeable scene. If one seemed to be brewing he would crack some joke so as to change the mood of those present. Or else he would suggest that the point at issue be laid aside until the next day, or failing that he would adjourn the meeting altogether. Firmness, however, was just as much a part of his success as his unfailing courtesy. When he made a decision there could never be any doubt that it would be carried out.

The whole experience made a tremendous experience upon young Lodge. Many years later he would write of General McCoy: "No man has had more influence on my life than he or has taught me more that has been of priceless value to me."

The Lodges came back from this adventure to start, very quickly, a much bigger one. They were going around the world, something very few people could ever hope to do at that time. They had been promising each other this odyssey as soon as Cabot had proved himself in his *Tribune* job. Now he had clearly done so. And if he was to editorialize about the whole world's problems, it was good that he should see far more of the world than he had done so far. The baby, George, was now old enough to be left with Emily's parents and her sister Jean.

On Saturday, Dec. 1, 1928, they sailed from New York on the French liner *Paris*. They were delighted to find Cabot's boyhood friend, Jerry Wadsworth, aboard with his wife Harty. "He is very nice and agreeable," Cabot typed that evening in his journal.

He had taken his portable along, determined to help pay for the journey by feature articles written en route for the *Tribune*. The *Trib* had given him some identifying letters: "Any courtesy that you are able to show Mr. Lodge will be greatly appreciated. . . ." And, in spite of the shock he had given Secretary of State Kellogg, that dignitary gave him an equally helpful letter of introduction to embassies and consulates. British Ambassador Sir Esme Howard gave him another. During the seven months they were gone, he wrote indefatigably, keeping a faithful journal as well as pounding out features for the *Trib*.

The trip was in a way their second honeymoon. Their marriage would prove to be an ideal one, singularly happy and unruffled. Many years later, on giving up smoking, Cabot said, "It's the smartest thing I ever did, except marry Emily." On the journey he yielded to her every whim.

"Emily," he confided to his journal on arriving in London, "likes saving money on what to me are the necessaries of life. . . . She insisted that we go to lodgings, over my remonstrance, as I had lived in them and know that they have no heat." Nostalgia guided him to Half Moon Street, where the boys had stayed with their mother while fleeing the war in France. "There was no heat," Cabot confirmed dourly, "and Emily being sensitive to cold anyway, and fresh from the tropics besides, suffered immensely. The bed with linen sheets was so cold as to be almost unbearable and there was no hot running water. She used to stick her feet into the sleeves of a sweater and wore one of my undershirts. . . . I suggested almost immediately moving to the Berkeley, but she refused. Finally . . . she began to snuffle and shiver. So I took command after a night in which I had visions of summoning medical assistance . . . and moved everything to the Berkeley—an expensive place, but where one certainly gets one's money's worth. I had all the steam heat turned on, the coal fires lit, hot water bottles placed at strategic points and this went a good ways toward thawing Emily out."

In London, all the doors of the senator's and Bay's old friends were open to them. They found Lord Charnwood's house "dark and absolutely crowded with pictures and furniture." They lunched with Lady Samuelson who had "that rare charm which . . . Mrs. Sears [Emily's mother] has to so great a degree and which I can find no word for. It is hard to believe that she is the mother of a 29-year-old son and another—killed in the war—older yet." With the younger son, Rupert, they went to the Café Anglais where "some extremely vulgar songs were sung by an extremely fat man. I have never heard such songs sung in a public way before. They probably would have been all right in French. . . . We had a fine time, though. . . ."

Cabot now found himself, to his surprise, making a political speech in England. Rupert Samuelson was standing for Parliament in Northeast Derbyshire, a futile gesture in a mining district heavily committed to Labor. But Cabot agreeably went along to help him, had his picture run (together with Emily and Rupert) in the Yorkshire *Post,* and spoke for Rupert in the Dronfield Town Hall. Rupert had warned Cabot that he was "going to build me up a great personage" in introducing him, and did so. "He said that I had come to England on purpose to address the people of Dronfield and conveyed the impression that George Washington and I were about on a par."

Cabot explained to the Dronfielders how an Administration could have a hostile Congress and why such checks kept things from being done. "In a country as large and diverse as ours it was the only possible system because one had to allow a much longer time for people to make up their minds. Slowness in government was essential—without it the country could not hold together. This, after all the silly talk of American speed and efficiency, naturally struck them as a new idea."

He pointed out that the year 1928 marked 114 years of unbroken peace between Britain and America and that this "constituted almost all of our history. . . . I was greeted with loud cheers and applause and Emily said it was the best speech she had ever heard me make."

The young wanderers pushed on to Paris. The London freeze had "killed Emily's idea of finding some pretty, cheap, picturesque place," and she now accepted without protest Cabot's dictum that "it would be better to go to the Princess, where we should be treated like kings."

They were caught up among many old friends and made new ones. They had Christmas lunch at the *hôtel* of the Prince Aymon de Faucigny Lucinge, meeting Prince Jerome Lucinge, "a delightful elderly man who has been forced by the hard times here now to go to work in a bank—which he is doing with much courage." They took a Christmas present—a radio— to an old family friend, Germaine Cossini, who once sang in the Paris opera. They went to St. Eustache Church to hear midnight Christmas mass.

They had a "most hilarious" evening with a friend of Bessie's, M. Met-man, director of the Musée des Arts Decoratifs, delighting in both "the impassioned kind" of conversation offered by Abel Bonnard, the author, and "the light, biting, screamingly funny kind" provided by diplomat Olivier Taigny, "telling us how Mme. Poincaré [the President's wife], in spite of the republic, always curtseys when she meets the Duchesse de Vendome." Taigny amused Lodge with his tale of an ambassador who became a father at 67 and was now "more than 'l'ambassadeur reclamé', he was 'l'ambassadeur étalon'—the stud ambassador. How differently these things sound in English and how impossible it is to put into written words the conversation of a clever Frenchman."

The Jerry Wadsworths joined up with them again. Cabot and Jerry went rabbit-hunting at an estate near Melun. ("The ferrets are stuck into rabbit holes and when they come to a rabbit they try to suck his blood out. The rabbit naturally tries to escape and then comes one's chance to shoot.") They saw twelve rabbits but shot only two. Cabot and Emily went to Chartres, where Bay had gone long ago with Henry Adams, and its "great purity of line took my breath away . . . the lines of the church impress me even more than the glass and statuary."

The tireless reporter found time to fire off frequent features to the *Tribune*. Cabot had lunch with Colonel Philippe Bunau-Varilla, one of his grandfather's and Teddy Roosevelt's old friends. In his sixties he had lost a leg at Verdun, and in earlier years virtually created the Republic of Panama, becoming its first minister to Washington. He had negotiated with Jerry Wadsworth's grandfather, Secretary John Hay, the treaty creating the Panama Canal. Now he was busy "Verdunizing" polluted streams of France, by the quick, simple method he had perfected at Verdun as Marshal Pétain's chief engineering officer. "The vast American investment in Germany," wrote Lodge, "strikes Col. Bunau-Varilla as an excellent thing for France and world peace. . . . We have replaced the warlike Prussians as the financial directors of the large body of peaceful Germans . . . and can keep Germany from becoming bellicose. 'Par la douceur,' he says, 'vous les dompterez'—by gentleness you will tame them." Lodge, neglecting nothing, took up the possibility of a Nicaraguan canal; old hand Bunau-Varilla warned him it would be destroyed by volcanoes.

At the Princesse de Lucinge's, they met a Rouchefoucald, as well as the Duc de Richelieu, who had some unusual theories of anthropology. He took advantage of the presence of two young American aristocrats to explain that "Americans who had three generations in America in back of them in every direction" had a larger cranial index than could be found anywhere except in fifth-century Greece. ("God knows why," Cabot noted skeptically, "not having sprung into being either in Canada or Latin America.") "He also told Emily that we had an older civilization than France, because ours dated from 1776 whereas theirs began with the Revolution, which, he declared, absolutely wiped out every trace of what previously existed." They met the Achille Murats who gave them "letters to French officials in Indo-China," and André de Fouqierres who gave them letters to Maharajahs in India. "What a wonderful collection of letters we have—to governor generals, ministers, consuls, admirals, generals, maharajahs, business men."

Every young Boston man had to have at least one night on the town in Paris. (One of Bay Lodge's had been so memorable that James Gibbons Huneker, who accompanied Bay's group of young bucks, wrote a vivid account of their night-long revels in his memoirs.) Jerry's wife Harty prepared for it by coming to spend the night with Emily. Thus freed, the temporary bachelors took in the Grand Guignol, spent some two hours at Chez Fysher's listening to "the very best of the Paris chansonniers," heard more singing at a place called La Perruche. They rambled on to the wicked Place Pigalle, "where a splendid opportunity for the release of surplus energy is afforded by throwing celluloid balls." Jerry threw them until his arm was so sore he could scarcely put on his coat. They ended up with a predawn feed in Les Halles, the market, at Le Père Tranquille. Instead of going home with Jerry as planned, Cabot decided to go back to the Princess and sleep on the sofa.

"What was my surprise," he wrote, "to find both sofas occupied, one by Susie Scott, the other by Harty Wadsworth. The two beds were taken by Emily and Anna Scott. They had played bridge and none of them had dared go home at night in a taxi. After the first moment of surprise I decided to go to sleep on the floor, and had just stretched myself out to do so when I realized that that would not be conventional. So I shut myself up in the bathroom and slept on the floor in there." Cabot ended this bacchanal with a proper puritan note: "A night like that is fun about once every five years."

On Saturday night, January 12, 1929, they left Paris on the Blue Train to spend a few days with Edith Wharton at her lovely house at Hyères, on a steep hill where it overlooks the town, the plains and the blue Mediterranean. Edith, since her divorce, lived there alone. Emily immediately fell in love with her house. She and Cabot, who were planning to build a home of their own on the Sears estate at Beverly Cove, decided then and there that they would model it on Edith Wharton's.

Cabot would have a hand in its planning. He was gifted at architectural sketching. Bessie had wanted him to become an architect. He frequently drew sketches of buildings which particularly interested him. Edith, knowing his interest, saw that they visited a nearby villa locally famous as "the epitome of all that is *art moderne*." The hardheaded Bostonian was not impressed, but his account of it gives an insight into his keen awareness of line and form:

"Externally, it looks like an assemblage of white cubes. . . . It reminds one vaguely of an outpost in the desert. . . . The rooms are formless caves, finished (?) in cement painted with Duco automobile paint. On the walls are meaningless daubs representing God knows what. He (Count de ————), about 33, was most agreeable, however attired in loud brown checked trousers. She (Miss ————) was quite agreeable and the guests looked like rather inferior mannequins." Cabot, seeing the nickel tables and chairs in the salon, was reminded of an operating room. "How nice to have your own first-aid station!" he was tempted to observe. "The whole thing was not only preposterous but absolutely unmodern. The essence of the modern is physical comfort. . . . They could have taken advantage of the marvelous new heating systems which give you just the degree of heat or cold. . . . They could have used Vitaglass instead of bad stained glass in cubist patterns. They could have had escalators instead of miles of waste space and dingy corridors."

They went on to Rome, then to Naples, thence via the *Ausonia* to Alexandria where they were wakened on a drizzling morning "by the mad screamings of the Arab porters." The ship stewards tried to wake them at dawn and bully them into packing and then wait around without breakfast for passport examinations. Cabot would have none of this nonsense. "The steamship company has to put us off," he told Emily, "and the officials have to visa our passports." So they slept late, breakfasted leisurely, and ignored the repeated calls to line up for passports. Cabot invariably replied: "Tell him to wait." "Finally they came to me and examined my passport without my even having to get out of my chair."

In Cairo, Shepheard's Hotel was ateem, in those last days of the great bull market, with Americans conspicuously consuming their paper profits. Cabot watched with fascination while a young man they had met on the train, Maynard Smith of Bay City, Michigan, haggled with the Indian who owned the hotel jewelry shop over a string of pearls priced at fifteen thousand dollars and a diamond bracelet priced at two thousand. Bargaining the pearls down to ten thousand dollars, Smith came out on the porch for a cocktail with the Lodges to decide if he really wanted them. Fortified, he returned to offer ten thousand for the pearls *if* they would throw in the bracelet. All four Indian managers argued vehemently, then yielded. "Instead of being elated with victory he looked sadly at the four speechless

Indians and said, 'Well, I guess I got hooked.' Having reduced their profit by $7,000 those Indians had the most wholesome respect for his business ability." Cabot bought Emily a set of star sapphires, noting sadly that he "got no reduction."

All sorts of interesting people were about: Loring Pickering, grandson of George Cabot's own friend Timothy Pickering who was George Washington's first Secretary of State. On the train to Luxor they met Countess Karolyi, daughter of Austria-Hungary's former foreign minister. She, in turn, introduced them to the Aga Khan who "spoke English with a grace of phrase which few of us possess. He is carried around Northern India and worshipped like a God. With the money from the faithful he goes to Paris and Deauville, buys horses, etc."

At Luxor occurred an event which might have startled Bostonians as much as Elizabeth Cabot's climbing the Great Pyramid. Cabot was challenged to enter a donkey race, against "a professional-looking boss in riding clothes." Cabot took the dare, even though he was wearing a derby hat and gray Brooks Brothers trousers. He noted objectively that this costume made him "an object of ridicule to the audience." Ignoring this, he spanked his beast on, bouncing brutally up and down until he had worn the skin off his thighs. He left the pro far behind and won the race, only to discover to his disgust that Emily and Countess Karolyi, having lost money on previous races, "did not have the sense to bet on me."

Countess Karolyi told them of a conversation with Count Leopold Berchtold, Austria-Hungary's foreign minister whose ultimatum to Serbia had set off the World War. "After sending it off," he told her, "I could not sleep the whole night, for fear the Serbs would accept it." Ruefully, she told the Lodges: "He is now gaily racing horses with no sense of guilt for the catastrophe." They met a Baron Von Klitzing who owned a great rubber plantation in Indonesia. "You must visit it," he said, giving them a letter to his manager in Java.

Cabot went to see Egypt's Prime Minister, Moehamed Pasha Mahmed, and informed his *Tribune* readers how this son of a fellah was "improving public health and has already [built] 150 hospitals in Egyptian villages and [filled] malarial swamps. He sees the need for more water and is working on a $120 million project for damming and irrigation." Noting that Englishmen felt they had to hold the whole of Egypt to defend the Suez Canal, Cabot saw no reason why a canal zone like Panama would not suffice.

On visiting the Luxor Temple he found himself outraged at "Anglo-Saxon hypocrisy" on discovering that "the best carvings and reliefs in the temple are Priapic depictions of Rameses. Yet of all the hundreds of photographs of the temple of Luxor which I had to study in college not one showed these things and I have never heard of their being shown in any other college. I can understand their being kept from children but why college students should not see them is beyond me."

Their next destination was to be Bombay, aboard the German steamer *Resolute.* They were piped aboard at Suez by four stout, red-faced German trumpeters, beneath a huge sign WILLKOMMEN DAHEIM—WELCOME HOME, with the German and American flags draped over it. "Was there ever anything more echt deutsch and more gemutlich?" The food was good, the beds comfortable, and they had a large outside cabin, "thanks to Eddie von Selzam (to whom I telephoned in Berlin to tell the company that we were personages.)" They arrived in Bombay on February 25.

They put up at the Taj Mahal Hotel, had lunch with Consul-General Allan Rogers, a fellow Bostonian, and were invited to lunch at Government House on Malabar Hill with Governor Sir Frederick and Lady Sykes. Lady Sykes, who was Bonar Law's daughter, knew of Cabot from her brother, who had also been a *Herald Tribune* reporter. He noted her quick sense of humor and infectious laugh. Sir Frederick, a retired major general who had helped organize the Royal Air Force, was much older. Lodge was fascinated by watching Lady Sykes and Mrs. Ian Fairbairn play ping-pong while military aides dashed about retrieving the balls. The Lodges left to much clicking of heels and a present-arms from the bodyguard.

On Malabar Hill they saw the Tower of Silence where the Parsees place their naked dead, to be devoured by vultures who reduce them to skeletons in ten minutes' time. "The sun soon dries and pulverizes the bones, the next torrential rain storm washes the powdered bones into the earth—and so it is 'ashes to ashes and dust to dust' back to Mother Earth whence all things spring." Cabot found a certain beauty in all this, nor was he shocked by the burning-ghats they passed later on: "In the tropics it is very important to dispose of bodies very soon after death, in fact the law requires [it] within 24 hours."

Young Lodge found his patriotic gorge being stirred occasionally by the British emphasis on class and caste. He was delighted to meet a young American, Frank Carr, who had risen from lowly origins to the responsible post of Allied Chemical & Dye's representative in India. "It is wonderful," Lodge noted, "the way in which our free air produces men who can move on equal terms and hold their own with the grandees of the old decaying countries." A European might say, Lodge added, " 'He is a cultivated man of the middle class.' Thank heaven we have no real classes and that we can merely say, 'He is an agreeable and cultivated man.' "

The sight of the Taj Mahal provoked the thwarted architect in Lodge. He found it enormous, when one stood right under it and looked up, yet "there is this marvelous lightness. It is ever on the verge of sailing away."

92   He tried to account for it: "The top of the dome is not perfectly spherical but has a delicate rise to it and this rise, I think, is what makes it seem that the next breath of wind would blow the Taj away." He drew an imaginary line across its top, following the line of a perfect sphere, "yet I could never see where the dome stopped being a mere geometric figure and became an inspired work of art." Afterward he and Emily sat in the lovely gardens "and watched the sunset turning the Taj to gold and lighting up in turn its windows and alabaster screens."

He had a keen eye for the strengths of the British, as well as some of their oddities. He found the Anglo-Indian a very special type, reminding him of Kipling's famous detective, Strickland, or even Kipling himself (whom Lodge had met at his grandfather's home): "He is intelligent, practical, fairly industrious and altogether quite solid. . . . I met a detective in Bombay who was Strickland's very counterpart." At the same time, while dancing with Emily at the Yacht Club, Cabot thought some of the members were "eyeing each other to make sure that none of their friends were really having a good time."

They went on to Delhi, where Lodge attended a session of the Indian Legislature. He met M. K. Acharya, best-known defender of child marriage. He wrote at length in the *Tribune* of the effects Katherine Mayo's book *Mother India*, had on shaking that custom, making "educated Indians . . . realize for the first time that a large and important section of the world's population thought they were not quite human." He dwelt on the bewildering multiplicity of India's ethnic strains. A representative from the large South Indian city of Madras "could not even make himself understood to the native waiters in the dining room. He could not communicate with many of his native colleagues except in English. . . . There is more racial difference between the Indian of the Punjab and the Indian of the South than there is between an Englishman and a Moor of Northern Africa. Neither of these men thinks of himself as an Indian. He says: 'I am a Punjabi,' or 'I am a Dravidian.'"

In New Delhi they dug out one of their many letters of introduction, and found themselves lunching at the palace of the Maharajah of Bikaner: a big man in Bond Street clothes, brown as a berry, and with huge mustaches. He introduced them to a short, gray-haired man in jodhpur trousers: "And this is my prime minister."

They got back to Bombay in time for the Governor's first state ball on Malabar Hill. House guests, the Lodges were ensconced in a suite of "two vast bedrooms, two equally vast bathrooms [the marble tubs were ten feet long and three feet deep, he meticulously reported] and two sitting rooms." At the ball, the dignitaries took up their position for the state quadrille. An admiral, plump face shining above his gold lace, tripped sedately across the

room. He, the Lord Chief Justice, and other dignitaries, now walked towards, now away, from each other, bowing and curtseying. Lodge, impressed, found the performance "a symbol of the stubborn English strength
which says, 'We've always done this—we're always going to.' "

Thus the last days of the British Raj, in the early twilight of empire.
Lodge saw it all in its late flowering, wrote of it with insight, and gave his
nod of respect to the tradition-bound British.

The weeks, the cities, the countries whirled by. Across a world that was
soon to end the young Lodges rambled on—from Bombay to Ceylon, to
Singapore and Java, to Bali and Siam, to Indo-China and the Philippines,
and to great, mysterious, struggling China. Everywhere, Lodge's keen eye
caught the odd and striking; often he sketched, quite creditably, unusual
architecture. He showed a sharp discernment for true values in unlikely
surroundings, and a high resistance to flapdoodle. Tirelessly he wrote his
features and updated his journal with uninhibited reactions which are a
candid mirror of a young Bostonian's mind, attitudes and character at age
twenty-six.

In Ceylon, at Macan Markar, the famous jeweler, when Emily fancied
a huge emerald priced at twelve hundred dollars, Cabot haggled the price
down to eight hundred but then, remembering Maynard Smith's disquie-
tude at Shepheard's, "decided not to buy it on the theory that it was probably worth still less." They traveled by train down the Malay Peninsula
with a young English couple, the Parrs, who became fast friends after a
slow warming-up. They went through the Sultanate of Johore all afternoon, and at Johore Station Lodge saw a sign: H. H. THE SULTAN'S PRIVATE
WAITING ROOM. He was prompted to a republican reflection: "I thought
Sultans and Highnesses never waited, but I suppose that if the British
railway officials force them to, they may as well have a private waiting
room to wait in."

At Singapore he found the noted and notorious Raffles Hotel "so jammed
with Americans of the *Belgenland* and a Dollar Line cruise that one could
hardly turn. In addition there were an unusually large number of English-
men who had come to the hotel on purpose to 'see the animals.' Whoever
said that if only people of different nations could know each other they
would like each other better?" To his chagrin, there was no room to be had:
they were told to try the Sea View four and a half miles away. Cabot sternly
flashed his letter of introduction from Britain's Ambassador in Washington,
Sir Esme Howard, "just to identify myself. A room with bathroom was
produced." Next day, they received the best room in the hotel, "with modern marble bathroom, view on the sea and everything."

They were asked to lunch by the Governor, Sir Hugh and Lady Clifford,
who wanted to know about the various members of Hoover's Cabinet. They

94 had never heard of Andrew Mellon. When Emily refused liquor at lunch, the Governor said: "There you are. You refuse it here where you can get it and at home you probably carry a hip flask."

They hired a rickshaw and drove through the Chinese quarter, consisting mostly of arcades. Lodge was captivated by the brilliant colors in the small and brightly lighted shops, the medley of strange music, banging pots and pans, and the clicking of clogs worn as shoes, "the strange effects of light on stranger faces, the sheen of brilliant silks hanging in the arcades, the pleasant motion of the rickshaw, and the smells, some delicious, others unspeakable. . . ."

For the *Tribune*, Lodge wrote at length of the Singapore naval base which the British were just beginning. In words that later seemed prophetic, he spoke of this base as of great moment in the Pacific "where in all probability the next decisive world drama will take place. What happens there may some day be of vital concern to every one of us," he wrote of this base which thirteen years later the Japanese took from behind because its guns could only fire seaward.

At Jakarta, the Lodges caught up with the *Resolute* and dined aboard it with shipboard friends, and after dinner, having heard that the native quarter "was teeming with all sorts of strange exotic vices," Cabot went to explore it with Dr. Kennedy of Port Chester, N. Y. The quest was disappointing. "We must have walked three miles . . . trudged through kampong after kampong and saw nothing which could not be observed at Beverly, Mass., at 10:45 P.M. Ninety per cent of the population were asleep, the waking portion either talking or finishing up a little work, or making love to each other. . . . Not a sign of vice." They returned to find the *Resolute* rather gloomy because a passenger had died; the others had lined the rail after dinner to see the casket carried off. "We left that ship at just the right time. Everyone was beginning to get on everyone else's nerves and many were already counting the days before they reached New York."

From Jakarta, the Lodges took a two-hour train ride to Bolang to visit the thirty-two-thousand-acre rubber plantation owned by Baron von Klitzing, whom they had met at Luxor. The manager, *Mijnheer* Halewijn, showed them his arsenal of twenty army rifles, with which the overseers practiced once a month in case of a native uprising.

Lodge was fascinated by the eating habits of the Dutch: "The essence of coffee is put in a little glass decanter, then filled with hot milk. The net result is a dream." The first time he saw the Dutch consuming their favorite dish, *rijstafel*, "I was sure someone had fainted. First comes the rice, then the various meats and sauces, then at least fifteen different varieties of peppers, spices and things resembling hors d'oeuvres. They are all piled on to each other and mixed—but not mixed so much that the whole will have the same taste throughout. It is washed down with beer. Sometime you can see the pink faces and bald heads of the Dutch over their high stiff collars turning to a delicate shade of purple as the enormous pile is gradually consumed and washed down."

Ascending the Bali hills, past rice terraces—some filled with water, others green with growing rice, others gold with ripe grain—Lodge found them "like huge, glistening steps down which some giant might walk or some angel ascend on his way to the sky. No wonder the people believe in devils and supernatural things." He drew a careful sketch of the unusual arrangement of pillars outside a temple entrance. This descendant of Jersey sailors had an eye for the peculiarities of island breeds, like the distinctive Balinese dog, resembling the Chinese chow but either black or white in color, and the cattle, which were uniformly tan in color but with a pure white rump. "Only on an island would such a special breed be possible. We owe the Jersey cow . . . to the fact that an island made pure breeding possible." He noticed that on the highest point of the island, Batoer, the dogs grew noticeably thicker hair.

Watching Balinese dancers enact a silent drama, he showed a keen appreciation of its subtlety, its "emphasis on form. . . . I suppose that in that play the appearance, the tone of voice and expression for a tragic character are immutably laid down and that he cannot deviate from them at all without the audience knowing it and disapproving. . . . The mere existence of such a ritual or convention means that the imagination is left freer than it is with us where every actor improvises." He noted the island's curious morals, "complete incontinence on both sides and the man does not mind," although he prudently files down his wife's teeth "so that she will not be able to bite her husband." He noted also the women's "fine, firm breasts, splendid erect carriages, long legs and narrow hips."

They went on to Sumatra, thence by small boat to Penang, then up the Malay Peninsula by train to Bangkok. Lodge was impressed by the Siamese, "the only Far Eastern people who have preserved their independence. They call themselves Thai—which means free—and they do so advisedly. They seem to be the only ones out here who have had the common sense to realize that some Western methods had to be adopted in this constantly contracting world and had the ability to translate that realization into practice. They had some great kings to carry out that idea, among them Somdet Phra whose history is one of the most romantic I know of [it was later told in *Anna and the King of Siam*]. . . . They have kept their art and their culture, their religion and their language, but they have called on the West to teach them to run their finances, their railroads, their army, their navy,

96 their sanitation, etc. The British taught them how to run the police and the navy, the Americans how to run their finances, the Germans how to run their railroad and their army. . . ."

Heading for Cambodia to see the great ruins at Angkor, they had to fill out endless forms at the French Indo-China frontier. "It was nice to realize that even in this desolate corner of the Asiatic jungle the French bureaucracy was still functioning. It was all a wonderful symbol of what Alphonse Daudet called 'une petite administration bien française et bien compliquée.' It gives some little chap in Paris a good job sorting and filing those blanks and helps to account for the seemingly large French bureaucracy."

The rest house at Battambang was a dirty-looking place, "kept by a still dirtier looking evil-faced Chinese. They were full up so they gave us a bed practically in the saloon." Trusting no one, Lodge strapped their luggage to their bed, carefully tucked his wallet, keys, and flashlight inside his pillow—with the pistol he prudently carried. They did better at Angkor, were put up in Government House, had "fine big bedrooms, Emily having that used by the King of Siam" when visiting, "I that used by Prince Henry," on its wall "a huge pair of buffalo horns given by the Bandahara of Bahang to the British. What a wonderful title!"

Possibly fearing the gimlet eye of Uncle John Ellerton Lodge, that famous Orientalist and art connoisseur, Lodge apologized for platitudes in trying to describe the ruins of Angkor Wat. "Unlike the Taj Mahal or our Gothic cathedrals there is nothing heavenly about the great temples here. There is even something wicked about them—but how majestic, how beautiful, how grandiose and how ominous. Their mystery is a part of their compelling fascination. They were seen by a Chinese in 1270 when Angkor was the populous seat of a mighty empire. They were next seen by a Portuguese in 1580 when they were as they are today—ruins struggling in the jungle's grip. What happened? No one knows. . . . Nothing can tell us, but there are mute signs that the work stopped suddenly. . . . There is nothing like this in the whole world—and I am a fool to attempt to describe it."

They left Angkor and reached Kampong Thom in time for lunch, by late afternoon were in Phnom Penh, Cambodia's capital on the edge of the Me Kong River. There they obtained a car and crossed "a ferry and several bridges" on their drive to Saigon, making the 150-odd miles in time for lunch. Years later, Lodge would find himself wearing a bullet-proof vest in Saigon itself; now he found the safety and pleasure of this drive a symptom of French colonial efficiency. "Your life and property are as safe in Indo-China," he wrote in his dispatch from Saigon, "as in the United States —safer, indeed, than in certain communities at home. . . ." He found "law and order, prosperity, health and education."

The jungles were ominous, and his description of them would seem, 97
years later, more ominous still:

*The jungles which fill Indo-China are the thickest, most persistent and
most hopeless ones which I have seen.*

However, they were made less so by the well-kept roads. "One can motor
to almost any point in that enormous country. You can drive the whole
length up to South China, where for obvious reasons the road stops, or you
can drive straight across from the sea to Siam." Torrential rains were forever washing parts of the road away, "but they are wonderfully kept up
and are surprisingly smooth, even those roads in deserted regions where
only one or two cars a day pass by. Taking these long motor trips you find
decent 'bungalows' where you can get as good a dinner and as good a bed
as you could find in most regions at home," and the roads were marked
with kilometer signs each kilometer "with the distance to the main town
written on it."

Lodge thought the white man's burden was being carried competently
with little sign of strain. "The type of higher French official in Indo-China
is very good, in spite of the fact that France, unlike England, has no pressure of over-population to drive good men abroad to earn their bread. In
the early days the colony may have been a resort of adventurers and
wasters, as Alaska was when we first acquired it. But now you see French-
men of the good sort on the streets of Saigon and even in deserted frontier
posts."

However, he found some weaknesses in this colonial structure. "The
evident flaw in the French system," he observed, "is that it deliberately
discourages—if it does not entirely prohibit—the investment of foreign
capital for the development of the huge and unplumbed resources of the
country. . . . This policy is, of course, designed to keep the wealth of
Indo-China as a sort of private preserve for France, but as things now
stand, there is not the capital in France to do what the combined capital
of the world could do were it given the chance."

Lodge concluded his Saigon report with some observations that seem
both perceptive and ironic in retrospect. "There is comparatively little un-
rest among the natives of Indo-China. The French, of course, never de-
luded themselves into the belief that the natives could govern themselves.
Some of the natives who have been educated in France return with revolutionary ideas [one such was Ho Chi Minh]. It is the old story which the
British have experienced with their educated natives and which we have
seen in the Philippines. Many of them cool off after their return, realizing
how destitute they would be if the French were to go. If it were not for the

98   French troops in Tong King [what is now North Viet Nam] . . . the country would be over-run with Chinese, who would drive out the simple Annamite as they drove out the Malay. Some Chinese now in Indo-China have been caught from time to time promoting policies of the Bolshevist school, but so far the French have had no serious disturbances. Their tenure is secure and they are doing a great deal to justify it."

If the twenty-six-year-old Lodge of early 1929 seemed to accept the imperialist status quo as the best of all possible worlds, not many other Westerners were questioning it at the time. At least, wherever he went, he looked at everything with the eyes of a skeptical realist—just as he had done on his own country's hopes of abolishing war by fiat—and he instinctively tried to avoid the greatest error of reporting—to find what you are looking for, to see what one wants to see.

In Manila, where he first encountered Douglas MacArthur, he was impressed, but he peered very closely to find the real man beneath the dramatic posturing and rodomontade: "He is young for a major general, and handsome, but he talks to one as though he were addressing ten thousand revivalists, marching up and down the room with rhetorical perorations." Lodge was touched to hear MacArthur's praise of his Uncle John Lodge, a schoolmate of MacArthur's in Washington, of whom he spoke "with great affection and at great length." He was more skeptical of some of MacArthur's praise of leading Manila politicians as incorruptible ("he cannot have believed any of that else he would not be a major general"). Lodge wanted to get to hard facts: "What I really wanted to talk about . . . his plans for giving military training to the Filipinos. . . . He said that if his plans were executed as he intended them to be there would be 500,000 trained reservists in the islands by 1940—enough to repel any likely power or combination of powers. That was interesting, but Japan is believed to have 5,000,000 reservists."

It was typical of Lodge's loyalty to his heroes that he should visit the Manila *Bulletin* and offer to write an article about General Frank McCoy, well known as Governor General Wood's former aide and whom he had just seen at work in Nicaragua. In the *Bulletin*, Lodge described that operation:

> *General McCoy had a large staff and very inadequate accommodations for them. . . . But through the cheer of his personality he made everyone cheerful and kept them interested and up to the mark. . . . He has that politeness which is of no one land, that straight-forwardness which all peoples appreciate. In a country like Nicaragua, which has been torn by revolution of the bloodiest kind, he succeeded in bringing rival factions together for discussion and in creating the utmost con-*

fidence in his decisions. . . . He is that rarest of combinations—a man of great intelligence who has not become a cynic. He sees, of course, what treachery there is in the world, he understands the motives of different sorts of men, but he welcomes everyone in a friendly way and expects them to be as honest and upright as he is. That attitude, so entirely devoid of suspicion, has often made men act as he expected them to. . . .

Another, and deeply human side, of Lodge is seen in his repeated visits to, and his appreciation of the true worth of an old man whom many Americans in Manila thought an eccentric crank half buried in the self-made dust and debris of his crackpottery. New England cultivates, rather than deprecates, eccentrics, and Lodge's friend McCoy had urged him not to miss Dr. H. Otley Beyer, digger in the ruins of Malayan and Chinese archeology, then resident in Manila.

"He is a short man, flat-chested, and with a skin and complexion rather yellowish but of a texture which makes it impossible to estimate his age," Lodge noted in his journal. "His white suits are full of holes and worn to shreds at the knees and elbow. His pockets are full of those little pieces of paper which street car companies provide for transfers. Ask him the name of a book, he will say nothing, smile mysteriously, pull out one of these slips, write the name of the book on it and give it to you. His pockets are also full of other pieces of paper, some of the well-known variety, which he uses to wrap up arrowheads and other archeological objects he happens to have with him. When he is talking he will pull out any old piece of paper from his pocket and wipe his face with it."

Lodge noted that the old digger never opened his mail, had left unopened invitations from Harvard and Princeton to join them as a professor. Harvard finally got General Wood to send an aide to inform Beyer of its offer. McCoy, of course, had told Lodge about this.

"Beyer turned his back on the aide, as he always does when he wants to think of something, brandished his huge cigar over his head before scratching it, turned around, the most irresistible grin on his face, and said: 'Oh, no, I can't go away now. They're digging up in the northern part of the islands. I certainly can't go.' That was all the reply Harvard ever got. Yet he has been very nice to Harvard in other ways, contributing many priceless books and manuscripts to it."

Emily and Cabot toured the Yazoo Market with Dr. Beyer—"full of the strangest native things, costumes, shoes, stoves, countless things of earthenware and wickerwork. He knew the purpose and history of everything." Next afternoon Cabot joined him for lunch in "a dirty little café while he ate a peculiar lunch in a still more peculiar manner." Cabot went home

100   with him and listened to him talk for more than four hours: "I could have stayed forever. The limpidity of his mind, the absolute lack of gaps in his train of thought, his reasoning and his information were stupendous. With the perpetual cigar almost as big as he is in his hands or mouth he walked around the room, most of the time with his back to me, talking, talking with occasionally a pause of sometimes a minute, after which he would go on. He sees the present in the light of his great knowledge of the past, he has no prejudices, he cares not what happens."

Lodge's dispatch to the *Herald Tribune* from Manila raised some questions which, in retrospect, would seem uncannily prophetic:

> *Shall we some day be required to go to these tropical islands as an expeditionary force to defend them against an aggressor? . . . As matters stand now it is estimated that a strong invading force from a country neighboring the Philippines could take the islands—except for Manila—in between two and three weeks' time. The taking of Manila itself would be a longer affair because the island of Corregidor at the entrance of Manila Bay is very heavily fortified. It is, in fact, the Gibraltar of the Far East. There are food supplies and ammunition buried on Corregidor which would support the garrison for a year. It is impregnable by naval gun fire and no ship . . . could get by it into the bay.*

On their way out of Manila for Shanghai on the S.S. *President Pierce* their own ship passed "right by Corregidor . . . I could see the barracks plainly, but the guns are concealed. However, searching around with my glasses in the dim twilight, I saw one monster, temporarily on its platform, rearing its profile to the sky."

They found Shanghai impressive and exciting. They left the steamer in a launch which sped them up the broad Whangpoo River, past merchant and war vessels flying many foreign flags, to the Bund along which the big red foreign consulates and banks were ranged. "The customs inspectors were White Russians and a bribe of one Shanghai dollar (50¢ U.S.) was enough to pass through all our extremely dutiable luggage without inspection."

Told, at the Majestic Hotel, that there was no room, Cabot again produced his letter from Sir Esme, and this time Secretary Kellogg's as well. He got a room plus a 10 per cent reduction "on account of diplomatic service." They found Shanghai, like Bombay, another outpost of Boston. Mrs. Bristol, wife of Admiral Bristol, who had them to tea at the French Club, proved to be "an aunt of Alice Pell's," while Lieutenant Commander Hamilton Bryan had known Helena Lodge's husband, de Streel, in Brazil and "spoke of him at great length and with enthusiasm."

Cabot, during his work in Labrador, had heard Dr. Grenfell tell about Feng, the Christian general who baptized his men with a hose. He heard new stories about him from George Sokolsky, an American who was a one-man intelligence agency for several clients: "Feng excites a popular interest greater than any other Chinese on account of [his] long and dangerous marches, his simple Chinese life . . . and legendary character." Cabot and Emily took in a concert, went to a night club where White Russian girls were taxi-dancing for fifty cents a turn, and to the Shanghai Wheel where four enormous roulette wheels were operated by an American with a Mexican front man. "Gambling of any kind has never amused me," observed Cabot. "I stayed about ten minutes and walked home." Emily came home later with her escort.

From a Major Bassett, he learned how difficult it was to insult crooked Chinese officials even when one wished to, because his interpreter "would not think of using insulting language to an official," but on the contrary would tell the major on leaving how grateful he should be that the interpreter had saved him from "making a spectacle of himself." They lunched with Hu Shih, a noted scholar who knew Uncle John Lodge and who expected soon to lecture at Harvard (he was later ambassador to the U.S.). "He is, I was told, about the only well-known Chinese to whom anything like freedom of speech is accorded." He also met T. V. Soong, the finance minister, "a Harvard man, 1912 I think . . . agreeable . . . able." Meeting a Mr. and Mrs. Yen, "she quite beautiful in a Chinese way," Cabot noted that she was "one of the many daughters of old Koo who made an enormous fortune in the Dutch East Indies," and was laden with "perfectly beautiful jade." He added, "One of the sisters is Mrs. Wellington Koo who does the big splurge in London and Paris all the time and is always in *Vogue*."

Early in May the Lodges set out for Peking aboard a thirty-five-hundred-ton river steamer, the *Ting Sang*. They could go up the river as far as Tangku, "only a railroad station in a desert of dust." The train took them to Tienstin, where Lodge visited the U.S. Army's Fifteenth Infantry Regiment which had been stationed in China since the Boxer Rebellion. He said hello to its commander, Colonel Taylor, whom he had known in Washington. By the time they reached Peking he could report it "an extremely hard place to get to," surmising shrewdly that was "why it was chosen for the capital."

Nevertheless, he was captivated by the place.

"Peking," he wrote, "has as powerful a fascination as any city I have ever visited. The immensity of everything is impressive. The walls and gateways are immense, the Forbidden City is immense, and the palaces and gardens are immense beyond belief. Then there is a feeling of mystery and of lurking danger. . . . The fact that the city itself and every house in it is surrounded by high walls causes this impression and the dust accentuates it, drawing its mysterious brown veil across everything from time to time and creating the weirdest and sometimes beautiful effects of light and color, especially when one looks through the dust at the brilliant polychrome of temple or palace. . . . All the mystery *and* the lurking danger which one feels among a people whom one can never fathom, never understand. . . ."

Inspecting the Temple of Confucius, Lodge realized for the first time that Chinese architecture depended a great deal on color for its total effect, something which photographs could not then reproduce. "The indescribable element consists of the rich yellows, delicate violets and mulberries and the reds and blues used in both walls and roofs and which must be seen to be believed. After being brought up in a world where the externals of architecture were always monochrome this Chinese architecture had a stunning effect on me. . . . It seemed to me that there was a whole new field, a whole new set of artistic possibilities and combinations which we had for some reason or other ignored. . . . I supposed we never knew how to apply color so it would last."

No Lodge could leave China without visiting Hong Kong. It had always been a chief port of call for his great-grandfather, Captain John Lodge, and all the other Yankee Clipper owners. It was a ritual for any new clipper to be portrayed there by Chinese artists who would catch, with perfect exactness, each spar, shroud and fitting of the ship. Skipper Lodge had framed his pictures in lovely rosewood frames brought from France on other of his voyages. These prized pictures hung back home at Beverly, and similar ones were cherished in homes all over New England.

They took a cruise over to another favorite port of New England seamen, Macao, the island controlled by the Portuguese. Lodge prowled its Protestant Cemetery, and was stirred by all the sons of Beverly, Salem, and other Essex ports whose stones he found there, together with those of such English "younger sons" as the one whose tombstone read:

Right Honorable Lord Henry Joseph Spencer Churchill, 4th Son of George, Duke of Marlborough

Lodge wrote a long feature for the Boston *Transcript,* recalling how Major Samuel Shaw of Boston had started the China trade, the beginning of the U.S. consular service, and the great missionary movement in China as the ultimate result of his first voyage to Macao and Canton in 1784 on the *Empress of China,* clearing thirty thousand dollars on the round trip.

He wrote of his visit to the cemetery, down "a broad and shallow flight of old stone steps. . . . Green moss is on the handrail," to the first terrace where lay "most of the Americans—men who came out to do a vigorous business or were sent out as missionaries to preach the gospel. I have said that the tropics deal harshly with man and here is eloquent proof of it, for scarcely a man or woman buried here ever reached the age of 40 and many graves of little children are pathetic examples of what these brave people must have suffered. Here is the grave of 'Thomas W. Waldron, Consul of the U.S. of America and Naval Storekeeper for the U.S. East Indies Squadron' who died in his thirties. . . . Beyond him lies Nathaniel Kingsland of Salem, Mass., who died in 1817 at the age of 18 and who probably had come out to China, his head high and full of hopes for great fortune."

Lodge was touched at how many graves he found of Endicotts, that sturdy family who first opened up the Bay State's Essex Coast. When Charles Woodbury of Beverly died in Macao in 1854, aged thirty-six, his tombstone was erected by J. B. and J. W. Endicott. In the cemetery's protestant chapel, "so like one of our little New England country churches," he found beside the altar a marble plaque to James B. Endicott, who had arrived in China in 1835 and died there in 1870, and two of whose children, Lilly and Rosalie, were sleeping in the cemetery (he in Hong Kong). The plaque calls him "an affectionate father, a faithful husband and warmhearted friend, a generous helper of all those who labored to extend the kingdom of our Lord and Savior Jesus Christ." It quotes also a verse from Romans:

Given to Hospitality

All this set Lodge in a nostalgic mood. "It really gives one a vivid idea of what he must have been like and how his 'hospitality' and 'warmheartedness' must have been appreciated in the pitiful foreign community which now lies buried in Macao. It is all very touching, these remnants of the past, so far away from home and so remote from the mainstream of life. . . . In Macao one can relive the past and realize those tragedies and griefs which are not in the history books but on which almost all of our great historical edifices rest."

But Cabot was now eager to turn his own face to the future and "the mainstream of life." Emily was dying to see the baby again ("I simply don't give a damn about seeing the world when I think of him," she had written her sister Jean, "SEND PHOTOS"). They were eager to get back to that Essex shore whence Macao's hardy voyagers came. After a brief visit to Japan, they boarded the S.S. *Taiyo Maru* on June 10, 1929, and Cabot began his last journal entry in jubilant capitals: GOING HOME.

CHAPTER SEVEN

Do you know that your state is desperately in search of a U.S. Senator? Jump right into the fight, announce your candidacy for the nomination on a wet platform and you can beat old man Butler easily. That being so, you would get the following and take the issue away from the Democratic candidate in the general election. After the primary, your personality, ability and incidentally your name would, I feel confident, make your election certain. Go to it. Best of luck. —Congressman Fiorello H. La Guardia *to Lodge, February, 1930.*

Lodge did not take that particular bit of advice, at least not then. But the three years following his round-the-world trip would see him make his first try for office.

They were years crowded with events and action. He settled down for a steady two-year experience at writing editorials which turned him from apprentice to pro. He found time as well to write thoughtful profiles and background articles, and to spend many weekends in secret, agonizing negotiations to buy a Boston newspaper. His second son, Henry Sears Lodge, was born. He took leave from publisher Ogden M. Reid to write a book, and ended by running for the Great and General Court of Massachusetts. A quarter-century and many careers later he would tell a younger publisher Ogden R. Reid: "Did you know I am still technically on leave from the *Herald Tribune?*"

With the editorial-page assignment, the Lodges moved to New York, into an apartment at 45 Gramercy Park. In the *Trib*'s 41st Street bullpen, where some six editorial-page colleagues worked, Cabot sat next to the redoubtable Walter Millis. He would join their frequent chinfests at Bleeck's speakeasy downstairs, together with such colleagues as sardonic city editor Stanley Walker and the sartorially elegant columnist Lucius Beebe, trying manfully to learn their arcane rituals and private language. The *Tribune* staffers were fond of Lodge, somewhat amused by his solemnity, envious that he could forget to cash his paycheck (thus confusing the bookkeepers), and sometimes ruffled by his enormous self-confidence. But they remembered him warmly for an unfeigned candor, directness and genuineness.

"It was a warm afternoon in the spring of 1930," Lucius Beebe later wrote, "and a *Herald Tribune* editorial conference had moved next door to Jack Bleeck's Artists' and Writers' Club, where hock and seltzer was being dispensed in green globular glasses holding approximately a quart. Geoffrey Parsons, the chief editorial writer, William Morris Houghton, his assistant, and even Walter Millis had removed their jackets and were appreciably more comfortable for it. Lodge kept on both jacket and waistcoat. Bill Houghton was reminiscing about the old days downtown, especially about Jim Knieram's Eats and Pilsner Sanitarium, where was invented the beer radiator—a device for serving the brew at the various temperatures required by true believers. 'I remember being introduced to Jim Huneker at that bar,' said Bill. 'I was on the city staff in those days, and Huneker shook hands with me and said, "Glad to meet you, Mr. Houghton. Glad to meet any newspaperman. Once a newspaperman, always a whore!" ' Everyone laughed except Cabot Lodge. 'Why, Bill,' he said after a minute, 'if I believed that, I'd never have joined the profession.'

"Another time on the same premises, Cabot was in learned professional converse with Stanley Walker. Some administrative villainy of uncommon proportions had just been perpetrated by a Republican Party leader, and Stanley was pounding at the bar and shouting that he'd be double-damned if ever he would vote for another Republican for President. 'But you'll vote for me, won't you Stanley?' said Cabot."

Certainly he was taking life most seriously, showing at times a trace of pomposity which Emily would as regularly deflate: "What does Henry Cabot Lodge have to say about that? Plenty, I'll bet!" And Parsons found that Lodge had a tremendous range of knowledge and information, and could be relied upon for editorials on almost any subject, from the Marines (he deplored the Navy's decision to reduce them) to the debt moratorium ("the most recent example of that friendship with all nations and entangling alliances with none which should ever be our policy").

A fellow reporter described him thus: ". . . an uncommonly agreeable and good-looking young man: over six feet tall, erect, with the build of an oarsman or a cavalry officer. . . . He always looked, even in the hot, suspendered days of summer, as though he had just left the shop of an expert tailor. Young Lodge is not [austere]. He is, I think, essentially serious-minded but he has an easy good humor about him and a ready smile. He is a fine laugher, hearty, infectious, flattering. People like him, and he likes people."

He had his own practical ideas about dress. MEN SHOULD ADOPT THE MESS JACKET, urged one of his editorials: this monkey-jacket "is only a short coat of white washable material, cut in the front like a dress suit, with a link to hold it together. In the back it terminates several inches above the masculine waistline in a demure point. It is cool and comfortable. Dancing with it on hot nights becomes a different experience from the miserable pirouetting which men must now indulge in with a thick coating of wool enveloping their trunk."

His signed articles utilized his grab bag of world traveler's lore. One discussed the "democratic centralism" of China's Executive Committee of 79, as described to him by Gen. Wu T'ieh-Ch'eng, a member: "I gathered that he meant the democracy was concentrated in the committee leaders. . . . By the time it reached the common man, there was very little democracy left."

Quite often Lodge wrote the day's leading editorial—the traditional leader. He studded these with learned comparisons: "There is the difference between Messrs. Hoover and MacDonald sitting on a log by the Rapidan in 1929 and the Kaiser and the Czar embracing on the deck of the imperial yacht in Baltic water in 1909."

In discussing the murder of union organizers in Gastonia, North Carolina, Lodge showed his awareness of the need for workers to defend themselves: "It can be fairly argued that unionism is an inevitable development in the South, and if it is not carried to a point where it drives out capital, unionism there may be a good thing."

His admiration for flyers and interest in airpower took him to the Cleveland Air Races. "The wind and the dust clouds," he wrote, "the mighty roar of engines and the screech of planes parting the air as they dived across the field created an impression never to be forgotten." Lindbergh, in a plane which he had never flown before, "did rolls and sideslips at vertiginous speed and flew the length of the field on his back while his two companions clung to him like leeches. . . . Aviation is still an infant industry, but it is a very lusty child, and these are things which help it to thrive."

Lodge sometimes turned his hand to book reviews. He took obvious delight in reviewing *Letters and Friendships of Sir Cecil Spring-Rice*, the British aide and subsequent ambassador who had known both his father and grandfather so well. Lodge's review showed a discerning eye for trenchant anecdotes. A New York machine politician told Spring-Rice there was only one class of Americans who couldn't be bribed—the poorest. "You could get Jay Gould but you couldn't get that man [pointing to a cab driver], he's a follower of Henry George." Lodge quoted Spring-Rice: "As far as the rich are concerned by this state of things, their life becomes intolerably dull. They are separated from the poor by so deep a gulf that they have no influence as politicians or landlords. As the chief enjoyment derived from money seems to be power they have to go to Wall Street to find a field for ambition. They can't be rich enough. And with all this they are intolerably dull. The young men, if born rich, become drunkards . . . it is the dullest country in the world to be rich in and the bitterest perhaps to be poor in." In singling this out, Lodge reflected his own inheritance of Bay's contempt for pelf and privilege. Indeed, he could be outraged by special privilege shown to the rich and powerful, as was shown by his editorial on Harry F.

Sinclair's ability to take joyrides in Washington while "jailed" for contempt
of the Senate in the Teapot Dome scandal:

> *Whoever reads the account of this leniency must feel sick at heart.*
> *His trial and sentence did something to restore public confidence in*
> *American justice. His treatment under sentence will foster the cynical*
> *belief that American courts dare not punish a rich man. If the Wash-*
> *ington authorities wish to restore some confidence in American institu-*
> *tions they will see to it that Sinclair is treated as a convict and nothing*
> *else.*

Lodge did not share the belief, so common to the Hoover era, that success
in business was automatic proof of a man's ability to run the government.
Lodge was quite well aware that they were two different things, requiring
different orders of ability. "So loudly have political leaders sung the praises
of 'a business administration,' " one of his editorials noted, "that the public
has almost come to believe that businessmen are ideally equipped to hold
high public office and to deal efficiently with military, naval and foreign
affairs. Because they direct efficiently and successfully one special form of
undertaking, the impression has been created that they are in all things
supermen. . . . When businessmen leave the familiar stamping grounds
and venture into fields where public opinion and political forces come into
play, they are rather like children."

Ever the political animal, Lodge plunged with relish into the tangled
affairs of New York City's mayoralty election of 1929. As he had done with
Tom Walsh, he now did a thoughtful profile of Congressman Fiorello La
Guardia, the Republican candidate: "Every generation, fortunately, sees a
certain number of men and women who are more interested in serving the
community than in advancing themselves—persons who do not adopt that
attitude consciously but are born that way. La Guardia was born that
way. . . ."

Lodge was indignant when Joseph Pulitzer's New York *World* decided
that Tammany and the ineffable James J. Walker were unbeatable, and
supported Socialist Norman Thomas as the best way of registering protest.
Lodge's editorial flayed the *World*, and flayed the *Times* as well for supporting Walker by its silence:

> *No informed person denies that the only candidate having a chance*
> *to defeat Mayor Walker is Major La Guardia. No one need have any*
> *illusions concerning the latter because he is frankness itself and his*
> *past is an open book. He is not consistent, he is not tactful, he is not*

always sound, but he is honest, courageous and ready to admit his mistakes. The Herald Tribune *does not maintain . . . that he is the country's greatest statesman or that he is a faithful Republican. That is not the point today. What it does say is that his presence at City Hall would give the City a badly needed cure. What is most needed now is change, and that Major La Guardia can be counted on to provide. The* World *and its followers profess an earnest disapproval of Tammany, but they evidently do not want to change it. That is the difference.*

Lodge found time, as well, for some imaginative features. He wrote to Calvin Coolidge, in retirement at Northampton, for an interview. "I saw something you wrote from Asia," Coolidge replied, "which I thought had a fine literary merit and have been wondering when you would return. If you and Mrs. Lodge are in Northampton we should be delighted to see you. . . . Call my office when you reach town." The result was a mood piece, MR. COOLIDGE'S HOME TOWN: "Into this flinty and compact landscape the personality of Mr. Coolidge fits like the proverbial square peg into the square hole. . . . He is in harmony with the little isolated schoolhouses, the swaying leafless elms and the granite courthouse where he began his career. . . . Every morning Mr. Coolidge goes to his office. Sometimes he arrives as early as half past eight, driving down in the limousine which he used as President. He does not practice law but passes a good deal of his time in the tedious business of answering his mail and declining invitations to attend or to speak at public functions. His recreations are simple. He takes a walk; in the summer he fishes; sometimes he goes to Boston." He was also silent: the interview had no Coolidge remarks whatever.

In the fall of 1929, the nation lay stunned under the impact of the stock market crash. The first of what would be an endless and deepening series of international crises also began to arise. Soviet Russia was now strong enough to start nibbling at its ill-defined borders with Manchuria. China appealed to the great powers for assistance against Russia under the Kellogg Pact. Lodge was against meddling, not because it was wrong but because the U.S. had let its military power decline to where it could use little but words. Said Lodge's editorial: "It would do no good and would help no one if we were to tell the Russians . . . to let China alone, when we know and the world knows that we are not prepared to follow up such an attitude with action. In this affair, as in all others, there should be the closest correspondence between our words and our deeds." The new Secretary of State, Henry L. Stimson, said he was "astonished" when a note to the Soviets drew an angry rebuke. Lodge added his own rebuke: "Foreign offices should not be astonished. They should know. That is why they exist."

The roaring twenties ended and gave way to the fearful and uncertain thirties. As the new decade began, Lodge was in London covering the World Naval Conference. He was now moving with unquestioned ease among the movers and shakers of the world. From 10 Downing Street came his invitation to a state reception, at Lancaster House ("Evening Dress with Decorations") by "The Right Honourable Prime Minister and Miss Ishbel MacDonald." His impeccable French and his long acquaintance with France's new Prime Minister, André Tardieu, who was one of Edith Wharton's old friends, gained him easy access to the French mission at the Carlton. He reported: "The French are scattered through this hotel and they work in their bedrooms. Tardieu smokes the Maryland cigarettes of acrid black tobacco which are so popular in France. With no ceremony at all a young man would dash in and say: 'Where is Briand?' There was no question of 'Mr. Briand' . . . no Anglo-Saxon deference."

Lodge thought he smelled some intentions to revive the old League's Article X, his grandfather's *bête noire,* in the new guise of a "consultative pact," and when Stimson turned his back upon such efforts, Lodge editorially applauded this "wise decision" against a pact "having as its ultimate end the committing of the U.S. when a European war threatens."

His experience was now global; his attitudes were still aggressively insular.

In the midst of elections, air races and naval parleys, Lodge had also found time to launch negotiations to buy the Boston *Transcript.* The paper had been teetering on the edge of insolvency for years. After the market crash, three or four major owners were willing to sell their *Transcript* holdings to raise badly needed cash. Lodge, recalling the Essex Junto, in which George Cabot had formed many a sly alliance with Theophilus Parsons, doubtless thought it fitting that he and Geoffrey Parsons should form a new junto to acquire that paper which more than any other spoke for the old Yankee aristocracy. They sounded out the *Herald Tribune's* business manager, Howard Davis, as a possible ally. He came in eagerly. All three moved very secretly, lest the Reids think them disloyal for even thinking of moving to another paper. Actually, they were all fiercely loyal to the Reids, but even more fiercely wanted to be their own masters. They had no doubt of their ability to raise the money. Cabot could tap any number of sources in Boston. Parsons knew many well-heeled Republican financiers in New York. Davis' high reputation as a hardheaded business manager would free them of any suspicion of being mere pipe dreamers. Parsons was able to wire the returning Lodge on the *Ile de France:* CONSORTIUM PROGRESSING CONFIRMATION AND AID FROM UNEXPECTED SOURCE AWAITING YOUR RETURN. He had landed a millionaire, named Dodge, who would bankroll them.

As soon as Lodge returned, he had numerous meetings on weekends with his old boss and friend, *Transcript* publisher George Mandell. Mandell was willing to sell, and proposed various combinations of down payments, promissory notes and preferred stock. At a leading Boston brokerage, Cabot's Nahant playmate, Malcolm W. Greenough, a big bear of a man who had been captain of the Harvard football team, worked out plans to float a million dollars' worth of securities. Lodge was to be publisher, Parsons editor, Davis manager. Lodge detailed some of his ideas for editorial improvements:

> *The development of a larger and stronger local staff under an able city editor should rank first on the list of agenda. . . . All news of wide human appeal must be well covered, murders included. Any sort of story can be carried without offense if written with taste and discretion and not too conspicuously displayed.*

Lodge's prospectus showed that despite his newness in newspapering he had already developed a shrewd understanding of the business and the requirements for success. As in national policy, actions must speak far louder than words:

> *It should be realized that the execution of newspaper policies is more important and far more difficult than the formulation of them. If a paper plan were made of the paper's present editorial policy it might not appear shockingly bad, but the execution. . . . is inefficient in the extreme. There is at present a lack of initiative, a failure to plan and anticipate, and an inattention to details which can in part be attributed to laziness and stupidity, and in part to the feeling which must by this time have permeated the staff that the paper is not growing, that the mechanical facilities are not at hand and that excellence is therefore wasted. These things do not so much call for planning of policies as they do for imbuing a new spirit throughout the staff.*

However, the closer the Junto got to solid plans, the more the owners kept raising the ante. The Junto finally concluded that the terms were too high, and gave up for the time being. A year later Parsons was lamenting: "I always thought that keeping the Junto intact would be the hardest labor. I may be an awful fool but personally I have not lost faith in the *Transcript* and should tackle it with great enthusiasm and confidence provided, of course, you and Howard were along. . . . Howard remarked yesterday that in his guess the *Trancript* will ultimately sell for the value of its AP franchise, which is practically nothing." Within a few years the *Transcript* went to the wall. Lodge remained convinced that he and Parsons could have saved it.

Lodge went on writing editorials between his trips to Boston. His name now appeared in magazines also. In *Harper's*, he expanded his theses against the Kellogg-Briand method of "abolishing" war by words, and in another article suggested the U.S. simply was not temperamentally suited to govern the Philippines. He advanced the idea that we should trade such liabilities for genuine assets, such as British bases in the Caribbean. Henry Luce, who had just begun his fledgling *Fortune,* published a Lodge article on naval power which would have rejoiced their mutual kinsman, Commodore Luce, who had backed Captain Mahan's radical theories of seapower. Lodge's argument: Genuine parity of seapower with Britain must include bases and merchant marine as well as warships.

His precocious concern with actual power, in fleets and armies, as distinguished from moral shibboleths, led him to perceive, far earlier than most, the revolutionary impact of the aircraft carrier on naval warfare. In mid-1930, noting that the new treaty just concluded at London allowed the U.S. to increase its naval strength by some 400,000 tons, Lodge wrote in the *Trib:* "Naval aviation is something in which Americans seem to excel, as anyone who has observed the flying from aircraft carriers can testify. There is certainly a strong case for devoting a very large proportion of the [new] tonnage allowed us to these ships."

The potentials of aircraft carriers made him regard the Philippines as all the more hazardous when ill-governed. He predicted that aircraft carriers would make it possible for the Japanese to seize the Philippines, and attack the West Coast as well. "It is possible for the *Lexington* [an early U.S. carrier] for instance to make a quick run and bomb a European city after having eluded the foreign fleet on the way over. . . . It would be equally possible for a Japanese carrier to elude our small Asiatic force, cross the Pacific and bomb San Francisco. This one new element of warfare—the aircraft carrier—shows how mid-Victorian it is to talk of 'offensive' and 'defensive' wars and to say that the nation whose 'coasts are protected' has all it needs for security. Here again the question is 'protected against what?' If that 'what' be aircraft carriers, then our 'defensive' force should be capable of acting in the enemy's home waters—at those bases whence the carrier springs."

La Guardia had lost his first battle against Tammany. The defeat merely spurred Lodge into renewed assaults on the Walker regime's corruption. Samuel Seabury's investigation of Walker had already begun. One of the witnesses before his commission, Vivian Gordon, a prostitute who told of

112 police shakedowns, was suddenly murdered. Lodge wrote a leader on this murder:

> *If any single event can arouse the public conscience it is the strangula-*
> *tion and beating to death of Vivian Gordon, whose bruised body was*
> *found in Van Cortland Park on Thursday morning. . . . Civil moral-*
> *ity has already sunk pretty low when the main question before the*
> *community is not the stoppage of corruption but merely the ascertain-*
> *ing of how much corruption exists. . . . New crimes are committed*
> *to cover up old ones. . . . Throughout the city at this moment are*
> *countless men and women who are so badly frightened that they will*
> *not tell what they know and who in a free city would willingly tell. . . .*

Such indignation led ultimately to Gov. Roosevelt's removal of Walker.

When he wanted to make demands or assaults the *Tribune* was not willing to endorse, Lodge sometimes resorted to letters-to-the-editor, often using the pseudonym of Ajax. When Britain and France were about to default on their war debts, Ajax suggested some shrewd Yankee trading for their Caribbean bases. "The way to deal with the reparation question," he wrote, "is to start conversations at once looking toward the acquisition of the British and French possessions in the Caribbean in exchange for the U.S. canceling the debts those nations owe us. . . . The time to take steps to this end is now. If we wait until default is at hand we shall be in an inferior bargaining position. . . ." Ajax cried in vain. Not until World War II would a U.S. President see the wisdom of seeking such exchanges.

Ajax was outraged over the Hoover Administration's handling of the long-awaited Wickersham Commission's report on the pros and cons of Prohibition. Lodge was strongly anti-Prohibition, and had never been a Hoover admirer, in part possibly because Hoover's closeness to Wilson made Lodge question the sincerity of Hoover's Republicanism. As with Eisenhower later on, the Democrats had often talked of running Hoover on their ticket, before Hoover clearly identified his Republican leanings. In any case, Ajax felt that the Administration's summary of the Wickersham Report— a report which was clearly an indictment of Prohibition—had twisted its true meaning almost 180 degrees. All that most Americans saw was the summary, since the full text was issued only to a few metropolitan newspapers. This (cried Ajax) "created the impression that the report is dry, which is of course by no means the case. . . . It is of course one thing to form public opinion by a straightforward presentation of the facts and by honest argument. It is another and very different thing to form public opinion by not telling it things which it must know before it can see the whole truth. . . . The first method is honest, proper and healthy. The latter is a mere devious trick, to be exercised by the meanest government clerk. It renders free opinion impossible. . . ." Years later Lodge would have a harsher quarrel with Hoover over similar matters of principle and ethics.

In another letter, "Republicanis Senescentis," which he signed himself, he warned, quite accurately, that unless Hoover took the leadership against Prohibition the party would lose the Presidency in 1932.

Congressman La Guardia, smarting over his defeat for mayor, was nevertheless grateful for the loyal support of his young *Tribune* friend. In February, 1930, he wrote Lodge urging him to run for senator in his home state. The situation there was that Republican Senator Fred H. Gillette was retiring at the end of his term, and former Senator William M. Butler was the leading contender. Cabot's Republican Associates had supported Butler in 1926, though Cabot's Aunt Constance had helped defeat the former senator because of his humiliation of the senior Lodge in 1924. Now Butler was claiming that the old senator had wanted Butler to succeed him. Cabot denied this, and announced that he would campaign for Eben S. Draper, Butler's chief opponent for the nomination. "The movement against the old guard headed by Butler is in full swing," reported the Boston *American*. It listed Christian A. Herter and Sinclair Weeks, son of Coolidge's Secretary of War John W. Weeks, as Lodge's fellow rebels. Butler succeeded in winning the nomination against their efforts, but was defeated by Democrat Marcus Coolidge. Nevertheless, Lodge had helped stir up a Young Turk movement among younger Republicans who felt their party needed new leadership and new ideas.

In May, 1931, Lodge went off to Fort Bliss, Texas, for two weeks of maneuvers with the Eighth Cavalry, serving as its adjutant. As one who had constantly editorialized on the need for military preparedness, he believed in suiting his actions to his words. He had urged that "legislation authorizing mobilization of men and resources in time of war [be] enacted in time of peace," and wanted it to conscript wealth as well as men, "to purge war of profiteering [and make it] seem as obsolete in the future as the Civil War right of a man to exempt himself . . . by simply paying a certain sum." Since qualifying for his cavalry commission, he had maintained his active reserve status. Now, from Fort Bliss, he sent daily dispatches to the *Herald Tribune* on the "war" between Colonel Walter C. Short's "Browns" and the "Whites" in New Mexico commanded by Colonel Ola Bell. In one night march, the Browns "swept along 50 miles of blistering desert north of El Paso. . . . Horses were hanging their heads after a day in the red sand without water." They bottled up the Whites in the Sacramento Mountains. "This maneuver," wrote combat correspondent Lodge, "which dealt the death blow to the 'Whites' and which surpassed anything of its kind hitherto accomplished by American cavalry consisted in taking an entire squadron up a mountain 10,500 ft. high over the famous Bug-scuffle Trail, which rises 5200 ft. and has gradients which are never less than 35 degrees and at many points are as extreme as 40 degrees. . . . On approaching a ranch word was brought back by a breathless rider on a lathering horse that a detachment of enemy troops was ahead. Major Willis Crittenberger and the writer galloped ahead, dismounted under a tree and crawled forward. Ahead of us was the silvery wooden stockade of a ranch. . . . We heard single rifle shots and presently the rattle of the machine guns, already dismounted and in action. We were crawling ahead with cocked pistols when the umpire waved his white flag and we learned that our advance detachment under Lieutenant Henry B. Crosswell had captured 15 'White' troopers and horses and one machine gun . . ."

Back from his Army maneuvers, Lodge was soon in the midst of an editorial crusade on behalf of the frigate *Constitution*. It had been restored by the pennies of schoolchildren, and would leave Boston Harbor in July for a tour of the U.S. Lodge was shocked to learn that it would be towed. "Surely the cost of enough sail to move her along is not prohibitive," he wrote. "We have already been told that there is an abundance of men who would make a handy crew. . . . What sight could be finer than that of the 44-gun frigate with towering canvas cutting through the blue waters of Massachusetts Bay. . . . Let Charles Francis Adams himself, the Secretary of the Navy, take the helm!" All over the country, supporting articles and editorials appeared in a flood; sail was donated; the navy announced that a crew of Annapolis midshipmen would man the *Constitution* next year. Fittingly enough, young Lodge was elected a director of the Navy League, together with his publisher Ogden M. Reid, Senator James W. Wadsworth and the son of T.R.'s sister, Corinne, Theodore Douglas Robinson, former Assistant Secretary of the Navy. More and more, Lodge was being projected into the public eye. He was no longer an anonymous editorialist. He was asked to speak in a symposium on disarmament at the Hotel Astor, drew some boos and a few No's when he asserted that Congress was doing more to reduce arms than any treaty could, and that the Army was approaching its "disgraceful pre-war stage of unpreparedness." *The Army and Navy Journal* expressed the hope that "others of the courage of Mr. Lodge [would] tell the people the facts."

Because of Lodge's interest in preparedness, the new *Fortune* assigned him to do an article on M-day, the industrial mobilization that would take place, under War Department plans, in a war. Assistant Secretary of War Frederick H. Payne worked with him on the article, together with his aide, Major Eisenhower. The article never ran. Years later *Fortune* archivists found this note from Payne to editor Parker Lloyd Smith, concerning photo-

graphs for the article: "If you like I would be very glad to send . . . Major
Eisenhower, who gave Mr. Lodge most of the information, to New York any
day to have an interview with Mr. Lodge and you." Curiously, neither Lodge
nor Eisenhower, who worked together in later years, remembered this early
collaboration.

However, Lodge had long since become a particular favorite of the
Army's professional officers who were desperately trying to maintain any
sort of military establishment under the starvation budgets of the Coolidge-
Hoover years. He had become close to Major George S. Patton, a staff
officer in the War Department, while covering that department in Washington. Patton, who believed himself the reincarnation of ancient warriors,
was given to a life style of dramatizing even the most prosaic episodes. One
evening, when the Lodges were leaving after dining with the Pattons in
their apartment, Patton grasped a carafe around the neck and lifting it off
a nearby table, remarked, "The carafe, they tell me, Mrs. Lodge, can be a
very deadly weapon when properly used." Testing its balance, his eyes
sparkling, he continued: "My grandfather used one to kill the Governor of
the Bahamas." Lodge assumed he simply made that up, on the spur of the
moment.

Patton was given to equally capricious adventures. He lived at Hamilton,
not far from Cabot's own home at Beverly, and they often rode together at
a nearby riding club. Patton also often took him sailing on his eighty-foot
auxiliary sloop, *The When and If*. In the middle of one afternoon, Patton
suddenly challenged Lodge to sail with him down to New York. He accepted, though thinking it a bit late to start. They had only reached the
Cape Cod Canal by the time darkness overtook them.

Soon they were in pea-soup fog so thick that Lodge had to lie out on the
prow with a flashlight, watching for the channel buoys as they crept along
at snail's pace.

The fog did not lift until sunrise, by which time they had reached City
Island near New York.

Lodge, exhausted from the ordeal, asked Patton why he had picked such
untimely hours for the trip.

Patton grinned: "I just wanted to test your courage muscles."

Much later, the two would serve together in the Second Armored Division.

Lodge's concern over the dangers of American military weakness led him
to take leave to prepare a book on the subject, elaborating and extending
the arguments of many editorials. Publisher Ogden Reid gave him a year's
leave of absence in the fall of 1931.

He chose as title for his book, "The Cult of Weakness." He was still

116 hard at work on it, the following March, 1932, when he took time to urge Publisher Reid to hire a young friend of his, Joseph Alsop, who would be graduating from Harvard that June:

> *He is a grandson of Mrs. Corinne Roosevelt Robinson, a grand-nephew of the late President, and a nephew of our mutual friend, Teddy Doug- las Robinson. I am not, however, recommending him because of this family inheritance although he has his full share of the Roosevelt energy and ability. I am bringing him to your attention because I be- lieve him to be first class material for newspaper work. He writes easily and well, he is a voracious student of public affairs. I have never rec- ommended a man for the* Herald Tribune *who is as young and inex- perienced as Alsop but he has impressed me so favorably that I feel that it would be very good policy for us to take him on . . . Unless I am very much mistaken he would . . . become a very valuable man in the Washington bureau . . .*

Alsop was hired.

Houghton Mifflin published *The Cult of Weakness* that October. It sold a grand total of 350 copies, and its author would soon find himself trying to buy up the remainder for reasons he had not even anticipated. But some of its argument for 1) preparedness, 2) economic self-sufficiency and 3) an end to rule by organized minority pressure groups, still make pertinent reading:

> *Some critics of government, tired of mediocre professional politicians, looked with a secret favor on a dictatorship and a better, if not a larger bureaucracy, or spoke openly of businessmen in government. Appar- ently lawyers, bankers and engineers could not become doctors or baseball players overnight, but they could become statesmen. Yet must we not admit the unpalatable truth that much of the furtiveness in government and much of the worship of expediency is due to these doubtless able men of no experience whom we have thrust into poli- tics? . . . Clearly able professionals are what the situation demands. No branch of private activity or appointive office gives a man a train- ing for public life which can equal politics itself.*

This sounded much as if young Lodge was giving serious thought to taking up politics himself. Certainly he had been giving serious thought to what was required of the pro. "The politician," he wrote, "must not only know the people; he must periodically bare his soul to them. He has to do what no man enjoys doing, and which most men in private life must only do very seldom—commit himself in public. . . . Every decision is pre-

ceded by the deepest thought of which the man is capable for the simple
and binding reason that these decisions affect his own personal career. To
be sure, his thoughts may be influenced by mere personal advantage, but
he cannot afford to ignore the real merits and demerits of the measures
confronting him. In the immortal Tammany phrase, he must 'pander to the
better element' as well. . . . A lifetime of this public commitment not only
develops convictions; it also breeds a healthy skepticism of miracle-working
devices. It should, in a man of proper type, give rise to a habit of public
courage."

At its heart, his book, like his *Harvard Advocate* piece of a decade before,
is an argument for realism and against "political sentimentalists." He dis-
misses extreme pacifism as "a symptom of the belief that anything that
should be done can be done. Classic examples of this belief are the assump-
tions that Americans can by legal devices be stopped from drinking, that
Malays in the Philippines can successfully administer an Anglo-Saxon
constitution, that prosperity can be achieved without work—and that the
human race by an elaborate series of written devices can be stopped from
ever fighting again." True, throughout its history, America had achieved
"the astonishing paradox of victory without preparedness," but the school
of "peace by unpreparedness" was "old-fashioned and reactionary," unsuccessfully tried by Wilson, while preparedness itself was "forward-looking
and progressive since it is a method the U.S. has never tried before."

Lodge's views provoked attack and support as diverse as the two schools
he described. Perhaps the most violent review was Quincy Howe's in *The
New Republic:*

"In the city of Boston there is a thoroughfare called State Street which
connotes locally what Wall Street connotes nationally. Young Mr. Lodge
belongs to State Street by birth, by temperament and choice. When, therefore, he speaks of 'America as we have learned to know and love it,' the first
person plural is editorial or royal, not universal. 'We' crushed the Shays
rebellion, supported Hamilton against Jefferson, advocated secession in
1814, stoned William Lloyd Garrison, hissed Robert Gould Shaw as he led
his Negro troops past 'our' Somerset Club on Beacon Hill, attacked Woodrow Wilson for keeping 'us' out of war, and electrocuted Sacco and Vanzetti.
The whole Adams family from John to Henry despised State Street; so did
the self-reliant Emerson. For State Street has unfailingly violated the
American dream by preserving the American nightmare." *

Whatever else this diatribe was, it was irrelevant to Lodge's book, which

---

* Many years later, in his sixties, Lodge observed: " 'Young Mr. Lodge'—and now
old Mr. Lodge—has never belonged to State Street—neither I, nor my father, nor my
grandfather. We have never had any connections with State Street. We have never
been in business or banking."

118 one Adams, Charles Francis, praised for "its generally sound reasoning," and Robert Gould Shaw's own descendant, Robert Shaw Barlow, hailed for its "self-restraint." H. L. Mencken was delighted: "You say a great many things which should have been said long ago. . . . You complain of the lack of a magazine setting forth the preparedness view. . . . *The American Mercury* throws itself into the breach. . . . I'd like very much to print a full-length denunciation of all the pacifists, world-savers and other such muggletonians. . . . I hope you move into Congress." In *The Bookman,* Hoffman Nickerson wrote: "Since the reviewer has long believed that the errors castigated in this book have helped make the last century and a half the bloodiest in human history, he submits that the author has deserved well of the republic."

By the time the book was done, so was Cabot and Emily's lovely new home on a grassy slope leading gently down to the sea at Beverly Cove, close to the great rambling summer home of Emily's parents. Modeled partly on Edith Wharton's, it was an L-shaped brick affair, its great front rooms, opening out on the sea, and it was walled on all sides with ceiling-high bookcases for the old senator's enormous classical library. A smaller sitting room to its right held Sargent's painting of the old senator. On the grass patio outside were some of the gigantic seashells, big as bushel baskets, which China Merchant John Lodge used to bring back in his clipper ships as ballast.

Approached from the rear, the house opens on a long marble hall, at one end of which is the oval dining room, and a spiral staircase to the bedrooms above. In its middle the hall yields to the slightly lower living room, beneath which, almost underground, was Cabot's large office, his father's portrait on the wall, and, beside his desk, the great iron chest,* locked by an enormous iron key, which John Lodge took with him on all his ocean voyages. Soon that office, indeed his whole house, would be swarming with politicians as Lodge set out to become one of those "able professionals" his book extolled. He would have to overcome such myths as Cabots speaking only to God. But he had already made a good beginning. While still on the *Tribune* he was made an honorary member of the Society of Polonia Restituta and given a great sunburst medal which caused a copy boy to call him "the Polish horseman" while Cabot merely giggled. The honor had provoked a Boston newspaper parody which proved prescient:

> *Here's to the city of Boston*
> *The home of the bean and the cod*

---

* This chest contained detailed journals of all his trips, to the Spice Islands, France, Portugal and many other ports, and a ledger entry of all goods bought and sold, with their prices.

Where the Lowells speak only to Cabots
And the Cabots speak only to—Filipowicz, Massalski,
Lepowski, Tomaszewski, Witkiewiez et al.

The year Lodge entered politics was the beginning of the Roosevelt Era that would revolutionize the U.S. economy, change the whole political spectrum, and doom the Republicans to a quarter century of minority struggle. Though Lodge would later find much in Roosevelt to admire, at the outset he saw him as simply another politician. Returning to the *Tribune* long enough to cover the Chicago convention which nominated Roosevelt, Lodge had much the same view of him as Heywood Broun—"the corkscrew candidate of a crooked party"—and as Lippmann, "An amiable man who is wealthy and good-looking and for some inexplicable reason thinks he is qualified to be President of the United States." At Chicago, Lodge thought Roosevelt showed "ruthless personal ambition" in support of his own nomination but "flabbiness where any general issue was at stake." He showed the ruthlessness in seating Huey Long's contested delegation in an effort to break the two-thirds rule, but flabbiness in failing to use his power on the platform committee "to secure the adoption of his own view on Prohibition. The last straw [Lodge wrote a friend] was the application of third-degree methods to the delegates by insisting that they be kept in all night sessions in the hope that due to physical exhaustion and desire to avoid a deadlock, enough extra votes would go over to him"—as they did.

Lodge renewed his friendship with Mencken at the convention. Prohibition was still on and Chicago was the center of both bootlegging and gangsterism. Mencken, kidding the undertakers who call themselves "morticians," said the bootlegger did so much good that he ought to be called a "bootician." He and Lodge prowled the dens of sin together. In one of the brassier nightclubs, a crooning piano player annoyed Mencken's musical sensibilities. "I'd like to shoot that bastard," he said. The girl behind the bar reached under the counter, took out a Thompson submachine gun, and laid it in front of Mencken on the bar. "Go ahead," she said. Offered the ultimate weapon of criticism, the Baltimore sage for once was silenced.

Back from Chicago, Lodge was ready to launch a campaign of his own. For months before, under the tutelage of John Trowt, an auto dealer at Beverly Farms who had worshiped Senator Lodge, he had been going to community gatherings, lecturing about his travels to business and fraternal organizations. Trowt saw to it that Lodge met the small businessmen, mechanics and insurance salesmen who ran the Republican Club. It met over a drug store on Cabot Street, Beverly's main stem.

One spring evening in 1932, Trowt dropped in for a long talk but not till

120   he was leaving did he casually observe, "You know, Cabot, there's going to be a vacancy in the Legislature. I think you ought to run."

Lodge, who felt that he now had acquired enough experience in public affairs to seek office in his own right, agreed. He announced his candidacy two days later. He worked at it night and day, spoke at "house parties" where supporters brought in a few undertaker's chairs. He mapped out the whole area street by street, and taking a section at a time, rang every doorbell. "My name is Henry Cabot Lodge," he told the answering housewife. "I'd like to get your views on the election." Few had encountered such a handsome door-to-door salesman, and they were visibly brightened by his wanting to know their thoughts.

Always systematic, he was trying, he told friends, to reduce politics to an exact science. He kept a card index of the names and addresses of everyone he met. The opposing candidate was hard-put to assail him; the worst epithet he could find was "carpetbagger from Nahant." But after all, Beverly was where George Cabot lived, and sailed his privateers. He had even built the bridge across the inlet linking Beverly with Salem. His three-story brick house on Cabot Street, where George Washington had come to breakfast with Mr. Cabot, was now the city's Historical Museum.

"I don't believe in trying to camouflage public issues," Lodge told the Boston *Globe*'s veteran political reporter, M. E. Hennesy. "The Republican Party can afford to be frank in all public matters. It was founded on human rights and we must not relinquish our great heritage." Lodge topped his nearest rival in the primary by fourteen hundred votes.

What would otherwise have been a minor local election caught the national eye because, as T.R.'s sister Corinne Robinson wrote, "another Henry Cabot Lodge is now going to be prominent in the service of his country." Both Walter Lippmann and Arthur Krock sent congratulations. Geoffrey Parsons paused at the Century Club to scribble this note: "Somehow I feel confident that the top of the world—for young and old alike—is destined to be yours." The note from Charles Poletti, Harvard classmate ("I wish you an astounding success, one that will carry you to the very highest rungs of the ladder"), was a curiosity; it came on the letterhead of the Democratic National Campaign Committee in New York. Corliss Lamont, reminded Lodge that he had declined Lodge's "standing offer to pay me $100 for speaking against you." His reason: "We radicals are most anxious to have you in office; it will give us such a perfect symbol of pure, consistent, autocratic Toryism. . . . We really admire you so much more than these muddled, mouthing, mitigating liberals who fool the workers into believing that they will do something for them. If we can't have radicals, we'd much prefer reactionaries." *

* Lamont added a postscript which disclosed the stillbirth of one of the most unlikely

With the New Year, Lodge took his seat, under the gold-leafed dome of
the State House on Beacon Street. He kept quiet, as a freshman legislator
should, impressed his elders by doing more listening than talking. He got
some friendly help from Speaker Leverett Saltonstall, in return for the
brash advice he had given Saltonstall a decade before when, as Saltonstall
recalled, "he hardly looked old enough to be allowed to work." It was hard
to get any Republicans to serve on the Labor and Industries Committee.
The Speaker told Cabot: "If you want to do a job and put yourself in a position to get some publicity and a reputation for open-mindedness on the
labor question, why don't you go on this committee?"

Lodge did so—thereby fooling, not the workers, but Lamont's estimate
of his "Toryism." He tackled labor problems with such thoroughness and
fairness that the following year he was made the committee's chairman,
and as such enacted some far-ranging reforms.

As journalist and pragmatist, Lodge saw clearly what escaped many of
his conservative friends—that the nation was undergoing a fundamental
social upheaval. Amid the collapse of the whole banking system, the
ominous rise of such demagogues as Huey Long and Father Charles Coughlin, the spread of such grassroots movements as Dr. Townsend's crusade
for fifty-dollar-a-month pensions for the old, the emotional fervor greeting
Roosevelt's effort to reorganize prostrate industry under the short-lived Blue
Eagle of the NRA ("We Do Our Part")—amid all this Lodge perceived the
need for constructive reforms. Rather than oppose needed changes, he felt
that the true role of a conservative was to give change a sound and coherent
structure.

In the House Labor Committee, until then a graveyard for any Republican politician, he got his chance.

For years, efforts to provide modern and adequate workmen's compensation laws in Massachusetts had been quietly sabotaged by employer lobbies.
Under Lodge, some thirty-odd bills were finally enacted, including one requiring that any totally disabled worker be paid the rest of his life. "I have
been on this committee for three years," cried New Bedford's Democrat
Representative Leo J. Carney on the floor, "and this is the first time an
honest effort has been made in behalf of labor. The chairman sat up until
three in the morning working on these bills." Lynn's Democrat Republican
Michael Carroll, who was also an official of that city's powerful Shoe Workers Union, praised Lodge's fairness and indefatigability so highly that fellow
Democrats rebuked him. In return, the Lynn *Item* rebuked them: "Mr.

---

publishing combinations in history: "I often think of our evening with young Hearst
and how jolly it would have been had we accepted his suggestion that he, you and I
run a newspaper together."

122 Lodge is one of the outstanding figures of the Legislature. . . . Why not admit it?"

Lodge's handling of the thorny field of workmen's compensation was typical of his thoroughness. He persuaded Samuel Horowitz, a leading expert who had written textbooks on the subject, to donate his services. Then he got representatives of both labor and employers together and with Horowitz at his elbow hammered out compromises both sides would accept. Employers praised his fairness. As for labor, Lodge was invited to be chief speaker at the fiftieth annual convention of the Massachusetts Federation of Labor. William Green, national A.F. of L. president, praised his legislation as national models.

Far from being a lackey of State Street, Lodge felt, like his father and grandfather before him, that the mere fact of being rich did not make any man automatically right or entitle him to immutable privileges. He felt that his party had been betraying its progressive origins in "simply sitting back and saying no" to every proposal of change, and fighting such experiments as NRA. "In the administration of this gigantic and revolutionary law," he told Essex County's Republican women at their annual garden party, "the difficulties may be so great that the attempt will fail." Nevertheless, it was headed in the right direction. He startled some by his own view of what that direction should be: "a nation in which there will be fewer very rich persons but . . . fewer who will be very poor. This should give us a more stable society and a greater amount of leisure which, if properly applied, should add immeasurably to the richness of life and the sum total of human happiness."

Lodge then launched into an attack on poverty as a social waste which indicated how deeply he had been pondering this problem. "For generations we were a people whose material activity consisted in skimming off the cream. . . . During our most prosperous years the majority of our people never earned 70% of the minimum necessary to decent subsistence. If the social injustice of this condition makes no impression, we should realize the expense which [it] finally brought upon the . . . taxpayers. . . . Poverty and unemployment reflect themselves in increased welfare costs and consequent increased taxes."

He warned his listeners not to suspect subversion in the theory that strong central government should have power of industrial control; it "stems from the mind of Alexander Hamilton, the spiritual father of our party." Let Republicans review "some of our own inspiring and now forgotten traditions."

In time the Supreme Court killed the NRA as unconstitutional. When some New Dealers introduced Constitutional amendments to limit the court's jurisdiction, a meeting was held at Fanueil Hall to "defend" the

Thudding sea *against the craggy rocks of East Point (above) was the first sound to meet Cabot's ears when he was born July 5, 1902, in the huge rambling old summer home of his grandfather, Senator Henry Cabot Lodge, Sr. The boy was 5 months old when this Christmas photo was taken (right).*

Poet father, *George Cabot Lodge, in his ensign's uniform after liberating Ponce, Puerto Rico, from the Spanish. He wrote love poems to his bride, Bessie (right). Both are shown with their three children, Cabot, John and baby Helena.*

Statesmen, scholars, sportsmen, *Cabot's forebears include President Arthur's Secretary of State F. T. Frelinghuysen (shown, left above, with granddaughter, standing, who became Cabot's mother), and slain Lincoln's honor guard, Admiral Charles Davis (shown at left of Lincoln's casket at New York's City Hall). Father of Senator Lodge's wife, Davis captured Memphis in Civil War. An avid horseman, Cabot's grandfather takes the jumps at Lynn. Cabot's literary-minded parents were often at Edith Wharton's "The Mount" where they are shown with Teddy Wharton, the novelist's husband.*

William Charles

In Paris, *Cabot learned both flawless French and tough French foot-boxing, savate, at Ecole Gory, whose master ran Cabot's anonymous photo (boy at right) in his school ad. Cabot was 10 (below) when he went to France, was 12 in photo on his Dieppe exit visa (below, right) when outbreak of World War I forced family to leave. His uncle, John (above), helped take the place of his dead father.*

BOXE FRANÇAISE (PRISE DE JAMBE SUR COUP DE PIED DE FIGURE)

ÉCOLE GORY
18, Rue Matignon
(A 150 mètres du rond-point des Champs-Elysées)

Directeur **G. GORY,** Docteur ès-Lettres

Programmes Officiels des Lycées
et Exercices physiques dans la même maison

GRANDES ET BELLES SALLES
DE
GYMNASTIQUE
Gymnastique méthodique et complète ✻ Tous les jours et pour tous
BOXE FRANÇAISE, LUTTE, SAUT, MOUVEMENTS D'ENSEMBLE

RÉPUBLIQUE FRANÇAISE

Département de la Seine-Inférieure
VILLE DE DIEPPE
LAISSEZ-PASSER

Nom : *Lodge*
Prénoms : *Henry Cabot*
Sexe : *masculin*
Nationalité : *américaine*
Résidence : *Dieppe villa Mouette*

M. *Lodge Henry Cabot* est autorisé à se rendre
à *Havre (aller - retour)*, département de *Seine Infre*
Départ le *5 Août* 1914, à *1* heures.
Délivré par Nous (2) Maire
de la commune de Dieppe.

Le *5 Août* 1914.

(1) La photographie doit être oblitérée par le cachet et la signature du Commissaire de police ou du Maire qui délivre le laissez-passer.
(2) Commissaire de police ou Maire.
(3) Signature et cachet de l'autorité qui délivre le laissez-passer.

Prep school days at Middlesex find Cabot solemnly lounging against tree at age 16 (right). At 17 he is a "machine-gunner" (below) at military camp where tough ex-Marine taught boys military discipline. At 18, Cabot makes Middlesex Debating Team (above, with G. R. Perera at right and L. B. Lockwood, at top, and A. S. Rogers, bottom).

Harvard days *find Cabot (rear row, second from left) on Freshman Rowing Crew. Already solemnly advocating Republican policies, he is nevertheless close friend of Kentucky Democrat, John Mason Brown (on right, with Cabot and John Lodge in photo at lower left). A year after graduation he is deep enough in G.O.P. activities to be in front row at Essex Club's picnic for President Coolidge year after old Senator's death.*

Wedding *comes in June, 1926. Cabot and his bride, Emily Sears, are shown below on wedding day. Emily's parents, Dr. and Mrs. Sears are shown (above left) with Emily's younger sister, Jean. Their huge old shingled home on the sea at Beverly Cove (above) was famous for good music, good wines, good friends and hospitality.*

Wedding breakfast *is held under umbrellas where grassy lawn of Sears' home slopes to the sea (the Irish butler, "Carty," carries champagne). By this same site, Cabot and Emily built their lovely brick home (right, below), modeled after friend Edith Wharton's villa at Hyeres (left, below), where they stayed on honeymoon tour.*

Fatherhood *finds Cabot proudly holding first-born George on porch of Sears home. Later, leaving baby with Emily's sister, the young Lodges journeyed around the world, posed together on camels near the Pyramids. They returned to their new home at Beverly. Soon their second son, Henry, was big enough to join George on his slide. The proud parents and sons sat on brick wall at their new Beverly home for a family portrait.*

Fun and formality, *in 1933, find Cabot up to his neck in sea (above, right) during Caribbean cruise with friends, bachelor Robert Cutler, and the Chandler Bigelows (above, left, Mrs. Bigelow, Emily, Chan, Bobby and Cabot enjoy shipboard costume party); Cabot is solemn and formal (below), as he takes George to Boston State House lawn for unveiling of statue of H. C. Lodge, Sr. Cabot was just entering politics for two-term stint in General Court of Massachusetts.*

Senator, *elected despite Roosevelt landslide of 1936, Cabot is shown rejoicing with wife, Emily, and his mother, Bessie. At 34, big victory in a national Republican disaster brought talk of Presidential possibilities. A new career also had begun for brother John, who became a Hollywood star (Shirley Temple's father), and Broadway lead in 1941's prize-winning "Watch on the Rhine" (he is shown with Lucille Watson).*

Fred Fehl, New York

In Senate, *young Senator is closest confidant of G.O.P.'s ablest elder statesman, Floor Leader Charles McNary (above). He quickly proved himself skilled, shrewd, resourceful politician, as adored by South Boston Irish as by Back Bay Brahmins (below, right, he marches in St. Patrick's parade of 1939 as South Bostonians give him the big hurrah). Lodge's shrewd counselor, Tom White, became his Senate aide (below, left).*

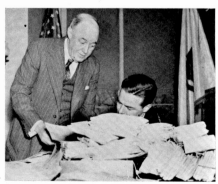

A liberal, *Lodge backs many New Deal measures, is friendly with Roosevelt's Vice President Garner (above, left), and admired by long-time G.O.P. liberal friends like La Guardia (right, with Lodge at 1942 Madison Square Garden mass meeting to denounce Nazis' Jewish atrocities, just then beginning).*

Presidential Campaign *of 1940 finds Lodge on Wendell Wilkie's campaign train (above). As war came to U.S. he donned Cavalry captain's uniform for Ft. Benning maneuvers with old comrade Col. Crittenberger (second from left) of horse-maneuver days on Bugscuffle Trail. On right is Maj. Paul Harkins, later commander in Viet Nam.*

Wide World

Tank Commander, *Cabot goes from 1940 Ft. Knox maneuvers (above) to first U.S. tank action in Egyptian desert (1942), then to armored action in Italy and to France as U.S. liaison with French (left, below, his team included Chan Bigelow and British Majors Aly Khan and Anthony McComas). Home during brief illness he had reunion with Navy volunteer George Lodge (right), returned to European fighting (below, right, he is briefed at front with Generals Edward Brooks and Anthony McAuliffe, famed Bastogne commander).*

As victory nears, *Lodge briefs Eisenhower, Bradley (partly hidden), Devers at First French Army front as De Lattre watches. Fluent in German, Lodge translated surrender terms to German commanders (below) who surrendered to Devers' Sixth Army Group.*

De Gaulle *greets Seventh Army's commander General Patch
(above) as Lodge acts as aide. Below, First French Army's
De Lattre pins Croix de Guerre on Lodge.*

Constitution. Lodge was asked to speak. He gave little comfort to those, like a retired Chief Justice of Maine, who declared that most New Deal reforms had been unconstitutional. Again, he reminded Republicans of their own liberal past:

"After all, it was Abraham Lincoln who said, 'We think the Dred Scott decision is erroneous. We know the court that made it has often overruled its own decisions and we shall do what we can to have it overrule this.' As President he later declared that 'if the policy of the government, upon vital questions affecting the whole people, is to be irrevocably fixed by decisions of the Supreme Court, the instant they are made in ordinary litigation between parties in personal actions, the people will have ceased to be their own rulers, having to that extent resigned their government into the hands of that eminent tribunal.' . . . The life of the law, as the late Justice Holmes remarked, 'is not logic but experience.' Because we have used our Constitution in a deliberate manner, amending it in most cases when experience clearly dictated the need of change, it reflects and transmits our accumulated knowledge and wisdom as a people. It sets high standards of public conduct. If the people are unequal to these standards, the Constitution cannot survive. It cannot by itself guarantee democratic government; it is we who by giving constant proof of the practical advantages of democracy must do that."

When occasion rose in the legislature, as elsewhere, to demonstrate political courage, Lodge never failed to respond. Only a handful of five legislators, for example, voted to ratify the Constitutional amendment to abolish child labor, and Lodge was conspicuous among them, doubly conspicuous because the opposition (it included Cardinal O'Connell and Harvard's President A. Lawrence Lowell) was so respectable and so powerful. He also fought the sales tax sought by the Democratic governor, Joseph B. Ely, believing it would soak the poor. He urged Ely to issue a proclamation suspending foreclosures on home mortgages, and cutting home mortgage rates to 5 per cent. Moreover, determined to preserve the gains for labor achieved under the NRA, he took an active role in promoting an Interstate Conference on Labor Compacts, whereby a group of states would accept uniform labor standards and the federal government would use its interstate commerce powers against goods not made in conformity with those standards.

In all these wide-ranging activities, he did not overlook the first principle of politics: "Do something for the folks back home." During his first term in the legislature he secured authority for the Beverly Harbor Master to shoot an occasional sea gull to frighten the birds away from the fishing boats, and got through a resolution calling upon the Health Department to investigate sewage pollution in Salem Bay.

Although it appeared trivial on the surface, this resolution was the opening wedge in a political maneuver which tells a good deal about Lodge and his methods. Its background was the pollution of the bay for more than forty years by the leather manufacturers of neighboring Salem and Peabody, both industrial towns, to the detriment of Beverly, a summer resort. Beverly had vainly protested the flood of grease from the tanned hides, which solidified into nasty, hairy little balls and floated back to the beaches.

In his second term, reelected by a large majority, Lodge used the Health Department's findings from its investigation to justify an awesome array of sewage bills, about a dozen in all, which would have cost the manufacturers millions of dollars. One required a pumping and purifying station, another a nine-mile conduit to carry the outfall far to sea. Two much milder measures merely forbade the dumping of grease in the sewers, and required $250,000 worth of sludge basins to clear the sewage of unavoidable greasy residues.

Alarmed, the manufacturers called mass meetings of their workers, and threatened to move South. Lodge came to meet with them in the ancient Peabody City Hall. After listening to an hour or so of their anguished complaints, he said, "I guess some of my bills *are* a little expensive. I don't want to ruin you. I'll withdraw them, if you'll just accept the two to stop dumping grease and build the sludge basins." The tanners accepted this proposition with obvious relief, and the bills passed without opposition. It was, of course, all that Lodge had wanted in the first place, and these two bills accomplished what the tanners had refused to do for four decades. Some pollution remained, but the beaches were notably cleaner.

Lodge spent part of every summer on maneuvers with the cavalry, and he kept in practice riding near Beverly as well, borrowing Major Patton's polo pony Barbara. Patton himself was at the Army War College, where he reported to Lodge that as part of his work he was writing a thesis on "the probable character of the next war as viewed from the standpoint of tactics and equipment."

As Lodge could see, the cavalry in which he was a reservist was a remnant of other wars and would probably not figure in the next war Patton was anticipating, at least in its traditional form. At the El Paso maneuvers of 1933, Lodge reported to the *Herald Tribune* "a long and dusty column of trucks and trailers" rumble into Fort Bliss, having traversed 630 miles through "the virtually roadless Big Bend desert country to Terlingua and back to El Paso," establishing the value of "transporting mounted troops by motor to those remote regions where the horse is still the fastest mode of travel. . . ."

By the time of the 1935 maneuvers, the First Cavalry was mechanized, and First Lieutenant Lodge was writing from Fort Knox, the new armor center: "The most modern regiment in the U.S. Army clattered out of its station one night last week under orders to repel an imaginary threat to the City of Louisville and in two crowded hours had spread itself like a huge claw over central Kentucky, gripping the road so as to make any immediate attack impossible. . . . It proved that it could bring its 175 vehicles into action more quickly than man had ever done before. It showed that it could, for example, leave New York City at sundown and launch a full-strength attack on Boston next morning."

The executive officer of this assault was his friend Crittenberger, now a lieutenant colonel. By now Lodge was known to all the top Army commanders, and admired by them. His book had become "must" reading at West Point, and Lodge himself was invited to address the cadets in 1935. It was the kind of speech the West Pointers did not often hear. "Whether you like it or not," Lodge told them, "the national defense is a political question and must be handled by political means." He cited the Oxford pledges not to fight in case of war, and refusals to salute the flag, as not "parts of dark and intricate plots to submerge the ship of state . . . but prompted by the highest motives. That is what makes them dangerous." He spoke of the Army's need to understand "something which you cannot see or touch . . . as wild and elusive as the wind . . . but powerful and fundamental . . . public opinion," which was as essential as bullets to victory.

By now he had begun making speeches everywhere in Massachusetts, and was becoming widely known. His message in these speeches was always the same: "The Republican Party has a future," and that future lay with capturing the independent voter—prophetic indeed. It had, he said, "always been the party of individual liberty and only recently has come to be regarded as a party wedded to special interests and reaction. This was never so before. It need never be so again."

By the summer of 1935, Lodge had made such a name for himself that his wise old friend, John Trowt, once more stopped by to see him. He found Lodge sunning on his front yard beach, and again talked to him in his amiable, leisurely way for a long time until he got to the point.

"Cabot," Trowt said, "I think you ought to get out and run for the United States Senate next year."

CHAPTER EIGHT

Don't press Cabot's suit every time he takes it off. Find one of his oldest suits, and don't let him wear another until after the election. And when he takes it off for the night, for the love of heaven don't let him hang it up. Throw it on the floor and let it lie there until he puts it on again.
—Thomas White, the Old Pro

Tom White had been a political adviser to Calvin Coolidge, who made him Boston's Collector of Internal Revenue. He was enormously wise. An admirer of his once said, "Why, he can think of thousands of things; nice things, clean things, beautiful things, things that cost you nothing and get you everything." He was a retired elder statesman when young Lodge came to seek his support for the Senate nomination. He had never known Lodge before, but looked him over carefully, and decided he had promise. He became Lodge's manager.

For the rest, Lodge's entourage was on the amateur side. Robert Cutler, bachelor, lawyer, banker, raconteur, wit* and author (*Louisburg Square*), was finance chairman. Malcolm W. Greenough, Cabot's chum from Nahant, his underwriter in the abortive *Transcript* purchase, and now his neighbor at nearby Pride's Crossing, was a tower of strength in many jobs. Chandler Bigelow, another neighbor and old friend, made endless telephone calls to possible supporters, addressed letters and made himself ubiquitously useful. Mason Sears of Dedham, a wise and weatherbeaten fellow legislator of Cabot's, a second cousin of Emily's, and a man of deep political savvy and wide political acquaintance, gave advice and counsel. Lawyer Charlie Barnes, Cabot's Middlesex classmate, did useful chores. "We didn't raise much money," finance chairman Cutler later confessed. "Most of it came from the Sears family. However, you didn't need to spend much in those days—telephones, mostly."

The Senate seat at stake was that of Marcus Coolidge, who had just died. He was the Democrat who defeated Butler in 1930. Almost certainly the Democratic nominee would be James M. Curley, who had been mayor of Boston time and again, and was currently governor. The Republicans, for the first time—and what proved to be the last—would choose their nominee, together with those for governor and other offices, in a state convention with duly elected delegates.

In view of Roosevelt's tremendous popularity, few Republican pros were

---

* His congratulation on Cabot's 1932 nomination: "Many happy returns of the day (rather appropriate, don't you think?)!"

126

willing to try for what seemed a hopeless assignment. Sinclair Weeks, mayor of Newton, decided to try—and urged Lodge not to. Cabot thought that over, then went down to the Beverly *Times* and announced his candidacy.

His delegate-hunting was confined to weekends because of his job in the Legislature. Every Saturday that winter he set out over icy roads, with a pail of sand, a towrope and a shovel in the back of his car, to seek out potential delegates in town after town. Each place visited he marked with a red thumb tack on his big map. When any area still looked glaringly white, he wangled an invitation to speak there.

His secretary went along, and would take down names as Lodge shook hands after the meetings. The secretary was Francis McCarthy, self-effacing, urbane, efficient son of the Sears' butler, Frank McCarthy. Francis had gone to secretarial school in Lynn, and was like a member of the family. On the way home from these trips, Lodge would tell him, "Write Schmitt I appreciated his views on freight rates," or "Tell Gulbenkian his views on pistachio tariffs is most interesting," not committing himself to support either. All the names went into his card files.

By the time Cabot, Tom White, Cutler, et al., descended on Springfield for the convention, that June of 1936, they figured they had personally met almost every one of the seven hundred delegates. Sinclair Weeks, Lodge's opponent, brought a hundred-piece brass band. He had favors for the ladies, and National Committeeman Joseph Martin working for him. On the morning of the voting White instructed Lodge:

"Get down to the hall a little early. Stand out in the lobby and shake hands. Be sure to smile—then they'll think you've got it in the bag. Just before the vote, walk across the platform slowly—let the boys see you're there. That'll make it harder for them to doublecross you."

It was a bitter, hard-fought convention. Leverett Saltonstall was opposing John W. Haigis for the nomination for governor. "Sinny" Weeks, though a Harvard classmate of Saltonstall's, threw his support to Haigis—who won by a single vote. That made Weeks look like the convention strong man. Many delegates believed that Haigis, in gratitude, wanted Weeks as his running mate. Accordingly the delegates were startled when Abe Glovsky, chubby Beverly lawyer, in a seconding speech for Cabot, cried: "Lodge has made a deal with Haigis!" Silence awaited the details of this deal.

"The deal is," said Glovsky, "that Haigis won't interfere with Lodge's campaign, and Lodge won't interfere with him!" Haigis nodded his assent to this neutrality. Glovsky later claimed his little maneuver stripped Weeks of thirty bandwagon votes.

Meanwhile, Cutler, whose hometown delegation from Brookline was solidly for Weeks, did some missionary work on a young lawyer member,

128   Maxwell Rabb. The delegation's head, Erland Fish, who was also a political power as president of the State Senate, warned his members: "No one here will vote against Weeks." Rabb, who was wavering, told him: "I want to keep an open mind."

Afterward, Rabb explained his thinking: "I liked Lodge's looks, he had a liberal record, and labor liked him. He could win a lot of independents and Democrats. Weeks was too conservative. I didn't think he could beat Curley." Rabb went to Weeks and told him he was going to vote against him.

Rabb then really began to get the pressure. Joe Martin got him downstairs and told him he was throwing away a promising career. Another man told him he would never be able to show his head in state politics again. Richard Saltonstall, Leverett's brother, came over to tell him: "I just heard you're going to vote for Cabot. It's a brave thing to do." Rabb's thinking began to spread. Horace Cahill, manager of the Saltonstall forces, told him: "I'm going to do the same thing."

When the roll was called on the first ballot, Brookline came early. Rabb was the first Weeks man to defect. Then Cahill and Dick Saltonstall announced their defection. The rush began. Delegates began to break all over. Lodge won by thirty-seven votes.

"Weeks' big band was waiting outside," Bobbie Cutler recalls, "ready for the triumphal entry. It had to go home without even sounding taps. It was 4 P.M. when we won—we had balloted right through the lunch hour. We were starving. We all rushed over to some restaurant, only to find the god-damn thing closed. But a big crowd was cheering the new 'Senator' so the owner came to open it up. We ordered bottles of champagne and chicken salad—Cabot, Emily, Mrs. Sears, Tom White, Chan Bigelow and I—and began drinking toasts. We were a bit delirious, you might say, because we had put the boy over."

"We didn't really," Chan Bigelow interjected modestly. "Put him over, I mean. The delegates did that."

The two old comrades, now both presidents of Boston banks, were reconstructing these heady events nearly thirty years afterward. They sat in the living room of Lodge's untenanted house at Beverly, at a time when Lodge himself was in far-off Vietnam. But the empty marble hall seemed to echo with memories of those exciting days. Bigelow had only to go down the basement stairs to pull out the handy card file, just as they had used it then. All afternoon they recalled the excitement of the long-ago battle.

CUTLER: Then came the campaign against Curley, Cabot speaking every night. I never came into this house but what Cabot had some politicians in here. He just loved it. I never saw anyone love politics so much.

BIGELOW: He drove a hundred thousand miles. I personally drove him

four thousand miles in the last month. He'd be at it from four in the afternoon till two in the morning. Cabot would never drive the car himself, he
always got somebody else to do it. He was afraid somebody would frame
some accident on him.

CUTLER: Curley was a very extraordinary man. I was corporation counsel for the city when Curley was found by the Superior Court to owe the city
$44,000. Jim petitioned that he didn't have any money and couldn't pay. He
lived in a great big beautiful house out Jamaica Way—had a better car than
I did—I used to see him eating in the fancy restaurants. But he claimed he
was penniless. He had a big new boat, a small yacht really, which he named
Maica Way, after his home. I thought that showed a nice sense of humor,
considering what he made away with. [He paused while other memories of
Curley came welling up.] Curley was very handsome. He had a beautiful
speaking voice.

BIGELOW: He had an Oxford accent, really. It was like hearing Shakespeare.

CUTLER: He could quote the Bible, Whittier, Lincoln, anything, in that
great organ voice of his. If you didn't hold on to yourself you'd be carried
away by this man. He went to jail because he took a civil service examination for a friend, and many people admired him for that. And he was a good
mayor, at first. Wilfred Doyle, who was city clerk for nearly thirty years,
told me Curley made a very good mayor. But we have Back Bay people
who did not like Curley.

BIGELOW (with an air of recollection): A lot of people liked Curley. My
mother-in-law, Mrs. Porter, always liked him. They had the Bazaar for the
Allies in 1918. Mrs. Porter was in it, and met Curley there. Twelve years
later she was in the Ritz having lunch, and here came Curley again. He
recognized her immediately. "Why, how do you do, Mrs. Porter," he said
with his charming smile. She always remembered that.

CUTLER: He was a very good mayor for two years—he was trying to
recompense for the hoosegow record. Under the recall procedure, the Back
Bay citizens tried to recall Curley. They failed, but they made Curley angry.
Wilfred Doyle told me Curley's face turned black as thunder. "Wilfred," he
said, "if those sons of bitches think I'm not good enough, I'll show them." So
after that he rooked the city, and when he was governor he rooked the
state. He decided to go for the Senate. It was thought that no one, nobody
at all, could beat Curley at that time. Still, a lot of decent Democrats were
outraged by his conduct. In the final election they got together and ran an
independent Democrat against Curley—Tom O'Brien, district attorney of
Middlesex, a fine lawyer, Harvard Law, friend of labor, and he got 140,000
votes from decent Democrats.

BIGELOW: Curley called Cabot Little Boy Blue—"blue-blooded, hand-

130   some and a boy," I'm quoting that last. Cabot never mentioned Curley by name. That was Tom White's idea, not mentioning him. Another thing burned Curley. When Cabot was in the legislature, Curley got behind this movement to make the teachers take an oath of loyalty to the Constitution. Meaningless sort of patriotism, but the veterans were steamed up for it, the Hearst papers were drumming for it, and Harvard, of course, was annoyed. Curley thought Cabot would be annoyed, too, but Cabot was smart enough to see they were trying to put him on the spot. He fooled them, he voted for the bill.

CUTLER: I thought the whole thing was a lot of crap. I've taken so many oaths so many times it's perfectly harmless to take another one.*

BIGELOW: Curley attacked Cabot's grandfather. That burned Cabot up. Cabot used to say, "My opponent attacked a dead man."

CUTLER: Cabot was very handsome, still is. Old biddies from South Boston would scream for him. Curley was fifteen years older, his hair beginning to gray. Cabot was a fresh, attractive figure, like Kennedy later.

BIGELOW: Curley claimed Cabot was posing as his grandfather.

CUTLER: Tom White was the most remarkable man. I told him I was worried about the Back Bay voters. He said, "Bobby, you don't have to worry about the Back Bay voter. Next to the Australian bushman the Back Bay voter is the most unintelligent person in the world. If they tell you they are going to vote for X, you can be sure Y will win in a walkaway." Curley tried to knock Cabot off the ballot, claiming he had no right to use his own name.

BIGELOW: A lot of people I suppose did think they were voting for Cabot's grandfather.

CUTLER: I'm sure they did. Curley brought legal action before the Ballot Commission. He claimed that Henry Cabot Lodge, Jr., was not his proper name, because Junior means a son. We were frightened. Charlie McGlue was as close to Curley as Chan here is to Cabot—and he was chairman of the Ballot Commission. For all we knew, McGlue might rule Cabot off the ballot, and we might never get him back on in time for the election. I got Bartholomew Brinkley, one of the most distinguished Boston lawyers, to represent Cabot before the Commission.

BIGELOW: In Webster's, "Junior" means just "the younger."

CUTLER: Anyway, they gave up on that. The Junior was right there on Cabot's birth certificate. The funny thing was that Curley's birth certificate —we checked that too—was different. He didn't have the middle name, Michael, on the certificate. But we didn't attack him on that.

---

* Thomas Reid Powell, Harvard's famed professor of Constitutional law, and well-known wit, welcomed the oath thus: "Why shouldn't I swear to support the Constitution? It's supported me for 25 years!"

Lodge himself summed all this up in a speech at Methuen on October 19,
1936:

"Since this campaign began attempts have been made to ridicule me because of my age, the color of my eyes and even my complexion. It has been insinuated that I am too young to take a seat as U.S. Senator in spite of the fact that the Constitution says that 30 is the age and I am well over that limit. An attempt has been made to take my name off the ballot because I have a Junior after my name so as to prevent any confusion between me and my grandfather. When this failed I was attacked on the ground that I was masquerading as my grandfather."

Lodge lashed out at Curley "reaching into the grave" to call his grandfather's record "mean and low." Retorted Lodge, "I suppose he is sorry that we are not involved up to the hilt in the hatreds and rivalries of Europe. . . . I believe the fathers and mothers of today's first voters will not agree. . . . He led the fight to prevent millions of Americans from ever shedding their blood on foreign soil by American entanglement in the League of Nations. If this record is mean and low let my opponent make the most of it. I am proud of it." The English-baiting Irish of South Boston roared with delight.

Lodge worked day and night. He let his suits get just as rumpled as old pro Tom White could desire. Lodge ran the campaign in Boston and sometimes met late at night in the basement office of his new home in Beverly. The numerous politicians running up and down the stairs were suitably awed by the familial relics hanging all about them—George Cabot's parchment commission from John Adams as the first Secretary of the Navy; Trumbull's painting of Alexander Hamilton, which Hamilton himself gave to his boon friend George Cabot; the embroidered Great Seal of the United States, surrounded by small photos or engravings of the whole puissant clan, with small typed legends of their identity:

CONSTANT FREEMAN, *captain of artillery, Continental Army, 1757-1816, great-great-great-grandfather of Henry Cabot Lodge, Jr.*
JONATHAN MASON, *U.S. senator from Massachusetts, 1752-1831; great-great-grandfather of Emily Sears Lodge.*
ELIJAH HUNT MILLS, *U.S. senator from Massachusetts, 1776-1829; great-great-grandfather of H.C.L., Jr.*
JOHN DAVIS, *U.S. senator from Massachusetts; governor of Massachusetts, 1787-1854; great-great-grandfather of H.C.L., Jr.*
FREDERICK FRELINGHUYSEN, *U.S. senator from New Jersey; colonel, Revolutionary War, 1753-1809; great-great-grandfather of H.C.L., Jr.*
FREDERICK THEODORE FRELINGHUYSEN, *U.S. senator from New Jersey; Secretary of State, 1817-85; great-grandfather of H.C.L., Jr.*

132   HASBROUCK DAVIS, *1827-1870, brigadier general, Civil War; great-grandfather of H.C.L., Jr.*
GEORGE CABOT LODGE, *1873-1909, ensign, War with Spain; father of H.C.L., Jr.*
THEODORE FRELINGHUYSEN, *U.S. senator from New Jersey; adoptive father of Frederick Theodore.**

By the foot of the stairs, the roving ward heelers could see the handsome photo of Teddy Roosevelt inscribed to the old senator's wife, "A.C.M.L. from T.R., Xmas, 1908," and one of Senator Lodge himself inscribed, "To Henry Cabot Lodge Jr. with Best Love from his affectionate grandfather." They gaped at the bright brass cannon which Capt. Charles Henry Davis took from one of the Confederate ships his flotilla destroyed at Memphis, and inscribed to the elder Lodge (his son-in-law) in 1876. They looked long at the photo of Captain Davis standing beside Lincoln's open casket at New York's City Hall, Lincoln's face just barely visible.

All this, indeed, gave the air of an ancient family seat. Actually Lodge was a beloved squatter on the fief of Dr. Sears, whose land this had long been. The Lodges even shared the Sears' gardener, Ralph Mitchell, who dwelled next the old coach house at the entrance to the estate. He had been born in that house, and his father had been the Sears' gardener before him. Mitchell's own family was one of the oldest in Beverly, and gave the town two acres for the Common to train volunteers in the Civil War. Ralph was already the hero of Cabot's two young sons. He gave them their first pipe, and never told on them when they broke the windows of his hothouse. He loaned them his cider press, which his grandfather bought in Marblehead in 1820. Their other hero was "Carty"—Frank McCarthy, the Sears butler, who had been buttons for Consuelo Vanderbilt's husband, the Duke of Marlborough, then for Edward Wharton before joining Dr. Sears. Carty taught the boys how to chew tobacco, smoke, play checkers, and cuss. On the other hand, he taught them manners. Carty was a great help in the 1936 campaign. He knew how to deal with all situations.

One example of Carty's imperturbable presence of mind became legendary at Beverly Cove. In the days when Joseph Alsop was still a fat young Harvard student, there had been a gay party at Dr. Sears', and Alsop, a weekend guest, had gone for a midnight swim to clear his head. When he reached shore, he flopped down, exhausted to regain his breath. He was sleeping there in angelic nudity on Sunday morning when Nurse Nellie

---

* Henry Clay's running mate for Vice President in 1848, when a campaign song went,

        Hooray, Hooray, the country's risin'
        For Henry Clay and Frelinghuysen.

Chapter Eight

McKenna brought little George and Harry Lodge by for their swim. She carried a cane, and prodded Alsop with it in his behind. He groggily betook himself to the front door, only to find it locked. He stood there, stark naked, ringing the bell. McCarthy, beholding this apparition at seven in the morning, opened the door and said calmly: "I think you need a very dry martini, Mr. Alsop," adding, with emphasis, *"in your room!"*

Now Carty watched in serene indifference the motley politicians trooping in and out of the Lodge preserve next door. He did, however, notice that young Mr. Lodge, faithful to Tom White's orders, looked unusually unkempt.

Well rumpled and well advised, Cabot campaigned in unlikely places. He startled grizzled old fishermen on the wharves of Boston and Gloucester by invading their chowder houses. He went to Lowell and spouted limpid French at the French-Canadian millworkers, who claimed with delight that he even had a Canadian accent.

He attended Syrian picnics, invaded C.I.O. meetings, German turnvereins and Polish sokols. To Italian meetings he took along his brother, John, and his Florence-born wife, Francesca (of Boston's musical Braggiotis) who sang Italian songs beautifully, and was beautiful herself. In 387 days, Cabot traveled 43,000 miles, made 680 speeches and in a single night in Boston spoke to 14 different groups of voters.

Sometimes, he tried to be—or seem to be—all things to all men. Lodge well knew that Dr. Francis E. Townsend's "Plan" to give $200 a month to every person over 60 was preposterous and unworkable, but he wanted the votes of the good doctor's thousands of fanatic followers. When they demanded he publicly support the plan, he agreed to "consider it very carefully." After a good deal of waiting and stage management, he put out a statement whose general tone was of great sympathy with Townsend aims, and a solemn pledge to give wholehearted support to their ideal to the limit of his ability—and "to the extent considerations of prudent finance permit." This proviso was tucked on so inconspicuously that a great majority of Townsend followers voted for Lodge. Afterward, he regarded this demagogy as one of the less creditable performances of his life. However, he was up against a master demagog, who fought with no holds barred.

Curley called Lodge "a young man who parts both his name and his hair in the middle." He harped on Lodge's youth: "Don't send a boy to do a man's job." Or, "When my youthful rival was still wearing diapers I was serving the Commonwealth of Massachusetts in the halls of Congress." Mike Hennesy of the *Globe* suggested Lodge might well reply, "When I was still wearing diapers, my opponent was serving a six-month sentence in Charles Street jail," but Lodge stuck to White's dictum never to mention his rival. Curley, that Biblical scholar, familiar with Job's lament, "O, would that mine adversary had written a book," was gleefully aware that his own adversary had done so. He dug out *The Cult of Weakness,* and smacked his lips to discover that Lodge had ended it with a somber and reflective passage remarkably apt for quoting out of context: ". . . there is a grim parallel between the [American] dream and the quest for peace, for if we allow the dream to fade, America, as we have learned to know and love it, may be gone. Then peace would not be worth preserving and America would not be worth fighting for." Curley would produce this book and read that "unbelievable" last sentence. *"Can you imagine any young man saying America is not worth fighting for?"* It disconcerted the young author so that he undertook to buy up all the unsold copies he could still track down in the book stores.

But Curley's attack on Lodge's youth backfired on a lot of young voters who had just come of age. Moreover, his own Irish Democrats defected in large numbers. There had always been a great many Lodge Democrats among the Irish, because of two traditions. First was the fact that in the days when fugitives from the potato famine had been stoned on the streets of Boston by workers fearing their competition for jobs, a gentle physician, Dr. Giles Lodge, had sheltered them in his house and treated their bruises. Dr. Lodge, brother of Senator Lodge's father, never married, lived on among the Irish as they took over his neighborhood, and willed his house to them (it became the first hostel of the Society of St. Vincent de Paul). His name was well remembered and beloved by the Irish, who liked to vote for his kin. Then there was the fact that old Senator Lodge himself was (in the words of Arthur Krock) "more Irish than Daniel O'Connell" and endeared himself to the Irish by such labors as getting the duty removed from the imported stained glass windows for a big Irish church. All this unquestionably helped young Lodge, who won by a landslide, in spite of Roosevelt's own landslide which buried Landon under an all-time record low of eight Republican electoral votes. F.D.R. carried Massachusetts by 174,000 votes, but Lodge beat Curley by 135,409.

His victory plunged him at once into the national spotlight, for he was the only Republican coming in who would displace a Democrat. Moreover, in a Senate whose Republican side would shrink to a lonely handful of seventeen, the handsome and confident face of the junior senator from Massachusetts would stand out like a lighthouse in a fog.

"I am a practical progressive," Lodge said on taking office. "I intend to remain silent until I have something worthwhile to say. My aim is to work for legislation which will achieve the results intended, not legislation which merely looks good on the surface." Lodge faced a hard task to build any sort of creative record from a party which was not only in opposition, but in a dishearteningly small minority. Such a position almost forces a man—

if he has great talents as a political strategist and tactician—to use them in isolated hit-and-run forays, much as Stonewall Jackson had done to "mystify, mislead and surprise." Lodge realized this and soon adopted that Jacksonian strategy as his own. He had the shrewd help of Tom White, who came with him as his secretary. Lodge was not devoid of constructive ideas. He could never understand why an Administration, which properly regarded unemployment as the No. 1 domestic issue, had never taken the trouble to find out how many unemployed there actually *were.* "There is a machinery of record for the stock exchange, for election returns . . . births, deaths, marriages and baseball games," he said in his book, "there is no such machinery for equally important matters like unemployment. . . . The finding of unemployment facts [seems] beyond the power of the government." In his first week, he introduced a bill to use the mailman, who visits everybody, to make a census of the unemployed. It made eminent good sense, and was promptly defeated.

Lodge quickly became a leader in opposing the White House effort to pack the Supreme Court. Just as he had refused, in his Constitution Day talk, to enshrine the court's decisions as immutable scripture, so he opposed any attack on the court itself. Enlarging it, as Roosevelt sought, merely to achieve a transitory aim, might "establish a precedent which could be used to destroy this republic," he told the Senate. "A ruthless man might some day come, taking advantage of the precedent which the President now proposes to establish, and appoint puppet judges. . . . Thomas Jefferson implied it was better to toss a coin and to abide by the flip of heads or tails than to put your faith in the hands of a puppet judge." Lodge made a nationwide broadcast against the bill. "Shall we say to every future presidential candidate, 'What sort of court do you have in mind, how many members do you want to add or take away . . . ? If you propose some fundamental change in our government, do you want to amend the Constitution or do you want to amend the court?' If, as some say, it is reactionary to oppose this program then the word reactionary has no meaning."

The Nye Committee's famed investigation of "merchants of death" (international munitions merchants) had produced the Neutrality Bill, forbidding the U.S. to sell arms to any nation except on a cash-and-carry basis. Lodge, one of the lonely six who voted against it (ninety approved), attacked it as "putting the country automatically on the side of the power controlling the seas in a war between weak and strong nations." Soon after, when Japanese armies had seized Canton, Nanking and Hankow, Lodge pointed out: "If the President was to invoke the Neutrality Act it would put us on the side of Japan because Japan has the sea-power and the money and China has not. This law was passed at the request of the Administration and it is not being invoked by the Administration which fathered it."

136   Lodge quickly became the most trusted lieutenant of the minority floor leader, Senator Charles McNary of Oregon. McNary had been a protégé of the first Senator Lodge, and made the second his own. The two men made a smooth-working team, McNary giving the advice on timing and detail, Lodge doing the rough work on the floor. "In the past session, young and inexperienced as he is," *Herald Tribune* correspondent Joseph Alsop was writing by 1938, Lodge "made more trouble for the Democrats than any other man on his side of the Senate." Hoover's Secretary of War Patrick Hurley asserted, "He is making the greatest impression of any Republican in the party at the present time." In the last days of the 1937-38 session, when the Senate was debating a big relief and pump-priming bill, Lodge whispered to McNary, whose little blue eyes twinkled and leathery cheeks wrinkled in a grin. Lodge scribbled out a note and sent a page to the rostrum to read an amendment. He rose to explain it: "This amendment merely increases the benefits under the Social Security Act by one-third. I know that the proposal will appeal to every old person throughout the country. . . . A few weeks ago the Senate refused to reduce the payroll tax which has been put upon the tired backs of the poor people of this country in the name of old age pensions." Pointing out that this tax would more than pay for the increase, he said: "I now submit that the people should receive their own tax money in the form of old-age pensions. No new tax money is involved."

"Instantly a wild pandemonium broke loose," wrote Alsop and Robert M. Kintner in describing the scene for the *Saturday Evening Post.* "Old George Norris of Nebraska, always ready to help the Administration out of a tight spot, jumped to his feet to ridicule the Lodge motion. Smart, witty Jimmy Byrnes of South Carolina had a sharp word to say, bumbling Majority Leader Barkley made a solemn statement which, unfortunately, revealed an inadequate understanding of the Social Security Act. Suddenly Byrnes moved that the Lodge amendment lie on the table—a parliamentary trick to end debate. Barkley and his followers tried wildly to prevent a record vote. But Hiram Johnson of California, ailing though he is, was too quick for them. With all the mock indignation of which he is a special master, he trumpeted his demands: 'Mr. President, is there no fairness in this body to give us the ayes and nays?' The record vote was ordered. The amendment was defeated 39 to 30 and the incident was forgotten save by the 39 men who went down the line for the White House. Claude Pepper, the pretentious, logorrheic New Deal coat-tail rider who had just won the Florida primary, was so terrified of the old folks that he voted with Lodge. Many of the 39 faithful would have liked to follow suit. From Alben Barkley, timorously facing a hard primary against Gov. Happy Chandler, through the maladroit Bulkley of Ohio they all realized that Lodge's amendment might cost one or two of them their seats."

Lodge staged a similar Stonewall Jackson-type raid when New York's Senator Robert F. Wagner had introduced a bill to help encourage low-cost housing construction. Wagner, father of the Wagner Act, which put government sanction behind collective bargaining for the first time in history, was virtually the patron saint of organized labor. To Wagner's horror, Lodge introduced an amendment to the housing bill which would require any government-financed project to pay prevailing union wages. Paying union wages would have vastly increased the cost of the housing projects. But the fearful senators, their eyes on union lobbyists in the galleries, approved the Lodge amendment by a large majority and then quietly proceeded to kill it, 4 to 2, in conference committee. When the bill came back to the floor, minus his amendment, Lodge leaped to his feet to read a telegram from A.F. of L. President William Green supporting his amendment and ending: "Urge you to read my telegram to Sen. Wagner and to members of the Senate." Senator Wagner looked as if he were sweating blood. "When a body of Congress passes an amendment without a dissenting voice," cried Lodge, "and the committee in conference knocks it out on a 4 to 2 vote, that is a travesty on democracy. The elected representatives of the people are defying the will of the people who elected them, in secret and behind closed doors." Wagner complained that Lodge had never brought up his amendment in committee but sprang it from the floor as "a surprise to everybody." "Why shouldn't I offer it on the floor?" demanded Lodge. "This is my forum." With harsh sarcasm, Indiana's Sherman Minton said, "The Senator from Massachusetts knows what is in the woodpile, he put it there. This man whose heart now bleeds for the working man never mentioned this in committee." "The whole point is," Alben Barkley interrupted, "there are no galleries in the committee room." The President himself had to intervene in person to get his housing bill through without the Lodge amendment. Barkley was forced to make a strong speech, which he later tried to cut out of the permanent record. The conference bill barely squeaked through, with a majority of two.

Having learned how, Lodge spent the rest of the session sharpening other such demagogue traps. He so infuriated Roosevelt that the President denounced him by name, to his Business Advisory Council, for playing "unjustifiable politics." That, of course, meant politics upsetting to Democrats.

Lodge proved himself equally astute at fulfilling his campaign pledge to "get more" federal funds for Massachusetts. He inspected the Springfield Arsenal, where he found a handful of workers turning out the Army's new semiautomatic rifle by antiquated, virtually handmade means. He remembered this when Springfield's congressman sought his help in getting the

138 Arsenal's rifle quota raised from 2,500 to 5,000. "Why ask for so little?" said Lodge. "Why not 7,000? And there's a lot of talk of moving the arsenals inland. Springfield badly needs retooling. And if we get some real money spent there they won't move it during our lifetime." Alsop and Kintner relate the sequel:

Lodge appeared at the next meeting of the Senate Sub-Committee considering the War Department supply bill. He made a little speech about the need for retooling in Springfield and asked for $1,200,000. The late Senator Copeland of New York was in the chair. Before anyone could say a word he snapped out, "Without objection it is so ordered." Then he turned to Lodge and revealed that he was sure the Senator would now support a large appropriation for New York Harbor fortification. Lodge promptly replied that harbor fortifications were well-known to be the most efficient defense, but pointed out that Boston was as sorely lacking in them as New York. Copeland peered down through his spectacles at the report on the table. "I see $750,000 here for Boston," he cried with an air of pleased surprise. "Why, that's splendid, Senator," said Lodge. And so the Springfield Arsenal was retooled and New York and Boston harbors were handsomely fortified.

"In the Senate, his aim is to get things done," these writers observed. "He has worked incredibly hard. He has voted sensibly. . . . His best moment of the last session came after the final disposition of the Housing Act when a friendly Senator came up to him, clapped him heartily on the back, and remarked: 'Cabot, I wish to God you'd go back to Massachusetts where you came from.' The day after adjournment he did go back to Massachusetts and the same evening spoke to two big Boston meetings. He was gratified to observe that large majorities of both cheering audiences were Democrats."

Lodge, on his thirty-sixth birthday, urged the Republican Party be purged of reactionaries. "It must become a party of the people. It ought to go back to Abraham Lincoln and get some real liberality."

Lodge was more than a hit-and-run raider. His long experience at clarifying complex problems in newspaper editorials gave him a rare ability to talk common sense, in ways that were perfectly clear to the average citizen. It was exemplified in his efforts to reform the Social Security system. He pointed out that this act called for an eventual reserve of $47 billion, which was "four times more than the whole world's gold supply." He called for putting it on a pay-as-you-go basis, with Congress providing needed reserves as payments came due.

Moreover, he would sequester the social security tax payments by workers and employers so they would not be spent for other purposes. "The wage earner has been misled," said Lodge. "His tax payments do not become a reserve, but are converted into an IOU for $47 billion, representing a permanent debt owed to the people. In addition the present national debt is $38 billion. In spite of the excessive taxation required to build this reserve, the taxpayer will be asked to pay [again] when the major payments fall due. This is a striking example of Peter robbing Peter to pay Peter."

He kept on introducing bills for an unemployment census, and they kept on being defeated. He urged that the U.S. negotiate with defaulting war-debtors to provide strategic materials for defense stockpiling in lieu of payment. Not long afterward the Administration did begin a program of international barter of farm surpluses for certain strategic materials useful for stockpiling.

Lodge kept on trying, as well, to raise the old-age pension. This was not merely a political device. He believed that America was rich and strong enough to provide for the old age of its citizens. And he continued his work, begun in the Legislature, to back wage-and-hour minimums, was the only Republican to support the first wage-and-hour law all the way through.

There were lighter moments. When Joseph P. Kennedy went to England as ambassador, he determined to abolish the undemocratic practice of selecting each year, some favored few applicants to be presented to the King and Queen. He arranged with Lodge, whom he knew and admired, to use one of the Senator's applications as the basis for the turndown. Arthur Krock devoted his entire column to the resulting hullabaloo. "Both men agreed completely that the system is undemocratic, and Mr. Lodge being a good politician was pleased to share in the glory of its abolition. Then promptly came to him an experience familiar to mice and men. He was represented in some newspapers as having been sharply turned down in his autocratic attempt to present a Boston damsel of blue Back Bay blood by a sturdy red-haired Irish Bostonian with true democratic instincts. He read that the Kennedys and the Fitzgeralds had shown the Cabots and Lodges what real Americans should be."

That was the last year when such trivia could seem important. The world rushed headlong and seemingly helplessly toward war. Spain flamed in civil war, Japan's warlords invaded China, Mussolini occupied Ethiopia and Albania, Hitler gobbled up Austria and brought Britain and France to their knees at Munich.

Through all this Lodge held steadily to his belief that a strong America could stay out of war. He called for preparedness and continued to set his own example by spending more and more time in Army maneuvers. When Roosevelt, in 1937, asked that we "quarantine the aggressor," Lodge urged that the U.S. "keep out of war by not taking sides in foreign quarrels." As the crisis deepened he was the first to demand compulsory military training, and, when war did break in Europe, he vigorously pushed Roosevelt's $1.3

140 billion expansion of our armed services and production. He was the first, as well, to call for a Senate watchdog committee on procurement which became the Truman Committee and led its chairman eventually to the White House.

At the 1940 Republican convention at Philadelphia, Lodge helped write the platform, and boiled it down to his own clear summary: "Mr. Chairman, delegates: I am going to give you the shortest speech of the convention—the highlights of the Republican platform: The Republican Party strives for Americanism, preparedness and peace; no foreign war; an air force, army and navy so strong that no one unfriendly power can successfully attack America or its essential outposts; the following ten brief points [enumerated] . . . and finally, No. 11, no third term for President. Thank you."

For three weeks he rode Wendell Willkie's campaign train, wrote an article in *Life* about the trip, made a nationwide broadcast pointing out that Willkie, a buck private in World War I, "has looked war in the eye—he hates it!"

In 1941, he met his greatest political ordeal—an inner struggle over Roosevelt's Lend-Lease Bill. Thomas E. Dewey said the bill "would abolish free government," Robert A. Taft said it would "authorize the President to make war on any nation without congressional approval," and Lodge himself asserted it would create the risk of an "internal dictator." The struggle went on even in his own family—Harry Lodge recalls, at age ten, telling his father at breakfast that he should vote for the bill.

Lodge vacillated all over the place, in a manner he would be ashamed of later. Like his grandfather, he had always drawn heavy support from the Boston Irish, who understandably had no love for the British. Their hatred was whipped to a fever heat by the Boston *Herald*'s Columnist Bill Cunningham, who gloried in a reverse form of Know Nothingism—and by the fulminations of Father Coughlin's *Social Justice*, whose rantings were openly pro-Hitler. Both had large, angry followings in Boston, and the sentiment was exacerbated by Ambassador Joseph P. Kennedy's dire prophecies that Britain was "doomed"—sentiments that soon forced F.D.R. to remove him. Lodge, hesitating to offend this anti-British sentiment, diddled and dawdled.

He took the line that if the British and French empires could not stand without our help, we should not try to prop them up. He believed, like most of his Army friends, that Hitler could not conquer Paris or London: he remembered General Hugh Drum, during the 1940 Louisiana maneuvers crying at the news of Hitler's sweep through France: "Why, that's impossible! The French are the best artillerists in the world." But after Hitler did take Paris, Lodge realized that the U.S. faced a serious threat to its own security. In an agony of indecision, he would write up lists of arguments in favor of Lend Lease on one sheet of paper, and on another the arguments against it. For the only time in his life, he lay awake at night worrying over a vote. What decided him was the advice of Chief of Staff General George C. Marshall, a soldier whom he trusted totally. "In my opinion," Marshall wrote him, "the prompt enactment of this bill into law is a matter of great importance to the proper and expeditious development of our measures for national security. The munitions program in prospect presents a colossal task which can only be accomplished under the most favorable circumstances, meaning absence of confusion, and simplicity of procedure. This bill has been drawn with this in mind." On this assurance, Lodge, in the showdown, parted from his devoted co-isolationist Vandenberg, from his grandfather's staunch old ally Hiram Johnson, and from Taft, to join the sixty Senators who made H.R. 1776 into law.

That summer he took part in some three months of military maneuvers. In May he went to Louisiana, to join Major General George Patton's Second Armored Division in its epic hundred-mile sweep through Texas to outflank the "enemy" and capture his capital at Shreveport. Lieutenant General Ben Lear commanded the Second Army of which they were a part, opposing Lieutenant General Walter Kreuger's Third Army, whose chief of staff was one Dwight D. Eisenhower (identified in a news picture as "Eisenberg"), a temporary colonel.

Lodge heard Patton say "I'll give fifty dollars to anyone who captures a sonuvabitch named Eisenhower," and decided he must be quite a soldier. He sought him out and they became friends.

In July, Lodge went to Fort Knox to command two hundred men and nineteen scout cars in the reconnaissance company of the First Armored Regiment. "His fellow officers here," reported the New York *Times*, "say he probably knows as much about tanks as any member of the Reserve. His day starts with an hour's foot drill beginning at 7 A.M. After that he and his men make their cars ready for tactical exercises. Then they are off in cross-country sprints over the wild terrain of this 33,000-acre Army reservation. The captain supervises the tricky business of maneuvering cars across ditches, through underbrush and whatever conditions the countryside presents. Afternoons are spent in machine gun practice, radio-training or map school."

In August, he joined the Second Armored again for maneuvers in North Carolina. He rode in a scout car as aide to his old friend of the Bugscuffle Trail, Willis Crittenberger, now a brigadier general commanding a brigade of tanks. They would sleep by their car on one side, their driver and radio operator on the other. The division made a three-hundred-mile forced march

142 back to Fort Benning with only one long halt of two and a half hours. Their march ended on December 2, 1941. Patton reported the division had "met every test short of war."

The following Sunday Cabot and Emily spent a pleasant day at Groton School where fourteen-year-old George was a third-former. Late that afternoon, driving back to Beverly, they stopped for gas. "Can you beat what the Japs did?" said the attendant, shaking his head. It was the first word of Pearl Harbor. Cabot switched on the radio. Emily remembered the grimness and whiteness of his face as they sped home, listening to the blaring news. In Beverly, reporters with microphones were seeking him. The ex-isolationist went on the air saying all Americans would unite and fight as one. He caught the midnight train to a totally different Washington.

Pearl Harbor forced Lodge to ponder his own future. His term would expire the next year. His preference was to go to war immediately with his unit rather than stand for reelection. But the choice was not wholly his. The veteran officers of the Army, like Marshall, Patton and Crittenberger, had regarded Lodge through the years as the one senator who knew the Army inside and out; not only was he totally sympathetic to its needs, but totally familiar with these needs in all their complexities. They had been through mighty lean years. Patton, who had proved what tank breakthroughs could do in the Argonne, had seen the Tank Corps abolished in 1920, because the Army's total budget for tanks was an incredible five hundred dollars; he returned to cavalry instead. Such men knew how Lodge had fought such pinchpenny treatment, as journalist as well as senator. They regarded him as the Army's "own" senator as much as Massachusetts'. The Army would have been aghast to lose such a friend merely to gain one more officer, however capable. Lodge decided that he would stay, at least until there was actual tank-fighting where he could serve. But he decided also that he would spend much of his time visiting the expanding units in training and learning at first-hand their needs. His old friend of Hoover days, Colonel Henry Stimson, was now Secretary of War, and Bobby Cutler— commissioned as a colonel—was one of Stimson's key assistants. They found plenty for Lodge to look into. Moreover, his Democratic colleague on the Military Affairs Committee, Chairman Robert R. Reynolds of North Carolina, was glad to have Lodge be the eyes and ears of the committee: "It would be most helpful . . . if you were able to make a personal inspection of our military units," he wrote Lodge on February 5. "I believe that continued first-hand reports from you would be of great value to us in our effort to do everything possible for a decisive victory." Lodge promptly prepared for such tours.

There was, however, the fact that his seat was up for election, and Congressman John McCormack had his eye on it. So did Ambassador Kennedy's father-in-law, Boston's former Mayor John Fitzgerald. Kennedy gave a thousand dollars—and so did his sons Joseph, Jr. and Jack—for Honey Fitz's campaign, but popular young Congressman Joseph E. Casey won the Democratic nomination. In the primary battle, however, Honey Fitz had denounced Casey in a most thorough and categorical way. Shrewd old Uncle Tom White had a recording made of Honey Fitz's denunciation, and played it frequently during the final campaign to let the voters know what one very prominent Democrat thought about their nominee. Nevertheless, Lodge had to face a tough campaign, President Roosevelt himself was looking forward to knocking off his Republican gadfly. Moreover, voters would understandably resent a senator-soldier who was not being wholly either.

In an editorial entitled "Toga and Uniform," the Fitchburg *Sentinel* observed on March 2, 1942: "Mr. Henry Cabot Lodge should make up his mind and be either a soldier or a Senator. He should not try to be both, shuttling back and forth between the Senate and the field, donning and doffing the toga and the uniform as if he were playing in a quick-change act." Charlie McGlue, Curley's friend on the Ballot Commission who had pondered Lodge's right to his own name, was now writing a column in the Lynn *Telegram-News*, "McGlue's Views on Political News." In it he complained that "the same person cannot hold both a military and a civilian commission as U.S. Senator." He noted with glee that Minnesota's young Governor Harold Stassen had already resigned to join the Navy. Therefore, "Cappy Cabbie," as he called Lodge, "cannot very well afford to claim immunity from Army service and hope for any great support at the November polls. It's just dastardly!" Roslindale's *Parkway Transcript* was less positive than McGlue. "While some of the experts on Constitutional law assert that a man cannot be in both Congress and the Army," it observed, "the best proof that it can be done is that Lodge is doing it." The paper added that the War Department had ruled that soldiers might even run for office if it did not interfere with their duties. "A lieutenant colonel on armed duty in Australia is conducting a long-distance campaign for a Senate seat in Montana. The mayor of Garfield, N. J., a second-lieutenant at Fort Eustis, Virginia, is trying to run his city by airmail and has his constituents in a state of bewilderment. Lodge received an opinion from the War Department and the Attorney General that it would be perfectly proper for him to be in both the Army and the Senate. . . . If [the voters] don't approve it they [can] elect someone else."

Columnists Drew Pearson and Robert S. Allen, noting that Representative Lyndon Johnson of Texas had gone off to serve as a lieutenant commander

144　in the Navy, raised another question: "When a member of [Congress] joins up, it means that his district is left without representation in the Government. So the President and his advisers frankly feel that a Congressman best serves his country by remaining in Congress. Therefore Administration leaders on Capitol Hill have requested War and Navy . . . to reject further enlistments of Congressmen." Lodge imperturbably showed up to address the Bristol County Bar Association in New Bedford on "Why Are We Fighting?" and just as imperturbably told them "now as in the Civil War and the World War, the chief business of Congress is to check on the conduct of the war."

Such nonchalance drove Charlie McGlue into a near-frenzy of rage: "Do not be surprised," he wrote on May 17, "if you see Capt. Lodge on a secret military mission in Massachusetts," noting that he had just performed one in New Bedford. "Cappy Cabbie would have done much better for himself if he had organized a secret group of Commandos at the New Bedford Bench and Bar dinner . . . and sailed away on one of the old whaling ships and taken possession of the Cape Verde Islands, or even grabbed a toe-hold on the Azores."

To McGlue's outraged chagrin, a few days later the Boston *Globe* announced: "U.S. Senator Lodge, member of a U.S. tank outfit, has appeared on the scene of the now raging crucial Middle East battle in Libya as an observer." It quoted Tom White, Lodge's secretary, as saying "As far as I knew Mr. Lodge was at Fort Knox only 10 days ago."

McGlue was not to be thus lightly fobbed off. "Just what he is observing, of course, is a military secret. . . . Is he at Tobruk, or at Tripoli? Is he located at Bir Hacheim or Bengazi? Is he stationed at Elgazala or at Alehamza? Is he doing his observations at long range from Alexandria, Pt. Said, or Cairo? It is an amazing situation wherein Capt. Lodge can cover political assignments, such as the Bench and Bar Dinner at New Bedford . . . and then the next month you are told he is on the Libyan front as an observer."

Like Stonewall Jackson, Lodge was indeed managing to "mystify, mislead and surprise" his opponents. "It looks as though Senator Lodge has won the first round," observed the Springfield *Union*. "The whereabouts of Lodge are the more intriguing in that the Administration has picked him out for special attention because of his pre-war isolationist attitude." President Roosevelt took hasty steps to recoup this error. On June 26, he issued a directive to Secretaries Stimson and Navy's Frank Knox: "All members of the House and Senate who are now serving in an active status will be placed on inactive duty July 1, 1942, or immediately on returning to the U.S., except those who wish to remain on active duty for the duration of the war." The Worcester *Telegram*'s Washington correspondent speculated that "Lodge might

remain with the army overseas all summer without any announcement of
his intentions."

Lodge had told no one about this surprise mission. Lieutenant General Jacob L. Devers, who had been put in charge of all armor at Fort Knox, recalled afterward that he had just received enough new tanks to equip the Second Army that Patton was training in the California desert when he got a call from General Marshall. "General," Marshall told him, "Mr. Churchill is in the room with me and I'm sorry I have to order those new tanks you've just received out to the desert. They're in great need." Devers told him, "I have a request to make. Could I send 200 officers and men with the tanks? If they don't have top maintenance they'll go bad. It'll accomplish two purposes—get the men blooded and the tanks all broken in properly." Marshall said, "I'm sure Mr. Churchill will agree to that."

About the same time, Senator Lodge paid a visit to General Eisenhower, then a major general in charge of Army operations in Washington, to discuss some active combat assignment. "He advised me to wait a month and then get in touch with him again," Lodge wrote his friend Patton in Indio, California. "He is an impressive man and a great admirer of yours." Eisenhower had just had some discussions with General Sandy Galloway, chief of staff of the British Eighth Army. Because of the terrible toll exacted by German submarines, none of the armored regiments which had now been fully trained were yet being risked on the seas. Eisenhower, mindful of General Devers' request to Marshall, suggested that picked tank crews be taken from each trained division and sent to Libya for ten days or two weeks at the front. They would draw American pay, but be under British orders.

The relationship was a potentially delicate one. General Crittenberger, who had succeeded Patton as commander of the Second Armored Division, recommended Lodge to head this mission. Since Lodge was both a thoroughly trained tank officer and a man of wide governmental experience, he seemed ideal for the job. Lodge, now a major, flew to Cairo in late May, joining three company officers and twelve tank crewmen; his travel orders to Matruh for "onward despatch" to the Eighth Army bore the date of May 28.

By coincidence, his men and tanks arrived near Tobruk just in time for one of the worst battles of the war.

With the three tank crews in a training area far to the rear, Lodge reconnoitered the front, which consisted of a huge mine field of varying widths which the British had laid, (they called it "the wire"), then extending from the Mediterranean seacoast south about forty miles. That forty miles was considered far enough, because after that, it was the limitless desert and armies ran out of gas. In effect, therefore, the battlefield was a long, thin strip running east and west with the Mediterranean on one side and the vastness of the Sahara Desert on the south. It was considered impossible to go around the mine field's flank.

General Rommel, using minesweepers on a large scale for the first time, lifted a way through the middle of the British mine field and drew the British Army up around him at a place known as "the cauldron." He made a few feints and then withdrew. Lodge could tell by observation of dust clouds through field glasses that there was much movement to the south on the German side.

Lodge was getting extremely uncomfortable. The British Army was so short on food that Lodge never accepted the hospitable invitations to eat at the various messes, knowing they did not have enough for themselves. He therefore was subsisting entirely on food out of a can and had had nothing hot to eat for about a week. Also, he had had no chance to wash, having only a little brackish water for drinking purposes. He had to borrow undrinkable water for the radiator of his jeep.

It was in this state of mind that towards the end of one afternoon he arrived at Thirtieth Corps Headquarters to which he and the American tank crews were attached. Thirtieth Corps Headquarters was at the southernmost end of the line. In fact, on its left (or south) there was nothing but the trackless wastes of the desert. It was seven or eight miles behind the mine field, and one felt quite "far back" as far as the front was concerned. Lodge looked at the situation map. He did not think it contained information on all the events which he had witnessed: bits of information were late in getting posted onto it.

But he was looking forward to some physical comfort. He received the equivalent of a frying pan of water, and with the aid of some soap and a small rubber sponge, he gave himself a very thorough washing. He then shined his shoes, got his one clean khaki uniform out of his musette bag and began to feel quite human. In addition to washing, the other thing which he had had on his mind was sitting down on a chair with his legs under a table and eating something hot. The Thirtieth Corps Commander, General Willoughby Norrie, had invited him to the mess that evening. On his way there, he met the general's aide Lieutenant Grant (later killed), who offered him a drink. Lodge and Grant were sitting on big empty gasoline cans having a drink when a Ford station wagon of the type then used as command vehicles by British Army officers came through the area heading east. Close behind it was another one. Lieutenant Grant stepped up and stopped the second vehicle, asking him where he thought he was going.

The driver was an Indian and could only exclaim: "The Germans are coming!"

Grant said: "Nonsense, we know where the Germans are. Get on back
to your unit."

After the drink, Lodge went to the general's mess which was in a canvas lean-to attached to the side of the truck in which the food was carried and prepared. The mess sergeant was a most personable and courteous man, who had worked for General Norrie in private life. Lodge sat down and started to eat.

It all tasted delicious. One of the things that he had looked forward to was getting suet pudding for which the British Army was so well known— so liked by some and so disliked by others—which consisted of a concoction vaguely resembling library paste on which jam was piled up. Lodge had looked forward to eating this.

When supper was almost through, the men at the table suddenly heard a very rapid fire on a low note, not like the chatter of a machinegun automatic, but low.

General Norrie had finished his dinner and had lit his cigar. He was an extremely charming, always courteous, man who spoke in a very gentle voice. He wore the closely clipped moustache which all officers in the British Army wore at that time. With his cigar in his teeth, he turned to Brigadier Dennis, who was the corps artillery officer, and said:
"I say, Dennis, isn't that a twenty millimeter?"
"Yes, I rather think it is," Dennis said.
"How far away do you reckon it is?"
"Oh, surely not more than two miles."

At that point, the general got up, and stooping down, went out through the side of the mess tent, a blackout tent so that people could come in and out without the light showing. Dennis followed him, as did Colonel Ray, the corps engineer. This left Lodge and Grant at the table.

Lodge had learned to recognize 20 millimeter fire at Fort Benning when he was being trained and he had recognized it here. He knew it was closer than two miles, and that it meant German tanks. And yet, he was hungering for the dessert. So he stayed while the mess sergeant brought the dessert to him. While he was eating it, Dennis stuck his head through the fly of the tent and said. "Has anyone any field glasses?"

Lodge had his on him, and he took them out of the case and handed them to Dennis. He then finished the dessert and went out of the tent.

When he got out, dusk had fallen. It was that moment just before complete darkness sets in, when the sky still has some light in it. Off in the distance, he could see black silhouettes of tanks, but could not tell with the naked eye whether they were our tanks or not. Ray and Dennis were standing side by side looking through the field glasses. Ray handed the

148 field glasses to Dennis and Dennis handed them to Lodge, and through the field glasses he could see plainly that it was the German Mark III tank with the gun on one side.

Dennis said quietly into Lodge's ear: "I think we had better move." Lodge's jeep which was in very poor order wouldn't start. But he got a lift.

It turned out that these tanks were the probing finger of Rommel's great sweep around the southern end of the mine field, which eventually resulted in his taking Tobruk from the east, taking thirty thousand prisoners from the cream of the Union of South Africa's army. These tanks were his reconnaisance, and when they came around the southern end of the mine field, the first thing that they found on the British side was not another combat unit, but this corps headquarters, which had been securely safe and well behind the lines as long as the battle was going on an east and west axis. But when the battle started coming from the south to the north, it was the first thing the Germans ran into.

As Lodge departed, he could see the tracer bullets being fired. They set fire to the truck out of which the mess had been served and killed the most delightful and personable mess sergeant.

While Lodge himself was narrowly escaping death or capture, the American tank units found themselves engulfed in the German attack, and joined the British in holding a desert ridge between Knightsbridge and Acroma to protect the withdrawal of South African units from the Gazala area. Shortly after dawn they were attacked by eighty-five German tanks; the battle raged all day and the ridge was held; Lodge's men knocked out nine tanks. After the battle, these tank units were ordered out of action, and returned with Lodge to the States to impart their battle experience to new tankers training at Fort Knox.

During the battle of Tobruk there was no mention whatever of Lodge in the daily streamer stories. British censors had a "stop" on any mention of Lodge or his tanks. No one, including columnist McGlue, knew just what Lodge was "observing" until Lodge himself popped up in Washington on July 6 at the same time as eight-column headlines blazoned AP correspondent Edward Kennedy's delayed account of the first action and victories by American tank crews in World War II.

Lodge himself was interviewed in Washington, and AP's John R. Beal quoted him as saying: "I must lead a charmed life. Men were killed within a half-dozen yards of me. Once I was nearly taken prisoner." He recalled one attack in which a man within eighteen or twenty feet of him was machinegunned from a Nazi plane. "I leaped into a little hole and lay flat. Believe me an experience like that makes you think—and it isn't about politics either."

Two days after Lodge's return, Secretary of War Stimson wrote him:

"Your eagerness to continue your military service as a major in the Army   *149*
is easily understood. You have rendered fine service as a commissioned
officer and doubtless would continue your useful contributions if retained
in the service. However, through your experience in Libya, you have gained
a knowledge and understanding of military and strategic considerations
which will greatly enhance your usefulness to the country as a U.S. Senator. At this critical juncture, skilled legislators who fully comprehend the
requirements of the military service are as important to the Army as soldiers in combat. . . . I feel impelled to direct that you be restored to inactive duty status. . . ."

Of course, this action was required by F.D.R.'s own order of June. But
it quickly dawned on Massachusetts Democrats that "Cappie Cabbie" had
mystified and bewildered them again; he had been in combat, yet he was
still a senator, and he was being both praised by the Secretary of War himself and ordered to stay where he was—all in all, a politician's dream.
Beside himself, Representative John McCormack denounced Stimson for
"pernicious political activity," and Representative Casey attempted—as did
columnist Drew Pearson—to question the validity of Lodge's exploit. Lodge
simply retorted: "A slur directed at me, insofar as that expedition is concerned, also slurs the brave men who carried their country's flag across
shell-torn desert sands and into the smoking mouths of enemy guns. And
I resent that, too." Certainly the Army seemed happy with his work. He and
his men were called to Fort Knox to give a play-by-play account to some
two thousand non-coms and later to a thousand armored officers. "Somewhere in their training," the New York *Times* reported, "these non-coms
may have been told that it was not proper to applaud an officer about anything . . . but this admonition was forgotten and 2,000 men stood up and
cheered and not just with their hands."

So did the voters of Massachusetts: Lodge 721,239, Casey 641,042. He
even carried the Democratic citadel, Lowell, the first Republican ever to
do so.

CHAPTER NINE

We have really been having trying times since the 17th and will prob-
ably be continuing to do so. Yesterday we really had a big battle in
which we smashed the 10th Panzer very effectively but took a good
loss, excessive I believe, in our SP-TDs [self-propelled tank destroyers].
This was partly due to terrain which afforded no cover and partly due
to the teaching of their school. It was also partly due to the German
Air. It is clear, I think, that the TDs must not go into a slugging match
with tanks unless they expect to come out at the little end of the horn.
If you are with Critt give him my best regards. . . . Since writing the
above I went to the front and a low-lifed hun shelled me and frag-
ments hit my jeep but not very hard. I was most provoked. I wish you
would pass a law against shelling Lieutenant Generals. —Gen. George
S. Patton to Lodge from Tunisia, March 24, 1943

Lodge, newly returned to the Senate, now gave his whole attention to
the war. He followed every bulletin of the landing of his old outfit, the
Second Armored, with Patton's Western task force that November. American armor, five months after Lodge saw its first action near Tobruk, was
now in major action on its own, and old comrade Patton kept him informed of its progress. Patton was also elated at his reelection: "I admit
that when the Senate gained you, the I Armored Corps lost a damn good
Lt. Colonel, but probably, or I should say certainly, the Country has
gained."

That December, Lodge saw his father's gifted and beloved brother, John
Ellerton Lodge, to his grave. He had been extremely close to him ever since
his father's death, and had relied on him as much as on the old senator for
masculine advice. Since coming to Washington, where John had run the
Freer Gallery of Art since 1931, Cabot had seen much more of him and his
Nova Scotian wife, the former Mary Connolly, sister of a famed Jesuit
priest. John was almost a recluse, as he had always been, seeing few other
people in Washington save the Eugene Meyers, who were patrons of his
gallery. He had never composed again after his *Agamemnon* musical drama
was produced at Harvard Stadium; the critics had called it very professional, but John merely commented: "I had the decency to master the
technique." While still Curator of Asiatic Art at the Boston Fine Arts Museum he often played the piano in his apartment on Hemenway Street. He
stopped playing after a woman next door told his wife how much she enjoyed it, and that she invited people in to listen whenever he played. Now

his lean, solemn visage—rather resembling Eugene O'Neill's—would be seen no more.

For Lodge, a whole era was passing with his uncle. The old summer house at East Point where Cabot was born had gone to Uncle John as the old senator's surviving son. When war came the Army commandeered it as a site for coast artillery. Its strategic position, jutting out into the ocean, made it an ideal fort. Finding the house in its way, the Army simply bulldozed it down, and made a bonfire of it. Later Nike antibomber missiles came to take the place of the guns. In a way this symbolized the transformation of America from the impregnable fortress the old senator thought it to a possible target for air armadas from across the sea.

Lodge was sworn in to his second term that January, 1943. He tirelessly sought means to press the war more effectively. The committee which he had sought to check on the war's efficient prosecution was becoming very active, under its vigorous chairman, Harry S. Truman of Missouri, and was already putting burrs under the saddle of procurement. Lodge regarded no cause too trivial to press if it could help assure that the American fighting man was supplied, clothed and fed to the fullest capabilities of the American people at home. Soon his prodding would lead to a first-hand senatorial inspection of the war at close range.

In the meantime, as Patton's letter indicated, Lodge had pursued the perfection of his own training in armored warfare, at the side of General Crittenberger who had been sent to Camp Polk, Louisiana, now that the Second Armored was in battle, to train a whole new Armored Corps—the III.

Patton's historic landing had succeeded even more perfectly than anyone dared dream. On January 14, 1943, President Roosevelt, Winston Churchill, Generals de Gaulle and Giraud began their meetings in newly liberated Casablanca. In the midst of such gatherings Patton found time to write his friend and neighbor, Lodge, one of his inimitable sprightly notes:

The other day his majesty the Sultan presented me with the Grand Cross of the Order of Ouissam Alouite which is the top flight order in this country. For formal evening wear you have a pumpkin colored sash going across your manly bosom from right to left, with a large rosette and medal hanging from your left hip. For less formal occasions, you have a sunburst similar to that worn by Theda Bara, except that she has to wear two. This is worn on the left side in the vicinity of the navel. For country lounging wear, you have a normal ribbon with a self-starter sitting on a gold background. The citation has something about the fact that when I walk about in the evening the lions are so frightened that they cower in the rear of their dens. I have never been able to put this to the test as the last lion in this country was killed about 400 years ago. I also received from General Eisenhower a second DSM or rather an Oak Leaf cluster to the one I already had. . . . If you can find any reason to investigate the morals of the Arabian women or the amount of sugar necessary to maintain this country on a sounder Republican basis, come and pay us a visit.

P.S. S.M. the Prince Imperial (aged 14) wants me for his Grand Vizor when Allah takes his father he will provide me with a palace and harem but that will be too late.

In the Senate, Lodge began prodding the overloaded government bureaus to prune their surplus manpower and help fill the ranks of the armed forces. While newspapers were being cut back on newsprint, tons of needless government releases were flooding newspaper offices: "It's just junk," cried Lodge, holding aloft a batch, "and a shameful waste of paper." He had a merciless eye for the slightest arrogant intrusion by any agency on the rights of the ordinary citizen. Nobody else minded when the Treasury began using the term "forgiveness" to describe Beardsley Ruml's plans for pay-as-you-go income taxes—i.e., "forgiving" one year's taxes to collect the next year's in advance. Lodge favored the bill. But, who, he demanded, was "forgiving" whom for what? He read the Senate the dictionary definition of "forgive"—"to pardon, as one's enemies; to forgive a wrong." Was the Treasury aware, he demanded, that "Congress, the people, set the taxes"? The Treasury had no vested right whatever in taxes, and nothing to "forgive." All it had was "a mere assumption that taxes will be continued by Congress. Nothing is decreed until Congress decrees it." The Treasury quickly dropped the term like a hot potato.

Lodge had no particular admiration for the chairborne admirals and generals who were being commissioned from civilian life to high-flown desk jobs in Washington. He thought that bestowing high rank so lightly denigrated the combat officers who had earned it. He chivvied an Assistant Navy Secretary, Ralph Bard, on the point. Bard remonstrated that all these officers were, in theory at least, subject to sea duty. Snapped Lodge: "You take the star worn by the Navy; that is worn by officers who would never walk on a deck." "Sure," Bard agreed. "That cheapens it," said Lodge. "It isn't fair to the man out at sea." Curiously, his great-grandfather, Admiral Davis, in a Civil War letter to Admiral du Pont, took the same position: "In no case is the position of an officer at the department, that of chief of bureau included, so important as a command afloat. A navy officer's pride of place is on the quarter deck. The business of most bureaus can be performed with little special training by a citizen as well as by a naval officer.

But it is only the latter, and the best specimens of the latter, who make a good commander-in-chief afloat."

General Patton had moved on from Morocco to Tunisia and had finally brought his armor into combat against the German master, Rommel himself, in the mountain passes between Gafsa and Gabes. After Rommel's initial victory at Kasserine Pass in February, Patton had taken over the II Corps and slugged it out with the Tenth Panzers, as described in his letter to Lodge. In the fifteen days that followed there was fiercer fighting culminating in his victory at El Guetar. Patton wrote Lodge on April 21 enclosing his General Order No. 28: "Due to your united efforts and to the manifest assistance of Almighty God, the splendid record of the American Army has attained added lustre," and added: "Usual bull! Don't put in *Congressional Record*." He described the fighting, and how their mutual friend, Captain Jenson, Patton's aide, was killed by a Stuka bomb by his slit trench at Patton's command post while Patton himself was up forward. Killed by concussion, he was not mangled. Patton went to the cemetery with his body, on a stretcher and rolled in a shelter half. They uncovered his face, while Patton and his men kneeled to say a prayer. Patton then kissed his brow and covered him up. Afterward he sent a lock of Jenson's hair to his mother. Patton asked Lodge if he could suggest a good officer to replace Jenson. Lodge wrote back that Bobby Cutler's nephew, Elliott Cutler, Jr., his own first appointee to West Point, had finished fifth in his class and was a fine soldier. By then Patton had already chosen another Bostonian, Major Charles Codman, a dashing World War I veteran, as his new aide. "We did have a very nice fight and were wholly successful," Patton wrote to Lodge of El Guetar. "My usual luck held, first, in getting command of the show, and secondly, in winning the battle. We actually had a good many more men than fought on either side at Gettysburg. . . . However, we did have quite serious casualties, particularly in the field officers. . . . As a result of this war I have had three changes of heart—I believe in female nurses, I believe in heavy field artillery; and I am strong for telephone wires instead of radio."

Patton described some close calls. "My car got hit while I was in it. A 155 shell hit the spot I had been sitting on two minutes after I had left it, and another salvo threw mud all over me. An Arab just missed me—unfortunately I just missed him, etc. I also forgot to say that on two occasions enemy planes pursued me down the road, which is a form of sport I am not interested in. Also, in going through a mine field I got through all right but the next vehicle blew up." He had lost five pounds. "Instead of being scared stiff I was scared thin. But really, this thing of being a Corps commander cramps one's style for the true pleasures of combat."

154   Lodge was zealous to right any injustices for servicemen, and sought a 15 per cent increase in the twenty-eight-dollar monthly allotment to their wives and the forty dollars to families. Traveling soldiers, he wrote Chief of Staff Marshall, should have the same right to berths as civilians. Marshall demurred: "In this instance, I feel that the tactical situation requires the more uncomfortable mode of travel," just as a soldier has "to sleep on the ground while the civilian is in a house or in a hotel."

Lodge was growing less isolationist; both he and Vandenberg were among the thirty-two "undecided" in a poll of senators on the need for a postwar international force to preserve peace; Ohio's Taft was among the thirty-two opposed. But Lodge was chary of the growing hero worship of the Soviets, though he shared the admiration for the Red Army's great feats against the Nazis. When President Roosevelt scoffed at any notion that the Red Army might stop once it had cleared the Nazis from Soviet land, Lodge said: "Russia will do whatever the interests of Russia dictate. The government of Russia is definitely pro-Russian."

In June came a chance to see the war again at first-hand. General Marshall advised the Senate leaders, Barkley and McNary, that he could provide transport for five senators to inspect the African and Southwest Pacific War areas. Barkley designated Georgia's Richard Russell, Kentucky's Albert B. Chandler and New York's James Mead for the majority. McNary chose Lodge and Maine's Owen Brewster. Lodge and Chandler represented the Military Affairs Committee, Brewster and Mead the Truman Committee which was checking the management of the war effort. They took off on July 25 in a four-engined converted B-24 Liberator bomber. During the next nine weeks they traveled forty-one thousand miles, crossed five continents, visited American troops in England, Casablanca, Marrakech, Sicily (Lodge alone was allowed to visit the front), Cairo, Basra, Calcutta, Chungking, Australia, Guadalcanal, the Fiji Islands and Honolulu.

Wherever they went, Lodge made it his first order of business to learn the chief gripes of the men in the ranks—what was wrong with their food, their supplies, their recreation or lack of it, their commanders and their treatment. He was well aware that the man at the front is at the farthest end of a supply line whose rear echelons often get first call on the things the combat soldier needs and deserves most—waterproof boots and ponchos, warmer jackets, even cigarettes. He kept careful notes on all these details, and turned them over to Marshall's office at the end, where they got prompt attention.

On the same day they returned, September 30, Lodge, on behalf of all the others, made a full-dress report to the Senate which drew frequent applause from both the Senators and the crowded galleries, for its movingly eloquent stories of brave deeds and sacrifices by innumerable Americans, as well as its carefully phrased criticisms of deficiencies. "I do not pretend to speak as an authority," Lodge told the senators. "Luckily for me, I was a working newspaperman for many years, which has given me some training in asking questions, and my military service has given me a wide personal, first-name acquaintance with members of the Army." As a senator, he had "access to all the higher military leaders; and being a civilian and a public servant, I had access to the enlisted personnel on a more intimate and franker footing than an officer would usually have." He had acted, primarily, "as a reporter."

He proved that he was still a first-rate reporter. As in his round-the-world trip of '29, he had pecked out careful notes each night on his portable, from which, on a brief stayover at Hawaii, he had prepared his hour-long address. Portions of it were stirring epics of heroism:

> *I think of Bernt Balchen, a great aviator, who went up in a plane and made a search for the crew of another plane which had been forced down on the Greenland ice cap. When he finally located them, they were in a very remote spot, and it was obvious that immediate rescue was necessary if their lives were to be saved. . . . The only place where he could possibly land his seaplane was in a slight depression in the ice cap where the ice had melted just enough to form a thin film of water. . . . Even if a successful landing could be made . . . there was only the slightest chance of being able to take off again from such a small area of melted ice. Nevertheless . . . he landed his seaplane there, and kept it circling on the surface of the water so that the plane would not stick in the slush ice which lay immediately below the few inches of water. Each time he went past the group of marooned men he reached over the side of his plane and pulled in one of them. Only his extraordinary strength enabled him to perform the feat of pulling into his [moving] plane men who were so weakened that they could not help themselves. One by one he pulled all of them into his plane, and . . . by great skill, was able to lift the plane off the water, and fly the men back to the base.*
>
> *I think of one boy in Sicily whose back was broken and who had just been placed in a plaster cast which reached up over his chin. Steel clamps were in his skull in order to exert traction on his spinal column. He was destined to lie this way for six months and then his recovery was not sure, but when I spoke to that boy he answered me with a joke. I think of another one whose face was horribly burned—there are a great many horrible burns in this gasoline war—whose eyelids had to be lifted up for him by a nurse, and who only had a hole for a mouth. But out of that hole came the strong voice of courage.*

I think of a Lieutenant Miller, of Alabama, who was washed up on a beach in the South Seas. He felt so weak from the explosion of the ship that he had been on that he could hold nothing in his stomach, and thought he was going to die. So he took off his shoes and gave them and his equipment to brother officers, thinking that they might need them to save their own lives. He lay down on the beach. In the morning he drank some rain water and found he could hold it on his stomach. He concluded he was not going to die. He stripped a Japanese corpse that was washed up on the beach and, gathering some Japanese hand grenades, made a camp for himself in some thick bushes on the island. When a Japanese party sought him out he destroyed them with the grenades and armed himself with their pistols. After 42 days he was found, but declined to leave the island until his captured Japanese documents . . . as well as his weapons had been safely removed.

I think of Lieutenant Jack Kennedy, of Massachusetts, son of our former Ambassador to Great Britain, whose PT boat was cut in two by a destroyer, who drifted for 18 hours in the hull, and finally reached a small island. Every night that young man would swim out to the channel, and supported by his life preserver, would signal with a flashlight all through the night to attract the attention of an American boat. He finally succeeded in doing so, and thus, by means of his brave conduct, the other members of his crew were rescued.

I think of a gunner in a B-24, a boy from Pennsylvania whom I saw in Port Moresby. His whole right side was a mass of gunshot wounds. He had been wounded at 3 o'clock in the afternoon. He had lost his right eye. I saw him at 10 o'clock the next morning. We know what happens to a man in civilian life who loses an eye. He is seriously weakened, if not prostrated in mind and spirit. But when I spoke to that boy, his voice came back as strong as mine is now, and he said, "The thing that bothers me is that they probably won't let me fly any more."

Lodge's day-to-day journal of the trip showed his attention to the smallest detail of unfair treatment of the GI. At the Newfoundland Base Command, he noted that non-coms had a fine service club, but privates none whatever. At Goose Bay, Labrador, and at an Iceland air base, he noted the troops had a lower death rate than civilians at home, but was disturbed that one-third had to be sent home for "arctic madness."

From Colonel Balchen, the army's Greenland expert, he heard the tale of the rescue, and also of Balchen's fifteen-hour flights, armed with 20-millimeter cannons and bombs, to blast out the German soldiers who kept establishing weather stations on the Greenland coast. In the naval hospital he

found a sailor, Lally, whose brother had been one of Lodge's tank crewmen   157
in Libya and was now with Patton's Second Armored. Since a German plane
had been over Iceland when the senators came in, they flew out with twenty
P-38 escorts, into a thick fog which lasted until they reached Scotland's coast.

At Prestwick, they got a sample of the V.I.P. treatment which would meet
them everywhere. A de luxe train was waiting, to take them to London with
stops on the way. After lunch on the train, they motored to Clyde where
the cruiser *Augusta,* which had landed Patton in Africa, was in dock with
some merchant ships full of German prisoners. They visited American
troops who had just arrived on the *Queen Mary,* and dined on a transport,
the *Santa Elena.* In London, Ambassador John G. Winant met them at the
Paddington Station. Averell Harriman took them on a morning's tour of
London's bombed-out areas. They inspected supply unloading at the docks,
then lunched with General Ira Eaker at his Eighth Air Force headquarters.

Lodge studied the reconnaissance photos after recent bombing raids. "I
was tremendously impressed with the pinpoint accuracy of daylight bombing." Occasionally, his notes reflect a wry bit of humor. The boys of Bomber
Command were sleeping in High Wycombe, a former girl's school, where
a sign was found by each bed saying: "Ring twice for the mistress." "The
bells rang all night," Lodge reported. He observed—after meeting and talking with members of the bomber crews who had made the great raid on
Kassel—that "the lead navigator was Capt. Nutter of Massachusetts who
was the first Harvard man to fly over Germany." And proudly added: "Perhaps the most impressive statement made is that at no time since the
Americans started to fly from the United Kingdom has any American plane
returned before completing its mission because of action by the enemy."
At Debden, the senators saw American fighter pilots being briefed before
beginning a sweep over Germany. Young Lieutenant Colonel Don Blakelee
nonchalantly stepped up to the map.

"He was dressed in old trousers and leather jacket," Lodge recorded, "had
his cap on the back of his head and a cigarette in his right hand. He had
one of the most determined chins and aggressive expressions I have ever
encountered." He noted also a sign on the wall: "Remember when you bail
out don't give out information," as "an example of the way terrifying things
become routine."

At a dinner given by General Jacob Devers, Lodge heard Lord Mount-
batten describe his commando raid on Dieppe. Sir Dudley Pound, First Lord
of the Admiralty, gave an encouraging report on progress in destroying
German submarines. Sir Alan Brooke, British chief of staff, discussed high
strategy.

At Buckingham Palace, King George VI agreeably signed Lodge's short-
snorter, and asked Lodge to sign his. Anthony Eden gave them lunch at

158 the Savoy. Then came a high spot of the trip—their visit to Churchill at 10 Downing Street:

> *We went through his conference room with its long tables and book-cases done in white and gold. In the ante-room are hooks for the hats of the ministers, with the name of each minister over each hook. He took us into the garden and talked very frankly. He wants to bear down hard on Germany. He is not at all disturbed about Russia getting too strong. He looks forward to the day when British and American fleets will use the same bases, that the joint chiefs of staff will keep on working together for 10 years, and there will be joint British and American citizenship.*

Churchill, however, was not above slipping a private message to the Republicans—just in case they won the 1944 elections. Only Lodge and Brewster, the two Republicans in the party, were invited to dinner by Minister of Information Brendan Bracken, who wanted to tell them the British Government could work just as well with conservatives as liberals, should the Republicans win next year. Lodge was spellbound at Bracken's description of Churchill's flight to France just before the fall:

> *The weather was bad and the RAF set itself strongly against any flying. Neville Chamberlain, calling Bracken by his first name for the first time, implored him not to let Churchill go. The decision was finally placed in the hands of Mrs. Churchill who said that if it was really vital, that Winston should go; that he had had 60-odd years of life whereas young boys were dying every day. Before leaving Churchill insisted on taking a loaded pistol with him so that he could have a crack at any enemy pilot that sought to attack him.*

An eight-hour flight took the senators, in early August, to Marrakech. They left London at midnight to lessen the danger of attack. Lodge was surprised to find that his brother John, an American naval liaison with the French fleet, had been flown in to serve as his aide. The party was put up at the villa where President Roosevelt stayed after the Casablanca Conference. They had a nine-course meal at the palace of El Glaoui, pasha of Marrakech, who later took them into a private room to tell them that Morocco wanted to be under American protection when the war was over. "Above all they wanted to establish an American university in Morocco similar to Robert College in Turkey."

Senator Russell, as chairman of the group, was handed a letter from General Eisenhower, commander of Allied Forces in Algiers, regretting that he could not invite the committee to go to Sicily because it would be too dangerous. Patton's invasion had already cut swiftly across the island to take Palermo and his tanks were now hammering their way toward the Straits of Messina. General Montgomery's Eighth Army was also fighting there.

Lodge, as a reserve Army officer, offered to go on the committee's behalf, and they agreed this was the best solution. He flew to Algiers, only to be told by Eisenhower's chief of staff, Major General Walter Bedell Smith, that he could not go to Sicily, reserve commission or not. The Americans would welcome him, but Montgomery flatly disapproved any visitors.

Lodge, through means he did not disclose, evidently pulled some influential wires. He had flown on to Tunis to attend General Carl (Tooey) Spaatz's meeting with his staff, and listen to briefings by "a tall, fine-looking man with a wonderful grasp of his subject, a general at the age of 37" —Lauris Norstad. After the meeting he was "pleasantly surprised" to get a call from General Smith that he could leave for Sicily next morning.

Lodge flew in a B-25, the fast medium bomber, with two fighters as escort. As they flew over Pantelleria the navigator said, "We used to bomb it twice a day, every day." The landing strip at Palermo was short, the field surrounded by steep mountains on three sides, and by barrage balloons on the fourth. There were cracked-up planes on the field as they landed, braking hard.

Lodge found Patton's headquarters in a palace, "equal in cubic space to the Senate Office Building, full of beautiful courtyards with arched balconies." Patton himself was up front at his command post, near Stefano. Lodge lunched with old friend General Geoffrey Keyes and Major General John P. Lucas, who then took him forward in a reconnaissance car.

He found Patton in great spirits and full of his usual salty talk. Lodge greeted other old Army comrades, Brigadier General Hobart (Hap) Gay, Patton's chief of staff, and his deputy Colonel Paul Harkins. He also greeted Major Charlie Codman, the aide who had replaced the dead Captain Jenson. Codman, like Harkins, was a fellow Bostonian.

They all dined together. Afterward Lodge said he would sleep on a bedroll, General Spaatz having loaned him his own. The old ground soldier Patton snorted at such Air Force generosity. "You aren't depriving him of anything," Patton said, as Codman recorded. "Spaatz never slept in it and never will."

Next day they were up early. Patton invited Lodge into his command car and took him forward toward the fighting at Orlando. As they passed through a town all the Italian carabinieri, letter-carriers, etc., stood at attention to salute the fabulous American general. One gaudy fellow in black boots and red striped trousers felt disinclined to do so, and sat, legs crossed,

160 in front of a café. Patton slowed the command car, leaned out over the edge with his piercing eyes flashing through his bushy white eyebrows, and snarled, "Stand up you sonuvabitch and salute!" The officer leaped up as if someone had knifed him.

At the next town, houses on both sides had caved in from bombs and shells so only a trail big enough for a single vehicle was left in the rubble. A platoon of U.S. soldiers was digging out the road. Patton stopped and yelled for the lieutenant. "You fellows have worked hard enough," he cried. "Get these local bastards to dig this out." Their faces shone with gratitude.

They passed some Third Division infantrymen who, to their own surprise, had become cavalry. Patton had cunningly brought six hundred saddles with him from the States. Sicily's rock-gorged roads often made it impossible to envelop them with tanks. So Patton had made amphibious landings behind the Germans to envelop them on the left, as they retreated toward the Straits of Messina. To envelop them on the right, he saddled up Sicilian mules and sent his infantrymen trotting off up the rocky files. The mules crossed the island faster than anything else could have done.

Now Lodge saw wrecked German vehicles, M-4 and M-7 self-propelled guns, knocked out by armor-piercing shells. A bit further they passed dead Germans who had been lying there for days, dead mules, and reached a company of The 301st Regiment's Third Battalion. A German lad killed a half-hour before lay sprawled on his stomach, his automatic rifle still aimed at an exposed curve in the road. Others, all very young, lay sprawled in the grotesque attitudes created by high explosive. Sicilians had begun to strip the bodies, and were stopped by the soldiers. A group of thirty Italian prisoners came by, looking cheerful; with them were six Germans looking glum. Lodge saw no American dead. One boy, however, was wounded so badly he did not look as if he would live. The forward medics had dosed him with morphine so he was not suffering.

"I cannot describe the impression made upon me by the infantry company," Lodge wrote in his journal. "They had no sleep for two days and were eating their first food in 12 hours. Patton asked me to talk to the soldiers, which I could do more informally than he. I talked with 25 or 30 individually. Their spirit was good but they were hoping for the 45th Division, which was resting, to relieve them—and that was soon done."

Patton proudly ticked off some of the achievements of these men. One parachute regiment marched sixty-eight miles in forty-eight hours. The Seventh Infantry Regiment of the Third Division marched thirty-six miles in less than twenty-two hours. The Second Armored and a composite division composed of two parachute regiments and one combat team of the Ninth moved faster against opposition than the Nazi blitzkrieg had moved in France in 1940. Lodge talked with Third's commander, General Lucian

Chapter Nine

Truscott, at his command post, saw General Troy Middleton of the Forty-   *161*
fifth Division, and General Omar Bradley, II Corps Commander.

Two German ME-109's attacked his car at a crossroads, but the bombs
hit four hundred yards away. When he and Patton got back to the forward
C.P., they were taken back to Palermo in separate Cub L-5 spotter planes.
Patton took him to see the Palermo docks, "a terrifying sight. One ocean-
going merchant ship had been lifted bodily onto a concrete pier. Sunken
ships were all over the docks and Army engineers had built wooden bridges
across the wrecks so that unloading ships could come right alongside and
be discharged in trucks. Divers were working on the bottom of the harbor
to clear its wreckage. Amphibious trucks ('Ducks') were unloading supplies."

Patton, so fond of flamboyance, now had a bit of comic opera to spring
on his friend. He took him to the royal palace. "I occupy the King's bedroom," he said. "I've assigned you the Queen's." He then produced a bottle
of cold champagne. They finished it between them, "a fitting climax to a
memorable day."

Next day Lodge went to visit his old Harvard classmate, Charles Poletti,
now a colonel bossing military government in Sicily. Lodge was delighted
to see Emily's brother-in-law, Captain Archibald Alexander (who had married her sister Jean) and was now one of Poletti's aides. So was an old
Washington friend, Morton Eustis. Later he went out to have supper with
his old outfit, Second Armored. Its commander, General Gaffey, sent his
aide Captain Burke with two motorcyclist M.P.s to drive him to the headquarters at Partenico. "What was my delight," Cabot noted, "to find that
the two motorcycle riders and the driver were all men with whom I had
served in the Second Armored. We had a fine reunion. We went out through
Palermo to the West with the sirens screaming." He found the division in
an olive and grape plantation. Its band was playing. Gaffey, Colonel Red-
ding F. (Speed) Perry and I. D. White "were all shined up to greet me—
who was extremely dirty."

Lodge did not let the attention from the brass cause him to neglect the
G.I.'s and their gripes. "There is no chocolate in the Post Exchange," he
carefully noted. "The movies are so old that everyone saw them at home
before they left." The G.I.'s had a great need for American radio, being fed
up with hearing nothing but British victories on the BBC, and their own
exploits described as those of "other Allied forces." He was careful to check
also on the local effect of Office of War Information broadcasts in Italian.
Cultured Sicilians told him these were "bombastic, ineffective and delivered
in a very bad Italian accent."

He got back to the palace late, fearful he could not find the Queen's
bedroom in the dark. Numerous MP's challenged him, but Patton had pro-

vided a password easy for him to remember: "Calvin Coolidge." He found the room, and slept fine, only to discover next morning that the Queen's bed was full of bedbugs. He was bitten all over.

Once more the B-25 winged him over the Mediterranean, one of the P-38 escort's pilots doing aerobatics around it to show off his stuff. He visited the hospital in Tunis to talk to wounded American flyers who had managed to get back from the inferno of their raid on Rumania's Ploesti oilfields, a raid in which 54 of the 164 Liberators were lost. Careful to note any deficiencies of America's allies, Lodge recorded: "If we had been able to base our planes in Russia for the Ploesti raid, we might have saved many lives." He had noted in Algiers that "the British are overcharging us for coal," and reminded himself to check into the British monopoly of cable communications east of Gibraltar as a possible source of some helpful reverse Lend-Lease. When he got to Cairo, to rejoin the other senators, he had a long talk with British Minister of State Richard Casey about it. "I pointed out that the OWI, although supposedly a war agency, was being charged cable tolls for transmission of their material." Casey promised to look into this.

In mid-August the senators reached Abadan, where American engineers were funneling 196,000 tons of supplies a month to the Soviets—102,000 by rail, the rest by truck. "It takes five days for a truck to reach the border, and two days later it is at the front," Lodge noted. Some two hundred planes a month were moving to the Soviets. "We saw them taking off, with the bright Red Star painted on the side. . . . Our boys are moving the stuff up so fast that the Russians get clogged up." He inspected an airplane assembly plant turning out six fighters and two bombers a day. In the terrible heat, "which would come up through the soles of one's shoes," the men worked in the cooler parts of the day, and soaked their cots with water so as to be cool enough to sleep.

They flew on, over the hot, greasy-looking Persian Gulf, to Karachi, in the semiarid Sind Desert ("but after Iraq as refreshing as Boston after Washington"), on to New Delhi, then up the Brahmaputra River to Chabua to don oxygen masks to make the dangerous flight "over the Hump" to China.

All along the way Lodge carefully checked on servicemen's conditions At Karachi he noted that someone had unloaded thousands of cans of beets ("which of course no one likes") on that mess, while there was a marked shortage of canned fruit and fruit juices which "are the most palatable and healthful foods in this climate." At Delhi, where "officers commanding service troops do not live with the men," morale was "the lowest yet," worse than Iraq which had had almost no creature comforts. He also had a pleasant reunion in Delhi with General Sir Claude Auchinleck, who was commanding in Libya when Lodge was there, and was now Governor General of India. They lunched at his vast Flagstaff House, Happy Chandler noting Churchill's desire for common citizenship. "If he becomes Senator from Kentucky," Chandler told Auchinleck, "I want your job."

After flying the Hump and coming out of the clouds, they saw "the bright green and purple, velvety-looking mountains of China, with the rivers running like orange ribbons. We landed at Kunming, a beautiful fertile plain surrounded by hills, at an altitude of 6000 ft., with the best climate since I left Beverly!" They were met by the Flying Tigers commander, General Claire Chennault, and the theater commander, General "Vinegar Joe" Stilwell. Lodge was pleased to see a familiar face smiling over Chennault's shoulder: Joe Alsop, now an Air Force captain on Chennault's staff.

With the aid of ace reporter Alsop, reporter Lodge soon found himself steeped in Fourteenth Air Force logistics—and astounded by all that Chennault's men had accomplished.

They had six auxiliary fields around Kunming to defend the air transport into China from possible Japanese attack. They had other fields in Kwangsi, operating only three hundred miles from Hong Kong. They were building a new one north of Canton, at Suichuan, which would take the huge new B-29's and make possible the bombing of Kobe, Kyoto and Osaka in Japan—as well as neutralize the Japanese spearhead on the Yangtze. They had thirty-six operating fighters (out of ninety), thirty-two heavy bombers and sixteen mediums—the whole effort entirely supplied by air. Lodge studied Chennault carefully, thought him "one of the most impressive human beings I have met, with his hawk-like face, his piercing brown eye, and his gentle Southern drawl; there is a fire and brilliance about him which inspire men to follow him."

Lodge found Stilwell apprehensive that, with Indo-China only 250 miles away, Japan might send four or five divisions from there to take Kunming —"then the whole structure collapses." Chennault countered that they would have done it long ago if it were so easy; if they tried it he could destroy the supply line behind their advance. They had not even been able to take the railroad from Hankow to Canton.

Once more, Lodge found the sights of China stirring tribal memories from his Old China Trader heritage. Visiting Stilwell's training center, "a miniature Ft. Benning," he passed through "noisy, smelly Chinese villages. I was once again impressed with the attractiveness of the Chinese people. They have vitality, they are polite, they have a sense of humor and they have an odd democratic feeling among them." In Kunming he attended the "Ding Ho Follies," put on by the 308th Bombardment Group which in July alone sank twenty-five thousand tons of Japanese shipping. "There was a fine American show, some beautiful singing by fine-looking young

164 Chinese student aviators. In front of us sat a Chinese flyer with a Chinese flag and Chinese inscription sewn to the back of his leather jacket. If he comes down anywhere in China that will be his passport to safety."

Lodge took a long walk with Alsop and marveled "at the intricacy of the irrigation system and at the industry of the people. They are fundamentally democratic, simple peasants. They have a system of town government where all questions are decided by majority vote." Nevertheless, Lodge could see deeper trouble ahead for these simple people:

"The Communists hold the Northern provinces, and when the war in the West is over and the Japanese are confronted by the full strength of the united nations, the Chinese Communists, if supported and aided by the Russians, should easily be able to extend their control into Manchuria. If the Chungking regime dared, they would probably try to wipe the Communists out. But the task is too big, and too dangerous in its probable repercussions abroad. So things are likely to rock along as they are until the Russians finally become the arbiters."

Back across the Hump to Chabua, they encountered Eric Sevareid, CBS correspondent, who had parachuted with twenty-one others into the Burma jungle after their C-46's engines failed. The Medical Corps parachuted three men in to aid them—the doctor, Lieutenant Colonel Donald Flickinger, gave morphine to one who had broken his leg, and set it. A chair was constructed so the others could carry him. "They walked 140 miles through precipitous mountains and jungle," Lodge noted. "Sevareid said that the headhunters whom they met were very kind to them and only once mentioned that their heads might be cut off. Apparently they preferred the heads of their own people." Lodge took care to record that a Boston man, Lieutenant Andrew Lebonte, had led them out of the jungle after making a five-day, double-time march, with troops and weapons, to find them. The senators flew on to Calcutta which they found stricken with incredible famine. "The human suffering in that city is undoubtedly on a par, if indeed it is not greater than, the sufferings of war. Famine, cholera and death are omnipresent." Lodge also found *Time-Life* correspondent James Shepley "extremely critical of the narrow censorship" followed by the British, "which he is sure will foster cynicism, disillusionment and lead to hostile feelings against our Allies." Lodge promised to try to remedy it.

They flew to Ceylon and the governor took them to Queen's House for tea. Some of the party also stayed there. Lodge preferred the Galle Face Hotel, remembered from his 1929 visit, "right on the ocean and ventilated by a very strong ocean breeze." He dined with the U.S. naval liaison in Ceylon, Lieutenant Commander Bryce Goldsborough, and noted that with

Singanese fallen to the Japanese, Colombo was the only big naval base left   *165*
to the Allies between Africa and the east coast of Australia.

From an RAF field, cut out of the jungle of ebony some ninety miles
northeast of Colombo, on September 5 they began a flight which marked
a new milestone in air progress—the first time a land plane had attempted
nonstop the thirty-two-hundred-mile flight across the Indian Ocean to Australia. "We had beautiful weather, with all the stars visible, and a bright
half-moon. Light clouds did not obscure the sea, which we flew over at
10,000 ft. We passed south of Christmas Island and north of Cocos Island
observing radio silence because we were in a Japanese area." Some fourteen hours and fifty-five minutes after takeoff they were over Australia, and
landed at Carnavon on its west coast. They were surprised at the air's cool-
ness after Ceylon's oppressive heat.

That evening they danced square dances with people at the local parish
house. Next morning a six-and-a-half-hour flight across badlands brought
them to the 380th Bombardment Group's headquarters north of Darwin.
That group had flown ninety missions the previous month, and dropped
250,700 pounds of bombs. Lodge noted that a B-24 killed a kangaroo on
takeoff that morning. Ever curious, he drove out to see some huge, twenty-
foot anthills.

Another six-hour flight brought them to Townsville, on the Pacific. The
senators met with lend-lease, economic warfare and OWI officials. Lodge
carefully recorded that, although the U.S. was providing Australia ten
times as much aid as the British, the latter were getting zinc and beryllium
at cheaper prices.

When they landed at Port Moresby, they were met at the plane by General MacArthur. MacArthur reminded Lodge of their discussions at Manila
fourteen years before.

"General MacArthur is a big man with a magnetic personality," Lodge
wrote in his journal, "and a splendid ability to express himself. He has a
dramatic sense which makes his statements extremely impressive. He does
not look his age, and appears extremely healthy and vigorous."

MacArthur had some gripes of his own to let off.

"No one," he said, "cavils with the decision to get Hitler first and to hold
the enemy elsewhere. The trouble is we have done neither. We have gotten
Mussolini first and have not made enough available in other theaters with
which to hold."

MacArthur paid his respects to the Japanese fighting men.

"Not a single Japanese prisoner has been taken who was in sound mind
and body. While we have cut their tentacles as they spread eastward, the
fact remains that they are very well dug in. With 500 heavy bombers, I

166 could be in Mindanao [the Philippines] and drive the Japs into Japan in a year."

After supper with the senators, MacArthur told Lodge it would take not less than one million American casualties to defeat Japan—unless the U.S. got access to the maritime provinces of Siberia. Clearly, he longed for these as bases from which to bomb the Japanese.

MacArthur sent the senators to some of his advanced airfields, where they could see the remarkable achievements of Army engineers in building them. "They try to pick out a place where the grass is fairly dry," Lodge wrote. "It grows 10 ft. high, and it is necessary to burn it before they land. They then come in and land in this unimproved place. The engineers get out of the plane, and the infantry deploy in the event there should be any Japanese lurking around. The engineers, with the small tools which they have brought along, carry on the important grading operations and get the rocks and other obstructions out of the way. Another plane comes in and brings a section of a bulldozer. Another plane comes in and brings other sections until the bulldozer is complete and ready for operation. Before long the crew is at work and the bombing area is advanced that much farther. In a short time another fighter strip would be in operation."

At one such forward field, at Buna on New Guinea, the senators could smell Japanese corpses moldering nearby. They saw swamps along Entrance Creek "where a man can sink out of sight" among the sago palms, and where the 127th Infantry had moved north. Back at Port Moresby, at base hospital, Lodge at MacArthur's suggestion pinned the Purple Heart on Lieutenant Leroy Miller of Pennsylvania, the B-24 gunner who had lost his right eye and was fearful he could not fly again.

Lodge left for Milne Bay in MacArthur's luxurious plane, "fitted up with all the smartness of a private yacht and containing an ice box." An old friend of many past Army maneuvers, Lieutenant General Walter Krueger, met him there and took him off sightseeing in a jeep.

"Milne Bay is the biggest port in the South Seas," Lodge noted in his journal. "It handles 250,000 tons a month—bigger than anything in Australia, bigger than San Francisco in peacetime." He found it impossible to describe what the engineers had accomplished in three months. "The trees have been cut down, the jungle soil pushed to one side with bulldozers, gravel has been brought in from the stream beds and the whole northern shore filled with all types of military equipment. Ocean-going vessels come right up to the shore and tie up to coconut palms."

He flew to Kiriwina, where ten thousand American troops were stationed only a hundred miles from a Japanese base, and were building a field capable of handling heavy bombers. Lodge was equally fascinated by the customs of the seven thousand natives: "They do not believe that love has

anything to do with having babies. When a woman wants to have a baby
she stands in the middle of a stream with a stone in each hand and
squeezes the stones." At the island hospital, he found the doctor was a
brother of Boston's Monsignor Minahan. "One of the field artillery messes
had some excellent chocolate cake."

Admiral William H. Halsey arranged for Lodge to go on a cruise with
one of the PT boats. It was here he first heard of the stirring adventure of
young Lieutenant Jack Kennedy of Boston. At 3:30 A.M. the day of his
departure from the Solomons, he saw some excitement himself. "A Japanese bomber was caught in the beams of five searchlights. He was at
20,000 ft., but stood out clearly against the vast inky blackness of the sky.
An American P-38 went after him, firing 20-mm tracer ammunition, which
made a red chain of fire, which struck the Japanese and set his left engine
on fire. The American made another pass. This time a huge sheet of flame
came from the enemy plane. . . . This was the third Japanee bomber
that particular American boy had shot down during the night."

On September 13, the senators flew to Brisbane in a plane with some
soldiers. One soldier was carrying a small black native dog which had accompanied him on nineteen aerial combat missions. One of the men said,
"Another six missions and we will give him the DFC."

Thence they flew on to Hawaii, and after a layover while they recapitu-
lated the lessons of the globe-girding odyssey, they flew home.

Lodge had now seen more theaters of war, and talked at first hand and
in detail with more of its combat soldiers and commanders, than any other
member of Congress—indeed, more at that point than General Marshall
had done.

If any man was now qualified to judge, improve and criticize the conduct
of the war, Lodge was that man. No senator in any war had been better
qualified to help guide it.

The trouble was that he was eager to be in it and fighting himself. He
would not be long in Washington.

CHAPTER TEN

You were the real thing in the war, a soldier serving overseas in combat, with a record that will be a source of satisfaction to you all your life. —Secretary of War Robert P. Patterson to Lodge, July 22, 1947.

The Senate floor, the galleries and the press gallery were packed to capacity on September 30, 1943, when Lodge rose to make his report on the tour. Many, remembering the isolationist battles of his grandfather, feared Lodge would turn the occasion to attack plans for postwar cooperation. Others expected partisan tub-thumping at Administration errors and oversights. What they heard was a calm weighing of good and bad in tones of hard-headed realism.

Lodge did not spare the Allies where he felt them carrying less than their share: "The United States, with less than 25 per cent of the oil resources of the world, was furnishing over 60 per cent of the oil being used to fight this war." The huge British refinery at Abadan, which could supply Australia far easier than could "the distant and unfortunately dwindling oil resources of California," was working at "little more than half capacity." Nor did he neglect the British control of cables: "The question of international communication is of the first importance. There are large areas of the world where our British allies have complete control of the cable system." Many higher commanders suggested the need "for reverse lend-lease."

He expressed great admiration for the Red Army and understanding for Russia's "unwillingness to open a war on other fronts. . . . But it is also true that the whole character of the Pacific War would change if the United States had access to the Pacific coastal area of Russia. For reasons of security I shall not say how many American lives would be spared if we received this aid [later headlines leaked MacArthur's belief that it was 1,000,000]. I can say that it is a major factor in the whole Pacific picture. It is one of the biggest military facts staring us in the face."

One note he struck again and again: the tremendous future importance of international air routes, the imperative need for America to nail down postwar uses of the bases it was building all over the world. He cited the senators' own historic thirty-two-thousand-mile Pacific flight: "Certainly, if it is so simple to make such flights in the year 1943, it should be easier to fly even greater distances in the near future. The situation has implications for the future security of our country which no responsible American can ignore." Yet it was being ignored:

Perhaps one of the most striking physical phenomena to a modern world traveler are the huge airfields which have been constructed. . . . Estimates of the amounts expended . . . run as high as $500,-000,000. So far as I could learn we have no post-war rights to any of them. We do not seek dominance; we abhor imperialistic domination over native people. . . . The places I have in mind can be secured for us without violation of this principle because they are all so sparsely populated. . . . American blood has been shed to get these places. Some of these places must remain in American hands.

Lodge, experienced soldier and student of arms, was the first to stress the great need for unification of the armed forces, citing "lessons learned in the white heat of actual combat experience. The fact which is most striking is the close integration of forces in land, sea and air. None can exist without the other." But there was a contrast between MacArthur's headquarters, where all were separate entities, and Halsey's where "Army, Navy and Marine officers are so intermingled that it is difficult to know to what service a man belongs." One outfit ". . . is commanded by a major general in the Army with a captain in the Navy as chief of staff, and a Marine Corps colonel as operations officer. All three, it should be noted, are flyers. Senior offices of both the Army and the Navy are deeply impressed with the need for unity of the services when our new military policy is framed . . . a single department of war, with autonomous land, sea and air services coordinated at the top by a joint staff. . . ."

Lodge lashed out at the "censorship and propaganda policy of the Government" as a source of dissatisfaction among soldiers, who criticized everything from "cigarette advertisements which always portray soldiers as clean-shaven and neatly-pressed, to . . . the practice of portraying all our allies as being perfect," all "completely out of tune with the realistic attitude which our young men have toward this war." He was equally critical of British broadcasts underplaying the role of American forces. What he demanded—above all—was "a clear national policy."

His report was widely praised. In the New York *Times*, Arthur Krock called it "especially constructive and clear. He spoke as a good reporter writes, in the light of high journalistic standards, having had his pre-Senatorial training in that field." "I listened from start to finish," wrote Senator Arthur Capper of Kansas, owner of the Topeka *Journal*, to Lodge. ". . . I think your statement is outstanding in character because of your previous experience as a newspaper reporter."

Moreover, Lodge got quick action on his suggestion that Britain was supplying less petroleum and rubber than it might. President Roosevelt announced that he was requesting a complete report on that situation. His

170 concern over the airfields struck home in distant Omaha, where Turner Catledge of the New York *Times*, feeling the pulse of the heartland, found an increased "skepticism . . . and a questioning as to whether the American administration is adequately looking after American interests in the military and diplomatic field. . . . The concern of the people out this way is that our own officials are not primarily interested in or capable of looking after our own interests."

Walter Lippmann rebuked Lodge for talking of a second Russian front on the eve "of the momentous conference in Moscow," while the President was "unable to talk back" to such rashness. However, the President did talk back. Russia, he told his press conference, wasn't ready to go to war with Japan because she had something more important to do, she had knocked the Germans down three or four times and maybe if she knocked them down three or four more times they would stay down.

Winston Churchill also took an oblique swipe at Lodge. "As soon as the war is ended," he told Commons, "the soldiers will leave off fighting and the politicians will begin. . . . Perhaps that is rather a pity but at any rate it isn't so bad as what goes on in some countries which I shouldn't venture to name where the soldiers are fighting abroad and the politicians are fighting at home with equal vigor [laughter]." Righteously, the London *Daily Mail* urged this slogan on the senator: "Careless Talk Costs Lives."

Lodge plunged again into the work of the Senate. Soon he had to come to defense of his friend Patton, now being pilloried by various columnists because he had slapped a malingering soldier in Sicily. Patton recorded it all in his diary. He had stopped at an evacuation hospital and talked to 350 newly wounded. "One poor fellow who had lost his right arm cried; another had lost a leg. All were brave and cheerful. . . . There also was a man trying to look as if he had been wounded. I asked him what was the matter, and he said he just couldn't take it. I gave him the devil, slapped his face with my gloves, and kicked him out of the hospital. Companies should deal with such men and if they shirk their duty they should be tried and shot." A fortnight later, after "a very nasty letter from Ike," Patton apologized to the soldier in front of the doctor, nurses and soldiers who had witnessed the slapping.

Many demands were being made for Patton's dismissal. For a time it looked as if he might be sent home. Moreover his promotion to the permanent rank of major general—up from colonel—was being endangered.

Lodge did not excuse Patton's conduct. But he told reporters that Patton had saved many lives by pushing his men so hard. "He was trying to maintain pace and momentum so that the enemy could not rest and reorganize. To do that he had to inspire his army to overcome the natural desire to rest.

If a general imposes such strategy he must overcome the natural human   *171*
instinct to rest—his own as well as that of his men. He drove himself as
well as his men. Leadership like that shortens battles and saves lives of
soldiers."

When Patton's nomination for promotion came before the Military Affairs
Committee, the general's wife, Beatrice Ayer Patton, wrote Lodge from
Green Meadows, their estate near Lodge's own home:

Dear Cabot:
Since the slapping incident broke I have had the most wonderful let-
ters from people I've never heard of: wounded men, noncoms, mothers
—all sorts, and all saying in different ways "more power to General
Patton." Would you like me to send them to you to show to the Mili-
tary Committee? If they are interested in popular sentiment, I can
really produce it, from every walk of life.

It did not prove necessary. Both Lodge and Senator Chandler defended
Patton so staunchly that his promotion was approved without difficulty.

Patton, after taking Messina on August 23, had been called to England
to spend long months training his new Third Army for its great sweep to
come across France. But there had been no real major tank warfare since
the fall of Tunis. As the New Year arrived, Lodge felt sure that the big test
for America's growing armored legions would soon come. This was where
his own training lay, and it was time for him to put it to use again.

Cabot's old commander, General Crittenberger, had finished training
several new armored divisions. He was being ordered to England with the
XIX Corps. On the eve of his departure, January 13, he stayed overnight
with the Lodges in their Georgetown home. The two old comrades sat up
late, talking about horse-cavalry days on the Bugscuffle Trail—and about
Cabot's future.

Critt said he would like to have Lodge with him in battle, both as an aide,
and as assistant chief of staff to help direct operations. Lodge agreed to
join him shortly, if he could arrange it, and swore Critt to secrecy. Crittenberger saw his men embark from Brooklyn, and then flew to England on
January 17.

Under the order which President Roosevelt had issued in June, 1942,
during Lodge's Libyan mission, Lodge could not resume active duty without
resigning his seat in the Senate. His only fear, if he did resign, was that
some political enemy might condemn him to innocuous desuetude—like
William Vanderbilt, former Republican Governor of Rhode Island, who had
volunteered and then been assigned to the Panama Canal.

Cabot talked the problem over with Colonel Bobby Cutler in Stimson's office. He talked it over with Stimson, too. He also saw Chief of Staff George Marshall, telling him about Critt's desire to have him in combat.

"Lodge," said Marshall, who seldom first-named anyone. "I think you should make all the preparations to go, and then ask to see the President and tell him about it. If you have his approval nobody can send you any-where else, and I am sure he would gladly give it to you."

Lodge did exactly as Marshall advised. The President gave his blessings and his praise.

Major Lodge found General Critt at his new XIX Corps headquarters, at Warminster, ninety miles west of London. This outfit, which embraced the new III Armored Corps, was preparing for the Normandy landings, engag-ing in practice amphibious assaults. At that time, the Pentagon decided that whole corps of armor were an overemphasis, and that armored divi-sions should be blended with infantry divisions in a "type" corps. Such, on paper, was the newly created IV Corps, headed by Major General Alexander (Sandy) Patch, fresh from Guadalcanal fighting. When Patch arrived in England the Corps was little more than himself and a few staff officers. Before the Corps itself could be activated, Patch was detached to reform Patton's Seventh Army, which had been inactive since Patton left Sicily, and prepare it for the Anvil landing in Southern France—scheduled at that time to coincide with Normandy.

General Critt got orders to proceed to Allied Force Headquarters in Al-giers, where the British general, Sir Henry Maitland (Jumbo) Wilson, had succeeded Eisenhower as supreme commander, and General Devers had become his deputy. Devers had a new assignment for Critt.

Critt took Lodge with him to Algiers. Bedell Smith, Eisenhower's chief of staff, told Lodge they would like to have him on that staff, but Lodge wanted to be with Critt. In Algiers, Critt learned that his new assignment was to take over IV Corps from Patch. He had to build his staff from scratch. He asked some of his old officers at Warminster to join him, including his two chiefs of staff, Colonel Lawrence Ladue and Colonel Curtis Nance. "We went to Oran," Critt recalled afterward, "to look over the officers of the Second Cavalry Division, which was being broken up. A guard of honor met us, and Lodge, nodding toward their leader, told me, 'That fellow looks like a good officer.' He was a captain, and I was looking for senior officers, but I asked for him. It was Graham Purcell, who had a distinguished combat record with our Corps."

In late February, 1944, Critt and Lodge flew with the staff to Lake Averno, ten miles north of Naples, to set up headquarters. The corps itself was not scheduled for major action until the Rapido could be crossed, the Anzio beachhead forces could break out, and the seizure of Rome could open the flatter land to the north for tank operations. Italy's fiercest fighting was then raging in the craggy hills at Monte Cassino, and at Anzio itself where the whole beachhead was under artillery fire. The IV Corps officers began going to Anzio to get their first taste of real war. Lieutenant Colonel Edward A. Stephenson, of G-3 (operations), made such a visit, and recalled that Lodge did also, although he had already seen desert warfare. "We all looked up to him as a veteran, he had already had his baptism of fire."

Along with these learning missions to Anzio they went through the tedious business of setting up the staff headquarters and assigning the new units of the corps as they arrived. In mid-April, Lodge's digestive system conked out—possibly from dysentery, as he thought, or the recurrence of an ulcer of twenty years before. His pylorus simply refused to let food pass. He was flown back to Walter Reed Hospital, where his old friend Colonel Cutler thought he was dying. Cutler alerted his surgeon brother, Eliott, to rush a top specialist, Dr. Sam Levine, down from Boston. Levine, consulting with Walter Reed's Dr. Fred Rankin, stopped the intravenous feeding and other treatment Lodge had been getting and fed him steak. He perked up again, and after a brief convalescence got back to IV Corps just as it was starting the advance along Italy's boot on the west coast. "Critt used Lodge as his eyes and ears," Colonel Stephenson recalled. "He always wanted to know where every unit was, and he would send one of us in a Piper Cub to spot the farthermost units we could find and report back to him. Sometimes I would go, sometimes Lodge." Once, when a unit bogged down in the face of fierce fire from a German Panzer division, Lodge flew up to the front to investigate and brought back a blunt recommendation that the commanding officer be relieved. He was.

Lodge was a troubleshooter. His job was to get up front, see what was going wrong, and make whatever arrangements he could on the spot to set it right, and get back quickly with recommendations for whatever more needed to be done.

On arriving at Ponsacco, Lodge climbed to the top of a church steeple to reconnoiter with his glasses. The road from Ponsacco, north to Pontedera was a raised one, some four or five feet higher than the fields on either side. After that the road ran level through little villages. The Germans were on both sides of the road and were shooting across it, but were not quite strong enough to prevent the Americans from using it.

Lodge got up to Pontedera, a deserted town, and proceeded on foot. Because of the artillery fire, he had to walk through the houses, and in and out of holes in their walls. Finally, in a baker's abandoned shop in the main square he found the U.S. company command post. Lodge was able to tell the commander of elements of strength on both sides of him, so he would know he was not cut off, and that more help would be coming. On the way back, Lodge came into the open to cross a street, pistol in hand, and round-

174 ing a corner almost bumped into a German similarly stalking. Lodge fired first, missed, and the German ran.

Captain Graham Purcell, who later became a Democratic congressman from Texas, recalled that Lodge sometimes organized expeditions of his own to speed up advances. Approaching Livorno (Leghorn), one corps division did not seem to be making much headway. "Lodge went out reconnoitering," Purcell said, "and was convinced it could be successfully reached over a certain road. He came back and began organizing a volunteer commando out of cooks, clerks and other troops assigned to corps headquarters, to lead them into Livorno at dawn to show it could be done. He had to call it off because during the night another division began laying down artillery fire on the road he planned to use." Purcell, who was decorated for valor, recalled that Lodge was one of the finest officers he had ever seen. "He was utterly without fear."

Takeoff hour was approaching for the Brazilian Expeditionary Force, moving in to replace some of the VI Corps troops being taken out of the line for the landing in Southern France. They had not been in combat before, and their first fighting was important for diplomatic as well as military reasons. Critt sent Lodge and Stephenson to be with them at H-hour. They helped them execute the taking of a hill, removing a bulge in the Allied line. Lodge's functions were those of a deputy chief of staff, though he had no such formal place in the corps table of organization. "He was very good at sizing up situations," Stephenson recalled later, "and recommending the action to be taken on this salient or that. He was in on all the staff conferences, where the G-3 leaders would make their recommendations. Critt put high value on his estimates."

"He was always with me when I was in my battle station," Critt himself recalled. "Most of the time he was operating at the Chief of Staff level. He was frequently under fire, was strafed and bombed by planes, and often had to travel through mines."

They had taken Livorno, the biggest port yet to fall, and were bucking the Gothic Line above the Arno when General Devers sent word to Critt that he was going to need Lodge for his own landing in Southern France. Lodge flew to Corsica around August 1 to head the liaison section for Devers' Sixth Army Group, which on D-plus-15 would take joint command of the Seventh Army under Patch and the First French Army under General Jean de Lattre de Tassigny. Liaison with the French forces would be of the utmost importance and Devers wanted the best man he could get. It was Devers who, as chief of armor, had sent Lodge to Libya and he knew how well Lodge had carried out that assignment, which also called for delicate teamwork with an ally. He also knew Lodge's intimate acquaintance with France, its countryside, its people and the language. Crittenberger reluctantly released

Lodge and awarded him a Bronze Star for performing duties which "required his exposure to enemy fire and the traversing of mined roads and areas. He rendered infinite service in the submission of complete detailed and accurate reports of conditions along the front line and contributed greatly to the success of combat operations."

On D-Day, August 15, the landings were made by the most battle-tested troops in the U.S. Army, the Third Division—which had hit the beaches with Patton at Fedala and in Sicily, and had made the Salerno and Anzio landings—the Forty-fifth, or Thunderbird Division, which had fought in Sicily, Salerno and Anzio, and the Thirty-sixth Texan Division which had lost so heavily in the attempted crossings of the Rapido. (Before they were done, the Thirty-sixth would capture Hermann Goering, and the Third, having "surrounded" the Alps, would be almost back to Italy again.) Their three task forces hit a thirty-mile stretch of beach just above Toulon from Cavalaire to Agay. The landings knifed through relatively light opposition and quickly fanned north along the Route Napoleon toward Grenoble, and cut off both Toulon and Marseilles. Lodge hit the beaches with General Magnan's Ninth French Colonial Infantry, the first French unit to land in Southern France.

The beaches secure, de Lattre's forces came in from Taranto and Brindisi on D-plus-1 and took up positions on the periphery of Toulon. De Lattre set up his command post in the little town of Pierrefeu. There, just a few miles from Edith Wharton's well-remembered house, Cabot first met him, on August 19. He came with Devers. The original timetable, which anticipated much fiercer German resistance, allotted three weeks for taking Toulon. "We told de Lattre to forget the time table," says Devers, "and to get moving. He did, too. He did a real job." De Lattre's *goumiers*, crack Algerian mountain troops, found all the hilly trails and passes in the hills about Toulon, and came down them like so many Indians, while American artillery pounded away down the coastal highway. By August 23, they took Toulon. One of de Lattre's armored units attached to the U.S. VI Corps romped all the way over to Arles and captured an intact bridge across the Rhône (all the rest were blown, far beyond Lyon).

Lodge was shuttling back and forth between de Lattre and Devers. "He made an immediate impression upon de Lattre," writes de Lattre's biographer, British General Guy Salisbury-Jones, "who summed him up not only as a man of exceptional intelligence but of great uprightness of character. Cabot Lodge understood de Lattre better than most of his American compatriots, and was to render a great service, not only to de Lattre, but to the greater cause of Allied cooperation."

With his forces across the Rhône, de Lattre wanted to advance up its west bank. His original assignment called for his army to protect the Seventh

176 Army's right flank, along the Swiss border. Lodge urged—and Devers agreed—that de Lattre should go up the Rhône as he wished. German units were fleeing along it, trying to get out of Southern France and Spain, but most of the country was already in the hands of some fifty-eight thousand maquisards armed with Allied weapons dropped by air.

American troops were pouring up the Rhône's east bank as de Lattre went up the west. When they met up north of Lyon, quite a traffic jam and great confusion was in prospect. Devers and Lodge foresaw the problem, flew up to a field near Lyon, and Lodge, issuing oral orders for Devers in French, directed the movement of de Lattre's forces between the spaces of various advancing American units. Armies usually move on written orders. "Whose orders were those we were following?" de Lattre asked Devers. "They were mine," said Devers, "but they were oral." Devers said afterward, "I couldn't have handled it as well if I had been able to speak French. I had the benefit of another man's mind which was well-equipped to do the job."

They tackled another problem, to keep the maquis from becoming undisciplined bands disrupting the rear. Nazi warehouses captured in Lyon bulged with German uniforms. Lodge asked de Lattre if he could get them dyed to outfit the maquis. They were dyed and trucked to Fréjus, where de Lattre's army issued both uniforms and officers to these units. They were thus brought under organized discipline and responsibility.

De Lattre moved his headquarters to Aix-en-Provence, which was more the location for an Army attacking to the North than one protecting the coastal flank. When Lodge called on him, de Lattre made no bones about his violent distaste for his assignment. He had come to fight, not to do guard duty. Lodge returned to Devers and discussed the whole situation. Devers decided to allow the French to move on north to Besançon and take positions to attack the historically strategic gap at Belfort, a trough between the Vosges Mountains and the Jura Alps that is the main passage into France from the Rhineland. Its forts had withstood a great siege by the Germans in the Franco-Prussian War and the area had tremendous sentimental associations for the French.

As November came on, the Seventh Army had hacked its way north through the Vosges, through St. Die, Rambervillers and Baccarat, crossed the Meuse and was poised to plunge through the Saverne Gap into the Alsace plain, where tanks would at last have open country to envelop Strassbourg and reach the Rhine. Devers drew up plans for a double-pronged offensive on November 13, when the Seventh would drive through Savern and the First French through the Belfort Gap. "We were well-prepared for all this." Devers recalled afterward, "but I could never get de Lattre to say he would jump off. All of a sudden, four days before jump-off time, I received word that Churchill and de Gaulle were going to visit de Lattre and would be there

the very day of the jump-off. I was certain their visit would slow things up.   *177*
I couldn't speak French, moreover I had to be with the Seventh in the North.
I told Lodge to go down and tell de Lattre to treat him as if I were right by
his side, giving the orders—and for Lodge to give them."

A terrible snowstorm was raging when Lodge set forth on his mission. At
de Lattre's headquarters, Churchill greeted Lodge warmly. "I remember
meeting you in Washington," he said. "And I have since noted your decision
to resign from the Senate for military service. This is a patriotic and un-
selfish act which you will never regret."

Lodge, Devers relates, "managed somehow to get both Churchill and de
Gaulle out of there and on the train by midnight before the jump-off day.
And he got de Lattre to agree to jump off at noon the following day, right
through the snowstorm. Lodge called me with the pre-arranged code word
that signified the jump-off, and when. They killed the German corps commander and captured his aide with all his papers. These clearly showed
that nobody was expecting an attack in that weather. De Lattre's forces took
Belfort and went right on to Mulhouse and hit the Swiss border. As far as
I'm concerned, Lodge was more than my liaison that day. He was acting
in my place."

Both prongs of the U.S.-French attack pierced both gaps. The Third Divi-
sion drove across the Alsace Plain, clearing the way for General Jacques Le
Clerc's French Second Armored Division to have the honor of liberating
Strassbourg as it had already liberated Paris. It did so, and swept on toward
Colmar.

Because of high water and heavy fighting, the French Army was unable
to close the gap at Colmar, which the Germans heavily reinforced. Some of
the heaviest and most savage fighting of the war raged in the Colmar
Pocket, which was not eliminated until weeks later. At this moment of great
crisis, de Lattre's biographer relates, Lodge recommended to Devers that he
give General de Lattre command of the new U.S. Corps which had been sent
in to crack the Colmar Pocket once and for all. He urged this on the grounds
that de Lattre was universally recognized as a competent professional who
would handle the American troops effectively, and, moreover, that giving
him their command would also give him the strongest possible incentive to
drive his own French troops as hard as possible. This would be advantageous
to the Americans, Lodge argued, because the French would make their own
maximum effort.

At the staff conference to discuss this project, there was strong opposition
on the part of all the senior American officers present. "They felt," wrote de
Lattre's biographer, "that Gen. Devers would never be able to explain to the
War Department at Washington how he had been able to agree to American
[troops] coming under a French general who belonged to an Army still

178   under the cloud of the defeat of 1940." The course of least resistance would have been to agree, but Devers had the imagination, vision and moral courage to do the bold thing. The whole XXI U.S. Corps was put under de Lattre. The results soon vindicated Devers.

During the battle of the Colmar Pocket, General Marshall came down to visit the front. William C. Bullitt, former ambassador to France who was a major on de Lattre's staff, registered violent complaints about the supply situation. "They were trying to get General Patch," Devers recalls. "They didn't get him. Lodge was just the right man to straighten out Bullitt. He handled Marshall's talks with de Lattre and kept the facts in order. That was just before we finally took Colmar—it fell on February 2, 1945."

Lodge, by now a lieutenant colonel, had his own small staff as head of the Sixth Army Group's Liaison Section. On it was Prince Aly Khan, a British major. "Shortly before the landing," General Devers recalled, "Jumbo Wilson called me in one morning and asked me if I would take Aly Khan. He said Aly owned half of the south of France and had a half-million dollars' worth of horses the Germans stole over there, and would be invaluable for collecting intelligence in the south of France. He spoke seven languages. I knew he was a prince, and was also supposed to have a lot of surplus energy. I told Wilson I'd take him. I thought his knowledge would be valuable, and that Lodge could help burn off the energy. He proved to be an exceptionally fine soldier. He was thoroughly reliable and carried out his instructions with enthusiasm and imagination."

When de Lattre was at Aix-en-Provence, Lodge found his old friend and neighbor Chandler Bigelow doing what he could to help the war as a captain in the service command of the Twelfth Tactical Air Force. "Cabot had been trying to get a couple of people detached, and been turned down," Bigelow recalled. "He decided he'd try to get me. 'We might as well have some fun,' he said. One day my commanding officer sent me up. I joined Cabot and Aly at Vittel in November, 1943. Most of the headquarters people lived in the hotel. Cabot, Aly and I lived in a little house and took our meals there—had a very nice Swiss cook. I was in charge of the office. We only had two GIs, Sergeant Bok who was a good typist and orderly, and Seloviev, a chap from New York who was a real linguist and well-versed in modern art. Whenever we captured new towns, Devers had to entertain the mayors, and he always had Cabot and Aly to help him. Devers' colored orderly, John Turnipseed, would pass out the whiskey. Aly was very good with these dignitaries. He was a good soldier, too. It was the first time anybody had ever treated him as just one of the boys."

"Cabot," says Bigelow, "always liked to get up close where the firing was. I was scared to death once or twice when he took off to look at some of these places." Others also noticed this. General Edward R. Brooks, who succeeded

General Lucian Truscott as commander of VI Corps, recalled, "I remember **179** having to tell Lodge to get down. We were under German observation and he's such a tall fellow I was afraid he would draw fire. I asked him, 'What are you trying to do, get killed or just wounded?' He laughed and said, 'I don't suppose it makes any difference.' " Lieutenant William Hershey, who was Brooks' aide, recalled Lodge going out to visit numerous foxhole outposts under shellfire. "I asked him, 'Are you trying to get hit?' He grinned and said, 'I'll admit it would be a political asset.' "

When General Eisenhower came to the Sixth Army Group's front during his tour of the whole line in late October, 1944, it was Lodge's task to brief him on all the dispositions of the French forces, to go over the maps with him, Devers and de Lattre, and interpret among the Commanders.

Lodge had one curious brush with death which he did not know about. After the war, Lieutenant Colonel J. C. Lambert of the Adjutant General's School related the story.

Lambert was with a combat unit near Obermodern, Alsace, whose outpost line pivoted on a shoe factory which was used as an O.P. (observation post), and was under enemy fire. This factory was well stocked with new shoes when the Germans withdrew, and weary American soldiers had been helping themselves. "Looting!" the Free French complained.

American rear echelons sent up an inspector, in spotless trenchcoat. "Those clean-shaved, clean-clothed officers from the brass end were interlopers who never took a chance and were held in the highest contempt," says Lambert. "This one awakened men who had just come off outpost duty to question them. Within an hour the whole outpost line knew the story. The men in the foxholes were enraged; this inspector was not only accusing them of being thieves but preventing them from sleeping. What to do?" They figured he would have to inspect the factory, and cross the seventy-five yards of open space across their own—and the enemy's—line of fire. If he got hit, nobody would ever know by whom.

The inspector (Colonel Lambert related) apparently had a second thought because he decided to accept a pair of bedroom slippers and close the investigation without going forward of the command post. This was negative information and naturally did not filter through the funnel as rapidly as positive information. By coincidence, Lodge had just arrived at the command post on a liaison visit and was about to dart across the open space, between shellbursts, with the company commander, to visit the O.P. "The outpost men spotted his trenchcoat and trained their rifles on his tall figure. A squad leader used his field glasses. That could not be an inspector—his coat was almost as dirty as the company commander's. There was only a second to divert the rifles—he pushed the plunger on a series of defensive mines. There was a series of explosions along the reverse slope

180   of the ridge as Lodge leaped across the open space. The outpost line dropped back in their holes."

Devers had great praise for Lodge's work in Stuttgart, after that German city fell, as solving a situation of great potential trouble. The city was taken simultaneously by General Gullaume's Second Algerian *goums*, from the west, and a relatively new U.S. division, the 100th, from the north. The whole city was in disorder, with hundreds of liberated slave workers roving the streets. The *goums* were notorious for sacking captured cities.

An American correspondent who had once lived in Stuttgart came to Devers with stories that the *goums* had driven four thousand Stuttgart women into a tunnel and were raping them *en masse*. "Lodge and I flew in at daybreak," Devers recalls, "and I told him to run this thing down. The 100th Division, who really belonged in the town according to the boundaries we had drawn, were worked up over the atrocity stories that the Germans were spreading. Lodge came back and reported that there had been some rapings but the story was largely false. I needed Stuttgart for logistic support, but de Gaulle announced publicly to the world that the French would never evacuate Stuttgart."

Lodge found de Lattre, in bed ill at Karlsruhe, and in ten minutes time they worked out together an arrangement whereby the French flag would fly over city hall, but the Americans would use all the roads, warehouses, factories and other installations necessary for their logistics. The 100th Division was simply moved across the river. "Lodge wrote a report on this whole affair that saved me a lot of recrimination," Devers recalled. "Senator Eastland came through right after, under the impression that Negro troops had been raping white women. I had Lodge's report, with all the facts, to set this thing at rest. Lodge has tremendous ability, excellent judgment, a very high standard of integrity. He risked his life innumerable times, I don't know why he didn't get killed. He was always at the front. He rode thousands of miles through those mountains of the Vosges, ice everywhere, slipping and sliding, I can't say enough about his courage."

At last came the time, when the Third Division had raced all the way to Salzburg, and the 101st Airborne had taken Hitler's aerie at Berchtesgaden itself, that a whole German Army Group, G, more than 200,000 men, surrendered on May 5 just east of Munich. Devers took Lodge with him to accept the surrender. The German-speaking Lodge helped interpret as the German commander stepped forward in an old stone building at Haar.

Lodge noticed that the German text of the surrender document which had been sent down from higher U.S. headquarters used the words "conditions of surrender." Roosevelt; of course, had demanded "unconditional" surrender. Lodge had the word changed to "specifications"—*Bedingungen*

—rather than "conditions." Lodge later wrote an account of the surrender   *181* for the Army's records.

At noon General Foertsch, commanding the 1st German Army and holding powers from Field Marshal Kesselring to surrender all of Army Group "G," mounted the few polished black marble steps and stood in the open door. He wore the polished black boots and light field gray uniform of the German Army. Around his neck was the Iron Cross. On his shoulders were the gold braid knots, edged in red, indicating his rank. On his collar were red tabs, carrying the gold embroidery which showed that he was a general officer. He was tall, black haired, with a slight stoop, and in the prime of middle life. His eyes were brown; his expression was solemn. For a moment he stood in the doorway. With his heels together he bowed slightly and then advanced towards his seat. We all sat still and looked at him.

He was followed by the officers of his party, similarly dressed, although with less ornamentation. Of the five officers who sat at the table, four appeared to be under 35 years of age. There were among them officers with a ready command of English. Brig. General Mencher, Chief of Staff XV Corps, who had made the arrangements for the entire meeting, presented General Foertsch to General Devers and General Foertsch in turn presented his officers, each of whom stood and bowed when his name was called.

General Foertsch began to speak, taking up the paragraphs of the surrender document one by one. He spoke in a clear deep voice, very slowly and distinctly, so that every word could be understood by anyone having even a smattering of German. He never argued. He knew, of course, that he was beaten. He would often begin his statements with the sentence: I deem it my duty to point out . . . and then would show, for example, that the German troops were so scattered that it would take more than the contemplated number of hours to get the news to them. Or else, coming to the dumps of German weapons which were to be established, he asked that they be guarded by armed men, lest disorderly elements in the country steal the weapons and thereby threaten law and order. He hoped that officers and military police could keep sidearms in order to maintain tranquility. His suggestions were all of that type. He stressed the number of refugees and the lack of food in his area.

General Devers would respond, asking questions and giving his views. After brief discussions, each point in turn was taken up. Boundaries were settled, the time schedule was established. General Devers

*was insistent that there be no misunderstanding on the big points—
there was to be no "armistice"—this was unconditional surrender. Do
you understand that? he asked. General Foertsch flushed a little,
looked down for a moment and said: "I understand it. I have no choice.
I have no power to do otherwise."*

*At 2:30 the meeting ended. Americans went to IV Corps headquar-
ters. General Jenkins and I stayed behind to work on the final draft of
the surrender text. At 3:30 we went to IVth Corps headquarters with
the finished text. A few minutes later General Foertsch arrived in his
long overcoat, lined with red. He mounted the stairs of the little doctor's house and signed the document which stopped bloodshed for
hundreds of thousands of men and was followed soon thereafter by the
capitulation of German armies on all European fronts and the end of
the European war.*

Lodge stayed on with the occupying forces for some weeks after the war
ended. He was laden with well-earned honors. General Devers awarded him
the Legion of Merit. General de Lattre, who had pinned the Croix de Guerre
with palm on Lodge after the capture of Belfort, now presented him a scroll,
signed by General de Gaulle, awarding him the Ordre National of the Legion d'Honneur. On June 15, de Lattre paid his respects to his American
allies in a colorful festival at Constance, Germany, on Lake Constance. It
lasted from five P.M. until five the next morning.

It began with a gymkhana by a regiment of fierce Moroccan and Algerian
Spahis. One brilliantly clad troop after another swooped down over the
huge field, performing jumps and acrobatics. From the riding field to the
Inset Hotel, some five miles, the American guests passed along a road lined
solid on each side by cavalry and infantry at present arms. One of the
guests, Major William Galvin, described the event afterward for the Kansas
City *Star*. "We were greeted at the Inset Hotel by waiters bearing whiskey,
wines, brandies, champagne, liquors and pastries. . . . The guests [then]
assembled on a boat in Constance Harbor. It was to carry us to the east end
of the lake to Lindau, 25 miles away. To get to the boat we walked along
the beach several hundred yards on a flower-strewn carpet . . . lined with
immobile guards at present arms. At the dock near the gangplank were
assembled a French military band and an American fife and drum corps
which played each its own national anthem on the arrival of Gen. de Lattre
and General Devers who arrived last and boarded the boat first. Standing
motionless and immense at the boat end of the gangplank were two Senegalese from the personal bodyguard of Gen. de Lattre. These two frozen-faced
blacks, resplendent in their brilliant uniforms capped with red fezzes, tow-
ered over the tallest in our party.

Chapter Ten

"Somewhere along the north shore a beam from a powerful search light stabbed perpendicularly through the night sky. Slowly it was brought to a horizontal position in such a way as to spotlight a lovely medieval castle on the north shore. The first light was followed by others on both shores. The lake was ringed by columns of lights. . . . When the lights were done and turned off we could distinguish, in the direction of Lindau, a glow as of a huge fire. As we drew closer we could see that all of Lindau Harbor was outlined in the flickering lights of hundreds of torches each held aloft by a Senegalese."

Waiting cars drove them to de Lattre's villa west of Lindau on the lake shore. "Here, instead of soldiers at present arms, on each side of the road and at intervals of about 15 ft. from each other there were Senegalese, Moroccans, Algerians and French soldiers each holding aloft a flaming torch." At midnight they were guided by torch to a festive Moroccan encampment. "Visible in the fire-lit woods to the right of the road were hundreds of Goumiers, mountain warriors from Morocco, some engaged in their old tribal dances, others turning a whole sheep on spits over a huge fire pit. In one of their tents, beautifully carpeted, sat a ring of camp followers (sanctioned by the Army) brownskinned girls dressed in simple flowing skirts and blouses. Included in their circle were a half-dozen musicians with skin drums, crude violins and other instruments." As the tempo increased, one of the camp followers moved on her bare feet to the center of the ring and began a belly dance. "Then several of her companions arose and with great dignity served heavily sugared tea to all of us assembled there." At two in the morning the guests adjourned to a sumptuous feast in de Lattre's garden. A chorus of Ukrainian DP's liberated from the Nazis sang their ancient melodies, dancing their spirited gopaks. De Lattre rose to pay tribute to Devers, Lodge translating into English, and Devers rose to respond, Lodge translating to French. The small orchestra in the garden was echoed by another, on a huge raft offshore, "twinkling with subdued light, playing back, bar by bar, the music from the shore." So the feast went until the dawn.

Lodge came back from the war—he was mustered out at the end of 1945 —quite changed in his views of America and the world. Even as late as his global tour for the Military Affairs Committee in 1943, his view reflected considerable chauvinism, as well as suspicion that America would always be shortchanged in any international collective venture. Now he was as firmly convinced that collective action by the victorious alliance was essential to peace. In February, 1946, he made his first postwar speech, as an unemployed civilian, before the Minneapolis Foreign Policy Association, in the heart of the onetime isolationist belt. "The ideal of a provincial nation of simple, humble people, far from the beaten track, has given way to a realization that we have become the world's greatest power," he said soberly. "Even if we elected to do nothing whatever we would be inextricably involved in everything that takes place in the world. . . . The United Nations Organization is our best hope [and deserves] the best that is in us of intelligence, forbearance, farsightedness and faith. . . . We must give it things to do so that its muscles will grow strong by experience. Our relations with Russia at present overshadow all international relations. . . . We have each done much to insult, antagonize and thwart the other. In the past few months the loose talk has grown to proportions which seem to me dangerous. We must have an efficient working arrangement with Russia . . . this involves not only our diplomats, it imposes an obligation on all of us to think clearly and fairly and to speak with firmness and restraint. . . . We not only want a strong America—we want a kind and generous one." He was already foreseeing the need for the reconstruction which the Marshall Plan would soon bring. "Common humanity demands that we help. The question of economic loans should be decided on a broad and far-sighted basis. . . . Let the terms correspond with the facts and the probabilities. Such loans, even though they may appear to some to be unusually liberal, can in the end be helpful not only to the country which received them but to the U.S. as well."

On domestic issues, Lodge was even more opposed than before to a negative, reactionary nay-saying approach by the Republican party. He studied a document prepared by one Republican leader which saw the issues drawn between a New Deal becoming dominated by crooked labor leaders and a Republican party providing a last redoubt to save the freedom of the individual, ignoring the need for a positive approach to social issues. "I neither hope nor believe that the issue is, or ever will be, drawn as he has drawn it," Lodge wrote to Henry R. Luce. "I do not see our future in terms of a choice between an undynamic preservation of individual rights on the one hand and government by labor racketeers on the other. I certainly think that liberal Republicanism can be equally articulate." Shortly afterward he made a speech to Republicans in Oregon to which Arthur Krock devoted his column in the New York *Times,* telling them "the other party should be given credit for having a public program which contains many good intentions. It has proclaimed certain broad goals which conform to age-old human aspirations. But there is the widest kind of difference between favoring social legislation as a supplement to your economy [and] government action as your chief source of jobs. . . . Large-scale production is the quickest way to spread lots of good jobs throughout the land . . . a much better way than by government-made work programs—although we would not hesitate to use the power of government to combat depression if one should ever come again. . . . As Republicans we must always remember that we exist to promote the aspirations of the rank and file of the people. We do not exist to cater to the ambitions of any minority or vested interest no matter how powerful it may appear to be. . . . I know many Republicans who think our choice is between trying to outdeal the New Deal on the one hand or standing for what they call 'the fundamental rights of the individual' on the other. If we are restricted to these alternatives I fear for the Republican Party—for the Democratic party—and for the U.S."

If all this sounded like a man who was about to run for the Senate again, it was indeed. The seventy-three year-old David Walsh's term would expire at the end of 1946 and his seat was a vulnerable target for a young Republican fresh from a brilliant war career. In April, Lodge announced his candidacy, expressing regret that he would have to gun for an old friend. The first Senator Lodge had welcomed Democrat Walsh to the Senate in 1918, Walsh had won the right, in 1926, to serve out Lodge's unexpired term, and had himself welcomed the second Senator Lodge to the Senate ten years later. Walsh had always drawn many Republican votes, just as both Lodges drew many Democratic ones. "It is hard to be in a competitive situation with the present Senior Senator," Lodge said, "but public service is often difficult and the duties imposed by our two-party system must prevail over personal feeling." It would be a campaign without acrimony. Lodge would not once attack his opponent, but hammer at the Administration itself as a bunch of "old wheelhorses who are over their heads . . . dreadfully tired and in need of a long vacation." Furthermore, he had come home to a situation made to order for a skilled infighter. The most momentous issue around was simply the fact that people did not have enough meat. The Administration's misguided effort to preserve price control had driven all meat into black market channels, and even new shirts were hard to find.

"I did not expect on coming home from Germany," Lodge told Newburyport World War II veterans, "to see American women standing in line to buy essentials. There is no meat available even though there is more cattle on the hoof than ever before." At the State Republican Convention he said, "In a land which is richly endowed by nature with more than is needed to give all a good life, our government had adopted such a complication of so-called remedies that it has worked us into a critical state of poverty." Senator Saltonstall, who had succeeded to Lodge's old seat, said: "Bureaucracy has indeed been built up to a fine art. No sugar. No meat. No shoes. No shirts. Is that the Democratic idea of a high standard of living?"

The Providence *Journal* saw the battle as of national importance: "If Lodge can defeat the most consistently potent vote-getter in the history of Massachusetts then Republican leaders seeking Presidential timber for 1948 or later can hardly afford to overlook him. . . . Lodge is gambling his

186   immediate political future in challenging the veteran of nearly 50 years in public life. If Lodge wins he gains inestimable prestige as a giant-killing vote puller, and a spot in the national limelight. If he loses he faces at least temporary political oblivion."

Lodge won, 982,613 to Walsh's 653,260. The defeated old warrior said, "In such an overturn, no man may justly harbor a feeling that his own record has been repudiated." Lodge, equally gallant, said: "I recognize and pay tribute to the faithful service which has been rendered by Senator Walsh. The people of Massachusetts will long remember all that he did for our State and nation and the spirit of tolerance and justice in which he acted."

Back to Washington in January, 1947, went the new junior senator from Massachusetts—junior now to Leverett Saltonstall, who had succeeded to Lodge's seat when he resigned. Though Lodge was only forty-four, had it not been for his war hiatus he would now be, next to Vandenberg, the senior of all Republican Senators, including Taft, who had succeeded the late Charles McNary as Republican floor leader. The retiring Secretary of War Patterson, whose letter of thanks to Lodge begins this chapter, concluded it: "A tribute from you . . . is the highest tribute I could get and I am leaving my work with the thought that with a man like you in the Senate, who understands the problem of the national defense so thoroughly, the safety of the country will never be neglected."

That problem was no longer merely one of planes, guns and navies. National defense was now inextricably involved with a whole new revolutionary age—the jet age of supersonic flight, of guided missiles, of thermonuclear power, of interdependent economies and emergent nations struggling to enter the good life. Lodge would soon cross swords with Taft and his followers over what sort of Republican leadership this new age called for— whether to rise to the world leadership which America could not escape "even if we elected to do nothing whatever," or try to shrink the new colossus back into isolationism. Lodge would fight, year after year, for the first, lose many a battle but win the war in a splendid and dazzling victory. Yet, ironically, in defeating the Old Guard forces he would also—for the time at least—defeat himself.

CHAPTER ELEVEN

We were not put in office in order to turn the clock back. We were, in my judgment, sent there in order to wind it up, get the crumbs and rats' nests out of the gears and get it going again. In Lincoln's words, "We must think anew and act anew."

Lodge brought this Lincoln's Day message to Louisville in 1947. He feared his fellow Republicans might misread the meaning of the previous fall's election, which—besides electing Lodge and reelecting his old friend Arthur Vandenberg—gave the Republicans control of Congress for the first time in fifteen years. "We Republicans are on probation," he warned in Louisville. "Many people did not vote *for* us so much as . . . *against* the things they did not like."

Lodge warned that the voters were not "for reaction but for positive action based on the aims and aspirations of the people." Feeling that his own smashing victory gave him some right to propose such a positive program, he advocated 1) a continuation of a bipartisan approach to foreign policy and national defense, 2) the rooting out of waste and corruption from government and 3) public health, social security and scientific research measures to meet situations not adequately reached by the private-property economy. The man who had so familiarized himself with the problems of New England labor proposed a labor policy which would reflect "no hate-filled action" but "only honest treatment of labor and management for the good of all the people of whom labor and management are a part."

Lodge's speech made a deep impression around the country. Scripps-Howard's thoughtful columnist, Thomas L. Stokes, devoted his column to it, terming it "one of the most timely observations of the day." In distant Alabama the Montgomery *Advertiser* thought young Senator Lodge ". . . seems most nearly to have caught a vision of the real Lincoln who spoke and thought in terms of the common man—a language lost these last fifty or more years by the Republican Party."

Nor was Lodge merely "against sin" in attacking government waste and duplication. He thought he knew how to find it and how to root it out; any good reporter could. He stalked out of a confused Senate budget hearing that February, 1947, saying, "I think we could cut out ten or eleven billions . . . if we knew what we were doing." Without knowing, they were "like a man wielding a meat-axe in a dark room who might cut off his own head." He began doing the reporting, soon was citing flagrant examples of government ignorance of its own sprawling activities. The Postmaster General, for example, after submitting his annual report, discovered he had forgotten to list fifty-five thousand "lost" employees. The American Battles Monument Commission, often praised by Virginia's Harry Byrd because it had only "one" employee, discovered it had thirty-eight others who were traveling outside the country. As to duplication, Lodge cited twenty-nine agencies engaged in lending government funds, thirty-four others engaged in buying land, twelve in home and community planning, ten in forestry. Did this make sense? He thought not.

Lodge set to work to prepare a bill to attack this waste. He had a helpful ally in another veteran newspaperman, Representative Clarence Brown of Ohio. Together they produced the Lodge-Brown Bill calling for a bipartisan commission with six members from each party. It became law in July, and Speaker Joseph Martin sought and got the appointment of former President Hoover to head the commission. Over the subsequent years the Hoover Commission's special task forces recommended innumerable reforms in government procedure which saved untold billions—and would have saved far more had all their recommendations been scrupulously followed.

Lodge's reappearance in the Senate had raised some problems of seniority. Save for his war service, he would be senior to Ohio's Robert A. Taft, who had become the Number One Republican leader in the Senate. At the first Republican caucus, New Hampshire's righteous old Charles Tobey mentioned this fact, and formally moved to restore Lodge's seniority. A dead silence fell. If Tobey's motion carried, Lodge would outrank Taft, and would displace Taft's strong supporter Eugene Millikin as chairman of the powerful Finance Committee. Amid the silence, Lodge himself rose to say the action would not be fair: "I was only doing my duty, like millions of others. I therefore would be grateful if the Senator would withdraw his resolution." Tobey did so, to applause. Taft, as a gesture to Lodge, got him put on the powerful Foreign Relations Committee, whose new chairman was Michigan's Vandenberg.

This was a fateful move, because Lodge and Vandenberg, both newspapermen, both fact-minded and contemptuous of narrowly partisan actions, had long thought alike and worked closely together. Moreover, "Van" completely shared Lodge's views, as expressed that Lincoln Day, that the party had to liberalize and modernize itself to survive. In the months ahead, Van would apply this philosophy to shaping a Republican foreign policy in keeping with the need "to think anew and act anew." Throughout this battle Lodge would be his right arm, his eyes and ears, and—since Van, in the absence of an elected Vice President, had to sit in the Senate chair as President Pro Tem—as his chief strategist and captain on the floor of the Senate itself. These were to be historic days.

The first signs of what later would be known as McCarthyism were just making their appearance in the party. President Truman's nomination of David E. Lilienthal as chairman of the Atomic Energy Commission was seized upon by Wisconsin's Joseph McCarthy, by Indiana's William Jenner, as well as by Taft, to suggest some intrusion by Communist agents.

They regarded Lilienthal as fair game because he had already headed the Tennessee Valley Authority, long the favorite target of Republicans as the spearhead of "creeping socialism." He had shown himself, charged Taft, "soft on issues connected with Russia and Communism," and his confirmation would be "a real threat to national safety."

Dr. Karl T. Compton, president of Massachusetts Institute of Technology, wrote President Pro Tem Vandenberg that he was "disillusioned and disgusted" with the way Lilienthal's nomination was being handled. Compton warned that atomic scientists were already scarce; if they "become disillusioned or gain the impression that political or special interests are getting control of the program, I believe it will collapse into a rather hollow shell."

Lilienthal himself made such an eloquent statement to the Senate committee of his own beliefs in democratic freedom ("This I Believe") that it became an American classic.

Lodge, always the fact finder, had made a thorough investigation of Lilienthal's whole career. He made public a letter to President Truman: "I have come to the conclusion that accusations made against his character and patriotism are without proof and without foundation." Moreover, it seemed to Lodge that Lilienthal's experience at running the huge TVA made him singularly qualified to manage the even larger, more complex AEC: "I have also discovered that he is the only man in the U.S. who has ever administered a project anywhere near as large and as complex as that which he will be required to administer as chairman of the AEC."

Lodge and Taft now often found themselves at odds on other matters. One was the proper Republican approach to labor legislation. Lodge, as he had stated at Louisville, thought it should be nonpolitical, and simply in the national interest.

Lodge joined Vermont's Aiken, New York's Ives and Oregon's Morse (who was then still a Republican) and a coalition of four Democrats on the Education and Labor Committee to keep the writing of the labor bill out of Taft's hands. Taft, Joseph Alsop reported, was seeking a catchall bill which would provoke Truman's veto, giving Republicans a 1948 presidential campaign issue "for the failure to pass labor legislation at this session."

"Ives, Morse and Lodge," wrote Alsop, "strongly disputed the remarkable thesis that the aim should be not to pass the best labor bill possible but simply to put the President in a hole. Lodge especially [warned] against the poisons that could be generated by a political approach to the labor issue. One might have supposed that Senator Lodge's views would have carried some weight. He and Senator Saltonstall together rebuilt Massachusetts Republicanism from its ruins; he got the largest percentage vote in the last election scored by any candidate except Vandenberg, and he is one of the soundest practical politicians in the Senate. But Senator Jenner rather condescendingly reminded him that 'this was politics,' implying that Lodge knew little of this manly pursuit, and that the national approach was for visionaries and mollycoddles."

The same clashes arose over Taft's and John Bricker's determination to kill rent control. If the landlords were not taken care of, Bricker had said, "It would not be the kind of Republican Party I am used to." This provoked another comment by Alsop: "Unfortunately, the kind of Republican Party the Ohio Senator has been used to may not be the kind of Republican Party that can carry a national election."

The polls seemed to be indicating this was true, and affirming Lodge's warning at Louisville. In March, 1947, a Gallup Poll showed the Party had fallen 6 per cent in its popularity, and was again in second place. Vermont's craggy old Aiken blamed this drop on "irresponsible policy pronunciations" by G.O.P. leaders.

Lodge, meanwhile, was giving much of his thought to the challenges posed, for a responsible foreign policy, by the devastation and political chaos left after victory in Europe. At Boston's Clover Club, on the eve of St. Patrick's Day, he gave his views.

Many of the former great nations of Europe, he said, had ceased to be world powers, "and may not be able to stand up to Communist doctrines without outside help. That there will be demands on our generosity is almost a foregone conclusion."

Lodge believed the U.S. should respond to these demands by programs of loans, economic aid, "in the name of religion and humanitarianism" and because Americans, "the descendants of immigrants who sought to escape the curse of Europe, are a generous people." The aim should be to stimulate the recovery of these nations, "and not to remain prostrate in the belief that we will go on forever feeding them a minimum ration."

Then Lodge added a warning, which could well apply to Republican inaction and indecision in many other matters:

"One thing we cannot do is to avoid a decision, for refusing to make a decision in an affair of this kind is itself a decision."

Shortly thereafter he put himself behind President Truman's proposed aid to Greece and Turkey to help them resist Communist aggression. He introduced two restrictive amendments reflecting typical Yankee prudence: they could not use the money to pay the principal or interest on any loan from another foreign government, and they must begin realistic tax programs to finance their own national reconstruction from those most able to pay—lest "the poor of America . . . be made to support the rich overseas."

Lodge also was concerning himself with other long-needed domestic reforms. Americans had been complaining about the Electoral College from the beginning of the republic. Lodge pointed out that it was possible for a man to be elected President without receiving a majority *or* a plurality of the popular vote. Furthermore, he pointed out that on a popular-vote basis, Dewey, in 1944 would have won 245 electoral votes against Roosevelt's 286, a respectably close contest. Instead, the existing system gave Roosevelt 432 to 90 electoral votes, an apparent landslide.

Lodge introduced a bill to replace the Electoral College with the direct election of the President and Vice President. It passed the Senate with the requisite two-thirds majority—itself an event without precedent in previous attempts at electoral reform—but it failed to get the necessary two-thirds in the House. Almost twenty years later, this same measure was still being strongly advocated and debated.

Lodge, with his Boston ally Saltonstall, was more successful in other reforms. They worked together pushing two progressive measures, Saltonstall to create the National Science Foundation to finance independent research in medicine, biology and engineering, and Lodge to amend the Public Health Service Act to help states provide drugs, medicines and medical services to the needy.

As the debate on Greek and Turkish aid began, Lodge shrewdly saw that this aid could become the lever to prod Europe, not only to rebuild itself, but to federate itself in growing economic union. In a full-dress speech, he demanded that the whole problem of European reconstruction be approached as an integrated whole, with the realism, planning and leadership—"the clear national policy"—which he had urged in conducting the war. Its absence had let true victory elude us in this war:

In the large sense we have defeated the enemy, but we have not won the peace. We have killed off the German threat, and the Japanese threat to our existence as a people, but we have not achieved any of our positive aims. . . . Poland has not been liberated, democracy has not been established, autocracy has not been destroyed. . . . How is it that we can win the battle and lose the peace? . . .

We were utterly, completely and abysmally unprepared for the end of the war. . . . Our leaders did not tell us that it was absolutely es-

sential to the national well-being that the U.S. maintain armed forces after the end of the hostilities. . . . And so the people of the world beheld this sickening and astounding spectacle: the greatest military power the world had ever had, within a few short months, defeated itself by allowing its huge strength to dwindle away. The armies and navies which the best troops of Germany and the finest fleets of Japan had not been able to defeat were going to pieces because of the lack of comprehension and the lack of leadership at the head of the government.

Lodge then laid down four essentials, as he saw it, if similar mistakes were to be avoided in the future, the essentials necessary to develop a coherent, long-range program to "win the peace." He stressed again the need for a plan, whereby in exchange for our loans and aid, the nations aided would make themselves self-supporting, then go beyond that to "integrate themselves into an economic arrangement which has the possibility of life and growth," not merely "reconstruct the same old European crazy-quilt." In return, the Yankee trader wanted "the raw materials which we need and do not possess . . . a foreign-aid program which will also aid the American people."

To carry out this program, Lodge argued, would require a far abler, bolder, better trained Foreign Service. He returned to the arguments he had made long ago with Corliss Lamont, and more recently on his global inspection of the war—that the U.S. was being repeatedly outwitted and outmaneuvered by other nations because it did not train, dispatch and trust enough men of the caliber and intelligence necessary to exercise true world leadership. Either it staffed embassies with political hacks, or harassed true professionals as cookie pushers in striped pants.

"Even the best of them," said Lodge of the existing Foreign Service, "give the impression that in diplomacy it is more important to avoid a blunder than to achieve a success. We are in an era now in which we must be somewhat venturesome if we are to avoid disaster. Only the bold ever rise above mediocrity. We need an infusion of new blood or of new spirit or of both into our representation abroad."

We could no longer afford the political hacks. "It would be dangerous and reprehensible to select men to head our missions abroad on any basis other than that of fitness to do the job."

Having precipitated disaster by premature disarmament, he said, we must become and remain strong. We must counter the "materialistic and brutal verbiage of Communism with the Christian concept of the dignity of man . . . the strongest revolutionary force in the world. . . . It is the essential first step that we believe in ourselves." All these together would

produce "a strong America—strong in its economic life, strong in its enthusiastic faith in its own institutions, and strong in its armed forces on
land, sea and air, without which no foreign policy can be aught but mere
words."

As Lodge ended, the galleries broke into applause.

In June, 1947, Secretary of State Marshall elaborated at Harvard the
argument, which Lodge also had delineated, that Europe must organize to
help itself: "There must be some agreement among the countries of Europe as to the requirements of the situation and the part those countries
themselves will take. . . . The initiative must come from Europe."

His challenge provoked European moves toward economic unity and
produced what become the Marshall Plan. Both France and Italy seemed
on the verge of civil war; all Europe was haunted by the specter of hunger,
unemployment and economic stagnation; Communist strength was everywhere on the rise.

Both Vandenberg and Lodge supported Marshall's aims. Marshall, for
his part, had always trusted and admired Lodge. These men talked frequently. At the end of 1947 Congress was ready to provide $587 million
of interim aid for Europe. But Vandenberg, prompted by Lodge, wisely
believed that any larger program should be based on a careful setting of
the stage, through exhaustive fact-finding and exploration of all arguments
pro and con. Vandenberg and Lodge sought the same sort of nonpartisan
fact-finding that the Hoover Commission had undertaken. President Truman, on June 22, 1947, appointed three such committees to determine
what Vandenberg had specified, to wit, how much America could "safely
and wisely undertake, on what basis, with what reciprocal benefits," plus
a total balance sheet appraisal of the needs.

As part of the same prodding, similar action was begun in Europe,
whose sixteen nations met throughout the summer of 1947. They organized the Committee of European Economic Cooperation to map the first
steps toward removing trade barriers with each other, toward economic
cooperation with each other, and joint planning of specific goals for industry and agriculture. The first seeds of a United Europe began to sprout.

The hearings steered by Vandenberg and Lodge determined that these
targets could be achieved through four and a half years of self-determina-
tion at a cost of some $29 billion. By careful screening, the cost was pared
to a bare-bones $17 billion. Vandenberg and Lodge prodded forth invento-
ries, appraisals and stock-takings which overloaded a five-foot bookshelf in
the Foreign Relations Committee rooms.

From January 8 to February 5, more than ninety witnesses were called in
the most comprehensive public hearing on a foreign policy question ever undertaken. By patiently hearing every possible opponent, and seeing that

194   every intelligent argument got an intelligent reply, Vandenberg and Lodge did the Administration an incalculable service in smoothing the way for later passage. Lodge, ever a master of the art of the politically possible, showed Administration leaders the different ways of skinning the same cat. When the Administration sought the full $17 billion, Lodge and Vandenberg persuaded them to seek only a general authorization, with amounts to be determined each year—a program easier to get through the Taftites. When the Administration sought an initial $6.8 billion for the first fifteen months, the strategists persuaded them to settle for $5.3 billion for twelve months—an identical ratio, but a figure more palatable to tight-pursed senators. In each case, they worked to narrow down the possible targets for opposition. They sought, not the ideal, but the attainable.

They saw to it that the prudent, Yankeelike sections dealing with Europe's obligations to help itself were strengthened. The State Department assumed that it would control the European Recovery Program. The strategists thought a special, ad hoc body under a nonpartisan leader of impeccable prestige would be less subject to sharpshooting from the Neanderthal wing of the G.O.P. The committee consulted the Brookings Institution, whose proposal for an Economic Cooperation Administration, to be headed by an administrator of Cabinet rank, under final Presidential control, proved acceptable to all. By the time the committee voted on February 13, Vandenberg and Lodge had either anticipated or accommodated all objections so adeptly that the vote was unanimous—13 to 0. In fact, during the whole two years Vandenberg was chairman, and Lodge his chief strategist, every single vote in the committee—some 49 in all—was 13 to 0, reflecting their ability to reconcile differing viewpoints and reach a common ground on which all could stand. Lodge always gave the credit for this entirely to Vandenberg—"truly a noble thing and the mark of a real statesman. I always tried to remember and emulate his method."

Lodge ran the floor fight for the Marshall Plan as the Senate spent two weeks debating it, speaking a total of 335 times in its behalf. Since there was no Vice President, Vandenberg usually had to be in the President's chair. He could not handle the floor strategy. But Van was often engaged in cloakroom negotiation of important amendments to win more support for the bill.

Since Lodge had to parry the attacks, he was the chief target of the opponents. They were led by Kenneth Wherry, the so-called Republican floor leader who in fact savagely fought all positive party policies. Wherry questioned making a general authorization for the four-and-a-half-year period. Nebraska, he pointed out, did not do so in building its state capitol. Lodge called his attention to the fact that Czechoslovakia had just been scooped behind the Iron Curtain, and that such clear dangers might justify a departure from Nebraskan precedents: "We are meeting in the shadow of a world emergency." Wherry was not impressed.

MR. WHERRY: I am not a member of the Foreign Relations Committee.
MR. LODGE: But the Senator can read the newspapers . . .
MR. WHERRY: Does the Senator believe everything he reads . . . ?

Senator Fulbright confused the issue of economic aid by seeking inclusion of an amendment calling on Europe to form a political union, as well as economic cooperation. Lodge argued strenuously that such language would serve more to delay, rather than advance, political union. As the elder Lodge had once said of Bryan, Fulbright seemed to think that words could serve as deeds.

MR. FULBRIGHT: It seems to me that the simple amendment will assist in bringing to fruition . . . a strong, united and free Europe.
MR. LODGE: If the most that we could achieve would be simply to reconstruct the European crazy quilt, simply to rebuild the watertight compartments of Europe, which cannot support life, but which have created death twice within our lifetime, I would be tremendously depressed. . . . I believe that if we include his language it will tend to defeat our purpose; but I heartily agree with him that the purpose which he so eloquently describes is the one toward which the Marshall Plan should move.

Senator Kem of Missouri wanted to hamstring the Administrator, with a flat prohibition of aid to any European nation which traded with Russia. Lodge urged that this be discretionary with the Administrator.

MR. LODGE: I think we are getting a very simple thing confused. It is obvious that we shall never get Western Europe on its feet and off our backs unless it receives from Eastern Europe some of the things it needs. If we can develop trade with Eastern Europe, if we can wean a part of it away from Communism and enlarge the borders of the non-Communist world, that is one proposition. . . . The second proposition is that we must not sell a nickel's worth of anything behind the Iron Curtain if it would strengthen and help Communism. As I understand the bill, the Administrator, in view of Russia's present frame of mind, would interpret the provisions to prevent France trading with Russia. But if conditions should change and it should appear that trade between France and Russia could be carried on in such a way which would be advantageous to the purposes of the plan, it could be done.

196   Floor Leader Wherry wanted a flat prohibition against trade with Eastern Europe. "To me," said Lodge, that "means that we shall have to support
Western Europe for the rest of our lives." Wherry retorted that he would
not "subscribe to any appropriation which would permit steel to be fabri-
cated into an implement of war to be sold to Russia." Kem chimed in that
the British government, being Socialist, would try to increase trade with
Russia. Lodge answered both.

MR. LODGE: This proposition is so simple that it surprises me that we
can whip it around as much as we have done this afternoon. Under certain
conditions trade with Eastern Europe is desirable and in the interest of
the U.S. Under certain other conditions trade with Eastern Europe is not
desirable in the interests of the U.S.

We would be the greatest fools in the world if we were to write language
into the bill prohibiting trade with Eastern Europe, just as we would be the
greatest fools in the world . . . to write language into the bill requiring
trade with Eastern Europe.

If the British were to take steel and convert it into forks and spoons, and
if it were deemed by the Administrator, the Senator from Nebraska, and by
nearly everyone else—as it might be— that it would be very advantageous
to send forks and spoons to the Russians in exchange for wheat which
Europe needs because we have a bad crop here . . . the Senator from
Nebraska might be the first to say that it would be a good thing to send
English-manufactured forks and spoons, made from American steel, to the
Russians. In fact, there might be fewer Communists if they began to use
those particular implements.

It would be a very silly thing for us to tie the hands simply because
there is a bad possibility. If the Administrator is a fool and a knave, then
it makes no difference what we write into the bill. The administration of
the law is to a great extent dependent upon the caliber of the Administrator.

Nevada's Molly Malone came up with what he thought was an exciting
discovery. He found that the amount of appropriations asked for corre-
sponded exactly with the balance of trade deficits of the countries to be
helped. This struck him as sinister.

MR. LODGE: The fact . . . is not a coincidence. It is deliberately arrived at. What we are trying to do is to bridge the gap in foreign exchange
which has been caused in large part by the war. There is not any mystery
about it. We have not uncovered a corpse here. It is exactly what we are
trying to do.

Kem of Missouri wanted to know if helping the Socialist government of England was "sound policy" to stop the spread of socialism. Lodge retorted that Europe's railroads, telephone, telegraph had always been operated by the government. "The fact that the European and American do not agree on . . . whether government should operate the telephone industry does not mean that they cannot agree in opposing Communism."

MR. WHERRY: Should we furnish money to a recipient country that is doing business with a satellite country, or one that does business directly with Russia?

MR. LODGE: Let me say that if the bill were to succeed 100% and if it were to live up to the fondest hopes of all its proponents . . . there would be a flourishing trade all over Europe between East and West everywhere. That would mean . . . that the Iron Curtain had broken down: and that would be the greatest accomplishment that could possibly be hoped for from the program.

These colloquies were followed by a Gallagher-and-Sheen act by Malone and Indiana's William Jenner.

MR. JENNER: [Is] ERP really for the purpose of financing socialism in Europe?

MR. MALONE: That will be the effect of it. . . .

MR. JENNER: It may be that it is also financing Communist strikes in Italy and France.

MR. MALONE: Those nations are financing social security, unemployment insurance and various other activities with the money which would not be available had it not been for the help we gave them.

MR. JENNER: Will the Senator tell me the difference between Communism and socialism?

MR. MALONE: I am unable to explain the difference . . . the end . . . is the same. . . .

MR. JENNER: What will happen to ERP if Austria and Italy fall to Communism?

MR. MALONE: They would be cut off the dole, or world WPA.

MR. JENNER: The only way that they can stop Communism over there is to have the will to stop it.

MR. MALONE: It occurs to me that Great Britain, France . . . that much of the material we are sending to these nations can be compared with the cattle coming off the Nevada range and being fed in transit. . . .

So went the attack by all these minor statesmen on what would prove to be the most farsighted and successful act of American leadership in the postwar period. No attack was too asinine for Lodge to meet it with calm patience and cool, articulate logic—and occasionally humor. When Wherry urged "force" as the way to stop Communism, Lodge expressed surprise at

198   his "rattling the saber" when the U.S. was ill-armed. "Will not the Senator from Massachusetts smile a little?" asked Wherry. "Yes; I smile whenever I look at the Senator from Nebraska," said Lodge, amid laughter.

When it came down to votes, Fulbright's well-intentioned amendment was beaten. Taft, who had made no frontal assaults on the bill while Wherry and Malone did the hatchet work, now made a flank attack upon it. He moved to cut $1.3 billion from the first year's appropriations. This was the exact amount which had been discussed as Britain's needs. It was therefore a way of articulating the oft-expressed dislike for helping Britain's Labor government.

Lodge marshaled his forces, beat down the Taft amendment by 56 to 31.

Then, at five minutes past midnight, on March 14, 1948, the final vote came.

Wherry, the Taft floor leader who had marshaled the fiercest attacks upon it, managed to rally sixteen others to oppose the Marshall Plan—including Jenner and Malone. Taft himself finally voted for it, in absentia, by leaving an aye to pair with another's nay.

By 67 to 17, the Marshall Plan came into being. As much as any man, Henry Cabot Lodge was one of its chief architects.

Lodge now faced a new challenge of leadership. When the Republicans met in presidential convention at Philadelphia that June, he was chosen chairman of the powerful Resolutions Committee, charged with drafting the party's platform. As for the Presidential candidate, he thought the party's best future lay with Vandenberg, who had just given such proof of his positive statesmanship. Though Vandenberg refused to become an active candidate, Lodge and Michigan's National Committeeman Arthur Summerfield ran the campaign on his behalf from a suite in the Hotel Warwick.

A year before, Vandenberg had led both Dewey and Taft in a poll of GOP senators, and during 1948 had kept climbing in newspaper polls. A *Newsweek* poll of fifty leading political writers predicted Vandenberg as the most likely candidate. "He is beyond reproach from his friends and, by the magic of bipartisanship," wrote Richard H. Rovere in *Harper's*, "beyond judgment by his enemies . . . it certainly puzzles a bystander to see [Republicans] enduring strife and discord in their search for a good candidate when all they have to do is draft the perfect candidate."

Vandenberg himself ignored the furor, and devoted himself to the foreign policy plank of the platform Lodge was preparing.

In this job, Lodge again showed his mastery of detail, and of systematic winnowing of all points of view. He called on Bobby Cutler, his old Boston friend, to be his chief of staff. "I got up at half past seven and worked till half-past 12 at night," Cutler recalled, "seeing all the members of the committee, getting the agenda worked out. Cabot did a superb job. We met at noon and didn't get done till 9 that night, Cabot presided. He was fair, and impartial, but he saw that the agenda was carried out. A lot of important people on the committee thought he wouldn't dare cut them off, but he did. It was a good platform. The best thing about it was that Cabot saw to it that it was short."

Vandenberg felt the same about Cabot's platform.

"I was prepared to fight to the finish," he wrote in his diary, "to protect the GOP against reversion to 'isolationism' or against desertion of the peace plans, including 'collective security' and the European Recovery Program. . . . It wasn't necessary—thanks to the superb job done by Lodge. . . . Before Lodge (Bless him!) went to Philadelphia he asked me for a working paper on a foreign policy plank. I gave it to him. He put it all the way through his sub-committee and his full committee and the Convention practically intact. I think it is of historical importance to nail down this fact. Before he presented the working paper to his Committee, Senator Lodge, with typical acumen, added four or five more extreme statements (all in harmony with this theme) for the express purpose of giving the little coterie of isolationists on his committee something to knock out.* One was a tacit condenmnation of the House Republicans 'led by Martin-Taber-Halleck' for having voted for the European relief and against necessary appropriations for it. In due course, the 'extras' were knocked down, just as Lodge planned, and he emerged with what I consider to be a miraculous performance. . . . Thus *my* platform was adopted by the Convention unanimously—which means that the Chicago Colonel [McCormick] and many bitter Congressional foes who were delegates must have voted for it. Life *does* have its amusing consolations. I did not need the nomination in order to be vindicated."

Nor would he get it. Vandenberg had some potent supporters—Senators Tobey, Chan Gurney, Wayne Morse, John Sherman Cooper, Homer Ferguson, Milton Young. Representative Clare Boothe Luce worked actively for him, as did the First Lady of progressive Republicanism, Helen Rogers Reid of the *Herald Tribune*. But the Dewey blitz was almost impossible to stop at the outset, when Senator Edward Martin withdrew as a candidate and split the big Pennsylvania delegation by supporting Dewey. The New Yorker shot across the 500 mark on the second ballot, 515 to Taft's 274 and Stassen's 149 (Vandenberg had 62 on both ballots). Stassen was ready to swing to Vandenberg, as was Indiana, but it was too late.

During the midnight lull between ballots, Helen Reid got William Robinson, *Herald Tribune* business manager and bridge partner of General Eisen-

* The same sly tactic he had used on the Beverly tanners.

200 hower, to make a last-minute effort to draft Eisenhower as a candidate. "I believe that the General would have accepted if the track could have been cleared for him," Vandenberg wrote in his diary. "But it could not be cleared for *anybody*." Dewey won on the third ballot.

Not only Vandenberg, but President Truman as well thought it remarkable that Lodge had been able to get the Republicans behind such a progressive, forward-looking platform. If they were going to seek power on such a platform, Truman thought he would let them support it even before election. He called a special session of Congress and challenged the Republican leadership—Taft in the Senate and Joe Martin in the House—to enact the Lodge platform. He shrewdly suspected that the top Republican leaders were merely giving it lip service—and he was right. They fiddled around for three weeks or so and went home. Truman branded them hypocrites, and the platform a fraud. All this helped him win a surprise victory over Dewey. Once more the Republicans lost their control of Congress. The new Senate had fifty-four Democrats to forty-two Republicans.

In the *Saturday Evening Post* Lodge asked, "What's the Matter with the Republicans?" and tried to give an answer.

> *The epic set-back of November may well be a blessing in disguise to Republicans. They now have an opportunity to clean house, to discard archaic concepts, and to mold the party to greater conformity with the will and the aspirations of the American people. . . . It is in defeat that the Republican Party will become a modern party and take its proper place in our political system. . . . The G.O.P. has been presented to the public as a rich man's club and as a haven for reactionaries. This is only true in that there have been some Republicans—and for that matter many Democrats as well—who have fought every piece of New Deal legislation with uncomprehending and myopic fury. But to say that these Republicans represent the rank and file of the party is in my view a gross untruth. It is little short of astounding to find the Democrats, with so large a segment of their membership comprised of avowed opponents of civil rights, making their claims to the title of being the sole party of progress.*
>
> *[The Party should not be] tenaciously anchored to a dead past. . . . There is far more hope for America and a basis for rejuvenating the party if the words of Abraham Lincoln are heeded: "The dogmas of the quiet past are inadequate to the stormy present. The occasion is piled high with difficulty and we must rise to the occasion. As our case is new so we must think anew and act anew." . . . Now that the Republicans are suffering from the reputation of being the party of the big shots let us recall the Republican Party's beginnings in the freeing*

of the slaves and let us remember the inspired radicalism of Lincoln.   **201**
*. . . The anti-trust laws, the regulation and rate-making bodies such
as the I.C.C., the conservation laws, were all largely the result of Republican action and inspiration. It was Senator Vandenberg who almost single-handed achieved the law for federal insurance for bank
deposits. . . . The Republican Party must take inspiration from this
progressive past.*

Lodge recalled the death of the Whig Party, which lost the confidence
of everyone because it refused to face the slavery issue, and warned the
Republicans they could not continue to alienate the whole American labor
movement by hostility to unions. The party "must make a vigorous, sincere
and successful effort to win the confidence of labor." He concluded: "So
great is the need for a living two-party system, so priceless are its benefits
and so tragic are the consequences of not having it, that I have both faith
and hope that we shall in Lincoln's words 'rise to the occasion.' "

He, at least, was determined to try.

When the new Congress met, Lodge found himself the leader of some
fifteen other progressive Republicans who decided they would try to oust
the Taft-Wherry leadership—a leadership which could give lip service to
a platform and then turn its back upon it. Senator Ives of New York, saying "Our feeling is that the party under Bob Taft is not going forward,"
announced the progressives would support Lodge to replace Taft as chairman of the party's Policy Committee in the Senate.

The rebels scarcely expected to succeed, as Arthur Krock noted. "But in
their view the fight is worth making if only to draw public attention to the
fact that a Republican *revolt* is under way after five successive defeats for
the Presidency and the loss of its Congressional majority gained only two
years ago."

Krock noted that the rebels could count on a minimum of fifteen votes for
Lodge (twenty-two were needed to elect him). "That is a block which on
numerous occasions could hold the balance of power on important matters
when Republicans and Democrats are divided." He added that Lodge was
determined to offer a fourth course to replace three which had failed: " 'me-
too' of outpromising the Democrats, that of blanket denunciation, that of
mere 'sweetness and light.' " Instead, Lodge would "take the ball and run
with it, offering in the party's name new, constructive and intelligent remedies for national and international ills that are conceded to exist." He
quoted Lodge: "There are millions of Republicans in this country who want
the party to engage in more than a rear-guard action."

Vandenberg, for all his admiration of Lodge, would not join the revolt.

"It would be best for the Party, and for Taft," he wrote, "if he [Taft] would voluntarily step aside." But if Taft sought reelection as policy chief, Vandenberg would not oppose him: "I deeply felt that he has rendered great Republican service; that he has been given a 'moss-back' reputation which he does not deserve; that we shall need his aggressive wisdom in the 81st Congress; yet that it would be best for the Party, and for him, if he would voluntarily step aside, but not otherwise."

Vandenberg did not feel the same way about Wherry, floor leader and party whip as well, who had led most of the sabotaging floor opposition to the unanimous reports which Vandenberg had steered so surely through his Foreign Relations Committee—particularly ECA. Columnist Roscoe Drummond pointed out that of ten ECA opponents who ran for reelection in 1948, only Wherry survived; Drummond suggested the party profit by the example of the other nine. Vandenberg told Wherry he would oppose him for floor leader.

What Vandenberg hoped to see, if Taft would step aside, was Eugene Millikin as a policy chairman whom both sides could accept, Lodge or California's William Knowland as floor leader, and Wherry kept on as whip so as not to be "kicked in the teeth." Wrote Vandenberg in his diary: "I deeply regretted that I could not vote for Lodge in this instance. He is one of my most precious friends. He has been of great assistance to me. He is a superb public servant." He added his conviction that Lodge would be "a Republican President of the United States," and his hope to live long enough to help put him there.

Taft won the showdown 28 to 14. The stubborn Wherry also won.

A far bigger showdown was approaching between the progressive and the standpat wings of the Republican Party.

The Marshall Plan was the cornerstone in what was soon to become a grander design of strength through unity as rebuilt Europe rose from the ashes.

First would come the North Atlantic Pact, and out of it, in time, the North Atlantic Treaty Organization with a multination army commanded by General Eisenhower. As with the Marshall Plan, Vandenberg and Lodge would be the principal Republican architects of this growing structure.

They would have to fight Taft, Wherry, Jenner, McCarthy, Malone & Co. every step of the way.

The master plan was laid down as early as the spring of 1948 in a series of meetings in Vandenberg's apartment at the Wardman Park, 500 G. Robert A. Lovett, Secretary of State Marshall's Undersecretary, would often stop to see the senator. Lodge often joined them. Some twenty-three Soviet vetoes had rendered the U.N.'s Security Council powerless. That March, the Berlin blockade, which would last for fifteen months, served notice of

Stalin's determination to push the Allies out of Berlin. It was clear that the
free nations would have to find means of self-defense "within the Charter
but outside the veto," as Vandenberg would phrase it.

When the U.N. was founded at San Francisco in 1945, Vandenberg himself had helped frame Article 51, stipulating that nothing in the Charter
impaired the inherent right of individual and collective self-defense from
armed attack. The three succeeding articles permitted regional arrangements for meeting such threats. The previous summer, at Rio, Vandenberg
had called them all into play to help draw the Rio Pact whereby the Amer-
icas pledged to meet an armed attack on any member—avoiding the veto
by making a two-thirds majority binding on all.

Van believed this same method held the key to organizing Europe's collective security against possible Soviet aggression. On long Sunday meetings, he tried out different phrasings of his idea on Lovett. Marshall was
kept informed. Thus was born the Vandenberg Resolution which would
make NATO possible. But it was so simply phrased that only the very far-
sighted could see the whole of its potentials. It would merely "advise" the
President of the "sense" of the Senate that the government, "within the
U.N. Charter," should pursue certain aims. These were to develop "regional and other collective arrangements for individual and collective self-
defense." And they were for the U.S. to associate itself with such arrangements as were based on "continuous and effective self-help and mutual
aid." Vandenberg, quite well aware that such a blank check for military
alliances could provoke a fight over sovereignty similar to the elder Lodge's
fight with Wilson over Article X, carefully added that this association must
be done by "constitutional process," thus guarding Congress's constitutional
power to declare war.

It was not so much a charter for NATO as a license for it. Lodge himself
explained it to the Senate that June:

> *The purpose is to show that we are in sympathy with the broad trend
> of strengthening the freedom-loving countries, but it does not commit
> us to anything. They must make the showing. If they make a good
> showing and if it is advantageous to our national security to help them,
> we shall help them.*

Few senators realized how broad a scope the resolution did provide.
After a single day of debate, it passed overwhelmingly, 64 to 6. Nothing
that flowed from it would ever have so small an opposition.

Less than a month after the resolution's passage, Lovett sat down with
the ambassadors of Canada, Britain, France and the Benelux nations. They
began the discussions that led to the North Atlantic Treaty.

204   The plans were well advanced by the time of Truman's inauguration. Dean Acheson, who succeeded the ailing Marshall as Secretary of State, kept the Foreign Relations Committee informed of the progress. A Democrat, Tom Connally of Texas, had taken over the chair from Vandenberg. However, Vandenberg and Lodge kept sharp eyes on the various phrasings of the treaty draft, and helped Acheson weed out needless ammunition for isolationist senators.

The ghost of Wilson's Article X surfaced again in a proposed Article 5, pledging each signatory to use armed force to repel an attack on any other. Lodge, of all people, knew what a red flag this would be to the Senate. He and Vandenberg helped rephrase this: each signatory would take "such action as it *deems necessary,* including the use of armed force," thus implying the sort of "reservation" the elder Lodge had sought for the League's police powers. They added another cautious proviso that the treaty would be carried out by the parties "in accordance with their respective constitutional processes."

Santayana said that those who fail to learn from history are doomed to repeat it. It was a measure of Lodge's stature that what he had learned from his grandfather's fight with one Democratic President was how to save another one from subjecting himself to a similar needless and self-defeating struggle.

Connally, Vandenberg and Lodge, working closely together, called some ninety-six witnesses during sixteen days of hearings after Acheson signed the treaty on April 4. Once again, they smoothly produced a 13-0 approval by the potent committee.

By the time the floor debate began on July 5, Lodge's forty-sixth birthday, the crucial Article 5 had already been so thoroughly thrashed out there was little more that could be said about it. Instead, the debate hinged on the military assistance program being planned to implement the treaty.

Lodge led the making of the case for that. "We should always remember . . . not only the moral phase and the legal phase of practical military implementation. . . . People like the Kaiser and Hitler are never as much embarrassed by words and phrases and good intentions as they are by their knowledge of the actual physical military means that are ready to be used in order to fight." He argued that we would help protect American lives by organizing and binding Europe's military manpower to our own.

Taft led the opposition. He opposed arms aid to Europe. He opposed the whole treaty. He called the pact "a tremendous mistake," and said it would provoke war rather than prevent it. If one accepted his premises, his reasons were logical, cogent and compelling.

Lodge did not accept them. He hammered with compelling logic of his own at the argument he had made all his life—that weakness, not strength, leads to war and provokes aggression.

Vandenberg, now failing from cancer, spoke for nearly two hours in what was to be the last full-dress speech of his life. He called the pact "a fraternity for peace. . . . It spells out, beyond any shadow of a doubt, the conclusive warning that 300,000,000 people, united in competent self-defense, will never allow an armed aggressor to divide and conquer them." Cordell Hull, former senator and former Secretary of State, telephoned to call it "one of the greatest speeches ever made."

After eleven days of debate the North Atlantic Treaty carried by a smashing 82 to 13 votes.

It left Taft, Wherry, Malone, Jenner & Co. so small a following as to raise chiefly one question: what was this "leadership" leading?

That summer Lodge returned to Harvard for his twenty-fifth reunion. He had been elected chief marshal of his class. In top hat and morning coat, he briskly led it across the beloved Yard. Like the others, he had been asked to sum up his interests for the reunion class book, the same task which provoked the late George Apley's observation that he was still trying to finish *The Education of Henry Adams*. Cabot Lodge had this to report:

My family life since graduation, as husband and father, has been marked by marvelous good fortune, for which I am deeply grateful, just as family life as son and brother have kept on through the years in the affectionate atmosphere of childhood. . . . Travels in journalistic and military capacities have taken me twice around the world and to almost every state in the Union. Hobbies are sailing, gardening and on rainy days, reading, writing, puttering around the house, and listening to music. But the harness which I wear (so gladly, and I hope, without harm to my fellow men) leaves little time for hobbies of any kind. Life as a legislator has on the whole made an optimist out of me —about both the U.S. and human nature. In the legislature, my experience as House Chairman of the Committee on Labor and Industries convinced me that the interests which men have in common and which bind them together are more numerous and important than those which drive them apart. The really evil politician is he who seeks to stress the things which divide. The cleverer he is at these divisive tactics the more evil he is. Because a united people can overcome all obstacles, it is a public servant's job to find the common ground and to unite. A public servant who seeks to divide the community is like a doctor who is trying to kill his patient. . . .

Despite all of Lodge's warnings against America repeating its chronic mistake of letting its defenses fall below the danger point, in 1948 Defense Secretary Louis Johnson had slashed the arms budget to a risky $13 billion. Lodge had led a successful fight to provide a seventy-group Air Force, but Truman had simply left the funds unused, held it back to forty-eight groups. Then Korea suddenly jarred the U.S. into awarenesss of its weakness. Truman fired Johnson, got ailing George Marshall to return, this time as Defense Secretary, to try to mend the damage.

"Every week or so after the war began in Korea," wrote Arthur Krock, "Lodge has demanded in the Senate to know why the Administration was mobilizing on the basis of 'politics and business as usual.' When it became apparent that our Korean airpower was inferior in numbers to that of the enemy, Mr. Lodge laid the blame on the Administration and got a letter from Senator Lyndon Johnson of Texas, Democratic chairman of the Mobilization watchdog subcommittee, agreeing that 'the performance record is poor . . . and our defense mobilization planners have devoted too much of our productive resources to non-essential civilian goods and too little to vitally necessary armament.' Not since the Democratic chairman of a similar committee, Mr. Truman, openly agreed on the Senate floor with Senator Vandenberg that the White House was responsible for a delay of 18 months in putting our Second World War Armament production into high gear has there been a comparable incident."

That same summer, Lodge got involved for the first time in the question of how to handle the charges which Joe McCarthy had begun making that the State Department was "riddled" with Communists. McCarthy kept altering his "facts" so frequently that they were patently irresponsible. Taft, who applauded the whole thing as an acceptable form of political assault, cheered McCarthy on and told him, "If that doesn't work try something else." Lodge, as a minority member of the Tydings sub-committee investigating McCarthy's accusations, saw clearly that such shotgun charges "tended to besmirch the reputation of innocent persons, hamper the work of the government investigative agencies, impair the position of the U.S. before the world, reflect unjustly on the many excellent persons in the State Department, and discourage other excellent persons from entering the service of the State Department." But he did not think the way to handle careless accusations was by an equally careless whitewash. When the majority report did precisely that, Lodge filed a dissent which showed what he thought the proper approach to be:

The fact that many charges have been made which have not been proven does not in the slightest degree relieve the sub-committee of the responsibility for undertaking a relentlessly thorough investigation of its own . . . An almost endless number of questions . . . have not even been asked by the subcommittee.

What officers were responsible for placing [Alger] Hiss and [Julian] Wadleigh in the State Department?

What person or persons were primarily responsible for sponsoring for employment 91 sexual perverts who were in the State Department and were reported as having been discharged as of Jan. 1, 1947?

. . . A real negligence reached a climax in 1945 and 1946 when over 4,000 persons who had been employed by the F.E.A., O.W.I., and O.S.S. and other wartime agencies were transferred to the State Department by a stroke of a pen and without any screening whatever. It was here that a large number of persons managed to get into the State Department who should never have been there at all.

Lodge demanded that the truth be established by a bipartisan commission of eight, two of whom would be senators, six others chosen by the majority and minority from a panel to be prepared by the President, and to function under a seal of secrecy, announcing its findings well after the 1950 elections. "This business will never end at all clearly or otherwise if the practice of having the majority party investigate the majority continues to hold sway. Nor will satisfactory results be obtained if the minority investigates the majority. The investigation must be non-political." Like his long-ago demand to count the unemployed, this proposal was entirely too sensible to be adopted. It was ignored, and McCarthyism raged on to fill the country with hatred, division and suspicion.

Lodge was constantly preoccupied with how the Republican party could break loose from the stifling influence of its Congressional leadership to win the White House in 1952. As far as he could see, the industrialists who controlled the party's sinews, and the county chairmen who dominated its state and local machinery, were determined to make Taft their nominee— and Lodge was equally convinced that Taft would lose. Lodge feared that a sixth Democratic victory, spanning a quarter-century, might end the two-party system, and that the G.O.P., which had long since become a minority party, might follow the Whigs into oblivion. Permanent one-party rule by the Democrats would, he thought, put the country in the hands of the arrogant and cynical second-raters who generally typified the lower echelons of the Truman administration, and be accompanied by an inevitable drift into a third-rate socialism. There would be no pressure on the Democrats even to nominate their best man for President. Investment would dry up, and the risk-taking elements of the community would lose their faith in the future—so Lodge gloomily feared.

208   What the party needed was a leader of such popularity that he could win away enough independents and dissident Democrats to be elected. It seemed to Lodge that only Dwight D. Eisenhower carried such a magic charisma. Lodge did not know if Eisenhower was a Republican; he knew the General had spurned the 1948 Democratic overtures from James Roosevelt and George Allen, Truman's court jester. In June of 1950 Lodge went to Columbia University to see Eisenhower for the first time since their wartime dinner with Devers and de Lattre in France. Lodge told Eisenhower that it might become his duty to run for President in order to preserve the two-party system.

"If that should happen," said Eisenhower, "it would be the bitterest moment of my life." He paced up and down the president's office on Morningside Heights. He was looking forward to a life of ease and retirement, writing more memoirs and playing golf to his heart's content. Nothing appealed to him less than the thought of entering the hue and cry of politics. But Lodge had used a word that a soldier could not ignore. "If it became my duty," said Eisenhower, "I would do it." He did not think it was likely to become so. Still, Lodge felt encouraged enough to state in public, that October, his conviction that Eisenhower should be the candidate. New York's Governor Dewey and Eisenhower's old Army friend, General Lucius Clay, also began publicly urging Eisenhower's candidacy.

In the March 1950 *Atlantic Monthly,* in an article "Modernize the G.O.P.," Lodge had tried to lay down a specific charter for the sort of party he hoped Eisenhower would lead. "Instead of scolding the darkness, let us light a lamp," he wrote. He proposed specific tax reforms to encourage enterprisers to start new businesses, an end to poll taxes and racial segregation in the armed forces, "a realistic civil rights program . . . a field in which the Democrats will always be weak, faltering, groping, and divided . . . a field in which we can be vigorous, effective and bold. We were born as the anti-slavery party and the party of civil rights . . . and it would be foolish and grossly negligent for us not to seize this issue again." He bespoke, as in the past, federal measures to help states and communities build new hospitals, provide drugs free or at cost to the needy. "We must press our own program—bold, different, practical, constructive . . . [to] create a climate in which the strength and self-reliance of the individual human being will grow and flourish."

That October, President Truman paid his respects to Lodge's foreign-policy leadership by appointing him a delegate to the 1950-51 session of the U.N. General Assembly, together with John Foster Dulles, Eleanor Roosevelt and Alabama's Senator John Sparkman. After some days of watching Russia's Andrei Vishinsky heap vituperation on every aspect of U.S. policy, Lodge rose to make his maiden speech before the U.N. Something of his striking figure, his powerful voice, his personal eloquence caused the delegates to lean forward with interest and attentive expectation.

I heard both the Soviet Union and the Polish representatives speak of America as monopolistic. Actually one of the great basic economic facts about America is that it is a competitive country in which monopoly is actually against the law. . . . In this country when you try to prevent competition you know you are doing something illegal and will be punished if caught. . . . The strange thing is that I think [they] actually believe parts of that strange grab-bag of news clippings about the U.S. from which they quote constantly. I saw the Polish representative waving a copy of an American magazine here a few days ago which contained an article which happened to put the argument he was making at that time. . . . If that magazine had appeared in his country I suppose its statements would have had the consent of the government. But in our country the magazine simply represents the editor's opinion and most Americans take full advantage of disagreeing with the editor. In fact the editor very often disagrees with the owner and the man who wrote the article. . . .

I think that some of you [Communist] representatives . . . really believe that we are monopolistic. You believe it because you come from the world's greatest monopoly . . . you just cannot believe that power is as diffused in this country as it actually is. . . . You keep looking around you all the time to see who is dominating the country. Well, there is no one.

You have made me wonder—and I say this in all sincerity—during the last few days whether you are really frightened. Maybe you are frightened of us. Maybe you are frightened of the plain people in your own country. But I know that a frightened man can be dangerous. I am sorry there is fright, and I hope and believe that the time will come when fear will disappear. . . .

Now I have been here since Sept. 18, and I have talked to many earnest, idealistic and sincere men and women—some of them in this room—who represent many different countries and who would like sincerely to have an efficient working arrangement with the Russian people. But you have rebuffed them; you have turned them down; you have made it impossible for people who would like to do so to cooperate with you. Your policies are certainly unpredictable, and there may be some tactical advantages in that fact, but I cannot think that the alienation of friends throughout the world is intelligent. You may be here as a member of the U.N. in a purely cynical spirit so that you can

*destroy it from within and thus promote your own form of world gov-
ernment. I get the extraordinary impression, however, of a mixture of
the conspiratorial and the childish.*

*As to whether all this helps your own ruling class I cannot judge. I
believe it is unquestionably bad for the long-range interest of the
everyday man, woman, and children of the Soviet Union. . . . I am
confident that the condition which exists in the world is not going to
last much longer because the people of the free world whom you have
finally aroused will, in a completely peaceful way, and within a very
few years, create a quiet and peaceful world in which disputes will
be settled by negotiations and other peaceful methods set forth in the
charter, rather than by the threat or the use of force. I think that that
time is coming.*

*We hope the day will come when the oppression of religion in the
Soviet Union will stop, when the creative energies of that brilliant and
gifted Russian people will be released, when the Russian people will
be able to mingle freely with people of other lands; and when the people of the rest of Europe will no longer live in the terror of the Red
Army.*

My advice is: stop being afraid.

*There has been talk here of the great powers against the Soviet
powers. We Americans are not a great power in the sense that we like
power or that we have sought it. We are essentially little people whose
ancestors came here from countries where they had been oppressed, so
that they could get away from power politics and live quiet lives of
their own. . . . We are becoming powerful, but we are not going to
use that power as some others have used it in the past. We will use it,
with the other peace-loving nations, to create permanent peace, and
whether the dictators like it or not, that will be a blessing to all suffering humanity, both in and out of the free world.*

Lodge sat down to thundering applause.

As 1950 ended, a new form of isolationism broke out in America. It was
provoked by President Truman's dispatch of General Eisenhower—on leave
from Columbia—to be Supreme Commander of a new European Army
which he would organize under a NATO shield. To the 100,000 U.S. troops
already occupying Germany—which included only two combat divisions—
the President planned to send perhaps four more divisions. He took for
granted that as Commander-in-Chief he had the same power to dispatch
land troops anywhere as he did to send the Navy or Air Force. No one questioned the latter prerogatives.

However, as 1951 began, former President Hoover made a nationwide radio address which called, in effect, for abandoning Asia and Europe to Communism and seeking to build the Western Hemisphere into "the Gibraltar of Civilization," essentially the same old Maginot Line concept which had brought Europe to the edge of destruction.

The titular Republican leaders in Congress caught up Hoover's theme. "I agree with many of the general principles he states," said Floor Leader Wherry. "The people are with him," said the Chicago *Tribune*'s Colonel McCormick. Former Ambassador Joseph P. Kennedy applauded Hoover and said that he would "enlarge the Gibraltar to include South America as well." Said Dwight Eisenhower, "I am convinced that to retire to our own country to wait for the end would bring sure defeat. I see no reason for the U.S. to act in an atmosphere of hysterical fear. . . ."

The burden of marshaling Republican support for Eisenhower fell upon Lodge. The dying Vandenberg, too ill to enter the fight, wrote Lodge that Congress should not challenge the President's Constitutional powers to deploy troops but the President himself should seek the consent of Congress whenever time and circumstances would permit. Wherry introduced a resolution which would flatly forbid the President to send any troops to Europe without Congressional approval. Lodge brought forth a resolution, approved 20 to 0 by both the Foreign Relations and Armed Services Committees, which would require the Joint Chiefs to "certify" each such assignment as "essential to the security of the U.S." and establish a Joint Committee of Congress to perform "continuous supervision of all steps taken."

On the Republican side, Taft and Lodge soon became the chief antagonists.

Taft spoke for two and a half hours, "cool, confident and precise as a mathematics teacher" reported *Time,* arguing again that the NATO Pact itself was "a tremendous mistake," and though we must fulfill our pledge to defend Europe if attacked, this implied no obligation to contribute American troops. He said the mistake had been compounded by the appointment of Eisenhower to lead a European army.

"The course which we are pushing will make war more likely. . . . If they [the Soviets] have any intention to attack, they obviously will attack before the Atlantic Pact forces are built up, and it will take at least three years to build them up. Why should they wait?"

For three months the Great Debate rolled on. Cried Indiana's Jenner:

If the members of Congress have a shred of courage and patriotism left they will lay down an ultimatum to the President demanding either a declaration of war or the bringing back of American GIs to home shores.

Cried Nevada's Molly Malone:

We should withdraw General Eisenhower from his military headquarters in Europe.

Said Lodge:

It is hard to understand how anyone can contend the development of a defensive holding force in Europe could look like aggression to such realistic men as the rulers of the Kremlin . . . I do not want to stand on the Himalayas nor do I want to fight on Cape Cod. We've got to pick the spots where we can bring our force to bear.

The most eloquent witness—who won the nation itself—was Supreme Commander Eisenhower who, after covering twelve capitals of Europe in three weeks, came back to answer the essential questions: 1) Could Western Europe be defended, 2) Had Western Europe the heart to fight? In the packed auditorium of the Library of Congress he told leaders of both houses that the U.S. *had* to join in; there was no alternative. Before a closed joint session of the two committees he said that within eighteen months Europe would begin to have a chance of success; to lose Europe would be to lose an industrial capacity second only to that of the U.S. and the skilled labor of 200,000,000 people. He opposed any fixed ceilings on American troops such as Taft sought, stressed the importance of sending them at once. "If we Americans seize the lead," he told the entire nation that night on TV, "we will preserve and be worthy of our own past."

"Eisenhower," reported *Time*, "had done for the President what Harry Truman could not do for himself . . . routed the calamity-howlers and the super-cautious—the Hoovers, the Kennedys, the Wherrys, the Tafts." That verdict was premature. The Great Debate still dragged on, new crippling devices were tried. McClellan of Arkansas brought still another amendment to require the President to get Congressional approval if more than the four divisions already planned should be sent. Lodge rose to question the whole concept of trying to tie Eisenhower's and Defense Secretary Marshall's hands:

Congress cannot function as the operations section of a General Staff and decide where and how and in what amount troops, ships, and planes should be sent to foreign lands. . . . Imagine a situation in which there are already two divisions overseas. If three more are sent the total of five might be successful whereas if the two remained they might be lost. In these considerations two and two do not always make four. If we doubled the number of divisions, we may increase our power by more than twice. If we cut the number of divisions in half we may reduce the power of our forces by much more than half. Men go to West Point . . . to learn how to make such decisions . . . something for which the Senate is not fitted either by training or experience or by its ability to act with secrecy and dispatch.

The McClellan amendment was defeated 44 to 46. But the isolationists hurried about, changing a vote here and another there, demanded a second ballot and carried the McClellan reservations by 49 to 43. Triumphant, Wherry then sought by a new amendment to embalm the whole NATO project. "The Senator does not want to do *anything*," said Texas' Tom Connally sourly.

MR. WHERRY: I do want to do something. I want to have mastery of the air.

MR. CONNALLY: The Senator already has mastery of the hot air.

Wherry's amendment was beaten 60 to 21—Taft voting for it.

So the debate ended. Lodge and his allies had won, at least in public opinion. What McClellan won, by his amendment, was never determined, for the subsequent occasion never arose to precipitate such a test of the President's powers as Vandenberg dreaded. That grand old warrior himself died as the debate was ending. Lodge was the acknowledged heir to Van's mantle of leadership for the modern Republicans.

Right at the same time came Truman's dismissal of General MacArthur from the command in Korea. "It is a great pity," said Lodge, "that due in large part to Administration bungling and lack of foresight, differences arose which made it clearly impossible for him to continue, but the civil power—even though we lack confidence in those who hold it—must, under our system of government, be supreme over the military." MacArthur appeared before the joint Committees and Lodge sought his views on the European issue:

GENERAL MACARTHUR: I believe we should defend every place from Communism. . . . The other fellow has the same problems that we do. If we have to work on two fronts or three fronts or four fronts, so does he; and if we can't meet him and defeat him, our ultimate destruction is certain.

MR. LODGE: Certainly then, you do not think we ought to withdraw from Europe. . . .

GENERAL MACARTHUR: I certainly do not. . . . The whole essence of some segments has been to say that if you defend in the Far East, you

214 sacrifice Europe, or vice versa. I think each of those concepts would be pernicious . . . we should hold our own in both places.

Senator Lyndon Johnson of Texas took up the questioning.

MR. JOHNSON: There is a school of thought which believes that we should confine the bulk of all our ground forces to the continental U.S. and that we should provide other nations with nothing but sea and air support in the battle against Communism.

GENERAL MACARTHUR: I believe that it is the gravest possible mistake in the use of the armed forces of a nation to try to draw the lines of demarcation between ground troops, air troops and navy troops. They are an integrated team. . . . It is impossible to make such a simplification in my opinion.

MR. JOHNSON: Then you would not favor legislative straitjackets that would place a limitation on the number of ground troops that could be supplied?

GENERAL MACARTHUR: Senator, I stand upon my answers. . . . That is a very heated, mooted thing that is being discussed in the chambers of Congress; but my own belief is that the elasticity that is necessary is not to be measured by academic or straitjacket formulas at all.

Ironically, the General would soon be supporting such straitjacket advocates for the future control of the Republican party and the nation.

All the events of the spring had convinced Lodge, more than ever, that the Republicans would plunge to their sixth successive defeat unless a truly national leader like Eisenhower could be found. On July 1, when he accompanied the Armed Forces Committee on an inspection of NATO, he had to see Eisenhower for that purpose, and took care to sound him out on the other. Eisenhower gave him no encouragement. Returning to the U.S., Lodge appeared on "Meet the Press" on August 5, 1951, and asserted that "nothing would destroy Eisenhower's military effort quicker than for it to get in partisan politics." But he added, "I certainly would be very happy to see him President of the U.S." Lodge got sufficient response from this nationwide TV appearance to make him believe a tremendous grassroots movement for Eisenhower could be generated without involving the General himself. NEEDED, A WINNER, declared the Boston *Herald* of Lodge's remarks: "He may have flown in the face of the party's reactionaries, but he just as surely put himself on the side of what the Republican Party most needs in 1952—a winner. . . . Will Eisenhower run? We think he will if the matter of approaching him is properly handled. In rejecting the nomination in 1948, he left the door open by saying that he would only consider such a political course in the event of a national crisis. What could be more of a national crisis in his opinion than

for Senator Robert A. Taft to become President and wreck the Western   215
European defense plan to which [Eisenhower] is dedicated?"

Bolstered by such arguments, and by the growing response, Lodge decided in September that the time had come to make a new appeal to Eisenhower.

CHAPTER TWELVE

Senator Henry Cabot Lodge came on Tuesday, Sept. 4, 1951, for a visit which turned out to be, for me significant. While many had preceded him, he was different in that he said he reflected the known views of numerous large groups, many of whom now wanted to start organizing a nationwide movement to present my name before the 1952 Republican convention. Cabot, an associate and friend of mine from wartime days, presented his plea with the ardor of a crusader. —Dwight D. Eisenhower, in *Mandate for Change*

Sitting in his office at the old Hotel Astoria in Paris that September day, Dwight Eisenhower tried to put his visitor on the defensive. "You are well known in politics; why not run yourself?" Without pause, Lodge answered, "Because I cannot be elected," and went on with his argument:

He started with a review of the political events [Eisenhower relates] in the last twenty years in the U.S., particularly in the five national elections of 1932 through 1948, all of which had resulted in defeats for the Republican Party. Cabot asserted that unless this one-sided partisan dominance could be promptly reversed, the record presaged the virtual elimination of the two-party system, which we agreed was vital to the ultimate preservation of our national institutions.

But beyond this danger he went into the performance record of the recent succession of national administrations. This record he called one of gradual but steady accumulation of power in Washington, increased "paternalism" in government's relations with the cities, constant deficit spending, and a steady erosion in the value of our currency. As a consequence he held, first, that these practices were becoming so alarming as to spell potential disaster for the country and, second, that corrective measures could not even be started unless we had a Republican victory in 1952.

On his opposition to centralization in the federal government and the cheapening of our currency I was in substantial agreement. . . . But now Cabot, sitting in my NATO office, turned to the subject of the Republican Party itself and its problems in attempting to cope with the danger which faced our nation. He felt that the regular Republican leadership, cast in an opposition role for 20 long years, inescapably gave the country a negative impression. The principal figures

216

of the party were, according to him, interpreted as saying that Americans faced the choice of doing the wrong thing under the Democrats or doing nothing at all under the Republicans. He also said that in 1951 the opposition of that part of the Republican leadership known loosely as the Old Guard to the sending of U.S. troops to Europe to serve in NATO had made the party appear unaware of the realities of the modern world.

Cabot believed that although the Republicans, during the past two decades, had nominated men with a variety of political opinions and beliefs such as Gov. Alfred M. Landon and Mr. Wendell Willkie, none of their candidates had been able to generate an appeal strong enough to unify the party and at the same time attract the independent and Democratic support necessary for election. Moreover the party was still blamed in many minds for the depression beginning in 1929. The Republican Party, said Cabot, must now seek to nominate one who, supporting basic Republican convictions—which had come down to us from Lincoln and Theodore Roosevelt—could be elected and achieve at least a partial reverse of the trend toward centralization in government, irresponsible spending, and catering to pressure groups, and at the same time avoid the fatal errors of isolationism. . . .

And then Cabot put forward the point of his presentation. "You," he said flatly, "are the only one who can be elected by the Republicans to the Presidency. You must permit the use of your name in the upcoming primaries."

To this I was not prepared to agree. But despite my protests he argued with the tenacity of a bulldog and pounded away on this theme until, as he left, I said I would "think the matter over." At the moment this general remark seemed inconsequential . . . but as I look back on that incident, my promise, indefinite as it was, marked a turning point. For the first time I had allowed the smallest break in a regular practice of returning a flat refusal to any kind of proposal that I become an active participant. From that time onward, both alone and through correspondence, I began to look anew—perhaps subconsciously—at myself and politics.

Lodge sensed, even more than Eisenhower, that the General could be persuaded, if a large enough and concerted enough effort could be made to persuade the soldier—as Lodge had first put it during his 1950 visit—that it was his duty to become a candidate. But Lodge also knew that the effort would have to be made, almost to the end, without the General's help —since he would never leave the NATO job until it was well in hand, and Army regulations would preclude his even discussing politics publicly.

218   Lodge came home, and on September 8 the Boston *Traveler* reported:
LODGE HEADS GROUP BACKING THE GENERAL. He was immediately attacked
by Taft's most vocal Massachusetts supporter, Basil Brewer, publisher of
the New Bedford *Standard-Times*. In an editorial, MISUSING EISENHOWER,
the paper asserted: "Four prominent Republicans seem to have constituted
themselves as managers of an Eisenhower-for-President campaign. They
are Gov. Dewey, twice nominated for the Presidency and both times defeated; Harold E. Stassen, who sought the nomination in 1948 and lost;
Senator Lodge and Senator James H. Duff of Pennsylvania. In the absence
of any spontaneous grass-roots demand that Eisenhower seek the Presidency, his ostensible backers are trying to start an Eisenhower boom."
Lodge himself would be up for reelection in 1952. The editorial accused
him of backing Eisenhower for his "own selfish political purposes." Lodge
wrote Brewer:

> *It is hard for me to understand why men cannot have honest disagree-
> ments about political questions without impugning each other's mo-
> tives. I do not impugn your motives in supporting Senator Taft and I
> think it is a great pity that you should question mine because I support
> General Eisenhower. . . . You infer that there is something discredit-
> able in the fact that I think General Eisenhower will be a "winner."
> When I think of the Republican defeats of 1936, 1940, 1944 and
> 1948, I say we have had enough losses and that a man who can carry
> the Presidency and help elect a Republican House and Senate will be
> good for the country. My support of General Eisenhower is in complete
> good faith as is everything I do in public life. For you to question my
> motives certainly does you no credit.*

The Chicago *Tribune*'s publisher, Colonel Robert R. McCormick, thun-
dered that "the Eisenhower Myth" was being foisted on Republicans by
people like Lodge who "are slipping." "Aside from such people the ballyhoo
for Eisenhower comes from New Dealers, New Deal propagandists, Europe
firsters and other brands of world savers. . . . Columnists and commentators playing the New Deal game are constantly whooping up Eisenhower.
So is the Un-American press in New York." *Look* sponsored a Gallup Poll
to see who, in case Eisenhower did not run, could attract most of the "28%
of the electorate which now classifies itself as independent." *Look* pointed
out that only 31 per cent of Americans now classified themselves as Republicans, 40 per cent Democrats and that the independent 28 per cent
were decisive. Among a list of ten men popular with independents, ECA
administrator Paul Hoffman rated first with independents, Lodge second;
among Republicans, Lodge first and Hoffman second.

In the midst of trying to start the Eisenhower boom, Lodge was giving attention to new Communist threats in Asia. Early in September his wartime colleague, Marshal de Lattre de Tassigny, now commander-in-chief of French forces in Indochina, came to the U.S. seeking arms and financial assistance for that effort. Lodge gave a luncheon for him which Vice President Barkley attended, accompanied him to a dinner given by Henry Luce, and arranged his appearance on the nationwide television forum, "Meet the Press", on September 16. Lodge acted as interpreter when needed:

LAWRENCE SPIVAK: Can you tell us now what the importance of Indo-China is to us Americans?

DE LATTRE: Indo-China is the keystone of Southeast Asia . . . it's of extremely great importance to all the future of the world. [His own son had been killed there May 13.]

LODGE: You mean if Indochina falls, all of Southeast Asia is lost?

DE LATTRE: Yes.

The cease-fire negotiations in Korea had already begun. Lodge on September 21 told the Senate it was possible that the enemy was using this respite to launch new assaults in Indochina. He termed the northern part of Indochina, Tonkin province,—whose capital is Hanoi—the strategic keystone of Southeast Asia. "As it goes so probably would go Siam, Burma, Malaya and probably India and everything up to the Suez Canal." That in turn would endanger the "ability of the free nations to hold even North Africa." The nation had little interest at that time in what happened in far-off Hanoi and Saigon. De Lattre himself died suddenly, shortly after his visit to the U.S., and the French soon were being chewed to pieces in strategic Tonkin province.

While Lodge was visiting Eisenhower, Thomas E. Dewey had met with a number of senators in Washington to sound them out on supporting the general. Taft had recently swung through New England and was making headway among those likely to be convention delegates. Lodge thought it was time to start some formal organization. He called Senator Frank Carlson of Kansas, who, together with Kansas Republican National Committeeman Harry Darby, had been building informal support for Eisenhower. Lodge called Jim Duff—his old ally in backing Vandenberg—and Senator Irving Ives of New York. Lodge, Duff, Ives and Carlson met in the Kansan's office. "What we need," said Duff, "is someone to head this thing up. We need an office, a staff, people to compile mailing lists, and send things out to leading Republicans."

Their first step was to set up a small office in the Shoreham Hotel. Governor Dewey, who was anxious that the movement should not seem to be a "front" for himself, preferred to have the others actively lead it. He

220   did send Thomas E. Stephens, secretary of the New York State Republican
Committee, to run the initial office, Lodge's friend, the political genius Tom
White, was dead, but the senator brought in his veteran Boston campaign
strategist, Mason Sears, who arrived with a shabby, battered, old-fashioned
suitcase which made him look like a carpetbagger. Sears' suitcase would
become a landmark of the campaign. Mrs. Irene White acted as secretary.
There was still no campaign manager.

Lodge had some meetings with his old *Herald Tribune* friends in New
York, Helen Reid and Geoffrey Parsons. They shared his enthusiasm for
Eisenhower, whom Mrs. Reid had tried vainly to draft in 1948. Now Parsons wrote a three-column page-one editorial, "The Time and the Man,"
which appeared on October 25:

> *At rare intervals in the life of a free people the man and the occasion
> meet. The opportunity for service that falls to a great party is matched
> by the appearance of a leader, wise and tested, capable of giving reality
> to what masses of men and women have dreamed. We believe that for
> the Republican Party the occasion has now come.*
>
> *We believe that Dwight D. Eisenhower is the man.*
>
> *By deed and word General Eisenhower has shown himself a keeper
> of the great liberties to which the Republican Party is dedicated. He
> knows that free individuals are responsible for every good and lasting
> accomplishment of our nation. He knows that the indiscriminate ex-
> tension of state power spells death. He is a Republican by temper and
> disposition. He is a Republican by every avowal of faith and declara-
> tion of purpose. . . .*

Actually Eisenhower's supporters did not know that he *was* a Republican. They were gambling that he must be because all of his public
speeches as president of Columbia had seemed to indicate a Republican
philosophy. In any case, the *Herald Tribune* piece overjoyed Kansas Republicans who were already organizing an "I like Ike" campaign with headquarters in Topeka. Henry Jameson, a newspaperman who had formed a
branch in Ike's hometown of Abilene, cried: "This is very fine news." The
grass-roots movement, still unorganized, gathered new momentum.

Lodge, now a full colonel in the Reserve, went off for two weeks of active
duty at Fort Dix, New Jersey. He had also gone to Camp Kilmer, in the
same state, to greet the first contingent of forty-four veterans of European
armies and anti-Communist organizations who had arrived for training in
the U.S. Army under a 1950 law known as the Lodge Act. After five years
of service they could become citizens. "It is hoped," Lodge told them, "that

you are the human material from which military leaders—either commissioned or noncommissioned—are made. It is believed that your knowledge of foreign languages, customs and terrain will be of great help to this country. But above all we want you to feel that you do not enter the U.S. Army as mercenaries or as a foreign legion. You are very definitely volunteers in the world struggle for human freedom."

Lodge had returned to Beverly when, on Saturday, November 10, he was telephoned by Dewey. "Cabot," said Dewey, "I'm trying to get the Eisenhower supporters together for a meeting tomorrow in my suite at the Roosevelt in New York. I think it's very important and I hope you can come." Lodge agreed to do so.

They had already had several discussions about the need for a campaign manager. There was a sort of unwritten understanding that he should be from Eisenhower's general Kansas area. Dewey had suggested Barak T. Mattingly of St. Louis, and Lodge liked the idea because Mattingly had served as a national committeeman and knew many Republican pros. Also, Lodge had faith in Dewey's judgment and admired his unselfishness in keeping in the background while giving indispensable help in the Eisenhower drive.

When Lodge arrived at the permanent suite that Dewey kept in the Roosevelt, both Dewey and Mattingly were there. So was General Lucius D. Clay, who had broken the Russian blockade of Berlin, and was one of Eisenhower's old and close friends. Lodge was to develop high regard for Clay's clear head and courage. Also present was Dewey's 1948 campaign manager, Herbert Brownell, whom Lodge later termed "one of the most intelligent men I have ever met." J. Russell Sprague, Long Island Republican boss, was there. Jim Duff arrived later.

One of the complications in choosing a manager was that Dewey and Duff actively disliked each other. Dewey had not forgiven Duff for trying to stop his nomination in 1948. Duff thought Dewey's ineptitude had lost the 1948 election. Duff refused to accept Dewey's proposal of Mattingly as manager. Harry Darby called in from Kansas to object to Mattingly also. Many other names were suggested, to all of which either Dewey or Duff objected. Duff had to leave the meeting before anything was decided. Finally Brownell suggested that Lodge himself become the campaign manager. Dewey took up the idea. "I'd never even thought of myself in such a role," Lodge said, bemused. "But if I'm the only man you can agree on I'll consider it very seriously."

Maxwell Rabb, who had been Lodge's administrative assistant until the senator's wartime resignation, was playing golf at the Belmont Country Club that Veterans' Day afternoon when he was called to the telephone.

"This is Cabot," said the voice. "I'm at La Guardia on my way home. Can you meet me at Beverly?" Rabb said he could.

"I remember thinking how fast he got there," Rabb recalled later. "By the time I got changed and drove to Cabot's home he was already there. Mason Sears arrived. Cabot told us they wanted him to head up the campaign. 'Of course,' Cabot said, 'we don't know whether we will have a candidate or not. And I have my own campaign to run against Jack Kennedy. He's going to be a tough man to beat and my own campaign will suffer if I do this. Should I take it on?' "

"It's pretty clear to me," said Rabb.

"I told him, 'You have always complained about being in the minority. You always felt your hands were tied by that. You have always wanted to get into a position where you could do more good than in the minority. If you can elect a Republican President you will be in that position. I think you've got to take a chance on your Senate career and do it.' Mason Sears felt the same way. 'Good,' said Cabot. 'We start on Monday.' "

Lodge called Dewey and told him he would take on the job if Duff also wanted him to. Duff soon telephoned to say he would be delighted. Lodge, Rabb and Mason Sears descended on New York—with Sears carrying his old battered bag. Dewey had set up Suite 922 at the Commodore, and Tom Stephens came up from Washington to run the office. Lodge called up Geraldyne Creagan, Senator Vandenberg's secretary who was eager for something useful to do, and brought her in as girl Friday. Van's son and namesake, Arthur Jr., came in to help.

Thus Henry Cabot Lodge took on the making of a President.

When the choice was announced on November 16, it was widely hailed. "An act of unity," said Arthur Krock of the *Times*. "Senator Lodge is a skilful politician. He can walk on eggs when he thinks that is indicated by circumstances and not break any. But when he is committed to a political enterprise he is a hard, bold and unremitting fighter. . . . Good looks, pleasing manners and a fine intelligence complete an equipment which should be very effective in this new undertaking." Citing Lodge's successful fight for troops for Eisenhower and his recent attack on the Administration's lagging supplies to the general, Krock said Lodge had in effect been Eisenhower's watchdog and "personal agent in Congress." Joe Alsop of the New York *Herald Tribune* termed Lodge "one of the ablest political operators of our time" and predicted the "once loose coalition will now be transformed into a tough and tightly knit phalanx with resources and ability to take on all comers." "No better choice could be made," said Clare Luce. "Senator Lodge is an extremely able politician, a man of enormous determination, conviction and ideals who will inspire confidence . . ."

With the New York headquarters functioning smoothly, Lodge went back to Washington to expand the original informal nucleus there. He opened an Eisenhower for President headquarters in suite 600-G at the Shoreham Hotel, spread bigger-than-life photos of the smiling general around it, and placed Wes Roberts, former chairman of the Kansas State Republican Committee, in charge. During these weeks Lodge was on the telephone all day and much of the night getting similar committees organized and functioning in every major city. Typical was the call to Allen Lowe, manager of Cleveland's Hotel Carter, who announced that he had accepted the "Ohio assignment" to see that General Eisenhower was nominated and elected. Sometimes the organization existed only in one man's hat or on a letterhead, or the founders could meet in a phone booth—but each group drew followers and grew. Enemies tried to prove that Eisenhower was really a Democrat. Walter Trohan of the Chicago *Tribune* dug out what he claimed was Eisenhower's "first public speech," on November 9, 1909, before the Young Men's Democratic Club of Abilene, in which he attacked the Republican Party as the party of "legalized robbery." President Truman claimed that Eisenhower had been a Democratic precinct worker in Kansas in his youth while Arthur Sylvester of the Newark *Evening News* reported that "Eisenhower has told friends in the presence of this correspondent that although his family has always been Republican he has voted in only one national election—for Franklin D. Roosevelt in 1944." But Truman's own court jester, George Allen, undercut this by observing: "I know General Eisenhower is a Republican because Lord knows I've tried hard enough to convert him to be a Democrat. I didn't have a bit of luck." The old China hand, George Sokolsky, asserted in a magnificent non sequitur that Republicans could not embrace Eisenhower because General MacArthur had "linked him with Dean Acheson in his address to the American Legion." Harold Stassen added a note of general mystery by visiting the general and announcing afterward that Eisenhower "definitely would not run," and that therefore, he, Stassen, would.

Piece by piece, the organization grew. Some typical memos give the flavor of the process. On Wednesday, November 28, 1951, Lodge met at the Commodore suite with Jim Duff, Herb Brownell, Russ Sprague, Tom Stephens, Barak Mattingly, Max Rabb, Mason Sears, Cam Newberry (a Little, Brown editor who had helped Lodge in various campaigns), Duff's assistant Lefty Lush, and Congressman Hugh Scott of Pennsylvania. The planners methodically went over the situation in each state, and chose assignments for each other. The following is a partial summary:

ALABAMA: *Brownell will supervise actively and keep in touch with Vardaman: Atkins, NCM [National Committeeman] and the NCW [National Committeewomen] are out publicly for Taft.*

ARIZONA: *HCL talked to Gov. Pyle. He will remain neutral for time being but says that he "is not at all unfriendly." HCL will see Pyle personally sooner or later. Feeling was that the Governor would respond to HCL more readily than to another emissary. The newspaper there is pro-Eisenhower. Gene Pulliam of Indianapolis influential here.*

CALIFORNIA: *Scott reports that Nixon's understanding is that the delegation will go for Warren but will have considerable freedom of action. All agree it will be a great mistake to go against Warren and HCL was to call him and let him know that the E. forces will do nothing to harm Warren's candidacy. Scott will advise Dana Smith that we don't want any activity for E.*

COLORADO: *Gov. Thornton told HCL that this is "an honor for us to be considered in connection with leadership in the E. movement," particularly because he is a new Governor. Rocky Mountain News for E.*

GEORGIA: *Harry Simmes, NCM, under great pressure from Taft. Simmes is a pretty sick man and doesn't want to fight with anybody. . . . HCL is to call Woodruff of Coca-Cola.*

MARYLAND: *Both Scott and Sprague will suggest developments. McKeldin says sentiment for E., but evidently he wants to be a favorite son. He would like to "second" Eisenhower and has VP ambitions. Congressman Glenn Beall is the closest adviser to McKeldin . . . HCL will drop a line to McKeldin indicating Sprague will be down there to scout around and we would appreciate any courtesies he could show.*

MONTANA: *Anaconda holds the key. Brownell will watch.*

MICHIGAN: *Sprague says Summerfield and Coleman very close so he thinks Summerfield is for Taft. Arthur Vandenberg says Summerfield claims he is neutral though Taft people put him down for Taft. Sec. of State Alger (candidate for Governor) for E.*

MINNESOTA: *Senator Thye told HCL he has publicly declared E. the strongest man but Stassen has delegates' pledge to him. It was agreed that this should be a favorite son state.*

MISSOURI: *Duff felt it was better to make mistakes than to do nothing at all. HCL is to talk with Darby and Roy Roberts regarding Kansas and Missouri to see if he can't push them on.*

MISSISSIPPI: *Three or four delegates. It was felt they should be permitted to stay with Taft. It was not worth the fight.*

NORTH CAROLINA: *Simm Delap is for E. Strong man in state. Says that he can insure a strong E. delegation. Delap is regarded as excellent and reliable. Bayley, State chairman, inclined toward us. NCM and NCW for Taft. This state is in good shape. Duff is charged with N.C.*

OREGON: *HCL called Ralph Cake who is for E. and he said the situation looks good for the delegation. Four different men around to lead E. bandwagon. Gov. Sprague is for E. Dewey men present were surprised and pleased to find that Cake would not be against them this time.*

SOUTH CAROLINA: *Can't do anything here. State Chairman Bates Gerald and Mrs. (according to Sprague) control the votes and have already gone to Taft—6 delegates. State chairman of the Republican Committee wrote Duff that he was favorable to E.*

TENNESSEE: *Mattingly says we may get something there but is not too optimistic. Only way we could get delegates is to get Congressional candidates to run and stir up a campaign. Lynn Hall can be helpful as well as Maxy Jarman who can raise some money there.*

TEXAS: *Successor of Col. Creager is for Taft. The meeting that Duff had there was one of the biggest that Republicans or Democrats ever had, with an attendance of over 600. Oil people in Texas for E. Hugh Roy Cullen and Sid Richardson for E.*

WISCONSIN: *Mrs. Peavey Heffelfinger wrote that it might be inadvisable to run E. in Wisconsin because 1) candidate must certify in his own handwriting and 2) most expensive kind of campaign and 3) thinks Stassen has strength. Gov. Dewey advises against going in. Sprague says "don't start any E. clubs in Wisconsin. Don't mention E's name in any official way etc." It was agreed that if favorite son could run it would be the best thing and that somebody should talk to Stassen which was another possible approach. Sprague agreed to confer with Stassen.*

WASHINGTON: *Scott reports that Gov. Langlie suggested that the various factions get together on E. and Senator Cain approves this.*

And so it went—dreary, detailed, tedious, the slow building of a movement to make a President.

Manager Lodge, who had wanted long ago to make a science out of politics, scrawled detailed memos to his staff. This one was marked "for public relations man":

Information which would be helpful to Eisenhower h.q.:

Where do governors stand?

The state chairman and vice chairman? The 1948 delegates? The Young Republican orgs.?

What newspapers are for us? What magazines? What columnists? What radio and TV people?

Many press friends will help us push the "party line." What is it?

226   Help came from the most unexpected quarters. The irrepressible Elsa Maxwell began plugging the general in her *Journal-American* column and acted to bring Lodge together with Arthur Godfrey who (she wrote him) "could do more toward his being elected than all of us put together for he reaches more than 10,000,000 people daily."

Again Lodge fired similar questions and observations:

> *Many influential people are committing themselves to the opposition through failure to hear from Eisenhower supporters (i.e., Jewett Todd, Jim Dewey, C. D. Atkins etc.).*
>
> *What prominent persons formerly in Taft, Stassen, Warren or other camps will issue public endorsements of Eisenhower upon request (i.e., Walter Judd, Lamar Tooz who nominated Warren)?*

On December 4, 1951, Paul Hoffman, who had been Vandenberg's successful choice for ECA administrator and had done an outstanding job, called Lodge with some ideas to help the Eisenhower movement gather steam.

"I think you ought to have a three-man strategy board," he said," "to lay out a thorough propaganda campaign, through publicity, through advertising, and through organizational activities in the congressional districts."

Lodge liked the idea and asked for candidates.

Hoffman, who had just become head of the Ford Foundation, suggested Earl Newsom, the public relations man who had been so successful in creating a new "image" for Ford and its young president, Henry Ford II. Hoffman also thought John Cowles, publisher of the Des Moines *Register-Tribune* and the Minneapolis *Tribune,* would be most helpful. He suggested James Young, head of Young & Rubicam advertising agency.

Lodge was able to reach only Newsom and Young but got them to meet him the following Monday at the Commodore. They later got together with Cowles and the three of them came up with some additional ideas. They mapped out a "two-phase program," the first being what they called "the jet takeoff" and the second "the sustained flight."

For the takeoff phase, they recommended the immediate formation of a national committee of two hundred well-known citizens which might be called "The People's Committee for Eisenhower" or "We the People for Eisenhower."

They thought the first step was to get the right person for chairman of the group. Young suggested Henry Ford II. Directing the publicity also would be important. Newsom thought his partner, Charles Moore, might be available if Ford would act as chairman. Ford, however, decided against it. Ultimately the group became Citizens for Eisenhower, and Vandenberg

and Mrs. Oswald Lord were named co-chairmen. Later, Paul Hoffman and   227
Walter Williams of Seattle, former president of the Committee for Economic Development, would head it.

Finances to pay the room rent, phone bills, office help, and travel expenses were a problem from the outset. The layman might expect the very
name Eisenhower to start a golden flood of money. However, men capable
of making large political contributions do not part with them quickly, or
lightly, particularly for men who are not even candidates. For quite a few
weeks money was a very real problem. Lodge turned for immediate help to
Emily's younger brother, Henry Sears, a New York investment banker, and
a wealthy one, who knew the main sources of finance capital in New York.
Sears formed something called the Manhattan Committee for Better Government to defray these initial expenses (Lodge turned in expenses of
$248.58 for October 24 to November 24, and $446.33 from November to
December 28). A more experienced man than Sears was available in Harold
Talbot, former finance chairman of the Republican National Committee,
but he had been Dewey's money-raiser. Lodge wanted to avoid giving the
Taft forces any ammunition to claim the movement was a Dewey front. He
sought the help of John Hay Whitney, multimillionaire capitalist and wartime friend and admirer of Eisenhower. Whitney helped set up an Eisenhower Finance Committee with Howard Petersen, a Philadelphia banker,
as chairman. Under this aegis Harold Talbot later put his talents to work
and raised a large part of the total. Harry Sears also helped throughout.

The first major move which could be made to advance Eisenhower's
chances would be to enter him in the New Hampshire primary, the nation's first, held in early March. However, Army regulations strictly forbade
the General's being a willing candidate, and if he should repudiate the
move, the whole drive would collapse. Lodge sought out Eisenhower's old
bridge-playing friend, William Robinson of the *Herald Tribune*. Robinson
flew to Paris and spent Christmas Day with the Eisenhowers. Lodge went
to New York and awaited Robinson at the Commodore impatiently.

"If we enter him in the primary," said Robinson, "the General won't repudiate it. He is willing to return in June, but he can do nothing publicly
before that time. And after that time he will not lift a finger to get the
nomination himself."

Duff and the others had insisted that Eisenhower would have to come
back and actively campaign if they were to have a chance of nominating
him. The prospects now seemed quite inadequate to Lodge. But he determined to make the best of it.

Shortly after Christmas he set to work drafting a letter to Governor Sherman Adams of New Hampshire to enter Eisenhower's name in the primary.
His job was complicated by the fact that some Democrats had already en-

228   tered Eisenhower's name swearing he was a member of *their* party. Lodge himself still did not know if Eisenhower actually was a Republican. But all the tenor of their past talks at Columbia led him to think so. Lodge's letter to Adams said Army regulation No. 600-10 prohibiting "any public activity looking to the influencing of an election," prevented the General from speaking, and added:

> *In the circumstances, therefore, I consider it incumbent to divulge certain conversations which I had with General Eisenhower while he was serving in a civilian capacity at Columbia. . . . Senator Duff and Senator Carlson and others have told me that they have had similar conversations. During these discussions he specifically said that his voting record was that of a Republican. He also pointed out that his political convictions coincided with enlightened Republican doctrine and that the family tradition was Republican. In these circumstances, the signers of the Republican petition are completely secure in their signed sworn statement that General Eisenhower is a member of their party. . . . The Democratic petitioners are swearing to something that is contrary to fact. . . . In our conversations . . . General Eisenhower . . . pointed out that he would never seek public office but would consider it a call to political service by the will of the party and the people to be the highest form of duty.*
>
> *I therefore authorize you to enter the name of Dwight Eisenhower in the primary election for the expression of the preference of Republicans of the State of New Hampshire for President of the United States. . . .*
>
> *Very sincerely yours,*
> *Henry Cabot Lodge Jr.*

Lodge mailed the letter to Governor Adams on Friday, January 4. On Sunday, January 6, he notified reporters that he would have an "important announcement" at the 600-G Shoreham headquarters in Washington. So many came that they overflowed into the hall. "In a room barely big enough to serve a four-passenger omelette," Alistair Cooke reported in the Manchester *Guardian*, "50 correspondents sweated like Calcutta bulls. Another score crowded a narrow corridor well beyond earshot. Two or three pretty but ineffectual young ladies, whose hearts belonged to Eisenhower, were passing out Eisenhower buttons in a cubicle with two typewriters which was meant to serve as a combination secretariat, press room, and powder lounge. Senator Lodge himself was reared up against a grinning mural of Ike like a brave suspect at a police lineup. Evidently the Senator had no idea that General Eisenhower is a man known far and wide."

This skeptical mood was shared by other newsmen. When Lodge made his "important announcement"—"I hereby announce that Eisenhower is a Republican, and we are entering him as such in the New Hampshire primary"—the reporters understandably wanted to know what authority he had to say and do this. Since Lodge had absolutely none, it was an embarrasing question. "Go and ask the General," said Lodge. "I assure you that I will not be repudiated." They promptly did so. It was already evening at SHAPE headquarters, and the officer of the day turned away all inquirers, denying them any access to the Supreme Commander. Finally, General Charles T. Lanham told the besieging reporters in France: "There will be no statement tonight. Early tomorrow morning we shall give the General a full report on Senator Lodge's statement and if he chooses to make some comment, then it will be made available . . . But there is no guarantee at all that the General will say anything for the record."

"That was a pretty grim Monday in Lodge's office," Max Rabb recalls, "just waiting around. It looked as if we were out on a limb. Reporters were still flocking around, complaining about his calling them out on a Sunday. 'You've got a story either way,' Lodge told them. 'If Eisenhower says he's a candidate it's a big story, if not I'm the goat.'"

Alistair Cooke had already made the latter conclusion. "As we rinsed off our perspiration and climbed back into our own shirts," he wrote, "the grumbles passed around: 'This is the first and last Eisenhower press conference,' 'He'll never do this again,' 'the guy does not know a thing.' 'Let's take him up on it, let's call Paris.' By the time Paris had coldly turned down any confirming words and thrown up a cordon of infantry and French gendarmes around the Eisenhower headquarters, the Senator had beaten a judicious retreat and 'gone for a walk in the woods.'"

Not until Tuesday morning did Paris respond. Eisenhower issued this statement:

> *Senator Lodge's announcement of yesterday as reported in the press gives an accurate account of the general tenor of my political convictions and of my Republican voting record. He was correct also in stating that I would not seek nomination to political office. I have frequently and publicly expressed my refusal to do so. My convictions in this regard have been reinforced by the character and importance of [my] duty. . . . I realize that Sen. Lodge and his associates are exercising this right in an attempt to place before me next July a duty that would transcend my present responsibilities. In the absence, however, of a clearcut call to political duty, I shall continue to devote my full attention and energies to the performance of the vital task to which I am assigned.*

Lodge could now come out of the woods.

One could scarcely predict the obstacles which would have to be hurdled, Lodge's group, unable to quote Eisenhower on anything connected with the campaign, had gotten together a reprint of his various remarks in the past—including one opposing loyalty oaths for teachers [shades of Jim Curley!]. One of the party's sturdiest and wealthiest East Shore pillars, Pierre du Pont, wrote:

General Eisenhower's comment . . . with respect to academic freedom is certainly mystifying to me and does not speak well for the analytic ability and judgment of General Eisenhower . . . There would seem to be various reasons why a special loyalty oath or other oath might be required of a teacher, and yet would be entirely inappropriate for a parent, or for a minister if his congregation felt otherwise.

Lodge patiently got off a reply:

The General has discussed this subject on many occasions. . . . He apparently has come to the conclusion that special oaths for faculty members are undesirable and impractical as a means of keeping subversive teachers out of the classrooms. He has stated, "Before appointing a man to our faculty, I would want to know all there is to know about his background. If I found he was a Communist, I would not appoint him." Presumably the General believes that a Communist would not balk at signing a loyalty oath, and that the way to deal with him is not to let him into the faculty in the first place. . . . Only the General, of course, can explain it in greater detail.

The next big event before the New Hampshire primary was a meeting January 17 of the Republican National Committee with California State Committee and State chairmen from ten Western states at the Fairmont Hotel in San Francisco. The committee invited all prospective candidates to make speeches or send their spokesmen. Taft had intended to come, but on learning that Lodge was scheduled to speak for Eisenhower, sent his campaign Manager, David S. Ingalls, instead. Ingalls was the dinner speaker on Thursday the seventeenth, Lodge spoke at lunch the next day, and Stassen at dinner the following evening.

Believing this to be the biggest and most important Republican gathering before the convention itself, Lodge wanted to start it off with some dramatic showing. He persuaded poll-takers to take a poll of Taft's own hometown, Cincinnati. It showed that four out of five people who voted for Taft for senator in 1950 would prefer Ike for President. He had the poll widely distributed in San Francisco. He flew out with Max Rabb, Howard Petersen, Harry Sears, Tom Stephens and Mason Sears, who carried his ubiquitous bag, and he brought a dozen other volunteers along to "surround" the meeting. They opened up their headquarters and spread big pictures around. Still, the atmosphere was not encouraging: "We felt really lonely," Max Rabb recalls. "All the pros were crowding around Taft's headquarters. Young people were enthusiastic for us but there was no real life in our headquarters. There was great life in Taft's. But that night we got our first big break—Dave Ingalls' speech."

Ingalls, a ruggedly handsome, gray-thatched World War I naval air ace, pulled no punches. "There need be no reason for the Republican Party to buy a pig in a poke," he asserted. Lodge stared in disbelief that Ingalls would liken Eisenhower to a pig. The party, said Ingalls, needed "a militant Republican rather than a mild variant of the leadership now in power." At this, the grin froze on the face of Earl Warren, a Republican whom Democrats adored. "Hero worship," Ingalls continued, "is no substitute for faith based on past performance. Neither is glamor or sex appeal." Then, finally, the prize line of the evening: The party should not "select a good-looking mortician to preside over its death as a political organization." Even hardened old pros, who had not blinked at the pig line, started a bit at the undertaker one.

Lodge had brought along a prepared speech which he had sent in advance to Dewey, Brownell and Duff: "typed triple space . . . mark it up as ruthlessly as you feel inclined to do, I shall certainly appreciate it." He stuck strictly to extolling Ike's unique qualifications and derogated nobody's. He interpolated a warning against "taking cracks at one another which will endanger cooperation" later on; he would not "take sly digs at other candidates."

"The whole atmosphere changed for us after that," Rabb recalls. "The crowds began to pour into our suite at the Fairmont. It marked a kind of psychological change. They no longer counted us as amateurs." Many key Republicans came to offer to help Eisenhower. The pros, who in many cases controlled delegates, recognized for the first time that the Eisenhower men were in earnest and had a capable organization in the making. They were gaining influential support. From his lofty empyrean of the Public Philosophy, Walter Lippmann wrote: "The case for Eisenhower is compelling for anyone who thinks as I do that the paramount problem is how, after 20 years . . . the Republicans can be brought to power without causing a convulsion at home and abroad."

They watched after a myriad of details. Even from San Francisco, Howard Petersen took time to wire Arthur Vandenberg at the Commodore his suggestions for Pennsylvania members of the national Citizens Committee: Raymond Pitcairn, maker of Pitcairn Autogyros; Robert L. Johnson, president of Temple University, Teddy Roosevelt, Jr. ("Cabot clears these names. First is almost a must and other two highly desirable"). Lodge bucked a request to RCA chairman David Sarnoff: "Jock Whitney . . . told me that you have an absolute genius in your organization, Manie Sacks, who can be extremely helpful," and asked for his services.

Back to New York they went. One of Vandenberg's notes, scribbled on Mason Sears' memo pad gives an idea of the organization's multiplying activities:

Assignments other than Lodge's arising as of January 25 meeting in New York.

TOM STEPHENS—*to visit New Hampshire and Vermont.*
WES ROBERTS—*to visit Oregon and Montana.*
ARTHUR VANDENBERG—*preparation of proposed stands for Ike to take on issues.*
SENATOR CARLSON—*start up AL and VFW kingmakers for Ike.*
  urge Youngdahl to pull out Lindquist.
  to ask Wes Roberts to go to Oregon and Montana.
GENERAL CLAY—*to pull out Bradshaw Mintener from Minn. to see Roy Roberts re Missouri.*
GOV. DEWEY—*to ask Gen. Clay to see Roy Roberts.*
  to call a man named Tom Heath re Idaho.
  to begin calling on telephone around Feb. 10.
  to write a letter to Queeny re Arkansas.
  to get Dulles to prepare Far East statement.
SENATOR DUFF—*to contact Sim Delap re Crusade of Freedom in N.C.*
  to call Lloyd and Gov. Thornton (Col.) about Gordon Weller, our Colorado contact.
MATTINGLY—*to check on John Kjellum of Jamestown, N.D.*
  to check on Paul Bellamy of Rapid City, S.D.
  to see Gov. McKeldin of Maryland.
  to pull off Dunn re Minnesota.
BROWNELL—*to find out re Lloyd Adams and Eberle in Idaho.*
  to offer through Bilby second speech to Gov. Pyle (Ariz.)
[*And the added scrawl*]: *Cabot—this is just for your information. Nothing here for you to do. A.V.*

Young Vandenberg, pursuing his preparation of Ike's proposed stands on issues, asked Gabriel Hauge, a gifted young economist and editor writer for *Business Week,* to produce what Hauge modestly called "a working paper which I hope the help of many heads and hands can whip into usable shape"; the paper turned out to be a minor classic of formulating the progressive Republican philosophy. "To this generation of Americans," it began, "much has been given. By the same token much is expected . . . Our political faith rests on certain foundation stones. It is of critical importance that we do not forget what they are . . . *First,* individual freedom . . ." Wisely, Hauge put the rights of individuals ahead of everything else.

Lodge sped up to Boston to address the State CIO Convention and won a big personal hand from the six hundred delegates who, nevertheless, withheld support of Eisenhower until his labor views were better known. "It is unfortunate that all Republicans don't think and act as you have," President Irving M. Simon told Lodge in a personal tribute.

Lodge, a systematic man, collected miscellaneous fragments of information on nominating and electing Presidents, such as this extract from *Paths to the Present* by Arthur M. Schlesinger, Sr.: "Abraham Lincoln, rounding up support for his candidacy, bought the Illinois *Staats-Anzeiger* for the duration of the campaign, thus helping the offset the *Staate-Zeitung*'s advocacy of William H. Seward as the nominee as well as securing a vigorous Teutonic organ in the post-convention battle. As President, he rewarded the editor with a consulate in Samoa."

On February 8, at 11 P.M., the Eisenhower backers led by promoter Tex McCrary, staged a big rally in Madison Square Garden, jamming it almost to the rafters with some fifteen thousand screaming, eager supporters, waving beneath an immense WE LIKE IKE banner strung across the whole cavernous hall, listening to screen and stage stars who had volunteered their talents. It was criticized as poorly managed and as frivolous, but the critics missed the point. Lodge thought that anything which brought fifteen thousand people into a hall at midnight nine months before election would impress politicians, the country and the General himself. Lodge arranged to have the whole jamboree put on film. As soon as the film was processed, an Ike volunteer, the aviator Jacqueline Cochrane, flew the Atlantic in her own plane to show the film to Eisenhower personally. "By the time she reached our house she had gone 35 hours without sleep," Eisenhower related. "The film . . . was shown in our living room at Villa St. Pierre in Marnes-la-Coquette. It was a moving experience to witness the obvious unanimity of such a huge crowd—to realize that everyone present was enthusiastically supporting me for the highest office of the land. . . . Mamie and I were profoundly affected. The incident had impressed me more than had all the arguments presented by . . . individuals. . . . When our guests departed I think we both suspected . . . that our lives were to be once more uprooted."

Shortly after the Cochrane visit, Eisenhower flew to London for the

234   funeral of King George VI. General Clay also came over to London and brought with him Sid Richardson, the Texas oil millionaire, and the ubiquitous George Allen, who had managed somehow to ingratiate himself as much with Eisenhower as with Truman. Ike met with them and agreed to run for President if nominated at the convention. At that point he was still imagining he might be nominated by acclamation without lifting a finger for himself.

At this point the whole movement hit its worst tailspin. Eisenhower's supporters in New Hampshire had bragged that the primary was "in the bag." Lodge got reports of growing Taft sentiment. The situation was dangerous, since the misguided boasting would make anything less than total victory look like a bad defeat. Moreover, Lodge's treasury was running low— and few new funds were coming in. Lodge decided to sink the remainder into the New Hampshire race.

He sent up Tom Stephens a month before the primary to work closely with the active organization Sherman Adams was building. Sig Larmon went up to help with advertising and posters. The ballot was complicated: the order of delegate candidates changed in each precinct. Nevertheless, Lodge got sample ballots printed for each of the 250-plus precincts, each marked to show where a vote for Eisenhower's delegates should be placed. A sample was sent to every registered Republican.

Taft was out barnstorming in Colorado and had been gaining votes there. Lodge was hopeful of drawing him into stumping New Hampshire, and tried a bit of psychological warfare to draw him in. Newspapers had been asserting that the most important thing was the popularity poll, not who won the most delegates. Lodge felt sure that the personal popularity of the fourteen Eisenhower candidates would win at least ten of the fourteen delegate positions. He was less certain of the popularity poll, since Stassen also was running and would draw away some of the "modern Republican" following. Lodge told newsmen he "didn't care about the popularity contest" —the delegate vote was what counted. This was interpreted as a sign of hedging against disaster. Taft took the bait. He cried that the Ike men were "on the run" and dashed up to New Hampshire to see if he couldn't clinch the victory which he thought he smelled. MacArthur helped out with a wire to a Nashua supporter, "SUGGEST YOU SUPPORT TAFT."

Until the Friday before election, Ike's backers had simply been pressing the case for Eisenhower. When Taft arrived, he began attacking Eisenhower as the absentee wonder, saying he should be there to state his own position on the issues, and that people would be foolish to vote for anybody without knowing where he stood. This gave Lodge the chance to open up on where Taft stood. He and Adams had a powwow in the corridor of Nashua High School. Lodge wanted Adams to handle the attack but Adams said Lodge

would have to provide the ammunition on foreign policy, and senate issues.
Lodge prepared a catalogue of the most glaringly reactionary positions Taft
had taken on foreign policy. However, instead of mentioning Taft, Lodge put
them down as positions Eisenhower would *not* take. Adams made this
analysis the basis for his final speech, which was spread all over the state
in advertising reprints, posters and press releases. The final vote: Eisenhower 46,497, Taft 35,820. Furthermore, Eisenhower walked off with all
fourteen delegates. Victory was total.

Not long after this victory came a surprise in Minnesota which had some
amusing overtones. Some of the staff memoranda cited above reflected an
original decision not to contest Minnesota, and to encourage Stassen; Clay's
assignment to "pull out Bradshaw Mintener" was to halt what the managers
thought a misguided write-in effort for Eisenhower there. Lodge himself
wired Mintener: "Hope and strongly request neither you nor anyone else
enter Eisenhower's name in Minnesota." In spite of all this, Mintener had
gone right ahead and led a statewide campaign for an Eisenhower write-in.
Stassen won with 128,605 votes yet Eisenhower, not even on the ballot, got
106,946. "They just wrote in Ike or whatever if they couldn't spell the name,"
Eisenhower chuckled many years later. "I was more impressed by that than
anything that happened." William Holbrook, secretary of the Minnesota
group, threw Lodge an understandable "I told you so," saying Lodge was
"close to a little number of substantial people but not to a substantial number of little people." Paul Hoffman came back from a series of visits with
Eisenhower saying the Minnesota vote would "remove the last vestige of
doubt in Eisenhower's mind that vast numbers of Americans want him to
run." Shortly after, Eisenhower said Minnesota might make him "reexamine" his early refusal to discuss a date for returning. Said Lodge: "Eisenhower will be in the right place at the right time."

It was high time for Ike to "reexamine." If he had any lingering thoughts
of being nominated by acclamation, they were soon dispelled. It would take
the hardest fight imaginable to win it—just how hard was indicated by the
tabulation which Mason Sears handed Cabot on the eve of the New Hampshire primary on March 12:

*While the delegates estimates are necessarily speculative at such an
early date they indicate the following:*
There are 1205 convention votes with 603 necessary to nominate.

TAFT	600
EISENHOWER	469
WARREN	76

As they stand, these figures mean that General Eisenhower cannot be nominated unless he is given the combined support of Warren, Stassen, and McKeldin, whereas Taft can be put across by any single one of them. To get away from a position where any one of these three men can throw the nomination to Taft, it will be necessary for the General to gain about 60 votes. The bulk of these could come from Michigan and Pennsylvania.

As a result of this memo, Lodge gave high priority to some proselytizing of Michigan's National Committeeman Arthur Summerfield, his former ally in the effort to nominate Vandenberg. Summerfield would not commit himself beyond staying neutral; that alone was a big gain. Herb Brownell began doing the same with Governor John S. Fine of Pennsylvania, who also got on the fence to stay. Lodge was now able to demand and get the full-time assistance of Brownell whom he called "a man of tremendous effectiveness." Brownell now became the chief planner and tactician ("cool, farsighted, effective, objective" as Lodge described him) for the Initial Advisory Group, as the Eisenhower managers modestly called themselves.

There were twelve men in this group, but their names had been published only once, on June 7, when they had lunched with Eisenhower at Columbia. They ran the national campaign, working closely with the important groups in the states. If their collective title seemed colorless, it was deliberately so. Lodge had chosen it carefully, so that no one who was not one of the twelve would feel that he was left out of the major planning.

On April 4 Lodge flew to Paris, where he was met by newsmen at Orly Field and held a press conference, followed by another at the George V. Next morning he rode out to SHAPE headquarters to see Eisenhower before lunch. The General had the long-awaited good news ready for him.

"I can tell you definitely," he said, "that I will be able to come home on June 1, return to private life, and I will accept the Republican nomination if it is offered." He still withheld one commitment. He refused to say whether he would be willing to campaign.

Lodge brought Eisenhower up to date on everything that had happened thus far. Michigan and Pennsylvania would be extremely crucial, Lodge said, and so would Texas, whose state convention was to take place at Mineral Wells on May 27, with thirty-eight delegates at stake. "Duff went out to Texas," Lodge told the General. "Everybody is wild about you out there, but the Taft forces control the state machinery. We may have trouble."

They lunched on fresh trout which Eisenhower had caught in the pool in front of his house. Officers on the staff, those from European nations as well as Americans, bombarded Lodge with questions about the political situation. That night Cabot had dinner at the General's house and reassured Mrs. Eisenhower: "The candidate should always get enough rest to be fresh and enthusiastic. I won't approve any program which makes your husband have to work too hard."

Returning to the George V, Lodge held another press conference. The French reporters were particularly pleased with him, because he could act as his own interpreter for them and for the newsreel cameras. They were not accustomed to such fluently bilingual American statesmen.

Back home again, Lodge began to make plans for Eisenhower's home-coming day on June 1. In doing so, he was pleased to observe that the money was now beginning to come in as a result of the success in New Hampshire. Already more than a half-million dollars had been collected for the campaign fund since the beginning, but unfortunately expenses had been considerable, and at the end of April the balance was only $63,751.44.

It was time, Lodge thought, that he went out and did a little campaigning himself.

"He and I went out most everywhere," Max Rabb recalls, "into every kind of meeting. In Utah, Nick Morgan turned out a band for us in that strong Taft territory—Nick owned the Salt Lake Bees—he has the Hawaiian team now. I got terribly airsick in Cheyenne. Lodge and I went to Houston and had breakfast at the Rice Hotel with L. F. McCollum, the big oil man. They were strong for Taft there but they listened, I'll say that for 'em. John Blafner, a young oil man, flew us in his plane to Dallas and to the Adolphus Hotel, where John Porter met us. He got rich people together in Dallas to listen to us. We went barnstorming through Colorado, Kansas, California, Spokane, Portland."

On May 2 young Vandenberg sent Lodge a memo on convention hotel arrangements in Chicago.

Confirming arrangements made at the Conrad Hilton for 39 rooms on the 11th floor, to be made by Tom Stephens, telephone arrangements by Howard Chase.

The suite directly in back of the floor checker is to be assigned to Senator Lodge. This suite includes Rooms 1100, 1101, 1102, 1101A and 1102A. This is all to be working space to be set up as follows:

1101A will be the general reception room requiring one desk and a telephone.

1100 will require two desks and two telephones.

1101 will be the office for Senator Lodge requiring one desk, one switchboard extension with two private lines.

> *1102 will require two desks and two switchboard extensions, and bridges from both of the private outside lines in 1101.*
> *1102A will be used as a waiting room and requires one switchboard extension.*
> *1105 and 1106 to be assigned to Mr. Brownell.*
> *1105A and 1106A to be assigned to Mr. Paul Hoffman.*

In the May *Harper's*, Lodge turned editorialist again to write an article called "Eisenhower and the G.O.P.":

> *The clue to General Eisenhower's political method is to be found, I think, in his concept of unity. He emerges from the military sphere without having been narrowed or deformed by the habit of command, because he has always known that obedience depends upon assent. . . . His greatness as a General rests on his having been able to submerge national differences in one command; his fame as a world statesman rests on his having brought about a greater degree of European unity than had been possible in centuries of stormy history. In these achievements Eisenhower learned the arts and developed the gifts which fit him perfectly for the Presidency. . . . As Supreme Commander . . . his task was defined by the Chiefs of Staff in these words: "History records how that directive was fulfilled. Today, framed in the inarticulate voice of the great masses of the American people, there is another directive, even more tremendous in its implications for the good of this country and the cause of peace in the world: 'You will take up the Republican standard [so it might be said to read] and with all who support true individualism will restore to our American government, in its policies at home and abroad, creative purposes and moral integrity." Can there be any doubt but that this mission too is destined to be fulfilled?*

John Hay Whitney wrote Lodge about his article: "How really thrilling I think it is. I felt quite clearly that long familiar tingle at the back of my neck as I read the last words. . . . You answer all the petty questions as would a flame thrower point blank at a beehive . . ."

Out in Oregon, Lodge had run up against some difficulties. For many years it had been the custom and the law there to require all delegates to vote exactly according to the results of the popular primary. He learned that the Taft forces had found an old law, commonly believed to have been repealed, which provided that if a candidate for delegate filed a certain type of petition he would not be bound by the results of the popular vote, but could vote as he pleased. Eight men had filed under this ancient law and all were strong supporters of Taft and popular in their own right.

Oregon's Eisenhower supporters were planning ads to tell their friends to vote *against* these eight Taft candidates and *for* any of the other forty-odd candidates.

"I don't think it's sound just to be *against* someone," Lodge told them. "We ought to have a sample ballot showing those they should vote *for*."

The Oregonians told him this was impossible since the only way to have an approved slate would be for many of the forty to drop out.

"Have you tried?" he asked. "Have you got the forty together and asked if some wouldn't drop out for the sake of the cause?" They had not. Finally a meeting was held, some did drop out, and an approved slate was drafted, with the result that Oregon gave all eighteen of its delegates to Eisenhower.

Meanwhile, some strange shenanigans had been going on in Texas, as precinct conventions were held all over the state to choose the delegates to the statewide Republican convention at Mineral Wells.

For thirty years, Republican leaders had been inviting "disgruntled Democrats" to join their party, and that April national committeeman Henry Zweifel of Fort Worth had specifically invited all those who were "sick and tired" of Truman to cross over. A good many did cross over, particularly those who were strong for Eisenhower. He was very strong also among rank-and-file Republicans, though Zweifel was for Taft, as was the state executive committee which he controlled.

In precinct after precinct, Eisenhower men began winning the elections. If Taft leaders had accepted the results, 984 delegates elected to Mineral Wells would have split 722 for Eisenhower and 262, or about 30 per cent, for Taft. They did not accept them. In precinct after precinct, the defeated Taft minority bolted to hold a second, rump election which they won—and sent rival delegates to Mineral Wells. At the convention, the Taft-controlled credentials committee "decided" these contests by simply throwing out the Eisenhower delegates from thirty-one counties on the grounds that the precinct conventions had been taken over by "Communists, socialists, CIO stooges and Democrats." Some fifty deputy sheriffs barred the hall to everyone except delegates with Taft buttons. All thirty-eight Texas delegates were then declared to be Taft's. It was, in plain words, a "steal"—and one Lodge would make Taft pay dearly for.

By now it was time to prepare Eisenhower's own triumphal return from Paris. He was arriving at National Airport on June 1, but would still be under Army wraps until he could wind up his SHAPE affairs. Lodge gave out this statement:

General and Mrs. Eisenhower will arrive in Washington Sunday morning June 1. During this period the General will be fully occupied with responsibilities incident to his retirement from active duty in the Army. His arrangements will be in the hands of the Department of Defense. Those of us who are presenting his candidacy for President will not attempt to discuss politics with him or to involve him in the campaign in any way during his visit to Washington. Politics will wait until Eisenhower is free to speak as a civilian at Abilene, Kansas, on June 4. This means that there will be no public reception for General and Mrs. Eisenhower at the airport on June 1.

Lodge drew up a "proposed schedule" for these next few dramatic days:

June 1—Sunday. 9 A.M. Arrive at Washington National Airport. Arrangements for the military ceremony at the Airport to be handled by the Department of Defense. Attached is draft of proposed statement by General Eisenhower at the airport.

June 2 and 3—Monday and Tuesday—Schedule in hands of Department of Defense. It is suggested that there be no official contact with any of the political groups for the three-day period of General Eisenhower's visit in Washington. A headquarters for his political staff will be established at the Statler Hotel during this period to answer the General's phone calls and to be available to consult with him at any time he wishes. It is suggested that a specific time be set aside by the General to receive a briefing from James Hagerty concerning political press conferences.

June 4—Wednesday—7:30 A.M. Depart Washington Airport in chartered American Airlines DC-6 for Salina, Kansas. Senator Lodge will be at the airport prior to the departure of the plane to greet Eisenhower publicly for the first time and to be photographed with the General who presumably will be in civilian clothes for the first time. For persons aboard the plane see Appendix D (Gen. and Mrs. Eisenhower, Col. Robert Schulz, aide; Senator Carlson, Tom Stephens, Kevin McCann, Robert Mullin, Vandenberg, research man, two secretaries.) Arrive at Salina 11 A.M., escorted directly to site of Eisenhower Foundation at Abilene.

Lodge did not include himself in this journey, historic though it was. Eisenhower's first speech, made in a drenching rain, began the campaign and marked the first time it had an actual flesh-and-blood candidate. Lodge stayed on in Washington to line up Eastern convention delegates and arrange to bring them to New York where they could meet Eisenhower, look into his own eyes and "press the flesh," that indispensable personal ritual so important to politicians as well as voters. The mere schedule of this bewildering parade or events shows how busy Lodge soon became:

June 7—Saturday, 1:30 P.M. Lunch at Columbia residence for Initial Advisory Group. Senator Henry Cabot Lodge, Gov. Thomas E. Dewey, Senator Frank Carlson, Senator James H. Duff, General Lucius D. Clay, Herbert Brownell, Jr., J. Russell Sprague, Harry Darby, Barak T. Mattingly, Paul Hoffman and Arthur Vandenberg Jr.

June 9—Monday. Visit to General Eisenhower of New Hampshire, Connecticut, Massachusetts, Delaware delegations. Senator Lodge is to entertain the delegates at dinner at the Waldorf at 7 P.M.

June 10—Tuesday. Visit of Alabama, Georgia, North Carolina delegates. Senator Lodge is to entertain the delegates at dinner at the Astor at 7 P.M.

June 11—Wednesday. Visit of Maryland, New York, New York upstate delegates. Senator Lodge is to entertain at dinner at the Plaza at 7 P.M.

June 12—Thursday, Visit of Virginia, Rhode Island, Maine delegates. Senator Lodge is to entertain at St. Regis at 7.

And so it went. The canny manager took care even to rotate the hotels where he entertained lest any banquet manager on this highly competitive circuit be alienated. Possibly he also had the vain hope of finding one banquet menu which would be better than the others. Care was taken to see that the delegates found good seats at Broadway hit plays.

In the midst of all this activity, National Chairman Guy Gabrielson asked Lodge for a meeting with Eisenhower to inform him of the plans for temporary and permanent chairmen, and other convention arrangements. Lodge arranged a session at Eisenhower's home on Morningside Heights. Gabrielson brought Ab Herman, political director of the national committee, with him. It was soon clear that Gabrielson, a Taft man, was there as Taft's emissary to "compromise" the Texas vote fraud.

"We hope it won't be necessary for the party to wash its dirty linen in public," said Gabrielson.

Lodge blew up.

"We have no dirty linen to wash," he exclaimed, "in public or in private. Your dirty linen has already been washed in public at Mineral Wells, and the nomination won't be worth your having unless you clean up that mess."

"That's just your opinion," said Gabrielson. "There was misbehavior on both sides." He said he had heard plenty of talk of questionable actions on the part of Eisenhower men.

"I challenge you to name one single instance of misbehavior," said Lodge, "and if you can I will publicly repudiate it. And I challenge you to repudiate what was done in Taft's name in Texas." Lodge went on to observe that their very meeting had been arranged under false pretenses—to discuss convention arrangements—and had turned into something quite different.

Eisenhower himself broke in to express surprise at the tremendous campaign of character assassination which had been spread about him, and Mrs. Eisenhower as well, in Texas and elsewhere by Taft supporters. (Lodge had already filled a large folder with this despicable material headed simply "Dirt"; it was the usual farrago of anti-Semitic nonsense, implying that Eisenhower was Jewish, Communist, and part of an international conspiracy.) When the meeting ended, Lodge felt that Eisenhower, who was just having his initiation into politics, seemed a bit melancholy and subdued. He thought the General might feel that his campaign manager had been too harsh on Gabrielson. Later Eisenhower told him he had handled it the right way.

Eisenhower went on to Mamie's old home at Denver, where he planned to stay until the convention, pausing only for a visit to Detroit where a vast turnout and hero's welcome augured well for his strength in a union citadel traditionally strong for the New Deal. Lodge and his staff now mapped their final plans for Chicago. The great battery of thirty-nine rooms was assured. But a quarter-century of familiarity with the Chicago stockyards—where Lodge saw Hoover nominated in 1932—made him aware of the difficulties of getting around fast enough in the convention hall, and finding places for quiet thought and secret huddles. He had already asked the National Committee for permission "to have a room actually in the auditorium. . . . If necessary we will construct a room which we can use for conferences. I am advised by the local authorities in Chicago that such rooms are available and that there is sufficient space to do this. . . . Please therefore give this committee the necessary clearance for that room. . . ." Lodge laid out eight thousand dollars to build a special plywood, air-conditioned office on the second floor which later proved invaluable. It also paid for itself; when the Democrats took over, Averell Harriman's managers paid the original cost to get it.

The Gabrielson episode was a signal that the Taft forces were worried about the repercussions of what they had done in Texas. They had just as brazenly appropriated other delegations. For example, the regular Georgia State convention had chosen fourteen Eisenhower men and three Taft, but the Taft forces—under the ailing Harry Simmes—had held a rump meeting and chosen seventeen for Taft which the heavily pro-Taft national committee was sure to recognize; similar shenanigans went on in Louisiana and elsewhere. Lodge was sure that Taft's managers had given him a moral issue on which many delegates who were not necessarily pro-Eisenhower could be united. Three weeks before convention he announced his strategy. He would ask the convention to prohibit any contested delegate from voting until his *right* to vote had first been cleared by the whole convention. Studying past convention minutes, he concluded this would have to be done at the very outset—when the customary motion is to adopt temporarily the rules of the last convention—by an amendment to change the rules. Brownell had just come to the same conclusion and was drafting an amendment, which Lodge found "a model of brilliance, brevity, apparent simplicity and yet great effectiveness."

The Taft forces were eager to prevent what Taft called "a final knockdown dragout fight." They brought pressure on former President Hoover, a Taft sympathizer, to smooth over this major issue. Lodge got wind of this and called on Hoover in the Waldorf Towers on June 19. He told Hoover precisely what had happened at Mineral Wells. Hoover suggested that if Eisenhower and Taft would each choose an "eminent citizen" to discuss the controversy, he would be glad to try to work out an agreement between them. Lodge told him there was nothing to mediate.

Girded for battle, Lodge and his staff descended on Chicago "I'll never forget," Max Rabb recalls. "Tom Stephens said he had bribed the Hilton to take Mason Sears' shabby old bag up the back elevator because 'we want to win this thing.' He didn't want them to think we were carpetbaggers."

They found the special office at Convention Hall equipped to their liking, as they did also two other rooms at the adjoining Stock Yard Inn where they could ply uncertain delegates with argument and refreshment. They settled down in their thirty-nine rooms at the Hilton and began working almost around the clock.

A week after his Waldorf meeting with Hoover, Lodge got a wire at the Chicago Hilton from the ex-President expressing "constantly greater anxiety" over the "acerbities in this pre-convention campaign" about the Texas issue and its "effect on Republican chances in the election." He renewed his offer to mediate. "I really cannot agree that there is anything to compromise," Lodge wrote back the same day. "The facts and the law are perfectly clear, and, if you will read the enclosed letter from Mr. Ingraham, who is one of Senator Taft's most active supporters, you will see that persons on both sides agree as to what the facts and the law are. Under these circumstances it is not only better to have the Convention clear the question up; it is absolutely imperative that this be done if the public is to have confidence in the integrity of the proceedings of the . . . Convention. Frankly I cannot imagine anything more undemocratic than for three men in a private meeting to arrogate unto themselves the power to disenfranchise many thousands of American citizens."

Lodge sent along a letter from Joe Ingraham, a Houston Taft leader, who described how the conventions had been set at nought. The letter's recipient, W. H. Worrilow of the Lebanon Steel Foundry, Lebanon, Pennsylvania, had released it and the New York *Times* devoted five columns to its text. Hoover thanked Lodge for it and sent back a column by Fulton Lewis, Jr., making much out of the fact that Democrats had voted in the Texas conventions, as Taft men had urged them to do. "Of course," Hoover replied on June 29, "I do not agree with your letter as I made no suggestion of compromise with evil but a method of arriving at right without emotional trimmings, which will do great harm in the election. However, knowing your zeal, I refuse to construe your remarks as an insult to my integrity." The exchange was not published at that point.

The next day the first battles began at hearings before the National Committee on the seating, not only of Texas, but of thirty-seven other delegates who had been chosen in equally irregular procedures. Lodge sought to throw these hearings open to live television and radio coverage. When the National Committee arrived they found TV cameras already set up. Rather than order them out, the Committee changed the hearing room, then voted, 60 to 40, to prohibit live coverage of the contests. Lodge cried: "They are afraid to have the public watch the proceedings. . . . They have shown a 'public be damned' attitude which will be resented wherever free institutions are prized." He ridiculed Taft's shifting delegate claims: "Last February Senator Taft himself claimed 654 delegates. On June 19 he claimed 588 delegates and two days after that it was back up to 603. Now the Taft campaign managers are telling people that they have 540. They are becoming more modest. Give them a couple of more tries and they will finally get their claims down to reality. Actually they will never reach the 500 mark."

On Tuesday the National Committee voted, 62 to 39, to exclude the Georgia delegation (fourteen Eisenhower delegates, three Taft) which had been elected at the regular state convention and to seat seventeen Taft delegates chosen by Simmes' rump meeting. It was now clear that the National Committee was so Taft-dominated that it would not only seat all these fraudulent delegates on the "temporary roll" but makes matters worse by letting them vote in the floor contests on the legality of their seating—in effect judge their own trials. That same day, Lodge got help from an unexpected source—the Republican governors attending the National Governors' Conference at Houston. Lodge's brother, John, who had been elected to Congress from Connecticut in 1946, then Governor in 1950, took the initiative in proposing a "manifesto" calling on the Convention to deny votes to disputed delegations lest they become "accused, judge and jury" all in one. New Hampshire's Sherman Adams and Colorado's Dan Thornton helped him push it. To their amazement, all twenty-three Republican governors at the conference agreed to back the manifesto, because they were meeting among Texans boiling mad at the Mineral Wells affair. The manifesto had a tremendous moral effect.

After the irregular Georgia delegation was seated, Senator Richard Nixon of California, a key figure of the potent Warren delegation, said the decision raised an issue of whether the convention would be "conducted with complete integrity and fair play," and that he was convinced the pro-Eisenhower Texas delegation would have to be seated "if the party is to survive."

Eisenhower himself, starting his two-day train trip to the convention, declared in Denver, "I'm going to roar out across the country for a clean, decent operation. The American people deserve it."

The barring of the press from the National Committee's shabby doings provoked this telegram to the Convention: ABSOLUTE FREEDOM OF THE PRESS TO DISCUSS PUBLIC QUESTIONS IS A FOUNDATION OF AMERICAN LIBERTY. HERBERT HOOVER.

Hoover, who had made that statement to an Associated Press lunch in 1929, denied sending this particular wire. A Wellesley senior later admitted sending it to show her contempt for Taft.

By Friday, July 4, Taft's managers began to panic on the Texas issue. They released Hoover's original proposal to Lodge (who promptly released his own replies), together with a new Hoover letter to Chairman Gabrielson suggesting that "the crux of all this is the Texas delegation" and that the National Committee should be able to reach "an amicable and equitable settlement." In this spirit of sweet reason, Taft offered a compromise to give up sixteen Texas delegates to Eisenhower and keep only twenty-two for himself. The National Committee then voted to split Texas as Taft prescribed. Said Taft "While I will suffer a delegate loss. . . . I am doing so because I think it is so generous that its equity cannot be questioned."

Obviously, as Lodge immediately saw, everything about the compromise was open to question, in equity, morals, honesty—and mother wit. For Taft had originally claimed that the "legitimate Republicans of Texas" wanted to be represented by twenty-nine to thirty-two Taft delegates and that this strength was properly and rightfully his. Now he was cynically offering to trade off seven or more of these delegates and disfranchise his own "legitimate" supporters. "They found themselves frustrated by their own cleverness," said a *Times* editorial. "They could no longer claim the Texas delegation as a matter of right. They could claim it only as a prize they had the power—the momentary power—to take." By instantly throwing it down, "Lodge and other Eisenhower spokesmen . . . left themselves free to come before the convention next week with their own hands clean. They have not sold any of their delegates or any of their principles down the river." Taft now complained that "rejection of my offer shows the ruthless character of the Eisenhower managers. Not being able to secure enough delegates, they are going to try to overwhelm the convention by the unlimited use of propaganda through a press and radio and TV system which they think they control. . . . The New Deal faction of the Republican Party and the Democratic press show their fear of the election of anyone who really represents the majority of the Republican Party." Dave Ingalls denounced the rejection as "the Stalinist tactic of the big lie."

Eisenhower arrived on Saturday proclaiming, "If they do give me this job, brother, it's going to be a slugging match from beginning to end." He and Lodge had dinner in Ike's rooms at the Blackstone. Lodge recalled to Ike some of his reporter's memories of the 1932 Democratic convention at Chicago. "Right at the outset," he said, "the Roosevelt forces managed to win a psychological victory. They pushed for the election of Senator Tom Walsh instead of Jouett Shouse as the permanent chairman. Walsh was popular with a lot of delegates who didn't necessarily want Roosevelt. They carried this issue by a big majority and created the atmosphere of victory that made them be regarded as winners." He explained that the test on Texas offered them a similar psychological opportunity.

If Eisenhower had thought he could just sit back and wait for the nomination to be brought in, Lodge was quick to disabuse him. "Senator Lodge and his associates," Eisenhower's memoirs recall somewhat plaintively, "now gave me a schedule for meeting most of the [delegates]; with no time whatsoever free. Two living rooms were provided; while I was meeting with one delegation, another group would assemble in the second room. This went on every day, all day, with breaks coming only when it seemed desirable for me to dash off to meet a group that could not be accomodated in my suite. The evenings were normally reserved for special conferences." Ike saw Dewey's foreign policy specialist, John Foster Dulles, who was trying to draft a foreign-policy plank for the platform which Taft would accept. "Cabot Lodge," wrote Ike, "kept a sharp eye on the drafting of the entire document to make certain I could accept it."

On Sunday night Lodge and Brownell arranged for Eisenhower to have dinner with the chieftains of those two key delegations—Pennsylvania and Michigan—which had preoccupied them since Mason Sears' memo of March. Pennsylvania's Governor Fine and Michigan's national committeeman Arthur Summerfield were still clinging to the neutralist fence where in fact, they would remain until the actual nominations Thursday night, However, the dinner left them visibly impressed with the Eisenhower magnetism and charm. Yet, as of that moment, Taft already had 530 votes to Eisenhower's 427 for the first ballot—and never had there been a candidate with more than 500 votes who had failed to win. But the key fact was that 75 of Taft's votes came from those malodorous, contested, rump delegations. If those were switched to Eisenhower—as by rights, they should have been—it would stand 455 for Taft to 502 for Eisenhower. The fate of the convention rested on these contested votes.

That same Sunday night the Eisenhower brain trust met in Lodge's big

1102 suite at the Hilton. They perfected their final strategy for the big test the following day, July 7, when the Convention would formally begin. Brownell had drafted the amendment for the rules change, with the help of Boston Lawyer Ralph Boyd. They now debated what to call it—the "clean politics" amendment? the "no deal" amendment? Pennsylvania's astute Hugh Scott spoke out. "Why not "fair play?" he asked. That was perfect. Governor Arthur Langlie of Washington was picked to introduce it to the convention. As the campaign manager, Lodge asked each member of the team what final detail they might have overlooked. "We're ready to go in," he said. "We've got our amendment, the strategy all prepared. Is there any way we can be caught napping, anything we haven't thought of?"

"I tried to think over the worst thing that could happen," Max Rabb recalls. "We were counting so much on the psychological effect of the show-down on the Fair Play amendment. The worst thing *would be for Taft to accept it,* to deny us the chance to *win* a vote on it. So when Cabot came to me I said, 'Just one thing. What if the Taft forces say they are ready to give in completely on Texas?'

"Cabot started and looked up. 'By God, that could be important!' he said."

The night dragged on. There was little sleep for the strategists. The whole hotel was seething with reports of various maneuvers and strata-gems. Like armies, each side had its scouts out, watching the major dele-gations, sending words of any important movements on the flanks. Over the grapevine at two-thirty in the morning came startling word:

"Senator Bill Knowland went in to see Taft fifteen minutes ago." Know-land was a key member of the Warren delegation. Governor Warren had already indicated he would support the amendment, just as he had sup-ported the principle in the Governors' Manifesto. Knowland had helped Lodge lead his 1949 "rebellion" against Taft. Nevertheless, he might be helping a compromise in the interests of a Taft-Eisenhower deadlock which might bring Earl Warren out the winner.

There was some fear that Chairman Gabrielson might somehow manage to avoid recognizing Governor Langlie to offer his amendment. "If that happens," said Tom Dewey, voicing one of the few witticisms of his life, "I'll go to the platform and grab the microphone myself—even if I am only the hind-titular leader of the Republican Party."

Monday morning, just ten minutes before the Convention opened, Lodge was sitting in his little plywood office at Convention Hall when Chairman Gabrielson telephoned to ask him to come to his own office just over the speakers' platform in the amphitheater. Lodge went, found Knowland there, together with Taft's big three—Dave Ingalls, Tom Coleman of Wis-

248   consin and Ohio's Clarence Brown. Knowland said California's caucus had agreed to support the Fair Play amendment, but if the same result could be achieved without a bitter floor fight he would like to see it done.

Brown said the Taft forces were willing to offer precisely that—to have the contested delegations agree not to vote on any contests until their right to their own seats had been determined. This was what the amendment demanded; they would cede it without a vote. Things equal to the same things were equal to each other.

"I think that's wonderful," said Gabrielson. He told Knowland, "Bill, you're entitled to a lot of credit if you can work this thing out peaceably."

What Hoover had failed to do, Knowland was trying in a different form.

Lodge remained silent.

"Well," said Ingalls, "none of you gentlemen have given me a proposition I can take back to Senator Taft."

"I'd like to be heard for two minutes," said Lodge. "I am certainly willing to discuss with my advisers any proposal from Knowland, Gabrielson or Taft. But I want you to bear one thing in mind. I don't think the way to avoid bitterness is to settle all this in a secret meeting. The delegates are thoroughly familiar with the issue. The way to avoid bitterness is to vote this up or down on the floor of the Convention. I have confidence in the delegates."

Lodge was dreadfully afraid that Ingalls would accept the Fair Play amendment itself without a vote.

"What's the matter with the proposition?" Ingalls asked, "It gives you everything you want."

"Well, Dave," said Lodge, "if that's true, why don't you fellows accept the Fair Play amendment?" Like Br'er Rabbit and the briarpatch, he reasoned the best way to get Ingalls to refuse would be to advise him to accept. He was right. Ingalls would not go that far.

"Gentlemen," said Gabrielson, "why don't we give Senator Lodge time to consult his advisers and meet back here again in fifteen minutes."

Lodge couldn't find any of his staff. Finally he reached Brownell on the phone. Brownell agreed they should refuse the deal. All this time the convention's opening was being delayed. On his way back to Gabrielson, Lodge ran into Christian Herter and Barak Mattingly and took them with him. Lodge told the waiting leaders: "It's too late to change everything now. I've got to get out on the floor and see that Governor Langlie gets recognized."

As they left the room a newsman stopped Brown to ask what the situation was. "We're so close together there's practically no issue at all," said Brown. Lodge had to dispute the co-author of his Hoover Commission.

"There will be no compromise," he said.

All the convention arrangements had been geared for a big Taft day.
General Douglas MacArthur was to make the keynote address, hopefully
to set the rafters ringing with his orotund eloquence, all heavy with Taftian
overtones. Joe McCarthy was to follow with his ever-ready clutch of damaging "papers" in hand to suggest that only ironclad patriots like Taft
could save the Republic. Sadly, these beamish arrangements had made no
allowance for a vote on the disturbing subject of Fair Play. Yet such a
vote now approached inexorably.

Clarence Brown made one last effort to stay it. An amendment to an
amendment always has priority, and now he offered one. It was to exempt
the seven contested Louisiana delegates from the ban against voting on
the grounds that they were chosen by a regular state convention. Had it
been accepted, it would at least have given Taft a victory on the first vote
taken. It was defeated. Then came the Langlie amendment. One factor
working strongly in its favor was the knowledge that the strong-arming of
Theodore Roosevelt's delegates in 1912 by William Howard Taft's forces
had set off the Bull Moose movement and elected the Democrats. Carlson
bet Eisenhower their side would get 600 votes; Eisenhower bet fifty cents
it would be nearer 650 than 600. Carlson agreed to pay double if it was.
Eisenhower was right. By a thundering 658 to 548, the convention approved the Langlie amendment. After that victory, MacArthur's pro-Taft
thunder seemed anticlimatic. "MacArthur's keynote speech was worth
about 50 per cent less than it had been two hours earlier," wrote Anne
O'Hare McCormick in the New York *Times*.

Arthur Krock wrote that Taft's whole strategy was "the kind of a blunder
that a witty Frenchman said is worse than a crime. Political managers who
build up and fortify the principal issue that stands between them and the
triumph of their candidate convict themselves of ineptitude if not of something that calls for a harsher word. These managers were from the start
outgeneraled by the Eisenhower group led by Senator Lodge."

Not only had Lodge outgeneraled Taft. In this psychological victory,
Warren had managed to deliver all 70 of his votes to the General. The
key states of Michigan and Pennsylvania had, together with Maryland,
come through with 121 votes. Dewey held all but one of New York's 96
votes for Eisenhower's side. The unmistakable sound of a bandwagon began to rumble. On Tuesday, the Credentials Committee, controlled by Taft,
voted, 31 to 20, to confirm the temporary credentials of the rump delegation from Georgia. Lodge's group announced at once that they would appeal
to the convention floor on behalf of the regular Georgia delegation.

Next morning, the Taft forces suddenly capitulated in a similar fight
over Louisiana and agreed to accept the delegation led by an insurgent,
John Minor Wisdom, who claimed to have won properly over John E. Jack-

250 son's durable old handpicked machine, familiar to innumerable Republican conventions. They hoped that this gesture would result in seating the Taft delegates from Georgia and Texas. The hope was doomed. Sherman Adams, the Eisenhower floor manager, challenged Georgia, and the convention, 607 to 531, seated the regular delegation of fourteen Ike men to three Tafters. Harry Simmes, the Georgia national committeeman who had put the Taft rump group together, cheerfully abandoned it when Adams, momentarily forgetting the moral tone of Ike's crusade, promised to reelect him. A roll call on Texas was now demanded. Suddenly Taft forces capitulated and moved the seating by acclamation of the delegation containing twenty-five Eisenhower men to three for Taft. Taft's men were now in almost total rout.

On Thursday came the nominations. The Eisenhower group had chosen Theodore McKeldin to nominate him, and the governor had accordingly released Maryland's twenty-four delegates to vote as they wished. The mellifluous Everett Dirksen of Illinois nominated Taft, launching into savage vituperation of Tom Dewey, pointing his accusing finger at him across the hall, for having led the party "down the garden path to defeat. We say unto you, we have been down that path before. Do not lead us down that road again!" It was nearly midnight when the nominations were finished. Lodge met with Governor Adams and his sixty floor captains in their rooms in the Stock Yard Inn. Lodge himself brought word that Arthur Summerfield was coming out for Ike and Michigan's forty-six delegates were moving their way, and so (Brownell reported) was Pennsylvania Governor Fine. Counting only delegates personally known to their floor workers, they came up with a sure first-ballot tally of 592 votes. "Five-ninety-two on the first ballot!" cried Ben Guill of Texas to Lodge in mock derision. "What kind of a campaign manager are you, anyway?"

Some of the Ike managers argued for a first ballot that night. Lodge decided against it. He was afraid they would barely miss on the first ballot and then an overnight adjournment would let some of the psychological steam of victory blow away. To adjourn now to the next day, amid an aura of victory, would give the victory psychology a chance to grow.

If they could swing Minnesota's nineteen votes from Stassen to Eisenhower on the first ballot, they would be able to make it. Lodge went out on the floor and told Minnesota's Governor Anderson what the Stock Yard Inn delegate tally had just shown, and informed him that Minnesota alone could swing it. He went back to his little plywood office and shortly thereafter Minnesota's Senator Edward Thye sought him out.

"Cabot," said Thye, "we've been making a count and we have a very accurate one indeed and we do not find that you have the strength for a first-ballot nomination."

Senate again — *1947s other new G.O.P.
Senators (right) pose with Lodge.
From left to right, Washington's Cain,
Indiana's Jenner, Pennsylvania's
Martin, Wisconsin's McCarthy, Cali-
fornia's Knowland, Lodge, and
Kentucky's Cooper.*

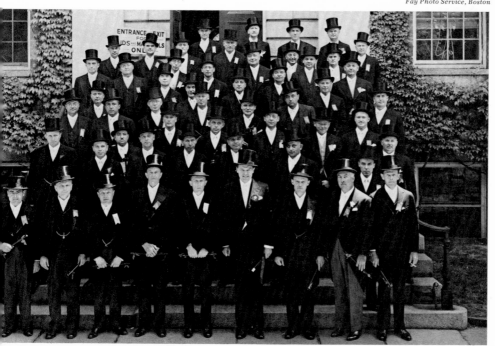

Harvard reunion, *his 25th, sees Cabot
(front row, fourth from right) donning
tails and topper as chief marshal of
Class of 1924. He also became a
Harvard Overseer. At New Orleans
for inter-American conference, Lodge
goes on sight-seeing cruise (right)
with Publisher Henry Luce (second
from right).*

Reluctant candidate, *Eisenhower is urged by Lodge to run for President (left). Lodge becomes his manager and leads Eisenhower forces to victory at Chicago convention, where Lodge is shown huddling with Massachusetts leaders Sinclair Weeks (left) and Senator Leverett Saltonstall. Manager Lodge joins successful nominees and wives as they come to Stockyards rostrum to be presented to the convention July 11, 1952.*

At White House, *Lodge accompanies President-elect Eisenhower for first conference with President Truman. Lodge acts as Ike's liaison for an orderly transition of two administrations.*

In victory, defeat. *Lodge fights so hard and so well for Eisenhower he loses his own Senate seat to young Congressman Jack Kennedy, shown above as two debated at Waltham High School. In new Eisenhower Cabinet (below), Lodge as U.N. Ambassador has protocol rank second only to Secretary of State Dulles.*

In United Nations for seven years, Lodge becomes one of the world's best-known figures, meets and deals with its ruling figures and chief crises. In Korea with Dulles (above, left), he is briefed as son Harry Lodge, serving in Korea, looks on from rear. General Maxwell Taylor is second from left. Above, right, he renews friendship with General MacArthur whom he first met in Manila in 1929. MacArthur was high school classmate of his Uncle John E. Lodge. As skilled debater, Lodge is always ready (left) for immediate answer to Communist attacks. At the Inter American Conference at Caracas in 1954, he listens intently as Dulles closes eyes in concentration.

To Ambassador Cabot Lodge with warmest personal regards. Soekarno. — June 1956

Ovation *greets Lodge (above) at 1956 Republican Convention in San Francisco which renominates Ike and Nixon. At right, above, Lodge greets Sukarno. At right, he greets Ethiopia's tiny Haile Selassie, below, left, he meets Germany's Chancellor Adenauer, and at the right, below, is cooly courteous to Soviet Foreign Minister Molotov.*

India's Nehru *on American visit has amiable chat
with Ambassador Lodge and his wife, Emily. Lodge is
host to old Senate colleague, Majority Leader Lyndon
Johnson who came to address U.N. in 1958. Lodge
wrote President of his effective performance. Lodge
also greets South Vietnam's President Diem on his
visit to U.N. in May, 1957 (left, below). He accompanies Secretary-General Dag Hammarskjold to
visit President at White House in May, 1959 (below,
right; Treasury's Dillon is on the left).*

Jim Mahan

Delicate mission *of showing America and the Americans to Soviet Premier Khrushchev is entrusted to Lodge by Eisenhower. Below, Lodge greets the Khrushchevs on arrival. Above, left, he arrives at Camp David meeting of President and Khrushchev, chats with Soviet Foreign Minister Gromyko and Secretary of State Herter. In February, 1960, Cabot and Emily make brief visit to Russia (above, right) and were entertained by Khrushchev, who genially called him "my capitalist."*

Ted Russell

Big surprise — *Answering Soviet spy charges after 1960 U-2 incident, Lodge astounds and amuses U.N. by displaying U.S. Great Seal from American Embassy in Moscow which Soviets had "bugged" with a listening device.*

At 1960 convention *in familiar Chicago Stockyards, smiling Lodge, fresh from stormy U.N. debate on Congo, greets convention with Presidential-nominee Nixon who has just designated Lodge his choice for vice president. Below, right, President Eisenhower joins his ticket in New York rally (Congressman John Lindsay is barely visible over Nixon's shoulder).*

Campaign begins *with Lodge eating hot-dogs at Coney Island with Gov.
Rockefeller and Attorney-General Lefkowitz (left). As paterfamilias, he is
shown (above) sailing with George and his children off Beverly home
and (below) with Emily and all their grandchildren on lawn.*

Arriving in Saigon, *Ambassador Lodge pays first visit to Presidential Palace, flanked by South Vietnamese Marines honor guard. At right, he meets President Diem.*

At White House, *Lodge briefs new President, Johnson, day after Kennedy's assassination while Rusk, McNamara and Under Secretary Ball listen. Diem also had been assassinated a few days before.*

Tribute in absentia — *New Hampshire presidential primary in March, 1964, brought unprecedented landslide write-in victory for Lodge, in distant Saigon, which snowed under Goldwater, Rockefeller and Nixon (cartoon, above). On field trip when news came, Lodge was smilingly non-committal at Saigon Airport (above, right). Herald Tribune cartoon (right) expressed feelings of many liberal Republicans. A 1950 Herblock cartoon (below) noted Lodge's long efforts to revitalize G.O.P.*

"Stand Up Like An Elephant"

"I WANT TO SHOW CABOT HOW I FEEL BUT I NEVER HAD A CHANCE IN SAN FRANCISCO"

Diem's successor, *General Khanh, makes grass-roots visits and fireside radio talks to people at Lodge's urging (right). Above, Lodge inspects Mekong Delta with Gen. Paul Harkins. On departure from Saigon, Lodge is given elephant-tusked dragon from Presidential Palace, and the gown and cap of honored Vietnamese scholar.*

Harry Redl

Republic of Viet Nam

Charles B. Carey, Boston Globe

After brief rest at Beverly, Lodge takes belated 1964 campaign trail in effort to stop Goldwater's nomination.

Larry Burrows, Life © Time Inc.

Returning to Vietnam *a year later, Lodge tours the front with Taylor (above), whom he succeeded. Left, he visits Marines debarking at Danang (Gen. Lewis Walt, left; Lieut. Col. David Clement, right), below, reports to Johnson's Cabinet on Vietnam situation.*

Visiting combat forces, *Lodge lunches at Danang (left) with Marine Commander Walt, Lieut. Gen. William Westmoreland, and South Vietnam's I Corps Commander, Gen. Thi. At An Khe (above), site of First Air Cavalry, Lodge is shown inspecting captured Viet Cong weapon, a Chinese copy of a Soviet 12.7 mm. anti-aircraft gun. Below, Lodge congratulates Prime Minister Ky the day after South Viet Nam's 1966 elections produced an 80% turnout despite Viet Cong threats and terrorism.*

Symbolic of Lodge's dedication *and sense of duty is this photo (below) of the Ambassador, incongruously garbed in straw hat and Mae West, helicopter-borne to visit U.S. warship off Viet Nam. His long career on world scene is typified by Lodge's repeated appearances on cover of* TIME *(above).*

"We think we will have 592," said Lodge, "and you know that when a candidate is that strong he is sure to make it on the first ballot."

"We have very accurate facilities for making a count," said Thye, "and we don't think you're that strong."

"Ed," said Lodge, "you have known me for a long time and you know that I make very careful statements. We just had a meeting of 60 of our floor captains in the Stock Yard Inn. There is not a delegate among all those 1200 who was not known by his or her first name to at least one of those 60 captains. Each one of them reported individually on the group for which he was responsible. Based on that canvass, we have reached the figure of 592. I believe it is completely accurate." Thye went away still not convinced.

On Friday came the dramatic moment of the first roll call. As state after state called out its vote, the score between Taft and Eisenhower seesawed close enough to be almost a deadlock. But gradually as the call of states progressed, Eisenhower forged slowly but steadily ahead. When Minnesota's turn came, Ed Thye arose to announce: "Minnesota casts nineteen votes for Harold Stassen." When all the states had voted, the score stood at Taft 500, Eisenhower 595—three more than Lodge had claimed the night before to Thye. Minnesota held a quick huddle. "Mr. Chairman," Thye announced, "Minnesota wishes to change its vote. Minnesota now casts nineteen votes for *Dwight D. Eisenhower, the next President of the United States.*" A great whistling scream filled the hall, vibrating the very girders. It was all over! Now one state chairman, now another, rose to announce changes in their voting. By the time the revised first ballot was finally tabulated, Eisenhower's vote had skyrocketed to 845, as against 280 for Taft, 77 for Warren and 4 for MacArthur. Then a Taft man rose to move that the nomination of Dwight D. Eisenhower be made unanimous. And so it was—almost.

There was one lone holdout. It was Lodge's old foe, Basil Brewer, publisher of the New Bedford *Standard-Times*. He was bitter about the whole campaign. He insisted on voting for Taft to the very end. It was an act symbolic of further bitterness to come.

Lodge, who had scarcely had more than four hours' sleep a night for the past ten days, wandered—groggily, joyfully, wearily—off to catch up on his sleep. Next day, when the nominee asked Republican leaders to help him choose a running mate, Lodge and Brownell agreed that Nixon was the best possible man and carried this view with the huddle on strategy that followed. Meanwhile, wires and letters came pouring in to Lodge.

International Bank's President Eugene Black: "It must be a source of real gratification."

Clarence Dillon: "A great job well done . . ."

Russell W. Davenport: "A wonderful job."

General Critt: "We salute you two incomparables in bestowing that traditional soldier's accolade: 'Well done.' "

Major General Bill Barriger, from distant Korea: "Nice going for an amateur!"

Rear Admiral James E. Arnold: "We who admire you realize that you compromised your political career on this convention."

Chan and Peggy Bigelow: "Jim Farley never had anything on you!"

General Patton's old aide, Charley Codman: "Dear Cabot sincerest congratulations on your conception, labor and delivery of Operation Ike. More power to you both."

Grenville Clark, the grand old defender of world law and civil liberties, wrote from Dublin, N. H.: "I have an impulse to send you a word of congratulation. . . . The decisive thing was the arrogant and cynical conduct of the Taft crowd at Mineral Wells—provided, however, that this issue was treated with firmness and without any compromise whatever. On that matter of standing firm, I surmise that you were the key figure throughout. It might be said that it was a simple issue. But I know that there must have been enormous pressure on you and for your firm resistance to it (in your letter to Mr. Hoover and at the convention), I think you deserve the utmost credit."

There was one jarring note, from one George Maroney of Boston, that proved quite prophetic. It read:

"We'll be very happy to retire you to private life in favor of Congressman Kennedy this coming November for your actions in this convention."

CHAPTER THIRTEEN

If ever this country needed a man, it needs you! —George C. Marshall
to Lodge, November 6, 1952

Lodge looked after Eisenhower's interests to the detriment of his own.
His political life was in danger, not only from the fresh and youthful appeal
of young Congressman Jack Kennedy, whose good looks and charm were
a match for Lodge's own, but from the defeated Taftites who were determined to revenge themselves upon Lodge, the instrument of their defeat
at Chicago. He faced a machine which the whole Kennedy clan had built
with computerlike precision and cool detail. He faced the enormous power
of their wealth. "Cabot was simply overwhelmed by money," Eisenhower
told the writer long afterward. "There was simply just too much money
spent." Kennedy committees, operating outside the state campaign, reported
$349,646 spent, compared with $58,266 raised by Lodge's supporters.

Even so, Lodge, always popular among the Boston Irish, could have won
had not the state's Taft forces worked openly for his defeat. Kennedy's
father, Joseph P. Kennedy, himself always close to Taft as to Hoover, got
a prominent Taft man to set up an Independents for Kennedy Committee.
Basil Brewer, Lodge's enemy from New Bedford, visited Publisher John Fox
of the Boston *Post*, to urge his opposition to Lodge. Fox, who shortly received a $500,000 loan for his ailing newspaper from Joe Kennedy, sup-
ported Kennedy's son in a front-page editorial.

Nevertheless, it was a friendly campaign. When the two men faced each
other before twelve hundred voters in a Waltham junior high school, they
argued politely, and paid some pleasant compliments to each other. "I
always found Jack Kennedy most likable," Lodge later recalled. During the
last week before election, when both candidates were going day and night,
chance happened to find their cars stopped side-by-side in traffic. Lodge
leaned out the window and called, "Jack, isn't this a hard way to make a
living?" Kennedy threw back his head and laughed. They gave each other
a wave as they parted. Years later, when Kennedy was President, he told
White House correspondent Hugh Sidey: "I've always been fond of Cabot."

Lodge once more showed the French-Canadian workers of Lowell that
he could talk their own language. He did the same with Italian-American
audiences. Among the Irish, he had a tacit ally in Jim Curley, who was
angry at Kennedy for refusing to sign a petition for his pardon when Curley
was serving a term in the federal penitentiary.

Kennedy's chief weapon was the tea party. In every city and town his   253

254 mother would give a reception, with engraved invitations to every house-wife with an address, and they would come, by the hundreds, to be handed their cup of tea and cookies and to shake the hand of the tall, magnetic young man who would lean with one indolent arm on the mantelpiece chatting informally about anything that came to mind. At the Commodore Hotel in Cambridge alone, 8600 cups of tea were poured in the course of one such afternoon. "I am told they are quite pleasant little affairs," Lodge would smile to his own gatherings, "and I am sure they are non-fattening."

"I accompanied [Lodge] on an auto tour of Cape Cod from Falmouth to Orleans," wrote Cabell Phillips in the New York *Times*. "In a dozen towns, at community halls, school auditoriums, and even on the town squares which were pretty rugged because of the autumnal fog and chill, he made brief, informal talks to groups from a score to as many as 150 citizens. It was 11 o'clock at night before he began the 150-mile return to Boston. In this instance he traveled alone except for the driver of his car, a practice he often follows. On other occasions he teams up with Rep. Christian Herter, the candidate for governor."

The traveling reporter found the various house parties for Lodge "a trifle stiff," imbued with awe of both the Lodge name and the prestige of the U.S. Senator. "But the Senator wandered informally into the kitchen for a brief chat with the husbands gathered around the ice-bucket and then into the living room to meet the wives. In a few minutes he was seated comfortably on the arm of a chair and talking casually about Korea, the federal housing act and the prospect of developing New England water resources. . . . Senator Lodge looks 10 years younger than his admitted 50 and evokes polite gasps of incredulity when he mentions that he is a grandfather."

Lodge's most effective tactic was the publication of a political advertise-ment in every daily paper in the state comparing the two men's voting records and their absentee records. Lodge was almost always on the Sen-ate's floor, Kennedy frequently absent from the House's. The advertisement was refused by Basil Brewer's New Bedford *Standard-Times*. "Undemo-cratic," cried Lodge. When the New York *Times* described Brewer as an "implacable enemy" of Lodge, Brewer replied: "It is not correct that I am an implacable enemy of Sen. Lodge—I have no personal grudge against Lodge at all. I am an opponent of his years of dissimulation and decep-tion. . . ."

Eisenhower wound up his own campaign at the Boston Arena on the night of November 4. There was no question that Eisenhower had a whirl-wind building for him in Boston and in Massachusetts at large. It was pos-sible that, had he tried diligently enough, he could have carried Lodge with him. Lodge introduced him. And Ike had prepared a high tribute to

Lodge at the beginning of his nationally televised campaign finale: "At the   255
end of the campaign it is fitting that I should be introduced to you here
tonight by Sen. Lodge. He was one of the very first seriously to suggest
that I might undertake this great crusade upon which so many of us are
now engaged. If on occasion I have singled out Senator Lodge to say how
much I will need his leadership in the Senate it is because I consider him
a man of courage and conviction . . . and because I have observed him
in the field of battle." This tribute might well have helped Lodge a great
deal. But Eisenhower's new managers, who had carefully timed his precious TV seconds, failed to allow for the tremendous and prolonged ovation
which greeted Lodge's introduction of Eisenhower. By the time Eisenhower
was able to speak, he had to skip over most of his tribute to Lodge to avoid
running overtime.

It was already clear that Lodge was going to suffer his major defections,
not from his strong Boston following, but from "station wagon" country—
the heavily Republican and pro-Taft suburbs. Ironically, despite Kennedy's
appeal as an Irish Catholic, Lodge would draw heavily as before in the
predominantly Irish precincts. It was Taft Republicans voting for Kennedy
who would damage him most. One of Lodge's lieutenants suggested that if
Lodge would ask Taft to come to Massachusetts to speak on his behalf, the
Ohio senator would undoubtedly do so out of party loyalty. John L. Steele,
later chief of *Time-Life's* Washington bureau, recalled that Lodge replied:
"I fought Taft with everything I had. I simply could not ask him to come
and speak for me. There are worse things than political defeat." Defeated
he was—1,207,105 for Kennedy, 1,138,352 for Lodge, a thin plurality of
68,753 for the thirty-five-year-old Congressman. Eisenhower carried Massachusetts by 206,879 and swept into the Presidency in a tremendous landslide. A photographer hung around for hours trying to get a picture of
Lodge looking gloomy. Lodge was so elated at the Eisenhower victory that
the photographer could only catch him smiling.

Of all the letters of regret, he received, the one Lodge treasured most
came in the firm, level handwriting of General George C. Marshall, who,
ailing and retired, was spending the few months he had to live at Pinehurst, North Carolina. On November 6 he wrote:

Dear Lodge:
*I am terribly sorry that the electorate failed you in your state. They
made a great error for you were among the most conspicuous statesmen in public office. I anticipated great things for you and maybe in
the curious workings of fate this misstep may be a turn for greater
things.*

Personally, I want to see you Secretary of State preferably. If not,
then Secretary of Defense. Some one tells me you came out against any
Cabinet position. I hope not. If ever the country needed a man it needs
you!

Faithfully yours,
G. C. Marshall

"I cannot tell you how much I prize your letter," Lodge replied. "My admiration of you goes back many years and for you to consider me worthy of occupying the high offices which you mention will always be a lifelong gratification to me. As far as my future is concerned, I will be glad to do anything that I can to be useful to the country."

Right after his defeat, Cabot took Emily down to Nassau for their first real rest that year. On top of the first half-year spent in the endless,wearying pursuit of the nomination for Eisenhower—"he never spent two nights in a row in the same bed," his son Harry recalls—Lodge had plunged immediately into his own day-and-night-campaign. He refused to dwell upon his defeat. "Senator," a reporter asked him, "in your own post-mortem do you blame your defeat on the Taft forces?"

"I don't engage in post-mortems," said Lodge. "I don't believe in looking backward. I have simply ended one phase of my career. Now I will embark upon another."

He was not at all sure what he would do as he went off to Nassau. He had several attractive offers from private industry and he was seriously debating one or two. He made no effort whatever to sound out Eisenhower for any job, Cabinet or otherwise. There is no evidence that General Marshall sought to impress his views on his own protege, Eisenhower. From the outset, Eisenhower had wanted John Foster Dulles to look after foreign affairs because he had such a walking-encyclopedia knowledge of them, including all the lawyers' minutae of their contractual, treaty and other involvements.

The job to which Eisenhower was giving most thought, as President-elect, was one which he would create, a totally new one—a carry-over from his military procedures. It was that of a chief of staff—the job filled for him by Bedell Smith in World War II and Alfred Gruenther in NATO. It was a job for an orderly and a deputy, for a whipping-boy and a strong right arm. In essence, its function was to solve, or at least divert, most problems before they ever reached the top man. Eisenhower immediately thought of Bedell Smith, and would have loved to put him in the spot—but quickly realized a second general would make the White House look terribly military. "My mind turned to two others," Eisenhower relates in his memoirs, "Sherman Adams and Cabot Lodge. Either . . . I thought, could

carry the responsibilities of the post satisfactorily, each had special abilities. The appointee would really be Assistant President.

"I was particularly interested in Cabot," Eisenhower later told the writer, "because I wanted someone who understood the staff system of operating. His military experience would give him that. He had both the political savvy, from his long experience in the Senate, and he had the military training to know the staff system. I think he would have been a damn good one. I always found him a keen observer and a man who had a helluva fund of common sense." In his memoirs he wrote: "I wanted both [Adams and Lodge] in the government and had been considering each for a possible Cabinet post. In November, Mr. Dulles suggested a change in the U.S. representation to the U.N. because of the age of the incumbent Warren Austin. He strongly urged that I consider Cabot for that job. I thought the idea admirable; Cabot's qualification seemed almost unique."

General Clay, who was acting as Ike's alter ego, got Lodge on the phone in Nassau and asked him if he would accept the post. He wanted him to come to Augusta, Georgia, where the President-elect was staying at the Country Club, to talk it over with him. Eisenhower told Lodge he had been considering him for the White House job but preferred to have him tackle the U.N. as a place of vital importance for which he was extraordinarily fitted by instinct, training and ability.

"Look, said Lodge, "you don't owe me a thing. Don't feel you have to give me a job."

"Oh, no," said Eisenhower, "I'm asking you because I need you."

Eisenhower was concerned that the Russians had been able to dance rings around the U.S. at the U.N. The American ambassador, former Senator Austin, was a dedicated and beloved man. But he would sometimes wait days preparing his formal reply to Russian accusations, which meantime captured the headlines. Eisenhower believed that Lodge, with his journalist's sense of the importance of timing, would be quick on his feet and to slug it out with them toe to toe.

"I regard this job," Eisenhower told him, "as next in importance to the Secretary of State. You will rank immediately below him, and have Cabinet status. And I'll want you to sit in on meetings of the National Security Council." In his memoirs Eisenhower wrote, "Cabot, delighted with this opportunity for service, accepted."

The President-elect had a more immediate task to ask Senator Lodge to undertake. President Truman had already been bombarding him with messages suggesting that the two of them hold an early meeting to discuss the orderly transfer of the powers of government. "Cabot," said Eisenhower, "I would like you to act as my personal liaison with the various executive departments. Everything except the Bureau of the Budget—I've

258   asked Joe Dodge to look after that." Lodge agreed. On November 9, Eisenhower—whose once friendly relations with Truman had become quite strained during the campaign—wrote a letter simply to "The President, The White House, Washington, D.C.," with no salutation:

> *With further reference to your several messages I am designating Senator Henry Cabot Lodge Jr., of Massachusetts, to serve as my personal liaison with those departments and agencies of government, other than the Bureau of the Budget, where liaison may prove useful in facilitating the transfer of public business from the old to the new administration. . . .*

Lodge went to Washington that same week and set up an office in the Statler Hotel. He called on his old friend, Bob Lovett, who had become Secretary of Defense. He had a talk with Secretary of State Acheson. He visited various old friends at the Pentagon. He called on his former Senate colleague, Lyndon B. Johnson, to hear his astute evaluation of major legislative problems. On November 18, he joined Eisenhower, who had flown in from Augusta for his first conference with Truman. After Eisenhower and Truman had seen one another in a rather chilly session, the two went to the Cabinet room where Truman sat in the President's chair, flanked by Acheson, Lovett, Treasury's John Snyder and Mutual Security Administrator W. Averell Harriman. Eisenhower sat opposite in the Vice President's customary chair, with Lodge on his right and Joe Dodge on his left.

Truman distributed a Treasury memo pointing out the imminent expiration of the excess profits tax and other emergency defense taxes. Acheson reviewed the Korean problem, and India's U.N. truce plan—which Britain and France had welcomed—that would permit forcible repatriation of prisoners, a plan strongly opposed by the U.S. Acheson urged the President-elect to speak out against the plan so as to prevent a split in allied unity. Eisenhower simply noted, "Call Eden [British Prime Minister] tonight." At the end, Truman produced a draft of a joint statement. Lodge read it and suggested striking the phrase, "we both agree that it is of the utmost importance to preserve the principle that prisoners of war should not be forcibly repatriated." Lodge agreed with this position, but objected to Eisenhower letting the outgoing Administration commit him to specific policies. As amended the final statement simply said the meeting and the liaison "furnished additional proof of the ability of the people of this country to manage their affairs with a sense of continuity and responsibility."

Eisenhower's great confidence in Lodge was reflected in his choosing Lodge's closest colleagues for high White House tasks. Bobby Cutler, who had been Lodge's right arm in so many past battles, and whom Eisenhower had asked to be his personal aide during the 1952 continent-crossing whistle-stop campaign, became personal assistant to the President for National Security Affairs. Maxwell Rabb, Lodge's former administrative assistant, came in as Secretary to the Cabinet. Later, in the pivotal job of looking after the affairs of minorities, he succeeded in getting the Navy to desegregate its Yards at Norfolk and Charleston. He was also instrumental in creating the President's Committee on Government Contracts, which did a tremendous job of eliminating discrimination by private employers holding federal contracts.

On January 12, 1953, the new Cabinet, with Lodge and Cutler both present, held its first session—a preinaugural one—in the South Room of New York's Hotel Commodore. Secretary of Agriculture Ezra Benson, a Mormon elder, began the meeting with a prayer. Mrs. Oveta Culp Hobby, the pretty, new Health and Education Secretary, was present. There was a discussion about wearing Homburgs (which Eisenhower favored) instead of the silk hats that had been inaugural tradition since Franklin Pierce's day. "Tradition is not involved," said Eisenhower. "If we were going back to tradition we would wear tricornered hats and knee britches." Bobby Cutler, the irrepressible bachelor wit, thought that over a moment, then drily observed, "If Mrs. Hobby comes in knee britches I want to be in the front row."

At the U.N. General Assembly on February 26 the Ambassador Extraordinary and Envoy Plenipotentiary to the United Nations rose to speak. It was not Lodge's first speech before that body, but it was his first as Chief of Mission, and he used it to set the tone of the new administration's approach to the U.N. itself. "Since the last meeting of the General Assembly, there has been a change in the Government of the U. S., a change in which the losers have neither been disgraced nor, may I say, liquidated. The American people wish to establish a lasting peace and regard the U.N. as a vital means to that end."

The truce negotiations in Korea were still going on. The Chinese Communists had just rejected the amended Indian resolution, which the U.S. now supported, against any forcible repatriation of prisoners of war (most prisoners from the Chinese Communist side did not want to go back). By this rejection said Lodge, the Chinese were telling the world, in effect, "We wish to continue the bloody struggle in Korea; and therefore tell you that you can only solve the Korean problem on our terms."

Lodge then turned toward Andrei Vishinsky, Soviet Foreign Minister. "The Soviet Union is actively assisting the aggressors in Korea on a scale which makes possible the continuation of the aggression and determines

260   its scope." He then cited "ten facts" to prove that the Soviets had both instigated, directed, and supplied the aggression. "The rulers of the Soviet Union can stop the war whenever they want to—and Mr. Vishinsky knows it."

Lodge had served notice that he intended to treat the Communists as the enemies of peace so long as they made themselves so. He pointedly refused to walk across the General Assembly Hall to pose for a photograph shaking hands with Vishinsky, and received a fan letter from an unexpected source—James Michael Curley, who now had a radio program over WBMS in Boston, and had praised his old rival for giving the Russians what-for. "It has been a very great pleasure for me to make you the subject of my radio talks during the past week," wrote Curley, "and it is likewise a very great pleasure to say that you not only have the administrative ability but the superior leadership that is required for the position of President of the United States which, I believe, you will attain some day." Lodge sent him warm thanks.

Vishinsky felt called upon to reply to Lodge's ten points about Soviet aid to Red China's aggression. He admitted that the Soviet Union was selling arms to China. Columnist Arthur Krock described what happened: "This reporter was present when Vishinsky made his opening oration. Two thoughts were uppermost, 'Does Vishinsky really believe this rubbish' and 'How and when will Lodge reply?' And the answer to that came the moment Vishinsky finished. The afternoon hour was late when the foreign minister of the Soviet Republic finished and the U.N. delegates had heard a lot of oratory. To have held them much longer would have been a tactical error, but to postpone rebuttal would have been another. Lodge solved this problem by speaking briefly, but pressing the advantage Vishinsky had lost in the preparatory drill by conceding that Moscow "sells" arms to Communist China as a matter of compliance with the Sino-Soviet treaty. The U. S. delegate dwelt on that for all it was worth in damaging Russia's position as a member of the very U.N. that had sanctioned international military action against the Communist aggression in Korea which is maintained by Soviet materiel. And, in the only remaining time he thought wise to use, he cited the facts against the old Soviet claim, stoutly reiterated by Vishinsky, that the aggression was [begun] by the South Koreans. . . . Giving Vishinsky a taste—which after previous experience with U.S. representatives in the U.N. must have surprised him—of skilled and vigorous riposte in simple words that will be clear to people in any country who may read or hear them . . . Lodge thus proved already how strong and effective the voice of the U.S. can be when it is raised as he is raising it."

On March 12, Lodge sat and listened while Vishinsky put on another of his performances of vituperation against the U.S. as "warmongers,

imperialist aggressors," and against the U.S. Army for alleged crimes of   *261*
brutality in Korea. This provided the first test of Lodge's ability to stand up
and slug toe to toe with the Russians, not waiting till "next week or the
week after" to answer, but answering them immediately and in their own
coin. While Vishinsky ranted, Lodge wrote calmly on a legal-sized yellow
pad as if writing a leader for the *Herald Tribune*. At last he rose.

"Mr. President, we have heard the representative of the Soviet Union
attack the U.S. Army and speak of alleged crimes and acts of terror committed by the U.S. Army. I would like to say to him here that the U.S.
Army which you have sought to smear here today is the same U.S. Army
that stood beside the Russian Army to defeat Nazism in World War II. The
men in the U.S. Army in Korea today are the sons and younger brothers
and in some cases they are the same men who made up the U.S. Army in
World War II. The U.S. Army was good enough for you in 1942, 1943,
1944 and 1945. It should be good enough for you now, and would be if
your country's position had not so tragically changed.

"Millions of Americans remember a time when the Germans made their
last great offensive (there was great joy when the Russians attacked during
the Battle of the Bulge). In those days, Mr. Representative of the Soviet
Union, your country was held in great respect. You had many friends. But
you have lost a great deal of that friendship and respect in the years that
have gone by. You have lost them because of the fear that seems to moti-
vate everyone in an official position in your country. This fear is not a
rational fear of attack from the outside . . . It must be a fear of their own
people, a fear that stems from the tyranny which they impose on the Soviet
people. In 1950, as a delegate to the Fifth General Assembly, I urged the
Soviet Union not to be afraid. . . . At the political Committee meeting
last week the Soviet representative said to me, 'You're going to lose Asia
anyway.' That astounding remark made me realize how far apart his view
of humanity is from mine. The U.S. is not trying to *get* Asia. We have
never thought of Asia as some sort of object inhabited by slaves which was
to be won or lost by outsiders. We believe that the people of Asia, like the
American people, have the right to live their own lives and to develop
themselves in their own way. If, instead of talking about Asia as some sort
of a prize in some game of power politics the Soviets would join us in the
economic and technical assistance required to help the people of Asia that
would help peace. But the only answer so far is a foreign policy consisting
entirely of violent words and violent deeds. This kind of foreign policy will
never bind up the wounds of the world and we look for the day when this
truth will be apparent to all, even to the rulers of the Russian people."

His sharp reply several times drew applause from the galleries and from
delegates themselves. The President had to gavel for order.

262   Cabot and Emily had moved in to the official Embassy Residence, a stately but bleak eight-room apartment on the top floor (42-A) of the Waldorf Towers. His neighbors included both Hoover and MacArthur. The annual rent was $30,000, and the Ambassador had an extra $17,000 allowance to entertain the 60 delegations then seated at the U.N. Lodge was usually able to turn back $2500 to $3000 of this allowance.

Lodge quickly fell into a brisk day-to-day routine. He usually rose by seven-thirty in his Waldorf residence, breakfasted on orange juice, toast and coffee, then would be off in his long, loping, distance-eating stride across the sixteen blocks down Park Avenue to the U.S. Mission (then at 2 Park Avenue). He would stride briskly into his office to the desk beside which stood the American flag and the flag of the Embassy. He tackled the day's work and let nothing pile up on his desk.

"He was an ABC type," said Nebraskan Rosemary Spencer, a U.N. secretary who watched the new Ambassador take over, and later became his private secretary. "He would take the facts one at a time, add them up and reach a decision very quickly. He wouldn't let things rest on a back burner. He knew what he wanted. He would ask for it and if you could provide it, you were 'in.' If you could not do what he wanted, he would go somewhere else. He got things off his chest. He liked people who stood up to him, even if he disagreed with what they had to say. His biggest dislike was indecisiveness."

He rarely went out to a restaurant for lunch. He either ate at his desk or walked home to lunch with Emily. When he ate in, a box of Portuguese sardines would do nicely. Since his wartime siege with his stomach, he had grown quite fond of baby food, and sometimes would spoon up a couple of cans of that for his lunch. At the hotel he often had cream soups made with baby food chicken or spinach. Almost a teetotaller, Lodge often had to go to three cocktail parties in the late afternoon—usually nursing one drink through the whole affair—and give or go to formal dinners night after night and week after week. He submitted to this ordeal conscientiously, in the belief that his task was to win as many friends as possible for America and its point of view.

At first, the atmosphere between Lodge and the eighty-odd staffers of the U.S. Mission was icy, even fearful on their part. Republicans taking over after twenty years of Democratic rule understandably felt that they were surrounded by staffs—most of them protected by civil service—whose political loyalties lay elsewhere. Often they were right. "Lodge arrived with a slight chip on his shoulder," Miss Spencer recalls. "He was convinced that we were overstaffed and he cut the staff by twenty or thirty. He let the extraneous ones go."

At the same time, he wanted men he knew and could trust close about him. He brought in the old friend and playmate of his youth, James J. Wadsworth, as his deputy, with the rank of Ambassador. An enormous man, both very tall and very fat, Wadsworth gave the superficial appearance of a genial, sleepy laziness, but he was polished and astute. "He's here not because I knew him when but because he's the best man I know for the job," said Lodge. They made a good team, not only at work, but sometimes singing duets together at the parties Lodge would stage at the Waldorf. John Mason Brown frequently attended those gatherings. "After dinner [he writes] the Ambassador often breaks the ice and solves the problem of the many unshared languages of his guests by drawing upon his endless repertory of songs—old or new, ballads or blues, sweet or hot, French or British but usually American—and singing them lustily alone or with [Wadsworth] his old friend and closest harmonizer. As examples of folk art, these duets are uninstructive. They may bewilder delegates from Pakistan and Saudi Arabia, but over the years they have created good will, reduced Sir Gladwyn Jebb (who is not easy to reduce) to tears of laughter, and prompted [Secretary General] Trygve Lie to say that if only everyone would sing like these two men there would be peace in the world."

Sometimes Lodge would render "She's a Personal Friend of Mine," his closest approach to ribaldry:

You can see she's not my mother because my mother's 49;
You can see she's not my sister because I gave her such a wonderful time.
You can easily see she's not my sweetheart because my sweetheart is so refined.
She's just a poor little kid, who forgot what she did.
She's a per-so-nal fri-e-end of mine!

Occasionally brother John would join him in the duets. Tom Dewey, who had professional training as a baritone, gave a solo. India's Krishna Menon, who refused to sing, always went to sleep—perhaps a form of criticism.

"It means a lot to have these delegates like you," Lodge said. "If they have a good time at your parties it's only natural that they may want to please you. Far from being rubber stamps most of these U.N. delegates have influence in their own countries. They're carefully chosen and highly regarded, and often they're powerful enough to recommend to their home governments that they be instructed the way they want to be." Many thought the rude, imperious Krishna Menon impossible, but Lodge took care to cultivate him, and Menon responded. "Menon thinks Cabot's great," Wadsworth once said. "He goes to see him whenever he's here."

U.N. correspondents, on the whole, did not share that opinion—at least,

264 not at first. For a man who had spent so many years as a newspaperman, Lodge had remarkably poor relations with the U.N. reporters in his first year or two. He played his cards very close to his chest, took few reporters into his confidence, seemed to most to be aloof to the point of arrogance. Finally they sought a showdown with him, arranged for him to attend a lunch where all the accredited correspondents one by one voiced sharp and candid complaints about his whole handling of press relations. Lodge was jolted. Later he persuaded the Associated Press correspondent, Frank Carpenter, a tactful, soft-spoken Tennessean, to join him as press officer. Thereafter Carpenter not only kept in close touch with reporters himself, but saw that Lodge became more available to them. If any editor called in the course of the day, Lodge always took care to call back, and whenever possible would provide background and guidance for editorials and interpretative stories.

Some reporters disapproved of his methods. They felt that his constant readiness for a rough-and-tumble with the Soviets detracted from the dignity of the world forum. "The first couple of years," Thomas Hamilton of the New York *Times* commented, "all that Lodge did was make speeches for the boys in South Boston. He was strictly playing for *The Last Hurrah*. He made the rafters ring with his denunciations of Russia. As an old newspaperman he was going to get the denial in before the attack could stick. Well, sometimes it was good, sometimes it was terrible. Obviously, the Russians paid no attention to it."

They paid some attention. They had never encountered anything quite like Lodge before and they were disconcerted. "Is he going to be this way all the time?" a Vishinsky aide asked one of Lodge's senior aides. "I guess he is," said the American. "Lodge gave the office excitement," said another. "He at once started to run the shop like a city room of a newspaper. Everyone had to operate by deadlines."

One day he was talking to the Greek ambassador in his office when the Yugoslav ambassador arrived outside for an appointment. An area officer sat with him in the reception room. When the Greek ambassador left, Lodge, preoccupied, turned to other chores and the area-officer failed to remind him that the Yugoslav was waiting; after a time the Yugoslav left in a huff.

"You know what this blunder means!" cried Lodge. "It means that now I have to go calling on a Communist!" He was furious.

One of Lodge's aides at the time told a newsman, "You learn three things right off around here. The first is that everything must be disposed of immediately. The second is that Lodge can't stand intrigue. Everything must be completely straightforward. The third is that he can't tolerate yes men. He wants you to tell him exactly what you think." One reporter attended a meeting at which Lodge read a paper he had worked on for hours. Another aide told him, "The paper is diffused, murky, unclear. Some of the writing is poor. I'm afraid it will require considerable reworking." Lodge calmly took notes of the criticism and revised his paper accordingly.

Lodge was always quick to catch the Russians up in any attitude that showed the hypocrisy of their proclaimed concern for "the working class." The Soviets were niggardly in meeting their full share of U.N. expenses. When a Soviet delegate opposed overtime for the U.N. cleaning women, Lodge shot to his feet: "The United Nations should set an example throughout the world for humane treatment of its employees. It should not support sweatshop labor. It is inhumane to say that time and a half pay for overtime and night-wage differentials for these women must be denied." To the Marxist's embarrassment, the other members voted with Lodge.

Beside being ready to answer Soviet attacks, Lodge felt that an equally important part of the Ambassador's task was to educate the U.S. public to the vital importance of the U.N. as a place to talk out disagreements before they led to hostilities.

His task was made harder by Senator Joe McCarthy's favorite sport of portraying the U.N. as well as the State Department as a nest of Communist spies.

From the time of his college days, Lodge had argued that the first requisite of American leadership in the world was the building of a first-rate foreign service at least as professional and competent as the British. He had hammered at this after his World War II visit to the war theaters as a senator. In the Senate itself he had consistently defended the foreign service, and opposed political appointments over those of able career men. He knew that McCarthy's wild attacks were demoralizing the service and making it doubly hard to recruit top-drawer men.

Max Rabb, who had become staff secretary for the Cabinet, recalls: "Eisenhower suggested that Lodge, Sherman Adams and Jerry Persons form a little subcommittee to dope out the proper stand on McCarthy." It was Lodge who with Adams, first heard Army Counsel John Adams' story of the efforts of McCarthy's staff to wangle special treatment for a former colleague, Private Joseph Schine, after he was drafted. It was Lodge who insisted to John Adams—who was reluctant to do so—that he make this pressure public and make an issue of it. The revelation led to the famous Army-McCarthy hearings, and ultimately to McCarthy's censure by the Senate.

Lodge, as part of his effort to shape public opinion behind the U.N., frequently wrote magazine articles about his work. "If there were no such thing as the U.N.," he wrote in the New York *Times Magazine* his first November, "men of good will would be demanding its immediate creation.

266   But we have it, and the result is that more is heard of its imperfections than its accomplishments." The start of the eighth session of the General Assembly was "a good time to take a hard look at what the U.N. means to the U.S. and to answer the claims of its critics . . . The U.N. is *not* a nest of spies, Communist or any other variety. If any proof of that were needed it would be found in the circumstance that the Soviets have not even filled their quota of employees at the U.N. headquarters. There is nothing at the U.N. to spy on, no military information or any other secrets. While American Communists should certainly never have been hired in the first place [one or two had been] it is worth noting that no U.S. citizen employed by the U.N. has ever been prosecuted for espionage and that every U.S. citizen employed by the U.S. has been screened within a few months by a process worked out by the civil service commission and the FBI. . . ." Second misconception: "The U.N. is *not* able to involve the U.S. in action against its interest. There is only one organ of the U.N. that can take action which *is* legally binding. It is Security Council and there the U.S. is protected by its veto power. No other U.N. decision can be anything but hortatory." Third misconception: "It did *not* involve us in the Korean war . . . instead it saved us two divisions—or about $600 million a year. . . .

"Let us keep before us what the U.N. actually is . . . a place where public opinion is developed. At the Eighth Session we are, for example, examining the brutal practice of forced labor as conducted by the Soviet Union and its satellites. . . . Public opinion can make things change in spite of the Iron Curtain." The U.N. is also "a communications center for the ideas of the world. . . . An agency for dealing with world economic development . . . the U.S. with only a sixth of the world's population but with much of the world's wealth has a great deal to gain by furthering the U.N. efforts to raise living standards in under-developed areas. . . ." Finally, it is "headquarters for developing whatever united action the world is capable of taking at any given moment in the face of an aggressor's threat to peace. . . ."

In the Cabinet meetings, Lodge urged the President himself to make greater use of his tremendous moral leadership in the world by personal appearances before the great sounding board which the U.N. provided. To Lodge the General Assembly's "low, rather sway-backed building . . . resembles a loudspeaker. And if the architect [so] intended it . . . he had the right idea. . . . If we have not got the gumption and the intelligence and the imagination to use this loudspeaker it is our fault."

On December 8, 1953, heeding Lodge's advice, President Eisenhower made a dramatic appearance before the General Assembly and proposd the creation of an International Atomic Agency as a way out of the "fearful atomic dilemma" in which "two colossi glower at one another across an atomic abyss." "The reaction in the free world was immediate and enthusiastic on all sides," Lodge reported to the President. "Leaders of such neutral countries as India and Indonesia hailed the proposal as an important step toward peace. The Soviet Union, surrounded by this universal attitude of acclaim, agreed after long hesitation to join the agency."

In his first year Lodge had become known to millions of Americans, not only through the headlines of his clashes with Vishinsky, but through the frequent televising of the U.N. debates. In his book *Diplomat Among Warriors*, former Under Secretary of State Robert Murphy, who at that time was Assistant Secretary of State for U.N. Affairs, describes these encounters:

When [Lodge] became American Ambassador at the U.N. he decided that every Russian attack should be countered sharply, and his method of immediately challenging Soviet misrepresentation had a salutary effect. . . . When Lodge and Vishinsky exchanged verbal blows, both contestants seemed to enjoy the match, and so did American radio and television audiences. Knowing that he was cast by American viewers as the villain, Vishinsky played his role with relish. Taunting "capitalist" governments had been standard procedure with Bolshevik orators, and Vishinsky adapted this tactic to the U.N. forum with considerable effectiveness. . . . In contrast to the public villain Vishinsky, the chief American delegate to the U.N. was well equipped to play a heroic role. Cabot Lodge, over six feet tall, youthful-looking and handsome, with a speaking voice well suited to television, became during his first few months at the U.N. one of the best-known personalities in public life.

In taking over the State Department's U.N. desk, Murphy soon discovered something else about Lodge: he did not stand in the usual relationship of an ambassador to the Secretary of State; the President had given him an independence and a rank unique among ambassadors. "I quickly learned," wrote Murphy, "that I would have to practice a form of diplomacy in my new post which I had not anticipated. During the Korean debates, a resolution was proposed on which the vote promised to be closely divided. There were discussions at the Office of U.N. Affairs in Washington about how the U.S. should vote, and after due consideration we decided that the American vote should be 'Yes.' We submitted our conclusions to Secretary Dulles and he approved it, so instructions were sent to the U.S. Mission in New York 'Yes'. But the next morning I was dismayed to read in the newspapers that Lodge had voted 'No.' As soon as I could talk to him by long

268 distance telephone I said, 'Apparently our instructions failed to reach you.' Lodge repeated, 'Instructions? I am not bound by instructions from the State Department. I am a member of the President's Cabinet and accept instructions only from him.' I knew that personal and official relations between Lodge and the President were exceptionally close. . . . But no one had warned me that Lodge regarded himself as independent of the State Department and I protested, 'But you are also head of an Embassy, and our ambassadors accept instructions from the Secretary of State.' After a moment's pause, Lodge replied, 'I take note of the Department's opinions.' I was flabbergasted. As an ambassador myself, I had acted under instructions for many years . . . 'This is a new situation to me,' I said, 'and I'll have to discuss it with the Secretary. Lodge replied cooly, 'Yes, do that. He will set you straight.' When I did report to Dulles, he listened carefully without comment until I finished, and then said, 'This is one of those awkward situations which require special consideration. If it happens again, just tell me and I'll take care of it.'

"My personal relations with Lodge were always agreeable. Once I understood that the Secretary of State did not choose to challenge the virtual autonomy which Lodge claimed for his Embassy at the U.N., I realized it was not appropriate for me to do so. A word from President Eisenhower or a call from the Secretary of State personally were accepted by Lodge in good grace, but there were explosions from time to time if instructions, or even strong suggestions, were sent by the State Department to the American Mission at the U.N. headquarters. Lodge would tolerate no poaching on what he considered his own preserve. He was as anxious as anybody to promote a consistent American foreign policy, but he interpreted his functions as much broader than those of an ordinary ambassador. . . . Of course the State Department made every effort to have him participate in policy-making."

Murphy's memory of these events does not agree with Lodge's. Lodge worked under instructions day and night for almost eight years, during his whole tenure at the U.N. There was one episode which occurred at the time of the Suez crisis when Secretary Dulles was ill. A group proposed a resolution which, while very cleverly worded, seemed to Lodge in effect to be backing away from the original Eisenhower position that there must be one law for all, and would make it possible for the British and French troops to continue to occupy Egypt. Lodge felt that on a matter of this importance, the President himself should be informed. Lodge received a call from Bob Murphy, who was then Acting Secretary of State, supporting this resolution and asking Lodge to do so, and Lodge said that he thought on a matter of this importance he ought to consult the President. He did so and the U.S. adhered to its original position.

Lodge was gratified to find that public support of the U.N. was rising. When the Associated Press held its annual luncheon in New York for member editors in April, 1954, Lodge was invited as the speaker. Lodge startled these newsmen for a moment by saying "the U.N. is not and should not be a good news source." He added: "When one of the world's insoluble problems gets on Page One, it is practically always because the news is bad." He warned that Americans, who had a "national trait . . . to solve problems and overcome obstacles," did not reflect enough "on the fact that all problems cannot be solved and that all obstacles cannot be overcome . . . We Americans make a mistake if we expect too much of the political and diplomatic tools which are available to us. We should not get impatient with the proceedings of the U.N. because they talk and do not reach basic solutions of some international questions. To many of these questions there is no basic solution under present conditions. In many of them the choice is 'talk or fight.' The fact that the talk may be boring or turgid or uninspiring should not cause us to forget the fact that it is preferable to war."

Lodge took advantage of this important audience to defend the State Department career men who were being impugned by McCarthy. "There has been so much publicity . . . about a few rotten apples that we have lost sight of the many excellent persons giving service that is not only faithful but skilful in a high degree and utterly indispensable to our survival as a nation." He cited outstanding examples: Robert Murphy; David Key, assistant secretary for U.N. Affairs; Livingston Merchant, Henry Byroade, Douglas MacArthur II. "There are 40 career ambassadors—people like George Allen in India, Charles A. Bohlen in the Soviet Union, Jefferson Caffrey in Egypt, James Dunn in Spain, Loy Henderson in Iran, John Cabot in Sweden, James Riddleberger in Yugoslavia, Harold Tittman in Peru and Fletcher Warren in Venezuela. All of these officers and others like them are rendering priceless service to their country in posts which call for the exercise of the most exquisite judgment. . . . If we did not have officers like them we would be in serious trouble. I wish we had more of them and I hope that young men and women of similar quality, from one end of our nation to the other will plan to make a career in the field of foreign relations, so that for the future of our country we will have a supply of these indispensable public officials."

As Lodge thus put himself on the side of McCarthy's favorite targets, the Senate itself was moving toward its final showdown with McCarthy, and later that year—by 67 to 22—passed the resolution of censure against him. The list of McCarthy's last-ditch defenders was reminiscent of Lodge's old floor fights for ECA—the ineffable Jenner, Malone, Bricker, Hickenlooper; also a new man, Barry Goldwater of Arizona. The vote which Lodge had

270 once cast for Massachusetts was not cast at all. It was a great moral show-down, of the type John Kennedy later made famous in a book, *Profiles in Courage*, but in this particular showdown Kennedy was ill from a serious back operation and could not be present to vote. He could of course have paired his vote, in absentia, but did not choose to do so.

Senator Kennedy was in a hospital not far from the U.N. Ambassador Lodge stopped by to leave his card, with a "get well" message written on the back. Jacqueline Kennedy, his wife, was touched by this gesture:

> *Dear Mr. Ambassador:*
>
> *I just wanted to tell you how much Jack appreciated hearing from you.*
>
> *It was the nicest thing I have ever heard of—your sending him your card—and you can't imagine how much something thoughtful like that means to people who are sick.*
>
> *I have just arrived in the sickroom with an armload of magazines—and am about to settle down with them for the day and read in* U.S. News & World Report *about you.*
>
> *Please give our very best to Mrs. Lodge—and thank you again so much.*
>
>

Very sincerely,
Jacqueline Kennedy

>

That June, Lodge happened to be presiding in the Security Council—a job that rotates among the Big Five each month—when a Soviet delegate, Semyon Tsarapkin, asked to be recognized. Lodge unconsciously lapsed into familiar Senate procedure.

"For what purpose does the gentleman seek recognition?" asked Lodge.

"I am not a gentleman," Tsarapkin bridled. "I am the representative of the Soviet Union."

"I had thought," said Lodge, "that the two were not mutually exclusive." Laughter rippled, then roared through the chamber.

The day after the interchange Lodge went down to the White House for a small dinner the President gave for Sir Winston Churchill, Prime Minister again, and Foreign Secretary Eden. "To jaw-jaw is always better than to war-war," Sir Winston said on his arrival. Lodge sat in place of Secretary Dulles who was out with his wife celebrating their forty-second wedding anniversary. Churchill had presented the President with a decoration which only Lord Alexander possessed—the British Middle Eastern Campaign Medal with two battle clasps, one for the British First Army and one for the Eighth. "I need a new decoration the way a dog needs a new flea," Eisenhower whispered to Lodge before dinner. Lodge recalled Churchill's visit to de Lattre's headquarters in France and how touched he had been that

Churchill not only recognized him but remembered that he had resigned
from the Senate. "I knew you were not only a great statesman but a great
politician." When they went in to chat after dinner, the President motioned
to Lodge to sit beside Churchill. As the small talk progressed, Lodge mentioned that his grandfather wrote in his diary that he had met Churchill in
an English country house when he was a very young man and had predicted
he would go very far. "Theodore Roosevelt," said Churchill, "never liked me
at all. I don't know what it was that I did. Maybe I lit a cigar at the wrong
time. But Alice Roosevelt always liked me."

Lodge came back to face a tough battle in the Security Council over
Guatemala. He had already discovered that "getting out the vote" behind
American policy in the U.N. was just as important—and not vastly different—from lining up votes in the Senate cloakroom for such measures as
the Marshall Plan. His long experience at such political footwork stood him
in good stead. It was a matter of pride with him that the U.S. was never
defeated in any significant political dispute in the U.N. But Guatemala
taxed all his talents.

After Colonel Jacobo Arbenz Guzman took power there in 1951, the
Communist Party virtually ran the country. In May, 1954, two thousand
tons of Czech weapons were shipped in as "optical goods." It was the first
Soviet effort to establish, as it later did in Cuba, a military base in the
Western Hemisphere. On June 29, 1954, a revolt led by Colonel Carlos
Castillo Armas, and assisted by the CIA, overthrew Arbenz. In the mean-
time Arbenz' representatives in the U.N. had made charges of aggression
against Honduras and Nicaragua—which had helped the rebels—and the
Soviet charged armed intervention by the U.S. It pressed for an investiga-
tion.

Lodge did not object to an investigation, but he insisted it be made by the
Organization of American States, which was already discussing Guatemala
under the Rio Pact that Vandenberg had helped to bring into being. The
OAS had already learned that Armas' forces had found warehouses
jammed with Communist propaganda sent directly from Moscow, and plans
for arming the populace to create a "proletarian revolutionary dictatorship."

To Lodge's dismay, he found Britain and France prepared to vote for the
Soviet resolution. These nations, which had never precisely rejoiced over
the Monroe Doctrine, saw no reason why the whole U.N. should not act
instead of the exclusively hemispheric OAS. The whole status of regional
organizations and their just jurisdiction was at stake. Lodge warned Eisenhower, who appealed directly to the British and French prime ministers. In
the showdown, Britain and France abstained. Lebanon, New Zealand and
Denmark voted for the Soviet resolution. Lodge mustered a majority with
China, Colombia, Brazil and Turkey to defeat it.

272   In the new year, Lodge would be preoccupied with disarmament—hear much talk about it, study and prepare position papers on it—but Soviet intransigence would make it nothing more than talk. On February 20, 1955, he flew to London for the preliminary disarmament talks, defining the U.S. objective as a "tamper-proof" plan of disarmament procedure and a "foolproof" system of inspection and control. It had been so since the first Acheson-Lilienthal proposal for international control of atomic energy—and Soviet rejection had been the constant problem. "What we will seek once again in London," said Lodge, "is a tamper-proof plan so we can reduce our strength with perfect confidence that the other side is doing the same thing at the same time. It is as simple as that. We can not run the risk of not doing something. We will not be fooled and we will never stop trying until we succeed." Lodge attended these meetings for three weeks. A "fresh air fiend," his habit of shutting off the radiators in his office, in the London Embassy and keeping the windows open, even in drifting snow, left a shivering impression on the aides who helped him. Russia's attitude toward inspection was still colder. He turned over the talks to Wadsworth, his deputy, and came home.

That July "a meeting at the summit"—for which Churchill had long pressed in the hope of finding some way to end the cold war—was finally held at Geneva. Eden came as Britain's new Prime Minister. Stalin had died the previous year, and the old Soviet warhorse, Nikolai Bulganin, was the new Premier. He came to Geneva accompanied by the new Party Secretary, Nikita Khrushchev, who soon made it clear that he was the new boss in fact. Eisenhower startled the Soviets with his proposals for "open skies," free aerial inspection by each side of the other. The discussions of these proposals were carried on by the Disarmament Subcommittee which resumed meeting at the U.N. in August. "I welcome you . . . to share in a great opportunity," said Lodge, reading again the President's proposal—'to give each other a complete blueprint of our military installations from beginning to end, from one end of our country to the other. . . . Next, to provide within our countries facilities for aerial photography to the other country—we to provide you the facilities within our country, ample facilities for aerial reconnaissance . . . you to provide exactly the same facilities for us . . . by this step to convince the world that we are providing as between ourselves against the possibility of great surprise attacks, thus lessening the danger and relaxing tension. . . .' The heads of government at Geneva instructed their representatives in the sub-committee to consider the proposals made at Geneva. . . . I do . . . here and now present President Eisenhower's plan. . . ."

That, too, got nowhere for the simple reason that the Soviets could easily hire, through dummies, commercial air or land reconnaissance of almost

every military installation in our free and open society. They saw no reason
to surrender the tremendous advantage of secrecy that their closed society
provided. Ultimately, Samos and other camera-eye satellites would to some
degree make all such questions of air sovereignty obsolete. The only immediate recourse against surprise attack was for President Eisenhower to
order high-priority and highly secret construction of the high-flying U-2
reconnaissance plane which soon afterward began overflying Russia at
ninety thousand feet and ultimately would figure so sensationally in U.N.
affairs.

However, Lodge could take some pride in the fact that he was winning
more and more public support for the U.N. Public opinion polls that summer showed that "satisfaction for the progress of the U.N." rose from 50
per cent in 1953 to 74 per cent in 1955—and the group that wanted to leave
the U.N. altogether dropped to a record low of 5 per cent. Lodge, "Appraising the U.N.'s Influence" in the New York *Times Magazine* that September,
cited Secretary General Dag Hammarskjold's successful mission to Communist China—made under a resolution sponsored by Lodge—where he
had negotiated the release of fifteen American flyers who had been held
prisoner there since the Korean War, thus achieving what "in all probability,
no single government could have done . . . by itself. In its first decade,
the U.N. has developed into the greatest single engine in the world for
mobilizing public opinion—a force which no government can withstand
forever, no matter how dictatorial it may be."

The year ahead would put that thesis to the severest test in U.N. history.
For 1956 was to be the bloody year of Hungary, the terrible year of Suez.

In ten days that shook the world, starting on October 23, Hungarian students and workers had overthrown the Stalinist regime of Ernö Gerö and
forced the accession of Imre Nagy—a Communist but an anti-Stalinist—to
the premiership. Russian tanks crunched into Budapest, but Hungary's
own Communist-created army rose to fight them. Even children fought the
Soviet tanks—with crude bombs made of gasoline-filled bottles. In the days
that followed, what pessimists had thought impossible occurred: a whole
people clawed its way to freedom, virtually with its bare hands, against all
the mechanized might of an alien police state. The people had seized their
own freedom and armed themselves. The whole question now was whether
the Soviets would dare crush this revolution with massive new intervention.
Already their use of tanks against students and workers had set off resigna-
tions from the Communist Party all over the world. In the U.S., Howard
Fast resigned from the Party. John Gates, editor of the U.S. Communist
Daily Worker, would soon resign in revulsion over the Soviet brutality. So
did Joseph Starobin, the *Worker*'s foreign editor. In France, Jean-Paul
Sartre denounced the Soviets.

274   On Saturday, October 28, Lodge joined Sir Pierson Dixon of Britain and France's Bernhard Cornut-Gentille in asking Secretary General Dag Hammarsjkold to call the Security Council into emergency session the following day. It met at 4 P.M. on Sunday. The question before it was the adoption on its agenda of "the situation in Hungary." Vishinsky was now dead; the suave Arkady Sobolev had replaced him. He rose to protest the inclusion of the Hungarian question on the agenda as "an attempt, in defiance of . . . the U.N. Charter, at gross interference in the domestic affairs of the Hungarian People's Republic." When the vote was taken, the agenda was adopted by a 9 to 1 vote, Yugoslavia abstaining. M. Kos, a Hungarian representative, joined the meeting. Sobolev then tried to obtain an adjournment. Only he voted for it. Lodge then rose to speak.

MR. LODGE: This urgent meeting . . . has been called to consider the situation in Hungary resulting from the violent suppression of the Hungarian people by armed force. The Hungarian people are demanding the rights and freedoms affirmed in the Charter of the U.N. and specifically guaranteed to them by the peace treaty to which the Governments of Hungary and Allied and Associated Powers are parties. . . . The convening of this Council reflects the deep anxiety and concern throughout the world regarding the bloodshed in Hungary. We fervently hope that the action taken in bringing this matter to the Council and the Council's decision to consider the grave events in Hungary will move those responsible for the repression of the Hungarian people to discontinue such measures.

Lodge then recited what was indisputably known about the events.

Sir Pierson Dixon recited more facts and was handed a new bulletin. "If the news which has just reached me is confirmed . . . early today two very strong Soviet armored units and air force ground troops entered the Debrecen area of Hungary from Romania . . . moving fast in the direction of Budapest. . . . The situation is even graver than it was when our U.S. and French colleagues and I, 24 hours ago, asked for [this] meeting. . . ."

The world's indignation against the Soviet outrage was so great that perhaps the U.N., though powerless to help Hungary physically, could have focused such moral pressure and condemnation as to make the Soviets withdraw. The confusion in Moscow's own councils was apparent in conflicting statements pouring from Moscow Radio, some to the effect that Soviet troops would be withdrawn.

At that very moment, as if events were no longer in the control of men, but in the grip of some malign fate, and moving to an inexorable doom, the tragedy of Suez burst upon the world. At the very time the Security Council was holding its emergency meeting on Hungary, Israel—which had been secretly armed to the teeth by the French with tanks and jet planes—asserted its inalienable right to self-defense by attacking the forces that Egypt, armed to the teeth by the Soviet Union, had been assembling on its borders with the openly proclaimed intention of destroying Israel.

On Tuesday, October 30, at 11 A.M., the Security Council met again, this time to hear Lodge's request for action on "The Palestine question: steps for the immediate cessation of military action of Israel in Egypt."

MR. LODGE: . . . It comes as a shock to the U.S. Government that this action should have occurred less than 24 hours after President Eisenhower had sent a second earnest appeal to the Prime Minister of Israel urging Israel not to undertake any action against its Arab neighbors. . . . Certain things are clear. The first is that, by their own admission, Israel armed forces moved into Sinai in force to eliminate the Egyptian *fedayeen* [assassin] bases in the Sinai Peninsula. . . . The Government of the United States feels that it is imperative that the Council act in the promptest manner to determine that a breach of the peace has occurred, to order that the military action undertaken by Israel cease immediately, and to make clear its view that the Israel armed forces should be immediately withdrawn behind the established lines [established after the 1947 Israel-Egypt war]. Nothing less will suffice. . . . I intend at the afternoon meeting to introduce a draft resolution whereby the Council will call upon Israel to withdraw and will indicate such steps as will assure that it does.

The situation was even graver than Lodge knew. By the time the Council reconvened at 4 P.M., Sir Pierson Dixon rose to announce that Britain and France had sent joint ultimatums to Egypt and Israel to withdraw to ten miles of either side of the vital Suez Canal—and that French and British troops were en route to seize the canal "for temporary occupation" at Port Said, Ismalia and Suez.

It was nearly midnight that same Tuesday when Britain was forced to use the first U.N. veto in its history to defeat Lodge's own resolution. All the rest of that week became like an endless nightmare to Lodge. Lodge found himself for the first time ranged with the Soviet Union against America's own chief allies. Then Yugoslavia moved to override the British veto by referring the case to the General Assembly under the 1950 "uniting for peace" resolution. Although the Soviets had fought this resolution originally, they were now glad to use it to embarrass Britain and France. Once more the inexorable events found Lodge voting with the Soviets and by a 7 to 2 vote the General Assembly was called, in effect to "try" our chief allies for aggression. Secretary of State Dulles flew from Washington to prosecute the charge, Friday evening, November 1, before the Assembly.

This writer was present that dramatic night. He will never forget how ill and ghastly Dulles looked. At times he trembled and clung to the podium as if he needed its support. He was actually dying of cancer, and before the week was over the cancer would be discovered in an emergency operation. But now he spoke his gloomy call to the Assembly to act against his allies:

"I doubt that any delegate ever spoke from this forum with as heavy a heart as I have brought here tonight. We speak on a matter of vital importance, where the U.S. finds itself unable to agree with the three nations with whom it has ties, deep friendship, admiration and respect, and two of whom constitute our oldest, most trusted and reliable allies."

But the President had already gone before the country to lay down his decision: "There can be no law, if we were to invoke one code of international conduct for those who oppose us—and another for our friends."

It was three in the morning of November 2 when the Assembly finally voted. By 64 to 5 it demanded a cease-fire and a stop to the movement of arms and military forces into the area. The U.S. had won, but at the expense of its allies.

That same afternoon, Friday, Lodge had to meet with the Security Council again, to renew the pressure on Russia over Hungary. Once more Sobolev demanded it be stricken from the agenda; this time, Yugoslavia, which had previously abstained, joined with the West in a 10 to 1 vote against Russia. The debate proceeded.

Finally a vote was taken on Lodge's draft resolution. Only the Soviet Union voted against it. Communist Yugoslavia abstained. Nevertheless, the lone Soviet vote was an effective veto.

Lodge promptly moved to call the General Assembly into emergency session under the "uniting for peace" resolution. Sobolev announced he would vote against the move, since a special session was already examining the question of the Suez cease-fire, and the Hungarian issue was a "smoke screen." Yugoslavia announced it would vote for it, thus dropping its neutrality. By 10 to 1 Lodge's motion was carried. The Assembly was called into session at eight the same evening. It voted, 53 to 8 (with seven abstentions), to urge the Soviets to withdraw their troops "without delay," for the Secretary General to send an investigating commission to the scene, and deplored the use of force. The Assembly then returned to the problem of Suez. Early in the morning on Monday it voted, 57 to 0, to create the United Nations Expeditionary Force to police the cease-fire at Suez. The following day Britain and France, brought to their knees by American threats of economic sanctions, put a cease-fire into effect; on November 8, Israel agreed to withdraw. The night before, Soviet troops broke the last pocket of resistance in Budapest and Communism's bloody victory in Hungary was complete.

Throughout this apocalyptic period at the U.N., Lodge played the most active role of any delegate, though stepping aside for Dulles at the Assembly

showdown on Suez. Does he deserve, on balance, praise or blame for his
role?

There is little question that the collapse of the Anglo-French-American alliance which led to the Suez fiasco marked the greatest failure of American diplomacy since the wartime failure to nail down access to Berlin. That failure was Dulles'. By the time the emergency reached Lodge at the U.N. it was beyond repair, and the only creditable role which the U.S. could play was to stand for "one law for all" and stop the shooting—both of which it did. Lodge accomplished what he had to do, and therefore succeeded. One severe critic—Herman Finer, who has written a massive study of "Dulles Over Suez"—says this: "Lodge was excessive in his prosecutions in the Suez affair. . . . What carried the most tragic consequences for the future of American relations with Europe was that the American spokesman did not privately approach the British and French to attempt . . . to find a way out that would at least save their pride." Finer, who interviewed all the principals, says Lodge "deliberately brushed Sir Pierson Dixon out of his way when the latter sought to converse with him." He argues that Dulles was "abjectly intimidated by the seething passions of the Afro-Asian nations, transmitted to him by Lodge, whose own personal susceptibilities amplified their hysteria." On the plus side, it must be argued that the U.S. emerged from this showdown with enormously heightened moral credit among the suspicious Afro-Asians who had always assumed we would back the "imperialists" in a showdown.

As for Hungary, this writer—who followed all the events closely in writing *Life*'s editorials in this crisis—felt at the time that the U.S. had let slip the one irrecoverable weapon, *time*—time in which the U.N. could still take some effective action before the Russians irrevocably committed themselves to crushing the Freedom Fighters. The editorial written then speaks for itself:

Time was the crucial factor in the Hungarian crisis. Had the U.N., with U.S. leadership, been able to act swiftly in the five days when Hungary was free, it might well have been able to forestall the subsequent Soviet invasion.

Some of the things that could have been done to help Hungary were outlined . . . by Franklin A. Lindsey, former chief of the U.S. Military Mission to Yugoslavia.* He starts with Nov. 2, the day Premier Imre Nagy proclaimed Hungary's neutrality, demanded withdrawal of Soviet troops and cabled Secretary-General Dag Hammarskjold asking for U.N. protection. . . .

* Now President of Itek Corp., Cambridge, Massachusetts.

Lodge could have immediately asked for an emergency session of the General Assembly.

The Assembly could have swiftly created a Hungarian observation commission.

An advance commission composed of U.N. member ambassadors in Vienna could have flown to Budapest by helicopter and been observing a full day before the massive Nov. 4, Soviet intervention.

Anna Kethly, Nagy's authorized representative, could have been installed as Hungary's accredited U.N. spokesman.

Nobody can say whether, had all this been done, the Soviets would have dared to slaughter Hungary anyway, right under the eyes of the U.N. observers. But had they done so the U.N. could have continued to recognize Miss Kethly as the true representative of Hungary and denied credentials to the puppet Kadar regime. In addition to all this, the U.N. could have issued a sort of habeas corpus *summons demanding that Russia produce the kidnapped Imre Nagy as the legitimate head of Hungary's government.*

[The editorial then cites Lodge's willingness, recounted above, to adjourn for the weekend when time was of the absolute essence.] Even four days later, for lack of a coherent plan of action, the Kadar delegates were seated. Miss Kethly, the only member of the legitimate Nagy government still free, was not even permitted to address the Assembly. At a time when the numerous Ambassadors already in Budapest could have been made U.N. observers, weeks were frittered away in vain attempts to get in. The whole record is a sorry one for the U.S. and the U.N. alike.

Lodge himself took sharp exception to every statement in this editorial and wrote a detailed answer to each point, which *Life* published. He concluded:

The record is not a sorry one. The record is a good one. Although it did not succeed in bringing about the withdrawal of Soviet troops, the U.N. has done things for the people of Hungary which no single country or other organization could have done. The steps which the U.N. has taken have played a useful part in preventing deportations; in bringing food to the people of Budapest; in helping 170,000 Hungarian refugees too find new homes; in persuading many Asian and African countries for the first time to vote to condemn the Soviet Union; and in dealing a body blow to Communism all over the world.

I presume that your editorial springs from the same human emotion of heartsickness that every American must feel at seeing heroes bru-

tally slaughtered and—for the present—defeated. I share that emotion. But we do not advance the interests of these people by wishful thinking.

In the Hungarian crisis it was U.S. policy to take every practicable step short of war. In pursuing that policy we left no stone unturned. Although the U.S. is powerful, it is not all-powerful. Although the U.N. is influential it cannot make its will immediately effective against the Soviet Union—any more than it could against the U.S.—without their consent.

/s/ Henry Cabot Lodge

Seen in the afterlight of a decade, the U.S. failure over Hungary still seems real. It was inevitably a part of the larger failure which flowed from Dulles' misconceptions. Dulles was a brilliant corporation lawyer, who had the lawyer's habit of seeing not only the holes in his own case, but of silently making the other side's case as well. He had a lawyer's respect for lawyer's devices, and in the midst of the crushing of Hungary was preoccupied with Russia's "rights" to intervene under its own self-made instrument, the Warsaw Pact. His world view was complicated by an intense religiosity which made him see policy in terms of a holy war, which justified deviousness of his own. It could be said of him as Lodge's Uncle Brooks Adams said of Samuel Adams, who provoked the Boston massacre: "A rigid Calvinist, reticent, cool, and brave, matchless in intrigue, and tireless in purpose, his cause was always holy, and therefore sanctified the means." His greatest failure, the collapse of the alliance, came because Dulles played so many lawyer tricks on Britain and France that in the end they lost faith in him completely and in the last fortnight before Suez shut off all communications with him, so that their actions both infuriated and totally astonished him. As Lodge wrote long ago in the *Tribune:* "Foreign offices should not be astonished. They should know. That is why they exist."

As for Lodge, within the limits of the possibilities open to him, he did the best that he could, and that best was of a consistently high order.

For seventeen days on end, during the whole crisis, Lodge scarcely got home. He met key people at his Park Avenue office or in his seventh-floor hideaway at the U.N. He went without sleep, grabbing catnaps when he could.

In the midst of the turmoil, Dwight D. Eisenhower was reelected President in another smashing victory. At the year's end he dropped this note to Lodge:

Dear Cabot:

As both 1956 and our first administration draw to a close, I want to

280   *express to you my appreciation of the outstanding job you have done as U.S. representative to the United Nations. Particularly in these last months of international crisis and great strain, it has been a source of tremendous satisfaction to me to know that you were so ably representing us in the council of nations, I truly cannot adequately express the proper measure of my gratitude for your tireless and dedicated efforts. At the same time I am aware that during the entire four years of this administration you have been extremely effective in your efforts to make the United Nations the instrument for peace that it must be; and I know that my own gratitude for all you have done is shared by people throughout the world. With all the best to you and Emily and to the members of your family for a fine 1957 (and, let us hope, a more peaceful 1957) and warm personal regards,*

As ever, D.E.

CHAPTER FOURTEEN

He has probably covered New York more thoroughly as a pedestrian than anyone since the late John H. Finley. . . . The Waldorf to the U.N. is a regular beat of his, and the day before we saw him he had loped 100 blocks up and down Park Avenue. He often zigzags along the side streets for a variety of window-shopping and architecture-gazing; Greenwich Village and the sections of town occupied by the foreign-born are familiar to his tread. As a television personality of commanding mien he is widely recognized and greeted by passersby. "That's Lodge," is an aside he often gratefully catches, and recently, whipping up his circulation on a street in the 50s, he passed a police-man who looked up from his chore of tagging illegally-parked cars, and said, "I pray for you every night for the good work you are doing."
—*The New Yorker*, March 9, 1957

There is an interesting contrast in the Ambassador's techniques," a Lodge assistant told *The New Yorker* reporter. "On the one hand he does a very mature, subtle, diplomatic job of negotiating and has held the support of more than two-thirds of the U.N. members by a course of moderation; on the other hand, he's a polished, literate, saloon-fighter. . . . He knows the tricks when no holds are barred."

The literate saloon-fighter came out slugging in October, 1957, when Soviet Foreign Minister Andrei Gromyko charged in the U.N. that the U.S. was inciting Turkey to attack Syria. He claimed to have discovered secret documents to that effect. "Here," cried Lodge, "is a government which has been condemned by the United Nations three times in the past year for its actions in Hungary . . . accusing the overwhelming majority of the hu-man race of wanting war. . . . Here is the chronic lawbreaker, not only seeking to be regarded as a good citizen, but actually trying to sit in the judge's seat and sentence the whole law-abiding community to jail. Here is the arsonist, trying his best to start another fire and demanding his right to lead the fire brigade."

His abilities at subtle, diplomatic negotiating were demonstrated in the strong vote of endorsement he got for the U.S. position on disarmament— the first time the General Assembly went on record on the subject. He spent the first ten weeks of the 1957 session advancing it.

Joseph Sisco, a State Department career man, flew up to Beverly one Saturday with the department's draft of its position. Lodge turned an old journalist's eye on its impenetrable bafflegab. "I don't understand it," he

282 told Sisco. "If I don't understand it, how in the world can we expect the U.N. to understand it? Let's see if we can't express our position in a nutshell."

Lodge tried to boil it all down to one paragraph. The two worked over the wording. This is what they finally agreed on:

We will suspend nuclear tests for an initial period expected to be two years but also subject to further extension, provided you, the Soviet Union, agree on establishing an effective inspection system, air and ground; on stopping production of fissionable materials for weapon purposes and reducing present stocks; on starting outer space missile control; and on reducing armed forces.

This oversimplified it a bit, but it was comprehensible.

During that same 1957 period, Lodge had brought his affable relationship with Krishna Menon into play to produce an American-Indian resolution on the withdrawal of Israeli troops from the Sinai Desert. The problem was to get a resolution which could win the two-thirds Assembly vote necessary to bring about an Israeli withdrawal and the stationing of a U.N. force in the Gaza Strip, with entry to the Gulf of Aqaba which the Israelis had closed.

To get support for it, Lodge met with three blocs of delegates. He addressed the entire European group, explaining and justifying the U.S. objective, speaking in English and French. He met with the twenty Latin American delegations, speaking in Spanish. And he met with the Arab-Asian blocs, speaking in French and English.

The action taken on this resolution, after it passed, has kept the peace ever since. "It was the one time Menon ever gave me his word," said Lodge, "and he scrupulously kept it. It proved you can get along with anybody whose word is good."

Lodge had developed a feeling of mutual trust and respect with his staff. "Cabot," said Jerry Wadsworth at that time, "has developed a far greater warmth and humanness than he had at the beginning, and is sympathetic to other views and suggestions. He is far more of a disciplined diplomat. He can be terrifically charming when he wants to be, and he is far more willing to be than when he started out. He has an appreciation of the job itself, aware that he can do the world a lot of good or harm. He has grown tremendously." Hearing of this compliment, Lodge said: "I hope to hell I haven't shrunk!"

As the only ambassador called on to debate in public, his mission was uniquely an "Embassy in a goldfish bowl." He had to deal with not one, but seventy-nine other governments, be a wheeler-dealer, trade and persuade, and—since he must do it in public—be an effective speaker. At the State Department, both the career men and the political appointees felt that Lodge had grown into all these qualifications to a superb degree.

Like a fireman, he had to be ready to answer any alarm, from the oddest places. He was attending the opera with Sir Pierson Dixon when the Suez crisis broke. The Mission sent a jeep for him and word that the President wanted him on the phone. He sped back, in top hat, white tie and tails to begin that 17-day ordeal. In July, 1958, he was loafing in old seersucker trousers and sneakers at the wheel of his thirty-nine-foot fishing boat, *Horse Conch*, off Porpoise Bay, Maine, when the ship radio crackled out the news of a military coup in Iraq in which King Faisal and Premier Nuri es Said had been murdered by pro-Nasser and "nationalist" Communist groups under General Abdul el Kassim (who eventually met a similar fate). At the time Lodge was on a leisurely cruise with Emily and her sister Jean's two daughters, Jean and Emily Alexander. When he heard the news Lodge knew that Lebanon would probably call for U.S. help—and Dulles would call for him. He was right on both counts.

Tiny Lebanon, tucked along the Mediterranean coast between Israel and Syria, and about evenly divided between Christians and Moslems, was torn by civil war, aggravated by the presence of 300,000 Arab refugees from Palestine. Nasser's Radio Cairo was calling for the overthrow of Lebanon's President Chamoun, a Christian, while Syria was flooding Lebanon with contraband arms and terrorists. The Security Council had sent observers there on June 11, but the Soviets were encouraging Nasser's indirect aggression. Thus matters stood when Lodge went off on his cruise.

Eisenhower had kept the Sixth Fleet near Lebanon, and had reinforced its combat-ready Marines. As soon as the Iraq coup broke, President Chamoun wired Eisenhower a plea for U.S. protection. Within twenty-four hours a battalion of Marines had taken over Beirut's airport and harbor.

While Lodge was getting back from Maine, the White House instructed Ambassador Wadsworth to request an immediate meeting of the Security Council. He did so shortly before nine that Monday evening, then drove out to La Guardia to meet the arriving Lodge, and fill him in. The Council was called to meet at ten the next morning, July 15.

Lodge was now in the toughest spot he would ever face in his eight years in the U.N. In a sense the U.S. had done what it had punished the British and French for doing two years before—it had used military, unilateral intervention, and bypassed the U.N. The fact that President Chamoun had requested it made a big difference, but Secretary General Hammarskjold was plainly unhappy; it was the only time he ever failed to see eye-to-eye with the American position. In a tense atmosphere, Lodge rose before the Council to state that position.

284 "Mr. President, the Council meets today to confront difficulties as serious as any in its history. The territorial integrity of Lebanon is under threat by insurrection, stimulated and assisted from outside. Plots against the Kingdom of Jordan which have been evident over the past few months are another sign of serious instability in the relations between nations in the Middle East. And now comes the overthrow—in an exceptionally brutal and revolting manner—of the legally established government of Iraq. . . . In all these circumstances the President of Lebanon asks with the unanimous authorization of the Lebanese government for the help of a friendly government so as to preserve Lebanon's integrity and independence. The U.S. has responded positively and affirmatively to this request in the light of the need for immediate action. And we wish the Security Council to be officially advised of this fact. . . . As President Eisenhower explained this morning our forces are not there to engage in hostilities of any kind—much less to fight a war. Their presence is designed for the sole purpose of helping the government of Lebanon at its request in the effort to stabilize the situation . . . until such time as the U.N. can take the steps necessary to protect the independence and political integrity of Lebanon."

Radio Cairo was already denouncing "another Suez." In Moscow there was vague talk of "volunteers not only from the Soviet Union but from many other countries" to oppose American "imperialism." In the Council, Sobolev introduced a resolution calling on the U.S. to "cease its armed intervention in the affairs of the peoples of Arab states." Warned Sobolev: "This action carries with it the threat of an acute deterioration of the international situation and can fling the world into the abyss of a new war."

Sobolev quoted copiously from New York *Times* dispatches to show that the U.S. was really intervening to prepare to restore a pro-Western regime in Iraq. He likened this to Hitler's "big lie" techniques.

"I greatly admire the New York *Times* as a newspaper," Lodge responded, "[but] I am sure they do not claim to be the official or unofficial voice of the U.S. Government. I assure Mr. Sobolev, once again because I know of his fondness for newspaper clippings—which in the Soviet Union, of course, are the voice of the government—I assure him that in this country newspaper clippings—they may be interesting—they may be stimulating—but they are not government policy. He has lived here long enough that I should think he would know that.

"Then Mr. Sobolev said that the U.S. was always against the U.N., that we talk in a hypocritical manner about justice, peace and freedom but that we were actually against the U.N. when the time came.

"This interested me very much because it comes from the representative of a government which has been condemned three times in the past year for its actions in Hungary. It comes from a government which has violated the express wishes of the U.N. more than 30 times in the past eight years, which has abused the U.N. veto power 82 times and they accuse the U.S. of always being against the U.N. I declare now that the U.S. has always carried out every single decision of the U.N. and the Soviet representative can not find a single exception to that statement. . . . Then the Soviet representative said that U.S. policy under President Eisenhower was like that of Adolf Hitler. . . .

"Well, I must defer to Mr. Sobolev in the knowledge of Adolf Hitler, because his government was once an ally of Adolf Hitler when Mr. Molotov made a pact with Mr. Ribbentrop of unfragrant memory. The U.S. has never been an ally of Adolf Hitler. So he knows more about that than I do.

"It is interesting, seeing that we are considering a subject in the Middle East, to remember that Soviet ambitions in the Middle East entered an active phase in 1939 when Nazi Germany and Communist Russia formed an alliance in this same Molotov-Ribbentrop Pact. In 1940 the Soviets sought to use this alliance to establish a sphere of influence in the Persian Gulf and the Black Sea regions. They even proposed to Mr. Ribbentrop, Hitler's foreign Minister, that this area be recognized as the center of the aspirations of the Soviet Union. These aspirations came to nothing but the Soviet Union pressed forward toward the same goals after World War II.

"We do think that the situation in Lebanon is part of a much bigger picture. We do not seek to deny that, even though Mr. Sobolev can not agree with us about that. . . . Now, Mr. President, before I yield the floor, let me just say that no country on earth is more friendly to Arab national-ism than is the U.S. and the U.S. Government has shown this on many an occasion. But we think there is a difference between normal aspirations of nationalism, which are proper and healthy and . . . can even be ideal-istic and forward-looking, and the subversion of the independence of small countries on the other hand.

"Mr. Sobolev creates the impression that Arab nationalism and subver-sion of independence are all one thing. Well, they are two entirely different things. We are in favor of nationalism and we are against the subversion of the independence of small countries."

All the time Lodge was speaking, Secretary General Hammarskjold looked steadily in the other direction. It was his quiet way of showing that he disapproved of the U.S. sending troops and then taking its case to the Security Council.

Sobolev introduced a resolution for the Council to brand the U.S. action "a serious threat to international peace" and call upon the U.S. "to cease armed intervention in the domestic affairs of the Arab States and to remove its troops from the territory of Lebanon immediately." Next day, Lodge introduced his own threefold resolution, to: 1) strengthen the U.N.

286 observation teams in Lebanon, 2) stop infiltration of arms and raiders, 3) make it possible for the U.S. to withdraw its forces.

The Japanese delegate then introduced a compromise resolution which would simply place more men in the observer teams and more authority in the hands of Hammarskjold to act on his own initiative.

When it came to voting on these proposals, Lodge, by quick foresight, managed to outmaneuver Sobolev. He realized that Sobolev would use the veto on the U.S. resolution, and failing to obtain its own resolution for the withdrawal of troops would press for an emergency meeting of the General Assembly under the Uniting for Peace resolution.

To forestall Sobolev slipping in such a resolution right after his veto, Lodge requested, and got a vote, requiring all three resolutions to be voted on before additional arguments could be made. When all three had been defeated, Sobolev found he could not get the floor because Lodge had already placed his own name on the speaker's list. Sobolev was disconcerted.

MR. SOBOLEV: I should like to say how surprised I was to learn, when I sent the secretary of the Soviet delegation to put my name down to explain my vote, that a list of speakers already existed. Three members were already on the list, and thus, unless I am mistaken, I shall be the fourth speaker.

He was not mistaken. The U.S. resolution was then voted on, the Soviets vetoing, and Lodge, first on the speaker's list, asked an emergency session of the Assembly under Uniting for Peace to consider the same action just defeated. That broke the back of the Russians on Lebanon right there. If there were any Assembly resolution, the U.S. resolution would take precedence. Lodge's Senate-born knowledge of parliamentary rules had enabled him to outwit and outflank the Russians.

As the Council approached a vote on the Japanese compromise, the Lebanese delegate asked a day's adjournment to consult his government. Sobolev insisted on voting right away. Lodge immediately saw the advantage this gave him, and pressed it:

MR. LODGE: Here is a small country, undergoing a great crisis, which wants a few hours to consider a debate which involves its existence. . . . The only explanation [for Sobolev's objections] is that the rights of a small country—no, I will not yield. . . . I have the floor and I intend to hold the floor. I guess I must be getting a little bit close to the mark [Sobolev was trying to break in]—my explanation of why he did this is because the rights of a small nation are involved and apparently it is a Soviet tradition to ride roughshod over the rights of small nations. . . .

MR. SOBOLEV: . . . With regard to the desire expressed by the representative of Lebanon, I fully respect it and precisely for that reason I withdraw my proposal that we should continue our work this evening.

In proposing that the Assembly act to prevent the overthrow of Lebanon by "indirect aggression," Lodge was drawing on his experience as a U.N. delegate in 1950 when Communist guerrillas, abetted by Yugoslavia, were trying to overthrow Greece. At that time he inserted a clause against "fomenting civil strife" in a resolution on Greece which established the recognition of indirect aggression as harmful. Lodge simply dusted off the 1950 principle for Lebanon.

"We face a great, rough brutal fact," he said in the course of the debate, "the fact is the fomenting of civil strife by assassins in plain clothes instead of by soldiers in uniform. Make no mistake about it, my colleagues, history will hold us responsible. We cannot avoid an answer to the question: Is the United Nations to condone subversion in plain clothes, controlled from outside a country? If the United Nations can not deal with indirect aggression, the United Nations will break up."

Action was deferred while various plans for a summit meeting at the U.N. of Eisenhower, Prime Minister Macmillan and Khrushchev were drawn, then canceled as the Soviets backed away. Finally, on August 13, Eisenhower addressed the Assembly on "A Plan for Peace," a six-point program for the Middle East, including economic aid, and pledging: "The U.S. troops would be totally withdrawn whenever this is requested by the duly constituted government of Lebanon or whenever, by action of the U.N. or otherwise, Lebanon is no longer exposed to the original dangers." Peace was restored, a new government established, and U.S. forces were withdrawn by stages until the crisis subsided. More importantly, having seen that the U.S. was prepared to use force—something Suez had made him doubt—Nasser pulled in his own aggressive horns.

In an interview with U.N. correspondent Pierre Huss, in February, 1959, Lodge gave his impression of his Soviet antagonists: "We should have no illusions about what kind of men they are. They are not soft. They are not stupid. They are not lazy. While their basic way of looking at the world must be described as malignantly irrational, they are very thorough and often clever in the methods they use to give effect to their fallacies. . . . Our greatest struggle is with ourselves rather than with the Soviet Union. We face the simple fact that enthusiasm for a bad idea can prevail over lack of enthusiasm for a good idea."

288   Before many weeks had passed, Lodge would face the toughest and cleverest of the Kremlin's leaders—Khrushchev himself. In September, 1959, the off-again, on-again summitry of the year before suddenly materialized in Khrushchev's decision to visit Eisenhower and see the U.S. The President decided that Lodge was the one man who could show America to him and at the same time effectively parry Khrushchev's propaganda.

On Tuesday, September 15, Lodge rode out to Andrews Air Force Base in Maryland to join the President and Secretary of State Herter in awaiting Khrushchev's arrival. His huge Soviet TU-114 turboprop transport, the biggest airliner ever built, loomed in the distance, looking closer than it really was because of its size. It rolled so far it nearly vanished at the far end of the runway, while three motocycles chased after to guide it to the red-carpeted dais. A specially built twenty-seven-step ladder was brought up, and down it clambered Khrushchev, a small, round, black-clad affable gnome, who vigorously pumped the waiting President's hand.

"Welcome to the United States, Mr. Chairman," said Ike.

"I am very pleased to meet you," said Khrushchev with a smile.

Madame Khrushchev came down the ladder next, in sensible black shoes, gray two-piece dress, black hat. "I am delighted to meet you," Ike told her.

When Khrushchev came to Lodge, in the receiving line, his cold blue eyes quizzically studied Lodge's face, with the respect of one good saloon-fighter for another whose prowess he has heard about. He gave him a cordial, lingering handshake. Lodge himself peered carefully into the face of a man whose constant companion he would be, morning, noon and night, from his awakening to his bedtime. No other American had ever seen a Soviet dictator so intimately for so long, as Lodge would see Khrushchev, and possibly no other could have handled this delicate, patience-trying, and potentially explosive, task as well. There were moments in it when a furious Khrushchev—the master of a formidable nuclear arsenal—seemed on the verge of virtually rupturing relations with the U.S. and going home in bitter anger. It was Lodge's tightrope-walking task throughout to save Khrushchev from offense while coolly rebutting his blatant propaganda.

After dropping the Khrushchevs at Blair House, the guest quarters across from the White House, Lodge returned in midafternoon to take Khrushchev to his first talk with the President in the oval White House office. Khrushchev sat in a straight-backed, padded leather chair to the President's left, Lodge to his right, flanked by Vice President Nixon, Foreign Minister Gromyko, and translators. Khrushchev, who had cannily timed his departure from Moscow with announcement of a Soviet rocket shot to the moon, beamed as he handed the President a replica of the Soviet moon rocket. Lodge had to admire his brass.

Chapter Fourteen

"Wouldn't it be a good idea," the President asked Khrushchev, "after you have seen our country, to take a small group up to Camp David and have really serious talks?" Khrushchev agreed, and added he would want to talk about "bases on foreign territory." Ike agreed, adding he would want to discuss Berlin, Laos, disarmament. "The Geneva conference on nuclear test suspensions," said Ike, "has laid the groundwork for real cooperation in this field, if you mean it when you say you want an agreement."

After the President took Khrushchev on a thirty-three-mile helicopter tour of Washington, Lodge took him back to the Blair House. After a brief rest, bath and change, Lodge returned in white tie and tails to take the Khrushchevs to the President's state dinner for them. Khrushchev, in a black suit similar to that of his arrival, wore a silvery four-in-hand as his concession to formal dress.* Mrs. Khrushchev was wearing a long, straight, dark blue dress of damask or faille, with a large diamond and gold pin at the bosom. In the East Room, the President escorted Nina Khrushchev, and Nikita escorted Mamie, to the dining room where the James Madison gold dinner service was set, a gold-rimmed place plate at each seat, a white damask napkin with "U.S." woven in its center. After dinner Khrushchev was introduced to CIA Director Allen Dulles who said, "You, Mr. Chairman, may have seen some of my intelligence reports from time to time." Lodge had to grin at Khrushchev's quick retort. "I believe we get the same reports," he said, "and probably from the same people." "Maybe we should pool our efforts," said Dulles. "Yes," Khrushchev agreed, "we should buy our intelligence data together and save money. We'd have to pay the people only once." Lodge took his guests home at eleven-twenty.

Next day Lodge took Khrushchev, Nina and their two daughters out to the Beltsville, Maryland, experimental station, where they saw cows which could yield 17,000 pounds of butterfat compared to the average 6,600. Khrushchev, examining some turkeys bred for extra white meat, jested: "If you don't give a turkey a passport you couldn't tell the difference between a Communist and a capitalist turkey." Lodge whirled him on to a National Press Club lunch, where Khrushchev had his first outburst of anger. President William Lawrence told as an introductory anecdote a "possibly apocryphal" story that Khrushchev, after he had denounced Stalin's crimes in 1956, had been handed a written question. It asked him

---

* The whole question of "proper" Communist dress is a fascinating study in Marxist ideology and psychology. The necktie was discarded after the Bolshevik revolution as a badge of bourgeois capitalism. It gradually came back. During World War II, Stalin dressed up the Soviet diplomatic corps in some of the world's fanciest formal uniforms, complete with red stripes, sashes and shoulder boards. However, both tuxedos and tails remained beyond the pale of Communist conformity; a light four-in-hand was as far as Communist usage permitted its chieftains to go when invitations called for "white tie."

where he was when Stalin was committing the crimes; Khrushchev supposedly demanded, "Who asked that?" and when nobody replied, snorted: "That's where I was when Stalin was committing those crimes." Khrushchev's face darkened as the story was translated. "I shall not reply to this question, which I look upon as being provocative." Another question on Russia's intervention in Hungary stirred Khrushchev's angry retort that this was "a dead rat . . . stuck in some people's throats."

Lodge stood always within arm's reach of Khrushchev, so that if any unexpected disaster should strike, the Soviets could have no suspicion that he had left their Premier unprotected. Any bomb thrown at Khrushchev during the whole tour would have killed Lodge as well. Lodge, his face set in courteous, impassive severity, carefully studied Khrushchev's personality and mannerisms. Here, it seemed to him, was a sharp and formidable figure. Though Khrushchev could draw a laugh when he wanted one, he was not the clown some had thought him. Even his apparent stumbles were perhaps artful: he apologized to the newsmen for accidentally calling them "comrades." He could be persuasive. His famous "We will bury you" threat had seemed almost a yearning for war to many Americans. Like a patient teacher, Khrushchev explained he had only meant that capitalism was "doomed," not from any action he contemplated, but by history's own evolution according to the "scientific proof" of Marx, Engels and Lenin.

Lodge broke off the questioning before it could get rougher. He took Khrushchev on a short tour of Washington. At the Lincoln Memorial, some two hundred tourists gaped while Lodge read aloud the chiseled lines of the Second Inaugural: "with malice toward none, with charity toward all." Khrushchev seemed awed as he stared up at the towering stone face. "This was indeed a man," he said. "He waged war against slavery. What more noble thing can there be in the world?"

As their motorcade swung past the Freer Gallery, Lodge thought of Uncle John Lodge's gentle spirit brooding there among his Whistlers, and wondered what that erudite soul would have thought could he see his cherished nephew escorting the high priest of Communism. Lodge guessed that Uncle John, student of so many oriental languages and religions, would certainly have asked the high priest in for tea.

That afternoon, after giving Khrushchev time to rest, Lodge took him up to the Hill for a meeting with twenty-six members and guests of the Senate foreign relations committee, Lodge's former stronghold. His old colleague, chairman William Fulbright, had tea and cocktails ready. Fulbright wanted to know if Khrushchev would be willing to accept the peaceful triumph of capitalism. Khrushchev promised he would be the first to favor capitalism if it should prove more able than Communism, but he would hate to choose between the Republican and Democratic Parties— "I don't think there's much difference." The senators laughed.

Majority Leader Lyndon Johnson pointed out that the two political parties present had the friendliest personal relations. "You run your Parliament and I'll run mine," grinned Khrushchev. Johnson later gave his size-up of Khrushchev: "A highly skilled, quick, smart leader. A hard, dangerous, evasive man." Minnesota's Senator Eugene McCarthy said: "He's a little like a candidate in the late stages of the campaign. He has heard all the questions many times, and his answers are sharp as hell."

Lodge got Khrushchev back to the Blair House in time for him to change his tan suit for his ubiqutous black one, to play host at the Soviet Embassy's return dinner for Eisenhower. It was a historic occasion, for Ike thus became the first U.S. President ever to cross the Soviet Embassy's threshold. Ike led Mamie, the Lodges and twenty-nine other Americans to join twenty-three Russians in caviar, fish fillets, stuffed patridges, perch soup, Ukrainian borscht, Sterlet in champagne, Caucasian shashlik, baked Alaska, and Soviet champagne. More toasts. More responses. Ike chided Khrushchev for his announced plan to go to Communist China on leaving America. "As for me," said the President with a twinkle, "I would not leave the Soviet Union for the sake of going to Red China."

Next day, Lodge got a closer acquaintance with Khrushchev's tough, sharp, cynical peasant wit and humor. He had routed the Russians out at 7:47 A.M. for their trip to New York aboard a special train, preceded by a pilot locomotive to guard against sabotage. As they sped through the continuous industrial complex along the Pennsy's tracks toward the perpetual fires of the Jersey marshes, Lodge tried to point out scenes of interest through their observation windows. Khrushchev seemed more amused in comparing Lodge's stern patrician face with that of his own abominable "no" man, the scowling Gromyko. Khrushchev's eyes lighted with mischievous humor.

"This train ride," he said, "reminds me of the two merchants who were each trying to figure out where the other was going, so as to get the better of him.

" 'Where are you going?' the first one asks. The second one thought it over, and decided to himself, 'I'll say I'm going to Byeletzekoff so he won't know I'm really going to Chokasy.' But then he thought, no, because he will know that I don't want him to know where I'm going, so he will be sure I am going to Chokasy. It would be better to tell him that I am going to Chokasy, even though I am really going there. He won't believe me. So the second merchant said, 'I'm going to Chokasy.'

"The first merchant was a shrewd fellow. He thought to himself, 'He doesn't want me to know where he's going. If he had told me he was going to Byeletzekoff he would know I would think he is going to Chokasy. So he has told me he was going to Chokasy hoping I will think he is going to Byeletzekoff.' So after all this thinking he turns to the first merchant. 'How long will you be in Chokasy,' he asks."

His anecdote finished, Khrushchev turned to Lodge and then to Gromyko. "Which of you is going to Chokasy?" he asked.

They all burst out laughing.

Khrushchev always had a homely allegory to illustrate the different national approaches to problems between nations. Take the matter of drinking, he suggested (something he had been rather noted for). "The French are used to drinking wine. When they drink whisky, they say, 'It burns.' When the English drink it, they say, 'We'll have a go at that.' When a Russian drinks it in a highball, he gulps it down and says, 'They've just invented it, and already they are diluting it.' "

In New York, Khrushchev spoke greetings to the "American toilers who create the wealth of society." His personal preference, however, was clearly for the society of those who controlled the wealth. He wanted chiefly to see and meet the men who ran industry—the "bosses" of capitalism, as he put it. Lodge arranged a session later in the day at the home of multimillionaire W. Averell Harriman, who had been F.D.R.'s ambassador to Russia and had visited Khrushchev there recently. First, however, Lodge took the Premier to the Waldorf Presidential Suite ($150 a day) and to Mayor Wagner's official luncheon in the Hotel Commodore's jampacked ballroom.

Introducing Khrushchev, Lodge, as he would do at endless lunches and dinners throughout the visit, gave a talk which served both to introduce Khrushchev to his audience and introduce the area to Khrushchev: "Most of the 40,000,000 people who have immigrated into the U.S. in 140 years have passed through New York City. Even today, one and three-quarter million of the people in this city were born in another country, including 314,000 who were born in what is now the Soviet Union. . . . Here in New York 8,000,000 people of every race, religion and color live side by side and for the most part all is peaceful. . . . Great progress has been made in establishing justice in this country—as the Constitution tells us to do—for all people regardless of color. But as long as one individual is discriminated against, a situation exists which we can't condone. We work without respite to solve the problem. And there is no doubt at all that, regardless of local obstacles, legal segregation will completely disappear. . . .

"There have been periods in our history when we felt so remote here between our two big oceans that we took our ideals for granted and some of us even forgot about them altogether. . . . I hope you will believe me

when I say that you, sir, have made us more conscious of the great ideals on   293
which our country rests—and we sincerely appreciate that. . . ."

Khrushchev arose in a genial mood, referred to Lodge, grinning, as "my
capitalist," and said: "He makes me suffer through this big program we
have, but at the same time he suffers, too, and that makes my suffering
easier." As for converting him to capitalism, his attitude was expressed by
the Russian saying, "Each duck praises his own marsh."

Back at the Waldorf Towers, an overloaded circuit-breaker suddenly
shut off the power in the elevator in which Lodge was taking Khrushchev
back to his suit. It stopped between the thirty-third and thirty-fourth floors.
Khrushchev feared no plot. "An example," he smiled, "of your marvelous
American technology." Lodge pried the door open to the thirty-fourth floor.
He suggested that Khrushchev get up on the little stool that was in the
elevator. As Khrushchev did so, Lodge pushed his massive behind until the
boss of all the Russias could scramble out on the floor above. Lodge, much
leaner, scrambled after him more nimbly. After a rest, he took the Premier
to Harriman's East Side mansion. Harriman had assembled twenty-seven
top industrialists, financiers and educators to meet him, and told Khrushchev bluntly that here was his chance to discover the views of those he
called capitalism's "ruling circles." Khrushchev sank back in a big chair
while Chase Manhattan Bank Chairman John McCloy, RCA Chairman
David Sarnoff, and General Dynamics Chairman Frank Pace assured him
they would be happy to give up defense profits to concentrate on the growing civilian economy. They made no dent on Khrushchev's view of the two
system's irreconcilable contradictions. "To argue differently," he said, "is
like the deaf talking to the deaf."

That evening Lodge took K. to a dinner of the Economic Club of New
York where an even bigger battery of high-powered capitalists was assembled. Lodge, speaking first, tried to educate Khrushchev out of his tired
old Marxist cliches about predatory capitalism exploiting workers:

*If robber baron is the definition of capitalist, then we are not capitalists
at all. In fact, on July 2, 1890, we declared war on monopoly capitalism when the Sherman Anti-Trust Act became law. That law is still
being actively enforced.*

*There are, for example, 14 million Americans who own shares in
American industry. In our country two-thirds of the gross national
product goes into consumption—food, entertainment, refrigerators,
automobiles, etc. Three out of four families own their own automobile.
Three-fifths of all homes in America which are not on farms are owned
by the families who occupy them. One out of every 10 families makes
$10,000 a year or more—triple the proportion of ten years ago. Family*

income, adjusted for change in the value of the dollar, has gone up 50% in ten years.

Economic humanism rather than monopoly capitalism perhaps best describes such a system. . . . American business prospers at the same time that the Federal Government, in ways large and small, pervades our lives—one adult in five gets regular checks from the Government and federal warehouses give out food to 5,000,000 persons and 2,000,000 persons live in government-subsidized housing. We live in a welfare state which seeks to put a floor below which no one sinks, but builds no ceiling to prevent man from rising. The plans of tens of thousands of independent producers lead to greater production, a more dynamic economy and a richer life for all.

It would be a mistake to think that business leaders are America's ruling class. There is only one ruling class in this country, and that is the American voter. And whenever the citizens have wanted to change the system, they have done so through the ballot. They can do so again whenever they want to. We have this system today because the rank and file approves it and because it has given them the highest standard of living in the world.

Even as Lodge was speaking, Khrushchev would sometimes break in to contradict him: "Only the grave can correct a hunchback." In his own speech, the Soviet leader was chiefly concerned with trying to whet the appetites of the businessmen for big export profits if the U.S. would lift its strategic restrictions. When the audience grew restive over his long-windedness, he mistook it for derision of his ideas, hurled a proverb: "He who wants to have eggs must put up with the hen's cackle." When heckling questions came, Khrushchev cried: "Gentlemen, I am an old sparrow, you cannot muddle me with your cries. If you don't want to listen to what I have to say, I can go."

On the hundred-mile visit to Hyde Park, the Khrushchev party was too late getting underway for Lodge to take them through Harlem, which Khrushchev had expressed a desire to see. Ambassador Menshikov, who seized every opportunity to needle Lodge, needled him about this omission. "You'll see Harlem on the way back," Lodge muttered grimly. After Khrushchev had laid a wreath on President Roosevelt's grave, and declined Mrs. Roosevelt's proffered coffee (merely grabbing a seed-roll, saying, "One for the road"), the party sped back to New York. Menshikov reminded Lodge that Khrushchev had to hurry back to the Waldorf to dress for a U.N. dinner that night. "In that case we'll go straight back," said Lodge. Menshikov again applied the needle: "Oh, so you don't want Chairman Khrushchev to see Harlem?" Lodge snapped: "Chairman Khrushchev will see Harlem if he never does another thing. We will all get up a little earlier tomorrow morning to go through Harlem."

Next morning, prior to a transcontinental flight to Los Angeles, Lodge routed everyone out at five, drove them through, in and around Harlem, on the way to the airport. It was a bright sunny morning. Much of the housing looked better than Moscow's. "This isn't so bad," said Khrushchev. "Bad or not," said Lodge, "it's coming down in the next few years because there is a tremendous slum-clearance project under way."

They were hurtled to Los Angeles effortlessly in five hours and twenty-seven minutes by a Boeing 707 jet. They had no sooner stepped out than Lodge realized Los Angeles would give him some trying times in his efforts to provide civil treatment for the visiting head of government. This became clear from Mayor Norris Poulson's studiedly insulting greeting: "We welcome you to Los Angeles, City of Angels, the city where the impossible always happens." Khrushchev simply put away his prepared arrival speech, muttered "Thank you," and turned away. Lodge sped him to a lunch at Twentieth Century Fox, where still other trials were in store. Shirley Mac-Laine, (who had boasted she was going to tell the chairman: "How the hell are you, Krush? . . . We're going to shoot the can-can number without pants"), actually made a little welcoming speech in Russian which she had practiced. That went well.

But Khrushchev, like all Russians, was very sensitive to heat, and the heat in Los Angeles was like that of an African desert. Worse, huge arc lights glared down so the luncheon could be filmed live on television. Spyros Skouras, Twentieth Century Fox president, already had nettled Khrushchev by drawing him into an endless and pointless debate about which poor boy, he or Khrushchev, had risen highest and fastest. "Shut up!" some of the audience were snapping.

Police Chief Parker, who had been hit by a tomato thrown at Khrushchev on the way in, came up to tell Lodge that he could not be responsible for Khrushchev's safety if he went, as Khrushchev very much wanted, to Disneyland. Lodge, under strict instructions from the President to safeguard Khrushchev's life above all, snapped: "If the police can't be responsible, they won't go." The chronic troublemaker Menshikov overheard this and ran at once to tell Khrushchev. Khrushchev hit the roof. "What is it, is there an epidemic of cholera there or something?" he cried to the luncheon audience, fists clenched, face darkening. "Or have gangsters taken hold of the place that can destroy me?"

He regained his good spirits after lunch watching Shirley MacLaine and her can-can girls up-end in their lacy pants. He apologized for losing his temper, and told Kim Novak that she had "wowed" Deputy Premier Anastas Mikoyan on his earlier visit.

Afterward, on a drive through Los Angeles, Khrushchev was curious about signs carried by pickets (One read: DEATH TO KHRUSHCHEV THE BUTCHER OF HUNGARY), and demanded to know what they meant. "Mr. Chairman, that is a woman who does not agree with your policy on Hungary," Lodge explained.

"If Eisenhower wanted to insult me," said Khrushchev, "why did he invite me to come in the first place?"

"Surely," said Lodge, "you don't mean to say that President Eisenhower would invite you to come to the United States and then arrange to have this woman on this street corner in Los Angeles to do this thing. We have free speech in America and anybody can say what they want."

"Well," said Khrushchev, "all I can say is that in Russia she wouldn't be there without my having approved it."

Khrushchev had several bodyguards. Among them was a vigorous, blond young Russian of about thirty-five, who only recognized the Russians, and took a long time to discover who Lodge was. Several times he mistook Lodge for a newspaperman or photographer, and would come up from behind and "lift" him out. It was Lodge's duty to be alongside Khrushchev at all times. Next time he saw, out of the corner of his eye, the young bodyguard reaching for him again, the fifty-seven-year-old Lodge whirled, grabbed the Russian, picked him up, threw him down in the corner, and told him emphatically: "Never lay your hands on me again!"

General Zacharov, Khrushchev's chief of security, rushed up to apologize to Lodge. Khrushchev, who had missed the episode, heard about it. Up to then he had been cool and reserved with Lodge. Now he had a warm smile, held his arms wide as to embrace him, and grinned broadly: "I hear you have been beating up one of my guards!" After this they were always on a very cordial footing.

At the civic dinner that night, Lodge again felt the trip was in danger of blowing up. Mayor Poulson resurrected the "we will bury you" line to inform Khrushchev, "You shall not bury us and we shall not bury you." Khrushchev reminded him that he had already explained the metaphorical meaning of this remark in Washington, and added if Americans simply wanted to insult him, "It took me about 12 hours to get here. I guess it will take no more than 10½ hours to fly back."

As a result of this blow-up, the President urged all Americans to be as polite to Khrushchev as they would to any guest in their homes. Consequently, when the party was proceeding to San Francisco on a streamlined train, the crowd that turned out at Santa Barbara was on its good behavior. The city is a mecca for retired millionaires, and Lodge recognized many rich friends from Boston in the sport-shirted crowd thronging the tracks. After Khrushchev made a little speech, they gave him hearty, prolonged applause. Khrushchev turned to Lodge, beaming from ear to ear: "You see, the ordinary people of America like me!"

In San Francisco, things at first went almost as badly as in Los Angeles. Labor leaders who attended an evening roundtable with Khrushchev felt called upon to needle Khrushchev to his face. One asked why the Soviets jammed Voice of America broadcasts. "What do you prefer for dinner?" asked Khrushchev. "Roast beef," replied the laborite. "I, borscht," said Khrushchev. "You continue to enjoy roast beef, I borscht." Suddenly Khrushchev leaped up and imitated the can-can he had seen in Hollywood, flipping his coattails upward to stick out his massive behind. "This is what you call freedom," he cried, "freedom for the girls to show their backsides. To us it's pornography. . . . It's capitalism that makes the girls that way."

When a brewery-workers' chieftain challenged Khrushchev to name a single instance where workers had welcomed a Communist seizure of power, Khrushchev snapped: "Is that all? Think it over. Drink your beer. Perhaps that will help you find the answer to your question."

Next morning, while waiting for union leader Harry Bridges to arrive at Longshoreman's Hall on Fisherman's Wharf, Lodge took the Khrushchevs for a tour of the harbor on the Coast Guard cutter *Gresham*. Khrushchev by now had fallen in love with San Francisco, and found Mayor George Christopher's warm courtesy more than amends for Poulson's insults. "Poulson," Khrushchev told Mayor Christopher aboard the *Gresham*, "was like a man who tries to let just a teensy little fart [squeezing his fingers together] then finds he has messed his whole britches."

After a cafeteria lunch at IBM's Santa Barbara plant, and a welcome by IBM President Thomas J. Watson, Jr., who recalled to Khrushchev that he had flown lend-lease bombers to Russia during World War II, Khrushchev relaxed: "You fed me so very well. . . . We will feed our people just as well as you're doing it." His brush with the union leaders made him think that he got on better with capitalists: "We each believe our system to be better . . . and it is only life that can show which one of us is right."

On a tour of a supermarket in Stonestown in San Francisco, Mr. K. patted a fifteen-month-old child on the head, moved along patting heads and melons, shaking hands ("he touched me!" squealed a teenager). Photographers were scrambling everywhere, one climbed on a display and tumbled it over, and another began grappling with a meat clerk. Khrushchev grinned like a gargoyle at the uproar.

Meanwhile, Emily Lodge and Mrs. Wiley Buchanan, wife of the State Department protocol chief, had sneaked Mrs. Khrushchev and Mrs. Gromyko, unobserved by press or crowds, out to a Sears Roebuck store for some shopping, and then to a school, gleaming new, where there were more Negroes than whites. The episode broke down the carefully studied indif-

298 ference which the Russians had maintained up to now. Mrs. Gromyko said frankly the sight of Negroes in such a fine school "made my heart feel good."

Next morning, as they passed endless streams of commuter-drivers, on their way to the airport, Khrushchev remarked at the "terrible extravagance, all these cars with only one person in them!" They soared off for the Midwest. The biggest crowd yet met them at Des Moines. After a quick lunch, their first stop was at Des Moines Packing Co., an automated place where cows came in at one end and hot dogs emerged at the other. Khrushchev ate his first hot dog, gobbled it down while Lodge was still gingerly nibbling his. "Capitalist!" he demanded gleefully, "Have you finished your sausage!" Someone asked if the pace was tiring him. "Life is too short as it is," said Khrushchev. "In 60 years you sleep 20 years. I have no right to get tired."

The following morning they visited the hybrid-corn farm of Roswell Garst near Coon Rapids. Garst had visited Russia, and also played host to the Soviet Agricultural Minister. No man was better prepared than big, friendly Roswell Garst to show Khrushchev the real America. "You don't have to treat him special," Garst had said beforehand. "He needs to know the simple things about America. We aren't a warlike people. We don't want any war. We want to get on with the worthwhile things like education, health, more leisure to enjoy what we've got. The most insane thing in the world is spending a hundred billion dollars a year preparing for a war nobody wants, nobody expects and nobody could survive. . . . With the techniques we now have—clearly proven and fully documented—it would be possible to erase hunger within ten years, so we can get on with the other problems of the world like better education, better health, greater convenience of living."

But Garst's genial dream of a peaceful world had not reckoned with the belligerent army of three hundred-odd photographers who were soon trampling his beloved cornfields. The cameramen, barred from following the official party into a cornfield reserved for Khrushchev's inspection, went through the tall corn in an encircling movement. They materialized suddenly under Garst's nose. "Get back! Get back!" he bellowed, surprised and angry. "Bring those horses in here!" he cried to his helpers, "Ride 'em down!" He began throwing damp, green ensilage at them, and kicked the scholarly New York *Times* reporter Harrison Salisbury squarely in the shin. Garst's son, Stephen, forgetting that Americans are not warlike people, armed three hired hands with pitchforks to set them on his own countrymen. Khrushchev, hugely enjoying this war on the disorderly American press, gleefully added a threat of his own: "We'll turn the bulls on you!"

On a drive to the State A. & M. College at Ames, Khrushchev poked more peasant fun at Lodge: "In all his life, Mr. Lodge probably hasn't taken in

as many smells as today." He liked the fat pigs he saw: "These Soviet and
American pigs can coexist, why can't our nations?"

After Iowa they flew on to Pittsburgh, arriving at night. The usual belch-
ing fires of open-hearths were absent; the plants were closed by strike.
But the city's lights blazed, and thousands choked the streets near their
hotel to give Khrushchev the biggest, loudest welcome of the whole tour.
Next day, at the Mesta Machinery Co., one of the steel mills still open,
Khrushchev questioned one worker about his wages ($80-$90 a week),
hefted tools, examined huge presses. When a steel worker offered him a
stogie, in a burst of generosity Khrushchev gave the man his wristwatch.
When a guide showed him a machine and said, "I'm sure that you have
better ones in your country," Khrushchev replied with rancor: "Don't be
so sure. We have better ones; we have the same kind—we even have worse.
I don't say that all you have is bad and all we have is good. We can learn
from you."

Late that Thursday afternoon, Lodge took him back to the big jet, for
the last, short hop to Washington. Under Secretary of State Robert Murphy
was on hand to greet them. Lodge dropped K. at the Blair House, hastily
showered and dressed for Menshikov's reception at the Embassy from 6:30
to 8, then escorted Khrushchev to the Sheraton Carlton for a dinner given
by Eric Ridder of the New York *Journal of Commerce* for some two dozen
businessmen. Once more Khrushchev sounded his familiar theme on building more trade.

Friday morning Lodge took Khrushchev on another tour of Washington,
pointing out various sights. In midafternoon he brought him back to the
White House for the most important part of the whole trip—the serious
talks at Camp David. Helicopters were waiting to take the principals to
this Catoctin Mountain retreat which Franklin Roosevelt had built as
"Shangri-La."

Lodge escorted Foreign Minister Gromyko to the first helicopter. They
were joined by Secretary of State Herter, Ambassador to Russia Llewellyn
Thompson, Ambassador Menshikov and A. A. Soldatov. President Eisenhower took off in a second helicopter with Khrushchev, Translator Troyanovsky, U.S. Interpreter Alexander Akalovsky, and the two security chiefs
—Soviet General Zacharov, Secret Service Boss Jim Rowley. Two Cadillacs
took them the quarter of a mile to the circular drive in front of Aspen
Lodge (Roosevelt had called it "The Bear's Den"). As they alighted they
were confronted by seventy-two pool reporters and photographers. "It's
lucky Mr. Garst isn't here," grinned Khrushchev. Everybody guffawed when
Troyanovsky translated his remark. "He would have tried to organize the
thing in his own way," Khrushchev added.

From the living room they could look down the slope of Catoctin Mountain to the Maryland farm valleys below. They sat down around a circular coffee table and began the first really private meeting of heads of the two governments since Harry Truman saw Stalin at Potsdam in 1945. These first exchanges were general remarks on the world situation, with specifics left to be dealt with the next day, Saturday. The talking continued as they moved in to the dining table before the huge fieldstone fireplace. Mess stewards served oysters on the half shell, then roast beef (or baked red snapper) followed by Key lime pie. After dinner a portable screen was set up and a 16mm. print was shown of a Navy film about the polar voyage of the nuclear submarine *Nautilus*. Khrushchev had expressed interest in seeing it. They also saw a western, *Shane*. There are four bedrooms in the lodge. After the film and some nightcaps at eleven, Ike showed Khrushchev to his, the third in line, Gromyko to the fourth, Herter to the second and retired to the first himself. Lodge, Menshikov and Thompson slept in an adjoining cabin.

Next morning, Lodge joined Chris Herter at the breakfast table. Khrushchev stuck his head in the door and said jokingly, "You two fellows are trying to eat up all the food before I get here!" He then sat down and had four eggs, eight sausages and six strips of bacon. Lodge commented that this was a rather hearty breakfast.

"I'm not usually allowed to eat this much," said Khrushchev. "When I'm away from home I give myself a good time."

The President joined them and some more exploratory talk began. At 9 A.M. they moved into the sun room where Ike sat in an easy chair across the coffee table from Khrushchev. Also present were Lodge, Herter, Thompson and Akalovsky. Vice President Nixon, who had driven up that morning, joined them. On a divan sat Livingston Merchant, State Department counselor; Eisenhower's son John; and Brig. General Andrew Goodpaster, White House staff secretary. Khrushchev had Gromyko and Menshikov on his left, Troyanovsky and Soldatov on his right.

The first topic was Berlin. Khrushchev did all the talking on his side and Eisenhower on his. It was mainly a restatement of each side's position —Khrushchev insisting that West Berlin must be neutralized and Communist East Germany recognized, Eisenhower insisting on free elections and a unified Germany. Only the previous November, Khrushchev had given a virtual ultimatum that if the West did not get out of Berlin he would sign a separate peace with East Germany and their rights would be forfeit. The talk then turned to disarmament proposals, questions of inspection and control. It was not getting anywhere.

At 10:45, Eisenhower suggested a break. Khrushchev, who had learned that Camp David had a bowling alley, wanted to see it. They walked a hundred yards from Aspen to the camp recreation hall and entered the two-lane bowling alley. They sat down and watched Yeoman Second Class John Halferty of Fennimore, Wisconsin, bowl a 218 game. He put together five strikes and one spare before getting a split. Both leaders congratulated him and autographed his score sheet. Khrushchev was fascinated by the automatic pin-setting equipment. They walked on north to Laurel Lodge, about a mile and a half over the camp's pleasant leafy, gravel walks, then back to Aspen at eleven twenty and sat down at the green-baize bridge table in the sun room for a private talk—with only the two interpreters present—which lasted until 2:10 P.M. There was a ten-minute interruption while Ike conferred with Herter, Lodge, Nixon, Thompson and his other staffers in Herter's bedroom. Then all sat down to lunch on boiled frankfurters and baked beans with Boston brown bread.

They were joined at lunch by some temporary visitors—Treasury Secretary Robert Anderson, Atomic Energy Commissioner John McCone, White House science adviser Dr. George Kistiakowski, Russia's cultural boss Yuri Zhukov, U.N. Ambassador Sobolev, and Soviet atomic-energy chief Vasily Yemelyanov. The conference resumed. Once more, when it seemed to be bogging down on specifics, Ike took Khrushchev off alone with just the interpreters, piled into the helicopter and flew him to his Gettysburg farm, a twelve-minute flight. They loaded into Ike's own two-tone green Dodge station wagon and drove over to the barns south of the main house. Khrushchev looked over Ike's Black Angus cattle, dropped by the main house to meet John's wife, Barbara, and her four children. There they reached at least one agreement: that Eisenhower's proposed 1960 return visit be made in the late spring, so the children could come and see Russia at its prettiest. They walked back to the helicopter and flew back to Camp David.

At 8 P.M. they sat down to a dinner of broiled grapefruit, loin strip steak, baked potato, chopped broccoli and hollandaise sauce, a Corton-Bressandes red Burgundy with a Pol Roger 1952 champagne with dessert. Ike, anxious to have as many of his staff as possible see the Soviet antagonists close up, brought in Assistant Secretary of Defense Thomas Gates, Attorney General William Rogers, Postmaster General Summerfield, Secretary of Interior Fred Seaton, Labor Secretary Mitchell and Lewis Strauss, former AEC head.

While they were at the farm, Herter, Lodge, Gates, McCone and other advisers talked over the problems of broader cultural relations, scientific exchange, and disarmament with Gromyko, Menshikov, Sobolev, Yemelyanov, Soldatov and Zhukov. The talks were friendly but inconclusive.

As before, the talks hinged chiefly on Berlin. Ike calmly but firmly took the position from the outset that the whole future of peaceful coexistence with the Soviets lay in Khrushchev's lifting of his ultimatum on the Western presence in Berlin. Nothing really could be achieved unless and until he did so. His position was, in effect, an ultimatum of his own.

Time and time again Eisenhower returned to this simple statement: "You have the opportunity to make a great contribution to history by making it possible to ease tensions. It is within your hands." Time and time again he returned to this simple demand:

> *You must remove all threats, implicit or otherwise, that the Soviets will ever try to impair our occupation rights or our access rights to West Berlin. You must give an absolutely clear guarantee that, at the termination of any interim agreement we make on Berlin, Western rights will remain unimpaired. All cut-off dates and threats must be dropped.*

The other negotiators had already reached virtual agreements on broader cultural exchanges, swapping of unclassified atomic information, closer work between atomic scientists. Saturday night Ike told his advisers he might even refuse to join in these unless the prime concession on Berlin was made.

On Sunday morning, Eisenhower rose early to drive twenty-five miles to the United Presbyterian Church at Gettysburg. He returned for the last, showdown round of talks with Khrushchev. They were supposed to wind up in time for a noon departure by Khrushchev. Instead, he stayed for lunch. The talk droned on. At last, Khrushchev conceded.

It was agreed that they would join in a formal communique announcing that 1) negotiations would be reopened on Berlin and Germany, that 2) Eisenhower would say publicly later in the week that Khrushchev had withdrawn cut-off dates and time limits on Western rights in West Berlin, and that 3) Khrushchev would issue a confirmatory statement in Moscow. Press Secretary Jim Hagerty flew to the waiting reporters at Gettysburg with the first news. At 2:12, Washington being foggy, the President drove Khrushchev back at a 90 m.p.h. clip for his final press conference at the National Press Club.

Eisenhower left Khrushchev at Blair House. Khrushchev changed his gray suit to the dark blue suit and silvery tie that constituted his formal evening wear, put on his familiar medals, and accompanied Lodge to the Press Club for his second appearance. President Bill Lawrence announced that the Embassy had requested all questions be in writing (no more "dead rats"). Gromyko screened them and passed the accepted ones along to Troyanovsky. "My esteemed fellow traveling journalists," Khrushchev began, drawing a laugh. "You will excuse me for this unusual form of address, but many of you have been traveling with me through the United States and therefore I look upon you as my sputniks, my fellow travelers."

He put on his glasses and read a statement thanking them, "the majority . . . tried as far as possible to be objective in covering our trip. I believe that the Communist pie is the best. We like to eat it and will be ready to share it with all who like to share it. . . ."

Khrushchev summed up the fruits of the trip as he saw it:

"I have no doubt whatsover that the President is sincere in his desire to improve relations between our countries. . . . I like your people. They, like the Soviet people, have one desire: to bring about peace and the prevention of a new war."

From the Press Club, Lodge escorted Khrushchev to the NBC studio where the pudgy premier addressed the American people for forty-five minutes. It was a deft propaganda performance, citing chapter and verse of the great material strides that Russia had made in industrializing itself under Communism. He even made an appeal to religious-minded people, saying they should not oppose the Soviet system because it was working for "the most humane and truly just relations in society." Lodge took him back to Blair House, where Khrushchev ate his final supper in the U.S. with his family.

At 8:48 P.M., when he emerged for the trip back to Andrews Air Force Base, Lodge had brought his oldest son, George, and his wife, Nancy to introduce them. George, who had been working with the International Labor Organization in Geneva, had become an Assistant Secretary of Labor. "These youngsters," said Cabot, "are the parents of five children." "You're real capitalists in that respect," said Khrushchev, beaming. "I wish you the very best."

Vice President Nixon arrived to accompany Khrushchev and his wife on the last ride (Mrs. Nixon had played host to Nina Khrushchev the day before at a private club), Lodge followed with the Gromykos. At Andrews the 125-foot red carpet again awaited, a 56-piece Army band played both nations' anthems, a 75 mm. howitzer again fired the 21-gun salute. The limousines drove out to the field, hard by the boarding ramp. Khrushchev shook Lodge's hand and thanked him for being "my capitalist" and invited him to come to visit him. Nixon gave a brief address saying the visit was a "significant step toward initiating a pattern through which these differences can be settled by peaceful means." "Thank you all," said Khrushchev, "from the bottom of my heart for your hospitality and, as we say in Russia, for your bread and salt. Let us have more and more use for the short American word, 'Hokay!'" He climbed the ramp the great plane rolled away and soared aloft. Nikita Khrushchev had come and gone.

What had it all added up to?

Lodge was sure of one thing. He had watched Khrushchev for nearly two weeks, closer and on a more intimate footing than any American before or since, and had studied his every mood and caprice. He was sure that in Khrushchev the U.S. confronted a man who was sharp as a razor, who missed nothing, who was quick to seize every propaganda advantage (like Poulson's insults) and turn them back upon Americans—yet a man calculating even in his anger; he never let it carry him to the point of forgetting his original design of "softening" the American attitude.

As to Khrushchev's motives, it seemed to Lodge that they must have been to make maximum use of America's own open press and radio for his propaganda—this he had skilfully done. Against this liability must be weighed the tremendous impression which America itself undoubtedly made upon Khrushchev—simply the tremendous size of it, the unguessed depth and richness of its prosperity, the surprising discovery that even the slums of Harlem were by Soviet standards "not so bad." Khrushchev would hesitate—as the events in Cuba would later show—to risk a test of strength with such a buoyant, ebullient and confident giant. This was a decided asset.

To whatever extent the visit would help build a modus vivendi between these "two colossi glaring at one another across the atomic abyss"—such understandings as indeed were later achieved at the signing of a nuclear test-ban treaty—that would be an invaluable plus big enough to offset all the disadvantages. Time alone would reveal how much it had done so.

In any case, Khrushchev kept his part of the bargain. He did announce, when he got back to Moscow, that there was no time limit or cut-off point on Berlin. He told the Russian throngs awaiting him, "I got the impression that Eisenhower sincerely wanted to liquidate the cold war and to improve relations between our two great countries. . . . I want to express my gratitude particularly to Mr. Lodge. He did everything in his power to make our trip pleasant and to acquaint us with the great people of the U.S."

Within a few weeks, back at the U.N., when the Soviet representative Vasily Kuznetsov was again assailing the U.S. for renewing its demand that U.N. observers be admitted into Hungary, Lodge let him have it straight from the shoulder.

"I took some notes during Mr. Kuznetsov's speech," he said, "and I noted some of these phrases: 'dirty work,' 'sordid assignment,' 'mouthpiece for slander,' 'puppet,' 'slanderous assertions and concoctions' in my letter [on Hungary].

"Now I am not fortunate enough to be familiar with the Russian language, and maybe these are ordinary, routine phrases in Russian. But I have some familiarity with English and with French, and I can say that in those two languages these are extremely violent words. If Mr. Kuznetsov is really

interested in lessening the cold war, he could very easily prove that fact by
using parliamentary language in a parliamentary assembly. I say that to
him in as bland a tone as I can use.

"Then he referred in his speech to the conversations between Chairman
Khrushchev and President Eisenhower . . . which . . . the other day the
Soviet delegation characterized as the 'spirit of Camp David.' Now Mr.
Chairman, we prize what was achieved at Camp David, and none are more
opposed than we to doing anything which would destroy it. One way to live
up to that spirit is to conform with United Nations resolutions.

"I feel that perhaps I have some right to talk about Camp David for the
simple reason that I was there. In fact I was present at all the meetings
which took place. . . . I can assert that there is nothing in [its] communique or in what happened at Camp David to justify the declaration that the
very modest action on Hungary which we are discussing today is against
the spirit of Camp David.

"What is against the spirit of Camp David, Mr. Chairman, is the subversion of small countries.

"What is against the spirit of Camp David are acts which turn a brave
little country into a moaning colonialist slum.

"What is against the spirit of Camp David is any behavior which makes
a veritable mockery of peaceful coexistence. . . . Nothing happened at
Camp David which requires us to pass by in silence on the other side of the
street when a brutality is being committed . . . from acting like human
beings made in the image of God when cruelty is being practiced.

"The spirit of Camp David was not intended to be a soporific to peoples
in the democracies, to put them to sleep in the belief that this dangerous
world, which we all hope may some day be safe, has actually been made
safe. . . . We can only build a peaceful world on deeds—deeds of justice
—and the spirit of Camp David never told us not to do such deeds.
. . . Why don't you do something to show that you really believe in the true
spirit of Camp David? Why don't you take down the barbed wire and the
observation towers which now divide the poor Hungarians from Austria
and the free world and which have turned Hungary into a vast human
cage? Why don't you chain up the savage dogs which roam along the border
to catch the miserable human beings who are seeking freedom? It is by
such deeds as these that we can best live up to the spirit of Camp David.

"Let me say in conclusion that the Camp David communique states that
'all outstanding international questions should be settled not by the application of force but by peaceful means through negotiation.' If, therefore, we
are really to live up to the spirit of Camp David, [U.N. Observer] Sir Leslie
Munro ought to be admitted into Hungary, the U.N. resolutions adopted by

306   overwhelming votes should be carried out in Hungary, and the Soviet Union, instead of working against the United Nations, should work *with* the United Nations. That would be really carrying out the spirit of Camp David."

CHAPTER FIFTEEN

It all simmers down to this: . . . if we want to make the people happy, it should be Lodge. —Thomas E. Dewey to the Republican chiefs in Chicago.

As the 1960 Presidential year began, and General Eisenhower prepared to return to private life, Lodge found himself pondering his own future—and that of his party.

As for the party, in spite of eight years of Republican rule, the big unanswered questions were the same ones which Lodge himself had asked so often in the past. Was the Republican Party at last ready to move into the future with a dynamic program of positive, constructive action? Or was it still so torn with political schizophrenia that it was doomed, like the Whigs of old, to destroy itself through its inability to achieve a clear political identity and a viable program?

As for Lodge, more than any man, in his thirteen years in the Senate, he had charted the principles on which that party, if it were ready to reorganize itself and act responsibly, could broaden its appeal beyond the dwindling minority of thick-or-thin Republicans. It had to do so to win a majority from independents, liberals and dissident Democrats who held the balance of power.

Lodge had led the party out of the wilderness of futile, sterile isolationism, of Fortress America obscurantism, into the real world of collective security, foreign reconstruction and freer trade. As the most articulate single architect of Party platforms he had charted the programs—of leadership in civil rights, concern for workers and for labor, practical health and welfare measures, extension of Social Security and pensions, elimination of governmental waste, electoral reform—behind which an intelligent, active conservatism could move forward. Moreover, in his eight years as chief spokesman for the free world before the sounding board of the U.N., his lithe, handsome figure had become better known than almost any other to a whole generation of housewives who had watched him through crisis after crisis as they performed their household tasks.

All this had made him so much the Number One Republican of his day —the one, moreover, with greatest appeal to independents and moderate Democrats, as poll after poll had shown; the one leader who looked every inch a President, and talked like one to boot—that it was remarkable he was not already the party's nominee-presumptive. Assuredly he would have been such had he played a similar role in the Democratic Party. In Eng-

308   land, a leader who had been the most active, articulate and effective leader
of his party for a quarter-century would long since have been Prime Minister.

Lodge, however, could expect no such recognition by the party which he
had served so well and so long. If he was clearly its outstanding leader, he
was a leader without a following. That was so precisely because he had
been taking the party in a direction where—whatever the wishes of its rank
and file, and of those independents and Democrats who had joined them to
give Eisenhower his two landslides—the professionals and party hacks still
dominating the Republican political machinery had never wished to go.

By and large, despite Eisenhower's unprecedented victories, this machinery was still in the hands of the very men Lodge had fought and beaten
at Chicago. They had forgotten nothing, learned nothing—and forgiven
nothing. Now, as then, they would prefer to lose an election with a man
sharing their prejudices and parochialisms than win with an antimachine
maverick they detested. They were like a man who would rather be wrong
than President.

Eisenhower, who could have done most to transfer the party's leadership
into younger, bolder, more pragmatic hands, had often done the contrary.
Sherman Adams related in his memoirs how Eisenhower had quickly forgotten a list that Lodge had prepared, at Eisenhower's request, of those who
had fought him the most savagely. Indeed, he had often given such men
preferment over those who had helped him win. Instead of using the incalculable moral prestige of his unprecedented landslides to demand, and get,
effective Republican leadership and a coherent Republican program in Congress, Eisenhower had stood ineffectually by while such party wreckers and
saboteurs as Joe McCarthy—attributing "treason" even to the President himself—all but destroyed his State Department and threw his whole Administration into confusion. Vice President Nixon and Majority Leader Robert
Taft, having applauded McCarthy in the past and become his boon companions, could not later oppose him, nor did they dare. It was the highest
irony that only the Democratic victory in the 1954 Congressional elections
saved Eisenhower from McCarthy by depriving him of the subcommittee
chairmanship that alone allowed him to make himself a one-man star
chamber and hanging judge. His loss of this strategic platform put him
well on the way to oblivion before the whole Senate's censure made it final.

Taft was a responsible leader—and unlike Eisenhower did his homework
on the great social issues which a responsible party could not avoid. But
after his death, William F. Knowland, his successor, seemed more often to
be the Administration's opponent than its spokesman. To compound the
irony, it was Democratic Majority Leader Lyndon Johnson who throughout
the remaining six years of Eisenhower's regime, gave him far more effective

leadership—in such vital matters as civil rights and defense reorganization
—than the nominal floor leaders of his own party.

There was a still greater irony. Throughout the twenty years of Republican famine, the party's biggest contributors, chiefly industrialists and financiers of the Far Right, had shrieked "creeping socialism" at every new Roosevelt reform. Yet Eisenhower, having fulfilled their dreams of a Republican reconquest of federal power, had not repealed an iota of the Roosevelt Revolution. Like a true conservative, he had consolidated and confirmed it. At the same time, the unquestioned, unlimited confidence of Big Business in Eisenhower had brought forth the biggest industrial expansion, biggest stock market boom, and greatest all-round prosperity in U.S. history. Even more ironically, this fact made it ever more unlikely that the Roosevelt Revolution—that curious, haphazard medley of welfare statism financed by the mounting profits of expanding private enterprise—could ever be repealed. It was here to stay because the American people liked it, had grown used to it, and wanted to keep it. Yet despite this the men still dominating the Republican Party's state and local machinery and coffers continued to have weird fantasies of undoing it, and gave ritualistic cry to their ancient shibboleths—much as doddering ex-Confederates, a score of years ago, gave quavering Rebel yells at their reunions until they tottered to the grave.

By virtue of all this, the situation, as 1960 began, was that Eisenhower, not having used his leadership, had no leadership to pass on. He had not, himself, regarded Richard Nixon as of Presidential stature ("He simply hasn't grown," Presidential aide Emmet Hughes quoted Eisenhower as saying), and in the 1956 uncertainty over Nixon's renomination had, first, suggested that he seek some other office; then later had praised him with faint damns by saying that, if he had a week to think it over, he could doubtless provide some examples of Nixon's high abilities.

Certainly Nixon had lukewarm following among rank and file Republicans. "The pros like him," Ohio's future Republican governor, C. William O'Neill, told the writer in Columbus in 1956, "because they think he is one of them, who thinks like they do. The rank and file don't like him because they do not trust him." Many independents shared this feeling. "Why is it the rich New York Jews dislike Nixon so?" Allen Dulles asked a prominent New York caller, who replied: "Because they think he looks like a Nazi storm trooper." Newsmen, by and large, shared this distrust; having watched Nixon close up they concluded his character was adjustable to situations. "Nixon," Walter Lippmann told a luncheon of *Herald Tribune* editors, "certainly is not of that generation which regards honesty as the best policy. However, he does regard it as a policy." But the Republicans pros wanted Nixon, and Eisenhower decided to let them have what they

310   wanted. By acquiescing in Nixon's renomination in 1956, he made him the
inescapable Republican nominee of 1960. "Nixon," said John W. Love, business columnist of the Cleveland *Press* and a lifelong Republican, "is like a
man who got on an elevator and found himself on the top floor by mistake."

That mistake would be costly to the Republican Party.

It was to be a swift-paced, tumultuous year for Lodge. He began 1960
with a trip to Africa—his third—to witness the birth of the Cameroons as
a new nation, to see President Tubman reinaugurated as President of Liberia, and to visit Dakar, capital of French Senegal. He and Emily were
housed in the maternity ward of a new hospital in Douala, Cameroon's sea-
port, and Lodge imperturbably termed it "as modern as any in the U.S."

On his return, it stirred the old reporter's pride to be singled out by the
New York Employing Printers Association for its annual Benjamin Franklin
Award. "Like Socrates in Athens," he mused, the free press's task was to
"be irritating and irreverent, to arouse, stir up and reproach," and he was
moved to quote Socrates' speech to the Athenian citizens trying him: " 'If
you put me to death, you will not injure me more than your own selves.
. . . For if you kill me, you will not readily find another such as I, who am
like some gadfly upon a powerful high-bred steed who has become sluggish
by reason of his very size and needs to be aroused. . . .' "

Khrushchev had invited Cabot and Emily to visit Russia. In February they
made a fifteen-day trip to the Soviet Union, but not as guests of the government. On February 2 he and Emily flew fifteen hundred miles from Moscow
to Baku. At Baku University, Lodge got a long briefing from the University
president and department heads, during which he asked many questions
on Soviet education and got eager answers. He stepped into a corridor
packed with waiting students who applauded him warmly and shouted
friendly greetings. On his way downstairs he stopped to shake hands with
them, saying: "My name is Lodge. I am an American visiting the Soviet
Union." Many voices called out eagerly, "We know all about you!" There
was more handclapping. He asked many questions. Was it difficult, he
asked one. "I am studying to be an engineer," the student replied. "It is
very difficult but we like studies here." He was grinning. "With that grin,"
said Lodge, "I can see you like it. You'll get along." To another group he
said, "Learning is power and it's the kind of power we all want in a peaceful world." When he got into his car, some student shouted, "We hope you
visit all our universities. Once we had very few of them, now there are
many, and we hope you stay in the Soviet Union a long time." In formal
offices, in kindergarten playrooms, in old mosques, they got the same
friendly welcome. As they halted in a playroom a five-year-old sang out, in
English: "Tell your children in America to come over here and we will all

play together in a friendly way." A nurse explained: "He thought that all up   *311*
by himself."

The next day they flew a similar distance to Tashkent where it was so
mild Lodge shed his coat. They toured collective farms, visited some more
schools. They flew on to Samarkand where they visited the ruin of the great
fifth century Registan—once a Moslem religious school—also called Tamerlane Cathedral after the great Mongol conqueror who ruled a vast empire
from the city more than five hundred years before.

They visited the blue-domed Bibi-Khanum Mosque, a 3½-acre wonder
built by Tamerlane in 1399-1404 in memory of his favorite wife (he had
eight). They were entertained by high officials of the Uzbek government.
They flew back to Moscow, where Khrushchev had several lengthy sessions
with Lodge. He carried on quite ecstatically about his U.S. trip. When
Lodge expressed regret over the Los Angeles fiascos, Khrushchev waved it
away airily. "It was nothing. These things happen." They had some further
talks about Berlin and disarmament. "There's absolutely no room for maneuvering on the Berlin issue," Lodge reported afterward. "Khrushchev is a
very tough bargainer, a shrewd bluffer and trader."

One night the Lodges went to the ballet to see Tschaikovsky's *Swan Lake*.
During the intermission, Khrushchev invited them to join him in a huge
room behind his box at the Bolshoi. He sat at the middle of a long table, put
Mrs. Lodge next to him, Lodge and Nina directly across. Caviar, champagne
and Ukrainian wines were served. The Lodges went on to Leningrad, visited
the Smolny Institute where Lenin ran his revolution.

"This is the same as your Independence Hall in Philadelphia," said the
guide. "Oh, no, it isn't," said Lodge politely but firmly.

Lodge came back to warn Eisenhower that Khrushchev was adopting "a
new tone about the summit," for which he had seemed so eager during his
visit. One reason, which only became clear later, was that the Chinese
Communists had already begun to accuse Khrushchev of "selling out" revolution for accommodation with the capitalists. Lodge himself was convinced
that the thing troubling Khrushchev was the incredible, surging, almost
hysterical welcome that Eisenhower had received a few months before on
his visit to New Delhi—a sea of millions that terrified the Secret Service trying to protect him. It was all the more marked in contrast to the cool reception Khrushchev had received there. Lodge believed that Khrushchev was
fearful that Eisenhower would receive a similar ecstatic welcome from the
ordinary people of Russia—and was seeking a pretext to cancel the invitation (a plane called the U-2 would soon give him one).

Lodge had been awarded the American Ordnance Association's Gold
Medal, named for Major General C. C. Williams, for his "outstanding service to the national defense," and was cited, among other things, for his early

312 articles on "the mechanization of modern armies." In the association's magazine, *Ordnance,* in March, Lodge wrote:

"Some Americans have been irked and annoyed because Chairman Khrushchev repeated so often that the Soviet Union was in competition with the U.S. and would win that competition. . . . I would like to broaden the competition to such things as free speech and the right to throw an administration out of office by free elections. I am afraid I can't tell you what he said to that. But that would be a contest, I think, in which everybody would gain.

"Nor do we need to take fright when the Communists say that in this competition their system will triumph over ours. There is not going to be any triumph of that kind. Humanity has no desire for a competition in which one side can reach its goal only by driving the other side to the wall. We have a different kind of competition—one in which all nations strive to develop the best in them without hurting each other. In that contest there is room not just for two systems but for as many systems as there are nations. . . .

"A country which thrives on competition the way we do in business, in politics, in sports, should not shrink from the idea of competition. A nation which sees what tens of thousands of plans of independent producers can create in the way of new wealth and new ideas need never worry about competition from a state which is run by the ideas of a few bureaucrats in a central bureaucracy. . . .

"A good ideal like freedom sitting passively in a fortress will certainly be defeated by a bad ideal which is on the march. But if bad and good command equal devotion and equal intelligence, Mr. Khrushchev's grandchildren will spend most of their lives in the Soviet homeland where the great central bureaucracy has diminished and where a much greater degree of individual freedom obtains and in a world in which the community of free nations will be flourishing and growing."

On March 16 Lodge traveled to West Point for an honor which was one of the proudest moments of his long career. The Academy's Association of Graduates had created, in 1958, the Sylvanus Thayer Award—named after the Academy's fifth superintendent (1817-33) who instituted the principles of academic and military training, based upon integration of character and knowledge, which are still followed. It is a gold medal, weighing about a pound, presented each year to an American for "outstanding service to the nation." The first award had gone to Dr. Ernest O. Lawrence, Nobel Prize physicist, the second to John Foster Dulles. The third was presented to Lodge on the 158th anniversary of West Point's founding.

At noon, he stood in a reviewing stand, hat over heart, while the Academy band played the national anthem and the whole "thin gray line" of the

Cadet Corps marched across the parade ground in salute to him. Afterward
he joined them at lunch in Washington Hall, the Cadet dining hall, where
his name would be inscribed on a memorial plaque. General McAuliffe, hero
of Bastogne and alumni president, read Lodge's citation:

> *A dedicated American who has devoted his life to the many facets of
> our government with constant emphasis on national security.*
>
> *He is unique in the breadth of his experience in the legislative, ex-
> ecutive, diplomatic and military branches.*
>
> *As a member of the President's Cabinet for seven years, he takes
> part in shaping the course of the nation. In his post as Permanent Rep-
> resentative of the United States to the United Nations, he enunciates
> with unceasing vigor the eternal truths and beliefs cherished by all our
> people.*
>
> *In his quick and effective defense of freedom, his stalwart voice is
> heard round the world.*
>
> *A Major General in the Army Reserve, he has had distinguished
> military service with combat units of the Army at home and abroad,
> in peace and in war.*
>
> *His contribution to our nation exemplifies his outstanding devotion
> to "Duty, Honor, Country." Accordingly, the 1960 Sylvanus Thayer
> Medal is hereby awarded by the Association of Graduates of the United
> States Military Academy to Henry Cabot Lodge.*

General McAuliffe also read a message of praise for Ambassador Lodge
from President Eisenhower, who himself would receive the medal the year
following. Lodge's eyes were understandably misty and his voice slightly
tremulous as he responded:

> *Whoever is mindful of the many times when West Pointers have saved
> our nation must feel a sense of awe to receive an award in this place
> and from the West Point graduates themselves.*
>
> *That this honor should be accompanied by a message from the
> President—himself a graduate of West Point—makes it particularly
> precious.*
>
> *This award bears the words "duty, honor, country." These are sum-
> moning words to me. Although fully conscious of my many inade-
> quacies, I have tried to live by these words.*
>
> *These are stirring words at any time. In particular they are the
> words by which our country should live today.*
>
> *I say this because we are in a contest with a small group who, hav-
> ing mastered the art of revolution, have acquired control of great re-
> sources.*

*They wish to be our adversaries in the name of a cult which teaches
as an unquestioned absolute that what they call "the science of history" prescribes that Communism must take over the world.*

*To meet this threat and deal with it we must first be able to neu-
tralize and nullify its military aspect. This is the first challenge. So
long as we have West Point and its counterparts I do not doubt our
ability to do this.*

*But Communist conquest of the world through its mastery of the art
of revolution and its ability to appeal to the minds of men must also
be prevented.*

*So it is that we will only prevail in the end on a spiritual basis—by
living up to our own great ideals: to those words in the Declaration of
Independence which tell us that all men are created equal and that all
men are entitled to life, liberty and the pursuit of happiness; to the
precept of brotherly love brought to us in the Christian religion.*

*To give life to these words we need: the unselfishness to do our duty
to humanity; the elevation and nobility of spirit to stand up for honor;
and thus to work for our country, since our country is what Lincoln
called "the last, best hope of earth."*

*In this spirit, humbly, and conscious of how undeserved it is—as
one of uncounted millions to whom West Point's ideals are a help and
a strength—I accept this award.*

Lodge returned to the U.N. to find the new nations of Afro-Asia in angry
turmoil over the bloody massacre of thirty-four blacks at Sharpesville, in
South Africa, by police who had simply shot them down in cold blood.
Lodge was president of the Security Council that month. The Afro-Asians,
nearly a third of the U.N.'s membership, demanded the Council place on its
agenda a charge that South Africa was responsible for "large-scale killings"
of unarmed demonstrators. Once more, the U.S. and the Soviet Union were
in accord, both urging its inclusion. Lodge dispensed with a vote and—by
a previous understanding—held that the decision to include it had been
taken in the absence of any objection. However, Britain, France and Italy
later took the floor to say they had reservations about the U.N.'s jurisdiction
in the matter. South Africa took the same position, and left the table while
the debate proceeded—with India, Ethiopia, Ghana, Pakistan, Guinea and
Liberia all joining Mongi Slim of Tunisia and Sir Claude Corea of Ceylon,
who were members of the Security Council. Mr. Slim likened South Africa's
treatment of natives to Hitler's treatment of the Jews.

"Let me say," Lodge told the Council ". . . the U.S. approaches this question with no false pride at all. We recognize that many countries, and the

U.S. must be included in that list, cannot be content with the progress which they have made in the field of human rights. . . . But we think there is an important distinction between situations where governments are actively promoting human rights and fundamental freedoms for all without distinction as to race, sex, language or religion, and situations where governmental policy runs counter to this."

Under Lodge's leadership the Council passed a unanimous resolution condemning South Africa's *apartheid* laws, asked it to change them, and requested Secretary General Hammarskjold to use his good offices to get them to do so. It was an act of rebuke and moral suasion rather than the economic sanctions the Afro-Asians sought. "It seeks to build a bridge," said Lodge, "and not a wall."

No sooner was the South African debate over than a new bombshell burst upon the U.N.

In May, on the very eve of the summit conference scheduled for Paris in June, the shooting down of a U-2 reconnaissance plane near Sverdlovsk, in the Soviet Union, and the capture of Pilot Gary Powers, a civilian employee of the C.I.A., provided Khrushchev the pretext he sought to withdraw the invitation to Eisenhower. For two years the Soviets had known of these high-altitude (70,000 feet) flights by the light, swift (500 m.p.h.) plane "kicked" by a single jet in its tail. Time and again our listening devices in Turkey and elsewhere had overheard the frustration of Soviet fighter pilots as they scrambled up trying to reach it, then running out of enough air to lift their wings. The flights, a precaution against surprise attack from intercontinental missiles based deep in the Siberian forests, were made necessary by persistent Soviet refusal to allow mutual inspection or "open skies." The whole elusive question of how "high" national sovereignty legally extends was involved; soon afterward, when camera satellites orbited the earth from heights of two hundred miles or more, no charge of trespass of sovereignty was made.

Nevertheless, Eisenhower handled the whole issue with incredible fecklessness. He allowed so many conflicting stories to be issued that the dignity and honor of the U.S. government was put in question, since some of these stories—e.g., a "weather plane" which strayed off course—were obviously false. So long as underlings did this, Khrushchev's own position was still tolerable, since governments traditionally disown their lost spies. But then Eisenhower admitted that he himself had ordered the spy flights and took full responsibility for them. This admission put Khrushchev in an impossible situation. He arrived in Paris to hold an angry press conference, saying he would meet with Eisenhower only if the latter made a full apology and promised that no future flights would be made. Eisenhower, now also in

Paris for the summit, did announce the termination of such flights but did not apologize. The summit conference, possibly as Khrushchev wished, blew up.

On May 24 Foreign Minister Gromyko, heading the Soviet's U.N. delegation, tore into the U-2 episode as evidence of American duplicity and betrayal. He demanded the Council censure such flights as a threat to peace. While extending friendship with one hand, he said, it was ferreting out Russia's military secrets with the other, as a prelude to aggression. Lodge was in an unenviable spot. His government's handling of the whole case had been bungling and amateurish in the extreme.

Lodge was badly in need of some dramatic way of regaining the psychological offensive against the Soviets. Years before, while Averell Harriman was still U.S. Ambassador in Moscow, some Soviet schoolchildren had presented him a large, carved eagle, a replica of the Great Seal of the United States, to hang in his Embassy. It had hung there for years until one day, a hunt for concealed listening devices had put the eagle under suspicion. Close examination revealed that the eagle was glued together in two halves, and when pulled apart, a hollow space behind the back contained a tiny electronic broadcasting device which would enable distant eavesdroppers to overhear all the Ambassador's conversations.

Lodge sent his security adviser, Richard Petersen, down to Washington to bring the carefully wrapped eagle back on a plane. At the next session the large, bulky object was carefully brought in and kept behind Lodge's chair. He was watching for the best psychological moment to present it. It was carried in and out of the chamber several times before Gromyko, in another slashing attack, presented the perfect opening Lodge was waiting for.

Earlier in the debate, Lodge recited a long list of Soviet spies who had been caught in the U.S., saying the U-2's intrusion of air space was no more aggressive than "the repeated violations of our American *ground* space . . . by Soviet spies." He gave chapter and verse on their offenses, such as that of Vadim A. Kirilyuk: "This agent Kirilyuk was actually caught in an act of espionage seeking data on cryptographic machines during the visit of Chairman Khrushchev when he was speaking from the rostrum of the General Assembly about disarmament."

On Thursday, May 26, Gromyko branded all these charges as "fabrications. . . . It belongs rather in the pages of a cheap detective novel than in the Security Council."

"Well, it so happens, "said Lodge, when he got the floor, "that I have here today a concrete example of Soviet espionage so that you can see for yourself." He held up the two pieces of the Great Seal, and showed how it was hollowed out inside.

"I would like to just show it to the Council. It is quite a beautiful piece of

carving. And you will note how it opens up into two pieces. Here is the
clandestine listening device. You see the antenna and the aerial and it was
right under the beak of the eagle. . . . It is really quite an interesting
device.

"I might add that in recent years the U.S. has found within its embassies,
missions and residences in the Soviet Union and the satellite countries well
over a hundred technical clandestine listening devices. . . . Our latest dis-
coveries . . . have been within the past month."

MR. GROMYKO: . . . I should like to ask the representative of the U.S.
to tell us from what play all this has been taken and when the play is going
to be performed.

MR. LODGE: . . . It is not out of any play. It is out of the Soviet Union.

The day happened to be Thursday when the members of the Security
Council met once each month for lunch. Lodge always attended these
lunches religiously. President Eisenhower thought it important to maintain
this regular contact with the Soviets, however little it might mean. At this
informal and relaxed lunch Lodge was sitting next to Arkady Sobolev. During a pause in the conversation, Sobolev, with a big grin, said:

"The next time we put one of those eagles in the American Ambassador's
office, we are going to put the microphone under the eagle's tail."

Lodge joined in the laughter.

The episode ended with adoption of a four-power resolution urging the
U.S. and the Soviet's to make new efforts to resume their discussions on
settlement of issues between them.

In June, Lodge, so recently honored by West Point, was invited to Annapolis
to address the 1960 graduates. "Yours is not a mothball Navy which sleeps
until war breaks out," he told them. "In the Mediterreanean and the Formosa Straits your ships and aircraft have accepted the risk of violence to
give sanctity to the treaties and pledges of the U.S. Your readiness is one
of the profoundest reassurances of peace that free nations can hope for in
this turbulent world. . . . It is not missiles which will ultimately save us,
but men. And it is not at moments of celebration such as this that men
prove their qualities, but in the hour of confusion and alarm. . . . The
American people look to you, the officers of the Navy and of all our military services, for the hard, steely resolve which can stand up amid disaster
and take command to save our nation. Thus, being ready for the worst, we
can pursue with confidence the path which leads toward the best."

In July, as the Democratic Convention was meeting in Los Angeles, the
Security Council became the focus of a new world crisis—the Congo. On

June 30, the day the Republic of the Congo became an independent nation, chaos and anarchy broke out which deepened into weeks of rape, anarchy and tribal murder, mutiny of the Congolese *Force Publique,* and intervention by Belgian paratroopers. The Soviet Union was making threats of intervening on its own if Belgium did not evacuate. Moise Tshombe's Province of Katanga was in revolt against Congo Premier Patrice Lumumba. Lumumba himself appeared before the Security Council to ask the protection of a U.N. Expeditionary Force. The situation held all the explosive possibilities of another Korea. Lodge took the leadership in getting swift action on establishing an expeditionary force. By coincidence, Lodge's face and voice were dominating the nation's TV screens whenever the broadcasting networks switched away from the routine oratory and delegate polling of the Democratic convention. By contrast with the convention's gassy meanderings and tiresome rigamarole, Lodge's arguments for troops and his sharp retorts to Soviet rumblings about a "colonialist conspiracy" seemed the real world.

"Speed is essential," cried Lodge in that night session of July 13. "The longer the present state of near-anarchy continues, the heavier the toll of lives, the greater the prospect of hunger and epidemic, and the greater the difficulties in future economic development. We confront a situation which is developing hourly—not daily, or weekly, but hourly. . . . It is not only futile but positively harmful to seek to apportion blame at this time for what has happened. What is required is an instantaneous response to the urgent request of the Congo government rather than ill-advised or malicious attempts to make political capital of the serious difficulties of the Congolese people."

Russia was threatening a veto if the resolution did not contain some censure of Belgium. France, Britain and Belgium were likely to oppose if the motion implied such censure. These three powers were seeking a twenty-four hour delay. Lodge refused: "My position," he told them, "is that we get action tonight if we sit through the dawn." He also insisted that the African members present the resolution. "The important thing is that Africans deal with Africans—there must be regional responsibility." His strategy succeeded. The Soviets did not dare veto an African resolution. At 4 A.M. the Security Council authorized the Secretary General to send out a U.N. force; at 5 A.M. the order went out for the first ten U.N. officers to enter Leopoldville. Soon a tremendous American airlift was created to fly Irish and other troops to the Congo as units of the U.N. force.

A fortnight later, when the Republicans were meeting in Chicago, Lodge was still dominating the TV screens. Cuba's complaint that the U.S. planned aggression, and a Soviet threat of rocket retaliation, had brought this response from Lodge on July 19: "Neither we nor the members of the Organization of American States are frightened by these threats, nor will we be deterred from our treaty obligations to prevent establishment of a regime dominated by international Communism. All we say very simply is this: Don't touch us; don't touch those with whom we are tied; don't seek to extend Communist imperialism. That's very simple and ought to be understood by everybody."

As the Convention itself was meeting, Lodge was on the nation's TV screens holding up photos of Soviet airplanes and ships making reconnaissance sorties off Alaska and the Atlantic coast, in the course of demanding an impartial investigation of Russia's shooting down a U.S. electronic reconnaissance plane, the RB-47, when it was more than fifty miles from Soviet territory and turning away. Lodge asserted that our electronic tracking devices could prove that a Soviet fighter had tried to force the plane off its course into Soviet territory, and, failing, attacked it. He forced the Soviets, who had claimed violations of their territory by the plane, into vetoing an investigation to get at the truth.

All these crises kept Lodge busy right up through the Republican Convention's foregone nomination of Vice President Nixon, and to the eve of the choice of his running-mate. Some three months before, Lodge had lunched with Nixon in the Vice President's office, and Nixon asked if he would accept the nomination for Vice President. His thoughts undoubtedly called up that moment in a plane, back in 1952, when Lodge and Herbert Brownell, running through the four or five likeliest running-mates for Eisenhower, had chosen Nixon as the one who would best add geographical balance, relative youth, and a brass-knuckled toughness to augment Eisenhower's blandness. Ironically, Lodge himself had turned down, at the time, the post which Nixon was now offering. "I'm not seeking it," he told Nixon. "I won't campaign for it. But if you need me, I'll take it. Don't commit yourself until you see whom the Democrats nominate." In the months since, Eisenhower had told many callers he favored Lodge.

At midnight Wednesday, July 27, nominee Nixon gathered some thirty-five other top party leaders into the Sheraton Room of the Blackstone Hotel in Chicago. Among them were four Cabinet members, three former national chairmen, a former Presidential candidate (Dewey), four state chairmen, five senators, three governors and five congressmen. The first-floor room was just three floors below the famous "smoke-filled room" in which the elder Lodge helped pick Warren Harding in 1920. On a small portable bar at the rear stood bottles of Scotch and Bourbon with plenty of glasses, ice, club soda and ginger ale.

Nixon pulled a chair up to the table and said he had four men under consideration for the Vice Presidential nomination: Lodge; Senator Thrus-

320   ton Morton of Kentucky, who was also National Chairman; Treasury Secretary Robert Anderson, a former Democrat; and Representative Walter Judd of Minnesota, a onetime missionary in China.

"I brought you here honestly," Nixon said. "I've talked to the President and either personally or by telephone with each of the four. But I have not made my choice and I will make it on the basis of the opinion expressed by you, my friends, who represent every section and every viewpoint in the Republican Party. . . . I'm entirely free to make a decision here tonight."

With that, Nixon started around the long table to sound out each participant. At first Lodge and Morton ran about evenly. The Cabinet members —Commerce's Fred Mueller, Labor's James Mitchell, Postmaster General Arthur Summerfield and Interior's Fred Seaton—lined up for Lodge, though with a tone of reluctance that they hadn't been asked to stay away as possible candidates themselves. Midwesterners, led by Illinois Governor William C. Stratton, argued for Morton.

As one after another spoke up, it was clear that a growing majority favored Lodge as the only real possibility—he was well-known, well-identified in the public mind because of his frequent televised appearances, he was famous for standing up to the Russians, and his whole record was a tremendous plus in a campaign where foreign affairs seemed likely to be the crucial issue. The chief argument for Morton was that he was Senator Barry Goldwater's choice and would help bind up wounds left with the Goldwater right-wing faction in their defeat on platform issues. Moreover, Morton himself had told Nixon that he felt Lodge could help most in the big urban states—New York, New Jersey, Pennsylvania—where Nixon most needed help.

Earlier that evening Nixon had seen Walter Judd, in Nixon's bedroom, and asked him who in his judgment, would aid the ticket most. Judd unequivocally endorsed Lodge. Judd pointed out that Lodge could woo votes from the internationalists, which the other three could not. He topped off his endorsement by offering to nominate Lodge. Nixon told Judd he had been swamped with phone calls supporting Judd himself—Clare Luce's among them—but Judd again urged Lodge: "He's very good in debate. I've watched him in action and he's a match for anyone."

It was after two in the morning when Tom Dewey summed up the "sense of the meeting" at the Blackstone: "It all simmers down to this: If we want to send the delegates home happy, we ought to agree on Morton. And, let it be said, he would be a good Vice President and one whale of a campaigner. But if we want to make the *people* happy, it should be Lodge. He would make a superb Vice President, and he would put the emphasis on foreign policy, where it should be." At 2:25 A.M. they agreed on Lodge and broke up.

Next morning, Lodge was reading the morning paper in his Waldorf suite and Emily was getting their breakfast when a call came through from Nixon. "Everybody in the group wants you," said Nixon. "Thank you very much," said Lodge. "I'm very touched and I'll do the best I can." When Emily came out of the kitchen and he told her of the call, she dropped the coffee pot, not in surprise at the news but because she hadn't heard the phone.

Lodge called in James Barco, his chief of staff at the U.N., to give him instructions for assignments in his absence. Later they lunched on some scrod and potatoes boiled by Emily. After lunch he set out with Emily for Idlewild, in a summer blue suit, handsome and buoyant. Emily was cool and immaculate in a lilac linen dress and blue linen coat.

Aboard the DC-8 jet to Chicago, Emily settled back with a new mystery, *Murder by Request,* Lodge with the *National Geographic.* Over a Scotch and soda he told *Time*'s Serrell Hillman—who would shortly join him as an aide—"Tom Dewey made a great mistake the other night attacking Kennedy's youth. Everybody who's that age gets sore at you."

At O'Hare Airport, they were plunged into a seething mass of several hundred placard-waving Republicans. For fifty minutes they rode in a long cavalcade to the Stock Yard Inn, so redolent of memories of Lodge's fight for Eisenhower eight years before. There they were ensconced in a three-room suite for the Ohio caucus, Robert A. Taft, Jr. seconded Lodge as a gesture of unity. As soon as Alabama had cast its votes for Lodge, they left for the International Amphitheater. They were popped into a blue-curtained-off recess until the nomination became official. Then, as the band played "Yankee Doodle Dandy," Lodge emerged, waving, and led Emily up to the platform to the winking of strobe lights. Pat and Dick Nixon joined them for the official photograph behind the respective Presidential and Vice Presidential seals. Then Lodge, in his deep-timbred, impressive voice, read the eight-page, triple-spaced acceptance speech—terse, pithy, tightly organized—which he had written himself. It was pitched, as he would pitch his whole campaign, on the overriding importance of foreign affairs and the threat of Communist imperialism:

> . . . *We could lose our country . . . all at once, by all-out nuclear war, or gradually by being isolated and nibbled to death.*
>
> *Of course, we are not going to lose our country. We are going to keep our country. More than that, we are going to advance, using the strengths and the talents which God gave us to build a world in which freedom will be secure; a world in which the rights of small nations will be respected; a world of open societies which practice tolerance and are truly devoted to the dignity of man. . . . Ultimately we will*

322   *win the world struggle on a spiritual basis—or victory will elude us.
. . . We have the most glorious purposes of any nation in history.
Purposes which, as Lincoln said, give "hope for the world for all future
time."*

The morning after his nomination, Lodge made a joint appearance with
Nixon at a meeting of the National Committee, and later at a press conference at the Hilton. Nixon looked extremely tired. "His jowls were flabby, his
skin gray, his eyes weary slits," a *Time* reporter noted. "Lodge deferred carefully to Nixon. He towers above him, makes Nixon look slight, hunched
and physically unimpressive. At one point, Nixon appeared to be trying to
stand on tiptoe to cut down the difference in height. Nixon embarrassed
Lodge at the National Committee meeting with an awkward crack that 'I
never thought I would have the honor of running with a Lodge for the
Presidency of the U.S.' Lodge visibly winced."

Bessie, Lodge's mother, was not destined to live to see the highest honor
yet to come to him. Long suffering from a damaged heart, she had died
quietly on July 2 in her apartment at the Sheraton Park in Washington.
Almost every week, during his eight years at the U.N., Lodge had managed
to visit her after attending the Cabinet meetings. She had usually joined his
family on the North Shore, staying with him at Beverly or at her own place
in nearby Manchester. Her passing left his acceptance deeply tinged with
sadness.*

After a week's vacation at Beverly, Lodge returned to the U.N. to serve
until the end of August. The Congo crisis dogged him to the very end. On
August 22, he was speaking at the Security Council at one in the morning
attacking a Soviet threat to send "volunteers" to the Congo, where Belgian
forces were still occupying Tshombe's rebellious and copper-rich Katanga
Province.

Dag Hammarskjold returned from the Congo to seek a new resolution,
pressing the Belgians to withdraw immediately, and pledging U.N. forces
to replace them in Katanga. At 4 A.M., a weary Lodge saw this resolution
carried. That struggle would go on until it would cost Hammarskjold's own

* In Washington, Bessie had always attended Washington Cathedral, whose rector,
Dean Sayre, was Woodrow Wilson's son-in-law. They were good friends. He was not
related to Wilson, any more than she to the elder Lodge, and felt none of the bitterness
those two had felt. On a previous Easter, while kneeling in the church, Bessie had
slipped and fallen, hurting her hip (it later proved to be broken). Dean Sayre anxiously
took her arm, helped her across the street to a stationery store where she could call a
taxi. As she waited she noticed a black Rolls Royce at the curb and suddenly realized
its occupant was Mrs. Woodrow Wilson, waiting for Dean Sayre. Despite her pain,
Bessie limped back to the car. "Good morning, Mrs. Wilson," she smiled. Edith Wilson,
hating all Lodges to the bitter end, simply turned her stonily frowning face away.

life, but on the night of August 31 Lodge gave his farewell reception to
fifteen hundred, guests—at the Waldorf residence and on September 2 said
his last good-bys at the U.N. On Saturday morning, September 3 he and
Emily met New York's Governor Nelson Rockefeller and took off in the
governor's plane to begin his campaign.

At Liberty Airport, in the heart of the Catskill borscht circuit, Cabot and
Emily stepped out of Rocky's plane into an area crowded with some 500,000
Labor Day weekend guests. At Grossinger's, they munched lox and kosher
egg rolls, shook hands with some 400 guests, moved on to Monticello and
to the plush fifty-dollar-a-day Concord resort hotel where Lodge made his
unflinching way through a lobby thronged with lively young things in
bathing suits and arrived at the huge second-floor dining room in the middle
of the soup course. He gave one of his briefest speeches and invaded the
kitchen, to add extra helpings of confusion to cooks and waiters caught up
in feeding some 2600 guests; nothing daunted, he shook every empty hand
he could find. He spoke from a street corner in South Fallsburg, then at the
Flagler resort hotel. At the Nevele, appearing on a sundeck above the
swimming pool, all were handed T-shirts which Cabot and Rocky good-
naturedly held up against their chests. Emily proved her true instincts as a
campaigner by slipping hers on. Back to New York, he spent Sunday working on a speech for Tuesday, then hit the campaign trail Monday morning
at a Hotel Roosevelt breakfast with 150 New York Jewish leaders where he
was introduced by Attorney General Louis Lefkowitz. That afternoon he
was pushed, mauled, shoved and jammed along the boardwalks of three
New York beaches in succession—Jones, Rockaway and Coney Island. At
Coney Island, he seemed to catch fire. He responded to the pawing hands
and clutching fingers in a relaxed, spontaneous way. He worked his way
through the crowd, dripping wet from his own and others' sweat, to
Nathan's celebrated hot-dog stand, gnawing a hot dog with gusto ("I really
like hot dogs, anyway"). On the way up a ramp to the boardwalk he stopped
and spent some ten minutes signing bits of paper offered by outstretched
arms below. He refused only to autograph a Kennedy sign (later, he would
refuse to sign a dollar bill, and a blank check). He was off with a bang.

Lodge then began a flying campaign tour that would take him from
coast-to-coast and as far south as Florida. Tom Wicker of the New York
Times, who accompanied him over much of it, and also accompanied
Lyndon Johnson's, wrote an appraisal which conveys its flavor. He quotes
Lodge's typical speech: "I come to you tonight after eight years at the U.N.
where I spoke for all the nation—north and south, east and west, regardless of party."

"Mr. Lodge," wrote Wicker, "so often begins his speeches on this note for
the simple reason the invariable response is long and prolonged applause,

324   sometimes even a standing ovation. Mr. Lodge brings a ready-made personality—a fully-created image—to the voters. Through the medium of TV which has brought into the pine-paneled game rooms his frequent rhetorical jousts with the Soviet representatives to the U.N., the handsome Bostonian has become something like the all-American boy defending American virtue and castigating Communist evil. It is a popular and profitable image and the former Ambassador is working assiduously and shrewdly to parlay it into votes. . . . So far from being identified as is Mr. Lodge with this sort of nonpartisan and instinctive patriotism, Sen. Johnson's image is entirely political and entirely Democratic, and where his work in the Senate is understood he has a reputation for cloakroom maneuvering—an activity which can be made to seem just short of subversive on some main streets. Lodge is reserved but surprisingly affable in a crowd, his steady smile offers something of the warmth of the famous Eisenhower grin. Mr. Lodge also seems to possess another Eisenhower-style asset: a considerable appeal to women. The teen-agers who shout 'We want Cabot to be vice-president' . . . seemed as charmed as the older women who flock around him. He shared the platform in Los Angeles with movie star Ronald Reagan and a breathless blond was heard to murmur, 'Aren't they divine?' Mr. Lodge seems to fire up an audience by his mere appearance, something Sen. Johnson cannot do. . . . When Mr. Lodge was greeted at a Skokie, Ill., shopping center by a roaring crowd estimated at 25,000 people and when he drew 14,000 whooping fans into Kansas City's cavernous municipal auditorium he responded with precisely the same speech—not a word more or less and with the same degree of vigor and effectiveness—he had been making everywhere he goes, sometimes to crowds numbering in the low hundreds. . . . He is going over big, and he is doing it with what amounts to a simple patriotic appeal couched in generalities and aimed with a motivation researcher's skill at the sensitive pulse of American pride. . . . He talks calmly, seriously, even grimly and tells no jokes but the flashing smile is always there when needed . . . 'That great soldier Dwight D. Eisenhower . . .' When the roars die down he talks about his eight years experience across the table from the Russians and asserts that what makes the world so dangerous is that the Soviet Union wants to take it over. 'Now my friends,' he continues with resolution echoing in his Harvard accent, 'no one is going to take over the U.S. and no one is going to take over the world.' This may be the most effective campaign line since F.D.R.'s Martin, Barton and Fish. In Kansas City it brought 14,000 people to their feet for a one-minute ovation. The Los Angeles Press Club broke into applause. Reporters who have heard that speech so often they mutter its phrases in their restless sleep have never seen it fail to produce tears. 'It touches something

fundamental in people,' Mr. Lodge told a reporter who wondered at the line's effectiveness. 'It is a reassuring line, a defiant line, in its way a bold line.' The speaker proceeds to demand civil rights action . . . keys almost everything to his U.N. renown. When a photographer dropped a flash bulb at a Chicago dinner, the candidate said of the explosion: 'Reminds me of the U.N.' to appreciative laughter." Wicker also found that Lodge had "stumbled badly. He supported Federal aid for parochial schools, in Harlem he pledged that a Negro would be appointed to the Nixon-Lodge Cabinet. When no support came from Nixon for either position, he was forced to back away from both."

The idea of a Negro in the Cabinet seemed like a blooper only because Nixon was concentrating on trying to win the Solid South away from Kennedy. Nixon, in concentrating on the South, neglected the Big Six states which could have brought him victory. Had he gone after the votes in the big Northern cities, as Lodge kept urging, the ticket might well have carried Chicago and Philadelphia—both with large Negro votes—and with them the election.

Lodge believed, and continued to believe, in the great merit of appointing a Negro to the Cabinet. (Six years later, a Southern-born President actually would do so). Lodge regretted what he concedes was an error; items caused by turmoil, confusion and fatigue in his inexperienced staff (an error for which he takes full responsibility), which resulted in a text being released which had not been cleared with Nixon.

On federal aid to parochial schools, Lodge had voted for this as a senator, and his position had to be that he had done so and his position had not changed.

Only after the campaign began did it become apparent that Lodge was more popular with the American electorate than any other candidate run by either party. A Gallup Poll showed Lodge was more popular than either Kennedy or Nixon, and far more so than Lyndon Johnson. Paul Hoffman informed the campaigners that Lodge's presence on the ticket had added at least 6 per cent to the ticket's potential vote. General Jacob Devers, who introduced his wartime aide, Colonel Lodge, to a Pennsylvania Dutch audience in York, Pennsylvania, his own hometown, reported that President Kennedy told him later that Lodge turned a normal 16,000-vote Democratic plurality in York into a Republican victory there. As awareness of his phenomenal popularity dawned on the party pros about the country, they made so many demands for him to appear that Lodge could not possibly have met them all. He stuck to his original determination "to stay in character" and not to tire himself to the point of becoming groggy and ineffective. He insisted on getting an hour's rest every day, and as a result was the only candidate who never lost a day of campaigning from illness. Yet some of the pros would later accuse him of "laying down" on the job, and giving a lackadaisacal performance.

Lodge was at his best in the quick give-and-take of TV interviews. On a "Meet the Press" program, NBC's Pauline Frederick asked why the U.S. was restricting the movements of Premier Khrushchev, who was planning to attend the new U.N. meeting. Lodge pointed out that Khrushchev had broken up the summit meeting and insulted President Eisenhower. "Why treat him like a bosom friend when he has made it clear he doesn't want to be treated like one? This is typical of Communist tactics. When they have done something wrong, they immediately accuse *you* of doing something wrong. It is the old Tammany motto—the old Tammany boss who said, 'Claim everything, concede nothing, and when defeated allege fraud.'"

MISS FREDERICK: If by some miraculous chance he was coming here with a serious motive . . . how do you think this might be affected . . . by realizing that he is going to be brought into a pier at the East River where no other ship has docked for a long time, that he is going to be restricted . . .

MR. LODGE: He'd think that is good, tough action of the kind he understands well and has meted out to many others and which he knows inspires respect in many people. He will not take it sentimentally, I assure you.

NBC's Huntley-Brinkley team had an interview with Emily in her Beverly home, and she proved quite an adept performer on her own. "It's been alleged," said Chet Huntley, "that there is one dictate that you have enforced in this home . . . politics only at breakfast and nothing after that. Is that true?" "That's right," said Emily, "But I'm the one that does the talking at breakfast and Cabot hides behind the newspaper and pretends to listen, but doesn't."

Huntley, speaking of their many travels, asked if any continent or country was her favorite.

"I loved them all," said Emily. "We went about four years ago to the Sudan when it got its independence and I'll never forget coming in over the desert. You see the Blue Nile join the White Nile right there in Khartoum, with its thin bank of green going along the river. And then you see these very small little white birds like doves flying right over the Blue Nile. It was perfectly beautiful. And the pilot as we were landing said the temperature was 104. And I thought of course I'd be slightly warm when we landed, but not at all because the humidity is 4%. . . . Oh, I'd love to go back there. And then we went to Libya and then just last year we went to the Cameroons on New Year's Eve. . . ." Speaking of their Russian trip, she added: "I'll never forget Samarkand, the place where Tamerlane lived and where his tomb is. And you can see the road and the mountain where they came and conquered much of the surrounding territory; the pass is exactly the way it was. And you get a sense of the past that I can't describe in that part of the world."

Wherever they went, Emily proved to be Cabot's greatest asset.

"Mrs. Lodge is a woman of gentle manners," wrote Neil McNeil of *Time* during the campaign journey. "Her face is open and candid, and her behavior on the stump, on the reception line, and in private is one of almost girlish enthusiasm, kept from mere silliness by her grace, her inherent sense of dignity, her quite obvious intellectual sensitivity. This woman has been a politician's wife for a third of a century and her mind and her manners are untouched and unaffected by even the suggestion of cynicism—a remarkable achievement.

"Emily Lodge has the graciousness to accept a dozen roses from a welcoming committees in a dozen different towns, as she has done this week (mid-September), and act as though these roses were the first anyone had ever thought to give her. Her pride in and affection for her husband are transparent and unadorned, charming in simplicity.

"She loves to tear Cabot's arguments to shreds, force him to strengthen them. [Like the old senator with Nanny, Cabot tried all his speeches on Emily, changed them to meet her criticisms.] She gets him up in time, sees that Cabot is properly fed, getting to him a glass of milk and a sandwich when he runs short of food. She sees that he gets some rest, making him take naps when he has a half-hour break during the day. She takes care of his clothes—Lodge has used only two silk suits so far, but she washes his socks, and darns those with holes (one heel came open at a recent meeting). Emily is an economical woman, who worries about wasting food they've paid for and can't take with them. This is nothing niggardly in her; rather it is the normal training of the Boston brahmins who have always carefully husbanded their resources. In her there is no awkwardness about campaigning—she loves it. Indeed, she has several times caused some tactical difficulties at receptions and platform appearances by Lodge, by wandering off to talk to people, utter strangers of course. She just likes to drift among a crowd, shaking hands and exchanging pleasantries. She talks with great affection of people everywhere, 'They're so friendly,' gets from these many multiplied experiences the sense that the American people all over the land are a good, kindly people. What she sees is a reflection of herself."

Lodge offended a good many local politicians by refusing to go to all the different hand-shaking affairs they had thought up. "I may seem ruthless and mean," he told an aide, "but dammit, I can't give in to these pros who want me to run myself ragged. I gave Eisenhower this advice in '52: 'There are just two things, stay in character and don't get tired.' I'm not going to

stagger across the finishing line. I want to stay fresh and stay in character."
To his staff, he laid down these rules for his campaign:

"No. 1) I must make sense in my speeches. No. 2) I must be good-humored. If I'm irascible, I might as well stay home. I hope I don't talk claptrap. The idea that the more you talk the more votes you get is fallacious. Being a politician is something like being an actor. You don't stay on too long. In a campaign you've got to think it's worthwhile, and then you've got to think it's fun, and then you've got to think it's funny."

The men who worked with Lodge in that campaign found him a wonderful companion, full of energy, full of good humor, full of hard-headed common sense. "It's a wonderful sign when a candidate wants to have his picture taken with you," he said. "In '36 I didn't want my picture taken with Landon."

Or, again to arguments that he should talk on more issues: "This idea that I ought, in Carlyle's phrase, to be professor of things in general, a latter-day Moses come to pronounce judgment, is silly. People don't expect me to do that—I've been working on the Congo. . . .

"I can't say what I'm going to say Oct. 18 any more than *Life* knows what it will print weeks ahead. As a seafaring man, I put my finger in the water and hold it up every morning. No man has more than one or two good speeches in his whole life. Say something that's true, that you believe, that makes sense. The truth doesn't change every day to make the A.M. and P.M. papers. You can't put out 40 or 50 major speeches, you save up something good for the end of the campaign."

He remembered some political tricks he had learned along the way.

"I was impressed when an officer started to arrest a drunk who was heckling a candidate in Massachusetts, and the candidate cried: 'Officer, take your hands off that man! He's an American citizen!' Then I learned the same guy was planted in every one of his audiences."

One critic said he wasn't hitting the Democrats hard enough.

"I won't attack the Democrats as such; I want and expect to get some of their votes. I've never been narrowly partisan. Let them present their case and we ours, and let the voters decide. Ther's no point in rebutting campaign oratory. You've got to stay fluid—in tactics, not in principle. Otherwise it's disaster."

He was always in good humor: "I feel like the old Boston lady who said, 'I expect to live till Spring—I always have.' "

Lodge turned to Serrell Hillman, *Time's* U.N. correspondent who had taken leave to work for him, and joshed him about the corrupting effects of political life on his journalistic ethics: "When you get back to *Time* you won't know a story if you see it. You'll play it down. But I predict you'll rise to the top—by politics, charm, conniving and blackmail—and then you'll wonder what you were doing all those years being true to yourself."

As they were traveling, Khrushchev had arrived in the U.S., and had made disparaging remarks about Lodge at the U.N. He had also banged his shoe on the table. "See!" gloated Lodge."I told you he was a friend of mine!"

Hillman's private log of Lodge's offhand remarks during the campaign provides a closeup of a jocular, fun-loving Lodge seldom seen except by intimates.

On one occasion, he dumped scraps of paper from his pocket into a staffer's hand and said, "Put this in your memory book with the dried flowers and pressed leaves of your youth." After a particularly wearying day, when asked if he wanted a drink, Lodge said, "I could beat around the bush. I could give you an elaborate and circumlocutory answer. But the short answer is yes."

When Nixon agreed to debate Kennedy, Lodge told his aides he would not have done it. "You don't debate when you think you're ahead. Curley thought he was behind and wanted to debate. We obfuscated, stalled and diverted the reporters till the idea got lost."

Lodge was under no illusions that eight years of Republicanism had appreciably altered the endemic inefficiency in Washington. "Some people in Washington don't want efficiency in government," he told Hillman. "They hate the Hoover Commission. They want to add employees and get bigger offices with a flag in the corner and hope by the time they're 58 they'll have a car and a chauffeur."

Hillman, who had voted for Stevenson in 1956, was gleefully repeating Adlai Stevenson's crack that no one since Lon Chaney had shown as many public faces as Nixon. "It amuses you," said Lodge, "and it helps Nixon. That's an ideal combination."

Something reminded Lodge of the story of Daniel Webster coming downstairs at the Parker House after a rough and drunken night. He met a bellboy who said, "Senator, here I get up at five o'clock every morning and work hard all day and I'm only a clerk. And then I see you, up drinking all night, and you're a United States Senator. It doesn't seem fair." Webster said, "The trouble with you, young man, is no matter how early you get up, you're no damn good."

Lodge admiringly reminisced about Curley as "an inventive, adroit, resourceful man." He was amused at his great audacity in trying to claim that Lodge was illegitimate and an impostor. "Was Curley right?" asked Hillman impudently. "Don't ask me a leading question," said Lodge. "You'll have to lead up to it, my boy."

At Knoxville he spoke at the airport in a pouring rain. Back on the plane,

330   he found Charles MacCarry, one of his aides, asleep. "Here's a man who was really moved by my oratory," said Lodge. "I'll award him the Order of the Silver Tongue." Knoxville reminded him of Tennessee's old Senator Bachman, and a story he had told Lodge of visiting a mountain hamlet and being greeted by a brass band. His host said, "Senator, I want you to meet my son." The boy was very polite and respectful. The Senator threw his arm around him and asked his age. "Eighteen, sir," said the boy. "Well," said the Senator. "Ain't that wonderful! Just think, three more years you'll be able to participate in government and exercise your franchise." "Oh, Senator," said the boy, "I been doin' that for a year already."

After a local congressman got through telling Lodge all the things that were wrong with his campaign, Lodge was reminded of Senator McNary telling Senator Jim Watson of Indiana how he stood back home. "The rich fat cats don't like you; they think you're a hypocrite. The wets don't like you because you vote dry. The drys don't like you because they know you take a drink. The professional people don't like you because they think you're a dunderhead. Labor doesn't like you because they think you're a reactionary." Watson thought all that over, then said: "Tell me, Charlie, where does Mrs. Watson stand?"

A man had called several times without reaching Lodge and would never leave his name. When Lodge finally discovered it was a national party leader, he was reminded of Wellington's meeting with his generals on the eve of Waterloo. As they were leaving, Wellington said, "They may not frighten the enemy, but by God, sir, they frighten me!"

One day Hillman had a slight case of flu. "It reminds me," said Lodge, "of the time the Prince Consort fell ill while on an official trip, and Robert Southey, the poet laureate, was called upon to compose a suitable poem. He wrote, 'Across the wires the electric message came, 'He is not better; he is much the same.' Think that over!"

Before going on a TV show in New York, Lodge told the broadcaster: "I'm a private citizen; I'm off the payroll trying to get back on. I'm not exactly private—at least I can't get any privacy—but I'm unemployed; just an angry taxpayer."

Lodge made his major address of the campaign—a half-hour on nationwide TV—on October 20 from Vocation High School in Minneapolis. "Two thirds of the world lacks the food, the housing, the industrial sinews, the social and economic foundation, to take full part in the adventure of the 20th Century," he said. "The people of the new nations demand a better life and they should have it. If they do not achieve it and achieve it quickly there is every prospect that the world will be plunged into further turmoil and instability, and inevitably impelled toward tragic tests of power between East and West, as the Communists try to exploit the discontent of the rising peoples." He called for bold international programs of cooperation such as the International Geophysical Year and the World Refugee Year, which were so successful. "At least one similar humanitarian program should be started each year such as the Eisenhower Food for Peace program, under U.N. auspices." He called for "a world campaign to reclaim the deserts," a challenge to the Soviet Union to move "toward an open world, free from secrecy and censorship. . . . Insist that all U.N. proceedings be broadcast to the Soviet people and that U.N. publications be made available to them." Turning to Khrushchev's own U.N. appearance, Lodge said: "I have been with Chairman Khrushchev in this country and I have met him in the Soviet Union and I assure you that he is no clown. He is a man who must never be taken at face value. There is a purpose in what he does—everything is figured out ahead of time—and his purpose in coming to New York was to destroy the U.N." Kennedy had made much of diminished U.S. prestige in the world. "The confusion about prestige," said Lodge, "arises from the belief that a country as large and powerful as ours can be loved. A nation as great and powerful as the U.S. can not be loved. But it can be respected. People can know that its word is good and its motives are noble. And people have this kind of respect for us—which is why no nation has higher prestige than we."

It was a photo finish but the Democrats won by the incredibly narrow margin of 112,000 votes, a plurality of less than 1 per cent.

Lodge wired his old antagonist Jack Kennedy at Hyannisport:

SINCERE CONGRATULATIONS ON YOUR ELECTION AS PRESIDENT OF THE UNITED STATES. YOU HAVE MY VERY EARNEST AND GENUINE GOOD WISHES FOR AN ADMINISTRATION FILLED WITH USEFUL AND VALUABLE ACCOMPLISHMENTS FOR THE AMERICAN PEOPLE. NOW THAT THE VOTERS HAVE SPOKEN AMERICANS SHOULD CLOSE RANKS AND PRESENT A UNITED FRONT BEFORE THE WORLD.

Kennedy missed this wire in the deluge. When he heard of it later from Cabot's son, George, an Eisenhower Assistant Secretary of Labor with whom Senator Kennedy had spent many an evening as a summer bachelor, the President-elect wrote his thanks. Lodge also wired Lyndon Johnson, who responded from Texas:

YOUR WIRE OF NOVEMBER 2 JUST DELIVERED TO ME UPON MY ARRIVAL AT THE RANCH LAST NIGHT. DEEPLY APPRECIATE YOUR FRIENDSHIP AND GOOD WISHES. MY PERSONAL REGARDS TO YOU AND MRS. LODGE.

And from the White House:

332   I SALUTE YOU FOR A MAGNIFICENT CAMPAIGN IN THE FINEST TRADI-
TION OF A GREAT AMERICAN FAMILY. I SHALL BE FOREVER GRATEFUL
FOR YOUR EFFECTIVE SERVICE TO MY ADMINISTRATION AND THE COUN-
TRY DURING THESE PAST EIGHT YEARS. PLEASE EXTEND MY REGARDS
TO EMILY, AND MY BEST WISHES IN WHATEVER YOUR FUTURE MAY
HOLD.   DWIGHT D. EISENHOWER

For the first time in twenty-eight years Lodge had literally become, if not an angry taxpayer, a private citizen again.

CHAPTER SIXTEEN

He had strong feelings about the United States of America. —President Kennedy, *in 1963, explaining why Lodge went to Viet Nam.*

In the year that followed the 1960 election, Lodge was at a loss how best to occupy himself. He had a number of flattering offers from industry, and for a time seriously considered some. He pondered returning to newspaper work as a commentator, but a long-ingrained sense of objectivity convinced him that a man so recently a candidate would have to wait at least some years before he could write a column that would not be discounted by most readers as some kind of disguised political ax-grinding.

His lifelong friend, Harry Luce, had invited him to join Time, Inc., as a consultant, so Lodge did so. In late 1961, however, a challenge came to him that he felt he could not refuse. A series of international conferences among world leaders deeply interested in creating both a United Europe and a transatlantic community linking it with the U.S. and Canada in common action had resulted in the formation of the Atlantic Institute. It was financed, in part, by large American foundations, in part by some fourteen participating governments. Its founders urged Lodge to take on its direction as Director General. President Kennedy and Secretary of State Rusk also urged him to do so. Lodge agreed, and flew to Paris to set the fledgling organization into motion.

His board of governors included Paul van Zeeland, former Premier of Belgium, as chairman, and, as vice chairman, Britain's Lord Gladwyn (a former opposite number at the U.N. as Sir Gladwyn Jebb); Germany's Kurt Birrenbach, a member of the Bundestag and active head of the giant Thyssen coal-steel combine; and France's former Finance Minister, Jacques Rueff. The governors included Paul-Henri Spaak, president of NATO; Canada's former Prime Minister Lester B. Pearson; Norway's Haakon Lie; Britain's Lord Franks; and, from the U.S., former Secretary of State Christian Herter, a Republican; and former Under Secretary Will Clayton, a Democrat. It was Herter and Clayton's joint study and proposal of a "giant step forward" that had led to Kennedy's program of across-the-board tariff cuts, America's biggest move toward freer trade since Roosevelt's reciprocal trade treaties.

Lodge, seeking a suitable headquarters for the institute, eventually found one in a large mansion overlooking the Seine in the Paris suburb of Boulogne; he had to pay $250,000 to buy it. (General Boulanger, nineteenth-

334   century leader of a Rightist plot against the Republic, had kept his mistress there.) To run the staff, Lodge recruited Pierre Uri as Counselor for Studies. A protege of Jean Monnet, Uri was an economist who had largely written the European Coal and Steel Agreement, as well as the economic sections of the Treaty of Rome creating the Common Market. Lodge set up a research staff under Marc Ullman, recruited from the Coal and Steel Community.

In the year that followed, Lodge organized a series of international conferences, whose aim was to achieve a consensus on a concrete program for action by the Atlantic community, and aimed eventually at creating some kind of interparliamentary councils among their governments. He named a working group on trade policy, another on economic and monetary policy, a third on agriculture, a fourth to discuss institutional arrangements (like the parliamentary councils), and a "rounding up" group to synthesize the views of the others. These groups included the ablest, brainiest economic and political thinkers of the participating countries. Lodge himself became a transatlantic commuter, shuttling back and forth from Beverly to Boulogne to arrange and direct these conferences. Through them all, Uri acted as *rapporteur*, and summarized the results of each conference. Out of them all, he then prepared a program for future action which the institute published as a book, *Partnership for Progress: A Program for Transatlantic Action*. The whole project had the active sympathy of President Kennedy. On June 12, 1963, Lodge called on him to present the book and explain its recommendations—now, for the time at least, rendered somewhat academic by President de Gaulle's studied disruption of Atlantic unity.

Thus Lodge found himself once more entering the familiar doors of the White House, where he had attended so many meetings of Eisenhower's Cabinet. Now, for the first time in his life, he was greeted by a President younger than himself, his old arch-rival from Boston. "Good to see you, Cabot," said the slim, patrician Harvard Democrat to the slim, patrician Harvard Republican. Lodge handed him the book and the President listened with interest while Lodge ticked off its high spots. Kennedy praised the suggestions. Then, abruptly, he said:

"Cabot, I'd like to persuade you to go to Viet Nam."

The request was not totally unexpected.

Earlier that year, Lodge, in January, had spent a tour of active duty in the Pentagon in his role as a major general in the Reserves. He had been briefed then on the situation in Viet Nam. He had raised a number of questions on the civil and political side of the problem. Some of the Army officers, impressed by his interest, asked if he might be willing to go to Viet Nam to study the situation at first-hand.

One officer in particular, Lieutenant Colonel John Murphy Dunn, a twice-wounded veteran of World War II and Korea, was struck by Lodge's unusual qualifications to oversee both the political and military aspects of Viet Nam. He talked to fellow officers about the desirability of getting Lodge to Saigon. On January 14, Lodge attended a big dinner at the Mayflower for Gen. Lauris Norstad, the retiring commander of NATO, and was spotted by President Kennedy who came by for cocktails.

"Why are you in town, Cabot?" the President asked. Lodge explained the tour of duty and Kennedy was surprised to learn of his military activity. On the way back to the White House he remarked to his military aide, General Chester (Ted) Clifton: "I didn't know Cabot was in the Reserve." "Yes, he's been active all his life," Clifton said. On January 18, at the President's suggestion, Clifton asked to see Lodge who suggested that they meet at the Army and Navy Club where Generals Devers and Crittenberger were giving a lunch in Lodge's honor. At the lunch, Clifton told him: "The President would like to know if you are available for an Embassy. "Well," said Lodge, "I'm not looking for a job. I have a job. But if something challenging and difficult arises where my experience could be useful, I'll be glad to accept." He had heard nothing more until the President made the direct request that June.

"If you need me," Lodge told the President, "of course I want to do it. I'd like first to see what my wife thinks about it. If it's agreeable to you, I think I should also consult General Eisenhower."

"By all means," the President said.

Lodge flew home to Beverly. Emily, recalling their long Pacific journey of thirty-five years before, said, "How nice to see it all again!" She knew it was apt to be dangerous, but as usual had a blithe attitude toward such things.

Lodge telephoned General Eisenhower at Gettysburg. The former President expressed admiration at Kennedy's political cleverness in getting Republicans to take on his most burdensome chores: Douglas Dillon as Secretary of the Treasury, McNamara for Defense, then John McCone to head the C.I.A., and now Lodge.

Lodge reminded Eisenhower that he, Eisenhower, had not hesitated to accept President Truman's call to head the NATO Army. "It was my duty," said Eisenhower. "I was a professional soldier, not a political leader." Lodge told Eisenhower that a sense of patriotic duty was no less binding on a private citizen than on a soldier. Eisenhower did not disapprove of Lodge's mission. It was clear, however, that he was not enthusiastic about it.

Lodge notified Kennedy he would go. "Dear Cabot," wrote Kennedy on June 18, "I am delighted that you are going to South Viet-Nam. This is a

336 most important assignment and I know you will do an outstanding job. We have today sent a message to the South Viet-Nam Government notifying them of your assignment."

Through most of July, Lodge found himself going back to school again. He had elaborate and extensive briefings at both the State Department and the Pentagon. In the course of this, he attended lectures at the Foreign Service Institute in Virginia. For State, the Saigon Embassy had become its biggest, and in many ways most important, operation. It embraced the biggest economic aid mission in the world. It was the most important single center for psychological warfare. It was the biggest single job of the U.S. Information Agency. For the Pentagon, it was the only place in the world where Americans were shooting and being shot at; it was the linchpin in the defense of all Southeast Asia. If South Viet Nam crumbled, then the tide of Communist power could well engulf India, the Philippines, Malaysia, perhaps Australia, and be immeasurably strengthened in its effort to sweep over the emergent states of Africa. To everyone concerned with all these tasks, Lodge's mission outranked all others in urgency and importance.

Some Republicans regarded Lodge's willingness to serve there as going over to what Kentucky's Thruston Morton called "the enemy." This was curious, because the Viet Nam struggle had equally concerned both Republican and Democratic Administrations. Indeed, at the time of Dien Bien Phu in 1954, Vice President Nixon had urged that the U.S. intervene. Eisenhower had decided against it on the urging of Chief of Staff Matthew Ridgway. Nevertheless, in July Congresswoman Frances P. Bolton of Cleveland, a longtime Republican member of the House Committee on Foreign Affairs, wrote Lodge:

> . . . I, *with so many Republicans here on the hill, am deeply disturbed that you should have accepted the Ambassadorship to this terribly difficult spot in Southeast Asia. . . . Red China is determined to get a foothold in Southeast Asia and the best one for her purposes is South Viet-Nam. . . . Should this happen during your incumbency out there, you know what they would do to the Republican Party. We would be blamed! Are you truly certain, my Dear, that you understand the complexities of these countries? Are you certain of your own capacity for patience, understanding, and really infinite wisdom? . . . This may sound as though I didn't trust your judgment and capacity. That isn't so at all! But I don't trust anyone in this Administration, and I believe they are perfectly capable of using a possible defeat in Southeast Asia to ruin the Republican Party.*

Lodge replied to Mrs. Bolton:

Service in any situation—foreign or domestic—which acutely involves American security must always be considered from a totally unpartisan viewpoint, without regard to party politics, important though party politics are.

A foreign situation which is the only one in the world where the cold war has become hot—a situation in which thousands of American soldiers, airmen and sailors are deeply involved—is assuredly such a situation.

If the Commander-in-Chief, in his official capacity, considers that any American can render useful services, and that the American obviously has relevant experience, then that American should render those services unless there is some overriding reason (such as health) why he cannot do so.

Under such circumstances, service is a patriotic duty as well as an honor.

As a lifelong Republican, who intends to remain so, I cannot believe that the course of duty which I have outlined will do other than redound to the credit of the Republican Party. How can service by a member of a political party, in a patriotic spirit, in what in many ways is a war theater, injure that party?

As far as praise or blame is concerned, I can only say that I will do my best. The President, of course, is the head of the Government and cannot escape ultimate responsibility for everything . . . I am by no means "certain of my capacity for infinite wisdom." In fact, I don't think I have such capacity at all. But I am willing to serve and expend myself, if need be.

Lodge appeared before the Senate Foreign Relations Committee on which he had served for six years; his confirmation was unanimous. On August 14 he spent the morning with Secretary of State Rusk and Under Secretary Averell Harriman, the afternoon with Secretary McNamara, getting their final views. He also saw a very prominent Vietnamese in Washington who told him that unless Madame Nhu and her fanatic husband, Ngo Din Nhu, who had been leading the attacks on Buddhist pagodas, left the country, "no power on earth can prevent Nhu, Madame Nhu and President Diem from being assassinated."

Lodge got endless inoculations—for smallpox, typhoid, typhus, tetanus, cholera, polio, yellow fever—and gamma globulin against hepatitis. On August 15 he had his final visit with President Kennedy, to get the clearest possible feeling of his wishes. He found the President much concerned at the trend of events in Viet Nam. There had been no effective government since May 7, when Buddhists in the city of Hué had been forbidden to fly

338   their flag, had marched in protest, and been massacred by Nhu's Special Forces: some of the marchers, including children, had been crushed under armored vehicles. On June 11, an elderly monk, Thich Quang Duc, 73, had burned himself alive in protest at a principal intersection of Saigon; the whole world's revulsion had been aroused by this event. President Kennedy had on his desk the now-famous photograph of this immolation taken by AP Correspondent Malcolm Browne. "Cabot," Kennedy said, "I spend more of my time on the Viet Nam problem than on anything else. I want you to study the whole thing carefully and make recommendations on what we should do."

Lodge flew back to Beverly to pack. He took little, knowing he could get good washable suits in Saigon, and that all he needed for ceremonies was a white suit, black shoes, black four-in-hand tie. He took one winter suit and topcoat in case he was called back. Two big suitcases held all he took, including some phonograph records ranging from Liszt, Beethoven and Chopin to Louis Armstrong and the Dukes of Dixieland. Emily took little more. On Saturday morning, August 17, they took off from Logan Airport in Boston, spent that night in San Francisco, went to church there the next morning, and took off that afternoon for Hawaii on a Pan American commercial jet. With them went Lieutenant Colonel Mike Dunn, whom Lodge had chosen as his right-hand man. Another passenger, by coincidence, was Eugene Burdick, co-author with William J. Lederer of the book, *The Ugly American,* which had torn so savagely at the ineptitudes of conventional U.S. "business as usual" diplomacy in the midst of Asia's revolution. Their hero was an "ugly American" who went out among the people, got down into the muck with them, and helped them find ways to help themselves. Lodge took care to seek the much-traveled Burdick's views on the problems ahead. Burdick's advice: rely on seasoned newsmen more than on Embassy officers.

At Pearl Harbor, Lodge spent Monday getting an extensive briefing from Admiral Harry Felt, Pacific commander-in-chief, and his staff, and flew on to Tokyo, planning to spend a few days there and in Hong Kong and Manila en route to Saigon. In Tokyo, Colonel Dunn began to get his first inkling of how pervasive and far-reaching was Lodge's knowledge of the Far East.

First, a Japanese Buddhist monk called at their hotel. He was thoroughly versed on the lifelong friendship of Lodge's grandfather with William Sturgis Bigelow, who became a Buddhist monk and was buried in Japan. The monk came to present Lodge with a photo of Bigelow's grave and the Buddhist shrine built above it. The monk also had known Uncle John Lodge, and talked of his deep interest in Buddhism. After his visit, a young Vietnamese Buddhist girl came to the hotel, threatening to set fire to herself because of the persecutions in Viet Nam. Lodge discussed Buddhism with

her in a reassuring way and talked her out of her suicidal frame of mind,   *339*
Colonel Dunn recalled later.

That same day events in Viet Nam rose to a frenzy which cut short their plans to tarry along the way. Through the past week, protests over Diem's suppression of the Buddhists had mounted. In Saigon an eighteen-year-old girl had tried to cut off her left hand. Outside the coastal city of Hué, a seventeen-year-old novice monk wrapped himself in a kerosene-soaked, six-color Buddhist flag and lit a match. In the village of Nin Hoa, two hundred miles north of Saigon, a young Buddhist nun set herself on fire in a Catholic school's playground. Then a seventy-one-year-old monk burned himself to death in the courtyard of the Hué Pagoda. Since the Ngo family were all Catholics, the Vatican grew concerned that the repressions made it seem, however unjustly, that the Catholic minority (about 1,500,000) was persecuting the Buddhist majority. Actually, the Ngo family spoke for the Vatican in no way at all.

That fateful August 21, Nhu proclaimed martial law and ordered his dread secret police, the Special Forces, into a series of actions clearly timed to be over and done with before Lodge could reach Viet Nam. They descended on the massive Xa Lai Pagoda in Saigon, and on the pagodas in Hue and other principal towns, shooting, clubbing, arresting Buddhist leaders left and right; at least eight were killed in Saigon and thirty injured. Two monks fled out of the Xa Loi Pagoda's rear into the nearby American A.I.D. mission and were given asylum there.

Lodge was roused out of bed in Tokyo in the middle of the night. The President wanted him to proceed to Saigon immediately. Mike Dunn was up all night arranging for a plane, got the loan of a general's specially fitted DC-6 in which they took off early next morning from Tachikawa Air Force Base. Lodge allowed four U.S. newsmen to go with him. At nine-thirty that night, amid Saigon's rainy season, they arrived in a city besieged.

Deputy Chief of Mission William C. Truehart and the U.S. commander, General Paul Harkins, an old comrade from Second Armored days, met them. The air was tense among the two-score newsmen who had gone out to meet Lodge. For months, they had chafed under the growing conviction that they were being fed little but half-truths and false optimism by both the diplomatic, military and CIA missions. Time and again, they had seen missions by Defense Secretary McNamara and others come out, hear glowing reports about the progress of "strategic hamlets" being built by Diem to defend against Viet Cong raids, and go back repeating such euphoric data. Meanwhile, they had seen the realities of Nhu's brutal repression against the Saigon populace reach such grotesque extremes that his Special Forces had even jailed grade-school children demonstrating against the Buddhist persecutions. The children were gradually released in the custody of their

340   parents, including numerous armed forces officers who went to the police stations in uniform to get the release of their sons and daughters. "Saigon was seething," U.S.I.S. Chief John Mecklin wrote afterward "and at least part of the stimulation was popular anticipation that Lodge had come to put things right, meaning to apply American power to destroy the Diem regime. A good many Americans in Saigon, perhaps a sizeable majority, felt the same way." Mecklin describes the electric atmosphere surrounding Lodge's arrival:

> *It was a somberly dramatic spectacle as the big plane lumbered up to the V.I.P. terminal at Saigon's Tan Son Nhut Airport, on that oppressively hot night. It was drizzling rain and there were puddles on the hardstand that glistened in the television flood lights. The airport observation balconies were dark and empty. . . . Straw hat in hand, wearing a dark suit, Lodge appeared alone at the cabin door. There were no cheers, only the whirr of cameras and popping of flash bulbs as he descended the gangway to be greeted by a small group of American officials, a protocol officer from the Foreign Ministry and and about forty newsmen who had come out in special buses escorted by armed police jeeps through the curfew. Lodge had radioed from the plane that he did not want to talk to the press upon arrival. When he saw the waiting newsmen, however, he stepped up to a microphone, regretted that he could not discuss substance, nor answer questions, and then talked for five minutes about the vital role of the press in American democracy and how much he welcomed any opportunity to help the newsmen do their jobs. This was the nicest thing anyone except the Buddhists had said to them in a long while and the newsmen were pleased. The effect was capped by the discovery that Lodge had allowed four more American newsmen to hitch a ride on his plane from Tokyo. This was a first glimpse of Lodge's masterful way with newsmen. As far as the U.S. Embassy was concerned, the so-called press problem ended then and there. . . .*

As they rode in from the airport in the Embassy's Checker limousine, they passed squads of Vietnamese soldiers guarding every intersection. No sooner had Lodge arrived at the two-story Embassy residence than an Embassy official asked to speak to him alone, then whispered intensely: "They have a plot to kill you. They plan to take you out, ostensibly to show you a strategic hamlet, stage a fake Viet Cong raid; in the confusion you will get shot." Lodge thought that over. "If these people intend to kill me," he said, "why do we have to whisper and be so careful about keeping their secret for them?" The episode reminded him of the man who told his dinner companion, "Don't look now, but that man over there is going off with your 341 overcoat."

Early next morning Lodge drove the two miles to the Chancery office at the inadequate, ugly U.S. Embassy Building at 31 Ham Nghi Boulevard, took the elevator to his fifth-floor office, and began his new career. He was not long learning how fearful and terrible the repression of Buddhists had been. When he heard of the two fugitive monks he strode down to the U.S. AID Mission and showed his sympathy by ordering that fresh vegetables be bought daily for these religious vegetarians.

He strode through a city where Nhu's heavily armed Special Forces guarded all main buildings, and mobile "anti-suicide squads" patrolled the streets ready to douse any new "barbecues," as Madame Nhu liked to call the immolations. Censorship had been imposed on all outside communications, blocking even the coded messages of Embassies (the U.S., of course, had its own direct radio communications with the Pentagon Communications Center and with Pearl Harbor).

Strict curfews were being enforced. David Halberstam, the young New York *Times* reporter, was cut off from any communications with his paper. So was Malcolm Browne of Associated Press, and Neil Sheehan of United Press International, the other two regulars in Saigon. Lodge promptly demanded that the censorship be lifted.

He had entered a situation where his predecessor, Ambassador Frederick Nolting, and the CIA Chief John Richardson had supported Diem and Nhu so completely that they had little leverage to influence their actions. Lodge clearly showed his displeasure with the whole setup. One of Nhu's proclamations was plastered on the door of the U.S. Information Agency. Lodge had it torn down.

Lodge was appalled to find that American correspondents had lost faith in anything being told them by the military mission or the Embassy. They felt that they were being lied to. Lodge, the old reporter, began dealing with them directly and frankly. A new feeling of purpose and command began to run through the American agencies. "I'm running things here," the *Times* quoted Lodge as saying when its dispatches flowed again, "and I intend to run them with a firm hand. If Washington wants a weasel for this job it can find someone else." (Lodge says he never made such a statement—"that's good journalism but poor government"—but it expressed what the correspondents hoped and believed he was doing.)

Lodge invited the three regular correspondents—Halberstam, Sheehan and Browne—to successive private lunches at his residence and carefully sought their views. "Except for his arrival and departure ten months later," wrote Mecklin, "Lodge gave no press conferences, no off-the-record briefings. Instead he met frequently but always alone with individual American

342 newsmen, thus at once flattering them and minimizing the risk of broken confidences. He was not an exceptionally good news source, but he knew how to talk to newsmen so they went away happy. Unlike Nolting and Harkins, he did not try to debate with them. Instead he invited their ideas, confided enough information to make a story, and treated them as equals— tried and true devices that should have been used much sooner in Saigon."

Emily Lodge, shortly after taking up this new life, had a new experience. She wrote frequent letters to her sons and grandchildren back home. "In the middle of dinner last night," she began one of these, "we heard machine-gun fire that couldn't have been more than 150 yards away. It's funny that I should live to be 57 years old and never hear machine guns before." Sometimes, as Viet Cong patrols made daring raids near Saigon, she also heard artillery fire. "We were dining with the ——'s last night," she wrote, "and heard rather heavy artillery fire during soup. This isn't really very strange because if you listen for it you can hear it almost at any time of day."

Lodge went to the Presidential palace to present his credentials to President Diem. As he strode up the broad stairs, he noticed, at the top on either side, carved wooden dragons with huge elephant tusks protruding from them, and admired their handiwork. Diem greeted him graciously. Lodge was anxious to get at once to the heart of the disintegrating situation. Saigon was still under martial law. Its relations with the U.S. were bad and getting worse. Lodge was extremely anxious to save Diem if it was at all possible, knowing that his fall would likely bring more chaos than it would help abate. But Diem was seeking to evade unpleasant facts. He rambled endlessly about his boyhood in Hué, and other irrelevant facts, until Lodge finally had to excuse himself and hurry back to his office.

Lodge told his Embassy aides, wrote Halberstam later, that "Diem couldn't possibly run the country; the President couldn't even speak coherently. While Lodge had ticked off American grievances and recommendations, his host had stared at the ceiling, and when the ambassador was finished the President poured out a babble of words about something totally unrelated. Lodge was told that this always took place whenever the Americans asked for anything." Halberstam went on to add:

> *Henry Cabot Lodge did not really switch policies when he arrived in Viet Nam but a new policy needed to be evolved. . . . Lodge is a handsome man, the image of the perfect American ambassador . . . but while he can be extremely charming, he can also be quite rude. He is a total politician in the best sense; that is, he is attuned to the needs, ambitions and motivations of others. Yet his background, coolness and reserve mark him as essentially different from other, more genial and backslapping politicians. . . . Lodge became known as a difficult, de-*

manding man to work for, but he had the respect of his subordinates and of the reporters. He turned out to be a shrewd, tough operator, very much a match for the Ngo family. He was absolutely single-minded, he worked hard and did his homework, and he had no illusions about the task facing the U.S. He quickly analyzed the situation in Saigon, and today in Washington he is considered to have been the best ambassador we have ever had there. Above all, he wanted to know what was going on in the country, even when it looked like bad news. He also played his hand very close to the vest. "He doesn't trust anyone," one aide told me, "and because of that he's never had any confidence broken." Sheehan, who comes from Massachusetts, said "Lodge is what my Irish mother would call a crafty Yankee."

Though Lodge did not believe the war was going well, or even being fought very hard, the fact that Harkins was an old family friend from Boston days placed him in a difficult position, since Harkins would never admit that things were not running smoothly.

As the repression of the Buddhists continued, the war against the Viet Cong was all but forgotten. "This wrecks the Army's efforts against the Reds," *Time* quoted a U.S. intelligence officer as saying. "They're too busy enforcing curfews to fight." Both in Saigon and at the State Department at home, U.S. hands talked openly of the possibility of a coup against Diem. There were rumors of impending cuts in U.S. aid to the regime. President Kennedy deferred any such action pending recommendations by Lodge.

Lodge, who could speak French as fluently as any native, quickly learned the true state of affairs in Saigon. He talked to people on the streets, in the market place, to pedicab drivers, He sought out men like Msgr. Salvatore Asta, the Vatican's Apostolic delegate, who was on intimate terms with Vietnamese in all walks of life; Patrick J. Honey, a professor from the University of London who had lived three months each year in Saigon for twenty years studying Vietnamese literature and art. He sought out the lower-echelon U.S. officers and helicopter crews who were up against the Viet Cong in the field and could discount the built-in optimism of headquarters. Moreover, he could see for himself the things going on: trucks with U.S. insignia but driven by Nhu's Special Forces taking school children out to concentration camps. He heard of teenage girls being questioned and mistreated by police; some had their breasts shocked by electricity. It was clear that Archbishop Thuc, Diem's brother, was the strongest influence in the whole government, and was inciting the persecution despite the alarm and concern of the Vatican itself. It was clear that Madame Nhu was equally an evil influence, ordering her own husband and his brother, Diem, to ever stronger measures. She seemed to take a diabolical joy in violence

344 and cruelty. *Time* put her on its cover, and reported her announced recipe for dealing with demonstrators: "Beat them three times harder." From all his sources, Lodge concluded that his earlier Vietnamese informant in Washington had been right—that unless Madame Nhu and her fanatical husband left the country, Diem could not be saved. He so advised President Kennedy.

In early September, President Kennedy discussed the situation in an unusual hour-long interview with Walter Cronkite over CBS television. He said Diem's government had "gotten out of touch with the people. The repressions against the Buddhists we felt were very unwise. Now, all we can do is to make it very clear we don't think this is the way to win." He added that "with changes in policy, and perhaps in personnel," the Diem government might win support of the people. "If it doesn't make these changes, I would think the chances of winning it would not be very good." But he was not prepared to cut U.S. aid to bring about these changes. "That would be a great mistake." In effect, observed James Reston, the President told Diem: "Change, or we'll string along with you anyway." Soon afterward *Time* reported that Lodge, putting his words in the most careful diplomatic terms, suggested to Diem that his brother and fiery sister-in-law leave the country until the crisis was over, and a rapprochement between the government and the population could be established, "hinting that their presence would 'endanger' U.S. congressional appropriations for Viet Nam. . . ." Diem expressed surprise and shock at Lodge's suggestion, coldly turned it down. Nevertheless Mme. Nhu shortly did leave the country, to attend an Inter-Parliamentary Union meeting in Belgrade, to visit Rome, Paris, and go on to New York where she had numerous speaking invitations. Archbishop Thuc also left the country, and when he reached Rome, was ordered by the Vatican to stop issuing his belligerent and controversial anti-Buddhist statements. Mme. Nhu did not hesitate to question the Pope's wisdom. After he had expressed dismay at the persecutions, she asserted: "Pope Paul is too easily worried. As a Catholic I am only required to believe in the dogma of my religion and the Pope. The Pope is only infallible when he decrees something *ex-cathedra*. I do not believe that he will put himself in his chair to disavow me, because that would be a very bad blow to Catholicism."

Every new headline she created seemed to stimulate Mme. Nhu to say still more shocking things. On September 25, she asserted that "young officers of the U.S. military mission are acting like little soldiers of fortune. They do not know what is going on." Back in Saigon, Lodge read this in a cold fury. On arrival, he had pointedly failed to call on Mme Nhu in his official visits. Now he decided to put the Dragon Lady in her place. "It is a shocking statement," he told correspondents in Saigon. "These junior officers are risking their lives every day. Some of them have been killed side-by-side with their Vietnamese comrades. It is incomprehensible to me how anyone can speak so cruelly. These men should be thanked and not in-sulted." His statement sent an electric feeling through the Americans in Viet Nam. More than anything else could have done, it symbolized that the bootlicking of the Nhus, the silent acceptance of their insults, was over: a new hand was in charge.

While these events were going on, some Republicans grumbled at home that Kennedy had sent Lodge to Vietnam to disarm Republican critics of his policies. At his September 2 press conference, such questions brought this strong retort from the President:

If he was as careful as some politicians, of course, he would not have wanted to go to Saigon—he could have looked for a safe job. He had strong feelings about the United States of America, and he put those ahead of any possible political advantage or consideration. His willing-ness to assume the duties of American Ambassador to Vietnam in these times of danger and difficulty was in the greatest tradition of distin-guished public service.

In early September, President Kennedy sent Joe Mendenhall, former No. 2 man in the Saigon Embassy, and Marine Major General Victor Krulak for an on-the-spot investigation. Mendenhall came back reflecting Lodge's feel-ing that Diem's control was disintegrating, Krulak shared Harkins' feeling that things were fundamentally sound. "Are you sure you two gentlemen visited the same country?" Kennedy inquired. He was so exasperated he sent McNamara and Joint Chiefs Chairman General Maxwell Taylor to see for themselves. Halberstam gives this version of events:

Behind all this double talk an absorbing behind-the-scenes struggle was taking place between Harkins and Lodge, each of whom was try-ing to press his views on the two visitors . . . as the two men were descending the ramp, Lodge assigned two of his aides to block Harkins so that the Ambassador would be the first to greet the Secretary. Har-kins was caught in a trap as the crowd surged forward and we could hear him shouting plaintively from behind a group of photographers, "Please, gentlemen, please let me through to greet the Secretary." Harkins had one advantage; the trip was under the auspices of MACV (Military Assistance Command, Viet-Nam) and therefore he could arrange the schedule of what the two visitors would see. On the other hand, the Secretary was staying with Lodge, and the Ambassador had the opportunity to work on McNamara each morning at breakfast and each night when the daily inspections were over. Lodge deliberately gave Harkins a head start: for the first three days the Secretary and his party flew to various corps areas where the military was in charge. With little variations he was given the standard briefing and statistics —except in the Delta, where the Americans were considerably more cautious. But midway through their stay Lodge began his campaign; he disagreed forcefully with the conclusions of the military and he expressed strong doubts about the progress of the war. Key civilian personnel working in the Delta in different capacities were quietly brought up to Saigon to meet the Secretary.

This conflict was something new to the Secretary. He had been to Saigon before, and he had met frequently in Honolulu with the Saigon team. Each time he had been given the team report: MACV would say that the war was being won; the Embassy would say the war was being won and that Diem was coming around; the CIA would say that things were going well and that the montagnards were coming around. Then, if it was a Saigon visit, McNamara would go to the Palace and be told in a five-hour monologue that the war was being won and that the Americans finally understood its nature. Lastly, he would visit a couple of specially selected sites where the news was good. Duly impressed with the effectiveness of the programs and the team, he would leave Saigon a less wise man than when he arrived. . . .

When Lodge disagreed flatly with Harkins, McNamara for the first time ran into real dissent from sources that he respected. The tipoff on the struggle between Harkins and Lodge came the next to the last day of the trip, when McNamara canceled a final military tour of the countryside, sent Taylor off by himself, and stayed behind for more talks with civilians. The next day when McNamara and Taylor left, the word was out; for the first time the Secretary had not only been briefed thoroughly on the political chaos of the country, but had been given a dark picture of the progress of the war. Lodge was satisfied that he had broken through (a high officer in the Embassy who did not like Lodge personally called it "a goddamn tour de force"). When McNamara returned to Washington he reportedly told Kennedy that the military had been wrong, that the war was not going well, and that the official version of military events was inaccurate. Out of this came a curious statement which expressed concern about the political situation, urged the Vietnamese to continue the fight and further said that the Americans hoped to bring home most of their advisers by 1965. Lodge was surprised by the statement, but in Saigon it was written off as election year rhetoric. What was important was that behind the scenes Lodge's viewpoint had prevailed. The Kennedy Administration no longer be-

lieved the war was being won, and the U.S. intended slowly to reverse its total commitment to Diem.

Lodge took all the reins of command tightly in his own hand. Some members of the Mission thought him arrogant, and said so behind his back. Others felt a grudging admiration for his masterful air of command. U.S.I.S. Chief Mecklin describes the air of tension in the Embassy:

Circulation of cable traffic to and from Washington was cut so drastically that even General Harkins, with responsibility for sixteen thousand American military personnel, was left in the dark on Lodge's activities and policies. . . .

Lodge also claimed for himself a monopoly on direct contact with top officials of the Vietnamese Government to the point where he ordered several senior Americans to cease working with Vietnamese whom they had known for years. This sometimes had the effect of delaying, or permanently canceling, projects because Lodge was too busy with other matters, and not interested. . . .

Lodge regarded the newsmen in the same category with cable traffic: as his private domain. "The leak," he said, "is the prerogative of the ambassador. It is one of my weapons for doing this job." Leak prevention was one of the main reasons for his blackout on information to his staff. He was uncomfortable if other U.S. officials even had social contacts with reporters. In his relationship with newsmen, Lodge not only repaired the dismal situation inherited from Nolting. He also converted the newsmen into disciples. "The correspondents," said a bitter official who had shared Nolting's ordeal with the press, "were patsys for Lodge."

At this point, Lodge was still trying to help the Diem regime to help itself. He was pressing, as before, chiefly for 1) expulsion of the Nhus and 2) reconciliation with the Buddhists. A White House statement of October 2, after McNamara and Taylor returned, offered all parties a chance to compromise without a loss of face: "We will adhere to our policy of working with the people and government of South Viet-Nam to deny this country to Communism," it said ". . . The political situation . . . remains deeply serious. The U.S. has made clear its continuing opposition to any repressive actions. . . . While such actions have not yet significantly affected the military effort, they can do so in the future."

This gave Diem a path of dignified retreat. With it, Kennedy and Lodge also began quietly applying pressure that was not announced: the suspension of several segments of U.S. aid to Viet Nam. One was the $4 million a year of condensed milk that the U.S. was supplying (Madame Nhu had told her New York audience that Vietnamese did not like this milk, so fed it to their pigs). The chief suspension was that of providing dollars for Vietnamese commercial imports, allocations normally made four or five months before the goods arrived. Hence the suspension would bring no immediate damage to the economy, but *would* bring an increasing psychological pressure on Diem to take such action as would end it. What began now was a war of nerves between Lodge and Diem, as to whether Diem could now unbend sufficiently to save his government before it fell apart.

Mecklin thought Lodge's handling of the strategy was superb.

"His personality exactly fitted the requirements of the job," Mecklin wrote afterward. "It was this performance that stirred many of his sourest critics among Americans in Saigon to grudging admiration."

Lodge had told Diem precisely what he wanted done, and had encountered the same irrelevant monologues as his predecessors. Unlike his predecessors, Lodge did not keep begging. He simply stopped making calls. Then Washington quietly began suspending the programs. "They have not done anything I asked," Mecklin quotes Lodge as saying. "They know what I want. Why should I keep asking? Let them come to ask me for something." Mecklin continues:

> *Instructions were circulated throughout the U.S. Mission that if anyone asked about the suspended aid the answer was to be simply that it was "under review." If a Vietnamese official requested U.S. assistance of any significance, the reply was to be that perhaps President Diem would care to take it up with Ambassador Lodge. The result was that our relations with the Vietnamese Government began to dry up at all levels, except for military operations. It became a standoff, a test of wills, with the odds heavily favoring Lodge.*
>
> *Lodge's strategy suggested a shrewd understanding of human nature. He knew that any approach to him from the Palace, especially in face-conscious Asia, could only be tantamount to surrender. The technique not only preserved but exploited American dignity, in effect turning an Asian characteristic against Asians, yet it never closed the door to reconciliation—on American terms.*

The last weeks of the Diem regime saw a surrealist, upside-down world. Thousands of people went to a lake near Hué, to look for a magical fish that was supposed to rise to utter prophecies. Other thousands were reported climbing a mountain in the central highlands where a Buddhist nun was performing miracles. In one of the Saigon pagodas a Buddha had reportedly been seen to weep real tears. The sun, it was said, encircled by a great ring of fire, had swung back and forth in the sky. The ineffable Nhu began trying to establish contact with the Viet Cong to use threat of a negotiated settlement with the Communists as a weapon against the Americans. He told a non-American visitor in mid-October he wanted all Americans to go home forthwith: "Without the Americans we could win the war in two or three years. With the Americans . . . perhaps never."

On October 7, the Diem regime itself broke the news of the aid suspension in its English-language hand organ, *Times of Viet-Nam*. Threats of assassination of Lodge, Mecklin, and others, spread; new rumors of phony anti-Diem coups in which Lodge would be killed. Mecklin reports that Lodge had supposedly told a top Vietnamese official: "You surely do not intend any harm to Americans in Viet Nam. If you do, of course, we will bring in the Marines. The Japanese tried to fight the Marines. On a lot of those islands in the Pacific there were not enough Japanese left to bury their own dead after the battle. You wouldn't like that, would you?" Mike Dunn recalls Lodge sitting grimly with a .38 police special on his desk, and a Smith & Wesson .44 Magnum—whose bullets have the impact of a Winchester rifle—in the nearby Embassy safe.

To many Vietnamese, any effective change in American policy would be measured only by what the U.S. did about Nhu's Special Forces, his little private army headed by Colonel Le Quang Tung. The CIA, which helped organize it originally, was paying Tung's forces some $250,000 a month. The CIA chief, John Richardson, was recalled to Washington for consultation with President Kennedy; he did not return. On October 19, Lodge notified Colonel Tung that his forces would receive pay only if they were used in fighting the Viet Cong, and then only if they notified their American advisers about every movement. About this time, according to Halberstam of the *Times*, three generals notified Lodge that they were planning a coup. "They did not ask for any assistance, but they said that the coup would be pro-American, and asked the Mission not to thwart it. In return the Embassy did not offer any aid, but it did make arrangements to stay in full communication with the rebels."

The Army plotters were emboldened by Madame Nhu's absence. She seemed to have a sixth sense detecting and thwarting plots. The Army leaders—as well as Diem himself—were literally afraid of her. (The American correspondents both feared and detested her. "Madame Nhu," Malcolm Browne writes in his memoirs, "tried to destroy the integrity of the free foreign press, and in the process she made life extremely dangerous and difficult for my colleagues and myself. I think if she had had completely free reign, she would certainly have arranged for at least some of us to die. . . . I always had the feeling that Madame Nhu despised and

350   hated men, including those closest to her.") Rumors of impending coups were open talk at the Hotel Caravelle Bar, the favorite meeting place for correspondents and other Americans.

Events were moving swiftly to an inexorable showdown.

Lodge still hoped that Diem would act in time. On Saturday, October 28, Lodge flew up with him to the mountain resort of Dalat, Colonel Dunn and Emily going along. They stayed in a palace built by the French as a cool refuge from Saigon's heat which is almost unbearable in April and May. The purpose of their trip was to visit a strategic hamlet, Quang Duc, on a high plateau, to see where Diem had moved people from the seacoast to what had been virgin lands.

That night the Lodge group and Diem all dined together, with the Mayor of Dalat and his wife. Diem discussed the U.S.'s new policy of withholding payments on Viet Nam's commercial imports. "I began to see a chance we might begin to get a different kind of behavior out of him," Lodge recalled afterward. Diem denounced the suspension. But he offered no compromises. He was a very proud man and very stubborn.

The following day they all flew back together. Lodge was still hoping that Diem might send Nhu away. He did not see Diem again until Friday, November 1, when Admiral Felt, making a routine visit to Saigon, was to make his official call at the palace with General Harkins. Diem sent word to Lodge that he wanted some time alone with him after Admiral Felt left.

"Harkins and Felt left shortly before noon," Lodge recalled later. "I stayed on. I was due to go back for consultations with the President, which Diem knew.

"Diem said, 'There's an old saying here that every time the American Ambassador leaves there is a coup against the government.'

"That had been true in 1960, when some rebellious pilots dive-bombed the palace.

"Diem was already getting rumors of plots, but there were so many different rumors he hardly knew what to believe. We talked on for a while about my impending visit. I went home to lunch. Mike Dunn's wife and two sons had just arrived from America and we were all lunching together. We were just starting to eat around 1:30 when I heard cannon fire, and recognized it as 20mm. fire and bombing. A coup had begun."

It had taken form during the Buddhist crackdowns. Lieutenant General Tran Van Don, acting chief of the Joint General Staff, and Lieutenant General Duong Van ("Big") Minh, together with other key generals, had drawn—so they stated later—a twenty-page proposal of proposed reforms aimed at getting the war against the Viet Cong back on the track. They presented it to Diem, who "agreed to every clause" (said one) but did

nothing whatever to put the reforms into practice. His determined inaction
—they said later—sealed his fate. One night late in September, Don met
in the Caravelle Bar with his old military-school classmate and drinking
buddy, Major General Ton That Dinh, 36, commander of the III Corps
which controlled Saigon. Dinh agreed to use his troops to overthrow Diem.
D-day was set for a Friday, when the top generals customarily met in the
morning with Nhu to review progress in the strategic hamlet program.
Then they usually broke for lunch together at the Joint General Staff headquarters, near Saigon Airport, which they controlled. They reasoned that
any generals not yet part of the plot could be won over at the lunch, or
kept under guard there until it was over. At twelve, when Admiral Felt was
leaving from the airport, General Don went out to see him off—a bit anxiously, knowing that the airport itself would be seized at one-thirty. Don
went on to the generals' lunch. At one thirty sharp, red-kerchiefed General
Dinh began barking the orders as the insurgents struck. Truck loads of his
Marines raced toward the heart of Saigon, surrounded police headquarters,
put pro-Diem officials under arrest. Rocket-equipped dive-bombers took off
from the airport to attack Navy headquarters, which put up a struggle, and
to bomb loyal naval vessels firing antiaircraft shells from the Saigon River.
At Joint General Staff Headquarters, General Don kept telephone lines
open, both to Diem's Palace and to the U.S. Embassy, in the hope of arranging a quick surrender by Diem and Nhu.

Lodge got his first word of what had happened when Deputy Chief Truehart arrived at the Embassy Residence to bring word of Don's messages
from rebel headquarters. "I decided to stay in the house," Lodge recalled
later. "I got one rumor that an attempt would be made to kidnap and hold
me as a hostage. I could reach the Embassy by telephone, as well as voice
radio. There was no telling how long the fighting would last. We had plenty
of beds, and food, so I decided it was best to stay there. With Truehart at
the Chancery, the U.S. would have two strings to its bow. Twelve American
MP's dressed in civilian clothes arrived to protect me—the biggest men
I've ever seen, armed with riot guns and tear gas. They were stationed in
the yard and at the upstairs windows."

About half-past four that afternoon, Lodge's phone rang. It was Diem.

"A group of rebels have started a coup," he said. "What will the attitude
of the U.S. Government be in this matter?"

"It's half-past four in the morning in Washington," said Lodge. "It's impossible for me to get any opinion from our government at this hour. I am
concerned for your safety."

The insurgents had relayed to Lodge a promise of safe-conduct out of
Viet Nam for Diem and Nhu.

"I offer you the good offices of the U.S. Government for your protection,"

352 Lodge told Diem. "I will provide you asylum in my residence. I can provide air passage outside the country. The generals running the coup have promised me their cooperation."

This was not at all what Diem had in mind. "I shall do what duty and good sense indicate must be done," Diem replied stiffly. "I am going to try to restore order." He hung up.

After that, Lodge relates, "the shooting went on and on. It got closer and closer. I didn't know how long it would go on. I decided the sensible thing for me to do was to try to get a little sleep. I had a very dependable man in Mike Dunn who would wake me if necessary. About nine o'clock I said, 'I'm going to take a little nap. You wake me up if you think you should.' I slept for three or four hours. The shooting began tapering off around 3 A.M. Around 4, I was standing on my second-floor portico when I saw a couple of my neighbors firing tracer bullets at each other from their houses up the street. Apparently they were using the coup to work off some private grudge. Next day I got word that Diem and Nhu had tried to escape, and had been captured and then killed. I was terribly shocked, and terribly sorry that Diem had not accepted American protection."

General Don called on Lodge with General Le Van Kim, to ask that American aid be started up again. "I stressed the importance of getting on with the war, and of no more persecutions," Lodge recalled. "I insisted that there be no reprisals against Christians for the recent oppression of Buddhists." The generals agreed, and Lodge agreed to resume all aid which had been curtailed.

In those crisis-ridden days, Lodge's lean, energetic figure and his rugged, determined face became again as familiar to millions of Americans as they had been in his years tilting with the Communists at the U.N. There had been a tendency, particularly among men who did not know him, to regard him as a sort of matinee-idol dunderhead. Keyes Beech, Chicago *Daily News* correspondent, termed Lodge an accomplished "switch-blade fighter" and quoted one "longtime U.S. official" in Saigon: "My picture of Lodge before he came out here was of a great big handsome zero. I soon changed my mind. That guy can be as tough and mean as they come."

U.S.I.S. Chief Mecklin, later writing his own impressions of Lodge at this time, says: "I was often struck by the contrast between his bearing in small, give-and-take gatherings, where he appeared bored and uncomfortable, and the way he behaved on a public platform. When the floor was his, even without prepared remarks, he was one of the most articulate men I had known. He could deliver his thoughts—and they were almost always penetrating thoughts—in succinct, often colorful language, with the polished manner of a professional orator. It verged on charism. His cables to

Washington, the few I saw, were written with exceptional literary persua-   353
siveness.

"In the barracuda world of government service, Lodge's protective shell
was an invaluable asset, enabling him to operate as he thought best with
serene ruthlessness—which is exactly what it often requires to get anything
done in the government. Right or wrong, he knew what he wanted. He
crushed the spirits of many of us, but he also disengaged the operations
of the U.S. Mission from the endless, agonized soul-searchings that prevailed before his arrival. He was a commander by instinct, in a situation
where resolute commanders had been hard to come by. Lodge expected to
be judged on performance, not on the affection of his staff."

In Washington the Democratic bureaucrats also began to discover some
unsuspected qualities in Lodge. "Praise of his performance before, during
and after the coup is well-nigh unanimous among our sources here,"
a *Time* correspondent memoed to his home office. "Contrary to normal practice, he has apparently been writing many of the cables from the Embassy
himself, in a succinct, lucid, clear-minded style that officials have learned
to recognize as the Ambassador's own. His reporting, highly accurate and
grounded upon a tough-minded analysis of what the U.S. wants and can
realistically expect in Viet Nam, has been much appreciated here. His personal performance on the diplomatic beat, sources say admiringly, has
been superb. From this poor perspective, it looks as if he has completely
absorbed Saigon press corps criticism of the Embassy. 'He looks very big
and tall right now,' one D.O.S. source states. His welcome at the White
House is certain to be a warm one."

Lodge, whose return had been delayed by the coup, was tentatively
scheduled to go on to Washington after a big strategy powwow on Viet
Nam which was held in Honolulu later in November. McNamara and Taylor again flew out, this time accompanied by Secretary of State Rusk, Presidential adviser McGeorge Bundy, his brother William Bundy (who later
took over the Viet Nam desk at State), and Foreign Aid Director David E.
Bell. Lodge and Admiral Felt discussed with them the whole post-coup
situation. McNamara was still hopeful that he could withdraw several
hundred U.S. servicemen from Viet Nam at the end of 1965, as he and
Taylor had predicted after their visit. Lodge set them straight. The situation was worse than anybody had realized. Diem and Nhu had told them
great stories of their success in fortifying some 219 settlements into so-
called strategic hamlets, stockades defended by armed militia. Many of
these hamlets had existed only on paper. In those that did exist, morale
was so bad that within two weeks of the coup, the militia in 169 hamlets
simply laid down their arms and refused to fight any more.

Such were the problems confronting the powwow in Honolulu.

It was agreed to step up economic and arms aid to Big Minh's new regime, in the hope of reversing the deterioration which had begun with the first attacks on the Buddhists in May. Rusk's party took off for Tokyo on another mission.

Suddenly word came of President Kennedy's assassination in Dallas.

Rusk's plane turned back in mid-flight. Lodge, shocked and saddened, made his Washington journey, not, as he had thought, to see Kennedy, but to say a silent prayer at his bier. He then consulted with the new President, Lyndon Johnson, whom he had long known in the Senate. They had managed to fight each other, for Vice President, on terms of mutual respect. Johnson also remembered gratefully how, after he had addressed the U.N. in 1958, Lodge had written Eisenhower praising his effectiveness. Now Johnson told Lodge how glad he was to have him in Saigon, and that he would depend upon whatever he advised.

While in Washington, Lodge also telephoned General Eisenhower at Gettysburg to pay his respects. He flew back to Saigon, concerned only with trying to get the fight against the Viet Cong back on the track and better organized. Nothing was farther from his thoughts than U.S. domestic politics. Lodge, at sixty-one, considered that he had run his last political race. He had had all he wanted of the Senate; if there were any more such races, his son George could make them, as he had done in 1962 when he did try but lost to Edward Kennedy. As he looked back upon his years, Lodge's chief feeling was that he had managed to live a life that had been full of challenge and responsibility. He so regarded his task in Viet Nam—onerous, dangerous, but stimulating and rewarding because it challenged all his skills and strengths. His motivations, now as before, were those that had become almost old-fashioned in American life, but which the men at West Point had recognized in citing him as exemplifying their unashamed dedication to duty, honor, country.

CHAPTER SEVENTEEN

What in God's name has happened to the Republican Party? —Lodge
to Osborn Elliott of *Newsweek* at the 1964 Republican convention.

That December of 1963, Felix Belair of the Washington bureau of the New
York *Times* went up to Gettysburg for a long chat with his old friend
Dwight D. Eisenhower ("I've always been fond of old Felix"). Eisenhower
talked about Republican Presidential possibilities. He said several good men
were qualified and expressed a hope that all of them would begin discussing
and debating Republican policies in the months ahead.

He talked a good deal about Lodge. He said he hoped that Lodge would
leave his post in Viet Nam and come back to participate in the discussion
of issues. He hoped that Lodge would do this in time to speak in Eisenhower's place on a closed-circuit forum of national Republican leaders
which had been scheduled for Lincoln's birthday. "I think they should all
talk common sense," Belair recalled Eisenhower saying. "If Lodge comes
back it will quickly become apparent that he talks more common sense than
anyone."

Eisenhower did not allow all this to be quoted, but the *Times* on Sunday
December 8 gave its page one lead story to the fact that Eisenhower wanted
Lodge to return to be a candidate. Two days later Richard Nixon hurried
down to Gettysburg to blunt the force of this endorsement. Eisenhower, apparently embarrassed, claimed he had been misquoted, but this, of course,
impugned the accuracy of his friend Belair. Eisenhower quickly wrote
Belair an apology for even implying any misquotation. Whether Eisenhower had done it calculatedly or not remains a mystery.

In any case, Lodge had assumed that his political career was over, and
felt that he could not leave Viet Nam at a time when new coups were being
rumored every day. Lodge himself tended to underestimate the tremendous
reservoir of political recognition and popularity which he had acquired
during the year-in-year-out televising of his confrontations with the Communists in the U.N. The Republican pros were even more unaware of
Lodge's tremendous popular appeal.

The first tangible symptoms of this popularity emerged when some amateur supporters of Lodge distributed 33,000 postcard ballots on outward-
bound New Haven commuter trains on the afternoon of December 23. A
surprising 12 per cent of the ballots were returned, and showed Lodge polling not only a majority of all votes, but more than the votes of Goldwater,
Rockefeller, Nixon, Romney and Scranton combined.

356   Lodge was busy with other things. He got word on January 29, 1964 that a new coup would take place the following day. It did. Pudgy, goateed little General Nguyen Khanh, commanding at the northern coastal city of Hué, capital of the ancient kingdom of Annam, came down and put Big Minh and Don and Kim under arrest. Shortly after, Khanh released Big Minh and made him a figurehead chief of state.

Lodge struck up an immediate rapport with the diminutive Khanh, who barely came up to his neck. The very morning of the second coup he breakfasted with Khanh at Colonel Dunn's apartment. "They hit it off well and immediately," Dunn recalled, "strange as the combination looks from afar, Lodge's French was a help—they seldom if ever spoke English together, and Khanh was always much more at home in French. Lodge's principal advantage with Khanh was his impressive credentials as a politician. Khanh was eager for practical advice in politics." As it turned out, he would need more advice than Lodge could give; he would be the first of a long succession of chiefs who would try, unsuccessfully, to achieve a stable government for beleaguered Saigon. However, Khanh tried hard. Lodge urged him to go to the people, to build grass-roots support, to make radio "fireside chats." Lodge patiently listened and gave him pointers on radio techniques. Khanh began going out among the people more than previous leaders had done, and shaking hands like any American congressman running for reelection.

Lodge also devoted a good deal of time and attention to the Venerable Tri Quang, the Buddhist leader who had taken asylum in the Embassy during Nhu's raids on the pagodas. Lodge, at President Kennedy's instructions, had steadfastly refused Nhu's repeated demands to surrender the Venerable Quang, who as much as any man had precipitated Nhu's and Diem's eventual downfall. This made Lodge something of a hero among the Buddhist leaders, who now became the most important single political force. His awareness of Buddhism, through his family, gave him perhaps a better insight into the Buddhist mental process than most Americans. One observer of that time felt that Lodge's good relations with the Buddhists helped stave off attacks on the new regime.

Nor did he neglect the Catholics, the second most important political force, and previously the chief source of Diem's power. He established close liaison with Bishop Asta, the Apostolic delegate. Bishop Asta and Khanh sometimes met together at Lodge's residence. Such meetings helped avert Catholic demonstrations which at that time were threatened against the Buddhist Khanh's rule.

Lodge was widely admired throughout Saigon. He struck everyone who saw him as a man who had absolutely no fear of the physical danger which was constantly around him. How close it could be was brought home in

May, 1964, when the U.S. Navy brought in the U.S.S. *Card,* an aircraft   357
transport to ferry home helicopters, and thoughtlessly anchored it right by
the opening of one of Saigon's sewers which empty into the Saigon River.
It was child's play for a Viet Cong to creep through the sewer and place
a plastic-explosive charge which blew open the *Card* and sank it in the
river. Next day Lodge went down to look over the damage and had just
walked away when a bomb was thrown into the crowd, killing two persons
and injuring eight others. It was clearly intended for Lodge.

On McNamara's next visit, when Lodge met him at the airport, he took
bullet-proof vests in the car, to bolster the floor against possible mines. Remembering Eisenhower's security advice for Khrushchev, that the surest
security is a last-minute change of route, he brought McNamara in from
the airport by a little-used route, and had an identical car take the usual
way. This car intercepted a Viet Cong agent who had placed a charge to
blow up the bridge over which the car would pass. The guards spotted and
caught another Viet Cong in a window, prepared to heave a grenade as the
Ambassadorial party passed beneath.

Lodge repeatedly subjected himself to risks as being simply hazards of
his profession. One day, with Dunn, he borrowed an old car and with two
Vietnamese for guides drove down some twenty miles south to Long An,
through territory infested with Viet Cong. Vietnamese commanders offered
him an armored car for escort. Lodge knew that this would just make an
ambush almost certain. He knew also that the Viet Cong molested only
official-looking cars, and not battered old jobs. He cannily chose a beat-
up old car, and made the trip without incident. On the way back, two armored cars were forced on him as escort. As soon as he put Long An behind, he signaled to the escort to pull over, got out and thanked them, and
sent them home. He proceeded back to Saigon unescorted and undisturbed.

He repeatedly made such trips into the field. He visited the Cao Dai Sect
in Tay Ninh, the Hoa Cao Sect in An Giang. He made numerous trips
with Khanh himself in the old two-engined DC-3 assigned to the Embassy.
On one trip back with Khanh, one of the engines failed while they were
over Communist-infested territory. Lodge scarcely paid any attention as
the remaining engine strained to get them safely home.

"If physical danger had any effect on him," Dunn recalled, "the effect
was exhilaration. There were constant assassination threats. I can see him
sitting at his desk with a pistol in the drawer, and a heavy Magnum in the
open safe. He used to talk about defending the Chancery as enthusiastically as a Knight of St. John."

Meanwhile, events at home began thrusting Lodge, without the slightest
encouragement from him, into the center of the political spotlight. With
their habitual astigmatism, Republican pros had not even discussed him as

358　a possibility. Dr. George Gallup, supposed expert on what the public is thinking, had not even listed Lodge's name on popularity polls. He believed, as he explained to one inquirer, "I can't imagine anyone could possibly be interested in Lodge." He was wrong, and so were the pros.

In January, 1964, a group of Boston political amateurs headed by Paul Grindle, forty-three, launched a campaign for a Lodge write-in vote in the New Hampshire Presidential primary of March 14. He was joined by David Goldberg, thirty-four, who had worked with him in the unsuccessful campaign of George Lodge, Cabot's oldest son, against Edward Kennedy, the President's youngest brother, in the 1962 Senate race. This primary, first in the nation, and the one which had set Eisenhower's candidacy in motion, is highly important for any Presidential aspirant to win. Consequently, both Nelson Rockefeller and Barry Goldwater were spending weeks on end stumping from one New Hampshire hamlet to another. Both spent tens of thousands of dollars on radio and TV broadcasts, pamphlets, billboards, and hiring local campaign workers. Rockefeller's grin and outstretched hand became so ubiquitous in New Hampshire that they became the subject of a *New Yorker* cartoon.

Grindle and Goldberg had no funds but their own, and only the hope to raise more. They rented an empty storefront in Concord, New Hampshire's sleepy capital. They were chiefly assisted by Sally Saltonstall, the senator's niece, and Grindle's wife, plus M. Richard Jackman, president of the large Rumford Press of Concord (which prints the *Reader's Digest*). Jackman agreed to head their write-in slate of fourteen candidates for delegate to the Republican Convention. The odds against this small band were almost insuperable. A write-in vote for Lodge and Lodge delegates was complex and difficult to make. Almost all of New Hampshire's top Republicans were running as delegates for either Rockefeller or Goldwater. Their own candidates were total political unknowns.

Yet, on the night of March 14, as returns began to pour into the New Hampshire Highway Hotel where election headquarters had been set up by all the managers, and for the press and TV, it became clear that the seemingly impossible had indeed happened. An incredible 33,007 voters had written in Lodge's name while only 20,692 had marked the regular ballot for Goldwater, 19,504 for Rockefeller; another 15,587 had written in Richard Nixon. Suddenly, Lodge, the supposed political has-been, was leading the whole field. And he had not lifted a finger in his own behalf.

As the Tuesday returns came in, it was already Wednesday forenoon in Saigon. Lodge was on his way north in a plane with Defense Secretary McNamara and Joint Chiefs Chairman Taylor (back for another visit), and Premier Khanh, for an inspection at Hué. On the way Lodge recounted an amusing tale. One sunny day in December he and Emily took a stroll

through the Saigon Zoological Garden with Emily's niece, Emily Alexander. They stopped to admire a magnificent male tiger. Suddenly, without
warning, it sprayed Lodge in the face, splashing his niece and his white
shirt. After the first surprise, he began to laugh uproariously. Solemnly, a
Vietnamese came up to tell him: "There is no better sign of good fortune,
in our country, than for a living man to be urinated on by a tiger. Tigers
usually do this on the body of a man they have just killed."

At the story, McNamara's press aide, Arthur Sylvester, observed: "You
can clearly claim to be the only Presidential candidate in history to have
been pissed on by a tiger." "That might be a slogan worth remembering,"
laughed Lodge. Neither Lodge, Sylvester nor anyone else had the slightest
inkling that he had just won the primary in a write-in landslide without
precedent in U.S. political history. When they landed at Hué it was raining
heavily. Lodge was hardly noticeable as McNamara shouted victory slogans
to a tremendous, surging crowd of soaking-wet but enthusiastic Vietnamese. Lodge sat quietly in the background of the stand. Not until they were
boarding the plane for the return to Saigon did a captain in the crew slip
him the message, which he read without a sign of emotion. Now the
startling news spread quickly. Just before landing, Khanh asked him, smiling, "When you're the President of the U.S., will you come back and visit
us again?" Lodge simply grinned. When they landed, reporters and photographers ignored McNamara and Taylor, clustered about Lodge for comment. He merely said, "It was a great honor and a great compliment, but
Foreign Service regulations preclude my commenting on political matters.
I have no thought of resigning my post."

Three days after the primary, over a light breakfast at the El Dorado country club in Palm Desert, California, former President Eisenhower told a
visitor that the surprise Lodge victory reminded him of his own in the
Minnesota primary in 1952. He said he was in almost the same situation
then as Cabot now, in France directing SHAPE just as Lodge was out in
Viet Nam. When admirers in Minnesota tried to enter his name as a write-
in, Lodge and all the rest said, "For God's sake don't enter any primary in
Minnesota," thinking it would be fatal to have a failure there. "But a couple
of fellows out there," Ike recalled, "Bradshaw Mintener was one, and the
Governor, thought it was damned important and said, 'We're going to defy
the whole organization and start a program anyhow.'" In spite of Stassen
being the favorite son, Ike got something like 120,000 write-in votes. That
clinched Ike's determination to come home and run.

Eisenhower discussed Lodge's deep sense of public service. He felt that
Lodge was tremendous in the United Nations—his mental agility, astute-
ness, and his understanding of the Communists had been a great asset **to**

360   the U.S. Ike's face took on a look of remembered admiration, as for a great golf game or any exhibition of excellence: "Old Cabot, you know, as Vishinsky or whoever would finish, old Cabot would get up and give 'em what for, and of course I liked that very much."

He recalled that he was considering Lodge for the top White House job that he later gave to Sherman Adams. He was particularly interested in him because Lodge understood the Army's staff system of operating, as few civilians did. He had as well the political savvy, from his work in the Senate, not to rub anybody the wrong way, and the knowledge of Congress. Ike thought he would have been very good in the job: "I always found him a keen observer and a man who had a helluva fund of common sense." He added that he so respected his work that he gave him a position right after the Secretary of State in Cabinet protocol. He did not think Lodge could be labeled, any more than himself, as either a liberal or a conservative. He recalled Bob Taft coming to see him to espouse three things—higher old age pensions, public housing, and federal aid to education—all of which Eisenhower opposed, and Eisenhower told him that he was puzzled that Taft, a supposed conservative, was favoring things that he, Eisenhower, a supposed liberal, opposed; it made Eisenhower seem far more conservative than Taft. Taft explained that the pressure for federal intervention was so great that one had to find a line he could defend—like a military commander. Eisenhower cried he was three times as conservative as Taft, and Taft, laughing, replied: "It's the newspapermen who pin the labels on you." By the same token, it was a mistake to label Lodge, who would support what he thought was right, on a pragmatic basis.

After Lodge's surprise victory, the pros had begun to whisper that he had "laid down" on the 1960 Vice Presidential campaign, and had slept every afternoon instead of going out to shake all the hands the local leaders wanted him to shake. Eisenhower expressed surprise at such talk. "It certainly wasn't true when he was campaigning for me. Nobody worked any harder." He reflected on the view of some Republicans that Lodge was a maverick. Eisenhower did not think that was just. "He's been a damned good Republican all the time I've known him."

Eisenhower cited Lodge's leadership in the 1952 battle for the Texas delegation as evidence of his moral courage. He could have compromised but refused to do so. The General quoted him as saying, "We are dealing with a simple question of the right and we won't compromise it." Of course, Eisenhower said, he could have lost everything. If the Convention had seated the whole Texas delegation it would have been a very close thing. This refusal showed Lodge's power of decision, and the courage to make difficult decisions.

Asked if Lodge would make a good President, Eisenhower saw no reason why he would not. He felt that he was so intelligent that he would get top men around him; the stronger a man is the stronger the assistants he can afford to have. He would have the strength to make his own decisions. He felt that Lodge had the three things any successful executive most needed: the courage of his convictions, the ability to recognize good people, surround himself with them, and listen to them; and a large element of humility, so that power would not go to his head.

"Cabot has all those things. He has always been a very valuable public servant. He has moral courage. He is always ready to listen to others. He is able to inspire others."

Eisenhower was determined, however, to support no single Republican above any other. Just as he had felt that it detracted from the Presidency for him ever to bring any pressure on Congress, so he seemed to feel that his unique role as public hero No. 1 precluded him from favoring any citizen above another. He was not yet aware that power, if left unused, tends to evaporate.

Off in Viet Nam, Lodge was unimpressed by any talk of his chances. "My position is so simple," he told *Time*'s Frank McCullough right after the primary, "I can't get anyone to believe it. I am not a candidate. I say without qualification that I have no intention of returning home to become a candidate. I can say with equal certitude that I have a big job to do here, and I intend to stay here and do it, period."

Even as he spoke, pollsters were detecting the same kind of groundswell for Lodge in Oregon, whose primary, to be held on May 10, was the next in importance. The admiration for this tough, duty-minded Republican was not simply a phenomenon local to his native New England. It was clearly national. It began to swell, too, in California, whose crucial primary would be June 1. At the New York World's Fair, the tabloid *Daily News* set up a battery of six voting machines, with signs inviting each day's visitors to vote for the Republican they would most prefer as Presidential nominee. From the first day, Lodge not only led the entire field, but his majority was greater than that of all other possible candidates combined. The same unmistakable clear showing began appearing in all the published national polls. Not only was Lodge the favorite, but he was clearly considered the Republican with the best chance of beating Johnson in November. As Walter Straley, president of Pacific Northwest Bell Telephone, put it in Seattle: "There is a general hunger throughout the country for a man that we are quite certain we can be proud of. I rather think that people are looking for a kind of impeccable background that represents a sort of dignity and a solid stable reputation that they can count on—and I think Lodge epitomizes that." One remark often heard was, "Lodge really *looks* like a President." The magnetism of his aloof appeal was nowhere reflected

362   more vividly than in John Mecklin's subsequent recollection that even those in the Saigon U.S. Mission who resented Lodge's methods were surprised to find their "resentment . . . mixed with reluctant admiration . . . some of the same officials whom he had outraged incredulously found themselves tempted to vote for this enigmatic man if he became a candidate."

In far-off Denver, *Time*'s Barron Beshoar found that many people saw in Lodge the same style they found in Kennedy—cultured background, wealth, urbanity, grace and charm. "He has a tremendous appeal for women," a Denver sales executive, William Van Voast Warren, Jr., told Beshoar. "But both sexes like him. When you look at him you can't help liking and respecting him. We are getting static from the pros who complain that he was a little flat in the 1960 campaign, but he wasn't running for the first place. He is just not a second place man. He is too much of an aristocrat for that." Mort Stern, editor of the Denver *Post's* editorial page, found "a lot of enthusiasm for Lodge among younger people of the type who organized for Eisenhower in 1952." F. W. Baumgartner, of the Baumgartner Oil Co., mailed a random sampling to Denver Republican and independent voters, and got back a tally of 40.1 per cent for Lodge, 10.7 per cent for Nixon, 8 per cent for Goldwater, 7.9 per cent for Rockefeller and 6 per cent for Scranton. Another Denver group sampling 208 persons found 138 for Lodge, 22 for Nixon, 20 for Rockefeller, 16 for Scranton and 12 for Goldwater. Yet, not least curious of the many anomalies of American politics, 14 of the state's Republican delegates were already lined up for Goldwater. Lodge had nobody for him but the people. In the Illinois primary in April, only Margaret Chase Smith opposed Goldwater on the ballot. She received a protest vote of 26 per cent from rank-and-file Republicans who did not want Goldwater. More significantly, without any campaign whatever in Lodge's behalf, 5.9 per cent of the voters wrote in his name on the ballot. All other write-ins combined, in this Republican heartland, totaled only 3.4 per cent for Nixon, Rockefeller, Romney and Scranton.

By April, it was clear that Lodge was far away the most popular single Republican, not only with rank-and-file members, but with independents and Democrats as well. Only a man who could appeal heavily to both independents and swing-Democrats could possibly have a chance against Johnson in November. Had Lodge been able to come home—something his sense of duty precluded—a great popular tide was ready to rise for him. In California, the Mervin Field poll, pitting various Republicans against Johnson, showed Lodge tops with 38 per cent of the votes, Nixon with 26 per cent, Rockefeller with 24 per cent, Goldwater with 23 per cent, Scranton and Romney with 21 per cent each. He was already the clear favorite in the forthcoming May 10 primary in Oregon.

However, popularity and potential votes were all that Lodge had. With   363
the inevitability of lemmings racing to the sea to drown themselves, one
after another Republican city and county machine was methodically choosing delegates pledged to Barry Goldwater, who totally lacked appeal to independents and to Democrats, and appealed only to the most extreme right-
wing splinter of the Republican Party itself. When it became clear Lodge
would not come home, enough of his supporters switched to Rockefeller in
Oregon for him to win the primary.

As for California, the rules of its primary had precluded the entry of
Lodge's name: the many thousands who wished to vote for him had only
Goldwater and Rockefeller to choose between. They preferred Rockefeller
to Goldwater, but without enthusiasm. A perverse fate decreed that Rockefeller's baby by his new wife should be born the same weekend as the primary, adding to the alienation which his divorce had already created
among many women voters. With thousands of Lodge supporters simply
failing to vote, Goldwater nosed ahead to win the California primary and
with it the almost certain nomination. With that, even if Lodge did come
back, it was too late to help himself. Indeed it was doubtful that, at this
late date, he could help anyone.

Eisenhower had hesitated until it was too late for him to help anyone
stop Goldwater. In June a desperate effort began to build a last-minute
drive for Governor William Scranton of Pennsylvania. Even then, Eisenhower, after having encouraged Scranton to make the race, failed to give
his open blessing. At the Governors' Conference in Cleveland he allowed
George Humphrey, the ultraconservative who had always wielded the greatest influence in his Cabinet, to persuade him to withhold his support for
Scranton. Everywhere, Republicans who felt that a Goldwater candidacy
would spell disaster, if not doom, for a Republican Party already a minority,
felt as if they were caught up in an ineluctable Greek tragedy with a fore-
doomed conclusion.

In Viet Nam, a young captain who was a battalion adviser to the Vietnamese, accosted Lodge in Saigon one day. "Sir," he said, "aren't you going
back to help Scranton?" The question troubled Lodge. He began to feel
that, with events having foreclosed any possible charge of his seeking to
serve his own interests, perhaps his greatest duty just then did lie in trying
to save the party which he had served all his life.

These feelings were strengthened by the fact that Emily's health began
to be affected by the terrible unrelieved heat and humidity of the climate.
She began running persistent temperatures in the afternoons. The doctor
said Emily ought not to stay there much longer. Lodge advised Washington
privately that he would like to come home as soon as it could find a satisfactory replacement.

364   Had there been any doubt that Lodge was occupying the nation's most important outpost, the reaction of the Cabinet to his news was sufficient evidence. Secretary of State Rusk was the first to volunteer to take his place. Secretary of Defense McNamara also volunteered. So did the late President's brother, Attorney General Robert Kennedy. So also did the President's chief assistant on foreign affairs, McGeorge Bundy. In the end the President called on General Taylor, the chairman of the Joint Chiefs of Staff, to take on what Max Frankel of the *Times* termed "the most difficult, delicate and potentially dangerous outpost of [U.S.] diplomacy." To assist him, Johnson reached into the highest echelons of State, where Deputy Under Secretary U. Alexis Johnson was the chief link between the separate mazes of military and intelligence commands, to ask Johnson to go to Saigon in the almost unprecedented role of Deputy Ambassador. Perhaps it was a compliment to Lodge that two of the top professionals of Army and State were both needed to take his place.

Lodge greeted his successors and saw them properly installed and briefed before taking his own farewell. Premier Khanh gave a formal reception in his honor, presenting him with South Viet Nam's highest civilian and military decorations—the Grand Cross of the National Order and the Cross of Gallantry. Almost dwarfed by the towering Ambassador, Khanh pinned these decorations upon him. Then he had a farewell gift brought in—the self-same carved wooden dragons, with elephant tusks, which graced the stairs of the Presidential Palace. Lodge gave his final press conference next day. Back home, Goldwater was sarcastically inviting him to "tell what went wrong in Viet Nam." "It's awfully nice of him to give me free advice," Lodge told the newsmen, "and his assignment, but I'm not accepting assignments from him and I don't accept his definition of what my duty ought to be."

He and Emily, accompanied by two puppies given to them as mementoes of South Viet Nam, drove out to the familiar Tan Son Nut Airport, to board the big KC-119 jet which had brought the new team to Saigon. A South Vietnamese honor guard and military band were lined up in his honor. A Buddhist delegation and all the leading Buddhist monks had come to bid him goodbye as did leading Catholics. Lodge paid his farewell respects to the gallant struggle of Viet Nam's people; Premier Khanh paid him a last, eloquent tribute—then unrolled still another surprise. He unfolded the blue silk tunic of an *ao dai*, the traditional robe in Viet Nam of a man of learning—"a worthy man"—and stood on tiptoe to drape it about Lodge's shoulders. He then placed atop Lodge's steel-gray hair the small black turban which accompanies it. Khanh then unrolled a scroll appointing Lodge an honorary citizen of South Viet Nam. The band struck up "The Star-

Spangled Banner." Lodge stood at attention, and remained so as it played
the South Vietnamese national anthem. Then, handing Emily inside, he
stooped to enter the great windowless tube, whose door was locked behind
him. As the big jet whined to crescendo and slowly rolled away, a sea of
waving hands saluted the man the shouting crowd could no longer see. It
lifted into the sky and toward home.

On his sixty-second birthday, July 5, Lodge left his Beverly home, after
a few days rest, to fly to Harrisburg, Pennsylvania, to take up the cudgels
for Governor Scranton for the Republican nomination. Arthur Godfrey
loaned Lodge his private plane for the flight. Scranton greeted him, and
the two appeared on TV together, addressed a rally at the airport, and flew
on to Chicago for a second one. Lodge left Scranton there and proceeded to
Wichita, trying to save part of the Kansas delegation from Goldwater. He
went on to St. Louis, to work on a couple of wavering Missouri delegates.

It was all too late. In a gloomy mood, Lodge flew on to San Francisco,
the Convention city.

On Wednesday, July 8, Lodge made an appearance in a familiar role.
He addressed the platform committee, which sixteen years before he had
headed. Once he had drafted the party's platform—a far-sighted, progressive program to bring his party abreast of the twentieth century and a
shrinking world. Now he was vainly fighting to save even a shred of this
viewpoint from a party leadership turned suddenly atavistic and savagely
reactionary. "He was brief," reported *Time*'s John Steele, "and very able in
his presentation. When he finished he drew a thirty-second standing ovation. He started out by declaring that 'having renounced all personal ambition for future political office, I talk to you here with really complete
frankness.'" Steele wrote:

> *Towering over the microphones and with his hair newly trimmed, he
> read a statement he had started to dictate in his Embassy in Saigon
> and then hacked away at with a lead pencil at his Beverly home over
> the July 4 weekend.*
>
> *It was keyed to a challenge: that of making the Republican Party a
> viable instrument for dealing with today's problems. It didn't mention
> Goldwater by name, but it consciously sought to draw a contrast
> with Goldwater's image.*
>
> *With 60% of Americans living in great urban areas, "we have not
> done enough about traffic congestion and the breakdown of mass
> transportation systems, about crime and juvenile delinquency." Then,
> quoting Bob Taft, Cabot said that unemployment had been fostered by*

"a fundamental failure to do enough in the field of education . . . disgraceful inadequacy at elementary and high school levels, and there is an unpardonable denial of opportunity to youth."

Then, in a neat kicker on the domestic front, he proposed a Republican-sponsored Marshall Plan for our cities and schools, much as Republicans in 1947 had backed the Marshall Plan for Europe's reconstruction.

"No one in his right mind would today argue that there is no place for the Federal government in the reawakening of America. Indeed, we need another Republican-sponsored Marshall Plan for our cities and schools. . . . Republicans must be the true conservatives who distinguish between conserving and hoarding and who know that it is possible to conserve when we are willing to innovate and to give every American citizen a chance by his own efforts to have something which he too will want to conserve.

"True conservatism starts a chain reaction of progress, which makes our system work—both our free economic system and our free governmental system. Both must be the instruments of change—of continuing peaceful evolution. Failure in this process causes people to turn to some kind of absolutism for bringing about the changes which they properly consider necessary."

Lodge, wrote Steele, was "emerging as the single happy warrior at the convention thus far." But he got nowhere with the platform committee.

Lodge came away from the committee to hold a news conference. He was hunting for some issue, like the Texas steal in 1952, to take the psychological advantage away from Goldwater and turn the tide toward Scranton. During his news conference, he spotted one such issue. The Boston *Globe*'s bright young political reporter, James Doyle, thrust the morning's New York *Times* at Lodge, with passages underlined in an article by Charles Mohr quoting an interview Goldwater had given to the West German news magazine *Der Spiegel*:

With all due respect to American military leaders, Germany would have won both World Wars if she had not been badly led.

De Gaulle should be supported in the development of French nuclear weapons.

"If necessary" Goldwater would favor using nuclear weapons to support anti-Soviet uprisings in Eastern Europe.

On each of the three points, Doyle questioned Lodge. Regarding military leadership, the old armored officer bristled. "I have great admiration for

General Marshall and General Eisenhower—Bradley, Devers and the
others. Such a statement rather runs down the role of American leadership." On nuclear arming of de Gaulle, Lodge snapped that a proliferation of nuclear weapons would be "an unmitigated calamity." On the use of such weapons, Lodge said it was "such a serious matter" that he wouldn't, in fairness to Goldwater, want to discuss it without seeing the full text. He added that Goldwater's remarks would make it certain that delegates would do "a great deal of soul-searching" before balloting, and that he sensed "a deep-seated worry" about assuring that there would be "a prudent, cautious man in the White House." The reporters found his flank attack sharp and telling, and filed columns on it; the delegates could not have cared less.

The more Lodge sought to win over delegates, the more he was startled by the change which had come over his familiar party, in its capture, at the local and state levels, by the Goldwater forces. Lodge had attended every party convention since 1924 (save 1944 when he was in combat). Now he felt himself among strangers.

Osborn Elliott, editor of *Newsweek,* visiting Lodge in his St. Francis Hotel suite, found him leafing through the roll of rank-and-file delegates. "What in God's name has happened to the Republican Party?" Lodge lamented. "I hardly know any of these people!" A party captured by unknowns was determined to nominate a man who cheerfully confessed to having a second-class mind.

Among those who should have been providing leadership to the party, there had been a failure all down the line. Rockefeller, with millions at his command, had done virtually nothing, a year or two before when headway could have been made, to win over the Southern delegations before Goldwater and his oil-millionaire friends got to them. Eisenhower had teetered and tottered in a magnificent display of nonleadership; a *Times* typographical error aptly called him "Eisenhowever."

Nixon, who could have fought Goldwater effectively, had cannily held off in the hope of a deadlock that would win him the compromise nomination. In Mid-June Nixon momentarily came to life, told the Governors' Conference in Cleveland "it would be a tragedy" for the Party to turn sharp right with Goldwater. But a fortnight before the convention, Nixon had phoned former National Chairman Len Hall to agree that Scranton wasn't getting off the ground and that Goldwater was a sure bet. Nixon asked Hall what he could do as titular leader to bring peace and harmony. Hall asked, "Dick, are you totally convinced now that you don't have a chance of getting this nomination?" Dick guessed he was. "Then," said Hall, "get Chairman Bill Miller to switch your appearance on the convention program. Forget your Tuesday speech before the balloting. Ask to be allowed to intro-

368 duce the nominee to the convention on Thursday." Nixon agreed. A friend called Miller, and it was done. The Nixon who flew into San Francisco that morning no longer thought Goldwater "a tragedy" but a man who would "have the largest and most enthusiastic supporters in Presidential history. . . . Despite the caricature in Europe we are not going to nominate some kind of nut . . . a wild man. . . ."

Eisenhower's total lack of leadership was even more pathetic. The man who became a candidate in 1952 to keep the Republican Party from being captured by the far Right seemed unaware that his inaction was now making a capture· inevitable. A hot-selling brochure of political satire at the convention depicted Ike as practicing "the Eisenhower Sway," to achieve which one must "carefully balance yourself, not incline to the left or the right. Sway back and forth. But end up in dead center." Ike described himself as "a politician emeritus" and played the nonrole to the hilt. His brother Milton would nominate Scranton; his former speech writer Malcolm Moos helped write the speech; son John was openly for Scranton.

Ike was for nobody.

He was simply a television commentator, and over ABC told Jim Hagerty and Bill Lawrence, about taking sides, "Personally, I think it would be completely inconsistent with all I have stood for for fourteen months. I have made it quite clear that I was hoping for a very healthy dialogue and debate among all of the leading figures in the Republican Party so that we could, if not achieve a consensus, certainly a broad understanding of Republican thinking . . . now as it happens things didn't develop the way I hoped they would . . . I may have made a mistake . . . when I decided to take this position . . . but in any event it is too late to change that . . . it would be completely a double-cross on my part to change that position. . . ."

When Ike addressed the convention Tuesday night, reading the speech he had written on his special train on the way out from Gettysburg, he himself seemed quite startled when he touched a raw nerve of the Goldwater zealots with a phrase which was almost a dependent clause of an incidental paragraph: "So let us scorn the divisive efforts of those outside our family, including sensation-seeking columnists and commentators . . ."

Ike could not finish the sentence. Almost to a man the delegates leaped to their feet in a roaring frenzy as they shook their fists at the press gallery. "We might get lynched before we get out of here," cracked Chicago *Daily News* reporter Bob Schultz. "We'll be using our pencils like swords to keep them off," said the *Herald Tribune*'s Douglas Kiker, slashing the air with his pencil. The ugly mood of delegates toward reporters that night helped build up an atmosphere which, culminating in the convention's booing of

New York's Governor Rockefeller, made the gathering more reminiscent of a Nuremberg rally of stormtroopers than the thoughtful deliberations of one of the two great parties of American democracy.

Lodge did not wait to witness Goldwater's nomination. He took an afternoon plane to Dallas, and spent the night in an airport motel so as to arrive next day in Boston at a decent hour.

During the ensuing campaign, Lodge devoted himself entirely to doing his best to elect the Massachusetts state ticket, and to help his brother John in his long-odds and unsuccessful campaign in Connecticut for Senator Thomas Dodd's Democratic seat. Lodge made four or five TV appearances on behalf of John Volpe, the former Republican governor of Massachusetts who was seeking a comeback, and for Edward Brooke, an attractive, magnetic candidate for Attorney General who happened also to be a Negro. Lodge had not been able to see a Negro put in the President's Cabinet, but he was able to help one sweep into the Attorney Generalship of Massachusetts. Volpe also was elected. They were two of the very few Republicans to win office in the crushing national defeat which was the most complete and devastating the party had ever suffered.

While the campaign was in progress, Lodge had occasion to go back to San Francisco, for a happier occasion than that of the frenzied Goldwater stampede. It was for the dinner of the Thomas A. Dooley Foundation, in honor of that selfless young doctor who had devoted his waning life to serving the homeless and the sick in Asia until shortly before cancer cut him down. In Dooley's honor, the Foundation had created an annual Splendid American award for Americans whose work had continued to give meaning to Dooley's own. Lodge had been chosen as the first recipient.

Peggy Lee, the singer and actress, who had taken a deep interest in the Foundation's work, read a number of remarks which had been made about Lodge, beginning with President Kennedy's of the year before ". . . he had strong feelings about the United States of America, and he put those ahead of any possible political advantage or consideration. . . ." She read President Johnson's at his resignation: "This nation has been most fortunate in having Lodge's distinguished and dedicated service in a post of vital importance in the past year."

Dr. Eugene Burdick, president of the Dooley Foundation, read telegrams of greeting from President Johnson, Pierre Salinger, Senator Jacob Javits, and a cable in French from the Vietnamese chief of state, General Duong van Minh: "This news rejoices all like me who have been witnesses to the constant efforts which you have deployed during your whole stay in Viet Nam for the amelioration of the conditions of life of the workers and particularly the rural peoples."

A message from Dr. Dooley's brother, Malcolm, was read: "It is impossible to find a man more alert to Dr. Tom's problems and loves than Ambassador Lodge. It is improbable that Americans will again have such a sensitive and responsible representative in Southeast Asia. Mr. Ambassador, I return to you the words you so beautifully stated at an honorary dinner for Dr. Tom in June, 1960—quoting Lincoln—you said, 'You are the better angel of our lives.' The appreciation, respect and the challenge of Dr. Tom are your gifts tonight. I believe and I know they are in good hands."

William J. Lederer, co-author with Dr. Burdick of *The Ugly American,* rose to present the award, a Steuben glass plaque. "This afternoon," he drawled, lighting his pipe, "a journalist nailed me and asked, 'Can you explain why Henry Cabot Lodge, who is the antithesis (get that, antithesis)—of what you and Bud Burdick wrote in *The Ugly American,* how come he is getting the Splendid American thing from you—out of your hands?' Now, if I can find a match, I'll tell you.

"First, it's necessary that you know what Bud and I meant by *The Ugly American,* who had a) integrity, and he went to Asia to help the United States to help the others to help themselves—with dignity. He was honest, this Ugly, and he reported what he looked at . . . exactly as he looked at it, even if it made him unpopular and he lost his job; b) he realized that a nation—and this is Asia and here also—is composed of many little people. And the Ugly American in this novel made it his business to see what their needs happened to be and to learn these needs from them directly by talking to them; c) he took steps to see that these fellows all over had their needs supplied—but on their own economic and technological level. And he was very modest, this Ugly. He volunteered for the job, and asked for nothing back, except for the satisfaction of doing the labor well.

"Now this Ugly is a sort of a kind, decent, effective (important, *effective!*) man. . . . He was a homely man but he was called 'Ugly' in contrast to the fancy-pants American, who spends most of his vitalities in cocktailing and maneuvering for the promotion of his own prestige . . . So you see . . . the Ugly American is really the Splendid American.

"Now, Tom Dooley was an Ugly American—the way we meant the expression. I knew him long and closely . . . in Laos and in Haiphong, and in Hanoi. . . . I loved him very much. He was one of the real Uglies, in the sense that we meant it—or shall I say that he was a Splendid Ugly? Now, Mr. Lodge over here is also a Splendid Ugly. He simply could not have obtained the knowledge, this understanding of the Vietnamese, without being, shall I say, a Tom Dooley Splendid Ugly, and digging deep into the heart and the small areas of Viet Nam.

"Some time back I was interviewing a large number of Vietnamese students from the plateau areas . . . a long haul from Saigon. None of them spoke English and I don't speak any Vietnamese. . . . One of the Vietnamese spoke Chinese . . . when he learned that I knew a little of it, he dragged out this [holding up a *Time*] this *Time* story on Lodge with his photo on it. And this Chinese-speaking Vietnamese kept pointing at that and saying, 'Oi yao dong pi tsa,' which means roughly 'I like that big-nosed foreigner.' [laughter.] And then he added, 'Ha po hi mung,' which means roughly, 'He gave us hope.'

"Now, at this moment, bless him, along came an American priest—a Father Murphy, from Boston—and standing in this group of Vietnamese was a Vietnamese priest. Father Murphy didn't understand any Vietnamese —but he went to the Vietnamese priest and spoke to him in Latin. The Vietnamese priest spoke to the Vietnamese in Vietnamese—and he spoke back to Father Murphy in Latin—who told me what they were trying to say. And in English, it went roughly like this:

" 'They say they like this man—*this* man [pointing to Lodge, amid applause] because even though he is important, he takes the trouble to find out what the villages need.' Father Murphy went on to say, 'They have high praise for three Americans—Lodge, Dooley, and Abraham Lincoln.' [Laughter and applause].

In responding, Lodge remarked that a man in politics seldom gets introduced in so flattering a way, and recalled a time when he was running for Senator and Leverett Saltonstall was running for Governor. Both arrived to speak at the same meeting, and the chairman began his introduction: "The man that I am about to introduce is a friend of the farmer, he's a friend of the laboring man, a friend of business and the professional man . . . a great expert on domestic questions . . . an authority on foreign affairs and national strategy, a great defender of the faith." The chairman then said, "Now which of you fellows wants to speak first?" As the audience laughed and applauded, he added: "So you see when I get grouped with Dr. Dooley and Abraham Lincoln, that's the kind of thing I'm not used to."

Lodge then became serious about the task in Asia:

"The men and women who worked for Dr. Dooley, and who are working now under his aegis, they live among the people . . . help them when they're sick. . . . They also train people, so that when the Americans leave, something durable is left behind. . . . We in the U.S. Government who have worked in Southeast Asia on the non-medical side, have learned much from Dr. Dooley—that in our work of pacification, of bringing in security, and law and order, we must never be content with hit-and-run tactics. But, like Dr. Dooley, we must always build something lasting—be it a citizen counter-terrorist committee in each precinct, or a village police force, or something which will then make it possible *immediately* to bring in medical aid and schools and agricultural help—which of course you

372 can't have as long as the terrorists dominate the community. Because all of us, in government and out, are, after all, trying to help the same man, and we must therefore consider the medical and the military, the psychological and the political, all together.

"Dr. Dooley's work, therefore, was not one of those gestures which are very nice but are really quite superficial. His work brought about irrevocable and permanent change for the better, and the Dooley Foundation carries on his work. . . . This work not only helps the sick of Asia, it helps America in *its* work of assisting these beleagured countries in Southeast Asia, especially Viet Nam, to achieve and then to maintain their independence.

"Now, why do we want to help Viet-Nam achieve and maintain its independence? . . . Let me give you a few fundamentals as to *why* Viet Nam is important and then a few thoughts as to *how* we can be successful there.

"Viet Nam stands at the hub of a vast area of the world, Southeast Asia, with a population of 240,000,000 people—extended 2,300 miles North to South, and 3,000 miles from East to West—farther than from here to Boston. The Mekong River, one of the ten largest rivers in the world, reaches the sea in South Viet Nam—and he who holds, or has influence in Viet Nam, can affect the future of the Philippines and Formosa, to the East; Thailand and Burma, with their huge rice surpluses, to the West; Malaysia and Indonesia with their rubber, oil and tin to the South. Japan would be deeply concerned. All this would affect Australia and New Zealand. It is part of a whole area where the Communists seek to undermine the Free World in order to spread their monolithic control and their suppression of freedom.

"In opposing this onslaught, much of the Free World has stood together for nearly two decades. One manifestation of our common determination to frustrate the Communist design to conquer Europe was the creation of NATO. This worldwide effort does not signify a desire to establish a new colonialism, or any kind of special position. The War of Viet Nam is not only the struggle of a small nation to exist, it is also an open encounter between the doctrine that Wars of Revolution, as the Communists call them, are the wave of the future, and our belief that, in the future, nations should be allowed to develop their own destinies, free from outside interference. . . .

"This effort has not been in vain. Although we are not yet victorious, much has been accomplished. *And they haven't won.* We haven't won but *they* haven't won. And sometimes I think we lose sight of that.

"We are learning by experience in a situation where Americans have no experience at all. We have to learn as we go. . . .

"Now, some have said, despite this effort, the war in Viet Nam can't be

won. Yet recent history shows that we have been fighting wars of this sort   373
for the past twenty years, and that the record is creditable. We, of the Free
World, won in Greece. We thwarted the Communist aggression in Korea.
We won in Malaya. We won in the Philippines. And we can win in Viet
Nam [applause].

"We must persist, and not play into the enemy's hands by counting on a
quick, sensational, easy way out, or by being discouraged. . . . *Of course,*
the problems are difficult. That's *why* we are needed. If the U.S. is going to
interest itself in nice, little, neat, quiet countries—which don't need our
help—and going to turn over all the rough places to the Communists—
we're very soon not going to have any place in the world at all. That isn't
my idea of America—and that isn't my idea of what it is to be a statesman
[applause]."

Looking out at some volunteer nurses who had been presented earlier in
the evening, Lodge added: "And all these splendid young Americans that
Dr. Chaney presented, that is precisely what America stands for—young
Americans who are willing to go into the tough places and the rough places,
where it's dangerous—because that's where we're needed, and that is what
we stand for [applause]. And that is why I'm convinced that the 'persistent
execution of the political and military plans that have been agreed to will
bring victory.' We must remember that these conflicts in far-off places are
precisely the ones which have often brought war and calamities to all of us.
Manchuria seemed far away in 1931. The subversion of Czechoslovakia by
Hitler seemed remote, in the United States, in 1938. Yet the result was an
untold outpouring of blood and treasure. Persistence and unity, in the face
of Communist pressure, have succeeded in Europe and in Southeast Asia—
and can succeed again."

CHAPTER EIGHTEEN

I know of no better way for a man to use his life than to spend it in the service of his fellow men. I know of no better way to serve our fellow man than in the halls of government. And I know of no public servant who has walked those halls more unselfishly than Henry Cabot Lodge.
—President Johnson, *in a toast to Lodge at a special dinner given in his honor at the White House on May 15, 1966.*

On his first day as the new White House press secretary, slender, black-haired Bill D. Moyers had some startling news to announce. Ambassador Maxwell Taylor, who had replaced Henry Cabot Lodge in Saigon a year before, had asked to be relieved. His successor would be Henry Cabot Lodge.

"The search for the best man . . . was neither very long nor very difficult," President Johnson explained later, "for the search led first to Ambassador Lodge. I thought he was the best equipped by training and by experience and by knowledge of conditions there. And when he was first asked, his first and immediate answer was, 'Yes, Mr. President.'"

The news broke on July 9, 1965. Six days later Lodge, though not yet confirmed or sworn as the new ambassador, flew to Saigon with Defense Secretary McNamara and General Earle Wheeler, Taylor's successor as chairman of the Joint Chiefs of Staff, to make an on-the-scene appraisal in Viet Nam. They conferred with Ambassador Taylor and Deputy Ambassador Johnson. Taylor, who had orginally agreed to serve only for a year, warmly welcomed his predecessor and old friend.

Lodge was heartened by the tremendous changes a year had brought. The biggest was that U.S. forces had dropped their "advisory" role and entered into the war as combat units. A few weeks before, McNamara had announced that twenty-one thousand new combat forces were being sent. Now the visitors saw the vanguard of these forces, some three thousand men, being unloaded at the huge new port of Camranh Bay which American bulldozers and construction crews were rearing overnight to handle the tremendous increase in men and materiel.

The sight brought back to Lodge memories of the enormous flood of men, guns, tanks and supplies that had poured in off the sea in the wake of our invasions of France. Watching the giant bulldozers slice hills into landing strips, and huge helicopters airlifting cranes and other heavy equipment, he was reminded of the awed observation of a witness to our Pacific landings: "To defeat the Japanese in the jungles, the Americans simply bulldozed the jungles away." He felt that he was witnessing, if not the beginning of the end of the attempted Communist seizure of South Viet Nam, at least the end of the beginning.

The Americans slogging into Camranh Bay, bringing the total U.S. forces in Viet Nam to 71,000 men, soon ended any hope the Communists had to cut South Viet Nam in two in the great 1965 monsoon offensive they had mounted to that end. A total of 25,000 Marines had already landed—since they first arrived in March—and were fanning out from their coastal base at Danang to "search and destroy" the enemy. They were already doing so.

On July 22 Lodge's group returned to Washington and reported at length to the President. A week later, the President went before the nation on television to reveal that he was raising the U.S. commitment in Viet Nam from 75,000 men to 125,000 (it would soon be raised to 250,000, and still more), raising draft calls from 17,000 a month to 35,000, and adding $1 to $2 billion to the annual amount of U.S. expenditures on the war.

Lodge was unanimously confirmed by the Foreign Relations Committee, and on August 12 went with Emily and a few close friends for the swearing-in at the White House Rose Garden. Secretaries Rusk and McNamara, the President's deputy for national security McGeorge Bundy, and General Taylor also were there. Lodge found it an event to remember. Few men were ever more highly praised by their President.

"Ambassador Lodge," said the President, "is one of the truly distinguished Americans of our time. He gave up his Senate seat to go into the Army in World War II. He was a soldier. He is a diplomat. He was the nominee of his Party for the second office of the land. He is a son of an honored American family. And he served his country and his times with very rare ability and effectiveness. His return to Saigon is a characteristic of a man that is motivated only by a great sense of duty to his people and his country. It inspires the respect and the confidence of all of his countrymen and the leaders of other nations in the world.

"I have known Cabot Lodge as both personal friend and as a political opponent. Whether ally or adversary, his wisdom, and his courage, and his decency, and patriotism have always had my admiration. I understand the yearning within him that leads him to seek again not the easy life, not the quiet life, but the active and useful life, the dangerous life of the duty to which he returns."

Lodge was quite moved as he responded.

He thanked the President for his trust, and added:

"Any American can consider himself lucky to have a chance to be of some help when young Americans are risking their lives in combat; when fine, young men from allied countries are doing the same things; when the Vietnamese, whose courage and stoicism I know and admire, need help to ward

376   off this aggression and to carry out their revolution for a new and better life.

"Our military are giving us precisely that opportunity and we must take advantage of it. Something brave, something noble is going on out there under your leadership, Mr. President.

"I am grateful to have a part in it, and I pledge you my very best efforts."

Lodge returned to Beverly for a last reunion with his sons and all their prolific brood—George's tribe now grown to six, Harry's to four. He had a farewell sail with some of them on the bay, and they had one of their favorite *al fresco* meals for the whole tribe on card tables on the stone patio, where Harry's lawn slopes down to meet his father's (George's house is between them in the distant rear). On the morning of August 18 Emily, who would not be seeing him for quite some while—American wives and children had been evacuated from Saigon some months before in fear of Viet Cong atrocities—drove him to Logan Airport with the whole family in trail. Among the close friends who came to see him off were the Chan Bigelows, General Bobby Cutler, the Richard Storeys and Colonel Mike Dunn, Lodge's former aide in Saigon, who was then resuming his career as a Regular Army officer. They saw Cabot board a big Presidential Boeing and wing off again for Saigon.

Actually, except for the time spent vainly trying to stop the Goldwater juggernaut, Lodge had been almost constantly on call from the White House since his return from Saigon. On August 12, 1964, he and Emily were invited to a White House state dinner for U Thant, Secretary-General of the United Nations, where Lodge was startled to find himself among four men the President singled out to introduce as representative of "all that is best in our country." The President cited two Democrats—Ambassador Adlai Stevenson and Foreign Relations Chairman J. William Fulbright— and two Republicans, Senator Dirksen of Illinois and Lodge. "Mr. Lodge," reported the *Times* "received the biggest round of applause from [the 140 guests of] the Democratic-oriented dinner party." It was at that party the President asked Lodge to undertake the first of what became several special missions.

This was to go to Paris, to speak to the NATO Council, and thence to all the capitals of the NATO countries, to acquaint their top leaders first-hand with the true situation in Viet Nam and the true nature of America's aims there—to get out as soon as the country could preserve its own freedom from external conquest.

Within a week of the White House dinner, Cabot flew to Paris for a rapid tour of a dozen capitals. He spoke to prime ministers, chiefs of state, leading parliamentarians. Many of the men he saw had served with him at the U.N.

Still others had worked closely with him in the Atlantic Institute. All gave   377
him respectful and attentive audience.

His trip seemed to get some tangible results. In Belgium, almost immediately after his talk with the Prime Minister, the Government decided to send
an ambassador to Saigon. In The Netherlands the Prime Minister announced that he would send young Dutchmen to Viet Nam to give technical
assistance, and would provide education for young South Vietnamese in
Holland. In Germany Chancellor Erhard, after talking with Lodge, promised economic aid to Saigon. In Spain the government promised technical
assistance, including medical aid. The Italian Government agreed to send a
nine-man medical team. In London men who had helped win Malaysia's
twelve-year-long struggle with Communist guerrillas arranged for police experts with rich experience in such struggles to go to Viet Nam as advisers.
In mid-September 1964, Lodge returned from his mission to report encouraging signs of a wider understanding in Europe of America's aims.

In the months ahead, Lodge continued to address public meetings, appear on television interviews, and defend U.S. policy before vehement critics—including a teacher-student "sit-in" at Oxford University in England,
site of the famous Oxford Pledge not to resist Hitler in pre-World-War II
days.

So it went through the Christmas holidays.

Then, in late February 1965, the President called him to the White
House again. Hell was literally breaking loose in Viet Nam. On both the
military and political fronts, the situation was going from bad to worse.
Grave decisions, such as carrying the war to North Viet Nam through
bombing, had to be made. The President wanted Lodge at his side in their
making.

From that time on, under the conveniently vague title of "consultant,"
Lodge was once more helping make and shape the big decisions that were
soon forthcoming on Viet Nam. The chief ones were, first, the launching of
the air war on the North, and second, the major commitment of U.S. forces
into the struggle to force it to a decision. Lodge endorsed both these moves.
He had been urging them before. He felt that the only alternative was a
Communist victory in South Viet Nam, and the ignominious necessity of
American forces to abandon the people they had pledged to save. Such a
defeat, he felt sure, would so encourage new Communist aggressions in
Asia as to make a third World War inevitable.

The previous months had witnessed a deterioration of General Khanh's
control of his own government in Viet Nam, and of Khanh's relations with
the U. S. Ambassador. At the same time the Buddhist agitator, the Venerable Tri Quang, began denouncing Taylor and trying to overthrow the
Khanh government.

378   President Johnson in March 1965 asked Lodge if he would return to Saigon as Ambassador. Lodge first wanted to consult Eisenhower. He flew up to Gettysburg in a White House helicopter. This time, Eisenhower raised none of the political objections he had previously. He felt the crisis clearly required any American to give whatever service he could render. Johnson himself was calling Eisenhower once a week to advise him of every contemplated move. Eisenhower had endorsed each one.

Neither Lodge nor Johnson told anyone else at that time that Lodge was returning to Saigon. It was one of the best kept secrets in Washington's memory.

Lodge spent his time, in the four months between his acceptance and the announcement, thinking through the intense experience of his first tour of duty and seeking the lessons from it to guide future U.S. policy.

He had insisted from the first that the *military* situation in South Viet Nam could be settled easily if the proper *political* climate could be established. He felt that this had to come in the villages, at the grass roots level. No government could claim loyalty from its citizens if it could not give them a good night's sleep, secure from atrocities. After the security of home and person must come a genuine chance for a good life—one's own land to till. This meant land reform, which in spite of several attempts, had never made real headway. And with land reform must come what the U.S. was superbly equipped to provide—massive aid of equipment, materials, technology and the technicians themselves to help the villagers build self supporting economies. And where the French had so deliberately denied education to the people, the U.S. must help build the thousands of needed schools and help prepare the teachers to staff them, and thus create the informed electorate on which alone some viable form of self-government could arise. At the same time, Lodge, wise in the ways of the Orient, was aware that "instant democracy" was neither feasible nor desirable in a land whose centuries-old tradition centered around family and village loyalties rather than national ones ("a sense of peoplehood but not the same sense of nationhood that we have" was the way he put it.)

In pondering these problems, which he rated more vital than the military, Lodge sought out the counsel of General Edward Lansdale, who had done so much to work out the strategy by which General Magsaysay of the Philippines had won the Filipino villagers away from the Communist Hukbalahap guerrillas.

Prior to Lodge's service in Saigon, back in the 1950's, Lansdale had studied the Vietnamese problem at close range, and in 1961 had made numerous recommendations for carrying the fight against the Viet Cong to the villages. He planned to do this with teams carefully trained in advance to lead a particular village, first, in protecting its own defense, then, in building its future. Lansdale's plan caught President Kennedy's imagination. However, it violated so many bureaucratic jurisdictions and stepped on so many bureacrats' toes, that it soon disappeared into velvet wastebaskets. Lodge lunched with Lansdale at Washington's Metropolitan Club and encouraged him to think about it anew. As soon as he was able to reveal his new assignment, Lodge would ask Lansdale to work with him in Viet Nam.

In April, while Lodge was thinking through Viet Nam's lessons of the past and trying to apply them to the future, President Johnson asked him to take on a second visit to the heads of nations—this time in Southeast Asia.

On April 15 Cabot and Emily went by helicopter to Andrews Air Force Base to board one of the familiar Presidential jets. A crew of seventeen Air Forcemen accompanied them, including four armed Air Police who stood guard over the plane at every stop. It was equipped with radio telephone and teleprinter, as well as cryptographic encoding and decoding devices. It provided instant communication with the White House, State Department, Pentagon, and, in fact, with anyone with a telephone anywhere in the world.

During the next ten days Cabot and Emily flew to Honolulu, thence to Australia, to Manila, to Taipei, to Tokyo, to Seoul, Hong Kong and Saigon. At each place, Cabot met with the premier or foreign minister, sometimes the whole Cabinet, and discussed America's Viet Nam policy for hours on end. Lodge talked with New Zealand's Prime Minister Holyoake, with Australia's Prime Minister Menzies, President Macapagal of the Philippines, saw both Generalissimo and Madame Chiang Kai-shek in Formosa, President Park of Korea. Premier Sato in Japan. Cabot spent several days in Saigon, where he told the press he had found that other Asian nations supported the U.S. bombing of North Viet Nam. He saw India's leaders in New Delhi, stopped at Teheran for a conference with his old Saigon colleague, Bishop Asta (who had since become papal delegate to Iran), flew on to Rome to give Pope Paul and the Vatican Secretary of State first-hand information on America's aims in Asia and to get the wise advice that they could give.

On his way home, Lodge sent to the White House, over the Presidential jet's radio teletype, some remarks made to him by one of the statesmen he had seen. This statement, in its simple eloquence, sums up what Lodge sought to achieve and what he and his nation stood for:

LODGE TO WHITE HOUSE IN TRANSIT

A highly placed political leader in one of the countries Lodge visited said this to him about the foreign policy of the U.S. since the end of World War II:

"The U.S. said: 'The Communists shall not conquer Western Europe'—Western Europe was not conquered.

"The U.S. said: 'We will not be driven out of Berlin'—and you were not driven out of Berlin.

"The U.S. said: 'Korea will not be destroyed'—and Korea was not destroyed.

"The U.S. said: 'The islands in the Straits of Formosa will not be captured'—and they were not captured.

"The U.S. said: 'Get out of Cuba'—and the interlopers left Cuba.

"Now you say you will not be defeated in Viet Nam, that you will not allow this small country to be thrown to the wolves.

"We believe that you mean what you say. We trust you, your sagacity and strength. On that trust hangs the hope of freedom and a peace in the world."

Nor did Lodge's mission seem unfruitful. After his visit, New Zealand promised to send—and did send—a battery of artillery to South Viet Nam. Australia committed itself to two battalions. South Korea had a twenty-two hundred-man engineering tank force, and agreed to send an infantry division. (They have since fought splendidly.)

Moreover, as Lodge reported to the President on his return—and shortly thereafter to congressional leaders—he found the private attitude among nearly all governments in Asia to be, "We are glad you are in Viet Nam, we hope you will stay there, we hope you will win." Most seemed in private conversation to approve of the selective bombing of North Viet Nam as a deserved response to North Viet Nam's invasion of the South—and the countless killings of its men, women and children by Communist terrorists striking them down mercilessly in the night. If there was any complaint, it was that we had failed to make clear how *much* guilt the North bore for these terror killings of the village innocent—thousands upon thousands.

Just prior to Lodge's tour, the President in a major speech at Johns Hopkins had asserted the U.S. was ready at any time to enter into "unconditional discussions" with North Viet Nam and prepared, as well, once hostilities had ended, to launch a huge developmental program for the whole area—including North Viet Nam. Lodge had carried this same assurance to Asia's leaders. Now, on his return, Johnson ordered the air raids on North Viet Nam suspended. The suspension lasted for six days, but provoked no hopeful response from Hanoi. It was met only with vituperation from Hanoi and Peking.

When Lodge arrived in Saigon on August 20, 1965, to begin his second tour of duty, he was driven to the same airy stucco villa he had left the year before. Very little was changed. His familiar cook, Can, met him at the door, smiling hugely. He knew what the Ambassador liked, and had laid in a

large supply of the PX baby-foods such as minced chicken which the ulcer-
wary Lodge liked to sip in bland, creamed soups.

Next morning, followed by a jeep-load of police, the Embassy Plymouth drove him the two-odd miles southeast to the five-story Chancery, where he found his office much the same as before; one window, however, had been walled up for fear of sharpshooting from a house across the street. The previous March, the Viet Cong had detonated a car loaded with 250 pounds of dynamite at the Embassy door, killing 22 persons in the vicinity and injuring 190. The month before, as General Taylor was attending a rally in Saigon, police had found, at the last moment, a mine intended to blow him to bits. Lodge had to consider himself the constant target of assassination. He would leave his home at a different hour each day and change the route each time. The Embassy Plymouth had replaced his familiar old Checker limousine; that had been blown up in the March explosion.

Ambassador Taylor had already gone, to become an adviser to the President; his deputy, Alexis Johnson, stayed on for several weeks and Lodge found him a tower of strength. Johnson returned to his previous post as Deputy Under Secretary of State, and William J. Porter came out as Lodge's deputy with the full rank of Ambassador. Porter was a battle-wise veteran who was consul-general in Jerusalem during the Arab-Israeli war, consul at Cyprus in the Greek-Turkish fighting and Ambassador in Algeria in the thick of that turmoil. General William Westermoreland, former 101st Airborne commander, whom Lodge had known as superintendent of West Point, now headed up all the military activities formerly commanded by General Paul Harkins.

The political situation in Viet Nam itself had changed a great deal since Lodge had left it. He found himself calling upon a new Premier, Nguyen Cao Ky, thirty-five, whom he had met the year before as Air Force Vice Marshal but had not known very well. He found Ky a picturesque character, fond of flamboyant scarfs, pearl-handled pistols, but also courageous—he had led the South Vietnamese bombers in the first joint raid on North Viet Nam, and had had part of his plane shot away. Ky, a black-eyed, black-mustached, handsome cavalier, had helped General Khanh survive a number of attempted coups and then finally had displaced him.

It was impossible to place the blame for what had gone wrong in Saigon, since the days when Lodge was patiently coaching Khanh in going before the people, getting to the "grass roots," making radio reports to the populace. The taste of power soon went to Khanh's head. For petty reasons, Khanh did not trust General Taylor as he had Lodge. One reason was that Khanh, although he had made "Big" Minh his figurehead Chief of State, was jealous of Minh's greater popularity with both the Army and the people. He was doubly jealous of the fact that Big Minh was an old tennis-playing partner of Taylor's from days when Minh was training in the U.S. Khanh wanted to get rid of Minh. A month after Lodge left in 1964 Khanh promulgated a new Constitution making himself President (as Diem had been) and abolishing Minh's job. Terrible riots ensued, egged on by Communist provocateurs. Khanh rescinded his Constitution and resigned.

He immediately came back as Premier, in a new triumvirate that included Big Minh. The great clamor from the public was for the military junta to turn over its powers to a civilian government. A High National Council of seventeen elderly leaders was named, charged with preparing a new Constitution and a civilian form of government. A second attempted coup against Khanh was thwarted by a group of young officers, chiefly Air Force Commander Ky and Sub-General Nguyen Chanh Thi, commander of the northernmost I Corps' First Division. Khanh now had to share his power with Ky and Thi.

In October 1964 the High National Council tried to establish a civilian government. It made its own chairman, Phan Khac Suu, a sixty-three-year-old unaligned agricultural engineer, the new chief of state. It chose as Premier Saigon's former mayor, Tran Van Huong, sixty-one. However, Khanh continued as Commander-in-Chief of the Army and as such the real power.

Through these upheavals, a somewhat sinister figure had emerged as the maker and breaker of governments. It was the forty-three-year-old Buddhist monk, the Venerable Tri Quang, whom Lodge had sheltered when Nhu's special forces had Quang marked for slaughter. Tri Quang had been uniquely conspicuous in the overthrow of the Diem government. He had organized the mass Buddhist demonstrations in his home city of Hué and later in Saigon. It was he who had stimulated the immolations of monks. Since the Buddhists were being brutally persecuted at the time, Tri Quang attracted much sympathy.

Later, however, it became clear that Tri Quang's true motives were to rule or ruin. When the persecution of Buddhists ended, Tri Quang insisted that it was continuing. Nobody knew what, if anything, he really represented. The vast bulk of South Viet Nam's three million-odd Buddhists, who have no central authority, had never heard of him; most would have disapproved, through the very tenets of their humanist religion, his tactics of instigating riots, setting hoodlums to assault Catholics, and persuading mental defectives to set themselves on fire.

Some thought him a Communist agent, others regarded him as a neutralist seeking to create a neutral Buddhist state which he could dominate as its *eminence grise*. In any case, he had come to exercise a sort of veto power over government actions, through his ability to summon up several thousand youths and rowdies to spread violence in both Saigon and Hué.

It also had become clear that his chief potential ally was General Thi,

commander of the strategic northern district around Hué where organized
Buddhists were most powerful.

Tri Quang, who had clamored for a civilian government, was not appeased when Premier Huong formed one. Quang immediately began trying to drive it from office "because it does not command the sympathy of the population." He began openly attacking the Americans for keeping Huong in power "against the just desires of the Vietnamese people and the Buddhist church." Huong stoutly resisted, saying "I cannot admit a state within a state."

In December 1964 Generals Ky and Thi mounted their own coup against the High National Council. They demanded that it fire some nine "Old Guard" generals and thirty other officers. When the Council refused, the rebels imprisoned its leaders, and created a new supreme body—the Armed Forces Council—with Khanh as its head. Actually, however, their aim was to clip Khanh's power over the other generals.

Ambassador Taylor, supporting civilian rule, advised Premier Huong to defy the purge of his High National Council. Khanh, in turn, began attacking Taylor as on a par with "Communism and colonialism" as enemies of the country.

Huong's civilian government survived, for a time, although the High National Council remained suppressed. Huong had to add four generals to his cabinet, including Ky. In late January 1965 the Armed Forces Council ousted Huong as Premier. In February the "young Turks" headed by Ky and Thi forced Khanh to leave the country as "ambassador at large." After a period of interim experiments with new civilian leaders, the Army junta coalesced into a ten-man National Leadership Committee, appointed General Ky, a Buddhist, as Premier, and, as chief of state, Lieutenant General Nguyen Van Thieu, a Catholic.

This was the government that Lodge confronted on his return, a government that had some impressive points of strength and determination, but one that was also besieged on all sides by Tri Quang and his followers, who were clearly determined to overthrow any government that would not obey their every whim and bidding.

Lodge settled down to his new duties in this greatly changed situation.
One big personal change was the absence of Emily. More than many men, the uxorious Lodge felt himself an incomplete person without the complementing love and wisdom of his wife. In time, Emily came out to Bangkok, in Thailand, where Lodge could join her one weekend in five or so (they would go to a beautiful beach called Pattaya). Later, as security improved in South Viet Nam, she managed to join him increasingly in the Saigon villa for special receptions and the like.

As noted, the greatest external change was the military situation. Only a few months before Lodge's return, the Viet Cong had been fielding more than fifteen hundred men in regimental-size assaults. They seemed clearly to be approaching the 1965 monsoon offensive with plans to mount ever larger attacks, hoping to cut South Viet Nam in two and perhaps capture some major provincial capital such as Hué. The arrival of U.S. Marines and other forces committed to direct combat, the attacks on the North, the deployment of B-52s in tactical raids, had now changed all this. No longer were the Viet Cong able to plan and strike at will. They were being hunted out and disrupted; more and more of their defectors complained of the lack of security anywhere in the jungle. Their prize tactic, proved over decades, of cutting roads and luring Government troops into expeditions to restore them, then flanking them in double ambushes—all this was going by the board as the great-winged American helicopters ignored the roads and set their troops down suddenly in the middle of nowhere—and often in the middle of surprised Viet Cong forces. Once more the Americans were proving their ability, in drastically altered situations, to apply Nathan Bedford Forrest's old Cavalry rule: "Be fustest with the mostest."

Lodge, the old cavalryman, felt an understandable nostalgic thrill when his old outfit, the First Cavalry, arrived for combat in Viet Nam. On September 13, 1965, he flew with General Westmoreland from Danang to Qui Nonh to see the First Cav arrive. In the harbor were five transports and the escorting aircraft carrier, U.S.S. *Boxer.*

This was a far different Cavalry from that which Lodge had trained with on the Bugscuffle Trail. It was now airmobile. Instead of horses, its mounts were helicopters—these strapped on the *Boxer.* But they still carried the same flag he knew—the bright yellow flag of the First Cavalry. Westmoreland and Lodge went down to the beach as a big LSU (Landing Ship Utility) came in. These are great, big, open ships that hold up to three hundred men standing up. The ship came in and gently bumped the beach and the ramp was let down. In the slight swell, the ship went slowly up and down.

The men came off. It looked as though they were twelve abreast. All were wearing helmets. The officers' insignia had been made dull so as not to catch the sun.

By great luck, Cabot and Westermoreland happened to arrive just as the unit which carried the Division colors was landing. These were unfurled just before landing, and they marched off by Westmoreland and Lodge—the Stars and Stripes on the right, and the bright yellow flag of the First Cavalry on the left—the Cavalry yellow of the stripe down the trousers of Sheridan's horsemen, which Frederic Remington used to paint.

Lodge noted one big change: what had been a bright yellow and black shoulder patch, with a diagonal black stripe and a black horse's head, had been made colorless and was simply stamped in black on every man's uniform.

As he watched this, helicopters were being assembled on the *Boxer* and flown directly off its deck into the Qui Nonh Airport. There were large trucks at the beach. The men walked from the ship up the beach into the trucks. The trucks took them on a five-minute ride to the airport, and ten minutes after landing, the men of the First Cav were in the helicopters high in the air, winging their way to the big camp they were establishing in the highlands at An Khe.

Lodge, watching them go, reflected that he was the only man there that day who had worn the same shoulder patch in older days. He alone had worn that patch astride a horse.

A few months later, the men of First Cav would send for him again. They had flown right into the heart of Viet Cong territory, and cut their own base into it. They had named it Camp Radcliff, after Major Donald Radcliff, who was the first officer of First Air Cav to be killed in action in Viet Nam. They asked Lodge to come to dedicate this camp.

Lodge flew from Saigon to Pleiku in a T-39 reconnaissance aircraft. First Cav had just been engaged in fierce action. Lodge spent an hour overflying the battle and operations areas in which First Cav had been engaged. He flew over the Ia Drang Valley, where the First Air Cav had met its great test of blood and mettle and had routed a division of North Vietnamese troops.

His helicopter landed on a hill dubbed Hong Kong Hill in the middle of the camp that contained the Division's communications headquarters. Only the night before, the hill had been attacked by a Viet Cong suicide squad. The area was still covered with blood. Several Americans and Viet Cong had been killed in the fight, Lodge inspected the site of the attack. He then took a helicopter down to dedicate the camp.

He made an address commemorating the camp. After flying back to Saigon, he wired the President his impressions:

The immense division size camp, with its 400 helicopters, its supplies of gasoline and ammunition, is right in the middle of enemy country. The Division had the night before successfully repulsed an attack and when I arrived had just found a Viet Cong body and a live prisoner. The hilltop on which their communications facilities are installed had been the objective of the attack. There is no access route to the Hong Kong Hill, except by helicopter and the hilltop area was cleared when a giant Chinook helicopter transported a large earth-moving tractor to do the work.

The First Cavalry Division is fighting with great skill, and really seems to have the initiative in Binh Dinh Province. I believe this is

having a favorable effect on revolutionary development (the new name
for pacification) because the Viet Cong in the second priority area
are probably cut off from the rest of the Viet Cong.

It was the First Cavalry Division which in Ia Drang met the Viet
Cong who had advanced in a virtually continuous line through our ar-
tillery barrage so as to attack us at close range because they believed
that Americans could not, physically and psychologically, endure hand
to hand fighting. But our boys shattered this Viet Cong illusion and
killed every Viet Cong in sight. It was this Division too which found
Viet Cong soldiers manacled to their machine guns.

In September 1965 General Landsdale came out to help Lodge in the
effort to move beyond military action into making the rural homeland in
Viet Nam a place willing to defend itself by giving it hope for the future.

Lodge gave top priority to Lansdale's programs, believing a truly revolutionary movement at the village level was needed to deprive the Viet Cong of
its sources of supply, recruitment and sanctuary.

Lansdale entered into close liaison with General Nguyen Duc Thang, the
Minister of Revolutionary Development, and also worked closely with Ambassador Porter, who was in charge—under Lodge's overall direction—of
all nonmilitary U.S. activities having to do with winning the war—activities
lumped together under the heading of "revolutionary development." Lansdale's title was Senior Liaison Officer and he kept in touch with a large circle of acquaintances going back to his earlier service in Viet Nam.

Lansdale became a key member of the U.S. Mission to Viet Nam. This
unprecedented mechanism of government—originated by Lodge and perfected by Taylor and Alexis Johnson—reflected the new realities of the Vietnamese war, a war which required many different types of effort.

It was, in the first place, violent and bloody; a truth which was reflected
in two facts: that it was a "military war" on the classic model known so
often in the West, and that it was also a "criminal-terrorist" war such as was
unknown in the West. This latter type of war used murder, kidnapping and
torture by men in civilian clothes and had to be dealt with by police-type
methods.

Also, in this war, when the Viet Cong military effort was unsuccessful,
the action often shifted from the battlefield to the field of political intrigue
and street demonstrations, with attempts being made to overthrow the Saigon government. Or an attempt would be made to win by savage economic
methods which, by creating scarcities and producing a wildcat, soul-eroding
inflation, were aimed at producing famine and a "night of the long knives"
in the big cities.

Winning such a war required more than military, and more than police, methods. It also required schoolteachers, doctors, engineers, agricultural experts. And it could depend heavily on what people were thinking.

Therefore, on the U.S. Mission Council over which Lodge presided, the two leading members were Ambassador Porter and General Westmoreland. Other important members were Charles Mann, the director of the U.S. AID agency, with its many economic and social programs; Barry Zorthian, the head of the American psychological warfare effort, and Leroy S. Wehrle, the brilliant young economic counselor.

Equally unprecedented was that, for what seemed to many like the first time ever, the *generalist* at the top of the entire U.S. Government activity in a foreign country—that is, Lodge—had the staff which could truly coordinate the whole U.S. effort with all its many superb *specialists*. Right-hand men to Lodge in all this were a Foreign Service officer of incisive mind and driving energy, Philip C. Habib, the Political Counselor; and Samuel V. Wilson, an effective executive on loan from the Regular Army, who held the newly created position of Mission Coordinator.

Thus the U.S. effort contained men with the rich—and indispensable—unconventional experience of Lansdale, plus the equally indispensable elite of the U.S. Government career services—those "able professionals" whose preparation Lodge was urging in his early letters and editorials.

The Ministry of Revolutionary Development, headed by General Thang, was allotted some $9 million for the year ahead, and the U.S., through AID, planned to spend some $400 million. Tangible targets were set: securing 987 hamlets, building 2,500 classrooms, resettling 41,000 families who had fled their villages, building 150 bridges and 600 miles of road, and adding an additional 14 per cent of South Viet Nam's population to the 50 per cent already made secure by Saigon.

The Ministry began creating the Revolutionary Development Cadre, whose teams were, wherever possible, recruited from the regions in which they were working, and were trained at the seaside town of Vung Tau. They were instructed in the arts of "self-defense, self-help and self-government," in everything from using a grenade launcher to digging a well and administering first aid.

No one was prouder than Lodge when Vung Tau was ready to graduate its first class. He radioed the President:

The first class of rural construction cadre graduated from the National Training Center at Vung Tau after ten weeks of paramilitary and political training. The 3,095 graduates included 119 women, and represented 15 southern and nine central provinces. This class had started training in November, 1965.

MACV reports that the greatest single request from the Vietnamese

*provinces, of all the requests for U.S. personnel, is for public safety
advisers. This would appear to me to indicate the pressing nature of
the criminal (as distinguished from the military) side of Viet Cong
violence, requiring police type measures to cope with it.*

The Revolutionary Cadres soon began providing such help and many
other kinds as well. In a few months, Vung Tau had trained and sent out
fifty-nine-man teams into seventy-six villages scattered among all forty-
three provinces of South Viet Nam. *Time* described the arrival of one team
in Tau Nghia, off the South China Coast, whose one thousand villagers for
twenty years had been "the helpless pawns of war: used and abused, taxed
and conscripted, sheltered and then shelled by first one army and then another in the march and counter-march of Viet Nam's wars." It had been in
Viet Cong hands for six months when Saigon troops recaptured it in the fall
of 1965. First South Korea's Tiger Division arrived and set up headquarters
in nearby Qui Nonh, providing a visible and powerful shield. In January
1966 the team of "revolutionaries" arrived. *Time* reported:

*It was a team with teeth: every man was armed and trained to fight.
But it was something else as well. "At first it had to be hamlet chief,
school-teacher and doctor," says a U.S. official, "a surrogate government in effect." A census of the villagers' needs and grievances was
taken, and within weeks they were being met. Roads were repaired,
loans granted to fishermen for larger boats, new nets. A school was
set up, a health center built, fertilizer trucked in, a new sewing machine sent from Saigon after the women were organized into sewing
groups.*

*Gradually, the village was organized to protect itself in a way that
gave every villager a sense of participation. Old women went to work
constructing punji sticks and booby traps for protective barriers
around the village. Teen-age boys manned klaxon alarms. Should they
sound at night, the women were taught to gather in the center of the
village with flaring pitch torches, while the men held back in the
shadows with the guns to ambush Viet Cong intruders. Last March, a
small Viet Cong propaganda team came, and nearly every villager went
to his assigned post. The Reds asked who the leaders were. No one
would talk to them, and the baffled and frustrated V.C. organizers
withdrew. So, too, has the pacification team, its mission accomplished,
with Tau Nghia now a village thriving, alive and ready to kick hard at
any Communist attempt to reinfiltrate it.*

Chapter Eighteen

The teams from the training base of Vung Tau arrived in the villages in black pajamas and black berets. One such team came to Binh Phuoc, an inland hamlet of rice and manioc farmers.

They started slowly, from the ground up, to win the villagers' confidence. First they drew a crude map of the village, its homes and road accesses. They ate in the local restaurants to get to know the people, took guard duty at night, began a census, used part of their first paychecks to buy cigarettes to give away. In three-man cells they visited huts and passed out sewing needles to the women, or went out in the fields to help the men cut manioc root. The medical cadres in white arm bands went out to distribute aspirin, nose drops, and to scrub down children. Within a month, the team felt sufficiently part of the village to call its first formal town meeting to organize against the Viet Cong.

Needless to say, such successful efforts brought redoubled efforts by the Viet Cong to assassinate the newly trained, newly encouraged village leaders. Such attempts continued, and sometimes succeeded. What was new, said former Marine Major Richard Kriegel, the U.S. adviser in Binh Dinh province, where great headway was made, was the attitude of the villagers: "The reaction of the people now is that this is going to happen, but they're ready to live with it, accept it—and fight back." Terror, the greatest weapon of the Viet Cong, was being visibly dulled.

Lodge spent much of his time giving general oversight and encouragement to these activities, which he regarded as all-important. He sought none of the credit, regarding that as belonging to those, like Porter, Landsdale, General Thang, leaders in the field like Major Krieger, who were planning and executing it. He felt that the big contribution he could make was to expedite it at every point, and keep it from getting sidetracked or sabotaged as was Lansdale's original plan.

Lodge's duties were widely different from those of an ambassador in a normal diplomatic post. Although a civilian, he was actually occupying the most crucial U.S. command post in the world, co-ordinating programs headed up by two-men of four-star rank—General Westmoreland and Ambassador Porter.

First, it was his responsibility to co-ordinate the whole U.S. effort. Washington considered this work the most critical. It required him to braid together the requirements of military fighting with those of fighting the criminal-terrorist activity, and with the creation of solid political institutions under which economic and social programs for the underdog could be carried out.

As part of this job, he presided over the U.S. Mission Council, which brought together regularly the heads of all U.S. agencies in Viet Nam and deliberated on all problems affecting U.S. interests. In this body, policy was not made by voting. Nor was it the usual loose consultation of a "country team." Rather, Lodge listened and consulted, but by authority of the President, the decision rested in his hands.

Daily, it was his duty to read the telegrams coming *from* Washington, as well as write the telegrams of greatest policy significance going *to* Washington. President Johnson, in an interview with the writer, told him how completely he relied upon Lodge's telegrams, and how forthright, lucid and accurate he had found them always to be. Lodge's long training as professional reporter and observer, blended with his even longer experience at dealing with governments, stood him exceptionally well in this important aspect of helping Washington frame its policies.

One such wire:

The U.S. military have perfected tactics of ambushing the ambushers. Last week the First Division sent an American unit down a road in Binh Long, near Cambodia. The Viet Cong, lying in ambush, attacked it; and then the Americans came in with more forces and troops.

I can't help thinking this could be a tremendously important development, since it does two things, both of which are of fundamental importance:

(a) It means that you find the enemy in a massed state instead of spread around like bread crumbs through the countryside.

(b) It means that when you deter the enemy, you have tried at least to open up the road. And if he gets wise to these tactics and stops making ambushes, then you have also tended to open up the road.

Roads are fundamental and have been one of our toughest obstacles. If roads are opened up and used, it is wonderful for troops, for civilian morale, for commerce, and it takes the pressure off the Air Force which would otherwise have to airlift.

As part of his duty to advise the government of South Viet Nam, Lodge visited Prime Minister Ky about twice a week. Lodge's secretary would telephone for the appointment, then Lodge would go to see the Prime Minister at his office on Thong Nhut Boulevard (the Champs Elysées of Saigon) or out to his house at Tan Son Nhut Airport, the residence assigned to him as Air Force commander.

Lodge also had to keep in touch with foreign diplomats, keep in touch with the press (at which he proved as expert as before), be in contact with other official Vietnamese besides Ky, and help conduct studies on long-range matters such as the evolution of democratic constitutional government in South Viet Nam.

Finally, an extremely time-consuming, yet vitally important, task was to receive and brief an endless stream of dignitaries, who had need to know about Viet Nam and could best learn by coming and seeing it. In less than a year after his return, he had been official host to Vice-President Humphrey and former Vice-President Nixon,* to four Cabinet members, seventeen senators, four congressmen, thirteen governors, fourteen sub-Cabinet members, twenty-six four-star generals, and some fifty other eminent visitors, American and foreign.

He organized trips for ambassadors accredited to Viet Nam, some based in Bangkok, to visit the front. And he also insisted on seeing the junior Foreign Service officers—men in their twenties trained in the Vietnamese language and history—whom he sent out in the field, to come in and tell him what they found. He believed firmly that to depend exclusively on information coming up through channels would, for the head of any big organization, make him miss many things.

In all his activities, Lodge kept coming back to the all-important necessity of giving the individual villager hope for the future. Lodge wired Washington:

> *As regards revolutionary development, [Ambassador] Porter reports that 90 more teams are now being inserted into the villages and hamlets and that these should be followed about Sept. 1, 1966, by 100 more. This infusion of personnel is concurrent with the insertion of the first police field force units who will work in the areas between the villages and hamlets, thus complementing the work of the Revolutionary Development teams inside those places. Together with the self-help programs, which are now functioning on a wide scale, it appears that by mid-September [1966] we may, with luck, have some interesting progress to report. This is all brand new and highly creative. In fact, if it actually happens, it would not be too much to say that nothing more imaginative than this would be going on in the entire field of government.*

To the successes achieved by these teams was added the creation of such supplemental elements as the Police Field Force Units under the leadership of a brilliant Australian officer, Colonel Ted Serong, who had had a rich experience in Malaya. Also, the police training help, which Lodge had been able to win from London on his 1964 visit there, made Lodge feel that such work had a far-reaching future significance. All of this involved help from AID, and the psychological warfare people. And, of course, the military had

---

* Who visits Viet Nam periodically for his legal client, Pepsi Cola.

392   to create the opportunity for any Revolutionary Development to begin.
Lodge could wire the White House:

> *A corps of men and a body of ideas and procedures are developing here*
> *[which] will be available for use elsewhere, to overcome subversion*
> *and terrorism and carry out the true revolution, in freedom, which will*
> *be more potent than the Communist revolution. If we succeed here, we*
> *will have men and measures for use in underdeveloped countries any-*
> *where in the world, and the downward spiral of world communism*
> *will have begun. The year that this blow at Communism is struck in*
> *Viet Nam may well be, in the history of Communism, on a par in im-*
> *portance with 1917—the year of its birth.*

Earlier in the year, while thinking out the lessons of his past experience in
Viet Nam, Lodge had made an intensive effort to look ahead to the problems
of the future—as a prime example, what sort of settlement should America be willing to accept?

Total victory was a cheap and easy cry for the ultra-hawks, for whom
America's unquestioned power to obliterate North Viet Nam was reason
enough to use it as the quickest way to end the war and to save American
lives.

Lodge could not find any of the problems quite that simple. James Reston, after a visit to Saigon toward the end of 1965, found him devoting
much time to pondering the various options for U.S. policy.

"What Ambassador Lodge is trying to do," wrote Reston, "is to anticipate
the problems that will arise if we ever get to the point of talking to the
Communists. He spent a number of years . . . at the U.N. where he had to
deal with the negotiating techniques of the Communists. He learned from
that experience that it is important to be prepared before talking to the
Communists, so he is being forehanded about the problem of urging his
associates in Washington to do the same.

"More important, Mr. Lodge is also trying to define the terms of a settlement that would protect the vital interests of the U.S. and the security of
South Viet Nam without creating a sense of insecurity—and therefore hostility to negotiations—on the Communist side.

"This is a very difficult but useful exercise, which is practical, not only for
the future of negotiations but for the present conduct of the war. For example, whom do you negotiate with if you decide on a policy of bombing Hanoi
and Haiphong and wipe out the North Vietnamese Government in the process? Would this not lead to counterattacks on the vulnerable ports of Saigon
and open North Viet Nam to the Chinese, whose expansion into Viet Nam is
precisely what we are trying to avoid?

"The definition of war aims has other implications for the conduct of the   *393*
war. Is our aim to destroy the Viet Cong and the North Vietnamese divisions
in a ground war? Would American public opinion stand for casualties involved in such a strategy . . . ? Would the U.S. achieve its purpose by
holding the populous perimeter of the Saigon area, and the coastal bases
and provincial capitals? Mr. Lodge is not, at this point, presuming to give
answers to all these questions, but he is doing something even more important. He is trying to bring thought to bear on action. He has been a
Senator, a soldier, and a diplomat; and he is trying to anticipate the rela-
tionships between fighting and negotiating, and between diplomacy and
politics.

"At the same time he is using his influence as head of the entire American Mission in Saigon to wage the war in the broadest possible terms. He
is working closely with General Lansdale on the pacification of the areas
under our control. . . . He is also paying attention to the problems of psychological and economic warfare in Viet Nam, in the hope of encouraging
desertions from the other side and denying the enemy essential supplies to
carry on the war. . . . Lodge is clearly working on the constructive aspects
of his mission and urging all his colleagues to do the same.

"Saigon is probably Lodge's last critical mission in a long life of constructive public service. He has overcome the partisan controversies of the past.
He is trying to serve his country in the best New England tradition. He is
working hard to concentrate, not on the mistakes of the past, but the constructive possibilities of getting out of the mess. And in this sense he is
acting in the best tradition of nonpartisan service to the nation."

Lodge looked for no miracles, no quick victories. Instead, he contented
himself with studying each week's evidence of the growing American ability
to keep both Viet Cong and North Vietnam forces off-balance, to detect and
break up their planned offensives before they could be formed, and increasingly to deny the Viet Cong guerrilla his greatest asset—the ability to hide
indefinitely and plan and prepare at leisure until fully ready to strike at
some point of his own choosing. Increasingly, as Lodge had predicted, the
guerrilla's favorite tactic of the ambush was being turned against him. A
Lodge cable to the President:

*The highlights of last week's military activity were two heavy battles
won by U.S. and Korean forces and a sparkling performance by the
Vietnamese Second Division which surprised a large Viet Cong force
with a midnight assault on its bivouac in Quang Tin Province. After
making the initial assault, the attacking force deliberately withdrew
and then re-attacked at 3:00 in the morning, catching the Viet Cong
survivors in the process of evacuating their dead and wounded. As a*

result, the Viet Cong lost 100 killed and 56 weapons, while the Vietnamese troops lost only two missing.

As 1966 went by, the year saw a summit meeting at Honululu in February between President Johnson and Premier Ky and Chief of State Thieu. Lodge escorted them to the meeting by Presidential jet, briefed the President on their views, acted as a catalyst at the sessions. It resulted in Johnson's pledge to see South Viet Nam through to the end, and to give the growing rural construction program the highest priority. He pledged, as well, to send in more U.S. experts of every conceivable kind to help the growing economic program at the village level.

Shortly after the Honolulu summit, on March 10, 1966, Premier Ky made a sudden move which many thought unwise. He ordered Lieutenant General Nguyen Chanh Thi, Tri Quang's chief potential ally, removed as commander of the I Corps in the crucial Hué-Danang area.

What started as a minor protest against Thi's dismissal was taken over by radical Buddhist elements under Tri Quang, who had helped overthrow both the Khanh and Huong governments. For years Thi, like any boodling politician in Tammany, had been building a political machine by making appointments to civil and military offices. With Thi gone, these jobholders' place at the trough was in danger. They had no choice but to resist. Tri Quang made a hasty alliance with these spoilsmen.

By late March, demonstrations, protest meetings, general strikes and other antigovernment agitation spread southward from Hué and Danang through Dalat, Nhatrang and other principal cities to Saigon itself. Violence threatened, and as many coup rumors were heard as there were Vietnamese generals. Government countermeasures were halfhearted and inept.

The city of Danang was seized by so-called struggle forces who seemed clearly under Viet Cong influence. The seizure was an object lesson in how terrorism operates. Under the nose of the U.S. Third Marine Amphibious Force, clearly able to defeat any large unit which might threaten it, a few men from Hué called on the chief of police of Danang, Viet Nam's second largest city. They told him they were determined to take over the city and to do it first by taking over his police force; they told the Chief that unless he turned over the police force to the "struggle committee" his wife and children would be kidnapped, his house burned down, and himself assassinated by six that night. He turned over the city. "The U.S. forces had a big net to catch whales," Lodge said of this incident, "but neither the Americans nor the Government of South Viet Nam had the fine-meshed net which was necessary to catch the small but deadly fish of terrorism."

The "struggle" movement demands purported to center on democratic elections and a change to civilian rule. The call for elections was plausible, however deplorable the tactics. Ky's government had already promised to hold elections in 1967, intending to have experts draft a Constitution to be submitted to the people by referendum. This scheme had the merit that such a Constitution would have been thoroughly debated and discussed from one end of the country to the other, and would consequently have the people's understanding and respect.

However, in response to Tri Quang's pressure tactics, Ky modified his plans so that elections would be held to choose delegates to a Constitutional Convention to draft the document. Lodge thought Ky's original plan at least as democratic as what was finally done—if not more so. But he concurred in the decision to hold the September 1966 elections.

For a time, it appeared that this concession would satisfy Tri Quang. He even made one of his rare public speeches in Hué on April 18, 1966, appealing for an end to demonstrations and other agitation. The Buddhist Institute in Saigon affirmed its acceptance of the government offer. A surface calm returned, even in the storm centers of Hué and Danang where the authority of the Saigon government had collapsed.

Tri Quang and his cohorts however, did not really cease their antigovernment maneuvers. They only changed the focus of their activity from public protest to quiet consolidation of their power. Throughout the country many Buddhist chaplains in the armed forces were spreading seditious propaganda. Students in Hué and elsewhere solicited "contributions" for the struggle movement from merchants and others, with implications they might find their homes in ashes if they failed to contribute. Although this movement represented only a small minority of the Vietnamese people (even in Hué where it was strongest), it was nevertheless able to erode the authority of the central government almost completely in the I Corps region and to a lesser extent elsewhere.

Although the struggle movement used many familiar Communist tactics, and although some Viet Cong did infiltrate its ranks, Lodge doubted that it was under actual Communist control. He acted accordingly. He refused Tri Quang's demands that the U.S., in effect, overthrow the government. But he did not consider the struggle movement as an element of the Communist aggression which the U.S. would help the government to smash with military power, although individual Communists agents took advantage of it by banners, signs and broadcasts over the Hué radio station.

By mid-May, General Ky recognized that he must make a difficult choice: he could either do nothing and watch Tri Quang gradually take over the country by default, or he could take strong action against the struggle movement. He chose the latter. On May 15, two battalions of loyal Government troops were airlifted to Danang, where they occupied the vital air base and began clearing the city of the small bands of dissident soldiers and armed

396 civilians which had been controlling it. Actual fighting was sporadic, casualties light. Tri Quang's propaganda claimed hundreds of Buddhists were killed; this was simply false. Ky's operation, using the minimum force necessary, was a remarkable success. Lodge got the news at a 2 A.M. meeting in the State Department, having returned to Washington on April 30. By the time of his return to Saigon on May 21, Danang had been brought fully under control by the Government troops, and Hué was the only remaining dissident stronghold. There were gathered Tri Quang, General Thi, and his allies Generals Dinh and Nhuan, with most of the other principal leaders of the struggle movement. Soldiers of Thi's First Division moved to seal off the airports, and block Highway One from Danang. Tri Quang sent his followers into the streets, creating roadblocks at every corner manned by grim-faced students with pistols and hand grenades. Communication of the U.S. Marine regiment stations ten miles south of Hué was threatened.

Then Ky moved. Strong forces of riot police were airlifted from Saigon, and support for the struggle movement quickly melted away. The city was brought back under control of the Government with no casualties at all. Many leaders of the movement were arrested and brought to Saigon. General Thi was allowed to leave the country.

Tri Quang had failed and Ky had won. Ky had shown great skill in his use of force, Lodge reported. He had avoided the fatal mistake made by Diem in the spring of 1963 of reacting violently and bloodily at the first sign of trouble. Ky had waited, he had allowed passions to cool; he had whittled away and split one area off from the other; he had moved in the middle of the night quietly and surefootedly. Relative political security was restored to the country.

Throughout the crisis Lodge had counseled moderation or action as the events demanded, carefully avoiding direct American involvement in a situation which was basically an internal Vietnamese affair. It was an extremely delicate situation, and a wrong move by the U.S. could have led to disaster. Lodge remained calm, did not yield to high-pressure tactics, and was able to witness the restoration of order and the resumption of progress in the war.

Lodge calmly watched and weathered the Saigon crisis. He ignored the American critics who said he should not have let Ky have planes for his movements. He equally ignored the Vietnamese critics who wanted the U.S. to intervene in the interests of "stability."

"It is ironic," Lodge wired the President, "that many Vietnamese are saying the U.S. should 'fix things up' without ever saying how, it being absolutely certain that if we tried to impose anything there would be first an 'anti-colonialist' howl from those with whom we differed and ultimately a howl from everybody.

"I do not, therefore, think that what is happening now will mean the end   *397*
of the world, or anything like it, But I wish to heaven that it wasn't happening."

As passions cooled, the Ky government emerged actually strengthened by
the showdown, Lodge went on about his daily task of seeking to build, stone
by stone, a better life for the villages. Education was a continuing concern:

By the end of May this year [he wired the President] *we had completed 43% of our program of distributing fourteen million elementary school textbooks throughout Viet Nam. This program, which
began in mid-1965, will be concluded in second half of 1967. The
books are distributed to the schools and lent to the students for the
school year. We hope to get three years' use out of each book.*

*The significance of this program and its impact on the system of
primary education is worth special note: for the first time, Vietnamese
children have textbooks which they can take home and read and show
to their parents. Content and illustrations have been carefully worked
out with leading Vietnamese educators and cover such subjects as Viet
Nam's history and geography, along with other standard subjects as
Arithmetic and personal hygiene and sanitation. I am providing a sample packet of these books separately, including brief descriptive com-
ments, as an item of possible interest.*
*Next to safety of life and limb, there is probably nothing more highly
prized in Viet Nam than education—perhaps greater even than land
reform.*

However, he kept a close eye on the problem of land reform, which had
never been satisfactorily tackled by previous regimes:

*We have agreed with the GVN (Vietnamese government) on a land
reform program for An Giang Province, one of the four national priority areas. The first phase of the program is to be completed in two years
and includes the distribution of 11,500 hectares of land, the surveying
of 42,000 hectares, and the distribution of 18,000 land titles.*

Lodge concerned himself also with the problem of the thousands of Vietnamese, including many women and children, maimed in the war. He
wired the President:

*This war has caused many Vietnamese to lose arms and legs, and
until recently, the facilities for helping these victims were very limited.
The National Institute for Rehabilitation had been painfully turning*

out a very few limbs and braces each month, using primitive hand methods. Mr. Juan Monros, of the World Rehabiliation Fund, who was brought here by Howard Rusk, has held a four-month training course which 43 student technicians completed on May 27, 1966, on the techniques of producing plastic limbs and braces. He expects that the Institute will now be able to turn out some 500 limbs and braces a month, which will be a great help in solving what has been a serious human problem. I recall your personal interest in making this possible.

Previous American missions had sometimes been deceived as to the true nature of land reform and other governmental measures through accepting as fact whatever reports Diem and Nhu had wished them to believe. Lodge took care to have his own reliable observers constantly appraising the scene at village levels. He created a new job category in the Embassy—a group of promising young Foreign Service Officers, known as "provincial reporters," who had been specially trained in the language, history and customs of the country. They were sent out into the provinces to do one specific job: look closely at the situation and report on successes and failures just as objectively and harshly as necessary. Often they brought Lodge good news, which he sometimes had to restrain others from proclaiming.

In this very strange conflict, we have many times seen individual situations in which we win but must not crow about it. On Wednesday, I reported the success which we seem to be having in —— Province. If, however, we publish to the world that we are having a great time in —— Province, and we bring in the journalists and the photographers and the TV men, then the Viet Cong or North Viet Nam will make a point of starting the trouble up again, and will pay a heavy price to do it, which, in turn, will exact a heavy price from us, and will mean that the people who have been successful will not be able to consolidate their gain—which they can do, if a little time goes by before our side starts putting out victory announcements.

Lodge, aware that most published maps of South Viet Nam show a large part of the country under Viet Cong control or influence, took care to show new Embassy arrivals his own special map, based on population density. This emphasized the relative unimportance of the highland jungles where Viet Cong could still hide and muster, and the all-importance of the rich Mekong Delta where more than a third of the people lived, and which supplied most of Viet Nam's rice. By mid-1966, more than 55 per cent of the Delta's people had been made relatively secure, through the mounting pressure of South Viet Nam's own forces. Moreover, the equivalent of five Viet Cong battalions had deserted.

"If you win the people over," Lodge told one group of new arrivals, "you dry up Viet Cong recruiting and the war is over. And so, in this war, you think more of people than you do of terrain and that's why I put this map here. You can see that about 50% of the people are in Saigon and the upper part of the Delta and about 35% along the Northeast Coast. If you have both areas, you have 85% and you're really on your way. We are making good progress toward that end."

He followed closely the joint Vietnamese-U.S. planning measures to rout the rest of the Viet Cong out of the labyrinthine swamps, marshes and canals of the Delta.

"I believe the Navy has established some kind of a record in rapidly developing a new type of boat," he cabled Washington. "In September they decided they needed a special boat to patrol the huge rivers—the Mekong and the Bassac—in the Delta. By December, they had it—a 31-foot fiberglass boat with two water-jet diesel engines. The Navy's plans for this watery region inspire confidence, as does the entire American military performance. In fact everyone—from Bob McNamara on down—can take pride in it."

When the September 1966 elections were held in South Viet Nam, fully 80 per cent of the people who were eligible to vote turned out to do so in spite of threats and terrorism by the Viet Cong. Lodge wired the President his view of their significance:

"1. The Viet Cong did its utmost, using hand grenades, ambushes, strikes, broadcasts, printed matter, and every known form of intimidation. Terrorism reached a high tide. And it didn't work.

"2. This election should end once and for all the notion which seems to be held in a few places that the Viet Cong is a socially-conscious group of liberals on the model of western socialism. This is a western idea which the Viet Cong, during my time here, has done nothing significant to promote. At no time has any enthusiasm been asked or given for any Viet Cong program. The Viet Cong emerges clearly from this election as an organized group of terrorists who, under western law, should be called 'criminals' since all of their methods are forbidden by the rules of land warfare and are crimes under western law. I refer to assassination, torture, kidnapping, etc. Without these crude methods there would be no Viet Cong. Without the Viet Cong there would be no recruits. And without the recruits there would be no war. In this election no public support for the Viet Cong was apparent. Had there been any votes in it, candidates would have been able to make ingratiating statements.

"3. For the Vietnamese people to have voted in such large numbers, in the

400   face of terrorism, shows their willingness to defy the Viet Cong in order to take a step which they believe is a step forward for their country.

"4. I have asked many Vietnamese in different walks of life why the Vietnamese want to move towards a democratic constitution, and the following answers always emerge:

    a. A constitutional democracy is a protection against despotism, to which they have been subjected in the past.

    b. For a Vietnamese to move towards a constitutional democracy is a step towards progress and a step away from coups. They have looked around them and have seen Korea and Japan and believe this is the way to go."

Looking at it in retrospect, Lodge wired on September 18, a week later:

"1. The Viet Cong went all out, both by violent deed and violent word.

    a. *By deed.* There were 166 Viet Cong deeds—acts of terrorism just before and including election day. This was about fifteen times the level of activity on an average day in August. GVN casualties from 6:00 p.m. September 10 to 6:00 p.m. September 11 are estimated at nineteen killed and 120 wounded. The Viet Cong casualties are estimated at eighteen killed, three wounded, and fifteen captured.

"The Government losses were small considering the all-out campaign of the Viet Cong because the GVN, on its side, went all-out too. It was high tide both ways. The Ky Government once again showed its talent in using force and handling troops and police effectively.

    b. *By word.* Then the Viet Cong, by word, made the issue, pumped it up, and unrestrainedly boasted about their certain success.

"In quite a miraculous way, the GVN suddenly seemed to grasp the technique of effective publicity. Certainly the posters, billboards, radio, television, and dragon dances were skillfully designed to work up interest and to do so in an honest and attractive way.

"All of this was observed by more than five hundred journalists, diplomatic observers, and Japanese and Korean parliamentary groups. In particular, the Vietnamese people were watching intently. The election was, therefore, as clean as such a thing can be.

"2. It, therefore, must be set down that the vote on September 11 was an immense vote of 'no confidence' in the Viet Cong. They asked for a verdict, and they got one. It is very big—on a par in importance with the departure of nearly 1,000,000 Vietnamese refugees from the North in 1954 rather than live under a Communist regime.

"3. The vote also indicates that the Government is capable of providing security for more people than we had thought.

"4. U.S. troops acted as a shield and prevented large units of the Viet Cong and the army of North Viet-Nam from interfering in the elections. For us, on our side, to destroy the redoubts, divide the main force units, and keep them off balance while the Vietnamese, on their side, do the face to face, elbow to elbow, work of population security is the ideal division of labor. What we have so often talked about actually happened last Sunday—and it worked. "5. The Vietnamese people showed amazing courage in the face of record-breaking attempts at terror. Embassy officers observed heavy voting at four Saigon polling places which were grenaded on election eve. An eyewitness reported that in Tra Vinh, the population trooped to the polls even while the area was under Viet Cong mortar fire. Only one polling area in the entire country suspended operations for security reasons."

Correspondent Charles Mohr, three weeks later, could report to the New York *Times:* ". . . The political atmosphere in South Viet Nam is probably better than it has ever been since the guerrilla war began six years ago." The 117 members of the Constituent Assembly, chosen to draft a new, demo-cratic constitution as a long step toward civilian rule, "had been chosen in the first really free and fair national election ever held here, and everyone was keenly conscious of this major fact. There was, almost literally, a clean smell to the air as the assembly gathered."

The elections encouraged Lodge to recommend that the President con-vene a new Pacific Conference, larger than the earlier one at Hawaii. Presi-dent Johnson called one for Manila, to which would come all the chiefs of government from the nations sharing America's concern over Communist expansionism—mostly the very same men Lodge had called on in his early 1965 visits to their capitals.

When the conference came, in October, 1966, Lodge was well prepared. For two months previously he had been working with Premier Ky and Chief of State Thieu to help prepare them for any kind of conference which might arise. They would have long sessions together to discuss the various ideas and phrases which would enter into the discussions of a peace settlement. He was determined that the Americans and the Vietnamese would under-stand the same meanings when they used certain phrases, and that Ky not repeat an earlier indiscretion of openly demanding an invasion of North Viet Nam—something the U.S. prudently feared could provoke World War III by driving Russia to drop its role of limited help to Hanoi, and bring in China also. When Manila came, the preparation worked well; Ky's moderate speech set the tone of limited aims, of conciliation and magnanimity for the conference's own communique. That Communique pledged American with-drawal six months after North Viet Nam ended intervention. It pledged the allies to postwar development of all Southeast Asia.

402   Prior to Manila, Lodge had urged President Johnson to extend his trip to a visit to American fighting forces in South Viet Nam. He argued that the security for this was as good at Camranh Bay, the huge American installation, as in Manila itself. He was supported in this by General Westmoreland, and by Bill Moyers. Lodge said it would do more for the morale of the troops than anything else because the President of the United States, whoever the man, has a meaning for American fighting men that is unique.

The final decision was made on the 25th of October at the somber old Spanish Malacañang Palace on the banks of the Pasig River in Manila. The Communique had just been adopted and a hasty conference was held in one of the sumptuous bedrooms of the Palace. Present were President Johnson, Secretary Rusk, Clark Clifford, Marvin Watson, Westmoreland, Moyers and Lodge. Speculation had been on a visit Oct. 27; instead they decided then and there to do it the next day.

Westmoreland hurried off to assemble token forces from all the services fighting in Viet Nam. On the morning of Oct. 26, Lodge zoomed away in the small T-39 jet he had at his disposal, a two-engine North American job with crew of three and seats for four passengers. He arrived early at Camranh Bay and went over all the details of the program with General Westmoreland and his associates.

Lodge says the scene was unforgettable. The air strip is located on a sandy peninsula some fifteen miles long. The sand dunes have been flattened by bulldozers and metal planking placed on it. The runway is 10,000 feet long. In the distance stood the purple mountains of the piedmont. The soldiers were standing, with their massed colors, on the metal planking which caught the reddish light of the setting sun.

First, in quick succession, came the Pan American chartered planes which carried the press, the soldiers being greatly cheered at the sight of the Pan American hostesses. Then came the Presidential's Air Force One. Lodge was at the foot of the ramp to present Chief of State Thieu, and Prime Minister Ky, to the President. They in turn introduced the Vietnamese officials, and then General Westmoreland took over. Afterwards came the ceremony, the award of decorations, the visit to the hospital, the visit to the mess hall and the talk with the Generals. After a few hours, the President took off; and Lodge returned to Saigon. The next day he received the following message:

For Ambassador Lodge   *October 27, 1966*
The following was sent from AF-1 in flight via the White House:
Quote. From the President to Ambassador Lodge:
I want you to know how much I appreciate your help at the Con-

ference—I shall always cherish the memory. Your good judgment was
again confirmed at the Cam Ranh affair yesterday.
    Signed: The President. End Quote.

So the war went on.

While some spokesmen were urging a million-man American force to
achieve some crushing victory of Communist armies, Lodge believed that
true victory would come on the day when enough Viet Cong recruits simply
decided to go home and not fight any more. When that day came, the invading North Vietnamese regulars, having no more support among the people
and no dependable lines of supply or information, also would have to withdraw or be crushed. Such a victory could not be achieved by any one mass
assault—whether of tremendous land armies, or of saturation bombing. It
would be achieved by constantly harassing and breaking up the Viet Cong
until he lost heart; and by forestalling and spoiling the planned offensives of
the North Vietnamese regulars, until they were disorganized and scattered. In such a war an Armageddon, or apocalyptic victory, was highly unlikely. The end might come, as in Korea, when the enemy suddenly decided
it had enough and sought negotiations. "Or the same thing might happen
that happened in Greece or Malaysia or the Philippines," Lodge told an in-
terviewer, "that they just decided it isn't any good and go home. That way
they don't lose face, that way they don't have to admit that they ever
started."

It is beyond the scope of this narrative, which is the story of Lodge, to go
into the merits or demerits of the Great Debate raging over whether the Viet
Nam war was a wise war, or whether the President had managed to get the
country into the position of Br'er Rabbit fighting the Tar Baby—unable to
win and unable to let go. Highly intelligent and perfectly sincere·men of
great integrity were at diametrical points of view about this, and the country
itself was more divided than it had been on any issue since the 1940 issue of
Lend Lease and aiding the Allies. Certainly every American prayed that the
end might come soon, and would welcome any opening for an honorable
and just cessation.

It was easy, in retrospect, for seasoned observers of Viet Nam's tragedy to
point to many an error of policy and many a missed opportunity. Some believe the greatest opportunity was missed in not helping Ho Chi Minh
against the French in 1945, when he was still friendly toward the U.S. and
the U.S. had influential advisers with him. Others felt that President Ken-

404   nedy's decision to back General Taylor's strategy and to depart from President Eisenhower's "advise and aid" policy to one of much larger commitment, was a tragic mistake which led from one escalation to another until the U.S. had found itself "fighting the wrong war in the wrong place." Still others felt that even if a U.S.-Red China showdown were inevitable, it would be foolish to bleed and bankrupt ourselves fighting a puppet rather than the main enemy, in the worst possible place, under the worst possible conditions. Others, like Walter Lippmann, argued persuasively that we had over-committed our resources beyond our powers and must give up trying to damp down every Communist flash-point in the world. Persuasive cases were made for all these points of view.

Lodge believed that whatever mistakes had been made, the issue had been irrevocably joined, and that if the U.S. failed to press it to a satisfactory end, Communism would engulf all Asia and provoke the larger war. Those who believed the Viet Nam struggle in vain might well consider some of 1966's events: Indonesia, which had been teetering on the verge of Communist seizure, almost totally obliterated its huge Communist Party, and moreover ended the Peking-inspired war Sukarno was waging on Malaysia. North Korea declared itself independent of Peking and so had the once pro-Peking Japanese Communist Party. In Seoul, the capital of an even bloodier war fifteen years before, the foreign ministers of nine free Asian and Pacific countries—Japan, South Korea, Taiwan, Thailand, the Philippines, South Viet Nam, Malaysia, Australia and New Zealand—met to launch cooperation on trade, development and other foreign common problems. Both Burma and Japan showed less fear of China. The new men of Asia, said Thai Foreign Affairs Minister Thanat Khoman, "are getting together without being influenced by any of the former colonial powers. Red China lost virtually all of its influence in emergent Africa." It seemed highly doubtful that this defeat, that such Free Asian initiatives, or the Indonesian upheaval, could have come about if Communist aggression had not been checked in Viet Nam.

With Manila, it could be said that the bi-partisan policy which Johnson and Lodge had evolved for Southeast Asia was beginning to resemble the achievements of the bipartisan policy that President Truman, backed effectively by Vandenberg and Lodge, had used to block a Communist guerrilla victory in Greece.

President Johnson's mid-1965 commitment of U.S. forces to thwart Communist seizure of South Viet Nam was similar to Truman's commitment of the U.S. to the defense of Greek and Turkey in 1947. By so doing Truman gave the region's non-Communist forces a center of power to rally around, and he also started a schism within the Communist camp itself between the Stalinists, who wanted to fight the Greek Civil War to the last Greek, and the Titoists whose eventual closure of the Yugoslav border to Greek guerrillas finally ended the struggle. It took 2½ years from the Truman commitment for the Greek Communists to realize that they could not seize the country by armed force—but they did realize it.

The Johnson commitment had given a similar rallying point for the six Southeast Asian nations represented at Manila—who were all contributing to the war effort in Viet Nam—and also as well for Japan, Formosa and Malaysia who were all members of ASPAC (Asian and Pacific Council) formed in June, 1966. Whatever the leaders of such countries as India said in public deploring American intervention, privately (as Lodge found in his earlier visits) they were glad to have the security of an American umbrella against the threat of an expansionist China now nuclear-armed. America's disavowal at Manila of any permanent ambitions in Southeast Asia made it easier, as well as necessary, for these Southeast Asian nations to move toward protecting their own mutual security, as Europe had done under the Truman shield. Moreover, the huge American deployment in South Viet Nam was itself now one of the chief bargaining counters for a peaceful settlement, since it forced Ho Chi Minh to choose between seeing South Viet Nam become another Greece (with American forces leaving), or another South Korea with a permanent American garrison on his doorstep. The latter prospect appealed even less to the Russians, who thus had an additional interest in finding doors to peace. Also, as in Greece, the American presence had split the Communists in Hanoi, Peking and elsewhere between hawks pressing for bitter-end struggle, and a growing dove faction seeking to stop it. In less than two years, the policy was beginning to pay off.

By the Spring of 1967, Lodge could look over the two years of his second tour in Viet Nam with a sense of fulfilment. No longer was there any question of military overthrow of South Viet Nam. A sense of defeatism spread among both Viet Cong and North Vietnamese invaders, and their defections to the "open arms" welcoming program had more than doubled. He prepared to end the most challenging, dangerous and demanding task his country had yet asked of him in a long life on active duty.

What new demands might come, he could not tell. At 64, an age when most men are ready for retirement, Lodge looks, as he always has, at least a decade younger than his chronological yars. He is as wiry, lean and sinewy as when he boxed with his feet at eleven, or knocked down the Tammany thug at Houston, or bodily "lifted out" Khrushchev's brawny bodyguard. He

406   is, in a word, tough—quite capable of being, as Correspondent Keyes Beech found him, "a switchblade fighter," yet graced also with the unstudied poise and bearing of a natural aristocrat. Since his almost fatal stomach attack of 1944, he has eaten so simply and so sparingly that he has the superb health that often accompanies the need to guard a bodily weakness.

Moreover, he is the cerebral type of man who pays scant attention to whatever he may be eating, except to finish it as rapidly as possible. He is so little concerned with food, or what others may think of how he eats it, that he slurps up his soup as noisily as some untutored goatherd, and after swiftly disposing of whatever bland food is on his plate, is as apt as not to vent a loud and rumbling belch without so much as seeming aware of it, much less offering apology.

Lodge has an equal intentness and preoccupation with whatever task he is engaged on. Though he is capable of gay, uninhibited conviviality at the occasional songfests he holds with old friends, he has little patience with small talk or light badinage, prefers to get to important matters and straight to the point of those; or, if nothing else affords, to spend his time boning up on problems that may soon require his attention. He is a glutton for facts, and files them on some indelible mental register. He is an instinctive organizer of ideas and synthesizer of their salient agreements, an equally instinctive setter of priorities on the work he has in hand. He has tremendous power of concentration, which shows itself in the orderly and methodical way he arranges and disposes of his tasks. He hoards his energy, retiring early, and rising early, and whenever possible works in a daily swim. He is a brisk walker, with long, lean, loping strides.

No attempt has been made, thus far in Lodge's story, to appraise his character or assess the meaning of his career. As Flaubert argued, character is best revealed in action—and certainly his story teems with that. It is, perhaps, proper to try to strike a balance on his strengths and flaws, to sum up his personality and his life style.

Few men know him really well. He has preserved from his lonely boyhood a certain aloofness of manner that keeps most people at arm's length. He is extremely close-mouthed and given to few confidences. He can be brusque, perhaps unintentionally so, to the point of near rudeness. He is a realist, and unsentimental about the ambivalence of men's nature and their vulnerability to the pressures of vanity, ambition, power, gossip and greed. He has never been a utopian dreamer, but his practical commonsense has always urged upon him the conviction that both the United States and his own Republican Party could order their affairs and evolve their programs much more sensibly and successfully than they have yet managed to do.

If he has had any single obsession throughout his life it has been the need

for America to be and to stay strong as the surest way of staying peaceful—
a conviction which he has yet to see tested by our leaders through any long
period of consistent and continuous practice.

The harshest epithet directed at him is that of arrogance. "His grandfather was arrogant," says Arthur Krock, who knew both well, "and he has
inherited some, but his heritage is minimal." "He displays the attributes of
tough-mindedness, decision, aloofness and arrogance," said the *Times* on
his reappointment to Saigon. "His critics are said to list these attributes in
reverse order." The judgment is sometimes contradicted. "He has never
been arrogant with me," veteran Saigon correspondent Keyes Beech wrote
the writer. "I'd heard all the stories about him being a snob, but the Lodge
we knew here was different."

To his underlings, that was not always true. During his second tour in
Saigon, Lodge emerged from his office one day to query his aide on the
whereabouts of a paper he had dictated the previous day. After a frantic
search of several minutes by the aide and Lodge's secretary, the somewhat
chagrined aide reported that apparently it had been lost. "Then you rewrite
it yourself," snapped Lodge, who had been in a foul mood all day. About
five minutes later, the missing paper was found, and the aide brought it in
to Lodge's desk without comment, along with a large stack of cables,
memoranda, letters, and other material. Later that same afternoon, Lodge
called in the aide to discuss a number of matters, among them the once
lost but now found paper. "Now this," Lodge growled, thinking the aide had
written the paper, "is just not right at all. I never begin a sentence with 'I',
and you should know that by now. And don't you realize that . . ." and
Lodge went on to point out several grievous faults in the paper. Finally the
aide, struggling to hold back laughter, said, "But you wrote it, sir. We found
your draft." After a moment of disbelief and a still longer moment of realization that what the aide had said was painfully true, a chastened and
slightly more humble Lodge boomed, "Well, I guess you've got me on that
one."

The charge of haughtiness particularly infuriates Lodge's youngest son,
Harry, himself a model of approachability and friendliness. Harry's own
view of his father's nature is that he is only completely happy and at ease
when at home and in the bosom of his family. "He's just not the sort of man
who likes to stop at the club to drink and gas with the boys," says Harry.
"He'd rather be out in the bay there, in a rowboat, with the youngest grand-
child wetting all over the seat or falling all over his legs. I've never seen
anybody who can read on as imperturbably as he does with half a dozen yell-
ing kids roller-skating through his hall. There are at least 16 of us when we
all get together for supper in the yard, and his laugh is so loud that Ralph

408 Mitchell [the gardener] tells me he can hear it all the way down at his house by the highway [some thousand yards away]. I'll never forget when Dag Hammarskjöld came here for the week-end and we taught him to play hearts with kids jumping all over him. I'd never seen him so happy. 'I feel like an uncle,' he said."

Lodge is objective enough to be candid about flaws of character, or mistakes of judgment. He regrets both his duplicity over Townsendism, and his expediency over Lend Lease. He also regrets the roughness of the tactics against Bob Taft in 1952. He greatly admired Taft's courage, particularly against the trial of war criminals (as *ex-post facto* law), and always cherished an admiring letter Taft wrote him on his resignation from the Senate. While he felt the Taft forces blamed him for much he did not do, he also felt that he could have used his influence more to prevent some of the strong language that was used. On Bob Taft, Jr.'s pre-election Viet Nam visit to Viet Nam in 1966, Lodge drove him to the Embassy for a pleasant lunch of combined current information and past reminiscence—including mutual memories of Alice Roosevelt Longworth's witticisms. Taft came away feeling that "most of the differences of the past have long since faded," and told the writer of his visit:

> *We then discussed my hopes for the visit in Viet Nam which was interesting. The Ambassador indicated that his feelings were that every candidate who had the nomination of either major party should be allowed to come to Viet Nam and review the situation at public expense. He indicated that the reason for thinking this was that this was perhaps the most important issue regarding the future of America and particularly the American foreign policy. It was interesting to note that about this time, the House Arms Services Committee was trying to get the Department of Defense to stop political candidates from visiting. However, throughout my trip, I had the utmost of cooperation from the armed services and from the various public affairs offices.*

Young Taft's later victory was part of a sweeping Republican comeback in the 1966 elections which heartened Lodge greatly—especially the phenomenal victory back home in Boston of a Negro, Edward Brooke, who would take Lodge's own former seat in the Senate, the same that he had turned over to Saltonstall in 1944. Brooke's campaign was successfully managed, against great odds, by Paul Grindle, the same amateur-turned-pro who had steered the unique 1964 write-in victory for Lodge himself. The Brooke victory seemed to Lodge a symptom that the Republican Party was finding its way out of the dead-end of Goldwaterism, and its thinly-veiled appeals to white backlash.

Chapter Eighteen

The writer, in the nine years he has known Lodge, has come to regard him as a man of essential simplicity. His most consistent quality is one of intense loyalty to his friends, particularly of his youth. The quality shows in his making a trip to Normandy, on behalf of the mother, to dedicate a memorial to Lieutenant Morton Eustis, his old comrade of the Second Armored Division, who was hit in the head by an antitank missile while standing in the turret of his own tank leading the way at top speed down the hedgerows of Normandy.

The same quality shows in Lodge's 1948 visits to the bedside of his dying friend, Mally Greenough, whose huge linesman's bulk was wasted with cancer; and his thoughtful letter to Mally's widow:

Dear Kathleen:

From the days of my earliest childhood Mally was such an intimate part of my life that it would be impossible ever to set down all the thoughts and memories that fill my mind. But for the sake of your two boys, I feel I should write this letter so that they may know a few of the things that he was and did, of which they might not otherwise know. . . . My memory goes back to the early days at Nahant when we were very small boys, taking swimming lessons, roaming over the rocks at East Point, attending each other's birthday parties, learning how to sail, going to our first dances at the Nahant Club, etc. Two memories stand out. Mally was always the best at any game or athletic effort and he was always the most popular. I think this was because of the kindly attitude toward people which he kept all through his life.

. . . Our life on the North Shore began and with it the wonderful help which Mally gave me in all my political life. I remember when I made my announcement to run for the U.S. Senate in the fall of 1935 we were all taking a Sunday afternoon walk around the Pingree's race track together, and Mally came up and offered to give me a hand in my campaign. He . . . was my active political mainstay from that time on.

Everything he ever tried to do—whether it was business or yachting or Navy—he did well and professionally. Political activity was no exception. It is so easy to make mistakes in political money-raising—so easy to accept money from wrong sources, on the one hand, or else not be able to raise the money on the other. His judgment, energy, wide acquaintance, tact and persuasive powers all came into play. Like every good treasurer, he was always on the alert to keep waste down. But I shall never forget one moment when we were alone in the '36 campaign when he said to me confidentially, "If there's something that you absolutely must do, go ahead and do it and we'll find the money some-

410   *where." That was the kind of treasurer and friend he was . . . I don't believe I ever knew a man who brought so much laughter, sunshine and delight into the lives of his friends. . . .*

Mrs. Greenough sought Cabot's help in choosing Mally's epitaph, and he suggested several—"The Good Man Never Dies" (Montgomery), and Plutarch's "The measure of a man's life is the spending of it, and not the length," but thought he liked best Shakespeare's

> *The kindest man,*
> *The best conditioned and unwearied spirit.*

He suggested also simply the Navy Seal, followed by:

> MALCOLM WHELEN GREENOUGH
> (dates)
> *Loving Husband and Father*
> *Joyful and Incomparable Friend*
> *Patriotic Citizen in Peace and War*

This quality in Lodge shows in the appreciation he wrote of General Frank McCoy when he died in 1953—first to the General's widow, and then at the request of Major General William S. Biddle, commanding First Armored Division at Fort Bliss, for *Assembly,* the West Point alumni quarterly:

> *. . . as a reserve officer I served a tour of duty in the horse cavalry in the Ft. Bliss area, which was notable to me because it involved a portee operation of horses from Ft. Bliss to the southernmost point of the Big Bend of Texas. But more noteworthy still was the fact that Gen. McCoy was in command, and to sit with him under the fly of his tent in those Texas summer evenings and hear his stories of the Philippines and of Cuba, of his doings at the White House as an aide to Theodore Roosevelt, of his contact with diplomats and the great of the world was unforgettable. . . . He seemed to me to regard life as a gift from God which was infinitely precious and infinitely wonderful. He seemed continually to marvel at the wonder of life, and consequently made life a wonderful thing for all those who knew him. . . . We are all better men because he was our friend.*

The quality shows also in his taking the time, in his busy schedule at the U.N., to write Henry Mencken on September 19, 1955, as he lay mortally ill in Baltimore of a stroke:

I have been reading all the newspaper stories about your birthday—an
*event which, I also read, does not interest you very much. But it did
make me think of you and of the times when we used to meet in Washington and at national conventions. I particularly remember one occasion in Houston in 1928 when the Texas Rangers invaded the room we
were in. . . .*

Mencken's secretary Rosalind Lohrfinck answered:

*Mr. Mencken was delighted to have your letter. He remembers with
the greatest pleasure the fun you had when you were working together
and he is sorry that he can't hope to do it again. . . . he laments that
there are so few men like you in the country. . . .*

Another striking quality in Lodge is an essential modesty which was first
brought home to the writer in discovering, only by chance, long-buried in
Lodge's "dead" correspondence files, a handwritten letter from General Marshall, which was an exceptional tribute (see p. 422) from that taciturn man
whose praise was as rare as it was treasured. Not only had Lodge never
made this letter public, or shown it to friends, but even his family was unaware of its existence.

Perhaps the strongest single trait in Lodge has been his quite simple and
single-minded determination to make some actual *physical* contribution to
America's defense, and, where need be, risk his life. Whether it was inspired
by his boyhood hero, McCoy, by the admonitions of his grandfather in that
long-ago letter of familial exhortation, or by the example of his Uncle Gussie Gardner, Lodge's determination to share the physical risks of his time is
still evidenced at this writing in the not inconsiderable danger of his daily
work in Viet Nam.

In a beatnik and Vietnik age, he is undoubtedly an old-fashioned man—
square in the sense that was once complimentary. Ours has been called a
time of disbelief when "certain words almost vanished from the American
vocabulary. Honor was one. Glory was another." Lodge is old-fashioned because he never ceased to believe in either.

It was Robert E. Lee, also an essentially simple man, who best defined the
deepest meanings of these much-abused and now unfashionable words.

"There is," he wrote down privately for his own guidance, "a true glory
and a true honor: the glory of duty done, the honor of the integrity of principle."

By these definitions, Lodge's life exemplifies the true honor and he has
earned the true glory.

Whatever new challenges lie ahead of him, whatever new callings or new

412 ordeals may face this essentially simple and dedicated man, he will perhaps be best seen and best remembered as he appeared that day on the blood-stained battle slopes of An Khe to make his brief and eloquent address to the men of his old division, First Cav:

"We name this camp Camp Radcliff. We dedicate it to the memory of Major Donald G. Radcliff, an officer of the Regular Army, who died as the result of enemy fire on August 17, 1965, having volunteered to fly to the relief of the Special Forces Camp at Chu Lai and whose heroic actions on that day have since resulted in his being awarded posthumously the Distinguished Flying Cross.

"Major Radcliff was 37 years old. By any standards, that is young. His life had meaning for him, for his wife and for his children. But it also had meaning for all of us—for persons like myself who never knew him, but who do know that the death of this skillful, courageous and patriotic man with many years of life ahead of him diminishes my country and diminishes me. We, therefore, have a tragic sense of a fine man being sharply and prematurely cut off. That is one reality.

"But there is another reality. It is written in the book of Ecclesiastes: 'There is a time to be born and a time to die.' And this should be considered in conjunction with the words of Solomon in the Old Testament: 'Having fulfilled his course in a short time, he fulfilled long years.' Major Radcliff was a professional soldier and a skilled aviator and he indeed fulfilled his course in a short time.

"A distinguished American, deepy moved by the thought of young men dying in war, once suggested that combat units consist entirely of middle-aged and elderly men, since they have their lives behind them and should be much more expendable. That seems like a fair proposition. The only trouble with it is that no man who is not young can do what needs to be done in combat. Even the healthiest among them would be useless by the end of the first day.

"The everyday citizen of America, therefore—in fact the whole of America—must look to its young men to lead them through the valley of danger. If there are no young men to do this, then the life of this nation has ended.

"Major Radcliff's widow has seen this clearly. She wrote to General Kinnard:

" 'Don was a professional soldier and died in the defense of a just cause. I am truly proud of him and your First Cavalry Division.' Mrs. Radcliff voices the spirit on which the life of the nation depends.

"But—let me close by saying—she also speaks in the spirit of Pericles who, 400 years before the birth of Christ, said this about soldiers who had died in war:

" 'They faced the foe as they drew near him in the strength of their own

manhood; and when the shock of battle came, they chose rather to suffer   *413*
the uttermost than to win life by weakness. So their memory has escaped
the reproaches of men's lips, but they bore instead on their bodies the marks
of men's hands, and in a moment of time, at the climax of their lives, were
rapt away from a world filled, for their dying eyes, not with terror but with
glory.

"'Such were the men who lie here and such the city that inspired them.
We survivors may pray to be spared their bitter hour, but must disdain to
meet the foe with a spirit less triumphant. . . .

"'They gave their bodies to the commonwealth and received, each for his
own memory, praise that will never die, and with it the grandest of all sep-
ulchers, not that in which their mortal bones are laid, but a home in the
minds of men. . . . For the whole earth is the sepulcher of famous men.'"

The Cabots and the Lodges: A Postscript

When the just-inaugurated President Washington made a tour of the Eastern States in 1789, he went from Boston along the Essex shore and stopped at Beverly for breakfast with his younger friend, George Cabot, who was then 38. In order to steal a look at the first President, Cabot's seven-year-old son, Henry, hid under the side-table and peeked while Washington ate and talked with his father. Years later, Henry Cabot told his grandson about it, and many other years later that grandson, Henry Cabot Lodge, told his own grandson and namesake about it.

This bridge across the memories of only two men shows how unbroken is the link which the present Henry Cabot Lodge enjoys with America's beginnings. In telling his story, the focus was kept purposely on his own deeds and time. However, a postscript about his forebears may lend that story additional continuity and perspective.

Lodge's earliest American forebear was Francis Higginson, the first minister of the Massachusetts Bay Colony. His direct descendant, Elizabeth Higginson, married Joseph Cabot, whose father John was one of three Cabot brothers who emigrated to Salem from St. Heliers, on the Isle of Jersey, about 1699. Like the Higginsons, they were sailors and fishermen.

Since 1784, the General Court of Massachusetts has kept a representation of a cod-fish in its chambers "as a memorial of the importance of the Cod-Fishery to the welfare of the Commonwealth." What tobacco was to colonial Virginia, the cod was to the Bay State. "The aboundance of Sea-Fish are almost beyond beleeuing," Francis Higginson himself wrote in 1630. The same boats that brought in the fish drew New England out toward the world. The American Revolution grew, in part, from the fact that New England built its own merchant marine to serve her fishermen. These same schooners, fitted out as privateers, became the first American Navy.

George Cabot, the seventh child of Joseph and Elizabeth Higginson Cabot, sailed as a cabin boy before he was 17, leaving Harvard in his second year when his father died, and by his 18th birthday commanded a cod-fishing vessel. At 23, he married his double-first-cousin, a second Elizabeth Higginson, and built his brick home in Beverly, across the inlet from Salem; later he built the causeway across the inlet. When war began he turned privateer. John Trumbull tells in his "Reminiscences" of taking passage at Bilbao in 1781 for Beverly on the *Cicero*," a fine letter of marque ship of 20 guns and 120 men . . . belonging to the house of Cabot," and having with her "a British Lisbon packet of 16 guns, which she had just taken as a prize." On arriving at Beverly Col. Trumbull saw "lying in the harbor 11 privateers, all finer than the *Cicero* and all belonging to the Cabots." A few weeks before the peace, two Cabot privateers captured in the European seas "several West Indiamen to the value of at least £100,000 sterling."

At war's end, Capt. Cabot's ships traded to the far ends of the earth; one carried the first American flag to St. Petersburg, in Russia, in 1784. From Beverly and Salem, the Yankee trading vessels took salted cod and rum to the west coast of Africa, brought copal for varnish from Zanzibar on Africa's East Coast, and rubber and crude overshoes from Brazil. "They picked up sandalwood in Hawaii or otterskins in British Columbia as currency for Chinese tea. Others played 'hide-and-go-seek'—finding cheap hides in South America or California to supply the new shoe factories back home. They sought out the best coffees in the Southern Hemisphere, brought Peruvian bark to make quinine against malaria, jute for gunny sacks, linseed oil for paint and ink, shellac for ships and furniture . . ." Salem quickly became the world headquarters for trade in the meat-preserving peppercorn, and prosperous native merchants on South Pacific Islands believed that Salem was "a country by itself, and one of the richest and most important sections of the globe."

At 29, young Capt. Cabot, world-traveled, self-taught, and wise beyond his years, was chosen a delegate by Beverly to the State Constitutional Convention, where he supported the more conservative James Bowdoin for Governor against John Hancock, who won (and who bestowed the term "Essex Junto" on Cabot, the Lowells, Timothy Pickering, Theophilus Parsons and others who opposed him). This "Junto" has been called America's first political party.

Cabot quickly learned French and Spanish in his travels, and became such a self-made expert in commercial law that all his friends sought his counsel, in political matters as well as business ones. His interests took him often to New York, where he became a close friend and ally of Hamilton. He also loaned Jefferson, on his way to Europe in 1784, his Spanish grammar and noted that Jefferson "mastered the language in the space of 19 days."

In June, 1791, at age 39, Cabot was chosen U.S. Senator from Massachusetts, and at once took a high position among the Federalist leaders in the national government. "Next to Hamilton, and side by side with Rufus King," wrote Henry Adams, "he was revered as the oracle of Federalism." He was shocked by the way the French Revolution developed, writing his friend Judge Parsons: "We have seen the Expression of the general will of a great society silenced, the legal representatives of the people butchered, and a band of relentless murderers ruling in their stead with rods of iron." He resigned from the Senate at 45, to tend his animals on a new retreat in Brookline where "the swinish multitude . . . more humane than those of Paris . . . are satisfied with milk instead of blood." When the imprisoned La Fayette's son fled to America for safety and protection, hiding in Boston under the assumed name of Motier, President Washington hesitated to assist him openly lest he strain America's relations with Revolutionary France. "I imposed upon Mr. Cabot," Washington wrote to young La Fayette, "a gentleman of character, and one in whose discretion I could place entire confidence, the agreeable office of assuring you, in my name, of my warmest affection and support, and of my determination to stand in the place of a father and friend to you under all circumstances." Cabot later turned Motier over to his friend Hamilton, who watched over the young exile until it was safe for him to join Washington's own family.

President John Adams, though he was irritated at the "Essex Junto" for preferring South Carolina's Charles Pinckney to himself as the Federalist choice for President, nevertheless sent George Cabot a commission as the first Secretary of the Navy, just then coming into official being. The Senate unanimously confirmed his choice. But when the commission reached Cabot at Brookline, he refused it ("my powers are inadequate to the work"), and went further into deliberate obscurity. Adams suspected Cabot, like the "retired" Madison, had deeper plans. "Mr. Cabot, I suppose," he wrote his wife, "after aggrandizing his character in the shade a few years, is to be some great thing . . . It is marvelous how political plants grow in the shade . . . His countrymen will soon believe him to be a giant in a cave, and will go in a body to dig him out of it." When Cabot at last emerged to preside over the Hartford Convention of 1814, during the unpopular war with England, John Adams cried to a visitor: "Thank God! Thank God! George Cabot's close-buttoned ambition has broke out at last. He wants to be president of New England, sir!"

While this convention has been accused of contemplating secession, Cabot himself told a younger man his job was to "keep you young hotheads from getting into mischief." Cabot, shortly before his death at 72, burned nearly all his own papers and letters, but the journal he turned over to the Legislature in 1819 as "a faithful and complete record" of the Convention, showed a final conclusion against secession. A witness to that convention, S. G. Goodrich, thought Cabot "the most imposing man among them . . . over 6 feet in height, broad-shouldered . . . his hair white . . . his eyes blue, his complexion slightly florid. He seemed to me like Washington, as if the great man, as painted by Stuart, had walked out of the canvas . . . In aspect and appearance he was strikingly dignified; and such was the effect of his presence that in a crowded room, and amid other men of mark, when you once became conscious he was there you could hardly forget him—as the traveler in Switzerland sees Mont Blanc towering above other mountains around him wherever he may be . . . When he began to converse, all eyes and ears turned to him as if eager to catch the music of his voice and the light of his mind." William Ellery Channing said Cabot was "consulted with the respect . . . paid to an ancient oracle, and no mind among us contributed so much to the control of public affairs . . . When we think of his whole character, when with the sagacity of his intellect we combine the integrity of his heart, the dignified grace of his manners, and the charm of his conversation, we hardly know the individual, with the exception of Washington, whom we should have offered more willingly to a foreigner as a specimen of the men whom America can produce."

Compared to the Cabots, the Lodges are relative newcomers to America. Giles Lodge, who was born in London in 1770, went to the West Indies at 21 as agent for his brothers who were merchants in London and Liverpool. He was caught in the slave uprising at Santo Domingo in August, 1791. The fact that he spoke French fluently enabled him to escape the general massacre. He took refuge on an American schooner which brought him to Boston, where he decided to stay, becoming an exporter and importer. In 1800, he married Mary Langdon, daughter of a Revolutionary war captain, John Langdon.

A stern man, Giles Lodge was not remembered lovingly by his son, John Ellerton Lodge. The father horsewhipped him for some offense, and the boy ran away from home in his teens, crying: "No man can do this to me!" He found his way to New Orleans, and stayed there for a decade. Little is known of his life there, but he had somehow acquired a fleet of 12 sailing vessels by the time he returned to Boston in 1835, aged 28. He built that up into a big fleet of Yankee Clippers, carried fortune-hunters to the Gold Rush in San Francisco, and made many voyages to China, to Lisbon, the Spice Islands, New Zealand, Sumatra. Always he took with him a huge iron chest, locked with an enormous heavy key. He kept a complete business diary, meticulously recording every voyage, every cargo bought and sold, the goods and the prices. His Clippers were made in Mystic and in Medford, from half-models which were first designed, then working models, then full-size enlargements of the models. Some of these models now hang on the walls of the homes of Henry Cabot Lodge, and those of his sons. The huge iron chest and the journal are in Lodge's home.

It was this Capt. John Lodge, the doughty China trader, who married Anna Cabot, daughter of Henry Cabot, the lad who had hid to watch Washington. They lived in Mr. Cabot's Boston mansion, where their son, Henry Cabot Lodge, was born in 1850. "He was over 70," the boy wrote of Grandfather Cabot, "when I first recall him clearly, a tall, erect, very fine-looking man who gave no impression of age or feebleness. When I asked him for money, he would pull out a handful of change and let me take my choice." The old man told him: "We do not talk about family in this country." Each day, the boy also was taken to see his Aunt Elizabeth, President Kirkland's widow, in her Summer Street apartments.

Capt. Lodge had become quite wealthy in his trading. When the boy was eight, his father bought for $50,000 the mansion at 31 Beacon Street which had belonged to Samuel Eliot, a former Whig Congressman who lost everything in the Panic of 1837; all his goods were sold at auction. Capt. Lodge raised a fund among Eliot's friends to buy in his library, and present it to him (his son, Charles Eliot, became another Harvard president). Capt. Lodge had his office in the granite block which stretched to the end of Commercial Wharf, and from his counting-room the boy could see the beautiful Clippers lying along the wharf. Some of them Lodge had bought—the Alfred Hill and Sarah H. Snow—but others, built for him at Mystic or Medford, he had named himself—his "luckiest ship," the *Argonaut;* and the *Don Quixote* and *Sancho Panza,* named from one of his best-loved books; and others with such adventurous names as the *Kremlin,* the *Storm King,* the *Cossack* and the *Magnet.* Young Lodge and his friends would prowl the great hogsheads filled with West Indian molasses, to run their fingers along the testing-sticks and scoop off the black molasses as a special treat. He made friends with the captains and the seamen, who brought him firecrackers from China, "and strange fireworks, fascinating in appearance . . . From them, too, came bronzes and porcelains and pictures and carved ivories . . . and ginger and sweetmeats and lychee-nuts (then almost unkown here), of which I used to partake with keen delight."

The boy would ride with his father behind a team of bays to the Medford shipyards to see the new Clippers under construction. He loved to drive with him, too, to their summer place at Nahant. On these drives, Capt. Lodge would recite to the boy long passages from Scott and Gray, and from his two favorite poets, Shakespeare and Pope. By his 10th year, the boy read all of Scott's Waverley Novels from beginning to end. "In the same way I was led to an early admiration of Macaulay and to a far earlier reading of Hawthorne, Dickens and 'Robinson Crusoe.' "

Young Lodge was thrown early among intellectuals. Charles Sumner, the great Senator and abolitionist, often dined at his father's house. The historian John Lothrop Motley was so close a friend he was "Uncle John" to the boy. His mother's cousin, Benjamin Peirce, famed Harvard mathematician, invented new games for Cabot and his sister Elizabeth to play. Longfellow often came, as did Louis Agassiz. His parents were strong Unionists and admired Lincoln from the first. The boy was thrilled to see Robert Gould Shaw lead his Negro regiment off to war. His father wanted to raise a Cavalry outfit, but an injury from a riding accident disqualified him. Cabot Lodge attended the funeral of a soldier killed in the war, the older brother of a schoolmate, and never forgot the sight of the young blue-clad body in its casket. He heard young Capt. Oliver Wendell Holmes, Jr., another of his mother's cousins, tell of his experiences at the front, where he was thrice wounded. He was 12 when his father suddenly dropped dead. His mother lived on at the Beacon Street mansion until her own death in 1900, after which Lodge used Dr. William Sturgis Bigelow's home as his Boston residence.

Had the first Cabot Lodge not entered politics, he would doubtless have become a Harvard professor. As a student at Harvard, he fell under the influence of Henry Adams, President John Quincy Adams' grandson, who, at President Eliot's suggestion, had come from Washington to teach medieval history, about which he knew nothing. Adams, living with his brother Brooks at the home of their aunt, Mrs. Edward Everett, taught his students by learning it with them.

During the seven years Adams stayed at Harvard, Lodge was his chief protege. At
21, Lodge married Anna Cabot Mills Davis, the daughter of Rear Admiral Davis (who
had founded the Naval Observatory and the National Academy of Science) and went off
to Europe for a honeymoon and a year's travel and study (their first child, Constance,
was born in Paris). But he was in constant touch with Adams, and two years later
joined him as his assistant at the *North American Review,* a quarterly of which Adams
was editor. Adams was a stern taskmaster. Lodge's first published writing—a one-page
review of Baxman's *History of the Popes*—was written eight times before Adams would
send it to the printer.

At Adams' urging, Lodge undertook a scholarly research on the ancient Anglo-Saxon
land laws, which won him the second Ph.D. that Harvard had ever awarded in history.
He also began to teach American history at Harvard. His lectures were published as
"A Short History of the English Colonies in America." Lodge soon became editor of
The International Review, and one of the first articles he accepted was "Cabinet Gov-
ernment of the United States" by Thomas Woodrow Wilson, then a senior at Princeton.
When Wilson applied for graduate work at Johns Hopkins, he cited his study of Dr.
Lodge's American history as one of the reasons why he felt competent to pass an ex-
amination in colonial history. Editor Lodge marked a second article by Wilson thus:
"R.R.R."—(received, read, rejected).

Lodge who loved children, also edited a volume of ballads and lyrics for boys and
girls aged 12 to 18, collected fairy tales for younger children, and by age 30 was
earning $3,000 a year (enough to live on handsomely then) from his writings and
lectures. He was embarked on new scholarly research which would see him, in time,
complete a "Life and Letters of George Cabot," edit the complete works of Alexander
Hamilton, write a biography of Hamilton, then of Daniel Webster, and a "Life of Washington." He might well have spent the rest of his life as scholar, editor, historian and
teacher had not Henry Adams and Senator Carl Schurz, the German emigre who was
Lincoln's friend and a Civil War general, got him interested in political reform. This
activity drew him, in turn, into running for the General Court of Massachusetts, then
(unsuccessfully) for Congress. At the age of 36 he did get elected to Congress, and
after a second term went on to the Senate to become the famous "scholar in politics."
He and Theodore Roosevelt later wrote, together, "Hero Tales from American History,"
whose introduction states its purpose:

> . . . to tell in simple fashion the story of some Americans who showed that they
> knew how to live and how to die; who proved their truth by their endeavor; and
> who joined to the stern and manly qualities which are essential to the well-being
> of a masterful race the virtues of gentleness, of patriotism and of lofty adherence
> to an ideal.

Roosevelt wrote on Daniel Boone, George Rogers Clark, King's Mountain, the Battle
of New Orleans, the Alamo, the Death of Stonewall Jackson, and "The Charge at
Gettysburg"; Lodge wrote on Washington, the Battle of Trenton, John Quincy Adams
as Congressman, Francis Parkman, Grant at Vicksburg, Robert Gould Shaw, Sheridan
at Cedar Creek, and Abraham Lincoln.

Roosevelt said Lodge was "my closest friend personally, politically and in every other
way and occupied toward me a relationship that no other man has ever occupied or
will occupy." Lodge once expressed to Roosevelt his inability to understand "why these
writers persist in calling me cold, and reserved, and a Brahmin." Roosevelt replied, "I
can tell you, Cabot—it's because you are."

The men of the Cabot and Lodge breed have been uxorious, home-loving men, who were singularly fortunate in finding wives as remarkable for their good sense as their good looks. Often they have been related to them.

George Cabot's wife, Elizabeth Higginson, "had all the firmness, vigor, resolution, penetration, capacity to form and express her thoughts in a strong, clear and masculine style which are found in men of the firmest, boldest and most elevated temperament and mind." So wrote John Lowell at her death in 1826, adding: "She had none of the advantages of early education afforded so bountifully to the young ladies of the present age; but she surpassed *all* of them in the acuteness of her observation, in the knowledge of human nature and in her powers of expressing and defending the opinions which she had formed. Without systematic knowledge, her mind was filled with information on every topic interesting to us in this world." It was her daughter, Elizabeth, who was the first woman to climb the pyramid at Gizeh and who married President Kirkland of Harvard.

Anna Blake, who married Henry Cabot, was a woman of such "beauty and grace, abiding charm and fascinating qualities" that her surviving friends spoke of them to her grandson, Senator Lodge, "with such emphasis and insistence that I frequently had an uneasy feeling at the back of my mind that they were thinking how unlike she was to some of her grandchildren.

Anna Cabot, the Senator's own mother, a cousin of Mrs. Oliver Wendell Holmes, Sr., was a "clever, high-minded, high-spirited woman." She read deeply. "It was from her," wrote the Senator, "that I first heard of Byron and Shelley. She was one of the early admirers of Browning in the days before his popularity."

The Senator's own wife, Amelia Cabot Mills Davis, was a distant relative of the Senator, and grand-daughter of an earlier Massachusetts Senator, Elijah Hunt Mills. Nannie, as she was called, was slim and pretty, with such arresting eyes that John Singer Sargent said of her, "Years ago I had the greatest desire to paint [her] portrait . . . I had such an unqualified regard for her that the odds were in favor of my succeeding in getting something of the kindness and intelligence of her expression and the unforgettable blue of her eyes." Theodore Roosevelt thought "She looked as queens ought to look, but as no queen I have ever seen does look." And Lord Bryce said, "She was one of those rare personalities in whom strength and elevation of character were united with sweetness, gentleness and a wonderful grace of manner."

She was her husband's sternest critic. Next to Henry Adams, she had the greatest influence on his political and historical writings. He once asked her to read a speech he had prepared for a local rally. She read it and handed it back "saying with charming frankness that it was very inferior stuff, would not do at all, in short was quite impossible." Lodge tossed it in the fire and wrote another. "Somewhat better," Nannie commented, "yet far from satisfactory. Really you ought not to stand up before an audience to read that." Lodge tried a third time, and Nannie said: "Better than either of the others, though not what it ought to be. However, I suppose it is as good as you can do, my poor boy." She gave him his deflating nickname of "Pinky."

When Bay Lodge, their son, married Elizabeth Davis—herself a distant relative of Nannie—she introduced some interesting new bloodlines into the family. Her father, Judge John Davis, had served as Assistant Secretary of State (he negotiated the American base at Pearl Harbor), and was the son of a Union brigadier-general, Hasbrouck Davis, who in turn was the son of "Honest John" Davis, a former Massachusetts governor and Senator. The Assistant Secretary married the Secretary of State's daughter— Sally Frelinghuysen, the belle of Washington in her day.

Through the Frelinghuysen line, the present Henry Cabot Lodge is a direct descendant of Theodorus Jacobus Frelinghuysen, "The Apostle of the Raritan," who brought
the Dutch Reformed Church to America, and whose son, John, founded the seminary
which became Rutgers University.

John's son, Frederick, the first teacher at Rutgers, served in the Continental Congress and in Washington's Army, at the Battles of Trenton, Princeton and Monmouth,
and in 1793 went to the U.S. Senate. His son, Theodore also became a Senator, famous
as "The Christian Statesman" (he kept a book of Scriptures by his razor, and for 40
years put aside 15 minutes at mid-day to pray aloud). In April of 1830 he spoke for
five hours, in a Senate speech spread over three days, vainly trying to halt President
Jackson's expulsion of the unoffending Cherokees from Georgia and North Carolina.
"I had rather receive the blessing of one poor Cherokee," he cried, "than sleep beneath
the marble of all the Caesars." In choosing Henry Clay's running mate in 1844, the
Whigs had to choose from among New York's Millard Fillmore, Massachusetts' "Honest
John" Davis or Frelinghuysen—and picked the latter on the third ballot. As president
of the American Bible Society, Theodore carried on endless correspondence with Clay,
unavailingly seeking to reform that gambler, high-liver and duelist. He became president of Rutgers in 1850 and served to his death in 1862.

The old Senator, at the death of his brother, Frederick, had adopted his three-year-old
son, Frederick Theodore, as his own, and trained him in his law office. In 1866 the
adopted son became Senator and joined the new Republican Party, taking on management of the Civil Rights Bill when Charles Sumner became incapacitated (the Negroes
of Washington named a school after him in 1917). He was instrumental, as a member
of the Electoral Commission, in deciding the disputed election of 1876 in favor of
Rutherford Hayes. As President Arthur's Secretary of State he let well enough alone
and sought no involvement in foreign disputes. "Mr. Frelinghuysen is understood to
hold," said the Springfield *Republican* "that the American eagle should not strain his
naturally fine voice by shrill and prolonged screaming on small occasions."

SAGAMORE HILL.

July 6ᵗʰ 1902

Dear Bay;

We are overjoyed; best-wishes for the boy, and warmest-congratulations for Bessie and you.

Affectionately yours

Theodore Roosevelt

1902: T.R. to Bay Lodge on Cabot's birth.

*1944: F.D.R. to Lodge on
leaving the Senate for
combat.*

423

THE WHITE HOUSE
WASHINGTON

February 1, 1944.

<u>PERSONAL</u>.

Dear Cabot:

I want you to know that I am awfully
glad that you came to see me this morning.
And I am writing this note to tell you that I
would do just what you are doing, if I could.

I missed being with the guns in
1917-'18. It's too late now. I envy you the
opportunity that is yours and I congratulate
you upon the decision you have made.

Good luck, and all best wishes,

Very sincerely yours,

Franklin D Roosevelt

Honorable Henry Cabot Lodge, Jr.,
United States Senate,
Washington, D. C.

*1952: General Marshall to Lodge on
his defeat by J.F.K.*

GENERAL G. C. MARSHALL
LISCOMBE LODGE
PINEHURST, NORTH CAROLINA

November 6-52

Dear Lodge..

I am terribly sorry that
the electorate failed you in your state.
They made a great error for you were among
the most conspicuous able men in
public office. I anticipated great things
for you and deeply deplore the circumstances working
to date. This misfortune may be a turn for
greater things.

Personally, I want to see you
Secretary of State presently. If not,
then Secretary of Defense. Some one
tells me you can't accept any cabinet
position. I hope not. If ever the
country needed a man it needs you!

Faithfully yours,

G C Marshall

THE WHITE HOUSE
WASHINGTON

December 28, 1956

Dear Cabot:

As both 1956 and our first Administration draw to a close, I want to express to you my appreciation of the outstanding job you have done as United States Representative to the United Nations. Particularly in these last months of international crises and great strain, it has been a source of tremendous satisfaction to me to know that you were so ably representing us in the council of nations. I truly cannot adequately express the proper measure of my gratitude for your tireless and dedicated efforts.

At the same time I am aware that during the entire four years of this Administration you have been extremely effective in your efforts to make the United Nations the instrument for peace that it must be; and I know that my own gratitude for all you have done is shared by people throughout the world.

With all the best to you and Emily and to the members of your family for a fine 1957 (and, let us hope, a more peaceful 1957) and warm personal regard,

As ever,

Dwight D. Eisenhower

The Honorable Henry Cabot Lodge, Jr.
United States Representative
   to the United Nations
Two Park Avenue
New York 16, N. Y.

1956: President Eisenhower to Lodge after Hungary and Suez.

1963: President Kennedy to Lodge on his appointment to Saigon.

THE WHITE HOUSE
WASHINGTON

June 18, 1963

Dear Cabot:

Thank you very much for your recent letter.

I am delighted that you are going to South Viet-Nam. This is a most important assignment and I know you will do an outstanding job. We have today sent a message to the South Viet-Nam government notifying them of your assignment.

With every good wish.

Sincerely,

John Kennedy

The Honorable
Henry Cabot Lodge

THE WHITE HOUSE
WASHINGTON

June 23, 1964

Dear Ambassador Lodge:

I accept with deep regret your resignation as Ambassador
to Vietnam. I hereby authorize you to make your farewell
call to General Khanh and to depart at your convenience
thereafter. I hope to see you at once on your return to
hear your final report and to offer best personal wishes
on your return to private life.

Your readiness to assume the duties of American Ambassador to Vietnam, in a time of danger and difficulty, was
in the great tradition of disinterested public service. Those
who carry on after you will find encouragement in your example.

Your departure will mean no change in the steadfast determination of the United States to support the government
and people of South Vietnam in their struggle for peace and
security, which means an end of Communist terror and an
end of external aggression. As you say, we will persist.

Sincerely,

Lyndon B. Johnson

The Honorable Henry Cabot Lodge
The American Ambassador
Saigon

*1964: President Johnson to Lodge on ending first tour
of duty in Saigon*

Acknowledgments

The writer thanks President Johnson and former President Eisenhower for personal interviews. He is similarly indebted to many others for interviews, reminiscences and valuable help.

In the Lodge family, he thanks Ambassador Lodge and his wife, Emily, for numerous interviews, and for access to hitherto unpublished letters, personal journals and photographs; George Cabot Lodge and his wife, Nancy; Henry Sears Lodge and his wife, Elenita; and former Gov. John Davis Lodge and his wife, Francesca, for many kindnesses.

Among Lodge's boyhood friends, classmates and other intimates the writer thanks John Mason Brown for much help and encouragement; J. O. Bangs, Charles Barnes, Guido Perrera, Chandler Bigelow, Gen. Robert M. Cutler; Francis McCarthy, Maxwell Rabb, Ralph Mitchell, Abe Glovsky, Senator Leverett Saltonstall, Corliss Lamont, Eugene Reynal, and Miss Aileen Tone, companion to Henry Adams.

Among newspaper colleagues of Lodge, he thanks especially Helen Rogers Reid, Ogden R. Reid, Walter Millis, the late Lucius Beebe, John Denson, Joseph Alsop, the late Howard Davis, and the family of the late Geoffrey Parsons; John Hay Whitney, editor, and Ben Price, picture editor, of the New York *Herald Tribune*.

Among Lodge's Army friends and wartime associates he thanks Gen. Willis Dale Crittenberger, Gen. Jacob L. Devers, Gen. Edward R. Brooks, Lieut. Col. Edward A. Stephenson, Capt. Graham Purcell, and Lieut. William Hershey.

Among Lodge's 1952 Eisenhower-campaign associates he thanks Gen. Eisenhower, Maxwell Rabb for his reconstruction of the events, George Lodge for his unpublished journal of their sequence, and Paul G. Hoffman. He also thanks Henry Sears.

Among United Nations associates the writer is grateful to Rosemary Spencer, Lodge's former secretary; Frank Carpenter, press officer; Richard Petersen, political officer; the late Adlai Stevenson, and Clayton Fritchey.

Among Lodge's 1960 campaign associates he thanks particularly Serrell Hillman, *Time* correspondent on leave as his aide, for making available his day-to-day journal.

Among Viet Nam associates he thanks Col. John Michael Dunn, his former aide; correspondent Robert Shaplen and his wife, June.

For help during the 1964 New Hampshire primary he thanks Paul Grindle and David Goldberg, Sally Saltonstall, and M. Richard Jackman.

For interviews he thanks Arthur Krock, James B. Reston and Felix Belair of the *New York Times,* and for assistance John Steele, Richard Clurman, Jane Scholl, Kenneth Froslid, Ruth Mehrtens, Jean Snow, all of *Time*, Philip Kunhardt of *Life*, and Thomas Winship of the *Boston Globe*.

He thanks Mrs. John F. Kennedy and Mrs. George C. Marshall for permission to use letters. He thanks Dean John Monro of Harvard College, Headmaster David Sheldon of Middlesex, and former Middlesex master Archibald K. Galbraith for assistance.

He is especially grateful to publisher James Heineman for initially making the venture possible, to Henry R. Luce for granting the leave to undertake it and for making available the invaluable source materials of *Time*, and to President Johnson, Bill D. Moyers and Assistant Secretary of State William P. Bundy for declassifying numerous Lodge cables from Saigon and so giving those chapters a scope and authenticity which they could not otherwise have had.

March 1967, Cincinnati, Ohio

Bibliography

Adams, Henry. *The Life of George Cabot Lodge*. Boston and New York: Houghton Mifflin, 1911.

Boorstin, Daniel. *The Americans: The National Experience*. New York: Random House, 1965.

Brown, John Mason. *Through These Men*. New York: Harper, 1956.

Chanler, Margaret (Mrs. Winthrop). *Roman Spring*. Boston: Little, Brown, 1934.

Codman, Charles. *Drive*. Boston: Little, Brown, 1957.

Davis, Charles H., Jr. *Life of Charles Henry Davis, Rear Admiral, 1807-1877*. Boston and New York: Houghton Mifflin, 1899.

Eisenhower, Dwight D. *Mandate for Change*. Garden City: Doubleday, 1963.

Finer, Herman. *Dulles Over Suez*. Chicago: Quadrangle Books, 1964.

Garraty, John A. *Henry Cabot Lodge*. New York: Knopf, 1953.

Hess, Stephen. *America's Political Dynasties*. Garden City: Doubleday, 1966.

Hoover, Herbert. *The Ordeal of Woodrow Wilson*. New York: McGraw-Hill, 1958.

Lodge, George Cabot. *Poems and Dramas of George Cabot Lodge*. 2 vols. Boston and New York: Houghton Mifflin, 1911.

Lodge, Henry Cabot. *Daniel Webster*. Boston and New York: Houghton Mifflin, 1883.

————. *Early Memories*. New York: Charles Scribner's Sons, 1913.

————. *. . . George Washington. . . .* 2 vols. Boston and New York: Houghton Mifflin, 1889.

————. *Life and Letters of George Cabot*. Boston: Little, Brown, 1877.

———— (ed.). *Selections from the Correspondence of Theodore Roosevelt and Henry Cabot Lodge*. 2 vols. New York: Charles Scribner's Sons, 1925.

————. *The Senate and the League of Nations*. New York: Charles Scribner's Sons, 1925.

Lodge, Henry Cabot, Jr. *The Cult of Weakness*. Boston and New York: Houghton Mifflin, 1932.

Longworth, Alice Roosevelt. *Crowded Hours*. New York: Charles Scribner's Sons, 1933.

Murphy, Robert Daniel. *Diplomat Among Warriors*. Garden City: Doubleday, 1964.

Roosevelt, Theodore. *Theodore Roosevelt; an Autobiography*. New York: The Macmillan Co., 1913.

Roosevelt, Theodore, and Lodge, Henry Cabot. *Hero Tales from American History*. New York: Century Co., 1895.

Salisbury-Jones, General Guy. *So Full a Glory; a Biography of Marshall de Lattre de Tassigny*. London: Weidenfeld & Nicolson, 1954.

Schriftgiesser, Karl. *The Gentleman from Massachusetts: Henry Cabot Lodge*. Boston: Little, Brown, 1944.

Vandenberg, Arthur H., Jr. (ed.). *The Private Papers of Senator Vandenberg*. Boston: Houghton Mifflin, 1952.

Wharton, Edith. *A Backward Glance*. New York: Charles Scribner's Sons, 1964.

Index

431

133; *Cult of Weakness* used against him, 134; wins Senate seat, 134; opposes packing Supreme Court, 135; infuriates F. D. R., 137; for retooling Springfield Arsenal, 138; on Social Security reform, 138; backs wage-hour minimums, 139; against U.S. involvement in foreign quarrels, 139; supports Willkie, 140; joins Patton's Second Armored Division in Louisiana, 141; at Fort Knox, 141; "soldier or senator?" 143; whereabouts unknown, 144; visits Eisenhower, 145; flies to Cairo, 145; with British Army in the desert, 146; narrow escape, 148; defeats Casey, 149; second term in Senate, 151; on allotment to servicemen's families, 154; report on brave Americans, 154; epics of heroism, 155-156; visits Churchill, 158; with Patton in Italy, 159; attention to GI's, 161; checks servicemen's welfare, 162; sees Chinese villages, 163; impression of Chennault, 163; on Chinese Communists, 164; comment on Milne Bay, 166; on war threats, 167; impression of MacArthur, 165; Purple Heart to Leroy Miller, 166; reports war tour, 168; on censorship and propaganda, 169; on unification of armed forces, 169; on international air routes, 168; defends Patton, 171; sees F. D. R., resigns from Senate to enter combat, 171-175; to Lake Averno, 172; troubleshooter, 173; to Walter Reed Hospital, 173; acts as deputy chief of staff, 174; fires at German, 174; Purcell: "L. was utterly without fear," 174; with French Colonial Infantry, 175; uniforms for maquis, 176; acts for Devers, 177; briefs Eisenhower, 179; account of German surrender, 181; awarded Legion of Merit by Devers, Croix de Guerre by De Lattre, Ordre National of Legion d'Honneur by De Gaulle, 182; first postwar speech, 183; mustered out in 1945, 183; speech to Oregon Republicans, 184; on price control, 185; candidate for Senate, 185; wins Senate seat, 186; Lincoln's Day message, 187; on Foreign Relations Committee, 188; problems of seniority, 188; defends Lilienthal, 189; at odds with Robert Taft, 189; on foreign policy, 190; on

domestic reforms, 191; speech on European reconstruction, 191; to "win the peace," 192; fights for Marshall Plan, 194; on trade with Eastern Europe, 196; chairman of Resolutions Commitee, 198; foreign policy plank, 198; *Saturday Evening Post* article, "What's the Matter with Republicans?" 200; recalls death of Whig Party, 201; on Vandenberg resolution, 203; Harvard reunion, 205; defends State Department against McCarthy charges, 206; convinced Eisenhower should run for President, 208; U.N. delegate, 208; maiden speech before U.N., 208-210; on defense of Western Europe, 212; on "Meet the Press" program, 214; letter to Brewer, 218; to Fort Dix, 220; on making of a President, 222; memos to staff, 225; letter to Sherman Adams, 228; reply to du Pont, 230; to Paris on Eisenhower campaign, 236; recalls Democratic Party convention, 246; liking for John F. Kennedy, 253; introduces Eisenhower on TV, 255; to Nassau, 256; takes U.N. post, 257; speaks before General Assembly, 259; reply to Vishinsky, 260; repertory of songs, 263; relations with U.N. reporters, 264; Yugoslav ambassador incident, 264; can't stand intrigue, 264; Joseph Schine case, 265; challenges Soviets in U.N., 267; defines U.N. role at AP luncheon, 269; message to John F. Kennedy, 270; debate on Guatemala, 271; Israel-Egypt war, 275; on Hungary; answer to Life editorial on Hungary, 278; on nuclear tests, 282; reply to Sobolev on Lebanon crisis, 284; meets with Khrushchev, 288; educated Khrushchev on capitalism, 293; reply to Kuznetsov, 304; thirteen years in Senate, 307; visit to Russia, 310; Benjamin Franklin Award, 310; Africa trip, 310; awarded American Ordnance Association Gold Medal, 311; with Khrushchev in Moscow, 311; U-2 incident, 311; to West Point—Sylvanus Thayer Award, 312; on Congo crisis, 318; on international Communism, 319; on a Negro in Nixon-Lodge Cabinet, 325; avoids handshaking affairs, 327; on political tricks, 328; on Khrushchev shoe-banging incident,

About the Author

William J. Miller literally grew up in journalism. At 17, on graduating from Asheville High School, he left his native North Carolina to join the Cleveland (Ohio) *Press*. For the next 16 years he served it as reporter, rewrite man, columnist and war correspondent. In Italy, he accompanied the U. S. Fifth Army with which Lodge served, and like Lodge landed on D-day in Southern France with the U. S. Seventh Army and First French Army. He witnessed the liberation of Toulon and Marseilles and the sweep to the Rhine at Strasbourg.

Miller's and Lodge's paths had crossed earlier—at Cleveland's National Air Races, which Lodge saw as a *Herald Tribune* editorial writer, and where Miller covered Orville Wright, James Doolittle, Lindbergh, Amelia Earhart, Ernst Udet, and took part himself in an unplanned spectacle—the mid-air collision of an autogyro and a 1910 Curtiss pusher, whose pilot was killed (the autogyro pilot and Miller, a passenger, escaped unhurt). Both Lodge and Miller also attended the 1936 Republican convention in Cleveland that nominated Landon. Miller also witnessed the nominations of Adlai Stevenson (1956), John F. Kennedy, Lyndon Johnson and Barry Goldwater.

Cleveland's famed editor Louis B. Seltzer termed Miller "one of the best newspaper writers Cleveland has ever had." Miller covered the social upheavals of Depression years—the bank crashes, eviction riots, auto sit down strikes, the Bonus March, the Little Steel strike, and interviewed scores of headline figures—Gen. Hugh S. Johnson of the NRA, Senator Pat Harrison, Tom Mooney, George Gershwin, Father Coughlin, Gertrude Stein, Earl Browder, Norman Thomas, Josephus Daniels, Frances Perkins, Lord Halifax, Alfred Duff-Cooper, and Senator Harry Truman. He won Cleveland's top awards for reporting and feature-writing, and a Heywood Broun Memorial Citation for a series on Negro housing. As a boy he had gone with his father to hear William Jennings Bryan, who summered in Asheville; later he interviewed Clarence Darrow (who in 1932 told Miller his advice to young men was "to jump out the window." He was a Nieman Fellow at Harvard. During World War II he saw at close hand Churchill, de Gaulle, Generals Eisenhower, Patton, Patch, Juin, Truscott and O'Daniel.

Joining *Newsweek* after the war, Miller wrote such cover stories as those on John L. Lewis, Chester Bowles, Eddie Rickenbacker. Shortly he joined *Time* where he wrote some of its best-remembered cover stories—the Hartfords of the A. & P., the Wallaces of Readers' Digest, Big Steel's Ben Fairless, Du Pont's Crawford Greenewalt, and Bob Kleberg of the King Ranch—as well as *Time*'s "Bull Market" covers. He began writing *Life* editorials in 1954, sat through the weary midnight U.N. sessions on Hungary and Suez, dealt closely with Lodge (Miller's eloquent *Life* editorials on "The Heroes of Hungary" are still remembered). As chief editorial writer of the *Herald Tribune*, his 1957 editorials on the Soviet Sputnik (*"The Lessons of Our Defeat"*) were voted New York City's best for that year, and helped rouse a sense of national urgency about America's deficiencies in space research, scientific education and defense duplications. Miller's keen sense of history comes, in part, from being the grandson of a Confederate officer who also was wounded as a teen-age volunteer in the Mexican War. A political independent, Miller was one of those who helped Ohio Democrat Frank Lausche become mayor, governor and Senator. He chose Republican Lodge as a subject in admiration of Lodge's own political independence and courage.